Mae Mallory, the Monroe Defense Committee, and World Revolutions

Mae Mallory, the Monroe Defense Committee, and World Revolutions

African American Women Radical Activists

Paula Marie Seniors

THE UNIVERSITY OF GEORGIA PRESS   ATHENS

© 2024 by the University of Georgia Press
Athens, Georgia 30602
www.ugapress.org
All rights reserved
Designed by
Set in 10.25/13 Freight Text by Kaelin Chappell Broaddus

Most University of Georgia Press titles are
available from popular e-book vendors.

Printed digitally

Library of Congress Cataloging-in-Publication Data

Names: Seniors, Paula Marie, author.
Title: Mae Mallory, the Monroe Defense Committee, and world revolutions :
   African American women radical activists / Paula Marie Seniors.
Other titles: African American women radical activists
Description: Athens : University of Georgia Press, 2024. | Includes bibliographical
   references and index.
Identifiers: LCCN 2023048943 (print) | LCCN 2023048944 (ebook) |
   ISBN 9780820366418 (hardback) | ISBN 9780820366425 (paperback) |
   ISBN 9780820366432 (epub) | ISBN 9780820366449 (pdf)
Subjects: LCSH: African American women civil rights workers—Biography. |
   African American radicals—Biography. | Black nationalism—United States—
   History—20th century. | Workers World Party. | Communism—United
   States—History—20th century. | United States—Race relations—History—
   20th century.
Classification: LCC E185.96 .S4246 2024 (print) | LCC E185.96 (ebook) | DDC
   305.48/8960730922 [b]—dc23/eng/20231122
LC record available at https://lccn.loc.gov/2023048943
LC ebook record available at https://lccn.loc.gov/2023048944

This book was funded, in part, by generous support from Virginia Tech Publishing,
the Faculty Subvention Fund, and the Religion and Culture Department.

I dedicate all my work on African American women radical activists to my scholar-activist mother and father for their unwavering love and support, and for their political and social activism. This work honors their lives.

To Angie [Justina] Thompson, the feisty little girl that you were, the daughter I always wanted. Angie, you have grown up to be a phenomenal woman and I am so proud of you.

To my daughter Shakeila. May you grow up to be a Radical Woman like your grandmother.

Contents

LIST OF ILLUSTRATIONS   ix

ACKNOWLEDGMENTS   xi

PREFACE   xvii

INTRODUCTION   1

Part I.   Histories, Influences, Activism and Writing Resistance

CHAPTER 1.   Mrs. Ethel Azalea Johnson: Motherhood, Self-Defense, and the Negroes with Guns Movement   9

CHAPTER 2.   Ethel Azalea Johnson: Mrs. Johnson and World Revolutions   35

CHAPTER 3.   Mae Mallory: From Georgia to New York, to Political Prisoner   55

CHAPTER 4.   Audrey Proctor: The New Orleans NAACP and the Monroe Defense Committee   82

CHAPTER 5.   Patricia Mallory: Awakenings of a Black Nationalist Rebel Girl   109

Part II.   Writing Resistance

CHAPTER 6.   Mae Mallory: Dream Escape at Twenty-First and Payne/"Pain"   137

CHAPTER 7.   Audrey Proctor Seniors: Motherhood and Writing Resistance   184

Part III. Internationalizing the Struggle

CHAPTER 8. Pat Mallory, Black Nationalist Rebel Woman: Social Political Awakening in Tanzania and Guyana   221

CHAPTER 9. Audrey Proctor Seniors: The Grenadian and Nicaraguan Revolutions   251

CHAPTER 10. Radicalized Daughters Speak   274

NOTES   295

BIBLIOGRAPHY   343

INDEX   383

List of Illustrations

Figure 1. Ethel Azalea Johnson 8
Figure 2. Harold Reape, Mae Mallory, Richard Crowder [Yusef] 11
Figure 3. "Support Monroe Defense Committee" march, Cleveland 56
Figure 4. Ella Baker, Clarence Henry Seniors 87
Figure 5. Audrey Proctor, high school graduation 101
Figure 6. Patricia Mallory, Miss au Naturale 126
Figure 7. "Mrs. Mallory Goes Back to County Jail" 136
Figure 8. Wilbur Grattan, Mae, Paula, Libby, Lumumba Kenyatta, Freedom House 193
Figure 9. Butch, "My Mother is No Kidnapper; Mae, "Save My Mother" 198
Figure 10. Paula, "Hell No We Won't Go" 203
Figure 11. Mae Mallory, national tour 235
Figure 12. Audrey Seniors at Women's Liberation march, 1969 250
Figure 13. Paula Marie Seniors, "Dancer as Athlete" 280

Acknowledgments

Pat Mallory Oduba

I am forever grateful to Audrey and Clarence Henry Seniors for their dedication and commitment, to the "cause" in general, and for helping save my mother's life in particular. I once got an opportunity to publicly give thanks to Audrey who, with Clarence and so many others, dug deeply into their hearts and activist souls to fight to save my mother's life. They proved that my mother's well-being was at the forefront of their efforts by moving with her when she was extradited from Cleveland to Monroe and you [Paula] were a baby. I was a teenager. My mother would often write to me about your milestones and the cute and/or naughty things you did.

I am forever grateful for your parents' many sacrifices made on my mother's and ultimately my behalf. Your family denied themselves many comforts in life given their dedication to the cause of African American liberation and Mae Mallory.

Paula, you have taken up the banner and followed their values in sacrificing economic gain and social pretention for the good of others. I am absolutely sure that Audrey would be very proud of you, as is Clarence. It is how they raised you.

I want to now thank you for telling the Mae Mallory story as a historian and from a firsthand recounting. I'd like to thank the Mae Mallory Brigade—Sophia Bandele, Robyn Spencer-Antoine, Mae Jackson, and Rudy Kofi Cain—for lifting and encouraging me to find new meaning and appreciation for my mother's strength and intellect in the struggle for humanity and for African heritage people. May you and Shakeila be blessed and our struggle victorious.

Paula Marie Seniors

I would like to thank everyone who made this book possible. I am especially grateful to Mick Gusinde-Duffy, who has shown faith in this book from the very beginning, and who took the time to help me in crafting the book. I am thankful to the anonymous readers, Anitra Grisales, Kenny Marotta, Gisela Fosado, Dr. Carole Boyce Davies, Dr. Robyn Spencer-Antoine, Lori Rider, and Dr. Akinyele Umoja, who offered valuable critiques and recommendations for the book. I am thankful to you all for helping me shape this book.

Bryan Parson's Photography restored images used in this book, for which I am thankful.

My aunt Doris Proctor Dubuclet offered unwavering love for me and my mother, Audrey Proctor Seniors. She offered me her remembrances and her love of her sister. Auntie Doris, I love and thank you. Pat Mallory Oduba shares this legacy of resistance learned from our mothers, making us sisters in the struggle. Pat offered love to me and my daughter, sustenance, and remembrances in interviews. I love and thank you too. Nadine Clark and her son Michael and niece Crystal have been a presence in my and my mother's lives since nursery school. I am grateful for our family connection and Nadine's friendship with my mother. I am so appreciative of Joan Gibbs's friendship with my mother and me. Maha holds a very special place, as she was my mother's friend and nurse. She loved my mother deeply and for that love and her kindness I am grateful.

I am grateful to Dr. Carol Bailey who like my mother was a brigadista in Nicaragua and who has never wavered in our friendship or in support of this book. Thank you to Dr. Marian Mollin whose upcoming book is about the Maryknoll Sisters who appear in this book. Who would have known that in Blacksburg I would befriend women connected to my research.

I would like to express my deep appreciation and gratitude to Dr. Denise Ferreira Da Silva, Dr. Sandra Angeleri, Dr. Gloria Dickinson, Dr. Carole Boyce Davies, Dr. Joanne Gabbin, and Dr. Yie Yin Foong for their encouragement and support in writing this book. Thank you always to Dr. George Lipsitz, Dr. Ramon Gutierrez, Dr. Ross Frank, Dr. Benetta Jules Rosette, and Dr. George Lewis.

Thank you to my family: Carl Proctor; Maurice Harvey and his children Felicia, Jen, Marissa, Maurice II, and Maurice III, and his grandchild Madison; and Shakeila's cousins, aunts, and brothers, Cheyenne and Malcolm Washington, Katie and Darius Schutz, and Jen and Jayden Tucker Eddins.

I am grateful to my Workers World Party family: Susie, Nina, Hindi, Mallory, Sara, Eric, Saul, Peggy, Eva, Ellen Catalanato, John Catalanato, Mary-Ann Weisman, Sharon Martin Eolis, Rosemary Neidenberg, Milton Neidenberg, Ruben and Joyce Kanowitz, Bill Kaessinger, Joyce Kaessinger, and Yuri Kochiyama.

I have a special appreciation for those who helped me through my mother's death: Dottie Zellner, Suzanne Shende, David Lerner, Sheldon, Lynda Elliott, Pina Mozzani, Sharon McFarland, Sheryl Rifas, Brenda Braye, Paul Crutchfield, George, Glen Hirata, Andrea Berry, Kharen Fulton, Derrick McGinty, and Cedric Mickels.

Thank you to my amazing friends Miron Lockett, Verna Hampton, Adriene Hughes, Ivonne Avila, Eddie Cacciocoppi, Bonita Williams, Sonya Ramsey, Sonya Donaldson, Nikol Alexander Floyd, Gregg Thomas, Jesse Benjamin, Janet Sims Woods, Andrea Dixon, John C. Tedesco, Sally Paulson, Corinne Noirot, Rob Blakley, Tracy Newton, Amy Splitt, Nichole Rustin-Paschal, Janet Splitter, Keith Driver and Lucy, Marianne Kubik, Debbie Hanley, Diana Dale, Amy Ballenger, Diana Williams, Jeff Barratt, Angela Cioffi, Eugena Gunderson, Cassandra Fraser, Aniko Bodroghkozy, Patricia Carubba, Katherine McNamara, Svetlana and Sergiy Dmytireyev, George and Stephen Guenzi Still, Zena and Tommie, Pam Chelette Picou, Dr. Rachelle Brun Bevel, Dr. Andrea Baldwin, Dr. Vee'tuh Parker, Dr. Ida Jones, Dr. Haiyin Zhu, Dr. Juliana Snapper, Dr. Stacey Vogt Yuan, Dr. Alicia Gonzales, Ray Zanick, and my San Diego mothers Janet, Jenny, and Mary.

I am grateful for the connections I have made with Monroe friends Woodrow Wilson III, whose grandfather and father were instrumental in the Negroes with Guns Movement and the Monroe Defense Committee; J. J. Phillips, who traveled to Monroe to support the Negroes with Guns Movement; and Veronica Ancrum, a devotee of the Negroes with Guns Movement who traveled with me to Monroe's archives.

Thank you to Drs. Rhea Lathan and Katherine Mellon Charron for sharing information and materials about Ethel Azalea Johnson; Drs. Seth Markle and Andrew Ivasca for sharing information and English-language Tanzanian newspapers; Dr. Rosemari Mealy for sharing photographs with me; Dr. Nishani Frazier for sharing my mother's connection to her family in Cleveland's CORE; and Dr. Ula Y. Taylor for your scholarship, which has guided me.

Thank you to the committed graduate students who worked as research assistants: Fang Fang, Yin Yuan, Stephen Jordan, Jennifer Mosher, Kacie Rowell Pham, and Amy Sorenson. I am especially grateful to Anamika Raj who courageously and gamely looked at Tanzanian newspapers on microfilm and found materials that appear in this book.

I am thankful to those who have kept me healthy: Drs. Charlotte Houston, Antoinette Thomas, Victoria Lewis, Laura Clarke, Francis Wong, and Steven C. Hendrickson.

In 2013 I became a mother, and that same year Dr. Robyn Spencer-Antoine invited me to share panels with her on Mae Mallory at the National Council of Black Studies and the Left Forum. Robyn taught me how to Mommy while being an academic. She has shown me steadfast support, reading chapters and inviting me to give talks at Brooklyn College and with Jeanne Theoharis at the historic Schomburg Center for Research in Black Culture. I am grateful for Robyn's friendship and lessons in academic mothering. Academic mothering came full circle with my friends Elsie and Ted Erwin. I met them nineteen years ago at the Association for the Study of African American Life and History. They have been on this journey with me and are my daughter's grandparents. I am so appreciative that Robyn, Elsie, and Ted are in our lives.

I have had the good fortune of giving talks about Mae Mallory and the Monroe Defense Committee in Grenada, Cuba, and the United States, invited by Drs. Reena Goldthree, Ricardo Guthrie, Ida Jones, Sonya Donaldson, Sara Rzeszutek, Emily Horowitz, Karen D. Taylor, and Jared Ball.

Dr. Joanne Gabbin, Ann Spencer, Dr. Hillary Holladay, Jeanne Nicholson Siler, and Dr. Rob Vaughan honored me with the South Atlantic Humanities Faculty Fellowship at the Virginia Foundation for the Humanities, and I took my sabbatical at VFH to work on the book. At VFH I made wonderful friends who encouraged me every day. I thank Judy Moody, Jeanne Palin, Caroline R. Cades, Elliott Majerczyk, Sarah McConnell, Ramona Marcia, Jamal Millner, Diana Williams, Emily Gadek, Brigid McCarthy, Lynda Myers, and Donna Lucey. I also thank the fellows for our long-lasting bonds: Drs. Hermine Pinson, Paula Barnes, April Manalang, Frank Brannon, Lynn Rainville, Corinne T. Field, Deborah A. Lee, Beth Taylor, Mehr Farooqi, George Greenia, Cathy Jackson, Thomas Kaspidelis, Catherine Jones, Jon Sensbach, Tatiana van Riemdijk, Drew Smith, Michael Jarvis, and Kiki Petrosino.

I have been honored with several awards that helped me write this book. The first came from Virginia Tech's Dr. Terry Kershaw—a one-year postdoctoral fellowship and research funds. I was also honored with Virginia Tech's South Atlantic Humanities Award, and Dr. James Hawdon awarded me funds that allowed me to publish my mother's iconic image "Women's Liberation in Support of Black Panthers."

I am grateful to Drs. Peter Potter, Ignacio Moore, Rachel Scott, Jason Crafton, Ashley Reed, Matt Gabrielle, Laura Belmonte, and E. Thomas Ewing, who awarded me Virginia Tech's Faculty Publishing Subvention.

I would like to thank librarians and academics who assisted me in the archives: Andre Elizee and Diana Lachatanere, Schomburg Center for Research in Black Culture; Elizabeth Campbell Young and Betsey B. Creekmore, Special Collections and University Archives, University of Tennessee Libraries, Knoxville; Mona Ramonetti, Kristin Nyitray, and Dr. Zebulon Vance Miletsky, Special Collections and University Archives and the Africana Studies Department, SUNY Stony Brook; Dr. Wendy E. Chmielewski, George R. Cooley, and Pam Harris, Swarthmore Peace Collection, McCabe Library, Swarthmore College; Marian Morgan, Heritage Room, Monroe, North Carolina; Susan Williams, Highlander Research and Education Center; Gypsy Houston, Dickerson Genealogy and Local History Room, Union County Public Library; Walter P. Reuther Library, Archives of Labor and Urban Affairs, Wayne State University; Bentley Historical Library, University of Michigan; J. Murey Atkins Library Special Collections and University Archives, University of North Carolina, Charlotte; Louis Round Wilson Library, University of North Carolina, Chapel Hill; Amistad Research Center, Tulane University; New Orleans Public Library; Louisiana State University Special Collections; Michigan State University Archives and Historical Collections, Archives and Manuscript Collections; David M. Rubenstein Rare Book and Manuscript Library, Duke University Libraries; Tamiment Library and Robert F. Wagner Labor Archives, New York University Library; Aaron Purcell and Marc Brodsky, Special Collections and University Archives, Virginia Tech; Cleveland State University Library; Dr. Ida Jones, Morgan State University archivist and former assistant curator at Moorland Spingarn Research Center, Howard University.

Preface

Mae Mallory, the Monroe Defense Committee, and Me

A Personal, Political, and Intellectual Journey

I was raised within a family of Trotskyist Black Nationalist activists—founders of the Monroe Defense Committee and members of the Workers World Party. My father, Clarence Henry Seniors, was a founding member of Workers World. My mother, Audrey Proctor Seniors, and I also belonged to the Youth Against War and Fascism and New York's Black Panther Party.[1] These organizations were sites of Black and ethnic studies learning where I was educated. My graduate school training in ethnic studies at the University of California San Diego prepared me for NOW, this moment in time. It gave me the solid foundation in research and critical thinking to write *Mae Mallory, the Monroe Defense Committee, and World Revolutions: African American Women Radical Activists (1955–1995)*. I realized later that my training was intrinsically linked to my life and upbringing. When I began graduate school, my classes startled and surprised me. We read and learned about family friends.

I recall a class about my mother's great friend, the Japanese American activist Yuri Kochiyama. I told no one of the connection; I was struck dumb as I grappled with what this meant. As a graduate student I bought very few books as they were already on the shelf. My mother bequeathed me her library in death, and my father shared his library in life. These libraries reveal my home education and my parents' commitment to ethnic and Black studies. They had books and pamphlets on art and culture; writings by and about Ida B. Wells, W. E. B. Du Bois, Claudia Jones, Carter G. Woodson, Arturo Schomburg, and Esther Cooper Jackson; books about Native American, Latin American, Iranian, Cuban, Japanese, Korean, German, and Chinese history. Our library overflowed with books written by and about socialist theorists. My parents maintained a library that reflected the precursor to ethnic and Black studies. These studies in academia unfolded at the same time Black and ethnic studies journals were being founded. My university training in UC San Diego's Ethnic Studies Department proved an extension of my home training.

This book combines personal and political family narratives to tell the story of Mae Mallory. Nishani Frazier argues that "historians used the curtain of "scholarly detachment" to cover and hide exercises of identity and power not at all "detached." She believes that scholars handpick specific quotations and documents and steer the narrative to their ideological frame. "Claims of distance and detachment hardly hid author[s'] power[;] [ultimately] the Self assert[s] its way into history creation in subtle and obvious ways."[2] Frazier holds up August Meier and Eliot Rudwick's work on CORE as an example.[3] She contends that they manipulated the story of CORE to tell the story of biracial cooperation and direct action, leaving out the Black Power CORE of her mother and family.[4]

Frazier also notes that they questioned Black interviewees as though they were state interrogators. They met with resistance, because CORE members knew the state surveilled them, and in those moments, they represented state surveillance.[5] Their book remains in conversation with Ruth Benedict's *The Chrysanthemum and the Sword: Patterns of Japanese Culture*, a highly contested anthropological study of World War II–era Japanese American concentration camp victims. Benedict argued that her study offered readers an accurate portrait of Japanese life, beliefs, and customs. She claimed this notwithstanding the reality that they were prisoners in their own country, living under stressful and abnormal circumstances. Their incarceration shaped their very being; it colored their responses and their behavior to Benedict. Benedict overlooked all of these variables, and like Meier and Rudwick she did not acknowledge the power she held over these human beings. She, Meier, and Rudwick never considered whether interviewees' answers were muted by the state surveillance that they represented. The Japanese American concentration camp victims, like the Black CORE interviewees, did not fully reveal themselves to Benedict.

Predating Frazier's work, W. E. B. Du Bois explored this in "The Propaganda of History," *Black Reconstruction in America*. DuBois challenged white supremacist historians' and teachers' revisionist history of Reconstruction by showing that their version was seeped in racism, racist ideologies, stereotypes, and mistruths concerning Black contributions to Reconstruction. This false history was taught for years. *Black Reconstruction* reenvisioned Reconstruction through meticulous research that contested the concept of intellectual distance. Du Bois conducted field research and interviewed former slaves. He also drew on his experience teaching grade school in rural Tennessee and living in Atlanta, where he taught at Atlanta University. He used all these experiences to tell the history of Reconstruction, challenging the idea of scholarly detachment.[6]

In telling the story of Mae Mallory and the Monroe Defense Committee, I am also recentering history with my knowledge of my mother Audrey Proctor Seniors's story. I offer historical analysis, based on information gathered from archives around the country and my own family's archives. I have conducted interviews with Pat Mallory Oduba, Mae Mallory's daughter, and attorney Joan Gibbs, my mother's friend and coworker at the Center for Constitutional Rights. This book offers a new model for writing, a new analytical and theoretical frame that I have created. Through the use of my unique vantage point I have broadened the knowledge of these African American radical women and their political movements.

This book models methodological creativity, interdisciplinary rigor, and analytical deftness. This work is not detached scholarship. I do not pretend that it is. I follow Nishani Frazier and Beryl Satter, who both reveal their personal positions in their books' introductions. I also follow Jennifer Denetdale's lead. In her *Reclaiming Diné History*, she places Native women at the center of their own history, rejecting the white supremacist male-centered narrative offered by many white scholars.[7] I situate my work firmly within these frameworks. In doing this, I intentionally use Majority World over Third World. Majority World indicates Africa, Latin America, Asia, and Caribbean countries who retain the majority of the world's inhabitants, decentering The West.[8] I also draw on Frazier's view that she situates her work "within the sphere of highly politicized scholarship," including Black freedom movement studies and Black Power history. This book sits at the center of ethnic and Black studies scholarship: political, politicized, and personal.

I must also acknowledge the precursor to ethnic and Black studies and their founding in the academy. In 1897 African American Victoria Earle Matthews founded the White Rose Industrial Home for Colored Women in Harlem, where she taught "race history" to Black women from the United States and the diaspora as well as Italian and Jewish neighborhood children. Matthews used her "collection of books written for and about the Negro in America" to teach these classes.[9] Similarly, Tennessee's Highlander Folk School, founded in the 1930s for labor activism, morphed into a site of civil rights activism training in the late 1950s and 1960s. My father and Pat Mallory Oduba, Mae Mallory's daughter, attended Highlander regularly. Guy Carawan led Black protest music classes at Highlander; they also taught Black history and ethnic studies history, and ran a Citizenship School.

In 1962 in Harlem Richard B. Moore offered the lecture series "The History and Culture of African Peoples" under the auspices of his group the Committee to Present the Truth about the Name "Negro." These lectures included "African Contributions in Mathematics and Geometry," "African Achievements in Astronomy and Architecture," "Africans in Medicine, Chemistry, Cosmogony," and "African American and European Contributions Compared."[10] My father regularly attended Moore's classes. The Nation of Islam also offered lessons in African and African American history and culture in New York and established a university in Chicago offering pre-K to twelfth-grade education.[11] My father attended the Nation of Islam intermittently. When his mentor, Dr. Cross, and other friends joined, my father refused membership, thus permanently rupturing these friendship and mentorship bonds.

Malcolm X's Organization of Afro American Unity and the Black Panthers, to which my mother and I belonged, also taught African American history. Our family's regular trips to Harlem's Liberation Bookstore rounded out my education. All of my parents' teaching offered me a strong foundation in African American and ethnic studies history and culture.[12] While they were teaching me, college students across the country were demanding change. The 1968 San Francisco State College strike marked the "Youth Rebellion" of the Third World Liberation Front, a coalition of Black, Filipino, Native American, Asian American, and Latin American student organizations at San Francisco State College. They demanded the founding of an Ethnic Studies College. This "revolutionary struggle" in which 80 percent of the students participated reflected the worldwide uprisings occurring against white supremacy, colonialization, and imperialism. As with the worldwide revolutions, these students were met with extreme state-sanctioned militarized police and National Guard violence. With Governor Ronald Reagan's approval, they used tanks and tear gas and beat them with batons.[13]

Professor Nathan Hare aligned with the students early on. Other faculty eventually joined the strike. The students demanded an increase in the number of Majority World students, and a relevant Majority World education. They wanted to study their history, "their contemporary real[ity]," and culture from an ethnic and Black studies perspective. They insisted on an "education that would prepare them" for service in their communities "as teachers, community leaders, and citizens."[14] These Majority World students rejected the retrograde history that white supremacist professors taught. They demanded professors who looked like them. They also insisted on the inclusion of community members in the university and their curriculum. At the end of the strike, the first College of Ethnic Studies in the United States was founded at San Francisco State College. The Third World Liberation Front's successful strike led to nationwide armed student protests for ethnic and Black studies departments. As the head of the Black Student Union at SUNY Stony Brook, Pat Mallory demanded the founding of Black studies and a Black dorm, both of which were created.[15]

After injury ended my professional dance and musical theater career, I chose to pursue ethnic studies guided by the head librarian of NYU's Bobst Library, Susan Hayes, and graduate director at Emory, Miss Kharen Fulton. I was unaware that the training would align with lessons learned from my parents. I also did not see my dance or musical theater experience contributing to my life in the academy. I envisioned a life as a scholar, almost rejecting my previous life as a dancer. But my dance and musical theater background inform my storytelling. This book was like mastering a very difficult piece of choreography, creating in my dancer's body a dance scene-scape, enchanting the audience, enthralling myself, and dancing to perfection. I hope to bring vivid moments to life in this book.

I was also unaware of how painful my experience teaching within the academy would be, with gendered racism, misogyny, patriarchy, and overt hatred of Black women. However, it helped me critically analyze what my mother, Mae Mallory, Mrs. Ethel Azalea Johnson, and Pat Mallory experienced with these same challenges.

In or around 1999, as an ethnic studies graduate student at University of California San Diego, I told Dr. Denise Ferreira Da Silva and Dr. Sandra Angeleri of my mother's life. I shared with them my mother's political activism; her membership in the Workers World Party, the Monroe Defense Committee, and the Black Panthers; and our family bond with Mae Mallory and her daughter Pat. I told them of my inception into protest as a baby—'the Youngest Freedom Marcher"—our political life of rallies and marches, my mother's active participation in the Grenadian and Nicaraguan revolutions, and her work in Namibia as an observer of their free elections when the people finally wrestled their country away from South Africa. I told Denise and Sandra about my mother's work as a legal secretary at the New York Civil Liberties Union and the Center for Constitutional Rights, where she was also the office manager. At the Center she befriended Dolly Filartiga, who sued Paraguay on behalf of her brother Joel after he was kidnapped and tortured in 1976.¹⁶ I told them how she worked on Filartiga's case, as well as the Panamanian invasion case. I shared my mother's adage "Today's liberal, tomorrow's racist," and then told them about my mother's illegal and humiliating firing as a disabled woman from the Center for Constitutional Rights by "white liberals" Arthur Kinoy, William Kunstler, and Michael Ratner, and African American executive director Ron Daniels. Joan Gibbs, my mother's friend and coworker at the Center, reminded me in a conversation that these men with deliberate and malicious intent canceled my mother's health insurance. I reveled in telling Denise and Sandra of the amazing support my mother received when the majority of the staff went on strike on her behalf. I told them how the strikers and my mother gained her reinstatement by obtaining the December 8, 1994, strike settlement. But given the hostile work environment she chose to retire and then died that summer at age fifty-three.¹⁷ They both urged me to write about my mother, and about our life. I didn't think we had led an extraordinary life and dismissed their suggestion.

In 2003 I met Dr. Carole Boyce Davies, chair of Africana studies at Florida International University, while I was a professor at Florida Memorial College. I shared with her my mother's life. Carole insisted that my mother's life was quite remarkable, and that my childhood was not an ordinary one. She insisted that I must write about my mother. Again, I set aside any idea of writing my mother's story.

In 2005 I met Dr. Gloria Dickinson, chair of the African American Studies Department at the College of New Jersey, where I was a professor. I told her of my mother's life. Like Boyce Davies, Ferreira Da Silva, and Angeleri, she too said that I must tell my mother's story, that it was not the typical family history, that my family background was incredibly unique.

Still raw, still suffering from the insurmountable pain of my mother's death, but with the urging of these four African-descended women, I began to work on this book, traveling to archives across the country and even to Grenada. In 2009 I began giving talks at academic conferences in the United States and the Caribbean. In 2014 my chapter "Mae Mallory and 'the Southern Belle Fantasy Trope' at the Cuyahoga County Jail 21st and Payne/'Pain'" appeared in *From Uncle Tom's Cabin to The Help*, edited by Claire Oberon Garcia, Vershawn Ashanti Young, and Charise Pimentel (Palgrave Macmillan). Keeping some scholarly distance as dictated by my historical training, I began to tell this story through the prism, the lens of Mae Mallory. Muted.

And then in 2009 I met graduate student Yie Yin Foong at Sarah Lawrence College. She contacted me because she was writing her master's thesis "Frame Up in Monroe: The Mae Mallory Story" and wanted some advice and suggestions.[18] Yie, a kind, gentle, and thoughtful young woman, was the first scholar to interview Pat Mallory Oduba, Mae's daughter. Yie was the very first person to get Mae's FBI files, and her master's thesis is very well written. I honor Ms. Foong. Yie idolized Mae Mallory and followed Mallory's path into the field of social work. After our correspondence, Carole Boyce Davies arranged for me to give a talk on Mae and my mother at Sarah Lawrence. Yie and I met before the lecture. At the talk, knowing of the Seniors and Mallory families' bond, Ms. Foong stood up and asked me in front of the packed auditorium what my relationship to Mae and Audrey Proctor was. At this early point, I used my mother's maiden name to mask my relationship to the research. I waffled and tried to avoid answering the question. Yie was having none of that and demanded that I reveal that the story I was telling was my own family history, my family legacy. She forced me to reveal this truth. A true moment of discomfort opened up—the Truth, THE TRUTH . . . For that moment and what has followed I am truly very grateful and indebted to Yie for pushing me, and for making it very clear that these women's stories, my family's story, could not be told from an academic or critical distance.

Mae Mallory, the Monroe Defense Committee, and World Revolutions

Introduction

I am not sitting here in jail holding my hands and crying either, I am fighting as hard as I possibly can with my pencil and through the media.... No Conrad, I am not sitting in jail feeling sorry for myself and licking my wounds. I am the same Mae Mallory I've always been perhaps a little wiser and more militant. I am as always For Freedom Now!
—Mae to Black lawyer Conrad Lynn, September 1962

In 1961 thirty-four-year-old Mae Mallory, an African American working-class self-defense advocate, traveled from New York City to Monroe, North Carolina, to provide support and weapons to the Negroes with Guns movement. The state accused her of kidnapping a Ku Klux Klan couple. After escaping to Cleveland, Ohio, she spent thirteen months in a jail there and faced extradition back to Monroe. In response, a group of what I call "African American Women Radical Activists"—my mother, Audrey Proctor Seniors, age twenty-one; Ruthie Stone (probably age twenty-one); and forty-five-year-old Mrs. Ethel Azalea Johnson, my adopted grandmother—along with my father, Clarence Henry Seniors, age twenty-five, and the Workers World Party, founded the Monroe Defense Committee (MDC) to support Mallory, with Ruthie Stone as secretary. Patricia Mallory, Mae's sixteen-year-old daughter, also took on an active role in the MDC. They were separated by decades and generations, yet they had a common goal: African American freedom, Mae's freedom. Mae's case bonded us to Johnson and the Mallorys as family. I did not know as a child the circumstances that brought the Seniorses and the Mallorys together as a family; I just knew that we were. These women fully rejected the public face of the mainstream civil rights movement of gradualism, a nonviolence/passive resistance movement, which resulted in images of African Americans' brutalization and death.[1] This movement never publicly showed the reality that in many cases the marchers and leaders found themselves protected by armed men and women. According to Charles E. Cobb, people like Martin Luther King Jr. maintained a home arsenal "just for self-defense," while encouraging youth from the Student Nonviolent Coordinating Committee to join SCLC and "commit to nonviolence as a way of life." Students rejected his proposal.[2] Most SNCC members were southerners who grew up with guns and knew how to use them. A SNCC member maintained that "acceptance of nonviolence as a way of life was not something we could commit to, and I think Dr. King made a mistake in asking us to do it."[3] This complicates our understanding of the nonviolence/passive resistance movement, for as Emilye Crosby notes, "Community-based movements often combined nonviolent protest methods with armed self-defense."[4] With all this, the conservative civil rights leaders like King publicly condemned the self-defense strategies of the Negroes with Guns movement. Ethel Azalea Johnson, Mae Mallory, Audrey Proctor Seniors, Ruthie Stone, Pat Mallory, and Clarence Henry Seniors defiantly signed all their correspondence "For Freedom Now," declaring their devotion to freedom, self-defense, and the urgency of the fight for civil and human rights.

For African American women radical activists struggling during this era, the idea of "For Freedom Now" took on added meaning and agency because it alluded to the gendered and racialized nature of white supremacist oppression that African American women suffered. In 1958, after the attempted rape and brutal beatings of two African American women by white men who were later acquitted, it was Monroe's African American women who compelled the president of the National Association for the Advancement of Colored People (NAACP), Robert F. Williams, to establish the Negroes with Guns movement. Black women, as this book will show, remained firmly at the center of this movement as active participants. My adopted grandmother Ethel Azalea Johnson helped found the Negroes with Guns movement. With Williams, she also established the Crusaders' Association for Relief and Enlightenment, a riff on CARE, the global humanitarian organization. CARE House distributed food and clothing to African Americans in need. Johnson also founded educational organizations: the Citizenship School, an adult education program, a preschool program, and a Head Start program. She edited the Negroes with Guns newspaper, the *Crusader*, and wrote the column "Did You Know." Johnson founded and was the first chair of Philadelphia's Revolutionary Action Movement. She was also an active member of the Monroe Defense Committee, and she created, published, wrote, and edited the newsletter *Did You Know*, the media arm of MDC. She published her work as Mrs. E. A. Johnson and also used the nom de plume

Asa Lee to mask her gender and to battle against white supremacists' language of suppression. White supremacists refused to call African American women "Miss" or "Mrs." They preferred degrading them, calling them "girl" or "auntie," or using their first names to maintain the social order and keep African American women in place. By using pseudonyms, Johnson ensured that whites would have no choice but to respect her.[5]

Mae Mallory fought through legal means to desegregate the New York City public schools. She founded the Crusader Family/Crusaders for Freedom in Harlem in support of Monroe's Negroes with Guns movement. Because of her activism, Mae became a political prisoner in New York, Cleveland, and Monroe. As a teenager, my mother, Audrey Proctor Seniors, joined the banned and notoriously radical and leftist New Orleans National Association for the Advancement of Colored People. She founded the Monroe Defense Committee, fought to desegregate Cleveland's public schools, belonged to the Trotskyist Workers World Party and Youth against War and Fascism (YAWF), and edited YAWF's *Partisan* magazine. My mother also belonged to the New York Black Panthers and fought to end the Vietnam War and other wars against communities of color across the globe.

Pat Mallory's life marked a place, time, and generational difference between Mrs. Johnson, Mae Mallory, and Audrey Proctor Seniors, who were twenty-nine, eighteen, and five years older than Pat, respectively. After a difficult childhood, at the age of twelve, Patricia Mallory found herself at the center of the lawsuit to desegregate New York's public schools. Not fully understanding the suit, not really engaged or wanting to participate, and overwhelmed by her mother's ambitions, she shrank into herself. She eventually found meaning for herself in high school where she came into her own. She became politically and socially involved in socialist, Black Nationalist, Yoruba Temple, Nation of Islam, and civil rights activities. In Cleveland, Pat and Mae met my mother and father, who were thirteen and nine years younger than Mae, and five and nine years older than Pat. In 1961 they became a solid family, and I joined them upon my birth in 1963. Pat looked to my mother (age twenty-one to Pat's sixteen) as an older sister, a mentor, a friend. Patricia worked with my parents on Mae's case through the Monroe Defense Committee and the WWP. She emerged as a Black Nationalist rebel girl.

These working-class women aligned themselves with a self-defense ideology that combined a range of leftist theories such as Trotskyism, Maoism, Cubanismo, Black nationalism, and African socialism. They fought for human and civil rights in the United States for African Americans, Majority World Americans, the working class, and the poor. Through the lens of socialism, African American women radicals connected African American oppression to European imperialist and colonialist projects in Africa, Asia, Latin America, and the Caribbean. Ethel Azalea Johnson, Mae Mallory, Audrey Proctor Seniors, and Pat Mallory fought to end colonialism and imperialism in the United States and around the world. They created cross-racial and class alliances, worked for peace through anti-war movements, and advocated for women's and children's rights. Notwithstanding their critical contributions, the historical narrative of the civil and human rights movement has largely excluded these women in favor of the palatable, preferably Black male revolutionary, Robert F. Williams, or the pleasant and pretty Black middle-class leftist revolutionary, Angela Davis.

Ethel Azalea Johnson, Mae Mallory, Audrey Proctor Seniors, and Patricia Mallory did not fit the prototypical model of African American women in conservative civil rights organizations such as the National Council of Negro Women, nor the leftist Black middle-class women's groups. These were everyday women. They publicly criticized conservative civil rights activists. They stood against patriarchy and misogyny. They adhered to radical leftist ideologies. They had public ruptures with Black males in the movement, including Robert F. Williams and other Black men. Charles Cobb and others advanced the notion that Black women activists are dead and unresearchable. All of these variables led to their deliberate exclusion from history books, by misogynistic and anti-communist historians. Their political stances made them more vulnerable to violence and persecution for their actions. Their working-class pedigree, devotion to self-defense, leftist ideology, internationalism, Pan-Africanism, and stance against patriarchy and misogyny, as well as Pat's connection to the Yoruba Temple and the Nation of Islam, marked them as revolutionary, defying categorization.

Disappointed with the outcomes of the civil rights movement and legislation that left the poor and working class behind, in the 1970s and 1980s Mae Mallory, Patricia Mallory, and Audrey Proctor Seniors joined international revolutionary movements in Tanzania, Grenada, and Nicaragua. The Mallorys worked in the Tanzanian government for five years, while my mother traveled to Grenada and Nicaragua and actively participated in these Marxist/socialist revolutions. Through her writing, Mrs. Johnson participated in world revolutions by advocating for the end of colonialism, imperialism, and war in the Majority World. These women connected the fight for African American civil rights to world revolutions.

In this book I offer historical analysis, archival research, sociology of art, textual analysis, and interdisciplinary studies, along with my personal remembrances. I also use Wilson Currin Snipes's character sketch and biographical exposition. I move beyond his definition of the "impersonal biography," given my personal relationship to this work and my assertion that "no historical record remains critically distanced." With all these methodologies, I holistically chronicle the radicalization and history of Ethel Azalea Johnson, Mae Mallory, Audrey Proctor Seniors, and Patricia Mallory.[6]

Through their writings and protests, and as socialist theorists, Mae Mallory, Ethel Azalea Johnson, Audrey Proctor Seniors, and Patricia Mallory emerged as what Antonio Gramsci and George Lipsitz define as organic intellectuals. They studied their world and disseminated "their ideas through social contestation," guiding the thoughts and desires of their "class" without an official intellectual position. These women personified Ula Taylor's community feminist, conjoining feminism and nationalism, to take on the role of leaders and helpmates in their communities. As Patricia Hill Collins's everyday political activists, they mirrored slave mothers and promoted and used the education of their children as a tool of liberation and resistance. They coupled organic intellectualism, community feminism, and everyday political activism with M. Bahati Kuumba's motherist frame. The motherist frame is the "justification for social action based on the mothering attributes of nurturance and responsibility for the family." Ultimately, Johnson, Mallory, and Seniors used their roles as mothers and wives as "justification for their resistance."[7]

The overarching question here is why these working-class African American women chose radical activism—Maoism, Trotskyism, Cubanismo, African socialism, and self-defense—to promote civil and human rights and justice in the United States. This book explores why they aligned themselves with revolutionary governments and linked the struggle for African American civil and human rights to world revolutions.

Part I
Histories, Influences, Activism and Writing Resistance

Fig. 1. Ethel Azalea Johnson, Audrey and Clarence Seniors Collection.

Chapter 1

Mrs. Ethel Azalea Johnson

Motherhood, Self-Defense, and the Negroes with Guns Movement

Mrs. Johnson always traveled with us from town to town for protest meetings as our babysitter for she loved her granddaughter. She had the best car and preferred driving. She knew everyone in North Carolina. Her friends welcomed us with first-class treatment and excellently prepared meals.... We spent hours at Mrs. Johnson's house working with her on "Did You Know?," drinking beer and listening to her extensive jazz collection, including Nina Simone's "Mississippi Goddam."

—Clarence Henry Seniors

Self-Defense Ideology

On August 8, 1959, Mrs. Johnson (age forty-three), secretary, eventual vice president, and founding member of the Negroes with Guns movement in Monroe, North Carolina, wrote:

> As the slaves rebelled again and again against their masters, with unyielding determination, [they did not] let up ... so must the Black race grasp the torch that Nat Turner and others have handed to us and hold it high by continuously fighting for freedom, with all the resources at hand. Rebel against all phases of injustice. Do not compromise with anything short of equality. If defeated in one effort, start another; if knocked in the mud in the freedom fight, let it dry[,] brush it off and go on.[1]

She published these words in her "Did You Know?" column in the *Crusader*, the literary arm of the movement. In 1963 she created the newsletter *Did You Know?* and published it with help from my parents, Audrey Proctor and Clarence Henry Seniors. She seized the torch of self-defense ceremonially passed down to her by Nat Turner, Harriet Tubman, and other freedom fighters. From the 1950s, beginning with the Negroes with Guns movement, to the 1970s, she cast down the gauntlet for African American warlike resistance against white supremacist terrorism.[2]

In 1942 Mrs. Johnson moved to Monroe from her hometown of Abbeville, South Carolina, an African American historical community of struggle and resistance. Her mother infused in her an ideology of self-defense. This ideology was cultivated through the ages by resistant militaristically combat-ready, intellectually gifted enslaved and free Africans. In Monroe she married Raymond Johnson, a Seaboard Air Line Railroad worker. They had a son, Raymond Jr. The FBI reported that as of 1953 Mrs. Johnson worked in Monroe at the Carolina Laundry and Cleaners, the Seaboard Air Line Railroad, and, for two years, at the Continental Insurance Company (n.d.).[3] Given her spirit of independence, selling insurance and merchandise empowered her, allowing her to work in a professional rather than a menial job. Her work environment remained free from the white gaze. Selling insurance buffered her from the constant barrage of white supremacist dominance because she worked exclusively for African Americans. Selling insurance and merchandise paved the way for her independent businesswoman status, meeting and politically mobilizing African Americans in Monroe, Charlotte, and North Carolina Black communities. The job, according to Timothy Tyson, gave her the opportunity to "pursue her community activism with less fear of white economic reprisals."[4] Because of her work travels, she saw Blacks' dire social and economic conditions, providing fuel for her activism.

Negroes with Guns

In 1955 Johnson became the lone woman in a position of power as the secretary and eventual vice president of Monroe's National Association for the Advancement of Colored People. It morphed into the Committee to Combat Racial Injustice and Negroes with Guns movement. She edited, financially managed, and published the *Crusader*, writing the column "Did You Know?," all under the leadership of African American president Robert F. Williams. Raymond Johnson joined in these efforts with his wife.[5]

Monroe native Williams married Mabel Robinson. He faced overt rac-

Fig. 2. From left, Harold Reape, Mae Mallory, and Richard Crowder [Yusef]. Paula Marie Seniors Collection.

ism as a soldier during World War II and the Korean War. After his military service, he received an education in Black militant and communist ideology while a member of the United Auto Workers and Congress of Industrial Organizations at Detroit's Cadillac Automobile Company. He attended North Carolina College for Negroes on the GI Bill. These experiences led him to radical activism as the president of Monroe's NAACP.[6] The wealthy African American Dr. Albert E. Perry (1921–1972) became the vice president. Perry married Monroe schoolteacher Bertha Mae Brooks. Dr. Perry, a devout Catholic, hailed from Austin, Texas, graduated from Meharry Medical School, and was a World War II veteran and member of the American Legion.[7] According to Akinyele Umoja, before the change in leadership Monroe's NAACP was just another elite Black social club. Johnson, Williams, and Perry transformed it into the Negroes with Guns movement.[8] The 1954 *Brown v. Board of Education* case and the white supremacist response to the NAACP's human rights efforts marked a change in Monroe's NAACP. The Ku Klux Klan, the Citizen Council, and white supremacist organizations escalated terroristic violence and economic sanctions against NAACP members. When Monroe's NAACP members successfully made demands that Union County hire an African American police officer and pave the Black district's Fourth Street, white supremacists forced the firing of Black teachers and members who worked for whites. They compelled banks and the state to deny NAACP members bank loans and building permits.[9] These strategies led to a huge drop in membership—to six, including Dr. Perry.[10] According to George Weisman, aka George Lavan, founder of the Socialist Workers Party, "Williams had almost despaired of the task [of rebuilding] when the idea occurred to him of building the branch without the social leaders of the community."[11] Williams wrote, "I was passing a noisy billiard parlor, [and] I decided to try recruiting among this most oppressed and exploited group.... I wrote six memberships on the billiard table and others promised to join. The ranks began to fill with construction workers, [farmers], the unemployed and domestic workers."[12] About his NAACP work he later said, "We ended up with a chapter that was unique in the whole NAACP because of [its] working class composition and leadership. We had a strong representation of returned veterans who were very militant, didn't scare easy."[13] In 1955 Johnson, Williams, and Perry built the organization from the bottom, with African American women, the working class, and the poor firmly at the center, discarding the Black elite's practice of excluding them. African American working-class women readily joined.

According to the FBI and Mrs. Johnson, in 1956 she and her husband became lifelong friends of the Williamses, a bond most certainly forged because they all lived on Boyte Street. The FBI reported that she was a "rabid follower of Robert F. Williams," was involved with "racial activities," and advocated for Black Nationalism.[14] The FBI did not at this time include her on the communist detention list, nor did they classify her as belonging to a "subversive group."[15] Ethel and other working-class Black women, the majority of whom were domestics, demanded weapons training because, according to Williams, "they wanted to fight." Mabel Williams noted that African American women "push[ed] harder than the men.... That is where the drive is coming from."[16] Johnson, the Williamses, and Albert Perry built Monroe's NAACP on the backs of combat-ready African American women with Mrs. Johnson and Mabel Williams at the center.

Monroe's NAACP was one of the most militant branches in the United States given the combat-ready working-class women and military veterans. Attempting to desegregate a swimming pool built with public money at a white country club led to an increase in Klan resistance. They regularly drove through the Black community in full regalia firing weapons at citizens.[17] These assaults led to the establishment of a defense guard, and an alert system of armed women and men who went to scenes of white supremacist violence. They also obtained a charter for a rifle club for NAACP members, and they used weapons they bought themselves or got from northern supporters—Julian Mayfield and Mae Mallory. Mallory founded Harlem's Crusader Family/Crusaders for Freedom to support them.[18]

My father, Clarence Henry Seniors, says that Dr. Perry owned a farm *and* "a palatial well-appointed house on The Hill," a few blocks away from the Williamses and the Johnsons. This inflamed the Klan, who believed that Perry subsidized Williams. They blacklisted Williams with employers.[19] According to Williams, "Dr. Perry had long been the target of insults by racists and city officials because he had built a home considered much too elegant for Afro-Americans on a choice piece of land overlooking a highway."[20]

Williams recalled the first time the Klan attacked Perry's home, when "over two hundred men and even some women, showed up armed with sticks, knives and guns."[21] October 5, 1957, a Klan motorcade attacked Perry's home. They came in contact with a home resembling a "military installation," with foxholes and sandbags. Williams wrote that "Afro Americans ran openly in the streets with arms, [charging] the police lines. . . . The police were afraid to enforce their unheeded orders." The defense guards met the Klan's gunfire with soldierly might, shooting low, not to kill but to rid the neighborhood of them. Williams recalled, "The Klan didn't have anymore stomach for this type of fight. . . . The next day Monroe's City Council banned Ku Klux Klan motorcades."[22]

The defense guard and the Rifle Club marked the foundation of the Negroes with Guns movement. They began training and raising money to buy advanced weaponry, steel helmets, gas masks, and high-caliber military surplus rifles. The attacks on African Americans subsided briefly, but unlike the Klan's retreat after the indigenous Lumbee victory, white supremacists sanctioned by the FBI would not back down when it came to Black self-defense.[23] To suppress the Black community, Chief Mauney told the FBI that Williams advocated for violence, purchased "a large volume of arms and ammunition, and recruited a number of teenage Negroes as followers."[24]

White supremacists amped up their efforts. In 1957 the state incarcerated Dr. Perry for performing illegal abortions, one on white woman malefactor Lillie Mae Rape. His Catholicism bound him from such actions. Armed Black women, one of whom most certainly was Mrs. Johnson, gathered at the police station in support of Perry, showing the state Black women's pugnacious might. Perry lost his license and found himself exiled from Monroe, with only his wife's teaching income to support them. Eventually, all charges were reversed, and Perry moved his practice to Charlotte.[25] On November 18, 1957, white supremacists murdered African Americans Mr. and Mrs. Clay of East Flat Rock, North Carolina, in their home. In 1958 Monroe's famous Kissing Case occurred. Police arrested, beat, and terrorized Hanover Thompson, age nine, and David Simpson, age seven, charged them with rape, and threatened them with the death penalty. The incarceration and brutalization of the boys in jail occurred because a white girl kissed Thompson. The girl's mother pressed for their arrest. The Kissing Case marked a turning point for Monroe's NAACP. The NAACP national office refused to get involved with the Kissing Case, willfully letting the boys languish in jail for two months. North Carolina's NAACP president, Kelly Alexander, distanced the state's branches from Monroe, fearing the label "communist." The NAACP's inaction and refusal to help at the local and national levels led Monroe's NAACP to establish the Committee to Combat Racial Injustice to help Thompson and Simpson. They hired the African American lawyer Conrad Lynn, and the case gained international attention. In 1959 the state released the boys to their mothers, who promptly moved their families to Charlotte.[26]

Mrs. Johnson: Motherhood and Negroes with Guns

In 1959 Monroe's NAACP took on two significant cases that centered on African American motherhood and womanhood, setting the self-defense tone of the organization as one that fully supported protecting Black womanhood. Mae Mallory wrote in *Memo from a Monroe Jail* that in 1959 Mrs. Georgia White, a mother of five, "a Black woman who worked as a maid[,] was kicked down the stairs of Monroe's local hotel. A white patron, B. F. Shaw, an engineer, decided that she was making too much noise."[27] A drunken white mechanic, Lewis Medlin, broke into the house of pregnant mother Mrs. Mary Ruth Reed and raped her in front of her six-year-old son and a white neighbor woman. Her son tried to "defend his mother," and Medlin beat him.[28] These white men participated in what Joy James defines as rape for game, a ceremonial and formalized activity marking communal solidarity in white manhood.[29] Monroe's Black women led the charge for justice. According to Robert F. Williams, "A lot of the Negro women wanted to get together and lynch that white man [Medlin]." They "wanted to go and machine gun his house, using the new machine guns that Julian Mayfield had brought to Monroe."[30] Black men were similarly outraged: "The brothers of Mary Ruth Reed wanted to go and blow his house up ... [and] kill her white attacker before the trial began," and several community members threatened to beat Shaw to death.[31]

In 1959 Mrs. Reed and Mrs. White courageously brought their attackers to court, only to face humiliation. At Mrs. Reed's trial the defense attorney debased her by displaying the defendant's wife as "one of God's lovely creatures, a pure flower." The prosecutor pointed to the attacker's wife and said, "See there sitting next to this man, the beautiful white flower of the South. This is what he has waiting at home for his return. . . . What does he want with that?" he asked, pointing at the Black woman involved in the case. "If this man touched that thing in any way he was probably drunk and having some fun."[32]

Consequently, they lost their cases.[33] But with their defeat, Mrs. Johnson and Monroe's Black women "vowed that 'never again, would a Black woman sit and be belittled before a crowd under the pretense of trying the assailant,'" for as Johnson would pronounce, from the inception of the Negroes with Guns movement, "The only alternative Black people have left is a self-defense policy."[34] "The [Monroe] authorities stopped at nothing legally or illegally to crush Williams's efforts. Members were imprisoned on false charges, harassed, and abused. Armed racist terrorist activities were encouraged by the local police. Getting no help from the law, Williams found that they had to 'meet violence with violence,' to protect themselves. Armed self-defense guards were organized."[35]

In 1959 this covenant led Monroe's African American women to force the NAACP, the Monroe Rifle Club, and the Committee to Combat Racial Injustice to transform into the Negroes with Guns movement, to protect women and children with arms. Williams noted that "Monroe justice has left Negroes no choice but to repel the spot attacks by white persons. The colored community has been armed for some time and it was their determination to defend themselves which succeeded in ending Klan violence last year." The retrograde accommodationist ideology of North Carolina's NAACP and the national organization led to this action.[36] The inaction of the state and the national NAACP, as well as the violent assaults on Monroe's children and women, led women to demand an ideological shift in the organization—to an armed Monroe NAACP and then to Negroes with Guns. With this action, the national NAACP leader Roy Wilkins suspended Williams.[37] Mrs. Johnson would not stand for this action: "We will not accept their decision. If it means losing our charter and going it alone we are prepared to do this. Despite continued reprisals against the colored community, the National office has given us no help, and everyone is angered by the leadership who don't know what it is to live in the South and expect us to lie down and cry before the race supremacists."[38]

Johnson vowed an allegiance to self-defense to protect Black girls and women, notwithstanding the NAACP's resistance.[39] Because of the NAACP's biracial nature, along with members such as white board chair Joel Elias Spingarn, the national face of the NAACP was that of passive resistance/nonviolent action. As a military intelligence officer during World War I, Spingarn headed investigations into African American loyalties under the auspices of the Military Intelligence Division. His early influence colored the NAACP's beliefs and their stance against Black self-defense. I contend that Spingarn's presence paved the way for agent provocateurs and informers in the organization.[40]

Crusader, "Did You Know?" and Self-Defense

In June 1959 Ethel Azalea Johnson, Robert F. Williams, and Mabel Williams founded the *Crusader* newsletter, the literary arm of the movement, "to educate and agitate."[41] They "felt a need for a southern journal that would reflect the sentiment of America's most ruthlessly oppressed class.... We wanted an autonomous people's journal that [focused] the attention of the world upon the captive people status of the American negro." The *Crusader* promoted an Afrocentric ideology and self-defense, coupled with an antiracist, anti-imperialist, anti-colonialist, and antiwar ideology.[42] Johnson's column "Did You Know?" appeared in the paper from its very first issue. She wrote under the alias Asa Lee, which she chose given southerners' pronunciation of her name Azalea, to hide her gender and defy the white southern custom of debasing Black women through the language of suppression. She infused "Did You Know?" with African-centered lessons, life lessons her mother taught her, and lessons she learned through Abbeville's historical community of struggle and resistance. Johnson suffused her columns with African-centered pride, taught her readers about her outreach and CARE programs, and charged readers with committing themselves to social action and self-defense. Ethel challenged them to rally and rise up against colonialism, imperialism, and racism in the United States and around the world.[43] The Negroes with Guns movement used the newsletter to promote self-defense, report on events in Monroe's Black community, challenge segregation, and actively oppose white supremacist violence against African Americans, the colonized, and the oppressed. The Williamses and Johnson compelled readers to demand governmental law and order to stop terroristic rapes, violence, and murders of Monroe's African Americans. They published stories on revolutionary movements in Cuba, China, Africa, Asia, and

Latin America; in this way they promoted cross-racial solidarity. Cynthia A. Young notes that Johnson and the Williamses worked "to forge an international network of radicals" and "disseminated news censored by the mainstream media," which led them to condemn censorship.[44] The *Crusader* reported news that the white press and the conservative Black press refused to publish. Mrs. Johnson personally called out Black conservatives and African American ministers for their attempt to maintain the status quo. She promoted self-defense and wrote stories that proved relevant to her community. The mission of the *Crusader* and "Did You Know?" mirrored that of Negroes with Guns' representation of working-class and poor members. The *Crusader* became the voice of the silenced.

In "All I Could Do Was Cry," Mrs. Johnson presented her case for Black self-defense. Johnson writes of an African American male passive resister who told a Monroe audience of his commitment to nonviolence, of passive resisters' brutalization by white fascists, broken jaws with brass knuckles, and water hosings. He told them of his own assault, not at a sit-in but while driving home—of the nightstick tearing at his hands, and spit and curses spewed at him. He recounted that although he had a gun in his back pocket, he pledged to "NEVER FIGHT BACK. He was very angry because he'd done nothing wrong and wasn't demonstrating." The young man's words elucidate how the act of demonstrating in a Black male body justified being brutalized. "The heavy blows caused excruciating pain, but [he said] "All I Could Do was Cry." Johnson continued, "Well, at this point of his story, everyone who was listening was expecting another type of ending, judging from the disappointed expressions on their faces. I walked away in deep thought. I wondered if the young leader thought he had acted noble. To me his actions in the incident was just plain stupid."[45]

Her critique brings to light questions concerning the effectiveness of passive resistance. NAACP member Dr. Hayling of Saint Augustine, Florida, recalled that in 1964 they adopted a self-defense strategy when confronted with white supremacist carnage.[46] Cynthia Griggs Fleming argues that many Black SNCC members struggled with the idea of passive resistance, given their parents' lessons of self-defense and their belief that women and men had the right to bear arms for protection and to practice self-defense. Some refused victimization by white supremacists protecting themselves with weapons.[47] African American scholar and SNCC member Joyce Ladner recounted that "all of our parents had guns in the house . . . and they were not only for hunting rabbits and squirrels, but out of self-defense."[48] SNCC's executive secretary, African American Ruby Doris Smith Robinson, expressed frustration in a 1964 meeting concerning their support of nonviolence. "In

1961 people had arms, but nothing was made of it," and exposing people to violence without a self-defense strategy proved counterproductive.[49] Mrs. Johnson noted, "The young leader has been, along with many more sit-iners, brainwashed. [They] will no doubt go through life, being pushed around because all the fighting spirit in them has been crushed. They may become a delaying force to immediate freedom because of their pacifist training, when they are violently attacked, "All They Can Do is Cry." Johnson reveals the idiocy of not fighting back when assaulted. She believed that the nonviolence movement would slow down the process for social change. She connected the U.S. nonviolence movement to the work of Mahatma Gandhi and questioned its success. "Have the conditions of the miserable people of India improved to the extent that they are free, with a better life for all?" She maintained that Gandhi's efforts did not uplift impoverished Indians, and a similar approach would not uplift poor Blacks. She argued that only the Black elite leaders and Blacks in power in the passive resistance movement would benefit, a presage of things to come: "Somebody has sold Afro-Americans the idea of turning the other cheek [to gain] social acceptance. Somebody has sold Afro Americans the idea that if you beg for your rights, you'll get them. 'Shake the moral thinking of the whites,' they say, 'worry their consciences.' What a laugh!"[50]

Johnson suggests that passive resistance did not originate with African Americans, and she was right, given the FBI's efforts to disrupt and destroy Black political movements. Ladner and others questioned the origin of the passive resistance strategy. V. P. Franklin notes that agents provocateurs infiltrated the Black Panther Party, including FBI informant and party member Richard Matsui Aoki, who gave Panthers their first guns. The FBI put in place disruption programs targeted at the Committee to Aid the Monroe Defendants, the Trotskyist/Maoist Workers World Party, and the Monroe Defense Committee to keep the groups in conflict with each other. They kept up heavy surveillance of Ethel Azalea Johnson, my parents, Mae Mallory, and her daughter Pat, hiring numerous spies and informants who reported on them *in every city in which they lived*. Consequently, Johnson's assertion that passive resistance tactics originated outside of SNCC, NAACP, and CORE is highly plausible, given the multiracial nature of these organizations, which most certainly opened them up to FBI infiltrators and informants like Joel Elias Spingarn, Richard Matsui Aoki, and countless others. This also gives credence to why Black members of these groups questioned passive resistance as a strategy.[51] Johnson continued her critique: "The 300 years of slavery didn't shake their moral thinking, nor worried their consciences. The many insurrections led by Nat Turner and others certainly played an integral part in showing the whites, how wrong slavery was." She proposed that slave revolts proved the only clear method for ensuring that white supremacists would honor African American rights. Thus self-defense proved the only real strategy for obtaining their rights. Holding Black civil rights leaders such as Martin Luther King Jr. and Black ministers accountable for passive resistance, Johnson asks, "Is there collusion between our African American national leaders and the rich capitalists, in all this? Afro-American masses need to start thinking FOR THEMSELVES. For as long as we allow our present national leaders to map our course of action for freedom, we will remain in bondage, because seemingly our so called national leaders, along with racist whites are dedicated to keeping the status-quo."[52] Her analysis is spot on because these conservative movements benefited Black elites and civil rights leaders who left the poor and working class behind, in crumbling urban centers, with no social services, inadequate education, and few opportunities except military service, while they moved to the suburbs and their children attended elite white institutions.[53] Throughout her writing career, Johnson charged African American conservative leaders with complicity with maintaining the status quo for personal gain.

> Yes, North Carolina's sophisticated brand of segregation is acceptable and being crammed down the throats of the states would be Militant Black youths by the state's respectable Black leadership, who are contented with loads of prestige and a few white-collar jobs for college grads that high school whites formerly held. They consider this freedom. They themselves would have militant minded Black leaders beaten, jailed or killed to keep the peace in the state.[54]

With this statement she undergirds her argument for self-defense and the Black elite's complicity in maintaining the status quo through passive resistance/nonviolent action. Self-defense was not a new proposition given the Louisiana Slave Revolt (1811); African Americans' defense of their community in Blossburg, Alabama (1899); Tulsa's paramilitary African Blood Brotherhood's sharpshooter military might during the Tulsa riots (1921); Grace Campbell's membership in Harlem's African Blood Brotherhood (1921); the 1944 murder by Lena Baker of her white rapist in Albany, Alabama; and eight-year-old Daisy Bates of Huttig, Arkansas, taunting to death her mother's rapist and killer. Like those before her, Mrs. Johnson fully supported and participated in self-defense. She wrote, "Since when is a struggle a peaceful nature? The U.S. Government's ears are deaf, and eyes are blind when Negroes demand protection against the white onslaught in Mississippi. The only alternative is a self-defense policy."[55] Like that of her kindred spirit Grace Campbell, Johnson's writing reflected her commitment to self-defense for Black women and girls. Johnson and Campbell held positions in their organizations and lived by the tenets of self-defense, which leads to the question of how Mrs. Johnson formulated her self-defense ideology. How did her upbringing in Abbeville's African American historical community of struggle and resistance, her mother's life lessons, and her own motherhood inform her self-defense ideology?

Motherhood and Self-Defense

Ethel Azalea Johnson was nurtured by her mother and Abbeville, a historical community of struggle and resistance, teaching her lessons in Black pride and self-defense. The gorgeously brown-skinned Johnson, my adopted grandmother, was born in Abbeville on January 31, 1916, to Sallie Guy and Hilliard Johnson. She had four siblings, and the family belonged to the Saint James African Methodist Episcopal Church.[56] Abbeville was the birth and death place of the Confederacy, a place where whites resisted African American humanity through extreme suppression.[57] In this location Blacks who came from Sierra Leone, Gambia, Angola, and Senegal participated in extreme physical, militaristic, and intellectual resistance to white supremacist violence, repression, enslavement, and its aftermath. In 1848 three Abbeville Black slaves killed their owners. They expressed insolence and remained resolutely unrepentant even while facing the hangman's noose.[58] "[They] said they had done right & expected to be forgiven for it & get to Heaven! They regard themselves as martyrs in the cause of liberty & say they cheerfully die to better the condition of the other [one hundred plus] Blacks on their plantation."[59] African American slaves learned of slave uprisings like the Denmark Vesey revolt (1822) when they traveled to different parts of the Piedmont region, where Abbeville was located. They disseminated the information broadly among themselves. Abbeville's African Americans, including Mrs. Johnson's slave grandparents and mother, taught their children through stories of repression, the triumph of fighting back, the power of insurgency, the lived and historical experiences of Abbeville's African Americans, and yes, of lynching. Johnson wrote, "Many times [my mother] talked to us about the oppressions that all Black people were enduring here in America. She relayed to us dreams and aspirations that her parents had hoped for their children. My grandparents were slaves."[60] Through these stories her family and Abbeville's African Americans cultivated a historical community of struggle and resistance passed down through the generations.

W. E. B. Du Bois writes that in states like South Carolina, where African Americans made up the majority of the population, true radical Reconstruction occurred. They held more power in South Carolina than in any other state, albeit fleetingly. By 1866 South Carolina's white supremacists' violent attacks led the national government to establish martial law, allowing for full Reconstruction. This progressive and equitable new government lasted a little over ten years, with Blacks gaining power. Some accumulated wealth and owned land.[61] By 1868 African Americans outnumbered white voters, put Black men into political office, and established schools, mutual aid societies, secret societies, and churches. They agitated for political change and the full rights of man.

Black power posed a serious threat to South Carolinians' white power, which led to the removal of federal troops (1876–1877), the loss of the vote, terroristic violence, the criminalization and murder of African American political officials, the shuttering of the integrated University of South Carolina's law school (1877), and the legalization of segregated schools, trains, restaurants, hotels, and facilities.[62] Notwithstanding the reversals, Blacks established Abbeville's all-African American collective agrarian community Promise Land, because as sixty-seven-year-old former slave Garrison Frazier stated, "We would prefer to 'live by ourselves' rather than 'scattered among the whites.'" Community members, sharecroppers, and landowners, including the wealthy Anthony Crawford whose formerly enslaved father bequeathed him 427 prime acres worth $25,000, kept socially isolated from whites.[63] Crawford educated his twelve children, gave them farms, and "deferred to no man Black or white," believing that he was both "the equal of some white men and the superior to others."[64] Community members, landed or not, established churches, schools, and mutual aid societies and shared in the leadership of these organizations.[65] The community's tenets—of communal resistance, community building, and self-defense, with a bit of religiosity—provided a model for Johnson's ideology.

Abbeville's African Americans saw education as integral to their growth. From 1866 on, using their own resources, they built and later taught at eleven schools, including Industrial Union of Abbeville County, Ferguson Academy/Harbison College, and Promise Land High School. South Carolina's white supremacists could not allow Black progress. They mismanaged Black schools and gave them little financial support, allotting $1.30 per Black child. In 1881 Abbeville's school term ran for only two months, Promise Land for three months; by the 1930s the school term ran for five months.[66] In 1910 white fascists burned down Ferguson Academy/Harbison College and murdered three Black male students. In 1930 they forced the closing of

Promise Land High School.⁶⁷ The majority of African American women and girls never received a full education and rarely advanced past the third or fourth grade.⁶⁸ Notwithstanding white supremacists' efforts, by 1900 education and literacy rates were high for African American cooks and domestics. Even with a short school term designed to force Black children into full-time service to fill the white demand for child labor, they arose literate. This most certainly accounts for Mrs. Johnson's mother's apparent erudition.

Not only was educational attainment a problem, but living conditions threatened Johnson's family. Her mother "was forced to live in a dilapidated third-class, segregated section of town," and the family lacked material resources. "I can remember many mornings she didn't have breakfast, there wasn't enough food for her after all of her children had eaten. She never allowed this to crush her spirit. She'd always say, 'someday things will be better.' But things never got better for her."⁶⁹

Life was made harder for the family by the disappearance of Ethel's father. He broke with the southern custom of accommodationist language by calling a white man a prevaricator. "I remember the sorrow of my mother when my father had to flee for his life, because he called a white man a liar." Staying in Abbeville meant the risk of lynching for himself, his five children, and his wife. He left the family to ensure their safety, yet the Klan came to the house looking for him. Mrs. Johnson recalled that awful night. "How [our mother] tried to keep us from seeing the white hooded men at the door. We saw them and heard the awful threats too." Johnson's mother stayed steadfast, courageously protecting her children, herself, and her home from the Klan invasion. Yet she was not able to protect the children fully, for they saw and heard the Klan threaten their mother. Johnson wrote that with their father's departure, the children knew the emotional and economic scars the incident left on them, and her mother's employer overworked her as a domestic and laundrywoman.⁷⁰ "My mother had to work so hard to support us. I remember the dim kerosene lamps and the huge pile of white folks clothing to be ironed. She worked long hours and lost her sight later in life, due (said the doctor) to years of eye strain."⁷¹ Johnson's mother's experiences mirrored those of 17 percent of Abbeville/Promise Land's Black women who found themselves single, divorced, widowed, separated, or never married, due to lynching and the mass exodus of African American men, as was the case with Ethel's father, who fled to Abbeville's sister city, Philadelphia, given the lynching threat.⁷² White supremacist bestiality meant the deprivation of the man in the family, breathtaking poverty, the loss of love, and the loss of masculine protection.⁷³

From the 1870s to the 1940s the majority of Promise Land's Black working-class girls and women held jobs similar to work performed during slavery. They made poverty-level wages as domestics, laundresses, cooks, and nursemaids, working long arduous hours; they were locked out of war industry jobs, factory jobs, and unions. The industry preferred white women.[74] This was the Johnsons' lot.

While her job proved brutal and potentially soul-killing, her mother found meaning in her life through her children. She taught them life lessons of revolt, resistance, and domestic labor, which Johnson published in two "Did You Know?" columns. In "As Relayed to Me by a Negro Maid" (October 1, 1960), she discussed her mother, a "widow" (in practice, due to the lynching threat) with five children. Her mother, who worked as a cook and domestic at a white church, found herself transfigured by racist "Christian" white women into a mutation, a thing, less than a dog. "It was a beautiful fall day in Abbeville. The parsonage was a galaxy of lovely fall flowers. . . . Everything was in readiness, awaiting the arrival of the new minister of the local white church and his family. . . . The cook [Johnson's mother] felt rather proud of the dinner, proud to show her culinary skill to the new family." The churchwomen, the minister's wife, "four children and a dog" arrived and Ethel's mother fed them. At the end of the meal "the pastor's wife mentioned the feeding of the dog. She and the other Christian white ladies began raking the leftovers into two plates and told the cook to take one of the plates of food and give it to the dog, and for her to 'sit down and eat your dinner.' [To the amazement of Johnson's mother, she] was given the other plate of leftovers. After she'd cleaned up the kitchen she was 'free to go home.'"[75] Johnson's mother sobbed given the maltreatment, for these "Christian women" believed her unworthy of the compassion they rendered the dog. "He ate his meal before her own."[76] She remembered the thoughtfulness of the pastor's wife's predecessor, who forwent an egg so that she could have a full meal. She treated her with dignity even though they could have gotten in "trouble with the members of their church, and the white racist populace of this small southern town." Wounded and numbed from the incident,

> she sat there thinking and silently crying. Finally, she slowly stood up, took her old coat and hat from off the nail on the back porch. She walked out the door and up the driveway. . . . Night was fast approaching as [she] continued on her way slowly homeward. Her feet ached. Her shoes were run over and needed repair. She didn't know what would become of her and her children now that she'd quit her job. One thing she knew—she'd never go back.[77]

She quit to save her dignity, claim her humanity, and protect herself against inhumane treatment. She went home with the knowledge that she defended herself against white supremacist "Christian" women. *She would not allow them to debase her ever again.* As an everyday political activist within the motherist frame, Mrs. Johnson's mother relayed this story to her children as a lesson in fighting white supremacy—a lesson in self-worth.

Johnson's mother's life work was as a low-wage domestic worker and laundress. As a product of Abbeville's historical community of struggle and resistance, her mother politically schooled her children and taught them life and family lessons, which had the intended effect of implanting seeds of rebellion and revolutionary thought. She embedded an insurgent spirit in her children.

> In her unpolished way, she planted the seeds of discontent in her children—discontent with any and everything inhumane. "Never rest contented," she'd say, "until all men are free." One thing the Jim-Crow laws and discriminatory policies of America did not do to her—break her spirit and lust for freedom. My mother never experienced living as a free person, but she was always free in her heart.[78]

Mrs. Johnson's mother charged her children with putting themselves at the center of fights challenging white supremacy and hegemony. Her mother infused her children with a moral obligation to advocate for social and political change for Blacks and all oppressed people. In 1961 Ethel would use her mother's life lessons to condemn the arrival of the Freedom Riders in Monroe.

Monroe Riot

Given the escalation of violence against Monroe's African American community and the NAACP's decision to arm and defend themselves as the Negroes with Guns movement, the national office of the NAACP, CORE, the Freedom Riders, religious civil rights activists such as Martin Luther King Jr., and SNCC, led by African American James Foreman, sought to teach the Negroes with Guns members the "effectiveness" of nonviolent/passive resistance. These leaders vehemently opposed Williams's self-defense stance and felt that he bungled the Monroe situation. Thus, in August 1961 CORE sponsored and sent the Freedom Riders to Monroe. The FBI reported that they sent eleven white men including John Lowry, seven Black males including Foreman, and one white woman. Notwithstanding their brutal defeats and incarcerations earlier that summer in challenging the Jim Crow transit laws and segregationist policies in public facilities, the Freedom Riders set out to teach Monroe's Black community the efficacy of passive resistance/ nonviolence.[79] That they ventured to Monroe indicates their stupefying ignorance concerning living under siege. Mrs. Johnson reported of Monroe's violence, overwhelming poverty, and Black youth unemployment.[80] She wrote of parents' efforts to prevent their children from joining Monroe's picket lines.

> What unthinking parents don't seem to understand is, that the fire of liberation has started in these youths and is rapidly spreading. These boys are so full of energy and ready to do almost anything for excitement. They are far safer on the picket line since most of them can't get work anyway. [If not for the picket lines] they would be roaming the streets day and night all summer with no organized activity to occupy their time.[81]

The Freedom Riders did not understand the constant threats that this community experienced.

> If Williams' children answer the phone, the whites curse them out. If Mrs. Williams answers, they curse her. When Robert answers, oh boy, then there is really a field day in profanity and threats. Have the white people who make these calls, ever considered that they are angry and ready to "kill" the Williams family, simply because Robert F. Williams desires the same things in life that they do? He hasn't broken any laws. He merely asks that people regardless of color, be permitted to work, eat, live, play and learn together.[82]

Just days before the Freedom Riders arrived in Monroe, Ethel noted that white supremacist violence escalated. On August 7, 1961, she wrote that an "Afro-American lady who had paint dashed in her face, by whites in a fast-moving car, still has the effects of the heinous attack, in her eyes." White supremacists shot into the home of an elderly Black couple not involved in political activities but whose "home nevertheless was not spared in the mounting intimidation of African Americans." Johnson wrote that white supremacists threw garbage cans on the porch of a Black family's home, brutally beat a man at a local restaurant, and used snipers to terrorize the Black community. She concluded, "And so, it goes in peaceful Monroe progressing under beautiful southern skies."[83]

The Freedom Riders knew little or nothing of the constant white supremacist attacks on Boyte Street where the Williamses and the Johnsons lived. They knew nothing concerning the way these families protected themselves with "spontaneous retaliatory firing with much heavier artillery," so that white supremacists who invaded and attacked them "haven't ventured another visit."[84] The Freedom Riders dismissed the effectiveness of the Negroes with Guns movement's self-defense methods, and their strategies of boycotting and sit-ins, *which worked*. These strategies punished Monroe's white racists, like the drugstore proprietors and the white owner of an "open-air market" who shot African American Amos Kiser. Johnson wrote in 1961 that the market "has gone out of business, [and] the drug store where Williams's sit-in case originated has gone out of business too."[85] By venturing to Monroe, the Freedom Riders dismissed Monroe's Black community's methods of survival, of fighting back. In August 1961 they traveled to Monroe bringing a cacophony of chaos and inciting white supremacist violence.[86] Mrs. Johnson, Williams, and Negroes with Guns members made a conscientious effort to de-escalate this very volatile situation.

> All of those who are human enough to believe in justice will join the ranks.... We ask all civilized people to support the Freedom Fighters who have joined us in our struggle. They have proven their dedication in Mississippi, Alabama and other points South. Let us match their courage and dedication!! We invite all Fighters everywhere to join us in our struggle for human dignity. WE WILL WIN

Riffing off of Theodore Roosevelt, they signed off as "Operation Big Stick."[87] The Negroes with Guns members anticipated that Monroe would erupt in white-on-Black violence due to the Freedom Riders' interference. They called for physical support from people all around the country—"Freedom Fighters"—which riffed on Ohio's self-defense organization to buffer the Negroes with Guns movement. They did not express outrage at the Riders' interference in Monroe and instead urged: "If you are a Freedom Fighter or Freedom Rider: Ride, Fly, or Walk to Monroe, the Angola of America. Join us in this noble undertaking for human dignity. We invite people of all philosophies who are dedicated to the cause of freedom. WE WILL WIN."[88]

The Williamses and Johnson made a clear distinction between Freedom Fighters—advocates of self-defense—and nonviolent Freedom Riders. They likened Monroe to the 1961 battle of independence the socialist People's Movement in Angola fought against the murderous Portuguese colonizers.[89] The Negroes with Guns movement called on their friends from around the country for physical support. Mae Mallory traveled to Monroe with Black writer Julian Mayfield, with "two submachine guns and ammunition, sophisticated military rifles," and weapons bought through the Harlem Crusader Family fundraisers. My father said that "Mae got the guns from a Harlem gangster who taught her how to use the machine guns and other weapons." Mallory recalled that Williams "called me up one day. He told me that they expected an attack by the Ku Klux Klan and that he would suggest that all the people that wanted to come down there come." So she did.[90]

In her "Did You Know?" column of August 21, 1961, Mrs. Johnson did not share her own views but rather published Charles M. Levy's "The Dangers of Non-Violence," which explains her stance on the visiting Freedom Riders.

> Once again the Negro finds himself on a slave block. This time he is being sold by non-violence. . . . Non-violence is only an excuse for continuing the conditions that made the Negro a second-class citizen (and this phrase has no meaning; anyone who is less than a first-class citizen is not a citizen . . . he is a first-class outcast). . . . Non-violence gives encouragement and excuses to mistreatment. There is encouragement when Whites know that neither the police nor the Negroes themselves will prevent attacks. There are excuses when the Negro says, 'Whites can't be blamed because they are mentally disturbed.' No group has ever before given its aggressor encouragement and excuses. [Passive resistance] has been widely praised by the white community in the North and even in parts of the South. This support indicates the worthlessness of non-violence activities.

There lies the crux of the problem of the Freedom Riders. Johnson ended the column with her own voice: "No wonder that Jesus Christ said, 'I came not to bring peace, but a sword.'"[91] With religiosity, a firebrand revolutionary spirit, and the gun, Ethel Azalea Johnson made her views concerning the nonviolent Freedom Riders, their visit, and her stance on self-defense crystal clear. She went rogue.

Williams hosted the Freedom Riders and Mae Mallory in his home. Mae did not participate in the marches, given her self-defense stance. They marched without incident every day until Sunday, August 27, 1961. Williams warned them not to march on Sunday. Ignoring his warnings, the Sunday march led to a horrible explosion of white supremacists' carnage as five thousand armed Ku Klux Klan members, including Chief Mauney and police officers, viciously attacked the demonstrators, arresting and beating a seventeen-year-old boy, James Foreman, and many others.[92] "When it became apparent that the vastly outnumbered Afro-Americans and their supporters were in danger of their lives, Williams's self-defense guard jumped into their cars and rode into town to rescue the picketers."[93] The Freedom Riders faced vicious assault, and following southern tradition, the police jailed them.[94] The police and the Klan invaded the African American community, where Blacks met them with superior military force: steel helmets, fortified "fortresses," sandbags, and, according to white Trotskyist actress Constance Webb, wife of C. L. R. James, "weapons [and people] of all descriptions."[95]

Monroe's African American community was at war. Joining in the white supremacist melee was the Ku Klux Klan couple Mr. and Mrs. Bruce Stegall. Mae Mallory wrote in "Monroe! Mississippi! Murder!" that the day before the riot, the couple paraded in the Black community with a banner reading "Open Season on Coons." Robert Williams wrote to Constance Webb that in 1957, when the Klan drove motorcades through Monroe's Black community, the Stegalls leased their land "for a giant Klan rally . . . [that] local papers reported drew as many as 7,500 racists." On Sunday the Stegalls returned to the Black community, and "the enraged masses recognized their car." The Stegalls sought shelter.[96] Mallory recounted in *Free Mae Mallory* that "those crackers beat Rob into his own house" where he allowed them to use the phone to call Chief Mauney. The Williamses gave them sanctuary.[97] *Jet* magazine reported that "Mrs. G. Bruce Stegall told [the] newsman she was not harmed by Negroes."[98]

The *Afro American* reported that Mrs. Stegall originally told "reporters that Williams had chastised his followers for flagging down the Stegall's car. Later she singled out Williams and Mrs. Mallory as ringleaders in the 'kidnapping.'" The Stegalls left unharmed.[99] From 1961 to 1966 the Stegalls changed their story; by 1964 Mrs. Stegall recounted the event like someone who had watched one too many 1930s gangster movies. She said that Mae, sounding like a gangster's moll, told her, "lady don't hand me that sob story. Don't make me get itchy fingers. She had the gun pointed right at me. Mae Mallory told me the quieter I was the longer I'd live."[100] Mallory writes in "Memo from a Monroe Jail" that after the Stegalls' departure, Mauney called them and threatened to "have us all hanging by our heels within thirty minutes."[101] My father says that "Mae and Robert had a huge fight." Williams disagreed with Mae's self-defense methods and strategies. He remained incredibly angry with her during and after the riots and melee with the Stegalls.[102] When they planned their escape from Monroe, Williams told Mae she could not go to Cuba with them. He drove her to New York and unceremoniously dumped her. The Williamses headed to Canada, then to Cuba. Julian Mayfield made his way to Ghana.

True to their word, the Monroe police raided the Williams home and found the house abandoned. The Committee to Aid the Monroe Defendants FBI file from February 2, 1962, noted that someone "was observed carrying boxes from Williams residence." This was presumably Ray Johnson Sr., because in a 1961 letter to Williams he indicated that he had burned the mailing list for the *Crusader* right after the riots, and the FBI found no "reports, mailing lists or any other material from Williams' residence."[103] The FBI arrested Mallory in Cleveland, Ohio, as well as Monroe youths Richard Crowder [Yusef], age nineteen, Harold Reape, seventeen, and white Freedom Rider John Lowry in Monroe. They charged them all with kidnapping the Stegalls, leading to the founding of Cleveland and New York City's Monroe Defense Committee to defend Mallory, Crowder, and Reape. Lowry hired white civil rights attorney William Kunstler. After the riots, Johnson promptly left for Philadelphia and published the *Crusader* there until January 13, 1962.[104]

Mrs. Johnson and the Revolutionary Action Movement

Between 1961 and 1963, Ethel Azalea Johnson traveled between Philadelphia and Monroe. Philadelphia, with its businesses, social organizations, and religious organizations, mirrored those of its sister city, Abbeville. A mass exodus of Abbeville's African Americans to Philadelphia occurred in 1916 given the brutal white supremacist murder of Anthony Crawford. Blacks continued to leave Abbeville between 1916 and 1923. By 1930, one out every two Blacks left South Carolina for Philadelphia.[105] During times of great stress and duress Johnson left Monroe for Philadelphia, where her relatives lived and where she maintained a friendship with nineteen-year-old African American Max Stanford. Philadelphia proved a place of solace and renewal for Johnson, who lived at 2942 French Street after the 1961 riots.[106]

Philadelphia also proved a place where she could continue her activism. According to the FBI, on Sunday, March 17, 1963, she spoke at a mass meeting for Mae Mallory and discussed "the conditions of the African Americans in Monroe." In Philadelphia she published the June/July 1963 *Did You Know?* newsletter. Most importantly, she cofounded and cochaired the Revolutionary Action Movement with Max Stanford, with whom according to my father "she had a good relationship." In 1963 the FBI noted that informants PhT-3 and CE-T told them that Mrs. Johnson "formerly of Monroe, N.C. is Chairman of a Negro organization known as 'RAM,'" that sixteen people belonged to RAM, and they hold discussions on the radio station WHAT.[107]

Although she was cochair, as my father and the FBI file indicate, the extant documents omit her name, exhibiting a masculinist identity with Stanford, Williams, and Don Freeman of Cleveland's Monroe Defense Committee listed. Johnson also published the *Uhuru* newsletter, the literary arm of RAM.[108] To understand Mrs. Johnson's role in RAM we must look at the organization's goals and tenets: "RAM was officially organized [in winter 1963] by Afro-Americans who favored Robert F. Williams and the concept of organized violence. Through a series of workshop discussions, the group decided there was a need for a 'Third Force or movement.'"[109]

RAM positioned themselves between SNCC and the Nation of Islam with the motto "One Purpose, One Aim, One Destiny."[110] Johnson left her stamp on RAM as they followed the tenets of the Negroes with Guns movement and promoted self-defense. Mrs. Johnson gave them the historical foundation of Black revolutionaries with a motto stating that they followed "in the spirit of Black revolutionaries" such as Harriet Tubman and others. RAM's writing resembled Ethel's, and they advocated Black Nationalism indicating her influence. Albert Luce noted that RAM supported China and "Chinese revolutionary philosophy" and saw China as part of the "colored world."[111] Under Johnson's guidance they promoted anti-colonialism overseas and protested the Vietnam War, refusing to fight against their "brothers." According to Stanford in the *Monthly Review*, RAM endorsed "a world revolution of [the] oppressed, [with] youth all over the world leading the revolutions of our people in Angola, Congo, Kenya, Cuba, and Vietnam."[112] This lined up with Johnson's internationalist and youth-centered ideology, for as she said in "Burn Baby Burn," "Black Leadership is not and has never been in the hands of the Big Four [Martin Luther King Jr., Whitney Young, Roy Wilkins, and James Farmer]. Like the Vietnamese Liberation Movement, leadership is in the hands of the people—the poor oppressed people."[113] From 1959 onward, her writings elucidated her alliances with Maoism and the Chinese Revolution, the anti-colonial revolution in Vietnam, Cubanismo and the Cuban Revolution, and anti-colonial movements in Latin America, Africa, Asia, and the Caribbean.[114] Ethel's radical ideologies and her encouragement of RAM to adopt them posed a serious threat to the state, who monitored RAM's and Mrs. Johnson's every actions. The state set about destroying the young people of RAM.[115] In Philadelphia she wrote of RAM's activism and their bellicosity against police attacks on demonstrators picketing for jobs in 1963. "Many Afroamericans after witnessing the attack on their relatives and friends on the lines, left but returned with 45's [and] straight razors."[116] This shows how her support and self-defense training of RAM's combat-ready youth manifested in real time.

Philadelphia offered Ethel Azalea Johnson solace. In 1961 she realized her hopes for nineteen-year-old Raymond Jr. He attended North Carolina College as "a star athlete in track and football, one of the best in North Carolina." As her mother had taught her, she taught Raymond Jr. that he must raise up the masses, not just himself; he must advocate for human rights for African Americans and the oppressed. *Workers World* described him as "one of the staunchest fighters for Afro-American liberation, [whose intellect would have led him to have] economically secure positions and prestige. His experience in Monroe led him to conclude that his life task should be to participate in the fight [for] his people for freedom."[117]

Following his mother's life lessons, Raymond Jr. became an active member of the Negroes with Guns movement and MDC. My father said that he "was one of the Monroe Defense Committee's most ardent supporters in Cleveland," traveling there to work with MDC frequently.[118] During one of his stints he wrote for Baltimore's *Afro American*. I share his article in its entirety to show how he learned his mother's lessons.

> I cannot understand why more of us have not taken an interest in the case of Mrs. Mae Mallory—that militant fighter who is being humiliated and abused in an Ohio Prison on an obviously trumped-up kidnapping charge.
>
> As an Afro-American, who was born in the South and who has spent the bulk of my life in Monroe, I have had nothing but the highest praise for Robert F. Williams, Mae Mallory and others who have had the guts to stand up and fight against the vicious attacks of racism in Monroe.
>
> Those of us who by our very backgrounds have had to put up with the daily stench of racial oppression feel in our dejected bones an earnest desire to be counted and recognized as human beings.
>
> What in the devil is now wrong with us? Let's face it. Can we continue to go on licking the white racists toes by doing nothing, or can we be counted on to let our voices be heard in the defense of Mae Mallory and other militants who are willing to stand up and be counted as human beings?
>
> It's up to us to save Mae from the KKK. We can no longer stand timidly by watching as law officials running rampant through the Southland preying on innocent Black men, women, and children, especially those who have the courage to defy their ruthless viciousness.
>
> I say, Black man—you who have the courage to say you want to be free—get on the ball!!![119]

His youth and his earnestness just bounce off the page onto our being. Raymond Jr. got on the ball. He testified in Cleveland on Mae's behalf to prevent her extradition. In court he brashly described collusion between Monroe's law enforcement, the Klan, and "likeminded people against the Afro-Americans of the community," in order to prove Mae's innocence.[120] In the summer of 1962 as a college junior, Raymond went to Raleigh to participate in voter registration drives.¹²¹ On August 9, 1962, he "drowned" in Raleigh in a "swimming accident" under suspicious circumstances. Clarence Seniors and Mallory believed that white supremacists murdered him.¹²² As Mallory wrote to Lynn and Williams, "You are very much aware of the accident that frequently occurs to those in opposition to the powers that be in Monroe. Most of these accidents are fatal! I am not yet convinced that Raymond Johnson's drowning was an accident. (In the true sense of the word)."¹²³ Mallory wrote to Mabel Johnson: "[I do not] believe that Azalea feels it is really an accident either. She is more capable to know and express her feelings better than I. Why no water in the lungs if he were drowned?"¹²⁴ Johnson told *Workers World* "that the whole system of segregation killed her son. Had there been lifeguards at the Jim Crow beach, he would still be alive today." *Workers World* vowed, "We must avenge this young fighters' untimely death by struggling all the harder so that other Ray Johnson's will be able to live out a full life."¹²⁵

The death of her son proved devastating. In 1962 Johnson moved to Philadelphia for solace and revitalization. Grief-stricken, she forwent publishing *Did You Know?* until June 1963. Ethel found meaning and strength in doing something valuable by working with RAM's youth.

Monroe Defense Committee

Sometime between 1963 and 1964 Johnson returned permanently to Monroe. FBI informant T-1 told them that she returned to Monroe indefinitely and planned "to work on Black nationalism. [She] is attempting to convince [redacted] a local negro youth, that he should stop working with a group in Monroe affiliated with the Progressive Labor Movement. She is attempting to persuade [redacted] to join her in her work."¹²⁶ Ethel returned to Monroe reenergized and with a renewed zeal to create real social and political change. Her work with RAM's youth refreshed her.

Before her permanent return to Monroe, the self-educated Mrs. Ethel Azalea Johnson, age forty-seven, joined in a political relationship with my parents, Audrey Proctor, twenty-three, and Clarence Henry Seniors, twenty-seven. From Philadelphia she advocated for Mae Mallory by joining my parents and African American Ruthie Stone of the Mothers Alliance and Workers World Party in establishing the Monroe Defense Committee. They worked for the release of Mae, Harold Reape, and Richard Crowder from jail on trumped-up kidnapping charges. They worked vigorously to prevent Mallory's extradition to Monroe.¹²⁷ We became a family: my parents,

Mae, Pat, and Mrs. Johnson, who claimed me as her granddaughter. Once MDC moved to Monroe, Johnson devoted herself to the organization, and to Mallory, Reape, and Crowder. Johnson along with my parents continued to build the Crusaders Association for Relief and Enlightenment (CARE) at CARE House, which she and the Williamses established before his exile. She dedicated herself to creating Monroe's educational initiatives, founding a preschool program, a Head Start Program, an adult education program, and the Citizenship School, all of which my parents helped her with. They fed, clothed, and advocated for poor African Americans.[128] She brought a new militant ideology to Monroe forged in Philadelphia. She founded Monroe's Revolutionary Action Movement and maintained her relationship with Philadelphia's RAM. RAM's *Black America* news magazine cited her *Did You Know?* as one of the "Centers of Black Nationalists Information and Activity."[129] The FBI reported that the "militant bi-weekly freedom publication *Did You Know?* [1963–1972] [was published and] edited by Mrs. E. A. Johnson, a long-time associate of the militant Robert F. Williams."[130] My father wrote of their good works:

> Dear Dottie [Ballan], Because of hours of leg work and button holding people, Black Monroe witnessed and attended our first forum this past Sunday. Unable to secure a church we used a funeral home. People packed the place. We had them on the outside listening. Everyone was pleased. Mrs. Johnson appeared overjoyed. We hope she will realize that in unity there is strength and as a unit we can put Monroe back on the map.[131]

The Seniors and Mrs. Johnson forged a firmly sealed family and political bond. In another letter to Dottie Ballan my father wrote:

> Mrs. Johnson asked us to help her get out DID YOU KNOW? She has also asked us to help her with a Community Forum which is being initiated here. As you will note from the leaflet. We helped her meet the deadline on the last edition of the newsletter. We helped on the leaflet and a letter sent out to local people. We suggested the Forum to her sometime back.[132]

My mother worked as the business manager and my father coedited Johnson's *Did You Know?* He wrote to Dottie, "We spend a good deal of time at Mrs. Johnson's getting out *Did You Know?*."[133] My parents and Mrs. Johnson wrote articles independently, collectively, and collaboratively. They received accolades from their great friends, Japanese American activist/Black nationalists Mary (Yuri) and Bill Kochiyama. "Your paper is wonderful!!! What you articulate is forceful and potent."[134]

With this family, this partnership of Ethel, Audrey, Clarence, Mae, and

Pat grew intellectually, committing themselves to radical activism and world revolution.

Mrs. Johnson and World Revolutions

Johnson, with guidance from my parents, learned about Trotskyism and Cubanismo, which she added to her ideologies. Brian Meeks identified Cubanismo as the "radical nationalist and state-building tradition ... which predated Marxism." Cubanismo combined armed struggle, "honesty and the need for morality in Cuban politics," coupled with José Martí's radical nationalist model of "deep reservations and hostility" toward the United States. It linked Cuban independence to African American freedom struggles and world revolutions, to argue for social reform and ending racial inequality, "as a necessary part of the independence movement."[135] Barbara Ransby described Mrs. Johnson as a woman schooled on Mao, conversant with Majority World revolutionary theory, and au fait on political scholars, evolved as an everyday political activist and organic intellectual trying to understand her world while fighting racism.[136] Johnson maintained an anticolonialist and anti-imperialist ideology, connecting the fibers of the African American freedom movement to that of world revolutions. She and her husband Ray proclaimed,

> We wish for all of you a new year filled with victories in the struggle for liberation of oppression. We wish continual victories in the international liberation struggle. Long live the great leaders of the international liberation struggles. Long live the people of the international liberation struggles. Our New Year's toast, may the eyes of the people on the local front be open and their ears unstopped, so that they may hear the roar of World Revolution and do what must be done, for the strength of the organized masses is invincible.[137]

Through her work Ethel Azalea Johnson revealed herself as a true revolutionary, connecting world revolution to Monroe and beyond.

Chapter 2 Ethel Azalea Johnson
Mrs. Johnson and
World Revolutions

Unlike Mae Mallory, Audrey Proctor Seniors, Pat Mallory, and Robert F. Williams, Ethel Azalea Johnson did not go to Cuba, Asia, Latin America, or the African continent; she participated in world revolutions through her writing and rhetoric. Thanks to Abbeville's communal lessons of resistance and struggle and her mother's life lessons of self-defense, affirming Afrocentricity, Black pride, and social justice, Johnson used Did You Know? *and her educational initiatives to promote and participate in world revolutions.*

Mother's Lessons

At age fifty-five "Mrs. Johnson wears her graying hair in Afro Style and wears colorful dashikis," signifying a great pride in her Black beauty aesthetic and her Black culture. In "Did You Know?" Ethel Azalea regularly used the terms "Black," "Afro-American," and "African American," signifying her African-centered pride, before the onset of the Black is Beautiful and Black Power movements. Burlage remembers hearing Johnson refer to Black people as "Afro-American," while Tyson contends that her pro-Black ideology became the main source of the Black Power rhetoric that permeated the *Crusader*.[1] This pro-Black rhetoric, the compelling argument to claim an African heritage, and African-centered self-worth resounded in "Did You Know?" Mrs. Johnson asked the African American community to reject the label "Negro," arguing that "the word 'Negro' was made by white supremacists for the definite purpose of separating the minds of Black people from any land country or nation, and from the dignity of manhood."[2] Johnson suggests that white supremacists used the word to enslave and socially kill African Americans. Ethel was writing a year before Moore's *The Name "Negro"--Its Origin and Evil Use*, and she identified what Orlando Patterson in 1982 termed "social death," the methodical strategy of creating a slave by defining them as outsiders, "domestic enemies."[3] Through the use of language, Europeans successfully maintained Africans in a low caste position by defining them as "negroes," "niggers," and "negresses" not worthy of the rights of man.[4]

Ethel Azalea Johnson drew on her mother's life lessons in her African-centered ideology to refute claims of Black inferiority. Johnson writes, "My mother was proud of her African heritage, and told us many stories about Africa, that had been handed down through generations, and incidents during slavery that her parents had endured. How families were torn up, never to see each other again on this earth."[5] Mrs. Johnson worked and fought vociferously to eradicate the use of corrosive language defining African Americans. "All races of men are named by two things; the land or country to which they belong and the race to which they belong. The word negro does not refer to any land or country. There is not now, nor has there ever been a place in the whole wide world called 'negro-land.' There is no such thing as a negro race." Johnson asserts that the dehumanization of African Americans and the chipping away of African-centered pride began when "white people schemed to keep Black people from calling themselves Black men and Black women (just as white people proudly call themselves white men and white women) by making the word *Black* a bad word." She maintains that this "brainwashing scheme" occurred at the inception of children's lives with children's books and lessons that taught children color symbolism, that "everything white is good . . . white means pure, clean, good, spotless and Caucasian people, and that everything Black is bad—Black symbolizes evil . . . a black cat, blackmail, and Black Friday—that the effort to debase Afro Americans was a deliberate act. Even the 1959 dictionary defined Black as "Negro. Dirty, filthy." She ended the column with Proverbs 29:17: "Correct thy son, and he shall give thee rest; yea, he shall give delight unto thy soul," conjoining religiosity with radicalism.[6]

Ethel Azalea asserts that "out of all this confusion that white people made, many Black people are ignorantly ashamed of the word 'Black' and gladly accept the caste name 'Negro.'"[7] She charges the readers to renounce "Negro" and proudly identify as Afro-American. Johnson insisted that her readers claim Black love and love of self. Her column exemplifies this effort. "Did you know that until all Afro-Americans in Monroe, realize that they are Afro Americans and stress the culture of the Black race, instead of imitating the white race, we will remain mentally slaves."⁸ Johnson challenged her readers to break the chain of cultural hegemony. She dared her readers to use pro-Black rhetoric, to define themselves in affirming language, and she liberally and proudly used pro-Black language in her writing unless making a point about nonprogressive Blacks. Johnson infused her columns with a pride in Africa, ultimately linking African Americans to the continent and Majority World countries, exposing colonialism in Africa, Asia, and Latin America. She aligned herself fully with the movements around the world as evidenced by the articles she wrote and published, beginning in 1959 in the *Crusader* and in 1961 in "Did You Know?" She wrote about anti-colonial movements in Cuba, the Dominican Republic, Kenya, the Belgian Congo, other African nations, China, and Vietnam. Johnson wrote about alliances between these movements and African Americans, as well as alliances between Africans, the Soviet Union, and Soviet Bloc countries.⁹ Her words suggest alliances built across the races and continents for Pan-African, Pan-Latin American, and Pan-Asian liberation.

> Down through the halls of Time,
> The echoes of a people
> Whom the whites have tried to keep in subjugation
> By trying to destroy their culture,
> Trampled their rights as human beings
> Under racist, greedy heels.
> The echoes of Black people in America and on the continent of Africa,
> Come together
> As one
> In the growing,
> Thundering cry of,
> "Uhuru, uhuru"
> (Freedom, Freedom).¹⁰

Her use of Swahili signified her commitment to African-centered ideologies as she linked African Americans to anti-colonial movements around the Majority World.

Johnson: Pan-Africanist, Anti-Colonialist, and Soviet Models

In 1959 Mrs. Johnson wrote articles that supported anti-colonial struggles using Pan-African, internationalist, and anti-colonialist ideologies coupled with an ideology of self-defense. She promoted newspapers such as the Pan-African Union of Journalists' *Afro Asia*, and she published articles such as the Dominican Liberation Movement's "Appeal to Human Rights."[11] Her ideological influences included Black nationalism, given her membership and leadership positions in the Negroes with Guns movement, Revolutionary Action Movement, and Monroe Defense Committee. Because of her affiliation within these organizations as well as the Socialist Workers Party and the Committee to Aid the Monroe Defendants, she added socialism to her ideology. She added Cubanismo, Maoism, and Trotskyism to her arsenal of knowledge, given our family bond and her close association with WWP, MDC, and the Youth against War and Fascism.[12] She added all these ideologies to her arsenal of political and intellectual frameworks, conjoining them to argue for African American and worldwide freedom from colonialism and racism.[13] Mrs. Johnson taught her readers about leftist ideologies and religiosity as supreme tools in fighting for human rights. Johnson advocated for world revolutions.

Johnson wrote of the cross-racial alliances that occurred between white socialist/communist countries and African countries: "The Communist dominated World Federation of Trade Unions has opened a training school for African labor leaders. A Hungarian trade union newspaper reports, 30 African labor leaders from 10 countries are attending the first course."[14]

This effort by Marxist/Leninist Budapest (1920–1989) was very much in line with efforts made by the Comintern in the 1920s to train anti-colonial leaders: Kenya's Jomo Kenyatta, Vietnam's Ho Chi Minh, Ghana's Nkrumah, and India's Nehru.[15] Ethel advanced her ideas concerning Blacks modeling after the Soviet Union in their quest for equality. "Just as Russia had to learn to use her resources, to become a strong and powerful nation, the Negro must become united and strong, if the Negro ever expects equality and recognition."[16] Johnson suggested that the United States should mirror the Soviet Union. She asked, "Did you know that American imprisonment rates [are] unmatched anywhere in the world? And that in Russia the crime rate is coming down, so much that they are tearing down some of the jails and replacing them with apartment houses and kindergartens?"[17] Johnson foretold the twenty-first-century scourge of massive criminalization and imprisonment of African Americans institutionalized after Reconstruction.[18] She offered the Soviet Union as *the standard* the United States should follow in building schools and homes for Blacks rather than prisons. Ethel suggested that the Soviet Union led the world in terms of social progress, a social progress that eluded Monroe, for she wrote, "I asked a ten-year-old boy a few years ago, why he wasn't in school. He replied that his mother had failed to wash him a pair of pants to wear to school."[19] Johnson reveals the abject poverty of Monroe's African American mothers and children, and that the hazards of poverty could lead Monroe's youth astray. "To-day this boy is in a correction institution."[20] By writing about the Soviet Union's initiatives, she offered an alternative Black liberation model of education over incarceration. By offering Soviet Bloc Hungary's initiative in training African leaders and the Soviet Union's building housing and kindergartens instead of prisons, Johnson offered important guidance for African Americans in their quest for freedom and equality.

Majority World Alliances

In 1959 Ethel Johnson drew the connections between African independence movements and African Americans. "Africa is no longer a hunting ground for Europeans, Tom Mboya, young brilliant dynamic, Kenya East African political leader told a capacity audience at Holman Methodist Church [in California]." She wrote that Mboya, general secretary of the Kenya Federation of Labor and founder with Jomo Kenyatta of the anti-colonial Kenya African Union, proposed that "Africa is ready to regain its independence," to rule themselves. He argued that African Americans "must play the leading role" in African independence and participate in cultural exchanges. This mirrored Soviet bloc and USSR initiatives.[21] By offering her readers a view into Kenya's anti-colonial movement, Johnson demonstrated her ideology, bringing Pan-African alliances to African Americans.[22]

Ethel discussed Patrice Lumumba and the Congo's independence struggle, challenging her readers to investigate the truth. "Did you know that it appears that the present United Nation Session is meeting primarily to find ways and means of keeping the Congo under the rule of whites?" She told her readers of the Soviet Union's and Cuba's role in supporting independence, notwithstanding Belgium's efforts to maintain colonial power over Congo. "Certain actions are trying to discredit Nikita Khruschev and Fidel Castro in the eyes of the world, because they are apt to expose the scheme."[23] In "Africa: Toms Tom's and Uncle Toms" (August 27, 1960), she and the Williamses eviscerated Moise Tshombe, the European-chosen dictator who replaced Lumumba, whom they described as an "Uncle Tom Puppet," a "Belgian fix." She reprinted Nicholas D. Ukachi Onyewu's "African Students See Khrushchev in New York" (October 8, 1960), recounting Khrushchev's discussion with the students of the Soviet Union's support of Lumumba's Congo and African independence. She wrote, "The United States considers herself the police of the world. Powerful enough to enforce the American way of life everywhere but the South of the United States.... She is demanding her special brand of government in the Congo and Cuba."[24]

Ethel Azalea Johnson's "Did You Know?" reveals her understanding and knowledge of Patrice Lumumba and the Congo's independence movement, the U.S. and UN machinations behind independent Congo, Lumumba's demise, and Castro and Khrushchev's efforts to support the Congo.[25] Writing of anti-colonialist movements across the globe and in the United States, she used her anti-colonialist, Pan-Africanist, Black nationalist, and self-defense ideologies to advance freedom.

Mrs. Johnson linked U.S. imperialistic projects in Majority World countries and anti-colonial movements to the African American freedom struggle. We see Johnson's political thought emerge through an intellectual conversation with Mao Zedong's anti-imperialist stance in the Majority World. According to Mao, "A revolution is not a dinner party, or writing an essay, or painting a picture, or doing embroidery; it cannot be so refined, so leisurely and gentle, so temperate, kind, courteous, restrained and magnanimous. A revolution is an insurrection, an act of violence by which one class overthrows another."[26] This undoubtedly resonated and appealed to Johnson as a member of Abbeville's historical community of struggle and resistance with its bellicose enslaved Blacks, free men and women, and their ideology of self-defense and resistance to white supremacy. She supported Mao's idea of a peasant-led revolution specific to the conditions of colonized countries—a revolution of people like African Americans whom Nelson Peery defined as internally colonized.[27] Mrs. Johnson educated herself by reading Mao to grasp how to battle racism in the United States.[28] She knew about Mao's aligning the Chinese Revolution to African American and worldwide anti-colonial freedom movements. Given her understanding of Maoism, Johnson adopted it as a theoretical model for African American freedom.[29] In advancing her ideologies, she published Robert F. Williams's essay where he proclaimed, "The Chinese people are blood brothers to the Afro-Americans and all those who fight against racism and imperialism."[30] By January 1969 Ethel included Mao's quotations on the cover of *Did You Know?*: "WE SHOULD SUPPORT WHATEVER THE ENEMY SUPPORTS." In her own handwriting she proclaimed, "He told it like it was on the international scene!"[31] Maoism fascinated Ethel. As an organic intellectual she shared Maoism with her readers and the organizations she belonged to: the Revolutionary Action Movement, the Monroe Defense Committee, and the Negroes with Guns Movement. She promoted an African American working-class revolution in line with that of the peasant-led Chinese Revolution. As an extension of her adoption of Maoism, Johnson found that the Youth against War and Fascism fit within her ideological frames. She connected the Vietnam War to the African American condition:[32] "Did you know that in 1965 the cost of fighting the war in Viet Nam appeared to be running at the rate of about $6 billion a year. About $16.5 million, daily? In the second half of 1965 it was found that employers in 32 Charlotte, N.C., area counties (Union Co. is only 23 miles away) paid their workers less than was required by federal law?"[33]

Ethel Azalea Johnson's ideology continued to evolve as she met new young people like my parents, of MDC and YAWF. They exposed her to new principles that she added to her battery of knowledge. As Trotskyists and Maoists, YAWF fully supported countries vying for independence from colonial rule. They tied the Vietnam War to the Korean War with headlines that read "Don't Let Vietnam Become Another Korea," "U.S. SUPPORTS VIETNAMESE DICTATORS," and "Join Our Demonstration."[34] Mrs. Johnson promoted YAWF's ideology in *Did You Know?* where she discussed their eighth demonstration at the Army and Air Force Exchange Service against U.S. Aggression in South Vietnam.[35] She reported that Monroe's youth "marched with "25,000 marchers Black and white, young and old . . . [making] up one of the largest anti-war March-on-Washington demonstrations to be held."[36] She also critiqued President Johnson's allocating money to "South East Asia" while "down in dear old Dixie, USA Black people were being brutalized by these same old bigoted 'Crackers.'"[37] Ethel cited the murder of twenty-six-year-old Jimmie Lee Jackson, an SCLC voting rights marcher in Marion, Alabama, by Alabama state trooper James Bonard Fowler. Johnson chronicled the brutal beating by the police of Jackson's mother and eighty-two-year-old grandfather. She told of Montgomery, Alabama, state troopers and police tear-gassing and billy-clubbing voting rights demonstrators "who defended themselves."[38] On November 7, 1964, she continued her denunciation of President Johnson's complacency, seamlessly connecting his inaction to Black brutalization, Black rights, and the Vietnam War:

> We must realize that "LBJ" as president hasn't enforced the recent so-called Civil Rights Bill he endorsed. (That's something to think about.) Yet he [pours] money and arms into some country 5000 miles away to help them gain their "freedom." Right in his back yard, here in America, Black people are victimized by the worst elements. Old Lindy seems helpless.[39]

Echoing Mao's denunciation of peaceful revolution, Ethel asked on April 24, 1965, "Since when is a struggle a peaceful nature? . . . The only alternative is a self-defense policy."[40]

Her "Continuing Psychological War" offered readers a critique of the war, the media, and their use of the heroic Black soldiers trope. She argued that television portrayed the Vietnam War's Black soldiers as "outwitting the Vietnamese people and crushing any form of liberation for them."[41] Fully integrated into the war effort, 30 percent of African American soldiers were drafted, compared to 18 percent of whites. Given the lack of opportunities like education, jobs, and other resources, African American soldiers re-enlisted at a higher rate than whites, remaining overrepresented in Vietnam.[42] Johnson noted, "It was recently confirmed that more Black soldiers are being killed in Vietnam than whites, and the daily papers throughout the South tells of the seemingly stepped-up plan to kill Blacks with or without reason."[43] Ethel perhaps referenced the wounding of African American activist James Meredith by a white sniper on U.S. Highway 51 in Hernando, Mississippi, the eruption of racialized violence in forty-three cities, and urban revolts in Newark, Detroit, and Watts in California.[44]

Mrs. Johnson noted that all colonized people against whom U.S. forces were sent to dominate—the Dominican "rebels" and the Viet Cong—"are in reality, people fighting for the same freedom we are fighting for. Our boys are helping in the slaughtering—to keep these people enslaved. What a glorious set up!" She ended the column proclaiming, "COMPLETE UNITY, DEDICATED STRUGGLE, TOTAL VICTORY!"[45] By 1966 Johnson merged her ideology of Maoism, Black nationalism, socialism, Trotskyism, Cubanismo, and Marxism into a fully formed ideological framework for ending the U.S. internal colony and colonialism overseas.

Cubanismo and CARE

Ethel Azalea Johnson seamlessly interwove her mother's lessons and Abbeville's community of struggle and resistance with the Cuban Revolution and Cubanismo, Monroe style. In August 1960 the *Crusader* ran "Sierra Maestra: The Face of Cuba" and "Cuba and the Negro," in which Robert Williams chronicled his visits to Cuba, where "we joined our voices in songs for FREEDOM." He met Afro-Cubans, university students, and an Afro-Cuban newspaperwoman who all achieved true equality. Williams saw firsthand how the Cuban Revolution "wiped out Jim Crow," and he and Johnson relayed his experiences to their readers.[46] The *Crusader* proclaimed, "SEE CUBA FOR YOURSELF," then announced their plans to sponsor a "group tour" of Havana.[47] The Johnsons would have gone on this tour, but the U.S. government halted the *Crusader*'s plans. Notwithstanding this setback, Ethel used Cubanismo and Castro's writings as a model for Crusaders' Association for Relief and Enlightenment and her initiatives.

Monroe's calamitous conditions mirrored those of Batista's Cuba, with starving children, poverty, deplorable living conditions, and unemployment. In August 1960 Johnson and Williams exposed their readers to the connections between African American poverty in the internal colony and poverty in colonized Cuba by publishing "Fidel Speaks to the Children," "Castro Speaks with the People of Cuba," and Cuba's "Agrarian Land Reform."[48] They unveiled the vast changes that occurred in Cuba due to the revolution. Mrs. Johnson quoted Castro's assertion that "you will see that with the help of you children [we'll] fill the entire island with fruit trees. There will not be a child unable to find a piece of fruit when he wants it."[49] With this pronouncement Castro's revolutionary government dedicated themselves to feeding the children starved and impoverished due to the Batista regime and years of colonization. They established the Agrarian Reform Law. The Ministry of Agriculture nationalized the farms and distributed land equally among the people. These initiatives provided food and shelter to poor families. They also relied on trade with Russia and Soviet bloc countries to alleviate hunger. Cuba's revolutionary government eradicated hunger, according to the World Food Programme, with "food-based social safety nets, including monthly food baskets for the entire population." They established "school feeding programs, and mother-and-child health care programs."[50] According to "Fidel Speaks to the Cuban People," the Cuban government dedicated itself to creating a Social Security bank, and to buying tractors and boats instead of Cadillacs for workers, farmers, and fishermen. It vowed to reinstate unions to end the exploitation of workers; to provide jobs, a living wage, and affordable housing; and to encourage planting of rice and cotton instead of importing these products.[51] Cuba's revolutionary reforms gave Ethel Azalea a model to follow for CARE to eradicate African American suffering in Monroe.

Johnson's articles bring out the stifling poverty and injustice afflicted on North Carolina's African Americans by white supremacist leaders. Jobs in new industries were denied to Blacks, although government contracts stipulated that companies must maintain nondiscriminatory hiring practices. Black women lived within the double bind of being confined to low-paid domestic work and denied aid to dependent children, as welfare was denied to African American women on a variety of pretexts. In addition, 68 percent of Monroe and Union County's African Americans were living in substandard housing.[52]

Because of the life-threatening conditions in Monroe, Ethel Azalea Johnson, Robert Williams, and the Negroes with Guns movement members did what the state would not do. She and the Williamses founded CARE House as a remedy for the state's complicity in oppression. They recruited volunteers and gathered donations. CARE offered food, clothing, shoes, a vegetable garden, and enlightenment to the desperately poor African American community, predating the Black Panther Party's free breakfast programs.[53] Mrs. Johnson noted that because of the lack of job opportunities, CARE was established "several years ago by four unemployable women who didn't want to go on welfare. They decided to sew and sell clothes at a low price. This developed into teaching young and old people in the community to sew." CARE mirrored Abbeville's historical community of struggle and resistance and Cuba's initiatives. By 1971 CARE was not receiving federal aid, with Mrs. Johnson asserting that "we must help our people learn to depend on themselves. We must control the destiny of our communities if we are going to survive. Each ethnic group has its own culture and desires and people who live together in these communities must control them."[54] CARE emphasized enlightenment, as Mrs. Johnson with help from my parents dispensed advice, material resources, and solace.[55] In each issue of the *Crusader* and *Did You Know?* Johnson asked readers to make donations. She reported on the donations received, including trailers of food, clothing, and shoes from the Monroe Defense Committee, the Committee to Aid the Monroe Defendants, Cornerstone Baptist Church (Brooklyn), and other organizations. She wrote that "many families are being helped and many children are returning to school, now that they have shoes and clothing" (11/11/61). Many in the African American community highly respected Williams and Johnson. They called on CARE daily for help, while others refused to see their good work.[56] According to Johnson, "CARE receives no cooperation from the Afro-American clergy and Afro-American professionals. There seemingly is collusion with them and racist whites to discourage and stop anything connected with [what] Robert Williams, organized."[57] Johnson relayed that an interracial contingent met at an "Afro-American church to discuss the work of CARE. After the meeting—they sent one of their Uncle Toms to me, to inform CARE that Monroe can take care of its poor people without outsiders help. The Uncle Tom slyly hinted that the clothing [and supplies], being received by CARE is coming from communists."[58]

One of the strategies used to destroy African American human rights movements included claims by the FBI, the Citizens' Council, and the government that human rights activities equaled communism, a plot to overthrow the U.S. government.[59] Black conservatives like this "Uncle Tom," the NAACP, and others condemned Blacks charged with communism in order to protect themselves. Johnson argued that his ilk worked to undermine and close CARE, and she pointed out that the Black Baptist church sponsored by white supremacists opened a store selling used clothing to undercut the organization because CARE freely gave clothes and supplies away. Ethel Azalea Johnson refused defeat. CARE sponsored a successful tea to buy shoes for poor children for Christmas. They helped ninety-six desperate families and gave advice and solace. Johnson proclaimed, "We are undaunted! We are determined!" She denounced Blacks who remained complicit in the maintenance of the status quo of white supremacy. "Amidst the suffering and oppression, there are Afro-Americans here who are selling their souls to aid our (and theirs too) oppressors."[60]

African American families took full advantage of the services offered by CARE. Mrs. Johnson knew that families who came to CARE "were legally and morally entitled to welfare assistance, [and] to Aid to Dependent Children." The state refused to help Black families. With the demographic shift from white to Black in the 1950s and 1960s, the state decreased welfare funding to prevent Blacks from receiving aid.[61] By 1965 Johnson noted that Monroe's government withheld federal food surplus from African Americans and offered "NO FEDERAL SURPLUS FOOD PROGRAM IN UNION COUNTY," notwithstanding several efforts by Johnson to secure a Monroe program. "Our elected officials refused to accept the program for Monroe and Union County's 4,446 families making $3000 or less annually."[62] Despite the state's efforts to oppress Blacks, the Johnsons, the Williamses, my parents, MDC members, and the Negroes with Guns movement gave food, clothing, and advice.[63]

Educational Initiatives

Ethel Azalea Johnson looked to Cuba's revolutionary government's reforms as a model for CARE's initiatives: "Cuba is the only country in the world that has been able to conquer a military fortress and convert it into a school. What do we need fortresses for? What we need are institutions of learning."[64] Castro's revolutionary government fed, clothed, housed, and educated Cuba's "neglected," impoverished, and illiterate children who suffered under the Batista regime—a regime that didn't "take the trouble to educate our children and to work for the good of the people"—Castro. Castro's government transformed Columbia Military Camp (1898) into "a scholastic center," opened an Institute of Science and Technology for all children, and in 1961 established a literacy campaign "with 270,000 literacy teachers," 19 percent of whom were Afro-Cuban. They achieved 99.7 percent literacy.[65] Castro gave children books, opened new schools, and provided ten thousand teachers.[66]

Just as Batista's regime neglected Cuban children, North Carolina's white supremacist government failed to provide education for African American children. In 1865 at a convention at the Loyal African Methodist Episcopal Church in Raleigh, North Carolina, Blacks demanded the establishment of schools and the hiring of Black teachers. Delegates voted this proposal down in favor of working with northern aid societies and the Freedmen's Bureau. The Black citizens sent their request to the all-white State Constitutional Convention, who promptly told them that Black children should work rather than go to school. The concept of work over education remained the long-standing ideology for education of North Carolina's African Americans from Reconstruction to well past the 1960s and Mrs. Johnson's time. With this ideology of education in mind, North Carolina established segregated schools. Black children attended dilapidated schools for six months and worked for six months. Their parents' taxes went to maintaining pristine white schools. By the 1930s no high schools existed for North Carolina's African American children. By the 1960s half the students dropped out of high school. In Monroe, 45 percent of Black adults lacked a high school education and hadn't gone past the sixth grade. An illiteracy problem existed in the state.[67] As part of her efforts to educate her readers concerning North Carolina's educational disparities, Johnson gave voice to what happened to Black children when their education was suppressed. "Because they can't read, they become the tools of white racist people. Why are so many Afro-American young men and women, unable to read or write? Part of the answer lies in economics and white supremacists who don't want Afro Americans educated."[68] Blacks had no choice but to "rely on their own resources" to guarantee the education of their children *and* themselves. They established their own schools and hired their own African American teachers.[69] Mrs. Johnson noted that "when Winchester High School uses the white high school football stadium, they have to pay at least $20.00 for the use of it, plus other expenses," notwithstanding that their parents' tax dollars paid for the "white school."[70] Like their forebears, Blacks remedied the stadium situation. In 1964 they built their own field and gym, funding it through "a basketball game between Western Union students and the alumni [on] November 19th in the new gym."[71]

Mrs. Johnson identified several other ways in which white supremacists blocked Blacks' educational ambitions for their children.[72] "There seemingly also is a planned scheme for illiteracy afoot. Reports continue to come to CARE of principals of Afro-American schools expelling students from school for long periods of time on the slightest provocations."[73] White supremacists also controlled who taught at Black schools, blocking progressive African American teachers who belonged to the NAACP, the Negroes with Guns movement, and the Monroe Defense Committee, as well as those who advocated for African American civil rights.

Mrs. Johnson's own educational initiatives—preschool program, Head Start program, adult education program, and the Citizenship Schools—would mirror those of the Cuban government. They acted as reminders of Abbeville's lessons—the schools established through Abbeville's community of struggle and resistance. In April 1962 Ethel attended Citizenship School classes in Dorchester, Georgia, invited by Septima Clark, director of education at Tennessee's Highlander Folk School.[74] Johnson was always willing to work with groups who did not share her militant political ideology in order to achieve her goals. With newly learned knowledge from Dorchester's Citizenship School, Mrs. Johnson ran Monroe's Citizenship School (1962–1965). In *Did You Know?* she advertised classes in "Voter Registration, Political Education, Economic Affairs, and Community Problems."[75] In 1962 she registered eighteen students in the adult education program.[76] Through these classes Johnson registered four hundred Blacks to vote and obtained Social Security benefits for illiterate adults.[77] She discussed community problems, including the Monroe Master Plan for urban renewal, put into place in 1947. On December 31, 1960, Monroe's city government began razing neighborhoods with "sub-standard housing," "clearing" blighted neighborhoods, "rehabilitating those deemed worthy of rehabilitation, and protecting neighborhoods against blight by enforcement of codes, zoning ordinance, and sub division regulations." The Monroe Master Plan claimed to offer displaced families assistance in finding housing with "the possibility of applying to the Public Housing Administration for construction of low rent public housing units." Monroe's Master Plan did not guarantee housing but only gave "the possibility."[78] Those who owned property would ultimately lose their land and their right to wealth accumulation. Mrs. Johnson foresaw this outcome: "We fear that [officials] will be preoccupied with expressways to transport shoppers into the town, with the clearance of land which many of us now inhabit to build industrial sites forcing us out of this slum and relocating us into substandard housing facilities that are EVEN worse."[79] The threat of urban renewal proved real. Monroe's African Americans, as Johnson pointed out, held no power in the city government, leaving the Black community vulnerable to the whims of white racists.

Johnson's efforts in the Citizenship School posed a threat. The FBI reported that she held her Citizen and Adult Education Program from her home to teach Blacks how to "press for integration of various county agencies" and "pass the required examination to register to vote." She "inform[ed] Negroes in the community about various federal programs, new trends in politics, and the implementation of any civil rights action."[80] Ethel Azalea was very serious in her efforts to uplift and educate Blacks—so much so that according to the FBI, on January 28, 1964, Ethel tried to rent and then buy Monroe's Old Royal Garden Café to teach Black nationalism. She was unsuccessful in purchasing the building.[81] Johnson had run into these types of stopgaps previously with white supremacists, Black ministers, and Black owners of property conspiring to keep her from moving forward in her programs. Undaunted, Ethel Azalea Johnson moved forward. She founded Monroe's Head Start.

Johnson's work with Head Start appears as an extension of her work with CARE, helping poor parents and their children, but this time she worked within the U.S. system through President Johnson's War on Poverty/Great Society programs. Ten days before President Johnson officially launched Head Start, a "comprehensive child development program" for poor children ages zero to three, Mrs. Johnson started Monroe's Head Start with Monroe native African American Dr. Hubert Henry Creft Jr., a Meharry Medical School graduate. Notwithstanding their ideological differences concerning self-defense, they worked together for the greater good. She announced her crusade in *Did You Know?* on May 8, 1965, promising "to service about 4,460 families (Black and white) [who] made less than $3000 a year." Using CARE as a model, she asked for volunteers.[82] By June 19, 1965, Mrs. Johnson had established a preschool program sponsored by the Citizens Adult Education Program, the North Carolina Council on Human Relations, and poverty program federal grants. They also sponsored her Head Start program. White supremacists who controlled education in Monroe worked to destabilize the programs. They used under-enrollment as a pretext to try to destroy Head Start. Each site was required by the government to have enrolled seventy students. Johnson says that she and her team complained only to be described by the local white press as "malcontents." Head Start and the Citizen Adult Education Program "help[ed] several struggling students to further their education, employ[ed] some of the unemployed, promote[d] a better feeling between the races with its non-racial policy; and portray[ed] the true image of need to Washington and the world of Monroe and Union county's poor. Project Head Start's enrollment of 5 and 6-year-old children of 250 to set up a unit with the present grant, employing 16 head teachers and 16 aides, custodians, and cafeteria help."[83]

In July 1965, as Mrs. Johnson began to get Head Start and the preschool program started, she faced opposition from the white-controlled school board, some Black teachers, and the Black elite. Ethel wrote, "I publicly asked previously, for someone to accompany me to the Monroe City School Board to request the use of school facilities for Project Head Start classes, which are scheduled to begin on July 6th. Not a Black man showed up." It appears that Dr. Creft was gone with the wind.[84] Johnson drew attention to the dual nature of racism and the participation of Blacks, for while Black men did not assist Mrs. Johnson and Monroe's children, they did want to take advantage of the Great Society programs for personal gain. "When applications for the $100 per week jobs were taken, over 100 persons signed up. Which points out the great tragedy of our people. . . . We want things, money and etc., but aren't willing to fight nor sacrifice for them." While African American men did not actively help Ethel Azalea, African American women stepped up to change the circumstances of Monroe's Black children. Mrs. Mildred Oxner, the "first Black woman to run for public office in Union County," accompanied her to the superintendent's office. They "sat, two Black women before a group of obviously angry white men we had helped to elect to office, asking permission to use a public school to have a federally assisted program for pre-school children." One furious white man stated, "We should have been consulted." The white officials suggested that they join their Head Start program with Johnson's. Ethel knew exactly what that merger would mean. "From past experience we knew their proposal of a 'merger' spelled doom for our program." She held her ground in keeping her program autonomous but discovered that some Blacks sabotaged her programs, "middle class traitors [who] worked hand in glove to defeat the program."

The elite set responded negatively to Johnson's radicalism, given her membership in the Negroes with Guns movement, the Revolutionary Action Movement, and the Monroe Defense Committee. It appears they feared she would infuse militancy into the programs. From Mrs. Johnson's politics we know that she would center her program on African American self-love and building African-centered self-image, which threatened the Black Elite Set. "These acts of division come at a time when every Black teacher's job in North Carolina is in doubt because of pending integration of schools." Mrs. Johnson foretold that with integration African American teachers would lose their foothold in education, as white teachers would ultimately replace them—the final nail in the coffin for obtaining education for their descendants. They ceded power and lost the right and the opportunity to teach African American children. Johnson warned, "Knowingly or not, these shallow thinkers [Black teachers] are going to need the support of all our people before the compliance with the law is completed." Ethel knew that Blacks must stand united. "We have no time to inject personalities into a liberation movement. We must think, plan and act as ONE huge force to survive the crushing blows of those who seek our destruction."

Mrs. Johnson held out hope, persevered, and successfully ran Head Start using CARE's strategies. She relied on volunteerism, and she gifted "shoes and clothing to pre-school children, enabling them to attend Project Head Start daily." Ethel educated her readers concerning the plight of Monroe's children and asked for donations. "As the opening of the fall term of school approaches, many poor children will be in need of shoes and clothing." Through pure grit, determination, and dedication, she worked to make Head Start and the preschool program a success.

Ethel Azalea Johnson knew of African American illiteracy and the loss of opportunity given white supremacists' schemes to keep Blacks ignorant. In 1959 she used "Did You Know?" to combat educational inequality. Johnson questioned the validity of an African American educational curriculum "[that] glorifies the white race, [like] George Washington the Father of our country. Not a word is written in the history books about the thousands of Black soldiers of the American Revolution who helped to make it possible for George to become the father of our country."[85] She questioned why "some local Afro-American high school students, didn't know who Harriet Tubman was." Ethel Azalea rallied for the inclusion of African American history in the curriculum. She encouraged Black parents to actively engage in demanding African American history and other courses not offered to Black students.[86] Johnson envisioned African American students leading the world. She taught a "Black history class each Sunday at CARE House to young people who crowd into the house to "gain a true knowledge of themselves, [and held] 'rap sessions' on 'Black identity theories.'" At CARE House she maintained a library of articles and books on African Americans, African diasporic people, and other cultures, noting, "There's more to read here than just about Booker T. Washington." Markers of Afrocentric pride punctuated by posters in CARE House including Leroi Jones's "Black is Beautiful, but not on the stuff (heroin)."[87] In 1964 Mrs. Johnson publicized educational opportunities for African American youth and young adults in Africa: "MALCOLM X SCHOLARSHIPS. 20 Stipend bearing scholarships to Al-Azhar University in Cairo, Egypt to be distributed among Afro-Americans from sixteen through thirty years of age. 15 scholarships to the University of Medina in Saudi Arabia to be distributed among Afro-American Muslims."[88]

Her articles advocated for the inclusion of an African-centered education in the public schools, and she taught her readers African American and African history. At a time when white supremacists removed Egypt from the African continent, she positioned Egypt firmly in Africa and taught its history to her readers. She wrote, "[Did you know] that Imhotep was the real father of medicine, a Negro?, [that] the art of catering and home economics was established in 2450 B.C. by Princess Nefertabet, a Negro? and that Africans invented 'luxurious African carriages' in 1710 A.D."[89] She positioned Africa and Africans at the center of civilization and advancements. "At the time of the invasions of Alexander the Great, the Black nations of Africa were already ancient and far advanced. They had populous cities, organized priesthoods, and an advanced state of agriculture, industrial arts, writing, and books so long known that their sources and origin is lost in time. Africans had religions which advanced philosophical and moral ideas that were highly developed."[90]

Through these examples Ethel Azalea Johnson claimed African genius, compelling her readers to embrace African pride. Johnson always taught her readers of African American heroes of resistance like Harriet Tubman, Denmark Vesey, Jack Bowler, Nat Turner, Gabriel Prosser, and Martin Prosser. She taught them of prominent African Americans in American history: educator Nannie Hill Burroughs, Crispus Attucks, Benjamin Banneker, antilynching crusader Ida B. Wells, choreographer and anthropologist Katherine Dunham, Manhattan Project professor J. Ernest Wilkins, and Harvard medical school graduate William A. Hinton, who developed the "Hinton test" to detect syphilis.[91] Ethel taught W. E. B. Du Bois's "militancy and brilliant writings," proclaiming that they were "indeed blueprints for Black liberation." Johnson defended him against those who condemned him for joining the Communist Party. In 1959 in "Did You Know?" Mrs. Johnson began to question the importance of educating her readers:

> I decided not to continue writing about the history of Negroes exclusively in my column, but so many readers have reminded me of the fact, that the Negro boys and girls are taught the history of the white race all the school year with the exception of one week, Negro History. There-fore I shall continue to write something praiseworthy and factual about the Black race. Maybe in doing so, our boys and girls will realize what a wonderful heritage they have and feel proud.[92]

She soldiered on in teaching African diasporic history in order to instill in her readers their beauty and self-worth, and the importance of Black contributions to history. She challenged the youth as she instilled the importance of African-centered education. "The Negro youth today must read Negro history for inspiration and encouragement, because most Negro adults today are so busy being like someone else, until they inspire no one. Be yourself, Negro youth, chart the course, and give the future the ideas that are latent in you."[93] She charged African American youth to Rise Up to greatness. She too took the challenge and Rose Up.

Friendships Fractured, New Friendships

Mrs. Johnson held steadfast to an unwavering commitment to equality in Monroe, the United States, and the world. She paid a heavy price for her ideas. In "Did You Know?" she illuminated her losses by sharing a discussion with an "old friend" who told her that "[I was] a changed person and my articles are too 'blunt' in referring to whites and their treatments of Negroes. According to my friend, I am a good person very much liked by a lot of people, but I've been associating with the wrong kinds of people. So much so until my friend fears for me and believes that if I don't stop, I won't have a single friend left in Monroe."[94] Five years after cofounding the Negroes with Guns movement and the *Crusader*, this friend stunned Ethel Azalea into silence. When she recovered her voice, she asked her friend how she *personally* felt about her. "'You know I've always appreciated our friendship. I don't believe all these things I've heard about you. I know you too well, but if I continue to associate with you, our friends will drop me too.' My friend and I parted, without any reference of future visits."

Mrs. Johnson watched her friend leave. Then her attention shifted, and she observed the scene of downtown Monroe unfolding. White people were chatting "gaily" as they left stores and banks. Unemployed "poorly dressed" "negroes" were sitting on benches in the courthouse yard. African Americans were exiting the drugstore with their sandwiches and drinks because they were prohibited from sitting at the drugstore lunch counter. As she watched the scene, Afro-Jamaican writer Claude McKay's "If I Must Die" "flashed across my mind."

> O, Kinsman! We must meet the common foe!
> Though far outnumbered, Let us show us brave,
> And for their thousand blows deal one death-blow!
> What though before us lies the open grave?
> Like men we'll face the murderous, cowardly pack,
> Pressed to the wall, dying but fighting back!

The poem invigorated Johnson at this sad moment, propelling her further into advocacy and writing as political activism. Ethel invoked McKay's militant history as a member of the paramilitary African Blood Brotherhood, and as a pan African and Pan Asian liberationist. She intertwined McKay's militancy to her own radicalism in the Negroes With Guns Movement, Revolutionary Action Movement, and the Monroe Defense Committee. She says that after the conversation with her friend, "I also thought as I walked away about how law-abiding I'd been. How often I've felt like sitting down [to] have lunch while downtown but couldn't because Negroes are refused service at drugstore lunch counters in Monroe. How often I've wanted to go to a movie but didn't because I had to sit in the segregated balcony. There are so many little injustices that I must face daily, merely because I was born Black." Johnson resisted hegemonic oppression, refusing to let white supremacists Jim Crow her.

> What is wrong with being born Black? Did not God create me in His own image? Must I bow to racist men, just because they say that I am inferior? Must I keep quiet about the injustices that I must endure daily? I was born in America, the same as my oppressors. The same constitution that protects my oppressors, is supposed to protect me too. If my oppressors continue to oppress me, I must continue to complain. I cannot hold my peace in the face of such senseless wrongs.

She continued,

> So, I've lost another friend, but I must do the things I believe are right. If to advocate goodwill toward all men, is wrong, if speaking out against the rich oppressing the poor is wrong, if my participation in the fight for a fair deal for a Black race that is discriminated against just because they are Black is wrong, then the teachings of Jesus Christ are wrong, for these are but a few of the things He said for us to do. The teachings of Jesus Christ, are what racist men call socialism today.

Ethel Azalea Johnson shed this friend and many others; she lived a satisfying life with new and exciting friendships sealed by activism *and* fun. She maintained a warm and supportive friendship with Max Stanford, the young people of RAM, my parents and me her granddaughter, and with Mae Mallory, Harold Reape, and Richard Crowder. She retained her lifelong friendship with the Williams family while they lived in Cuba and China. In 1969 the Williamses returned to the United States, and in 1971 through CARE Mrs. Johnson petitioned to overturn the kidnapping charges against Robert, "to let them know we think Robert was framed."[95] In the 1970s she moved with the Williamses to Detroit. Johnson gained new friendships there, which fed her hunger for knowledge and equality.

In Monroe the friendship with the "old friend" ended, and over time Ethel Azalea Johnson would lose many friends given her political ideology of African American human rights, self-defense, anti-colonialism, and anti-imperialism. Separated in age by decades, and bound together as a family through motherhood tropes, ideologies of self-defense, radical leftist activism, and Black nationalism, in 1961 the Mallorys, the Seniorses, and Mrs. Johnson made their way to each other in their fight for the Monroe defendants' lives. All of them were cast in the mold of African American women's radical activism, informed by their upbringing and their particular place and time.

Johnson's bond to Mae Mallory leads to the questions: Who was Mae and what drew her to the Negroes with Guns movement?

Chapter 3 Mae Mallory

From Georgia to New York, to Political Prisoner

Passive Resistance Never Liberated Any People.
—**Mae to Black comedian and civil rights activist Dick Gregory, June 1, 1963**

After Monroe we all moved to New York—Mae back to Harlem, we to Brooklyn, Lincoln Road, and then Ebbets Field. I thought I always lived in Brooklyn. My earliest memories of Mae and Pat revolve around Mommy and me visiting them regularly in their Harlem high-rise apartment. We rode the train sitting on orange-yellow woven wicker seats. We'd walk to their tall building and ride the elevator up to their immaculate apartment. Malcolm X's photograph was prominently displayed on the living room wall, as it was on our living room wall. The Mallorys and Mommy bedecked my childhood friend Hindi's and my heads with magnificent Geles, draping beautiful African fabrics around our little bodies. Gregarious and wonderful Mae had an infectious laugh; her warm arms that embraced me suffused me with love. Beautifully grown-up Pat with her Afro was fun to be around, even though I did not know the circumstances of why we were family. We just were. I knew my parents belonged to the Monroe Defense Committee but did not know what that meant.

Self Defense and the Harlem Crusader Family

Fig. 3. "Support Monroe Defense Committee" march, Cleveland, Illinois. Audrey and Clarence Seniors Collection.

Photographic relic—my mother took the photo because she is not in it. I am not born. Our great friend Mary Ann Weisman of Workers World Party stands in the center of the protesters with a sign that reads "Support Monroe Defense Committee." Black men stand in support of Black womanhood holding the sign "Mallory Has a Right to Be Free." A multiracial, multigenerational march. Photo album memories of long ago, always there at home. Too young to understand . . . our family album.

In 1959, Harlemite Mae Mallory, bred in Macon, Georgia, at thirty-two, eleven years younger than Mrs. Johnson and an avowed advocate for self-defense, supported Robert Williams's Negroes with Guns movement, because Black mothers were at its center. She recounts that Williams's words "made a profound impression on me and I vowed then and there to support this man in his efforts down South." She heard him in 1959 on the progressive Black radio station WLIB. They broadcast the NAACP national convention, where Williams argued against his suspension from Monroe's NAACP, given their armed self-defense ideology. Mae recounted, "When Robert Williams was there, brought up on charges by the national body for advocating armed self-defense. I heard it. I said My God, you know, this is only right. Instead of going to work, I got up and went in the streets and organized some support for Robert Williams."[1]

In 1959 Mallory befriended Williams, his wife, and Mrs. Johnson. She joined Monroe's NAACP and founded Harlem's Crusader Family/Crusaders for Freedom to support them with lectures, money, and guns. Her group participated in protests against Harlem's Woolworth's to support the sit-in movement, calling for "all leaders" to support southern youth fighting for civil rights. By 1960 other members included African American women activists Ora Mobley, recording secretary, and Parnella Wattley, treasurer.[2] Mae put all her energy into helping and building the Negroes with Guns movement. On May 7, 1961, under the auspices of the Crusaders for Freedom, Mae held a benefit concert for them at the Jazz Gallery on Eighth Street with an admission price of two dollars. The performers included African American drummer activist Max Roach, African American singer activist Abbey Lincoln, African American musician Charlie Mingus, and African American actor activist Ossie Davis.[3] On June 7, 1961, Harlem's Crusaders for Freedom organized a presentation by Dr. Lonnie Cross [Dr. Abdulalim Abdullah Shabazz] of Atlanta University on "The Correct Approach to the Afro-American Liberation Struggle." Cross was my father's professor and mentor.[4] Mae also organized rallies and fundraisers at her home when Williams called for help to buy guns for the Negroes with Guns. She also collected guns for them from a Harlem gangster with the help of African American Garveyite, Black nationalist, and radical activist Queen Mother Moore; African American writer Julian Mayfield; Sylvester Leakes, the African American editor of *Muhammad Speaks* (and the father of my Brooklyn Friends classmate, Gideon); African American historian John Henrik Clark; and Mae's friend and comrade, Japanese American activist Yuri Kochiyama.[5] The FBI targeted them all, blacklisting Abbey Lincoln, compiling a substantive file on Ossie Davis, and installing surveillance equipment in Mallory's home and tapping her private phone.[6]

Mae understood state repression and the threat that the African American woman's body posed to hegemony. She had experienced state suppression and the threat of state-sanctioned violence all her life. She knew that fighting back proved her only alternative. On June 13, 1961, at the United Nations protesting Patrice Lumumba's murder by the CIA, Mae Mallory used her body to fight state persecution. Well versed in the political movements in the Belgian Congo as the secretary of the African American Committee in Defense of the Congo, Mae participated in protests in support of Lumumba's overthrown government.[7] In her lawyer Conrad Lynn's *There Is a Foun-*

tain, he described Mallory in very disparaging terms: a "physical woman, a block of granite ... When the police waded in swinging clubs [at the UN protest], Mallory took two policemen and cracked their heads together and knocked them unconscious." When charged with assault, Mae hired Lynn. She won her case because according to him, the officers were too demoralized to admit that a Black woman beat them. Although he represented Mae, Lynn's words reveal an unrestrained contempt for her—a hostility she would experience time and again from the Black elite, some Black men like Lynn, and white supremacists.[8]

With the understanding of the impact a Black woman's body could have, she joined in sisterhood with Monroe's combat-ready Black women, who fought back. She knew of the 1958 Kissing Case, the rape case of mothers Georgia White and Mary Ruth Reed. Mae knew of the losses that Monroe's African American community had endured, how they mirrored her own dedication to self-defense and her experiences with white supremacy and the Black elite. This is why she put all her energy into the Negroes with Guns movement.

In August 1961 Mae Mallory traveled from New York to Monroe with Julian Mayfield to buffer Williams given the arrival of the Freedom Riders at Williams's home. At Williams's home she added domestic helpmeet to her self-concept. Mallory reconfigured conceptions of Black womanhood and motherhood as that of Black combat-ready women in defense of themselves.[9] "I never participated in any of the picket lines. Never did I intend to offer my head or a whipping without retaliation. I was a headquarters helper and no more. That's where the guns were and that['s] where I was!"[10]

She helped Mabel Williams cook and keep house for the Freedom Riders, and she offered her knowledge of first aid if the need arose, committing herself fully to guns and self-defense.[11] Mae Mallory reconceptualized African American womanhood. Her body represented armed protector, mother, nurturer, and caregiver. She refused to participate in the Freedom Riders' demonstrations, reiterating her self-defense stance.[12] "Not that I am against picketing; my trade union background will bear that out. But I cannot let someone hit me or kick me and remain passive. It was agreed by all that I should stay at home."[13]

As discussed in the previous chapter, on Sunday, August 27, 1961, the Freedom Riders marched, the police attacked, and the Klan couple invaded Williams's home. Mallory told the *Call and Post* (April 21, 1962) that "the couple asked for protection when they were stopped by an angry crowd of Negroes in the 'Negro section.'" The Williamses sheltered them. On their departure the Williamses and Mae left Monroe given the racialized threat.

The Williamses abandoned Mae in New York and escaped to Cuba. Mayfield escaped to Ghana. On learning that the authorities had charged them all with kidnapping, Mae fled to Cleveland by bus. The *Call and Post* (October 21, 1961) reported that "Mrs. Mallory successfully eluded a nationwide dragnet and went into hiding." The FBI described Mae as "a loud talker, violent nature; carried 22 pistol in brassiere . . . Considered armed and very dangerous."[14] How did the FBI learn of Mae's whereabouts? Mae wrote to Williams:

> [Conrad Lynn] persuaded my mother to tell [my cousin] where I was. Not knowing any better she told him. [Lynn] wrote me a letter "advising" me to give myself up. He claims he made arrangements for my safe conduit back to N.Y. Naturally I didn't go for this. Another cousin got served. . . . [He] had the feds waiting for me to come to his house. I no longer lived with [him] but used to call him from a public phone to check the mail.[15]

Patricia Oduba Mallory recalled, "My relatives who lived in Ohio, my grandmothers people let the FBI know where she was. She thought she could get lost in a large population. . . . I hated them for a long time. I found out that these family members turned her in when she was out of jail."[16]

Incarceration and Respectability

Because of the treachery of her relatives, when the state learned that the Williamses made their way to Cuba, as Mae Mallory recalled, "On Thursday night [November 11, 1961], twenty-five members of the FBI swooped down on my landlord's house to arrest me. It literally rained cops. They grabbed me up so fast that they nearly ran off and left a few of their men stranded without rides back to their headquarters."[17] Mallory spent thirteen months in jail and faced extradition to Monroe.[18] While incarcerated, she unsuccessfully sought help from various civil rights groups. Mallory wrote that the "so called respectable organizations slammed their doors in our faces." She told the *Call and Post* that "only one minister came down to see me." The *Call and Post*'s Al Sweeney wrote that "caution [was] displayed by many Negro Leaders."[19] The *Herald Dispatch* reported that "the NAACP, a Zionist-controlled organization with Afroamerican men and women stooging, refused all calls for help from Mrs. Mae Mallory [who] escaped from the hate-infested city of Monroe." Mae's lawyer, William Haffner, noted that "the NAACP seems to think Mae Mallory is the plague and the boogey woman combined."[20] In Cleveland, Ruthie Stone, a Workers World and Mothers Alliance member and secretary of the Monroe Defense Committee, wrote a letter to the NAACP asking for help to no avail.[21] Mallory's Black councilmen wanted her extradited; she did not fit their model of Black womanhood or motherhood.[22] In 1965 Jewish activist and newspaperman Harry Golden noted in a letter to Arthur Robinson, one of the lawyers for lone white Stegall kidnapping defendant John Lowry, "surprisingly, Mae Mallory has shown her contempt for the NAACP and a few of us do-gooders who, during the early stages of the trial tried to interest themselves."[23] As Golden's letter indicates, Mallory's comportment as an unruly African American woman prevented white activists like Golden from supporting her. So it is not surprising that Mallory exhibited derision for these organizations and for white "do-gooders" who while "liberal" one day could exhibit their racism just as easily the next when it came to the lives of African American women like Mae.

Mae: Motherhood and the Monroe Defense Committee

In 1961 in Cleveland, Audrey Proctor and Ruthie Stone, both twenty-one, established the MDC, with Stone as the secretary.[24] My father eventually joined them. They stood strong and undertook Mae Mallory's liberation, visiting her daily and bringing her fruit.[25] In March 1962 they fought her extradition to Monroe on the kidnapping charges, using motherhood as the framework for their arguments. The menace of the lynch mob and rape impended over Mallory's case. The committee, along with the exiled Williams, underscored the peril to African American motherhood.[26] Williams noted, "Tonight in the so-called free world, a mother of two children languishes in a dismal jail . . . deprived of the right and joy to give companionship and guidance to her teenage daughter."[27] MDC sent out flyers that included their "Free Mae Mallory" pamphlet.

> Mrs. Mae Mallory, Afro-American mother of two children and "a militant freedom fighter from way back," has always been ready to sacrifice herself in the cause of her people's liberation. . . . We demand that she should be freed. Let us prevent another Southern massacre. The State of Ohio must not become the friendly accomplice to racist mob violence and murder by sending an innocent mother into enemy territory.[28]

The Monroe Defense Committee conjoined motherhood and self-defense, centering Mae firmly within the cult of true womanhood, MDC-style. By shaping the case around motherhood, MDC rallied to protect her from the lynch mob and what Harold Bloom calls "southern erotic sadism," the containment and control of the Black female body through sexualized terror and violence.[29] MDC and Williams used the motherist frame and linked the protection of Black motherhood to liberation and social action. Williams illuminated how structural racism obstructed Mallory's motherhood rights and prevented her from physically caring for her children. The incarceration of her Black feminized body also prevented her from physically nurturing or mothering her children. This resonated with the history of slavery—forced separations of mother and child, and Black codes that criminalized African American women and legally sanctioned their jailing. MDC and Williams reconfigured the discourse surrounding African American women by defining Mae Mallory as the quintessential African American woman, the prototypical Black mother. After six months the committee raised the $15,000 bail and continued to fight Mae's extradition.

One must ask, how did Mae get to this point in her life? How did Mallory's early childhood and adulthood experiences lead her to this defining life moment? What experiences in childhood shaped her self-defense and radical ideologies? How did her ideologies move her to become a social theorist in the organic intellectual everyday political activist motherist frame?

Teenaged Motherhood: Erudition and Self-Defense

Place, space, and time informed Mae Mallory's life in a way that proved radically different from Mrs. Johnson's charmed life in Promise Land/Abbeville. Johnson learned lessons in Black motherhood, self-defense, the importance of education, and community struggle and resistance—ideologies that Johnson brought to Monroe, North Carolina. Mae was born in rural Georgia eleven years after Mrs. Johnson, to a teenaged single mother who, given her youth and personality, remained unable to express love and affection to her daughter—a fractured Black teenaged motherhood. Mae was born into a Black Southern Baptist, patriarchal, misogynistic, anti-intellectual family. All of these things should have stifled Mae's growth, but in fact they propelled her toward an ideology of radical activism, and self-defense. The *lack* instilled in her a keen desire to learn. Born in different decades, raised in two divergent working-class environments with divergent ideologies—Mae's and Mrs. Johnson's lives intertwined as organic intellectuals, with tropes of motherhood and womanhood, and as social theorists and radical activists.

In "Constant Desperation" (1962–1963), Mae proclaims "weighing in close to 10 pounds, I arrived on the scene that day [June 9, 1927])," at Bibb County Hospital in Macon, Georgia, to a working-class family consisting of a mother, Willie Lee Streeter; a father, William Clarence Range; and a grandfather. Mae's 1957 FBI file verifies her birth, birthplace, and parents' names.[30] In Malaika Lumumba's 1970 interview Mallory recalled:

> I came from a family of just plain average people. Like most people they were semi agrarian. My mother's grandfather lived off the land. He was a good farmer, provided a good home for his family. We were nonintellectuals. We weren't starving, you know, sharecroppers who didn't have food or clothes or anything like that. We weren't the doctors, the attorney kind of people either, just simple people.[31]

Mae informs us that she did not come from those who owned Macon's twenty-plus African American businesses: a printing firm, funeral parlors, real estate enterprises, a coal business, a hospital, the Liberty and Loan Investment Company, and Middle Georgia Saving and Investment Company. She did not belong to this social ilk, or to the sharecropper class. She came from plain, ordinary country people.[32] This family adhered to old Southern Baptist patriarchal beliefs that men should dominate women and girls. They believed that education would make you crazy and reading would ruin your eyes. They discouraged education of any sort.[33]

Class and caste appear as important themes in Mae Mallory's life and proved very important to her teenaged single mother, Willie Lee, who gave Mae the last name of Street. "How'd I acquire the name Street has never been explained to me. You just don't discuss [this] with an illegitimate child. . . . The nearest guess is simply since my mother was born Willie Lee Streeter; she did not want to bring her 'shame' on her fathers' name. She decided to give me only part of the name."[34] What a heavy load her family put on little Mae: *shame* for her birth to her single mother, *shame* that Mae's father, Clarence Range, died a month before her birth. Mae's mother's marital status proved an incredible embarrassment to Willie Lee. She passed that *shame* onto Mae.

> Her mother wasn't able to love her in that kind of nurturing way. Her mother was a little older than eighteen when she had Mae. My grandmother didn't marry her father. She was thrown out of the house because she was pregnant without the benefit of holy matrimony. There was a stigma attached to that. I guess she figured if it wasn't for the fact that she was pregnant she wouldn't have all these troubles.[35]

For the majority of African Americans, marriage connoted a trope of respectability, what Claudia Tate defined as an emblematic civil right. Mae's mother found herself denied the trope, which embarrassed and embittered her, causing an unsurmountable rift between her and Mae.[36] Pat says that her grandmother "was not a touchy-feely kind of person. I guess you could say cold. She wasn't mean, it's just she just didn't demonstrate affection, never smiling, she just couldn't show love."[37] This lack of a mother's warmth did not bode well for Mae's comfort or well-being. Mae described her mother as a "modest quiet and church going girl," meek and fearful of whites. She put all her faith in God, believing that he would take care of them. Mallory wondered why God did not provide for them and give her mother a larger salary so that they "could pay rent and have better clothes. . . . It seemed to me 'God' certainly could have taken much better care of us. Especially since my mother worked in a church and was always singing and praying. It is the same church John Birch, or his family belonged [to]." She questioned why God forced her mother to work so very much, making it necessary for her to spend long stretches of time away from Mae. Mallory bounced from one relative's home to another. Her mother came into her life sporadically, ultimately catapulting Mae back to a relative's home. Her mother moved to Macon soon after her birth and left Mae in the care of her father's oldest sister and her husband in the country. Perhaps Mae's mother placed her with her father's family because of the shame she brought to her family. Mae said, "The very first years of my life seem to have been spent with my father's relatives. My fathers' oldest sister assumed the responsibility of quite a few of the family's children because their mothers had gone north to find work, and the fathers had either died, were killed or simply took off." The family pooled their resources to raise Mae with three cousins at least ten years older than her, along with children from different families with absent fathers, and mothers who worked in the North.[38] Mae's family makeup mirrored that described by Sudarkasa, Gutman, and Heinecke, of shared parenting and socialization, single parentage, and fostering. Heinecke notes that it "addresses [families'] economic and social reality," offering a chance to escape lifelong poverty. This parenting style linked to literacy worked, given Mae's love of learning. Mae's family also reflected Frederick Douglass's childhood. He had formed familial relationships with Maryland slaves when sold away from his mother and grandmother.[39] Mae Mallory recounts that when living with her aunt and uncle, they exposed her to an extremely loving and warm environment. She held a special place in the family given their cultural beliefs that a child like Mae who never "saw" her father could cure childhood diseases.[40] During this time, when she moved to a different family, Mae formulated a self-defense ideology.

At the age of three, while living with her cousin Tempia on her mother's side, Mae used her child's body as a tool of resistance. Mallory recounted that a white female store owner, Mrs. Saloon, offered Black children maggot-filled cheese. Mallory recognized this as mistreatment and abuse.

> I slapped this garbage out of the woman's hands. She slapped me. I ran home crying. This cousin made me explain to her why I was crying. Somehow or another I told my cousin that this little girl, [the store owner's daughter] had hit me. She told me to go back and even if Mary Saloon crawled up her mother's dress to hit her or I wasn't going to come into that house. I went back to the store and Mary was behind the counter. I went back there. I popped her; you see. Then I ran home.[41]

Mae recalls that Saloon called the police on her three-year-old self. Fifteen motorcycle police came to the house "with sirens blazing" looking for the toddler, more specifically asking for "this little nigger who hit a white woman."[42] Saloon knew of the lynch laws that threatened lynching and death of three-year-old Mae, in order to protect white women from African Americans, even Black children. By calling the police, Saloon ensured that they would mete out white supremacist violent justice. Cynthia Skove Nevels asserts that white women lynched for power, to elevate their class status, and to claim whiteness and womanhood rights.[43] In 1930 Mae Mallory and her cousin fought back, refusing to tolerate abuse from Saloon *and* the police. Mae recalled that Tempia castigated the police:

> "Why you white people are so stupid. You mean you had to have 15 motorcycle cops come for this?" She held up this little round fat ball of Black flesh that was me. She said, "now don't you look ridiculous?" She really made them feel like a fool! They told her that she would have to teach me that I would have to respect white people. My cousin said that "you tell them that they have got to respect us."[44]

Mae remembered the events clearly. Mallory and her cousin evinced a sense of African American worth by demanding that whites show deference to them to gain their respect. Tempia's actions of publicly reprimanding and humiliating the cops who proposed deadly assault on Mallory proved successful. Neither the officers nor the white supremacists retaliated against the family, in a state that lynched African American children and women, ranked either number one or number two in lynchings from 1880 to 1930, and lynched 460 African Americans, six of them in Macon.[45]

This incident proved so potent that Mae Mallory recounted it almost forty years later, connecting it to her lifelong fight for human rights. While Mae and Tempia escaped harm, they left Georgia for Brooklyn soon after the incident, because as Mae states, "my mother could see that I wasn't going to make it so good in the South."[46]

Around 1930 or 1932 Mallory's mother married Mr. Brown, as Mae was taught to call him. She described him as older and illiterate—a "male supremacist of the worst sort," a moonshiner and WPA worker. Mae felt that her mother married him for "respectability or economic reasons." This allowed her to stay at home. Mallory surmised that her mother fell hard for this older man who wore fancy clothes and had traveled to New York. Her mother brought Mae into the marriage in Macon. He severely mistreated Mae and her mother.[47] Pat recalled that her grandmother "was abused by her husband and she was just afraid."[48] In 1967 Mae wrote to Ethel Johnson about him. "I hate the name Brown. I never was a Brown, he was my mother's husband a mean ignorant, and vicious man. You may write me by any other name."[49] This experience informed Mae's ideology concerning gender inequality, patriarchy, and misogyny.

Mallory recounts that in 1939 her mother eventually left Macon and her husband. She moved to Brooklyn to work as a live-in maid. Mae sardonically recalled that her mother traveled "north to Brooklyn, N.Y., to freedom, justice, and equality, and all the luxuries one can imagine easily bought on the enormous salary of $30 per month."[50] Black women in the North, even college graduates, found themselves blocked from factory jobs, relegated to domestic service due to racist hiring practices. Maid's work meant that her mother worked from sunup to sundown in white people's homes with little if any time to raise Mae, so she sent her daughter to live with her aunt Daisy in Atlanta. Aunt Daisy shared her home with Aunt Edna, her son Chavis, and his daughter Doris. Mae Mallory's mother's uneven parenting and frequent absence appear as a recurring theme in Mae's life, for after many months she sent for Mae. "I finally boarded the train going North. My Aunt Daisy took me to the station where the Travelers Aid Society was to tag me and turn me over to my mother in New York."[51]

In 1939, at the age of twelve, Mae Mallory experienced a political and social awakening as she traveled by train to New York. She writes that she saw Black shoeless workers, as well as Blacks and some whites living in shanties "with tin roofs and various tin sign boards advertising the virtues of the Woods Chewing Tobacco and Sweet Society Snuff." Mallory describes this stark image and how it contrasted sharply with fine homes owned by whites: "What did all this mean? Why was it I never saw a Black family in the beautiful houses, sitting a good distance back from the tracks. Why did the shanties that were so close to the tracks that you could actually see the newspapers that covered the walls, most always have Black people?" A panoramic landscape of inequality opened up to Mae. Her words reveal a young child's understanding of social and political inequity: "I had a strong feeling of the unfairness of it all and felt it was my duty to do something about it. What to do—I had no idea."[52] It was at this early time in her life that she formulated a holistic socialistic ideology of equality for all. Her principles mirrored the ideology of the Workers World Party and the Socialist Workers Party, who had aided her when arrested for kidnapping. Her words echoed the ideals of Maoism, Cubanismo, and the Black Panther Party.[53]

In New York Mallory lived with her mother in a Brooklyn brownstone with several other families in a multiracial community downtown near Albee Square, Hell's Kitchen. "It was very integrated. Italians, Jewish [people], Germans, Irish, a few Cubans. There weren't many Puerto Ricans, and Blacks." She recounts that she lived an isolated existence because her grandmother would not let her play with the Black children, believing they were dirty and unbathed. Mae did not play with whites because of their race.[54]

Isolated, her main outlet was educational engagement. Mae notes that she was intellectually precocious with an insatiable "thirst for knowledge." In Macon, at the age of three, she learned how to read, write her name and her mother's name, and the names and addresses of family members before she entered Macon's school. This proved an issue for her anti-intellectual, anti-education family. Mallory recalled, "I became aware of my problems as a person. I've always had a thirst for knowledge." Because of her educational desire, her family led her to believe that she was flawed. Their old Southern Baptist beliefs dictated this ignorance, believing that women and girls were low caste. Notwithstanding these ideas, Mae pursued education. "At the age of five I could read all the children's books that the Metropolitan Life Insurance agent distributed." With African American illiteracy rates in Georgia at 79.4 percent in 1920, it is noteworthy that Mallory was literate by the age of three. She recounts that in Macon she attended the rural Hazel Street School, with coal-fueled potbellied stoves to heat the classrooms.[55] Because of the lack of educational opportunities for sharecroppers' children, the students ranged in age from six to sixteen. While Mae Mallory loved learning, rote learning left her easily distracted. She quickly learned her lessons so that she could play games, which frustrated her teachers.[56] While the educational experience proved frustrating, Mae says that the Black woman principal instilled in them a sense of worth, that they must "stand tall" and "face the world with their heads high, their shoulders thrown back and walk to the tune of 'The World Is Mine.'"[57] Mallory states that the principal's words meant little to her then, but she remembered them, and they left an indelible imprint. Mallory's personality was imbued with an abundance of aplomb, which she drew on as a Brooklyn student.

As a child and a recent transplant from Georgia, Mae entered a Brooklyn public school system with Jewish, Italian, German, and Cuban immigrant children, as well as African American children. Although the Jewish and Italian population was subject to virulent stereotypes, nativism, and anti-immigrant sentiment, they assimilated and claimed whiteness by participating in racism and violence against African Americans.[58] Diane Ravitch asserts that Blacks "found a color line in New York, illegal, unwritten, but effective. They were, in W. E. B. Du Bois' apt phrase, 'marginal persons.'" By the 1940s the state and white parents had successfully segregated African Americans into separate schools. Despite the rise in segregation, however, a majority of Blacks attended schools with whites. This was the educational climate in which Mae Mallory entered Brooklyn's schools. She encountered white supremacist ethnic women teachers in public schools, which informed her self-defense ideology and her opposition to white supremacist racism.[59] Mallory learned that her southern Black body threatened her white ethnic teachers' concept of the social order. The teachers conveyed to Mallory and the students that she did not belong—that her very presence in the classroom imperiled white ethnic children *and* the white teacher. On her first day of elementary school Mae's mother sent her "scrubbed and just as shiny Black as I could be. You couldn't find a speck of dirt on me if you wanted to, how scrubbed I was. This was my family's way of telling white people we were different. We weren't dirty. We were proving things." Notwithstanding the family's efforts to literally buffer her through a sea of cleanliness, the northern white supremacist female teacher, like her southern storekeeper counterpart Mrs. Saloon, found Mallory's southern child's body menacing and wanted to wield control over her. "The teacher said to me, 'stand up in front of the class and tell them how much cotton you can pick.' I stood up, nine years old, and I said 'teacher, I've never picked any cotton.' She said, 'well aren't you from Georgia?' I said yes. 'Well, all negroes pick cotton in the South.'" With these words the white teacher defined Mae as alien with a degraded slave past, different from her northern white working-class ethnic classmates. Using lessons learned in Macon about resistance, Mallory fought this consignment. "I told her that she was lying. That I didn't pick any cotton." For this act of resistance "she told me to go home. Don't come back until I brought my mother." When she returned with her mother, Mae states the "teacher lied and didn't tell my mother that she demanded that I tell the class about picking cotton. She told my mother that I was impudent." Her complacent mother, whom she described as meek and passive when faced with whites, believed the teacher over Mae.[60] Mallory's experience with white supremacist women in Georgia, in Brooklyn, and in 1961 at Cleveland's Cuyahoga County jail proved a devastating experience.

In 1940, seventh-grade Mae did encounter kindness.

> I had an Irish teacher, mostly interested in an academic mind rather than the color of the skin. She hated everybody who wasn't Irish you see. It didn't make any difference whether you were Black, white, blue, green, or purple, if you weren't Irish then you were something funny with her. If you showed any indications of intelligence, she kind of dealt with it somewhat. I got along famously with this woman because I guess it was like her justification for being there. She had found one mind.[61]

Mae Mallory recalled that her teacher treated her with respect, cultivated her intellect, and taught her that she deserved womanhood rights and that she should expect people to call her Miss Street. Mallory notes that while the schools tracked most Black students into domestic service and trades, her teacher encouraged her to learn to sew as a career choice. She felt this profession would suit Mae. "She sent me to a so-called grade A school. I didn't get the academic schooling; I went into a vocation." Mae from earliest childhood longed for a scholar's life of reading and writing. While her teacher moved her away from domestic service, one must ask what it means that she encouraged Mae to choose seamstress over intellectual. While Mae felt the teacher appreciated her intellect, she still tracked her into demarcated Black women's work.[62] Mallory states that she was unaware that Black women could pursue any profession other than teacher, hairdresser, or homemaker. Mae longed to become a scholar. U.S. society conscripted her to work, using white immigrants like her Irish teacher to keep her in place.

In 1942, on her first day at Brooklyn's Commercial High School, Mallory arrived "new from skin out, head to toe, scrubbed to death," and sat where she knew she belonged by alphabetical order in front of a Jewish girl named Sharon Redsah.[63]

> As soon as the [white woman] teacher walked upstairs she saw this one Black face. She said "you," meaning me, "take the last seat in the last row." I said "hell no, I'm supposed to sit in front of Sharon. You don't even know my name." She said "oh, one of the fresh ones, huh. You go downstairs and see the dean. Don't come back until you bring your parents."

Mae returned with her mother. "The teacher said, 'Didn't I tell you not to come back here until you brought your mother,' speaking to my mother. I said, 'you see Ma this woman is a rat.'" Realizing her mistake, the teacher apologized to Mae's mother. Her mother "was very quiet, a pliable piece of putty [and] accepted the teacher's XX."[64] These incidents with white supremacist women teachers show that her mother lacked the mental dexterity to protect her daughter. She bought into white superiority tropes. What becomes apparent here is that northern white supremacist women participated as fully and with much vigor in repressing Black girls as their southern counterparts. The lessons Mae Mallory learned in public school were harsh ones. She learned from white supremacist female teachers that she was unworthy of education, respect, and the moniker "Miss," bestowed on her by her Irish teacher. Mae battled these concepts by demanding the proper address of "Miss." She remained resolute concerning her right to her place in the classroom and a proper education, rebuffing the teacher's command to sit in the last row. Throughout her life Mae Mallory pushed back against white supremacist women, refusing to sit in the last row of life.

Arranged Marriage, Arranged Motherhood

Mae's mother left her again after this incident. "I guess my mother thought I was absolutely too trying, so she ran off with a husband that I just couldn't stand." Her mother's abandonment follows a pattern, a theme in Mae's life: abandonment and shared parenting. We think of motherhood as African American women protecting their children from harm. Mae's mother, at age thirty-two, appeared incapable. An abused mother, she did not protect her fourteen-year-old daughter from her new husband, whom she called Mr. Will. Pat recalls, "Mr. Will severely abused his wife. The abuse was so bad that her sister, who believed in male domination[,] confronted him with a frying pan." Mae's experience proved brutal. Pat said that "Mr. Will was violent towards my mother, [and she vowed] that he would never do anything like that to me. . . . Now I know that he kicked me one time. I was just a small kid. [Mae] really hated him severely. . . . This wanton abuse, any old kind a way, what is that? To abuse me as a baby?" Mae's girlhood experience of abuse, violence, and misogyny led her to commit her entire life to an ideology of gender equality, anti-misogyny and anti-male supremacy ideology and rhetoric. When she became a mother, she tried mightily to infuse her children with this ideology, but with a family with retrograde ideas, it proved very difficult. Pat recalled, "*Let Resistance Be Your Motto* was her favorite book. I think my mother resisted a lot. She hated segregation, Jim Crow, racism. In the South as a child, she hated the situation, particularly in

Black families where women were not supposed to be rebellious, talk back, think, or certainly in her case be more than a wife."[65]

Mae Mallory maintained a lifelong commitment to education, cultivated in elementary school by Macon's African American principal, and by her Irish middle school teacher. Mallory retained her dedication to education throughout life. Her educational aspirations caused problems. She recalled that while living with her aunt, given her mother's second marriage, her family found her odd. "They thought I was kind of strange because I was fifteen years old, wasn't interested in boys. Every time I got a dollar I would buy books. They decided that something was wrong with me. When little boys [tried] to come around, I would chase them away." Before she finished high school, her family brokered an arranged marriage with Keefer Mallory on November 25, 1944. Her FBI file confirms this generational pattern. Mae was the same age as her mother had been when Mae was conceived.[66]

> By the time I was 17, just about ready to come out of high school, my family decided that I should get married. Not to a city slicker, but to somebody who came from the soil, who was used to working the soil, who would be interested in making a home for a wife because this was the kind of people they were used to. So, they picked for me my husband.

The couple were fundamentally at odds. "He wasn't interested in much, except the soil. Here I was interested in how come the soil. What made up the soil? Who owned the soil? These were questions the poor boy couldn't cope with. I was always trying to find answers, and reasons why."[67]

Mallory states that her husband and family decided her ultimate role in life would be as mother and wife. Three months after delivering Pat on June 9, 1945, Mae found herself pregnant again with Keefer Jr., known as Butch. Mae, age eighteen, revolted against the marriage, patriarchy, and normative Black motherhood. She left her husband, pregnant with a toddler in tow. Her FBI report noted that she divorced Keefer on September 12, 1953. They reported that her divorce was issued on the grounds of adultery in Perquimans County, Hertford, North Carolina.[68] Mae said, "Now I love babies, but I think there is something else in life besides having a baby and rearing it. . . . All I could hear around me, was all that I could expect during my childbearing years. Which would be numerous since I was only 17. I just couldn't cope with this thing. My husband and I just couldn't make it. I left him."[69]

Mae Mallory wanted to learn, to ask questions. She wanted more out of life than traditional roles. Her rebellion against marriage and children complicated notions of the role of African American women in arranged marriages and their assigned position as mother and wife. Mae became the primary supporter of her children. She worked in factories making jewelry, dolls, mattresses, and pillows. The FBI reported that they called her employers, contacted the Welfare Department, and called Mae's home. They found that she worked at Dusty Noisette (1947), as a domestic for Mrs. Solins (1947), at New York Feather Company (1952–1954), at Silver Novelty Company (April 1954), at L. Buckman Company (1955), as a domestic for Mrs. Provenzano (1956), at Easton Manufacturing Company (1958), at Braunstein Dress Company (1959), as a nurses' aide at Warchaeuer Haym Salomon Home for the Aged (1960), and at Brooklyn Hospital (January 1961). From the moment she left her husband, Mae dedicated her life to learning social and political activism, and teaching her children by example.

The Communist Party

In 1952 Mae Mallory discovered the Communist Party while working in factories supporting her children.

> Every time I raised a question of better wages, better working conditions and equality for Black people, the whole aspect of life, somebody would tell me that was communist. When I picked up the paper all I could read was McCarthy accusing somebody of being a communist. I couldn't understand how the communists were the only people who wanted good things. Here was somebody [McCarthy] who wanted them in jail. I decided I better seek out the communists.

She took to communism at the height of the Cold War, the McCarthy era, and its blacklist. But she stated, "I joined the Communist Party by accident, mainly seeking information. A friend of mine, I guess she meant well. She took advantage of my ignorance. She had me give a person a quarter without telling me this was my initiation fee into the Communist Party."[70]

Inexplicably, Mae distanced herself from her reasons for joining CPUSA. "I went to all these meetings. There these people sat, Black and white. Saying words like international proletariat, democratic centralism. It was a different kind of language. I didn't know what in the world those people were talking about." Notwithstanding her lack of knowledge concerning communism, she fearlessly took up the cause and rallied for communism in her union job. "I went out and I did all the things that good communists are suppose[d] to do. The boss hated me. I figured well, so what, the boss is supposed to hate the worker. [The] worker is supposed to fight the boss. The union is going to protect him. The communist union was the best of all."[71]

Mallory maintains that she committed herself to the Communist Party. White communists and the communist union did not commit to her. She felt that they refused to protect her in 1956–1957. She stated, "The boss fired me. The union let him." The union denied her a job "because only the Hungarians had to have jobs." Choosing white supremacists' ideas over race, the white communists and the communist-backed union opted to support and hire new Hungarian immigrants fleeing the Hungarian revolution over African Americans.[72]

Mae Mallory's experience within the Communist Party and in the communist-controlled union was not singular. White socialists and CPUSA maintained a long history of betraying Blacks. They wanted to maintain white power within a communist framework, with acquiescent nonwhite members. From the 1800s the white-controlled socialist movements opted for what Afro-Caribbean activist Herbert Harrison termed a "white race first policy." A mass exodus occurred with African Americans and Afro-Caribbeans founding the African Blood Brotherhood (1909) and other socialist/communist organizations.[73] In 1919, when the CPUSA was founded, African Americans joined to fight for human rights. Their numbers increased from the 1920s to the 1930s, due to the 1929 CPUSA resolution on the "Negro Question," which defined "Blacks as an oppressed nation, with the right to self-determination." Black membership also increased due to the dictate from the Communist International instructing CPUSA to involve themselves with African American issues and racism, issues that CPUSA neglected. The Black presence in CPUSA led whites to deliberately sabotage Black comrades. Whites argued that class trumped race, ignoring Comintern dictates to engage in Negro work. CPUSA relied on stereotypes, arguing that African Americans lacked organizational and leadership skills.[74]

Mae Mallory's Communist Party experience proved similar to that of early Black communists. Mallory found that communists "didn't really want to challenge the system. It was impossible for me to exist without challenging the system because the system denied my very existence, you see." Part of denying her existence included rendering the Black woman's sexual body impotent within the party. Mae discovered this at meetings. "There were all these Black men with white women and Black women alone and you know, I said, what is this?"[75]

The FBI began gathering information on Mae beginning in 1956, leading to a file that eventually passed two thousand pages. They characterized Mae as a "security matter—communist" and kept substantial tabs on her because she belonged to and attended meetings of the Communist Party and the Negro Women for Action, a "communist front" organization according to informant T-8. Millie McAdory Edelman, the chair of the Harlem branch of the Communist Party and Mae's friend, noted that Mae left Harlem's Communist Party in January 1958. The FBI interviewed Mae on May 28, 1958, and considered recruiting her as an informant. They concluded that she was "totally unreliable" because she accepted $1,040 while working under an assumed name, "allegedly threatened to kill a person at a former place of employment, and in general appears to be an agitator." FBI informants found no data pointing to Mae as a communist. They still watched Mae her whole life.[76]

Disappointed with the communists, Mae Mallory turned to the Black nationalists.[77] "I went to the Nationalist Movement just to listen. They talked a real militant thing, but nobody did anything. They didn't have any answers and the men had contempt for the women."[78] Like the communists, the Black male nationalists also rendered the Black female political and social body impuissant.

Mae found little comfort with formal conservative Black organizations. They judged her politics. When incarcerated in New York for fraud in 1957, a female FBI informant noted that someone told African American civil rights activist Ella Baker, chair for the Educational Committee of New York's NAACP, that Mae belonged to the Communist Party. Baker's secretary confronted Mallory and told her that "she was putting the NAACP on the spot."[79] This encounter with Baker and the conservative NAACP points to why Mae and others rejected them. Those who did not fit into the prescribed norms of Black middle-class respectability received little if any support from the NAACP and other conservative groups. Going it alone and marching to her own drum offered the only viable alternative for Mae as she became a radical African American woman political activist. Using the motherist frame, Mae positioned herself as an everyday political activist.

Desegregation Case

Mae worked to better the conditions of African American children in the New York City Public Schools, making her case on television.

> When *By Line*, the new T.V. afternoon show made its debut last Monday the first two guests were Mrs. Mae Mallory, the leader of the Harlem Mothers who are keeping their children out of segregated schools and Jayne Meadows. Mrs. Mallory did a wonderful job of presenting her case and ended with this

wonderful statement. "I don't want my child to sit side by side white children. I just want the same classroom with equal opportunity for my child to absorb what is being taught."[80]

The 1954 Supreme Court decision reversing *Plessy v. Ferguson*—the separate but equal doctrine—had little impact in northern cities such as New York, given the deliberate efforts by the state from the 1920s to the 1950s to keep the races separate. The North promoted anti-Black and minority sentiment among whites, through laws that dictated separate education. The Commission on School Integration and Diane Ravitch described "gerrymandering of school district lines" to maintain white schools. Ravitch and the commission discussed how New York State promoted "pupil transfers" in which administrators encouraged white students to transfer to white schools while blocking Black and Puerto Rican parents from transferring their children. They noted the use of discriminatory housing segregation, which led to educational segregation, "deliberately contrived by public school authorities." Housing segregation, the rise in suburbs, and whites sending their children to private and parochial schools contributed to northern school segregation. "Optional zoning" for communities whose racial makeup changed from white to Black or Puerto Rican enabled whites to send their children to white schools, while preventing Black and nonwhite parents from using optional zoning. The state created school zoning lines to maintain white schools. According to Ravitch, New York's schools maintained segregation by elementary schools sending their students to certain junior high schools and the city government's approach to site selection for building new schools.[81] When Mae Mallory's children entered school, she found that schools were more segregated than when she had attended.[82]

In "I Was One of the Harlem Nine" and her 1970 interview Mallory discussed significant incidents that led her to educational advocacy. She wrote of how her fifth-grade son Butch came home assigned to count pipes in the bathroom, to aspire to become a plumber. Pat says it "never happened because my mother objected."[83] She became involved with the PTA. Mae protested to school administrators: "I said whatever he is going to be he will determine it, you won't." This led to her efforts at school curriculum reform.[84] In 1956 her children attended PS 10 on Saint Nicholas Avenue between 116th and 117th Streets. Pat recalls telling Mae that "they shut the street off at lunch time so that children could play. A beer truck backed into the street and crushed this little boy [to death]."[85] Mae went to the white male principal to discuss the horrific death, to work toward solutions.[86] Like the *Moynihan Report*, which maligned working-class African American women for being single, poor, and mothers, the principal showed little concern for the child or his single mother.

> PRINCIPAL: You really don't have anything to worry about. Our Sunshine Club went to see the mother. We took her a bag of canned goods. Actually she is better off because she had so many children to feed.
>
> MALLORY: I couldn't believe that here a white man is going to tell a Black woman in Harlem that a can of peaches is better than your child. If you are alone your child should die anyway.[87]

Mae also learned why her children described their school as a pigsty and why they didn't use the bathroom at school. "Words cannot describe my anger at the condition of that building and the toilets." She discovered that steel from the school building regularly fell onto the playground, creating a hazard. The horrible odor of two substandard school bathrooms with nonflushing toilets for 1,700 children assaulted her senses. Pat recalled, "There was one slab of wood across a whole wall and holes drilled into the slab. That was the toilet. We never went." Mae wrote that the school building and the bathrooms were worse than anything she'd seen in Georgia.[88]

Confronted with all these inequities, Mallory went to Albany to talk to her Black congressman, meet United Parents Teachers Association members, and speak to the assembly. The association repaired the bathroom, after which the principal became enraged with Mae. At the height of the Red Scare, knowing the repercussions, the principal accused Mallory of communism. The FBI and like agencies actively engaged in surveillance and suppression of ordinary African Americans like Mae Mallory, advocates for civil and human rights, "racial political activists, Pan-Africanists," African American newspaper publishers, and union members. J. Edgar Hoover firmly believed that communists were central to African American activism, which posed a threat to the United States, and that they were a "potentially dangerous class of activists," more dangerous than communism. Hoover embedded these ideals into the FBI, informing the FBI's complicity in violence against African American activists. Theodore Kornweibel asserts that the FBI, by labeling African American advocacy as communistic, used the "'red' label to delegitimize Blacks' desires for peace and liberation from the racial status quo." The red label proved useful in suppressing change.[89] The principal's efforts were unceasing and damaging, for he equated Mae's advocating for educational equality with communism. He urged other parents to turn against Mae and block her access to the school.[90]

The NAACP resisted helping Mae because of her working-class status, fearful she would tarnish their shine, fearful they would face the communism charge. Notwithstanding the accusation, Mae Mallory organized and agitated for a new school building. In 1956, according to an FBI informant, she spoke at Bermuda Hall (402 146th Street) in front of the Harlem Communist Party under the name Comrade Mary ("for security reasons") to argue for a new building. She also "led a delegation to school authorities protesting the physical conditions of the school. [The informant] learned from Ella J. Baker that Mae Mallory was the leader in the fight for new facilities at Public School #10."[91] Mallory *did* gain the support of Thelma Lyons and the Reverend Eugene Callender of the Mid-Harlem Community Parish and the Church of the Master. They attended meetings with Mae at the Board of Estimate, the borough president's office, and the city council. They advocated for better conditions and were granted a new school building at 121st Street and Morningside.[92] Mae wrote, "I can't do justice to the story here, but getting that school was quite an achievement and gave me so much confidence in the fact that you *can* fight City Hall and win!"[93]

Mae's firsthand knowledge of inequities and racism within New York City schools, her mother's inability to protect her from white supremacist women teachers, and her knowledge of the hazard that the African American girl's and women's body posed to hegemony did not dissuade her. She chose to battle the school system on behalf of Black and Brown children. Although her family and husband forced motherhood on her, she emerged as an organic intellectual and an everyday political activist within the motherist frame.[94]

Mae wrote, "My daughter Pat filed the first case against the public schools of New York for discriminatory practices."[95] In "Mother Moves to Sue Schools," the *Amsterdam News* (June 29, 1957) noted, "The first step in a move to force New York City's Jim Crow schools into court was taken Monday by a [30] year old mother, and her 12 year old child." They attempted to enroll Patricia into the Joan of Arc School at 154 West 93rd Street instead of the segregated Wadleigh Junior High School on 114th Street. The FBI obtained a letter that Mae wrote to Marion Clark, assistant superintendent of schools: "There will be no opportunity to [interact] with children of other racial groups. The faculty of the school is [made up of] substandard inexperienced teachers. The physical plant [notwithstanding] renovations is still substandard." Mallory and Paul Zuber's lawsuit reiterated the arguments from Mae's letter. For their actions, the FBI maintained files on Mallory and Zuber, a law student at Brooklyn Law School. Mae's file included news articles concerning the lawsuit and her 1957 attendance at a Harlem Parents Club meeting. On August 20, 1957, informant T-4 reported that the NAACP Education Committee met to decide whether to support Mae in her fight against the school system: "'T-4 stated the purpose of the meeting as best as he could understand was a discussion of Mae Mallory's case, which was concerned with their fight to have a child entered in an 'all-white-school.' The Committee discussed the possibility of holding street meetings in sympathy with Mae Mallory's case in support of school integration."[96] Zuber and Mallory lost the suit at the Supreme Court, and the state upheld the zoning laws.[97]

On September 9, 1958, Mae Mallory and the Parents' Committee for Better Education in Harlem responded to the loss. Mae wrote, "About 100 of us agreed to keep our children out of school if we could not change their junior high schools." They founded a "Freedom School," hired a teacher, and held classes at the Emmanuel Sunday School, 126th Street and Third Avenue.[98] But "when the hour of decision came, all backed down for some reason. . . . I think it is only fair to say that most of us were getting reprisals in some way. The women, in the main, were all for the program, but many husbands faced losing their jobs. Since I had no husband or job, I stuck it out."[99]

The state charged the parents with neglect for taking their children out of school and founding the Freedom School. Mae Mallory and some brave women protected their motherhood rights by filing a million-dollar lawsuit charging Mayor Wagner, the Board of Education, and others with "'sinister and discriminatory purpose in the perpetuation of racial segregation' in five school districts in Harlem."[100] Despite state suppression, Mae Mallory soldiered on, unafraid and undaunted in her efforts.

Political Prisoner

Mae Mallory's advocacy led the state to target her and her family through the Counter Intelligence Program, COINTELPRO. In 1953 and 1954 the U.S. government, with the backing of the National Security Council, remained successful in overthrowing the leftist governments in Iran and Guatemala, respectively. In 1956 these efforts led the National Security Council and the FBI to turn their attention to oppressing U.S. citizens. J. Edgar Hoover established COINTELPRO with the mission to "subvert subversives," prevent spies from stealing U.S. secrets, and annihilate communists, African Americans, everyday people, and activists.[101] Tim Weiner wrote, "Hoover started watching the new leaders of the civil rights movement very closely. By 1957, COINTELPRO was primed as a weapon in the long struggle between Black Americans and their government." With the founding of COINTELPRO, they targeted numerous Black organizations and people.[102] They used dirty and illegal means, including informants, hate mail, "snitch jackets," electronic surveillance, mail interception, forged documents, tax harassment, trash inspection, and misinformation. They caused race riots and instigated and participated in the murder of African Americans and supporters, such as the murder of white activist Viola Liuzzo by white supremacists with an FBI agent present. People found themselves blacklisted and lost their jobs, their homes, and educational opportunities because agents contacted employers and schools. Their ultimate goal was to destroy human beings whom they saw as enemies. Mae Mallory found herself ensnared in their web.[103] COINTELPRO worked with the Internal Revenue Service using tax harassment and audits to target financially strained people. According to Tim Weiner and Rhodri Jeffrey-Jones, COINTELPRO's goal was to drive people to self-destruction and hopefully suicide, as they tried with Martin Luther King Jr., Robert F. Williams, and many others. They wanted "to instill hate, fear, doubt, and self-destruction within the American Left. . . . The goal was to destroy the public lives and private reputations of Communist Party members, and everyone connected with them."[104]

This was the strategy they used against African American activists like Mae. The *Crusader* (1960) reported that the state accused Adam Clayton Powell Jr. and Martin Luther King Jr. of tax fraud and used tax harassment against them. In 1962 African American lawyer Len Holt discussed the use of tax harassment to punish activists including Black civil rights attorney Samuel Mitchell. He faced tax fraud charges and a prison sentence "directly related to his efforts to protect the rights of Negroes in North Carolina." Unfortunately for Mae, Holt was not her attorney.[105] Mae Mallory's FBI file revealed the use of tax harassment against her. It noted that Miss Hedi Schulenklopper, the social investigator for the New York City Welfare Department, told the FBI that Mae was a "constant source of trouble to the Welfare Department." They considered "bringing legal action against [Mallory] in as much as Mallory, in the past has been drawing relief checks while employed."[106] The Welfare Department arrested Mae "on [a] grand larceny charge" on June 20, 1957, for working at Brooklyn's New York Feather Company in 1952 and 1954. Mae told the *Amsterdam News* that "she told the Welfare Dept [in March 1953] that she had been working, but nothing was said of it." She believed the city targeted her because she led the desegregation protests. Mae charged that they tried to force her to sign a document stating that "she accepted money under false pretenses. When she refused, the welfare representative complained to the District Attorney's office. She was 'invited' over to the Brooklyn District Attorney's office where" they arrested her. In 1957 they incarcerated Mae for accepting welfare checks totaling

$1,040 under an "assumed name." Callender freed Mae by providing $1,000 bail. The Welfare Legal Division told the FBI that Mallory "signed a 'confession of judgment' in the amount of $1042.15 which is the sum of money she fraudulently obtained from the Department of Welfare. . . . The 'confession of judgment' signed by the subject meant that should [Mallory] ever become self-sufficient, all the money she obtained by fraud would have to be repaid." In 1958 they again charged her with fraud for working at Easton Manufacturing Company and collecting $218.85 in welfare checks. The Brooklyn County Court found her guilty on January 30, 1958. She "received [a] suspended sentence and probation. [The Welfare Department] has [a] pending fraud case against subject and plans to prosecute."[107]

They also charged her and other parents with child neglect, to suppress their motherhood rights, and they targeted Mae's son Butch as well. In Mae's words, "[In 1957] I was thrown in jail, charged with grand larceny. I went before the judge. We had quite a hassle. I told him about himself. They picked my son up, tried to say he was a delinquent. The judge said I was trying to make something out of him that I wasn't. Whatever that means! They took my son away." Threatened by the idea that Mae was raising little radicals, ready to challenge educational segregation policies, authorities arrested Butch. They charged him with delinquency, placed him at the notorious Spofford Juvenile Detention Center, and upon his release gave Butch to Mae's aunt and her husband.[108]

In 1959 COINTELPRO's tax harassment strategy proved successful in Mae's case. They jailed her again at New York's infamous Women's House of Detention for thirty days. Mae *did try to pay the State back*—$318.[109] They incarcerated her anyway. Mae believed as do I that the state singled her out and arrested her for advocating for educational desegregation and equality. The fraud case was six years old, and conspiring correspondence between the Welfare Department and the FBI shows the effort to criminalize Mae. I firmly believe that the timing of her incarceration in 1957 and 1959, at the height of her efforts toward educational equality, is suspect. I contend that the state incarcerated Mae and harassed her family at the urging of the FBI because of her activism and affiliation with the Communist Party. In 1957 they classified her as a security risk, placing her on the communist detention list.

Mae Mallory used her wit to convey her feelings about the charges. "I told them I definitely would [pay them] as soon as they turned Manhattan Island back to the Indians. But until such time, like don't bother me." Mallory sought help from Black communist Ben Davis. The FBI reported that he did not "come when she was arrested." Mae recalled that he refused to help her. I suspect that due to his broken state from five years in prison and his recent release, he was in no shape to help Mae.[110] Mallory did get help from Pan-Africanist Communist Party member Ramona Garret. Garret hired a lawyer to gain Mae's release on $1,000 bail.[111]

Mae recounts, "They tried to make life miserable for me. I just fought back. I was disposed of the house I was living in. The whole world just crashed down. They try to pile as much on you as they can to see if you will snap. To see if you will break. I am determined that I'm not going to."[112] In 1957 and 1959 she didn't understand the machinations behind the scene working to keep her imprisoned—working to drive her mad, even to suicide. She didn't know of the numerous informants or welfare workers who fed the FBI information on her to keep her jailed. Since 1917 the FBI has used informants, infiltrators, and agent provocateurs who joined Black organizations to spy, report, and disrupt.[113] The FBI infiltrated the African Blood Brotherhood, the NAACP, the Black Panther Party, SCLC, the Monroe Defense Committee, and the Committee to Aid the Monroe Defendants, using Black and multiracial spies to cause chaos and mayhem.[114] They wiretapped people's homes and phones as they did Mae's. They covertly rifled through people's offices, and they confiscated and opened their mail as they did with the Negroes with Guns movement, the Monroe Defense Committee, and the Committee to Aid the Monroe Defendants. They contacted employers and forced people's firing. Even when the FBI made alliances with African Americans like the NAACP's Walter White and Roy Wilkins, praising their anti-communist stance, they still tapped their telephones and investigated them.[115] Mae did not know of the disruption program the government put forth to keep the MDC and the CAMD at odds with one another through a full-on campaign to keep her imprisoned for kidnapping. She knew they watched her, but she didn't fully grasp the extent of the FBI's surveillance. What she grappled with and understood was that the state was determined to keep her jailed. This proved extremely painful for Mae.

In 1957 New York, Mae found little help except from the Pan-Africanist communist Pam Garrett, and from Thelma Lyons and Reverend Callender. She found no solace as an incarcerated political prisoner in New York's most notorious jail. Her 1961 incarceration in Cleveland proved quite different. As a political prisoner there, Mae found a solid family of like-minded people. Separated in age by thirteen years, bound together by a common goal—freedom and human rights—Audrey Proctor Seniors and Mae Mallory made their way to each other under circumstances of unfreedom with my mother's unbending commitment to Mae, to see her free through the Monroe Defense Committee. Each woman came to radical activism under different circumstances informed by place and time. They found themselves bound together through the tropes of motherhood, radical activism, and a socialist–Black nationalist theoretical frame. In Cleveland they created an unbreakable kinship bond. One must ask, who was Audrey Proctor Seniors? How did place and time play a role in her self-defense and radical ideological frame? How did she formulate a self-defense radical ideology? What drew her to Mae? What did their bond mean? In the next chapter I will answer these questions looking at place—New Orleans circa 1958, the site of my mother's radical woman activist formation.

Chapter 4

Audrey Proctor
The New Orleans NAACP and the Monroe Defense Committee

In Cleveland, Miss Audrey Proctor sets quite a pace.
She may turn out to be the leader of the race.

—Charles Anderson, "Forecast Storm," 1963

A beautiful childhood. The magnificence of being raised by a dazzlingly gorgeous radical mother. Daily ritual: Mommy drinking coffee light, cream and sugar, smelling wonderful—reminiscent of a New Orleans childhood of toasted buttered French bread dipped in coffee. Perfume carried on the breeze of my mother's body onto mine, hugging me, kissing me, loving me. Getting ready for kindergarten and work. Mommy puts on her makeup, Gele, high-heeled shoes, black minidress with gold chain belt, and white mod tights, and off we would go, down the elevator, to our big shiny mezzanine. Walking in the big courtyard, past the playground jungle gym and swings, our gigantic high-rise rising behind us. Mommy lifting her head to the sun, breathing in the rays, smiling, holding my hand in her soft small hand, looking down at me with her deep black eyes, keeping me safely loved. Her heels clicking on the courtyard bricks, the warmth of her body next to mine. We arrive. The 41 bus picks us up in front of Bond Bread Factory's bread-fragranced air. Wetson's Hamburgers next door, Prospect Park, and the train station across the street. We wait for the bus. Downtown on the lumbering bus we go. Mommy drops me at the beautiful red-brick Brooklyn Friends School. After school we walk to her job at the beaux arts Board of Education on Livingston Street.

> She worked for Mrs. Alesi. Mommy sets me up with crayons, markers, paper, staplers. I play as she works as a secretary. Contentment.

In 1961 in Monroe, Mrs. Johnson, forty-five, worked as the secretary of the Negroes with Guns movement. In Cleveland Mae Mallory, thirty-four, was incarcerated. Audrey Proctor, twenty-one, worked in Cleveland to free Mae through the Monroe Defense Committee. Pat Mallory, sixteen, went to New York's Seward Park High School and joined the Monroe Defense Committee. Johnson was twenty-four years older than Audrey Proctor; Mae was thirteen years older, and Pat was five years younger. Place, time, and decades separated these women, yet they all worked toward a common goal: freedom. This collective objective intertwined them as family, as quintessential radical African American women activists.

The Mae Mallory Case

> Mommy dressed elegantly and I, age four, traveled by taxi from Brooklyn to Manhattan to the exquisitely ornate gold Grand Central Station. Through a dark cavernous tunnel we went, getting on the train riding to Cleveland. In Cleveland we stayed in a warm, inviting home with Mommy's Brown lady friend, a member of the MDC or perhaps Mommy's Auntie Gladys. I was gifted a lovely brown toddler girl paper doll with a colorful clothes set.

In 1958 my mother begged her parents to let her leave New Orleans. They refused. After her high school graduation Audrey worked for three years as a hat-check girl at the International House on Canal Street. In 1961 her parents finally relented, allowing her, age twenty-one, to move to Cleveland to live with her Auntie Gladys Winters, a bookbinder.[1] In Cleveland Audrey attended secretarial school and worked toward political and social change. With lessons learned in the radical New Orleans NAACP, she moved forward in her political, intellectual, and social thought, becoming a devotee of Robert F. Williams's self-defense movement. In 1961, when Mae Mallory sought help from civil rights organizations, they safeguarded themselves from Mae's taint of communism, radicalism, and the working class. Her Black councilmen supported her extradition because she did not fit the idealized model of Black womanhood or motherhood. Founded in 1959, the Trotskyist/Maoist Workers World Party in Buffalo offered her a lifeline. They sent African American Ruthie Stone and her infant daughter to Cleveland away from the safety of her Buffalo life with her white husband, Ritchie Stone. Stone belonged to the Mothers Alliance and the WWP, and she worked as a barmaid. As the secretary of the Monroe Defense Committee, Stone organized picket lines at Governor DiSalle's office on Mae's behalf.[2] Audrey joined Stone as a member of WWP. In 1948 white disaffected members of Buffalo's Socialist Workers Party took great umbrage with their political positions, their right-wing agenda, their complacency during the Red Scare witch hunt, and SWP's support of Stalin's repressive Russia.[3] Ideological differences also emerged because the disaffected members came from working-class stock and adhered to "a tradition of working class struggle, while many SWP members came from the petty bourgeois."[4] On February 12, 1959, Sam Marcy, Vincent Copeland, Jack Wilson, Ronald Jones, Dorothy Flint, and Fran and Ted Dostal joined with my father, Clarence Henry Seniors, a Morehouse College student; his African American mentor, Dr. Lonnie Cross, professor and chair of Atlanta University's math department; and Rosie and Milt Neidenberg, "the proletarian left wing of the Socialist Workers Party," to establish Buffalo's Workers World Party. Our friend Deidre Griswold described them as a "combat party based on the working class." They founded WWP to "openly fight for orthodox Trotskyism, which is the authentic Marxism-Leninism of today."[5] Introduced to the SWP by Dr. Cross, Daddy worked in Buffalo's car factories when off from school and lived with his friends Milt and his wife Rosie of Mothers Alliance and WWP. They were a decade older than he.[6]

> On seeing men from the African continent as a little girl, I asked my mother, "Why do they have those carved lines and designs on their faces?" "Paula, that is scarification. They signify their African country and their tribe. Scarification is part of their culture." Question answered, lesson taught. Onward in our day's adventure.

At age twelve I met the glamorous, sophisticated, fabulously Afroed, gorgeously dark brown-skinned fourteen-year-old Mikko at Brooklyn Friends. She lived on Central Park West in a posh high-rise. Her mother named her after a cherished Japanese friend. Oh, I adored Mikko!!! She taught me so much about friendship and life. I wanted to be just like her. One time Mikko and I rode the train giggling and laughing, engrossed in our teenaged revelry. A transgender Black man sitting across from us thought we were laughing at them. Scoldingly they said, "You should not make fun and laugh at me because I am different." Admonishments and reproaches abounded. Honestly, we were not even paying attention to them, so engrossed were we in our teenaged banter. Mikko's social worker mother worked with boys from children's homes. She raised Mikko better than that. So did my mother. We played with those boys different from us, went to Great Adventure Amusement Park with them. I remember Mommy and I as a little girl going to Manhattan's WW meetings, walking up three flights of stairs to the capacious space, with creaky wood-plank floors. Our WW friends were Black, Brown, Asian, Native American, and White, transgender, blind, sighted, disabled, nondisabled, gay, straight, wonderful people. Nobody cared about difference. We all worked toward a free equitable world, toward ending war and violence. We went to WWP friends' houses, reveled in their lives and accomplishments. We children played. I don't know if we apologized on the subway for the misinterpretation or whether we were struck dumb. I do know we talked about the encounter once by ourselves. Mikko and I learned a lesson to add to our arsenal of things our mothers taught us.

WWP's commitment to a just world led them to Mae and the Monroe Defendants. They helped establish Cleveland's Monroe Defense Committee, following the lead of Ruthie Stone, my mother, and Mrs. Johnson. My mother's lifelong friends Rosie Neidenberg and Jeanette Merrill wrote "Mae Mallory Unforgettable Freedom Fighter Promoted Self Defense," which detailed Mommy's initial encounter with WWP and MDC. They asserted that Audrey "worked in a coffee shop patronized by [MDC] members and enthusiastically agreed to receive mail, shielding it from the FBI. She took telephone messages to bypass the office tap." Audrey joined WWP and managed the office for MDC, "a group with a way-out philosophy of self-defense against mobsters [white racists]."[7]

MDC, CAMD, and the FBI

Soon after the arrest of Mae, African American youth Harold Reape, Richard Crowder [Yusef], and white Freedom Rider John Lowry, people established groups to help them. African American Calvin Hicks of the Trotskyist *On Guard* contended that "the initial response was made in the offices of Mr. A. Phillip Randolph. A conference had been arranged, at my urging by Mr. Bayard Rustin." Randolph, Rustin, Mr. Hope Stevens, Rowland Watts, and Freedom Rider David Morton established the first group, New York's Monroe Defense Committee, led by Hicks.[8] On October 2, 1961, the FBI reported that Mae's arrest a month after the riots led to the founding of New York's MDC. "Some may wonder why we have placed so much emphasis on Mae Mallory when there are a number of other defendants involved in the case. The answer is simple: In the absence of Mr. Robert Williams, the prosecution in Monroe, N.C., views Mrs. Mallory as target number one."[9]

New York's MDC worked to obtain Mallory's freedom from prison, prevent her extradition on kidnapping charges, and block her permanent incarceration.[10] In October 1961 they held benefits, reported on continued Monroe violence, raised legal defense funds, and gathered "food and clothing for the needy in Monroe, [because] many persons who followed Mr. Williams's leadership have been removed from welfare rolls."[11]

People also founded the Committee to Aid the Monroe Defendants, which Dr. Perry aligned with.[12] The FBI saw CAMD as a communist threat, linked to the Socialist Workers Party, "for the purpose of making a national and international issue" of the kidnapping charges against Williams. They wrote that the CAMD's sole purpose was to attract members to the SWP. They listed Berta Green, the secretary of SWP, and George Weissman, who founded the party in 1937, as members of SWP and CAMD.[13] The FBI charged that SWP "is currently attempting to organize branches of the CAMD throughout the country." With $15,000, CAMD bailed out Reape, Crowder, and Lowry to prevent their long-term jailing. The FBI reported, "In view of the dominating subversive elements within the [MDC and the CAMD], it is felt that the counter-articles would be extremely valuable in discouraging individuals from becoming associated with or contributing funds to the CAMD and the MDC."[14] The FBI established a disruptive program to keep the MDC, CAMD, WWP, and SWP at odds with each other. This program prevented the MDC and CAMD from unifying. New York's MDC was dismantled in May 1962 in favor of Cleveland's MDC.[15] Mae wrote,

> I have been held in jail here in Cleveland for nine long months without having been tried or convicted of any crime.... THE ONLY CRIME I AM GUILTY OF IS THAT I HAVE FOUGHT FOR THE RIGHTS OF THE BLACK PEOPLE AND THE OPPRESSED. My fight against extradition is the fight of all persecuted and hounded people. A victory for me against the racists will also be a victory for all the oppressed. I need your help in this important struggle.... [Cleveland's MDC] has been leading my extradition fight. They take care of my personal needs, even bringing fruit to my cell regularly each week. They desperately need funds to continue their work. Yours for Freedom Now, Mae Mallory.[16]

Fig. 4. Ella Baker (center) and Clarence Henry Seniors seated next to her, May 1960, Wisconsin Historical Society.

With this pronouncement my mother and Ruthie Stone led Mae's case and we all became family.[17]

In 1961 my father, Clarence H. Seniors, eventually joined them as chair. His mentors included Dr. Cross, Ella Baker, and Septima Clark. Seniors accompanied Clark as she accepted the Woman of the Year Award from the Utility Club at the Waldorf Astoria Ballroom on June 4, 1960, sitting on the dais as her honored guest. In high school in Tampa, Florida, he joined the Urban League, was president of the NAACP Youth Council, and participated in Tampa Public Library sit-ins. Seniors initially attended Tuskegee Institute but quickly transferred to Atlanta's Morehouse College. He was arrested with Martin Luther King Jr. and seventy-five others conducting Atlanta "sit-downs" in March 1960. That same year Daddy filed a million-dollar lawsuit challenging the segregation of spectators and white and Black defendants in the Atlanta courts. White supremacists burned a cross at his and Dr. Cross's homes due to the lawsuit.[18]

My father accompanied Ella Baker to Monteagle, Tennessee's Highlander Folk School, where he participated in workshops and taught classes. At her invitation he attended the conference when SNCC was founded. In 1959 his activism led to his dismissal from Morehouse, a bastion of conservatism and fear. Dr. Cross gained his admittance to Atlanta's Morris Brown College, where he befriended Robert F. Williams and Cross introduced him to

Malcolm X. Daddy graduated with a mathematics degree.[19] As a student, he wrote essays in support of Mae Mallory for *Workers World* under the name A. T. Simpson:

> This 35-year-old factory worker, once a dress maker, hospital worker, housewife, maid, and mother of two children has been courageously defending the honor of Black womanhood and taking a firm stand against the racist terrorists of both the North and the South. This is being done even in spite of the fact that when this fugitive from Southern so-called justice fled to Ohio last October seeking protection in the state, the Governor abruptly ordered her arrest and said that the woman has to go back to the Klan country to stand trial.[20]

As the chair of Cleveland's MDC, Clarence Seniors and the other members could not align with CAMD because of white resistance to Black power, which arose during CAMD's attempt to work with New York's MDC. Green wrote in CAMD's "Summary Report" that the Monroe Defense Committee's main objective included advocating for self-defense as a "mobilizing center" for satellite self-defense organizations around the country. She asserted that MDC felt the Freedom Riders were solely responsible for Monroe's melee and must not hold leading MDC positions "since they considered the Freedom Riders wrong in principle."[21] The New York branch's Calvin Hicks wrote that "even though the Freedom Riders precipitated the full-scale attack, and got the first brunt of it, it was the Monroe people who had aroused their ire—not the strangers from out of town." Hicks let the Freedom Riders off the hook.[22] In a series of letters Hicks's loyalty was called into question. Pat warned her mother Mae about him. Questions arose concerning funds donated to the New York branch.[23] Cleveland's branch held the Freedom Riders wholly responsible, cut them no slack, and expressed anger toward them. Green also contended that the MDC placed the Monroe Defendants' needs second and insisted on an all-Black organization.[24] Hicks wrote that white "liberals and radicals" wanted leadership positions over Blacks. Hicks noted that "progressives actually stated that they would not support a committee with only an Afro-American leadership." Hicks wrote that SWP's Green and Weisman wanted sole leadership roles in the MDC. They felt that African Americans could not lead. Hicks and New York writer MDC member Leroi Jones [Amiri Baraka] decided "that the leadership should be Black. Mr. Weisman and Miss Green vehemently opposed this makeup," even offering money so that whites could lead. When rebuffed they withdrew the offer.[25] In the "Monroe Defense Committee Bulletin" Hicks further articulated the Black leadership stance, stating that MDC members decided "because the fight in Monroe was essentially a Black led fight for Black rights, the MDC must be a Black led committee. However, it also determined that white people should and indeed, must participate. However, their participation must be that of an understanding and aware ally, rather than that of supposed ideological lord and master."[26] White communists and Trotskyists attempted to take over the defense of Mallory, Reape, Crowder, and Lowry.[27] Berta Green proposed to Mae's lawyer, Conrad Lynn, that Clarence Seniors conjoin Cleveland's MDC with CAMD. Green asserted that he could be the executive secretary as opposed to the chair. Implicit in Green's letter was that whites knew more about how African Americans should advocate for their rights and those of the Monroe Defendants than Blacks themselves.[28] Green's and Weisman's attitudes and the FBI's disruptive program ensured that the two groups would never come together.[29]

Cleveland's Monroe Defense Committee

> *My whole life, two extraordinary rifle knives lived on our bookshelves—always present, sheathed, heavy, and metal—relics from my parents' time with MDC.*

The FBI report stated that Cleveland's Monroe Defense Committee was founded "to act as an educational organization to inspire the Negroes to united mass action on issues affecting Negro rights and opportunities."[30] The FBI identified the MDC as a "Provisional Organizing Committee for a Marxist-Leninist Communist Party, aka the Workers World Party."[31] MDC maintained that they worked toward "the correct approach to the Black Liberation Movement." They proposed unity "to give the kind of leadership to the masses so that they can see the liberation of the struggle of the people of Asia[;] the practical liberation of Africa [links with] the struggle here."[32] Like New York's MDC, the Cleveland branch's key objective was liberating Mae from jail and preventing her extradition. As my father and mother wrote,

> Our drive to save Mae Mallory from the clutches of the KKK is gaining more momentum as we begin the new year. Mrs. Mallory is still in County Jail in Cleveland [fighting] extradition, [and] Southern so-called "Justice," because of her militant stand against Jim Crow oppression [in] the South. Mallory's extradition fight has come to the fore as one of Black America's most cele-

brated freedom causes. Protests against forcing her to return to Monroe for trial have come from China, Ghana, Mexico, Egypt, Jamaica, Czechoslovakia, Australia, and Cuba. These events coupled with our picket lines and demonstrations in the states here, successfully blocked her from being thrown to North Carolina racists by the defeated Governor Di Salle. Mae Mallory begins her twelfth month in jail, the danger of her being sent back is imminent.... Shall we count on you to join us with an active campaign for the freedom of this bold and gallant warrior? A freedom fighting Mother's life is at stake and your support can make a difference. Sincerely, Yours for Freedom Now, Clarence H. Seniors.[33]

MDC also worked on voter registration drives, school and job desegregation, equitable welfare rights for Blacks, and fair housing. My parents bonded as a family with Mrs. Johnson as she became my grandmother, and they assisted her with her educational programs and *Did You Know?*[34]

Cleveland's MDC members represented a multiracial coalition of local and national people from radical, formal, and religious groups, such as WWP, CORE, RAM, the Northern Negro Grass Roots Leadership Conference, the Cleveland Freedom Fighters, the Republic of New Africa, PRIDE, and the Group on Advanced Leadership. Our family friends, white activists Ted and Fran Dostal and African American Wilbur Grattan, belonged to these groups.[35]

Twenty-four years older than my mother, Grattan was born in 1916 in Alabama to an activist father, a "sympathizer of the International Workers of the World, a leader and organizer of striking [coal] miners." Grattan's father taught him to fight oppression, so they marched. Because of this training, at fourteen Grattan became a labor organizer at an Alabama hospital where he worked, leading to his departure from Alabama given the threats to him and his family. After hoboing (migratory traveling and working) and landing in Chicago, he protested in the "Spend your money where you can work" campaign against the grocery store A&P. He integrated the store as a worker and organized unions in "the cane fields of Louisiana." He moved back to Alabama during the Great Depression and formed the Congress of Industrial Organizations in coal fields. In the 1940s Grattan moved to Cleveland, became an insurance salesman, married, and had four children, three boys and a daughter, Iris, who would become one of Pat Mallory's close friends. The *Pittsburgh Courier* reported that in 1954 Grattan became "recording secretary and committee man of the Local 1250, UAW-CIO." The *Call and Post* reported that he was the president of the Cleveland Conference of Negro Trade Unions working to integrate the AFL and the IBEW (1956). Mirroring Mae's experience with the Cold War, Grattan wrote that he became "regional and local chairman of the Fair Practice Committee and Educational Committee of the United Auto Workers until the McCarthy Witch Hunt Period [when] I was officially removed from the Union [and left] the shops." Grattan participated in the Montgomery Boycott and the sit-ins:

> I played whatever role I could to destroy the illusion of non-violence as a revolutionary political posture.... I maintained a relationship to Clarence [and] Audrey Seniors, Mae Mallory, E. A. (Lovey) [Johnson], and other class-conscious groupings.... [I am] closely attuned to the mood of the Black community ... [and] the need for Black people to protect themselves through armed self-defense. To be sure it was at this point in our relationship with the white people in the country, that we knew there could be no turning back. May I say here that Mae Mallory, Clarence Seniors, [Audrey Seniors, and] Ethel Johnson have been in my opinion, the most forthright advocates through which this philosophy has been developed for the Black oppressed masses in the U.S.A.... I worked with the Monroe Defense Committee throughout the fight, which is not yet ended, and would like to say that I do not believe in male superiority, in regard to Mae as the foremost and most politically astute Black Freedom Fighter among the women of America.[36]

Grattan and Mae became leaders in the Republic of New Africa as the minister of foreign affairs and consul, respectively. Founded by Milton and Richard Henry (Gaid and Imari Obadele) in the late 1960s, RNA demanded that the U.S. government give Blacks five southern states.[37] Grattan became a leader in PRIDE and Cleveland's July 23rd Committee. It supported Ahmed Rashad, who founded Cleveland's RNA in 1966.[38]

In 1961 Grattan, Cleveland public school teacher Don Freeman, Johnny Rogers (who my father said "looked upon Audrey as a little sister"), and Rogers's white girlfriend all belonged to MDC. Freeman and Rogers acted as Proctor and Stone's bodyguards. The MDC sustained and buttressed Mae Mallory, gained her freedom from prison, and worked to prevent her extradition. They performed these same services for Harold Reape and Richard Crowder when they abandoned CAMD. John Lowry maintained his own representation with the famed white lawyer William Kunstler after breaking ties with CAMD.[39] Mae felt that this break was strategic:

> They were willing to save John Lowry and let the rest of us rot in jail.... In his summary for Lowry [Kunstler] said "The victims said they were kidnapped by some Negroes. Look at my client, he is a white boy. He was an emotional youth and did a very foolish thing." Without a doubt Kunstler is a

very clever lawyer, he does not wear that Phi Beta Key for nothing. However, I seriously doubt that he is as principled as he is clever and capable.⁴⁰

It remains interesting that Kunstler shamelessly displayed such anti-Black sentiment and white supremacist ideology in defending Lowry.

The FBI kept copious records on MDC members. They coerced Don Freeman's suspension from his teaching position, maligned him in Cleveland's *Plain Dealer*, surveilled him through Chicago's American Security Council, and claimed he organized Black gangs. They gathered thousands of pages of files on my parents, Mrs. Johnson, Mae, and Grattan, having surveilled Grattan since 1933. They followed and photographed them in each city in which they lived. J. B. Matthews, a conservative Methodist anti-communist missionary and director of research for the House Un-American Activities Committee, gathered materials on MDC, CAMD, RAM, WWP, YAWF, and other groups helping the Monroe Defendants.⁴¹

The repression proved unstinting and multifaceted. Matthews reported that Workers World Party

> engaged in an unending propaganda campaign to undermine faith in the American system in favor of Communist revolution. . . . [They gave] a great amount of space to the activities and pronouncements of Robert F. Williams . . . [and] urged the creation of armed "self-defense" organizations among Negroes while, at the same time disseminating blatantly inflammatory propaganda about so-called "racist cops." . . . [They] made common cause with the following Communist and pro-Communist organizations as part of the Communist united front effort—The Monroe Defense Committee [and] The Revolutionary Action Movement. [They went on to list many others.]⁴²

We see what a threat Mae Mallory and the Monroe Defense Committee posed to the United States. To combat them, in 1961 the FBI created the disruption program aimed at Cleveland's MDC, given their Workers World affiliation, and CAMD, given their Socialist Workers Party association. This worked to keep the groups in conflict and prevent "communist infiltration" into Black civil rights groups. This proves especially ironic because Proctor, Seniors, and Stone *were* communists, and Mrs. Johnson conjoined Cubanismo, Maoism, Trotskyism, and socialism into her Black nationalist ideology. No threat of infiltration existed because the foundation of the organization was firmly rooted in socialist ideals of equity and justice.⁴³ The FBI decided that their New York office "should immediately institute an investigation concerning the MDC. . . . The investigation should be directed toward determining all phases of the organization, its leadership, membership, degree of infiltration or domination, finances, and other activities in which the Committee may engage. Appropriate leads should be set forth where necessary with the instruction that the leads should be covered expeditiously."[44] The FBI sent "counter-articles," misinformation, poems, and letters and made anonymous phone calls to the MDC and the CAMD, their supporters, New York and Monroe newspapers, and the NAACP to ensure constant discord.[45] They sent a letter to newspapers and civil rights groups from "a Negro" supportive of MDC and WWP and distrustful of the CAMD and SWP. The FBI paid meticulous attention to detail in drafting this and other letters. On May 14, 1962, they asked the FBI informant to write a letter on commercial paper and advise the bureau of when the letter was sent, and "this should be signed a true friend and supporter of Negro rights." FBI reports from March 6 to April 3, 1964, state that they composed the letter from the viewpoint of a supporter of MDC and WWP, to obscure the FBI's hand.[46] Inexplicably, they felt that letter writing proved more effective than publicizing the groups' disagreements. The informant's letter begins:

> As a Negro who has seen his people pulled and pushed, set up and knocked down, and otherwise fooled by the white power structure, I used to feel that the future of my race would depend on the support of the working man and workers' organizations. As a fairly close observer of some recent happenings in a Negro defense case, I am disillusioned and disgusted by the way the "socialist" "workers" groups also betray the Negro. When efforts were first made to form a committee to defend the people in Monroe, North Carolina, who had been framed on a kidnapping charge, the Johnny-on-the-Spot was GEORGE WEISSMAN of the SWP, offering money, publicity, and the hidden fist inside the glove-control.

The letter actually echoes the main complaints that New York's MDC had against CAMD. The information was most certainly obtained by an insider, an informer in both groups. The FBI letter goes on: "[Weissman] was properly rebuffed, and a Negro-controlled committee, the Monroe Defense Committee, was formed. The SWP, however, regardless of the divisive effect, set up its own Committee to Aid the Monroe Defendants. And [look who] popped up as head of the CAMD, completely running the show, and most important, handling the money, BERTA GREEN."[47] The letter accused Green of running the CAMD for financial gain and charged the CAMD with withholding information about the defendants from New York papers and reporting falsehoods in Weissman's *Militant*. The FBI continued their efforts to discredit Weissman and Green by publishing and distributing a poem to the news media, MDC, and Black civil rights organizations:[48]

> Georgie-Porgie, down in Monroe,
> Found himself alone with the dough
> Called the cops, and what did he say?
> "Bad guys came and took it away."[49]

The poem portrayed Weissman as a thief, given the 1964 robbery by white bandits of Dr. Perry's home safe, which contained CAMD money. Weismann, Lowry, and Kunstler stayed at Perry's home for the Monroe defendants' trial. On the day of the robbery all attended court except Weissman, whom the thieves tied up.[50] The FBI noted on March 6, 1964, that WWP and SWP held long-standing hostilities against one another and rivaled each other to represent the defendants. The FBI left out the reality that they, the CIA, and other spy organizations fired up these hostilities to keep them in a fractious state with each other. The disruption program's efforts proved so successful in causing friction that many people, including Leroi Jones, Harold Cruse, Sylvester Leakes, and others, supported the Monroe Defense Committee over CAMD.[51]

The FBI disruption program ensured the imprisonment of Mallory, Reape, Crowder, and Lowry. It worked to build distrust for Reape and Crowder, who initially sought help from CAMD, repudiated them, and joined Cleveland's MDC.

My father told me that in 1961, after the dismantling of New York's MDC and the formation of Cleveland's Monroe Defense Committee, a Black radical group invaded their offices and brutally attacked members. They wanted to purge the organization of whites and take control.[52] They fought with the Black and white members and raped two white women. My mother and Ruthie Stone physically defended themselves. Don Freeman, Johnny Rogers, and Wilbur Grattan fought the militants and protected women and children. Thankfully Audrey and Ruthie came out of the melee physically unharmed, although my father says that my mother and Stone were a complete mess after the battle. Was this assault part of the FBI's disruption program?

Bobby Seale's *Seize the Time* identifies agents provocateurs as police and FBI agents who infiltrated the Black Panther Party to encourage illicit and illegal activities among members. If not encouraged by these provocateurs, the Panthers would not ordinarily have gotten involved with such activities. As previously discussed, Panther member and FBI informant Richard Matsui Aoki gave them their first guns. According to the Church Commission (1976), the FBI did this to destroy the Black Panther Party. The FBI also paid African American photographer Ernest C. Withers to provide photographs and information on Black civil rights movement activities and leaders, including Martin Luther King Jr., Coretta Scott King, Andrew Young, and James Bevel.[53] This bestial attack on Cleveland's MDC most certainly had the imprint of the disruption program, instigated by agents provocateurs to destroy MDC and cause mayhem and chaos. Weiner and Jeffreys-Jones make it abundantly clear that they used these types of assaults and strategies to crush the movement and destroy people.[54]

While severely shaken by the attack, Proctor and Stone escaped physically unharmed. Stone's experience of fighting off the Black militants proved emotionally traumatic. She abandoned Cleveland *and left her baby with my mother*. Stone eventually returned for her daughter, but she never returned to Cleveland's MDC, opting to continue her activism with Buffalo's Workers World and Mothers Alliance and seek a safer life with her husband, Ritchie.[55]

After the assault, according to my father, "In 1961 Workers World sent me to Cleveland to work as Chairman of the Monroe Defense Committee."[56] He "described himself as a science student active in the defense of Willie Mae Mallory."[57] He replaced African American MDC chair and member of the For Freedom Now Party Don Sharp. My father says, "I met, fell in love [with,] and married Audrey Proctor. I graduated from Morris Brown College in 1962 while chairing The Monroe Defense Committee."[58] The March 3, 1963, FBI file and the September 14, 1962, *Call and Post* reported that "Clarence Seniors, 25, 10516 Superior, [married] Audrey Proctor, 21, 8419 Decker." I was born on March 29, 1963. Or as my friend Dr. Tatiana van Riemdijk, reading the FBI files, exclaimed, "Oh, oh, OH, OHHHHH." I laughed. They named me after Paul Robeson, whose model of unrepentant political and social activism they followed. Like Robeson, my parents were fearless when faced with state repression.[59]

> *My father says our friends Mary Ann Weisman, Sharon Martin Eolis of WWP and YAWF, and Fran Dostal came to Cleveland when I was born. They taught my parents how to care for me. Sharon was a nurse.*

The attack on MDC led RAM's Max Stanford to "send down a fully armed security detail headed by Jomo Kenyatta." Kenyatta protected my parents and trained committee members in weaponry. On gaining her freedom Mae moved in with my parents, solidifying the family bond.[60]

FBI Harassment

My mother's membership within the banned New Orleans NAACP and her subsequent activism within the MDC caused the Proctor family in New Orleans to receive unwanted attention from the state.

Her parents loved Little Audrey
She joined the MDC
They protected her, you see
From the FBI, yes sirree
Never disowning Little Audrey.

My aunt Doris Proctor Dubuclet, and my mother's thousand-plus-page FBI file, confirm that the FBI visited the Proctors on Sunday, December 13, 1962. They ensured the whole family would be present. Doris believed that they picked Sunday to intimidate them. According to her, they told the family that Audrey belonged to a "subversive organization" and "if she did anything against the government she would be run out of the country (their words) and would not be allowed back."[61] The FBI file indicates that my grandfather revealed scant information in a bid to safeguard Audrey. My grandfather told the FBI that she moved to Cleveland in December 1961 to find work and married Clarence Seniors. The FBI file states that he "remained unaware of any information concerning his daughter's social or political activity in Cleveland, Ohio."[62] Unlike Mae's Ohio family, Audrey's family protected her.

Aunt Doris recounted that her parents were "very frightened and scared for their oldest daughter. To never see her again was something they could not comprehend." They sat at the kitchen table talking about African American civil rights activism around the country. Doris said, "My dad said he knew his daughter was smart enough to not get mixed up in something so extreme. The more we talked about it the more they started to understand that this was a scare tactic, yet we remained mindful that something terrible could happen to her." The Proctors knew Audrey's phone number but did not call her because they knew the authorities tapped the phone. They "didn't want to give their child's whereabouts away." Doris remembered that Bertha and Robert Proctor warned their children, "If anyone be they Black or white, friend or foe asked about Audrey's whereabouts that we did not know. We spoke in hushed tones around the house. Everyone was suspect including the neighbors. They waited until she contacted them maybe a day or two." Feisty, fearless, and twenty-one years old,

> Audrey assured them by phone that the government knew exactly where she was and if they wanted to pick her up they could at that moment. She also told them that the phone was probably tapped, and they were listening as they spoke. She told them she was not involved in any communist activities, and she was okay. My parents told her to call home often so they would know that she was ok. After that we did not hear from the FBI again.

Notwithstanding the reality of her communist affiliations—the Monroe Defense Committee, the Workers World Party, and the New Orleans NAACP—Audrey Proctor assured her parents that she did not involve herself in communist activities. Apparently my mother tried to spare her parents and siblings additional worry. FBI informant CV T-2 reported that my parents attended a Workers World Party conference at 42 West Twenty-First Street in New York from September 1 to 3, 1962, and that my father belonged to WWP's National Committee.[63] From 1965 to 1967 the FBI followed Audrey from Brooklyn to her job as a teletype operator at Manhattan's RCA Communications. From 1965 to 1973 the FBI and the Secret Service classified my parents as "potentially dangerous member[s] or participant[s] in the communist movement, under active investigation as members of a group or organization inimical to the U.S." My parents were placed on the Security Index from 1957 to 1973. My father was described as "[expressing] strong or violent anti-U.S. sentiment" and was "tabbed Detcom [Detention Communist List] on 5/2/66," to be detained in a concentration camp during a national emergency, given he was a National Committee member of the Workers World Party.[64] Airtel to the FBI director (April 15, 1965) indicated that they watched our family's arrival in Monroe. They knew that we lived at 605 Brown Street. They knew of my parents' efforts to raise bond money for Mae, gaining her freedom, and that my parents planned to establish the committee headquarters at their home.[65]

> *The aunties and grandma in Tampa, a siddity bunch*
> *Didn't like my mother*
> *Didn't like my aunt, of the migrant farmer stock*
> *They disowned my Daddy, the activist*
> *Disowned him when the FBI told them to.*

Many people involved in civil rights and political activities found that their families rejected them once they received a visit from the FBI. My father's family disowned and shunned him. My mother was *very fortunate*. Her family never abandoned her, standing by her and supporting her activism.

Working for Mae

Audrey Proctor's intellectual and political horizons expanded further when she joined the Trotskyist/Maoist Workers World Party and the Monroe Defense Committee. She aligned herself with Maoism, Cuban Revolutionary thought, and Robert F. Williams's self-defense stance. Before the attack by the Black militants, Audrey and Ruthie Stone ran MDC, with Audrey using her secretarial skills as the office manager. After Stone's departure, Mommy ran the MDC with my father.[66] She worked on the Monroe defendants' day-to-day activities, participated in fundraising activities and their legal defense. In 1961 Audrey petitioned for Mae's release and helped compose petitions for Mallory signed by people from China, Cuba, Algeria, and Ghana, as well as luminaries W. E. B. Du Bois, Shirley Graham Du Bois, and Bertrand Russell. In 1962 she created flyers and press releases distributed in the United States and the world, and she helped organize fundraisers.[67] In 1963 Audrey and Clarence created the pamphlet "Free Mae Mallory," which also appeared in the journal *Africa, Latin America, Asia Revolution*. Audrey and the committee organized a "Freedom Now" picnic on June 14, 1963, for the Youngstown Friends of Mae Mallory, in which my mother held membership.[68] While Audrey Proctor's immediate family supported her, Auntie Ruthie became fearful once she learned of Proctor's radical activism. She put her out of the house. Audrey lived with friends thereafter, and then my father.

Becoming a Revolutionary Socialist Theorist

According to Clarence Seniors, Audrey Proctor and Ruthie Stone were incredibly close friends. I believe that the Monroe Defense Committee, the Workers World Party, and her discussions with Ruthie Stone advanced her radicalization. I am most certain that my mother tied together her political education from Paul Robeson and the New Orleans NAACP with her theoretical discussions with Stone, which sharpened her political thought. The relationship between Ruthie and Audrey proved important given the support of women for women in the struggle for political, social, and womanhood rights. WWP "supported the struggles of oppressed peoples," which advanced her political ideology. As a ravenous reader with an insatiable appetite for knowledge, her library included the writings of Marx, Lenin, Trotsky, Engels, Mao, and Cubanismo, as well as books on Majority World and African American liberation movements. Her library included the many writings of Fidel Castro, Che Guevara, Mao Zedong, Sun Yat-sen, Wu Yu-Chang, Lu Hsun (literary mentor of the Chinese Revolution), Lin Piao, and Guatemala's Juan José Arévalo, as well as the constitution of the Communist Party. This all indicates her growing knowledge concerning socialist theorists and revolutionary thought. Her library also included books and pamphlets about racism and resistance. Her library speaks to her breadth of knowledge and her political intellectual growth.[69]

My mother emerged as an organic intellectual and a radical African American woman activist, making sense of her world.

Audrey: New Orleans NAACP and Radical Activism

Mommy was so glamorous and beautiful. I remember at four or five watching her in her bedroom before her night out, wearing her black sparkly hot pants outfit. Her awesome Afro, long dangly earrings, and high heel shoes, always high heels. I remember the smell of the makeup. A cloud of powder wafting the air, haloing around her face. Mommy kisses me, lipsticking my lips. Spraying herself with perfume, her inner wrists, behind her ears, imbuing the air. The softness of Mommy, sitting on her bed. Warm love-filled hugs, her heartbeat, the softness of her breast when I lay my head on her, ruining the crispness of her attire. She did not mind. Intimate moments, intimate shared space. My Mommy.

Let's explore Audrey Proctor's New Orleans radicalization, her ideological frame before Cleveland. How did the New Orleans NAACP and growing up in New Orleans shape her ideological thought?

In 1958 New Orleans my mother, age seventeen, emerged as an advocate for self-defense, an unrepentant socialist—what Antonio Gramsci and George Lipsitz define as an organic intellectual and an everyday political activist—given her membership in the banned radical and leftist New Orleans NAACP. She cofounded Cleveland's Monroe Defense Committee and joined several Cleveland groups: CORE, the Freedom Fighters, and the United Freedom Movement. She also joined WWP, the Trotskyist Youth against War and Fascism, New York's Black Panthers, and New York's Prisoners Solidarity Committee. She aligned herself with the anti-Vietnam War and prolabor union movements.[70] Audrey maintained a voluminous library, reading voraciously, analyzing Majority World radical revolutions, searching for a way to make real social and political change for all people.

Audrey Proctor was born on October 24, 1940, at Charity Hospital in New Orleans to Bertha Scott, a housewife, and Robert Proctor, a World War II veteran. Robert first worked as a postal carrier, ultimately becoming an auto mechanic. Audrey was the second of five children, three boys and two girls. According to Aunt Doris and Mommy's high school memory book, they lived in a four-bedroom Lafitte Barre Accent Home (a very nice housing project) with a green slate roof, at 2564 Lafitte Avenue. The state built them for Black soldiers returning from World War II.[71]

> *My grandmother loved her sons*
> *Her daughters not as much*

I recall as a child that Mommy and Aunt Doris often proclaimed in New York and New Orleans that "Bertha LOVED her sons." They left out the caveat: "more than us girls." Peals of sisterly laughter punctuated the air. My mother did recall real sincere moments of affection from her mother, a short, round, beautifully brown woman with eyes the color of black olives. Bertha played with little Audrey, perhaps teaching her the hambone as Mommy taught me. They baked together, which Mommy passed down to me as a mother-daughter ritual. Using my red-handled rolling pin and baking utensils, we baked oatmeal cookies shaped like Charlie Brown and Snoopy. We baked cakes as my mother did with her mother, infused with fun. Mommy's relationship with her mother remained a prickly, complicated one. Audrey adored her tall, good-looking father with his dazzlingly magnificent black skin, black eyes, and muscular frame. I learned of his mischief, merriment, and magic.

> *We visited New Orleans my Mommy and me*
> *I was four, five, or six, just a baby*
> *We visited my Grandma, Granddaddy, and teenaged Uncle Gary on*
>   *Bienville Street*
> *That shotgun house WOO*
> *Granddaddy gave me a crisp ten-dollar bill*
> *Whispered,*
> *"Don't let Grandma see"*
> *That crisp ten-dollar bill was especially for me*

Fig. 5. Audrey Proctor, high school graduation, New Orleans, Louisiana. Paula Marie Seniors Collection.

Unlike Mrs. Johnson, the Proctor children did not receive a political education but an education in protection from the state, sprinkled with love and heartfelt caring. The working-class Proctor children got the best segregated education offered in segregated New Orleans, including art lessons and athletic classes at Rosenwald's Gym. Doris had a chance at an elite education at the historically Black Dillard University. Audrey's childhood existence proved a stable and loving one, like Mrs. Johnson's, a far cry from Mae's chaotic childhood. Audrey and her siblings lived a working-class existence with middle-class striving. Time and place made a difference, informing the lives of Johnson, Proctor, and the Mallorys.

In 1958, seventeen-year-old Audrey—a diminutive five-foot-one, under ninety-eight pounds, a recent graduate of New Orleans Joseph C. Clark Senior High School, and an advocate for self-defense—took her initial steps toward radical activism. "My first involvement in the area of social and political change began in New Orleans, in the late nineteen fifties. Along with a number of my peers, I became a card-carrying member of the NAACP, which at the time was a very radical thing to do."[72]

Her high school graduation photograph offers a window in which to view and understand how she emerged and engaged in radical politics. At her home on graduation day, an effusive Audrey displays a magnificently brilliant smile that emanates from her joyous black eyes. She wears a Prince Valiant pageboy, white pearl drop earrings, and on her jewel, a three-strand white pearl necklace that lightly touches her collarbone. She is attired in a brilliantly white boatneck cap-sleeved dress with a fitted bodice and a voluminous skirt with a crinoline petticoat, de rigueur for the fashionable 1950s teenager. She wears a white corsage at her heart, with beautiful green ferns accentuating the flower's whiteness. A crisp pink and light blue ribbon hangs from the corsage, announcing "J. S. Clark High School, Class of 1958," in bold gold print. A well-appointed window with white lace curtains frames the scene. Audrey stands at the right side of a massive television on long legs, a marker of middle-class dreams and aspirations. It dwarfs her tiny frame. Her white lace gloved hand with a gold bangle bracelet rests delicately atop the colossal box. Her brother Robert's military photographs rest on a crisp white doily. One shows Robert in military dress uniform, the other in combat gear. The disharmonious image of the warring masculine soldier and the femininity of Audrey Proctor, the doily, the curtains, and the room should clash, but somehow everything belongs. My mother's other hand holds a white kerchief and displays the red leatherbound cover of her diploma. The image heralds Black feminine power. The abundance of brilliant white, white dress, gloves, corsage, earrings, and pearl necklace symbolizes a cheerful innocence, a celebration of Black girl élan, youthful wonder, and hope. The photograph communicates a collective pride in Audrey, a family effort to display all that is beautiful about my petite Mommy.

Audrey Proctor's display of glittering youthful virtue and guilelessness personifies her evolution from African American girlhood to womanhood. The photograph reveals that Mommy loved herself, and her parents truly loved her. Although working-class, Bertha and Robert Proctor made sure that my mother received all the things a well-appointed 1950s girl could want—poodle skirts, saddle shoes, and, in her own seventeen-year-old words filled with youthful glee, "nice wide dresses and pretty colors."[73] Doris recalled, "Audrey had a card at Goldrings Department Store that my parents gave her. So anytime she wanted to go someplace, she would use that card to buy an outfit at Goldrings. By the time it was my turn, I didn't get a Goldrings card. I asked my parents why and they said they couldn't afford it."[74]

Audrey Proctor received a fully rounded education with swimming, art, and tap dance classes at Rosenwald's Gym. There she learned to perform a mean time step, which she could execute throughout life and taught me. My mother told me that as a girl she loved the movie *Mighty Joe Young* (1949) about the misunderstood giant gorilla. Her high school memory book listed her favorite actors as Dorothy Dandridge and Nat King Cole, perhaps because *St. Louis Blues* (1958) played in movie theaters. As a 1950s teenager she loved music and dancing, and she knew all the latest dances, which she taught me. Throughout my childhood I delighted in hearing her tell me of her absolute and complete *love* for Buddy Holly, Chuck Berry, and Hank Williams. Her memory book listed her favorite singers and musicians: Berry, Bobby Freeman, and, as any New Orleans teenager would list, Louis Armstrong. She wrote that her favorite music was "Rock and Roll—all kinds."[75] Audrey signed all her 45 rpm records as young people did, and she enjoyed singing in a lovely voice, which is apropos because she listed in her memory book's Charm Chart "skills and talent—singing."

> *In the 1960s and 1970s my mother was exquisite . . . elegantly bedecked in her favorite color, red. My very talented mother could play the guitar, read music, and sing—lullabies, folk songs, and songs especially for me. Our own mother-daughter parties. I loved her. Mommy warmly offering me a welcoming shoulder as she sang my theme song in her delightful crystalline voice: "Hey, Hey Paula, I want to Marry You." Singing me to sleep in my pink room: "Hush little baby don't you cry / Mama's gonna buy you a mockingbird" . . . Playing her wooden guitar singing Joan Baez: "I'd hammer out Freedom, I'd Hammer out Justice" . . . Singing the anthems of the Movement just for me. We danced listening to 45's: "What goes up must come down, spinning wheel got to go around," "Attack, attack, say your love for me will last forever." Music filled the living room from our record player on the homemade wooden bookshelf and matching magazine rack, which Daddy had lovingly made, painted and shellacked to perfection. Our orange sofa, with the sublime painting of a stunning Black lady wearing an orange Gele and Charles White's artwork enhancing the living room. We'd watch* Laugh-In, Mannix, Ed Sullivan, *musical groups—the Honeycombs, the Fifth Dimension—on our black-and-white TV in my bedroom, never in the living room. My mother infused our home with love, art, and culture, learned from her parents. She shared this love—collecting artwork, going to museums, art galleries, music concerts, Broadway shows, social dances, and dance concerts. But what most conveyed her love for me was singing and playing her guitar.*

Concealed within Audrey Proctor's high school graduation image is her nonconformity. As a little girl and as I grew up, my mother told me the following story many times. Although her parents raised her Catholic, between the ages of eleven and twelve, the inception of her period, my mother lost her religion. Her period wreaked havoc on her tiny little frame. She suffered with horrendous, sickening cramps, cramps that wracked her body with nauseating, excruciating pain, so intense that she fainted each month. She prayed to God to stop the agony. God never did. Audrey became a nonbeliever until the day she died. Her FBI files confirmed this. Informant CV T-1 "overheard subject state that she does not believe in God and advocates 'Black Supremacy.'"[76] My mother's rejection of religion and her free thought concerning God marked a turning point in her life, a rebellion against conventionality. Her rejection of religion reveals Mommy's burgeoning thought and independent nature. The high school graduation photograph shows her smiling happily, eyes sparkling, glowing with pride in her dazzlingly white attire. Excavating the image exposes her expanding ideology, for she graduated from the segregated Joseph C. Clark High School, lived in the hypersegregated New Orleans, negotiated the racially and sexually volatile climate of the city, and joined the radical, banned New Orleans NAACP.

The NAACP, Communism, and FBI Surveillance

The "History of the New Orleans Branch, 1915–1990" notes that African Americans founded the branch in 1915 to fight the reversals of the gains Blacks made after Reconstruction. They centered their activism on fighting for the Black vote, which dropped over a twenty-year period from 130,000 to 500 by 1915. The NAACP advocated for the end of segregation on streetcars, and they rallied against increased racialized violence, police brutality, and the lack of economic opportunities. By 1941 the New Orleans NAACP leadership came from a more radical faction, "The Group," as they called themselves, who challenged the old guard. In 1941 the branch included working- and middle-class members of unions.[77] The FBI targeted and "identified" communists, including African American educator Mrs. Noelie Cunningham, a member of John Dewey's Progressive Educational Association, an organization that promoted child-centered education, "racial understanding, democracy, citizenship, and social justice."[78] On April 21, 1945, the FBI first identified African American Ernest J. Wright, director of the People's Defense League, as belonging to the Communist Party. They used the *Louisiana Weekly* to build a case against Wright. The *Weekly* noted that Wright spoke at Alexandria's NAACP branch. He encouraged attendees to "join hands with the freedom loving people of the world." Wright stated that "Negroes must vote in Louisiana but not until all of us in this State put it on the must list in our agenda in the church, labor, fraternal, social, educational, and civic affairs."[79] In 1958, when my mother joined the New Orleans NAACP, membership proved extremely radical. The FBI had surveilled the group beginning in the 1940s, keeping meticulous files. They regarded the group as seditious, because the leadership came from progressive Black women teachers who were NAACP secretaries and vice presidents and working- and middle-class union members of the CIO and ILWU, unions affiliated with the Communist Party. The 1950s saw FBI surveillance escalate as African American teachers participated in voter registration drives, paid poll taxes to vote, and rallied for equitable pay, overall equality in the segregated public school system, and more teachers in the Black community. They demanded the building of playgrounds and fought for African American history classes, music classes, and trade schools.[80]

Louisiana's NAACP proved a threat to the state and hegemony as African Americans made social and political advances in the 1940s and 1950s. Senator William M. Rainach of Louisiana's Citizens' Council, the Ku Klux Klan in suits, along with the FBI, equated communism with African Americans, the NAACP, and their battle for human rights. Rainach held hearings arguing that Louisiana's NAACP was a "communist front organization" and that "communism and integration are inseparable."[81] The Louisiana Citizens' Council ensnared the NAACP within the Red Scare, with fear-inducing articles such as "Birds of a Feather—Key NAACP Leaders Have 'Front' Records" (May 1957) and "'Freedom' Red Style" (February 1957), arguing that the U.S. Communist Party ordered members to infiltrate "Negro Organizations."[82]

Dudziak, Lewis, Layton, and Woods all contend that the southern Red Scare was connected to the massive resistance movement, whose main objective included tarnishing the civil rights struggle by, as Woods notes, "associating it with the nation's greatest enemy, Communism." The massive resistance movement argued that communism was a cover for racial integration. They worked to prevent Black social and civic advancement.[83] Lewis argued that by equating civil rights with communism, southern white supremacists deflected "culpability away from their own actions" of racialized violence, insisting that they acted to fight "ill-defined 'subversive' outside forces" and the Soviet Union. Southern white supremacists "depicted the South as the last bastion of true Americanism fighting against a single, un-American enemy."[84]

NAACP surveillance also intensified because the NAACP won court cases against white male sexual predators.[85] These victories proved the Louisiana NAACP's most important interventions, protecting African American womanhood against white sexualized brutality.[86] Unlike the majority of the

South, in 1927 and 1928 the Louisiana NAACP was successful in winning cases of rape and murder of teenaged Black girls against white men. The New Orleans NAACP's African American lawyer, Pierre Tureaud, also won cases that forced merchants to allow African American women to try on clothes before buying them.[87]

Similar to Mrs. Johnson's education by her mother and in Promise Land's/Abbeville's historical community of struggle and resistance, my mother's exposure to teachers and NAACP members put the finishing touches on her radicalization and politicization. She learned that Black women could lead and could fight back. Audrey learned of New Orleans's unjust system of education and how to advocate for better conditions. She learned that equalization of segregated schools was not enough. Desegregation could prove more effective. Her contact with NAACP communists and union members opened up a new dimension of thought for Audrey, leading her to become an unrepentant and unapologetic socialist/communist. Like Mae's political education in New York's workers unions that informed her radical thought, my mothers' connections with union members also informed her philosophy. Throughout her life she advocated for unions, living wages, fair and decent working conditions, and housing. My mother's exposure to the NAACP also taught her that African American women could fight back against white racialized and sexualized violence—that African American women could win. Audrey stood for self-defense and talked to me about it always. She told me often that she had no regard for Martin Luther King Jr. and his ilk and thought nonviolent protest was ridiculous. Like her idol and my namesake, African American actor, singer, and political activist Paul Robeson, she believed in self-defense. When asked in the 1940s if he believed in turning the other cheek, Robeson replied, "If someone hit me on one cheek, I'd tear his head off before he could hit me on the other one."[88] Audrey Proctor adopted this same ideology.[89]

In 1958 my mother owned a well-worn copy of Robeson's *Here I Stand*, which he wrote in response to his blacklisting by the U.S. government and his refusal to abide by the House Un-American Activities Committee's insistence that he state whether he belonged to the Communist Party. Audrey Proctor read of his stand for African Americans, the oppressed, and workers. She read of his blacklisting, the confiscation of his passport, and the support he received from international leaders such as Fidel Castro and the international community. She read of Paul Robeson's 1958 proposal for self-defense for African Americans against American fascists, and his call for "Negro Action" and "Negro Power," which predated the Black Power movement of the

1960s and 1970s.[90] Mommy knew that Robeson advocated for African independence from colonial rule through his and Du Bois's Council of African Affairs. She knew of his challenge against Spain, Italy, and Nazi Germany's fascism, his support of workers' rights worldwide, and his crusade against lynching.[91] My mother modeled her political life after Robeson, unafraid of state repression.

The battle for equal rights in which Robeson and the New Orleans NAACP engaged ignited the fire of political activism within Audrey Proctor and planted the seeds of radicalism, for all of her life she fought unjust conditions. Her exposure to Robeson and the radical women within the NAACP guided my mother in her activism, and her exposure to southern brutality instilled in her a dedication to self-defense. Like Robeson, Proctor and the members of the New Orleans NAACP found themselves labeled communists due to white southern supremacists' and legislators' strategies to dismantle civil rights organizations through what Jeff Woods defines as "Little House Un-American Activities Committees" and "little FBI's which dotted the South in order to weed out communists." The FBI maintained the belief that Communist Party members plotted to take over the New Orleans branch even though the "national leadership of the NAACP made constant anti-Communist statements."[92]

In 1956 the Citizens' Council cynically used the Fuqua Ku Klux Klan law, which required organizations to submit their membership lists to the state, to dismantle the NAACP.[93] They "authorized the dismissal of teachers" or public employees who belonged to the NAACP. The NAACP resisted handing over their lists, fearing that the state would publicize their lists. They believed that members would face retaliation, violence, and the loss of jobs, businesses, and income. The state successfully closed the Louisiana branches for ten years, suppressed the Black vote, and blocked the desegregation of New Orleans's Catholic schools.[94] In 1956 the New Orleans branch complied with the Fuqua Ku Klux Klan law, leading to the reinstatement of Louisiana's NAACP. Membership dropped from 4,750 to 1,300, members faced the communism accusation, they experienced economic sanctions, and Black women teachers could lose tenure for encouraging school integration.[95] In 1958, by the time Audrey Proctor joined the NAACP, they failed again to file their membership list. The state brought a legal case against them, making it again unlawful to hold membership. Proctor's name most certainly appeared on the membership list.[96] My mother's radical activism, like that of Mrs. Johnson and Mae Mallory, remained a threat to the state. Amazingly, Audrey Proctor embarked on a life of radical political activism, committing to social equity for African Americans and other aggrieved communities of color notwithstanding the perils that this would bring.

Pat Mallory: Generational Shift

A profound generational shift occurred with Pat Mallory. In 1956, at age eleven, Pat had difficulty navigating her mother's radical activism and aspirations—aspirations that included her but were not her own. Pat wanted a childhood unencumbered by her mother's activist life. During Cleveland's Monroe case Pat (age sixteen) found her way to my mother (age twenty-one) and saw her as a big sister. My mother helped her grow into her own person out of Mae's shadow. Pat learned to love herself, to find her own way to emerge as a Black Nationalist Rebel Girl.

A little girl to Pat's twenty-three-year-old woman self, I loved Pat, the awesome secure woman that laughed with me, spent the night at 220 Montgomery Street and sat on my bed next to me. A beautiful round-faced, brown-skinned beauty. She played with me with her infectious giggles. She gave me Afrocentric gifts, as she does with my own daughter. In her Afroed awesomeness Pat beamed enchantingly with youthful confidence and self-possession. She dressed in mod and hip clothes, a green minidress, silky orange head wrap, gold hoop earrings, and a gold ring on her finger. As an important ever-present family member, I assumed that Pat's childhood resembled mine, infused with Black pride, Black dolls, Black beauty, "Sock It to Me" pocketbooks, grown-up style ... marches, rallies, political pamphlet making at WWP and attending Black Panther meetings like me and Mommy. In my child's eye I just knew that Pat enjoyed these activities as a fun, natural, and normal part of her life, like in mine. I didn't know that our radical childhood daughter experiences were dissimilar and discordant. I thought everyone grew up with my life experience.

Patricia Mallory's experiences as a Black Nationalist Rebel Girl represent a major generational shift from those of Mae (age eighteen when she birthed Pat), Mrs. Johnson (age twenty-nine at Pat's birth), and my mother (age five at Pat's birth). The experiences of Johnson, Mae, and my mother, and their transformation into African American women radical activists, differed greatly from Pat's transformation into a Black Nationalist Rebel Girl. Time and place informed Pat's social and political metamorphosis.

Chapter 5

Patricia Mallory

Awakenings of a Black Nationalist Rebel Girl

Memory tableaus—Patricia. Beautifully dark brown skin. A wonderful soul, an infectious laugh, a grown-up. At sixteen Pat marching for Mae. Age nineteen, sitting in my room with me, age five, Daddy looking over us... Her shimmering smile lighting up rooms. Our family. Pat traveled to Guyana, to the mythic Africa, infusing herself with an African-centered persona, which my child's mind loved. Pat showered me with love. Family.

—*Paula*

Patricia Mallory's life as a Black Nationalist Rebel Girl marked a complete generational shift from the African American women's radical activism of Ethel Azalea Johnson, Mae Mallory, and Audrey Proctor. Pat was born in 1945 in New York, at the end of World War II, a war that Blacks hoped would equalize them—Double V for Victory and equality. Actually, World War II led to an increased onslaught of racism, violence, and continued poverty across the country. War's terror led to Japanese American citizens' incarceration in concentration camps. World War II visited horror on Japan as the United States dropped atomic bombs on Nagasaki and Hiroshima, propelling an anti-nuclear war movement that teenaged Pat joined. Patricia's birth year marked the Pan-African Congress in Manchester, England; African Americans' petition for civil rights at the newly formed United Nations; and anti-colonial movements in Ghana and Nigeria.[1] These political and social happenings informed Patricia's life, setting the stage for her teenaged years as a Black Nationalist Rebel Girl.

Pat's childhood did not mirror the charmed upbringing of Audrey Proctor or the magical political girlhood that Mrs. Johnson's mother and Abbeville's community of struggle and resistance offered Johnson at birth. Pat's girlhood in many ways mirrored Mae's, both products of teenaged motherhood. The shared parenting arrangement constrained Mae's motherhood efforts, but Mae's teachings allowed Pat to excel educationally. Pat's girlhood experience with mothering was quite different from Johnson's and Proctor's experiences. As Pat said, "No, no, I can't imagine being a mother at eighteen. It would be so ridiculous, so ridiculous, and impossible. Especially taking care of them by yourself!! Two at age nineteen!!! I guess I would have an attitude everyday too [laughs uproariously]."[2]

In Brooklyn in 1944, Mae Mallory's family forced her into teenaged marriage and motherhood. Resentful of the assigned position, she rejected the common model for motherhood, opting for a political life as an organic intellectual.[3] Like children of Black activists, Pat felt forsaken by Mae, who Pat felt chose the movement over her.[4] "My mother was left as a child to be raised by others. My mother had no choice but to leave us. She was a young girl. She abandoned me. I didn't understand the whole picture. I just felt my own personal feelings. I understood the movement was important, but I didn't understand that I was important too." Pat felt emotionally distant from her mother, unimportant in the great plan for social protest. She believed that activism trumped motherhood for Mae. "She had things to do, people to meet, and this business about children, it's in my way, you've got an aunt, you've got a grandmother, and their home. Make sure that you're fed, that you're housed, that you're clothed, that's it, that's it. Meanwhile, I'm going out there to save *EVERYBODY* [laughter]."

Patricia Mallory was born in Brooklyn on her mother's eighteenth birthday (June 9, 1945). Her brother Keefer (Butch) was born six days after Mae's nineteenth birthday. Pat said, "I don't know when my parents divorced, but they did." Mae left the childrearing to her aunt and her husband, the janitor of their New York apartment at 103rd Street and Second Avenue. Pat doesn't recall whether Mae lived with them. Perhaps Mae slept in the living room. What she remembers is her mother's constant contact with her children, when she wasn't working. Pat recounts that her aunt's "neighborhood was predominantly Italian or Irish or a mixture [of white ethnics]." Like her mother, teenaged Mae used shared parenting and socialization, unintentionally allowing them to teach the children old-fashioned patriarchal norms.[5] In Pat's words, "With the Great Migration, the values also came with them. They left the place. The mentality remained. There was always the thought that as a woman you're supposed to be second best. . . . My great aunt had those southern poor working-class values, Christian Baptist values. To her, sexism, there was no such thing as sexism. As a female you did certain things, and males did other things."

Although the family consigned Pat to the standard girl position, she formed a warm, loving relationship with her aunt, clashing with Mae's stance on education and her pro-Black woman and Black nationalist ideologies. Pat fondly remembers, "My aunt was the kind of person who was a very loving person. I wanted that maternal touch, that closeness that my mother did not provide." At eighteen, motherhood proved incredibly difficult for Mae. She financially supported her children by working in Brooklyn factories and as a housekeeper. "I genuinely didn't feel love from my mother. I thought she was mean, and my brother felt the same way."

Mae tried. She enrolled Pat in the Girl Scouts. Mae wanted her children to fit in. She tried to provide for them. Pat told me that every so often there were moments of tenderness and a political and social education, but not enough to counter the lack of maternal warmth.

> Every once in a while she would be a little cuddly, but not often. I remember we would all pile *in her bed*. She would read us Frederick Douglass's Fourth of July Speech.... Like those people who pledge allegiance to the flag, Douglass's speech was *Our Pledge of Allegiance*. My favorite part was "What to the American slave is your Fourth of July? ... A day that reveals to him more than all other days in the year the gross injustice and cruelty to which he is the constant victim. To him your celebration is a sham." That says it in a nutshell. Douglass's speech was my nursery rhyme, the basis, the foundation for my philosophical, political, and social beliefs.[6]

What remains wonderful about this moment is that Mae conjured it when imprisoned in Cleveland. She wrote about the speech in the *Afro American*, teaching her readers as she taught her children. "Now that the Fourth of July celebrations are over, the firecrackers have fizzled. I wonder if half the Americans really know what they're celebrating." She schools the readers, offering the same Black history lessons taught to her children. "Do they know that the first man to give his life for the independence of this country was a Black man, Crispus Attucks? Non-whites are still refugees in this land, their lives worth only the whim of the white man. Frederick Douglass made the speech exactly 109 years ago. The situation has not changed one iota."[7] Mae shared the full speech with her readers. Amazingly, embodying Collins's everyday political activist, Mae politically educated her children *and her readers*—always a political education, notwithstanding her girlhood, her youth, and her forced marriage.

Shared parenting did not work well for Pat *or* Butch, as the family undercut Mae's efforts. Pat said, "My relatives discouraged reading. They felt if you read too much you'd end up wearing eyeglasses, which is the worst thing in the world that could possibly happen [in the family's opinion]. [The] emphasis on education and all that studying would drive you crazy." In *A Voice from the South* Anna Julia Cooper contended that the expectation for girls was to mother and marry, forgoing education and dreams beyond the patriarchal model—Mae's family's model.[8] William Falk interviewed a Black family living between Alabama and Georgia. They followed the traditional agricultural family model that children forgo school to work, with boys working in the fields and girls working in the home.[9] This is why Pat's family rejected education and Mae's lessons. Embodying the motherist frame as an act of resistance against her family and as an everyday political activist, Mae tried mightily to counter these negative retrograde ideas. Mae's aunt and uncle's child-rearing ideology negated Mae's efforts. The family held retrograde ideas concerning skin tone that deeply affected Pat and Butch.

Corrosive Lessons

Pat's aunt and uncle treated Butch as a special child because of his light skin and gender, relaying to Pat that her lovely dark skin marked her as unworthy. The family fully embraced the color caste code that viewed light-skinned Blacks as superior to dark-skinned Blacks. This ideology, according to Kevin Gaines, Drake and Cayton, Bettye Collier-Thomas, and James Turner, emerged during slavery as a strategy to keep the slaves at odds with each other. Whites offered special privileges to light-skinned slaves over their dark-skinned brothers and sisters. After slavery, light-skinned Blacks emerged as the elite class, adopting a color caste ideology to identify who proved eligible for jobs, citizenship rights, and viable marriage partners.[10] Poor and working-class African American families like Pat's adopted color caste codes. Claudette Colvin, in discussing the color caste code, noted, "For some reason we seemed to hate ourselves."[11]

The color caste code proved devastating for Pat given her dark skin and her gender. She felt that some of the extended family treated her with disdain. Mae fully rejected these corrosive ideas and tried to counter them to protect and teach her children, but work impeded her efforts. Pat recalls the family telling her a story about herself and a cousin. "They'd put us in the same carriage and when anybody came to peek at [us] they would cover me up [so that the focus went to him] because he was light." The family conveyed that Pat was not a beautiful dark-skinned girl.

> Their behavior and their treatment of me made me not think of myself at all, but if I had to think of myself at all, I quickly eliminated any thoughts about my beauty or whatever.... No one ever said anything to me, but I felt it. The lighter-skinned children got the opportunities, were thought of as better. Look at *Jet* and *Ebony* magazine. Interestingly enough the title itself indicates Black: [laughter] *Jet*, *Ebony*. The contradiction. Come on, people!!!

Black-owned *Ebony* and *Jet* magazines (1940s–1950s) featured fair- to white-skinned Black women as the Black beauty ideal, rarely featuring dark- or brown-skinned women. They advertised skin-lightening and hair-straightening potions. As Pat's case illustrates, these color-caste beauty ideals proved incredibly destructive to those who did not fit the mold *and those who did*. These images and her family's behavior eroded Pat's self-esteem, blinding her to her dark-skinned gorgeousness.

> *I found it hard to hear Pat's experience with color caste. Beautiful Pat whom I loved, admired, and looked up to as a child had been traumatized by the ridiculous color caste. I remember the incredible sadness that overcame me to learn of such silly ideologies. I shared my feelings with Pat. Pat said, "You were born in a different time, your parents were conscious, they were involved in the movement, it was quite different. They knew how important it was to build you up, probably knowing how the rest of society acts."*

Butch was the favored honored child in the immediate family. The family dismissed Pat. Pat maintains, "My brother was allowed to go outside and play in the streets. I had to stay in the house, where I made up the beds and helped my aunt cook."[12] Because of the unsupervised freedom, as well as lessons in patriarchy and misogyny taught to him by his uncle, this intelligent, outgoing, mischievous boy grew into an angry, troubled youth. Pat recalls, "[In 1956] we moved to [27] Morningside Avenue. Mildred [McAdory] Edelman and Joe Edelman, friends of hers from the Communist Party, had an apartment and so we moved from my aunt's apartment on the East Side to Harlem—117th Street and Morningside Avenue."[13] Pat recalls that Mae tried to gain control of Butch. "He rebelled ... [refusing to do] homework, chores, things like that. My mother insisted and he wouldn't comply.... He was always running away. And where did he run to? My aunt." The damage done to Butch by the family proved irreversible. Butch lived a difficult life, attending Franklin K. Lane High School, having a daughter and an unsuccessful marriage, and fighting in the Vietnam War. He became an emotional casualty of war with, in Pat's words, a "certified card [saying] that he was totally nonfunctional, unpredictable, and violent." He and Mae would live estranged.

Abuse

Shared parenting in the family enabled the children's abuse. The living environment boded terribly for Pat, given the uncle's overt hatred of Black women and girls. The living arrangement presented an unhealthy situation for Butch, given the uncle's lessons to the boys in mistreating girls and women. The uncle operated under an ideology of Black male supremacy, that Black girls' and women's lives should be centered on motherhood and home.[14] The uncle taught these lessons to Butch and his male cousins, through the silent complicity of Pat's aunt. Pat noted that Mae hated the uncle, "especially since he was the one that corrupted my brother in terms of doing anything you want to a woman." Pat recalled a very misogynistic lesson: "My cousin picked me up, *threw me up in the air*, and when I came down he put his hand under my dress to catch me and told my brother, this is how you treat a woman. This went on in my aunt's house!!! That kind of stuff, the sickness."

Mae tried to protect her children. Pat remembers "she didn't bring a man into the household. She couldn't trust a man in the house with me and my brother. She was afraid of sexual abuse. She never married and nobody lived with us, I give her that much [laughter] because they are out there, so she was afraid of that and took precautions." Notwithstanding these safeguards, Mae could not fully protect her children because she worked. Pat recalled, "I was not carefully protected or looked after. At age seven or eight I was abused by the Puerto Rican custodian [who lived] next door to my aunt's apartment. I had a lot of fear growing up." The custodian abused Butch too. Pat recalls her mother's effort to obtain justice and help for them after the horrific abuse. Pat says, "I know I was taken to somebody who interviewed me. I know my mother did not let it rest. Because I was reticent, I could not express [what happened] at that time." Butch exposed the abuse. "He told my mother that we were working. This guy said that he would pay us to help him in the basement. That's how the information came out."

Sadly their experience was not unusual. African American women and girls experience high rates of sexual assault.[15] *Sarah Phillips* details an old woman's recounting of her rape at age twelve. Maya Angelou, Oprah Winfrey, and Dr. Lakeesha Walrond discuss their rapes as young girls by family members and family acquaintances. Abuse left Angelou mute. For Winfrey, abuse became "an ongoing continuous thing, so much so that [I thought] this is the way life is." The cycle repeated in Butch's and Pat's lives.[16]

Abuse by her uncle, family members, and the custodian shaped Pat's identity. Pat responded to her mistreatment by retreating into herself. "I was constantly afraid. I think my mother was probably afraid that I was going to be too much like her mother, who was very reticent and abused by her husband. So she watched carefully to make sure that I would be a strong Black woman, *which I was not*." Pat says Mae too "had no way of expressing [her feelings concerning what happened to them or] knowing how to handle [their abuse]." Mae used education to try to liberate them. She offered them actions and behavior that they could follow to overcome their injuries. She tried to teach them concepts of resistance. "She just constantly demonstrated through her behavior and activities and actions that this is how you behave." Mae rebelled against family and societal expectations. She fought back. She wanted her children to fight back too. Pat *could not do any of these things*. She, like Maya Angelou, became mute with fear.

The abusive treatment weighed heavily on Pat. Maltreatment can lead to a lack of self-esteem, promiscuity, failure in school, drug and alcohol use, incarceration, and jailing due to defending oneself against assault.[17] While Pat did develop low self-esteem, she defied some of these outcomes. She excelled in school. Pat remembers most painfully the rejection she felt from her family given her abuse. "My family blamed me. This is where I felt my mother could have been strong. She was not, as far as I could see. All I could tell was everyone in the family was talking about me." Pat's family held her responsible for the sexual horrors she and Butch endured.[18] New rules were put in place for them. "[My brother] did things and I was constantly afraid. I wasn't allowed to play outside and [the abuse] might have been the reason why. I was isolated in the family as a spectacle. I withdrew a lot." Her aunt who showered her with so much affection became distant. "I think she had to side with the adults, because of tradition. The victim was always wrong. I was a female and she believed in sexism. . . . When we were together she was more comforting when it was just the two of us." By isolating Pat, the family silenced her, following the practice of silencing victims to protect abusers who might be family members or friends. The family laid the "burden of fault" solely on Pat.[19]

Harlem Nine

In 1957 Patricia's life remained markedly different from the feisty Audrey Proctor, a recent high school graduate and member of the radical New Orleans NAACP, and different from the battle-ready Mrs. Johnson, secretary and eventual president of the Negros with Guns. In 1957 Pat, age twelve, was a scared, innocent, abused girl when Mae as an organic intellectual and community feminist filed New York's desegregation case on Pat's behalf. In the 1950s social movements and racialized events swirled around her world, touching her, influencing her, planting seeds of rebellion as she grew into the Black Nationalist Rebel Girl. The 1955 murder of fourteen-year-old Emmett Till in Money, Mississippi, in the name of lying white womanhood, profoundly affected Pat. Till's single mother, Mamie Till Bradley, exhibited Black motherhood in action by displaying his brutalized body to over a thousand attendees at the funeral and in *Jet*. Bradley's actions angered the NAACP, who urged her not to show her battered son's photograph.[20] The horrific image seared into Pat's memory at age ten, planted there for future reference, and as a weapon against white supremacy as she grew into a Black Nationalist Rebel Girl. McCarthyism, the blacklist, anti-communist hysteria, and the conflation that communism equaled Black activism had already touched Patricia Mallory. The Mallory family's state oppression resembled McCarthyesque Blacklist violence against Paul Robeson, W. E. B. Du Bois, and Shirley Graham Du Bois; African American CPUSA members Esther Cooper Jackson and Claudia Jones; and founders of the communist-inspired Southern Negro Youth Congresses, Dorothy and Louis Burnham. Mae Mallory's lapsed membership in the CPUSA, Mae's many communist friends, and her activism made her whole family targets for surveillance.[21] The country witnessed the civil rights activism of King's Southern Christian Leadership Conference and Ella Baker's Student Non-Violent Coordinating Committee, girding King by moving to Atlanta to establish SCLC offices. Baker saw her grassroots voting plans undercut by King and his supporters. Teenaged Black girls led the charge for change in Montgomery, Alabama. Claudette Colvin, age fifteen, and Mary Louise Smith, age eighteen, initiated the Montgomery Bus Boycott. They refused to give their seats to racist white women. Black girls of the Little Rock Nine led the desegregation of Central High School. The five-thousand-member Nation of Islam called for a Black nation, Black businesses, self-defense, and strict eating and drinking habits for better health. Ghana gained its independence. These actions set the political and social tone, unfolding on the edges of Pat's life, piercing through her world, impacting how she would develop. But in 1957 she was just trying to survive, to heal, to grow, to just BE.[22] Pat recalled,

> I was put in a grade for slow children in the fourth grade which my mother violently objected to [laughter]. It's like when you come from the South they put you back [laughter]. I went from that class to the top class.... My mother and some other parents organized. Out of that came the Harlem Nine. They took us out of school. We went to Freedom Schools, almost like homeschooling.... We went to the 369th armory's after-school programs and went there on Saturdays for tutoring.

Mae was denied a high school education that would have allowed her to become an intellectual—denied a university education too. Given an arranged marriage and forced into motherhood, Mae determined to give her children what proved unattainable for her—the education she longed for. While Mae politically educated Pat, like many activist parents she *did not talk to* Pat. Pat felt that Mae thrust her into the desegregation case without telling her what it was about or asking her whether she *wanted to be involved*. Mae could not join her need for political and social activism as an organic intellectual with teaching and nurturing Pat and Butch. Pat says that Mae did not talk to her about the desegregation case.

> I guess she felt that I just should have known. I didn't feel like I had any voice. I just went along with whatever was happening. Parents at that time didn't talk with you and explain. At least my mother didn't talk and explain. I just got bits and pieces of what was going on. That was one of the issues I had with my mother. You sort of learned by osmosis. Then too I didn't feel like I had a say.

Like other activists' parents, Mae did not tell Pat what was being done on her behalf. Martin Luther King III and Betty Shabazz's daughters Ilyasah and Attallah all recall that their parents did not give them a political education. Russell Rickford aptly notes that Shabazz "hoped to raise conscientious citizens, not race spokesmen or revolutionaries." For Shabazz, Malcolm X, Martin Luther King Jr., and others, education equaled revolution. Margaret Burnham recalled that her parents "rarely spoke about politics" but rather taught by example. Mae's friend Bob Moses, a mathematician and SNCC leader, raised his daughter Maisha Moses to be politically *and* socially aware.[23] Our friend Grattan recalled that as a child,

> I watched and marched with my father on picket lines in a long series of struggles to gain better wages, working conditions and federal safety reg-

ulations in the coal mining industry. My father explained these things to me.... I saw my father, as a leader and organizer of striking miners, beaten by company cops and left lying with a broken back, permanently [disabling him] when I was thirteen.[24]

My life as an activist child replicated Grattan's. My mother explained to me why we marched and infused my life with fun. We marched in a workers' strike at Manhattan's RCA where she worked. We attended Workers World Party meetings and parties, Black Panther meetings, Columbia University's May Day Festivals, parks, museums, Harlem's Liberation Bookstore. Mommy seamlessly conjoined fun, activism, and mothering.

Mae could not conjoin motherhood and activism.

Mae's Incarceration

I just knew she was in jail. It was something about working and receiving welfare or home relief.... I couldn't quite understand what that was about. I didn't know it was debtors' prison.

—**Pat Mallory Oduba**

The FBI used tax harassment and tax audits to imprison Mae, to destroy her life, because she dared to integrate New York City schools, was connected to the Communist Party of America, and was Black.[25] Pat recalled, "They probably talked about [her incarceration] in the family. They were very embarrassed by my mothers' activities [laughter].... In fact, I had one relative who said [to my mother], *"Ain't you scared?"* That's what she asked my mother because they were scared. My mother was just so forward with this stuff. *She scared them.*

With Mae's incarceration, Pat and Butch moved in with their aunt. Her aunt took Pat to visit Mae in prison.

> I remember that she was in the Women's House of Detention, the only thing I can remember. I remember it very clearly. I brought my mother some clothes, a nightgown; my aunt went with me. When I got there, you had to give it to somebody. They looked at it and said, *"this is not a hotel."* She was very nasty to me. I was hurt, she was not kind. What do I know of the prison system?

Like Pat, many children of the incarcerated found themselves treated mercilessly by prison staff.[26] Pat says, "My aunt, I don't know what she was thinking. She might not have had any information about the prison system. I had this real fancy nightgown, they wouldn't take, but also gave me a little tongue lashing. How would I know?" Pat was severely wounded by the hostile encounter with the prison guard, so much so that she recounted it to me sixty years later. "Instead of saying, look, 'that's very sweet of you to bring this to Mommy. We have certain things that they wear, and this is not one of them. You can bring her something else.' None of that, like I was a prisoner. Like I had committed some kind of crime. Like the next minute I was going to be in shackles, that's how I felt."

Mae was liberated from prison in 1957, forcing the family to move to the St. Nicholas Housing Projects at 212 West 129th Street, Apartment 12E. The state punished Mae and her children for her activism, punishment that imbued every aspect of the children's lives, including school. In 1957, because of Mae's political beliefs, Pat at age twelve experienced emotionally harmful treatment at school.

> The teacher in my class had a section of the classroom cordoned off for people who were "bad." So I was put there because I was talking. The teacher called that "Never Never Land." We were reading something in our books about Russia and from listening to my mother and talking with her Communist Party friends, Russia didn't seem a bad place.... I was telling a little friend of mine next to me, "You know, Russia is not bad." [Laughter] The teacher put me in Never Never Land.

Talking too liberally, too positively about Russia made Pat a threat to the school and to the United States, thus her banishment to Never Never Land. "Because I said Russia is not bad and because of my mother's activities, [my mother and the lawyer Paul Zuber] had started the suit against the Board of Education. I was not allowed to graduate with my sixth-grade class. While they did not ban me from coming to the school's graduation, they consigned me, my mother, and Paul Zuber to the back of the auditorium." Pat's experience resembled Cornell University graduate Paul Robeson Jr., who was unemployable because of his family's activism. It mirrored Esther Cooper Jackson's experience of unrelenting FBI surveillance and the FBI initiating expulsion of her daughter from nursery school.[27] Pat found herself victimized by the state and blacklisted at twelve.[28]

Notwithstanding this middle school tragedy, the loss of the desegregation case, *and* incarceration, Mae still held high hopes for Pat's intellectual education. Pat wanted to go with her friends to Wadleigh Junior High School at 215 West 114th Street, because the Wadleigh girls "looked cool."²⁹

> I used to see girls from Wadleigh coming home from school. *They were so fresh, and they did things.* I thought *I wanted to do those things too.* The ones that I saw that I liked used to stand on the corner with tight skirts and their hands on their hips. *And I wanted to do just that.* [Laughing] Stand on the corner with my hand on my hip. In fact, I did, until one of my mothers' neighbors saw me and *I sort of like, very slowly slid my hand down off my hip.*

Pat would not have a Wadleigh girl's experience of learning "how to cook and prepare for menial jobs, my mother wasn't going to have that." With the help of her communist friends and Ruth Russell, the head of the United Federation of Teachers, Mae sent Pat to the Downtown Community School at 235 Eleventh Street for the seventh and eighth grades. Russell helped pay Pat's tuition. It was an all-white progressive private school where blacklisted teachers and children of the blacklisted attended. Pat recalled that "Pete Seeger was the musical director at the time." Given Mae's political background, this should have been a perfect fit for the radical's daughter. It was not. The Downtown Community School was founded in 1944 as a "social reconstructionist school," a cooperative. It began at nursery school up to the eighth grade. Norman Studer, the director from 1951 to 1971, envisioned the school as a "politically radical democratic society, with students of different races, classes, religious affiliations, and ethnicities." Carleton Mabee claimed that although Jewish students made up the majority of the population, the school actively recruited nonwhite students. Pat's experience does not match Mabee's assessment. Gold's *Downtown Community School* indicates that the school didn't meet their lofty goal and ideals when it came to racial inclusion. The majority of the children in Gold's pictorial are white, except for one Asian and one Black student.³⁰ As the only Black kid at the school, Pat did not quite fit in. Pat was just learning the social norms of her Harlem school friends how to "sound"—'You think you're funny,' 'Yeah like Bugs Bunny.' You have to answer back in rhyme," Pat told me. Mae crushed Pat's hopes of becoming a Wadleigh girl and perfecting her "sounding" skills. Mae's plans for Pat proved far statelier than "sounding" and standing on the corner with hands firmly on her hips when she enrolled Pat into the Downtown Community School. Pat states, "Here I was at this white middle-class school with little, small classrooms, all that kind of privilege."

Pat could not wrap her mind around the class and racial differences as a working-class girl, having no concrete point of reference for this experience. Like other Black children who attend elite white schools, Pat found it difficult to adjust to the school environment. She felt alienated and marginalized.³¹ The white kids lived in Stuyvesant Town and Peter Cooper Village, while she lived in the St. Nicholas Projects.

> I was embarrassed by living in the projects—the class difference. I don't think my mother was embarrassed to be living in the projects. I was embarrassed with the white kids at school. I felt bad about being poor. My defense was like I'll beat your ass, I'll kick your ass . . . I always wanted to fight. So, in fact, that first day at school I did fight.

Pat did not dress like them, didn't have the money for the fancy clothes they wore. This further compounded her mortification. The regular tensions of teenagehood, of trying to fit in and navigate class differences, racial differences, and social and cultural hiccups were amplified for Pat, compounding her social self-consciousness and humiliating her.

Pat told me, "A Black girl came to the school in the eighth grade." She and Pat formed a tight bond. "I was like 'thank you Jesus.' We just caught on like this." She crossed her fingers. Although Pat came from the working class and this girl came from the middle class, they bonded due to their shared racial background and their social isolation at the school. Her Black friend's family knew the markers of middle-class acceptability in fashion. For graduation *"she dressed just like the white girls* in a nice cotton summery dress" from *Seventeen* magazine. I asked, "Did you tell Mae you wanted a *Seventeen* magazine dress?" Pat emphatically replied, "Nooooo, I didn't tell her. I came to graduation—*in a wedding dress* [laughing]. It had scallops, eyelets, satins, bows, all kinds of stuff. It was most embarrassing. I came down the aisle in that dress."

The Downtown Community School would not be Mae's last attempt at offering Pat a stellar education. In a letter to Mabel Williams in Cuba, Mae begged her to arrange a Cuban education for Pat. Mae wrote that "Julian [Mayfield] had suggested that you and Rob help with [the] kids' education. If you can get them to attend college in Cuba that is better than money. It will probably only be Pat, Butch, I am afraid is something like Ray."³² In 1963 Mae wrote to the writer Charles Anderson, who was living in Mexico, about educating Pat and Butch there on scholarships. Anderson wrote, "I am sure that because of political 'sympathy' or whatever word fits, (admiration) we will be able to arrange something appropriate."³³ When the Williams family moved to China, Mae asked them to arrange a Chinese education for Pat. Mae also asked her communist friends for help arranging a Soviet education for Pat. She never wavered in trying to gain an august education for Pat—the education she'd been denied.

Black Nationalist Rebel Girl

When Pat entered high school in 1959, white supremacists countrywide were running amok—raping four Florida A&M students and murdering Mack Parker in Poplar, Mississippi. A white woman falsely cried rape. White supremacists blocked interracial housing development in Deerfield, Illinois, and prevented school integration in Prince Edward County, Virginia. In 1960 in Greensboro, North Carolina, the sit-in movement was initiated by A&T students, sparking the movement across the country. It ignited white supremacist riots in Chattanooga and Montgomery and caused the expulsion of nine Alabama State University students for activism. Anti-colonial independence movements occurred: Ghana's independence, Puerto Rico's independence movement, and Vietnam's continued efforts to free themselves from French and American control. New York's Black nationalism blossomed: Lewis H. Michaux's African National Memorial Bookstore, Richard Moore's Frederick Douglass Book Center and classes, the African Jazz Art Society and Studios, and Mama Keke's Yoruba Temple, Moremi Bookstore, and African Market. New York was popping.[34]

At fourteen Pat metamorphized. "I considered myself a Black nationalist since a teenager." She became an organic intellectual and a community feminist. Pat describes a very exciting time in her life when she entered Seward Park High School. She emerged from the cloud of abuse and neglect and formed a leftist Black nationalist identity. "I was a wild woman at that school. I was coming into my own. After coming out of that Downtown Community School I had sort of found my feet." Grossman et al. point to self-care as a form of resilience and resistance to abuse. Singe et al. argue that healing takes the form of rebuilding one's self-esteem, gaining agency in one's life, and learning to use "problem solving skills" to self-heal. Black therapists encourage all of these strategies, adding listening to music, drawing, and creating poetry as self-healing strategies. Pat instinctively adopted these strategies, involving herself in many kinds of social, intellectual, and cultural activities, cultivating good, strong relationships.[35] Pat says of this time in her life:

> I'm beginning to put things together, I was still fucked up, but I was able to speak and express myself. I took leadership roles in high school. I was voted third-term representative in the general elections in school, I was the president of the Negro Culture Club, we went to the UN, I was a member of the Chinese Culture Club and attended Puerto Rican Independence meetings. I was living the idea of multiracial unity.

Pat began a journey of self-restoration. "I was just being wild, but going in a positive direction, not going to hang out at the juke joint. It was almost straight and narrow, but a little out there.... I'd get up at one o'clock in the morning and meet friends. I'd sing wildly at the top of my lungs in the park.... I had a lot of fun. It was totally wild." Her "wild" behavior led her to European folk dance with her best friend/sister Angela. "One time we said we were going to this folk dance club in the city. [To their surprise, when they arrived] Angela's aunt was there [laughter], making sure we actually went. You couldn't fool the aunt, our guardian angel. We weren't slick. We just were running the city having as much fun as possible. Go to Greenwich Village. We thought we were intellectuals. We thought we were really smart."

Pat joined the multiracial Symposium Club—her "mini version of being an activist." The club consisted of "mostly left-wing" Black, Puerto Rican, and Jewish friends. Their sole purpose was fighting against nuclear war and debating. "This business about the bomb. They would have us go outside somewhere. We protested hiding when the sirens would go off [nuclear bomb alerts]. [We protested the school] preparing for the bomb scare. We refused to participate in that activity because we were not trying to prepare for war. We didn't think it was necessary. We refused to participate in that."

The year 1959 was a time of intense nuclear war protest, given that people witnessed the atrocity of the nuclear bombing of Hiroshima and Nagasaki, saw images of Japanese people with their skin melting from their bodies, the utter death and destruction that the bombs brought to Japan. Mae's Crusaders for Freedom, the Workers World, groups to which Pat belonged, as well as the Negroes with Guns movement, actively protested nuclear war and advocated for peace, an anti-American stance according to the U.S. government.[36] These memberships informed Pat's anti-bomb and anti-war stance. Pat says that in the Symposium Club "we did our protesting and writing.... I learned to smoke, because that was the intellectual thing to do, smoke, drink coffee, read poems, and talk. I was being a mini Mae [laughter]. That's what I called being wild in the streets."

In September 1960, as a Black nationalist and proud supporter of the Cuban Revolution, Pat prepared for Fidel Castro's historic New York visit.[37] "I belonged to the Debate Club, a group of left-wing students. When Fidel Castro came to Harlem we were preparing to greet him, making posters and signs in our kitchen. I made a sign 'Give 'Em Hell Fidel.' My mother was so proud [laughing]. She puffed up like a peacock." At fifteen Pat became a steadfast supporter of Castro and the Cuban Revolution. Pat and the Crusaders for Freedom carried a sign that included Castro's oft-quoted phrase,

"We in Cuba have done in 18 months what you are still trying to [do] for 400 years."[38] Pat and Mae admired Castro's Cuban Revolution because they eradicated illiteracy and claimed to have also eliminated racism and discrimination. Pat venerated Cuba's revolution, which allowed an Afro-Cuban to become a doctor. Before the revolution he "couldn't get into a hospital as a patient, let alone become a doctor." Pat appreciated Cuba's revolution, which supported African, Latin American, and Asian anti-colonial movements and vowed to fight for the human rights of African American and African diasporic people.[39]

Pat attended Highlander Folk School's teen workshops in Monteagle, Tennessee, which had been founded in 1932 by white activist Myles Horton to train workers in the labor movement. In the 1950s it morphed into a training site for multiracial civil rights activists.[40] Highlander developed a "democratic community ... [of] labor leaders and workers of all races and colors." Through their "workshop programs" they brought about "peaceful but effective integration and democracy in the South."[41] They sought to break southern norms. The multiracial people lived and ate communally, breaking bread together in a vast dining room, a prohibition in the South. They successfully broke the chains of white supremacists' southern norms. Highlander ran workshops for teenagers: integration workshops, voter registration workshops, and Sing for Freedom Workshops, which white folk singers Guy and Candy Carawan ran. Highlander fully expected teenagers like Pat to go back to their communities and actively participate in human rights movements.[42] The Carawans were charged with bringing Pat to Highlander from New York. At Highlander she attended workshops with people like Fred Shuttlesworth Jr., the son of the civil rights activist Rev. Fred Shuttleworth Sr., who co-founded Alabama's Christian Movement for Civil Rights and the Southern Christian Leadership Conference.[43] About her experience at Highlander Pat recalled,

> Everybody was going to be talking about their experiences. Most of them were from the South; I was the only one from the North. We talked about segregation in the North and the South. We talked and *we partied*. *Those kids were really Hearty*. James Brown was popular then, and I learned some dances I had never seen before [laughter]. And their thick southern accents, it was an experience.

By sending Pat to Highlander, Mae tried to offer Pat a typical childhood infused with a political education, like many politically active parents, including the Burnhams, who sent their children to Communist Party summer camps.

A decade younger than Mae, Mommy sent me to camps, Brooklyn's YMCA. I went with my yellow Sock It to Me pocketbook, played with Gretel, took photographs on the roof playground, made movies, went to Jones Beach's big pool and Palisades Amusement Park, my Mary Poppins hat with shiny papier mâché cherries bought there. Something happened, and my Y camp summers ended. Did I spout racist rhetoric? Was I called a name? Mommy told me why. I don't remember, but that was it. Summers at the politically progressive multiracial Beacon, New York, University Settlement Camp. Hindi, Nina, Susie, Sara, and Eric went too. Singing Puerto Rico's "Que Bonita Bandera" and Cuba's "Guantanamera." Watching in awe as gorgeous, tall, huge Afroed Black woman counselor sang "Grandma's Hands" in the outdoor amphitheater. We sang and danced to "Soul Makossa," swam, went on hayrides to town for grinders, Pixie Stix, and wax soda bottles with colored syrup; slept on wooden bunk beds, broke rocks, getting at beautiful crystals inside. My Harlemite friend Sheri Z and I played skully with colorful bottlecaps. At age eight I walked backward, talking to an intriguing boy, and blackened both eyes when I walked into a tree. A decade apart, Mae and Audrey did everything to raise pro-African American radical daughters.

Black Nationalist Activities

Nationalism was ingrained in me, both the political and economic side. My mother's brand of nationalism [influenced me]. She tried to make us proud of ourselves, and to follow a course that reflected that pride.
—Pat Mallory Oduba

Singe et al. contend that in order to self-heal, one must resist stereotypes and "intentionally affirm [one's] racial/ethnic and gender identities." Pat healed herself from her childhood trauma by embodying a strong African-centered persona.[44] Patricia attended Harlem's Black nationalist activities with Angela. This enabled Pat to come into her own. She recalls, "We got very Afrocentric. We got our African names [from the priestess] Mama KeKe, [mine was] Ayoka, and the beads representing one god or another and that was it." Pat involved herself with New York's Yoruba tradition bearers: Mama KeKe's Yoruba Temple. "I hung out with a bunch of Yoruba people and attached myself to the Yoruba culture. . . . I just went for the fun of it; there was a lot of drumming, dancing, music, and ceremonies. So that's why I liked it—it was African culture." Her involvement with the Yoruba allowed

Patricia Mallory

This Miss au Naturale is Pat Mallory (or Ayoke Iyalode). She organized a limbo team last year. It was great, this year it should be better. All you guys and dolls on the Lower East Side can get your tickets from her:

377 E. 10th St.
phone 533-3663

Fig. 6. Patricia Mallory, Miss au Naturale, Women's Committee of the Harlem Unemployment Center, "Annual Steer-B-Que Bus-Outing & Dance Booklet, July 30, 1966," p. 4, box 2, folder 2-25, 1965–1966, Mae Mallory Papers, Wayne State University.

her to gain some separation from Mae, who "was not interested in any of that kind of stuff. I had that to myself." While she took on a Yoruba name and enjoyed going to their events, because of her atheist, Black nationalist, and communist upbringing Pat skipped initiation. Pat's Yoruba involvement points to a search for meaning and spiritual guidance. Pat sought religious experiences as healing balms with Harlem's stepladder street preachers and the Nation of Islam. Pat regularly attended the NOI's Temple no. 7 with no intention whatsoever of joining. She verbally sparred with Muhammad Ali, a student of Malcolm X, member of NOI, Vietnam War protestor, and 1960 Olympic gold medalist and heavyweight boxing champion of the world. She recalled, "Muhammad Ali was *such a loud mouth*."[45]

Pat immersed herself in the Nation of Islam. "I started getting involved in the nationalist movement with Malcolm around that time. . . . I used to listen to Malcolm on the corner a lot." According to Robyn C. Spencer-Antoine, NOI was a "community-based organization advocating Black cultural self-determination, [and] economic justice and dignity." Following Booker T. Washington's Black economic nationalism, they founded the *Messenger* magazine, the University of Islam for preschool to high school students, department stores, dress shops, dry cleaning facilities, grocery stores, restaurants, newspapers, and barbershops. They held conventions for nation-building and promoted the Black woman and the Black family.[46] Malcolm X was the leader of Temple no. 7 and the "fiery spokesperson" of the group. He traveled to Africa and the Middle East, including Mecca, met with activists and heads of states, and learned and talked about human rights.[47] Pat recalled, "[In 1964] when Malcolm X came back from Mecca, we were there in the Hotel Teresa making signs welcoming him back. I was just out there in the streets as per usual. . . . It was all political stuff I was involved in, and nationalist stuff. This definitely came from my mother." Pat's meek, apolitical grandmother got involved in Black nationalist politics. Perhaps because the family lived together in the Harlem housing projects and Mae held Crusaders fundraisers at the house, Pat's grandmother became acquainted with the people and the causes. Pat says, "Even my grandmother came around. In fact, she and Queen Mother Moore were very close. My grandmother belonged to Malcolm X's Organization of Afro-American Unity, so she was very much involved. I didn't belong to that." Queen Mother Moore attended all Crusaders for Freedom events, and this is most certainly where she befriended Pat's grandmother.[48] Pat says, "Most of my time was spent running the streets, listening to Malcolm, and the preachers in the street, and [going to] this demonstration or another." It's interesting that Pat did not join Malcolm X's Organization of Afro-American Unity (which he founded when he left the NOI), especially given that Pat couldn't abide by some of the NOI's ideologies. She most certainly would have enjoyed Malcolm X's commitment to teaching African American history at his Liberation School.[49] The Nation of Islam recruited heavily at the mosque, participating in "fishing contests," a recruitment strategy. Like Christian churches, the NOI encouraged people to join at their services.[50] Pat said, *"Ohhh, I'm not going that far, sitting there with those white dresses. No, not doing that. Mae Mallory would have a heart attack.* I wasn't joining none of that. *She was in my head all the time.* It was very hard to get her out of my head." As a Black nationalist feminist who rejected patriarchy and misogyny, especially after Mae's lessons concerning the evils of male supremacy, Pat could not join the NOI. The Nation of Islam maintained strict gender roles, modeled after patriarchal norms. They required women to excel in housekeeping, maintain a certain weight by following a strict dietary regimen, wear head coverings, and an "overgarment" so as not to "tempt men with your beauty in any form." Marriage meant that women had to be half the age of their potential husband, in order to be, as Malcolm X stated in 1957, helpmates to their spouse, good mothers and wives. Pat could not conform to these types of strictures as she learned to be a strong independent Black women. Given her lessons in color caste and retrograde beauty ideals, she would have agreed with their prohibitions against bleaching creams and hair straightening.[51]

Like the NOI and other Black Nationalist groups, Pat embraced Black nationalist women beauty ideals. She participated in the Marcus Garvey Day Celebrations sponsored by James Rupert Lawson's United African Nationalist Movement. "I remember going to the Miss Africa Contests and the Miss Africa Ball a few times. More frequently I attended the Miss Standard of Beauty events." Pat enjoyed attending Harlem's Miss Natural Standard of Beauty contests, founded in 1940 by Afro-Dominican Carlos Cooks. Cooks was a prolific Harlem street speaker who established Harlem's African Nationalist Pioneer Movement to keep Marcus Garvey's "legacy of African redemption and reclamation alive." Cooks worked to establish African diasporic hegemony,[52] which fit in with Pat's Black feminist nationalist identity. "I used to go to that every year. First of all, your hair had to be natural. . . . Miss Natural Standard of Beauty [was] like [the] Miss America contest. Every year they would put this thing on in one of the ballrooms. Everyone came in their African finery. The women [contestants] would be selected beforehand." This was Afrocentricity on full display. Sharifa Rhodes-Pitts and Tanisha C. Ford note that the contest occurred in August as part of the African Nationalist Pioneer Movement's Marcus Garvey Day Celebration. It was a beauty contest intended to rebuild pride and self-confidence in Black women, to help them reject the concept of white women as the personification of beauty.[53] An example of a typical Marcus Garvey Day celebration (August 17, 1956) included a parade down Lenox Avenue, a "Eulogistic Mass Meeting," the beauty contest, and "dancing to the music of Billy Hargraves and His Rhythm Masters" at the Renaissance Casino, Seventh Avenue and 138th Street.[54] Modeled after the Miss America pageant, Miss Natural Standard of Beauty contests added Black nationalist tropes to the bathing suit, evening wear, and question segments. The winner answered the questions correctly and fit the Black feminine aesthetic ideal of "racially pure" dark skin and nappy hair.[55]

> One of the questions I will never forget: "If you were in a boat and there was a young handsome white man and an *old snaggletoothed raggedy Black man* in the boat, and the boat capsized, who would you save?" [Laughter] So naturally you're supposed to say *the old snaggletoothed Black man*. As a teenager that's what I was fed. I know some of the stuff was ridiculous, but this was part of your pride and race-building. I learned to separate.

Embracing an African-centered identity and aesthetic as self-healing, Pat "decided to go natural." Pat recalled that singer/activist and her mentor "Abbey Lincoln in fact did my hair. She taught me how to take care of it. I don't know how or why I was at her house, and yes Max Roach [the drummer and

Abbey's husband] was there."[56] Lincoln sported and popularized the Afro. She and Roach, both Pan-Africanists and Black nationalists, belonged to the African Jazz Art Society and Studios, founded in the late 1950s by Black nationalists Elombe and Kwame Brathwaite with friends from Manhattan's School of Industrial Art and Design High School. Marcus Garvey and Carlos A. Cooks inspired them.[57] Pat attended the African Jazz Art Society and Studios and their Grandassa Models African-centered fashion shows. The Grandassa Models embodied an African diasporic body aesthetic of full-figured glory, with brown- to dark-skinned, natural-haired mannequins modeling African-inspired clothes. They moved away from the ideal of light skin, white features, ultra-thin body, and straight hair.[58] Abbey Lincoln helped the Grandassa Models introduce "Zulu Styles, Afro Puffs inspired by the Ethiopian 'Amharic hairstyles' and traditional South and West African hairstyles." Lincoln influenced Pat's sense of beauty.[59]

> When I started wearing my hair natural one of the guys who ran this thing [the Grandassa Models] came up to me. I was in Nedicks [hot dog restaurant] on 125th Street [and] Seventh Avenue with my high school friend Betty Evans. He came up to me and asked me, "Why do you wear your hair natural like that?" I didn't know who he was, and I, with my sassy self, said, "Ask her." He said, "I'm not asking her cause she fries her hair." *Well, excuse me!!!* I didn't know he was part of this thing. A couple of weeks later, I applied to be one of the models. He was there and reminded me of how I brushed him off [laughter]. That was the end of that. We became friends.

Pat recalled that the Grandassa model book featured a "picture of the Grandassa models, and me at a demonstration protesting the opening up of wig shops . . . and [protesting] Black women wearing these wigs. I had a good time in Harlem too. I enjoyed my life."[60]

While Patricia enjoyed her life, racialized carnage spewed in the United States. African American radicals and passive resisters demanded change. Unfolding in the South was a passive resistance nonviolent movement accepting of white supremacist brutalization, which led the Nation of Islam, Negroes with Guns, Monroe Defense Committee, and others to denounce them. Audrey Proctor, Mrs. Johnson, Ruthie Stone, Mae Mallory, and Pat Mallory all looked on incredulously at the Freedom Riders and others being assaulted by white supremacists. When the Student Non-Violent Coordinating Committee moved from direct action to voter registration, the Seniorses, Mallorys, and Johnsons remained horrified at the white supremacist murders of protestors. While all this action erupted around the United States, in New York Pat struggled to understand her mother.[61]

Abandonment

In 1961 Pat still found it difficult to understand her political mother. Like many children of activist parents, Pat felt neglected.[62] "My mother took up all the air. She filled up the whole space with all the people in the world but not me." During Mae's escape from Monroe the FBI determined to capture her. In Harlem they surveilled the family brutally, wiretapping their home and regularly harassing Pat, Butch, their grandmother, and other family members.[63] "The FBI used to come to the house [in Harlem] and ask my grandmother to let them in. I was furious; I would not let them in. I was actually kind of feisty at that time, especially with them.... They would ask where she was, they would ask our neighbors." At sixteen Pat was unafraid of the FBI and exhibited Black Nationalist Rebel Girl bravado and bravery.

> I didn't want anything to do with them and I wanted them to know that I was not voluntarily answering their questions. [I was] not cooperating. I was trying to live up to [my mother's standard]. I was trying to win her approval. "See, this is who you want. I'm being who you want me to be." Wow, but I was furious with the FBI. I told them, "You find the killers of Emmett Till." I was about sixteen [laughter].

The visits by the FBI could have proved physically dangerous to Pat *and* her grandmother, given that agents and agents provocateurs regularly brutalized and killed political activists. Pat and her grandmother thankfully escaped physical assault but experienced a constant barrage of psychological assaults by the FBI and police.

Mae's 1961 arrest and jailing marked another test for Pat: "When they finally caught my mother, it was Calvin Hicks [chair of New York's MDC] who told me. I was in hysterics because I didn't know what was going to happen. Hicks was like, 'Oh, come on, you know they were going to catch her.'" Pat involved herself with her mother's case by attending meetings and demonstrations with WWP, becoming active with RAM, working with New York's Monroe Defense Committee, and visiting her mother in Cleveland. Pat remembers, "My mother was concerned that I wasn't interested in the case anymore. I did detach myself somewhat. Life, living, high school."

When Pat visited, she arrived in a segregated Cleveland, housing the eighth largest Black population in the United States—a city in which one-fifth of the white population moved to the suburbs, leaving middle-class African American homeowners behind. Poor and working-class Blacks lived in subpar conditions, overcrowded housing, and segregated public housing.

Urban renewal wreaked havoc on Cleveland's Black community. It systematically destroyed African American housing, which wasn't rebuilt. Pat came to Cleveland where Blacks were locked out of skilled manufacturing jobs and unions. They worked as unskilled laborers. Many received welfare, as did their children. Education proved another obstacle given the overcrowding of Black schools and the lack of qualified teachers and resources, libraries, and playgrounds. The predominantly white and suburban-living school board refused to build new schools. They spent $500 per each white child, but only $300 per each Black child. In 1960 the average African American age twenty-five attended two years of high school, given the high dropout rates in middle school and high school.

The Black community was cognizant of Cleveland's and the world's social and political climates: the Red Scare/blacklist loomed large in Cleveland with the firing of Cleveland radio station engineer Rudolph Jones, who refused to answer HUAC questions. The Black population read of a United Nations unwilling to embrace Cuba and independent African countries. They learned of apartheid Rhodesia's refusal to enfranchise Black Africans and Rhodesia's refusal to enfranchise Egyptians. Black Cleveland participated in voting drives and read affirming stories of the *Washington Post* hiring two African Americans: Ellsworth Davis and Dorothy Butler. They read of Dr. John Wesley Lawlah's appointment to the Health Advisory Council, and of Thurgood Marshall's appointment to a federal judgeship. Pat entered a city with a clearly defined Black social order of sororities, fraternities, motorcycle clubs, women's clubs, elite NAACP, and sports activities—a city where Flora C. Green, the Olympic running champion and Jesse Owens's sister, gave a talk at her exclusive women's club, the Jewelites, about Universal Negro Improvement Association (UNIA) leader Lillie Mae Gibson. Pat entered a world of Black girls' clubs such as the Addison Girls League and Jacqueline Balthrope's lessons in "Correct Etiquette."[64]

In Cleveland Pat met the Monroe Defense Committee, and notwithstanding Mae's protestations, Pat *did* involve herself in the case. The *Afro American* proclaimed, "New York's Monroe Defense Committee announced that Patricia Mallory was the national youth organizer."[65] Pat recalled, "I would go back and forth to Cleveland during the year and sometimes in the summertime." Cleveland most certainly was not ready for the Black Nationalist Rebel Girl that Pat metamorphosed into: the Addison Girls League was teaching Black girls with straightened hair hegemonic standards of beauty, and Jacqueline Balthrope's "Correct Etiquette," proper dress for the opera. Pat's Black nationalist style, which she learned from the Grandassa Models,

National Standard of Beauty Contests, and Abbey Lincoln, most certainly did not conform to Cleveland's elite set.⁶⁶ "We went to some school my mother was speaking at, a Black school. We were walking down the hall and some group of Black kids walked by and said some nasty things. They called me Watusi. As if that was an insult. So, she made me straighten my hair and I was not for that. . . . She said, 'People are not ready for that.'"

Interestingly Mae, the rebel who conformed to Black social norms and Eurocentric beauty ideals in Cleveland, delustered Pat the Black Nationalist Rebel Girl. Curiously the *Call and Post* reported, "Mrs. Mallory prefers to wear her hair as 'God gave it to me,'" even though the accompanying photographs showed her with straightened hair.⁶⁷ While Mae's public persona professed pride in Black hair, her private persona warned Pat against natural hair. Why? Perhaps she did not want Pat or herself to experience any isolation or shunning. Pat says that young men in Cleveland found her attractive and were interested in dating her, but they knew not to "mess with Mae Mallory's daughter." In Cleveland Pat stayed with the Monroe Defense Committee member Wilbur Grattan, his wife, his three sons, and his daughter Iris, who was sixteen like Pat. They became fast friends.⁶⁸ Pat also met my mother. "Audrey was very proper. Audrey was just so fun-loving. She just liked to mess with us. That's how we knew her. Out of all the people my mother had [who were] always around, Audrey and Clarence were fixtures." Pat and Iris found my mother at age twenty-one worldly and glamorous. "Audrey was like an older sister to Iris and I. [Laughing] We admired her [laughing] because *she knew things*." They thought of her as an intellectual. They so admired my mother, her looks, her intelligence, her language, and her use of slang.

> She used to say "something was SKD—some kind of different." [Laughing] So we looked at her a lot as if this is how you act. We tried to talk like her. We would say SKD and nobody else knew what it meant. She used to do this [she indicates a fancy way to put on your earrings], which I still do; it just stuck with me. Audrey was very up-front. The only role model we had was Audrey.

Pat says that everyone else was older and could not relate to them. They followed Audrey's lead in working on Mae's case. Pat says that at the Monroe Defense Committee "she did put us to work because *she wasn't joking either too*. When she would tell you to do something, you would go on and do it. We would half-ass do it. If there were chores to do we did it. We would go on demonstrations and [we helped with] mailings." Pat and Iris received the typical training that children of communists and Black nationalists received: doing office work, collating, and putting together pamphlets for

Mae's case. Because they were teenagers, Pat said, "Most of the time [Iris and I] were into ourselves. We were trying to be serious. [We were] trying to listen to what [older people] were talking about, as much as sixteen-year-olds could listen. Audrey would get pissed off and call us 'TNT [typical nigger teenagers].'"

> *I found this funny, but I was SHOCKED. Growing up my mother taught me that "nigger" and "bitch" were the worst things that someone could call you. You had to fight them. My mother's use of this language is a part of her personality that she never revealed to me. I did not know this Audrey.*

My mother offered them true sisterhood and, for Pat, a source for healing. "She would listen to a whole lot of stuff [we told her]. *We could talk to her!* [Excited] We couldn't talk to our parents. So, you know, she was open like that. It was a release, a release from all the tension."

Pat looked to my parents' relationship as a model: "I guess just being impressionable, like I said Audrey was like a big sister. [I was] projecting my future, what the possibilities were. I didn't have a boyfriend at the time; none of my friends did." Pat suggests that if she had had a boyfriend, she would have emulated my parents' relationship:

> I often looked at people in the movement and their relationships. There were not very many that I saw that looked good. I thought your parents looked good. I was closest to them at the time. It was hard for me to understand how to behave in a marriage. Your parents were very sweet; they talked nice. I said, I don't know if I could talk like that. It seemed like it would be very difficult. I didn't hear my mother talk sweet to a man, like "honey," saying those kinds of words.

Pat says because she didn't come from a physically demonstrative family, it was hard for her to understand physically loving behavior. My parents worked side by side at MDC teaching Pat, Iris, and the other children at the office how to work. They took these children to Mae's demonstrations, desegregation marches, anti–Vietnam War marches, picnics, and parties.[69] As a teenager, Pat took this all in and was determined to have a relationship like my parents', built on activism, love, and fun.

By "running wild" and taking part in Black nationalist activities, Pat healed herself, becoming the quintessential African-centered persona, embodying a Black feminine and Black beauty aesthetic.[70] Notwithstanding the life-threatening charges against Mae, Pat found teenage joy, exuberance, and rebellion. Because of Mae's incarceration Pat found sisters in Iris and Audrey. She found joy. She found happiness. Pat, like the phoenix, emerged as a Black Nationalist Rebel Girl, an organic intellectual, and a community feminist.

Part II Writing Resistance

Fig. 7. "Mrs. Mallory Goes Back to County Jail,"
Audrey and Clarence Seniors Collection.

Chapter 6   **Mae Mallory**
Dream Escape at Twenty-First
and Payne/"Pain"

It's terrible that the crooks are on the outside and the good people in the jails.
—**Mae**, *Letters from Prison: The Story of a Frameup*

Mae Mallory spent from 1961 to 1963 in the Cuyahoga County Jail in Cleveland, located at Twenty-First Street and Payne. Dream escape writing offered her an important strategy for surviving incarceration and U.S. hegemony through what Carole Boyce Davies and Barbara Harlow identify as "prison blues" and "resistance literature," respectively. Boyce Davies writes that incarcerated women used prison blues writing to resist domination, class oppression, and patriarchal authority. Harlow defines resistance literature as an "arena of struggle," writing that challenges state repression aimed at those who resist hegemony.[1] Mae used diary entries (1962–1963), fantastical stories, correspondence, and published articles and pamphlets. "Of Dogs and Men" and *Letters from Prison*, with coauthor Clarence Henry Seniors, are examples of her writing. I define "dream escape" writing as a mode of escaping prison through dreams of better days, recalling these dreams through writing, writing herself out of prison through fantastical stories, sexual imaginings, prisoners' sexual encounters, and tales of fighting hegemonic oppression within and out of jail. Mae redefined what Katherine McKittrick and Clyde Woods call the politics of place to include jail as a Black geography, and therefore a site of positive transformation, social justice, "cooperation and stewardship," not a site of domination.[2] Mallory's writing offers us a window through which to view her inner life and personal experience as one of many children and women incarcerated at Cuyahoga jail. Her writing reveals several important themes: jail as a place, struggles with melancholy, and the use of dream escape writings to escape prison life.

During Mae's incarceration a national and international movement materialized around Mallory and the Monroe Defendants. Simultaneously this movement fought on behalf of human rights, liberation, and freedom movements in the United States and worldwide. These movements are significant as I consider how Mae's experience as a political prisoner mirrored those of African American performer-activist Paul Robeson, Irish American communist Elizabeth Gurley Flynn, and Afro-Trinidadian communist Claudia Jones. Studies of their work reveal how they used writing to survive incarceration.

Political Prisoners in the United States

> *Well-worn copies of Paul Robeson's* Here I Stand, *Robeson's "The Negro and the Soviet Union," and Shirley Graham Du Bois's* Citizen of the World *sat on our bookshelves. My mother told me to read the books when I asked about my namesake. At age eleven I wrote an essay about Robeson. I faced no repercussion at my Quaker school.*

A victim of the Counter Intelligence Program, Mae Mallory joined the long list of political prisoners of the Military Intelligence Division, the Red Scare, and COINTELPRO. These political prisoners were incarcerated for their political activism, their socialist beliefs, and the belief that Black people deserved human rights.[3] While Paul Robeson was not incarcerated in a brick-and-mortar prison, he was technically jailed in his own country when the U.S. government confiscated his passport, which prevented him from working overseas and being able to support his family. In his words,

> I have been in prison for seven years but for what crime? . . . What kind of country is this that says "This is a fine artist, but we are going to stop his career, even if we have to starve him to death? . . . I have been deprived of my livelihood, I have been stopped from functioning as an artist, which means I have been denied the right to be a full human being.[4]

Robeson was imprisoned following years of surveillance by the FBI, the Special Branch of the Royal Canadian Mounted Police, and Britain's MI5. He was surveilled for his belief in Black equality and Black Power, and for his political ideologies.[5] Through his and Louis Burnham's newspaper *Freedom* (1951–1955), his column "Here's My Story," and his autobiography *Here I Stand*, Paul Robeson wrote himself out of prison, which is significant to this chapter's theme.[6] The Smith Act imprisoned Elizabeth Gurley Flynn and Claudia Jones. They too wrote themselves out of prison.[7] At her trial Elizabeth Gurley Flynn proclaimed, "In all my long life . . . I never expected that I would go to jail for books. . . . If I return to my normal life of the last 47 years of working and speaking on unionism, democratic rights and against fascism and war, and on socialism, what happens, then, your Honor? . . . Does the whole thing start over again?" Flynn then declared, "I can be imprisoned. I cannot be corrected, reformed or changed. My body can be incarcerated but my thoughts remain free and unaffected."[8] Like Robeson, Flynn wrote herself out of prison: *I Speak My Own Peace: Autobiography of "The Rebel Girl"* (1955). On her release she wrote "Horizons of the Future for a Socialist America" (1959) and *My Life as a Political Prisoner: The Rebel Girl Becomes "No. 11710"* (1963).

Flynn's sister in the struggle, Claudia Jones, declared at her own trial:

> I proudly plead guilty . . . of holding Communist ideas. . . . You dare not, gentlemen of the prosecution, assert that the Negro woman can think and speak and write. You dare not read, because [my] article not only refutes the assertion that the ruling class will ever grant equality to 15,000,000 Negro Americans, but shows that what we are granted is unrequited force and violence. . . . The prosecution also cancelled out [my] "Women in the Struggle for Peace and Security"—it urges American mothers, Negro women and white, to write, to emulate the peace struggles of their anti-fascist sisters in Latin America, in the new European democracies, in the Soviet Union, in Asia and Africa. To end the bestial Korean war, to stop "operation killer," to bring our boys home, to reject the militarist threat that embroiled us in a war with China so that their children should not suffer the fate of the Korean babies murdered by napalm bombs of B-29s, nor the fate of Hiroshima. . . . Is all this not further proof that we were also tried for our opposition to racist ideas?[9]

Like Flynn and Robeson, Jones found herself facing incarceration for her writing, rhetoric, and radicalism. Like them, she fought back with words. Like Elizabeth Gurley Flynn, Mae Mallory learned that she could be imprisoned but not "corrected, reformed, or changed. [Her] thoughts remained free." Like Claudia Jones, Mae let readers know that African American women "can think, speak, and write." Her great friend Grattan wrote of Mae's intellect and verbal prowess to Robert F. Williams in China:

I want to mention in particular, in case you don't already know, the magnificent response of Mae Mallory when asked by the racist judge before he sentenced her if she had anything to say. In an unwavering voice [Mallory] told the court: "I am innocent. I am being tried and convicted because I am Black. I expect to spend the rest of my life in jail. The reason for this trial is that you hope to silence the voice of those who teach Black people the right of self-defense. You will fail. Even though I am jailed you will hear from me."[10]

In court and at Twenty-First and Payne, Mallory metamorphosized into a scholar like Phi Beta Kapa Paul Robeson, and into an organic intellectual like Flynn and Jones. While Mae remained eloquent in her dream escape in court and in prison, Black rebellious history marched on.

While Mae was imprisoned Black rebellion against tyranny unfolded. White supremacists retaliated. Mae wrote. In 1962 Ola Mae Quarterman, age eighteen, reignited the Albany Movement in Georgia by sitting in the front of the bus, leading to her arrest, bus boycotts, and desegregation efforts. White supremacists rampaged. From prison Mae wrote to Lynn and Williams that an Albany sheriff "cracked the skull of the Afro-American lawyer [which] indicated that this is more than a class struggle [for] Afro-Americans." Two white police officers brutalized pregnant mother Mrs. Slater King, who held her three-year-old on her hip as she took provisions to incarcerated demonstrators in Albany. Mae connected her case to theirs: "[The protestors] should know about [my] fight against extradition. . . . [People] understand that 21 year old woman blowing the head off that Klansman, wounding the others [which relates to my case]."[11] Mae conjoined her self-defense ideology to these women and girls defending themselves. In Birmingham, Bull Connor led brutal assaults on high school and college protestors using fire hoses and dogs. From prison Mae read with horror of white supremacists bombing Birmingham's Sixteenth Street Baptist Church, killing Addie Mae Collins (age 14), Cynthia Dionne Wesley (age 14), Carol Denise McNair (age 11), and Carole Rosanond Robertson (age 14); maiming Sarah Collins (age 12); and injuring twenty-two attendees. [12]

From Twenty-First and Payne/Pain Mae wrote to Dottie and Sam Ballan, offering Black resistance to trauma: "Behind the Birmingham movement there is an element of non-passivists. The element will help to bring about a turning point. It has already started only after policemen had been critically wounded (critically I hope) that the president saw fit to act in any way. I can't help to agree with Malcolm X on this."[13] She wrote to Robert Williams, "This is what I have learned about the people of Birmingham. Our people are no longer dependent on Passive Resistance. They are learning effective ways of combating vicious police dogs. They are even rendering the firehoses useless by cutting them up with the axes that they take from the fire trucks."[14] Mae wrote of self-defense as Black resistance to trauma not recorded in history books, books that document Black trauma over martial resistance. In jail Mae considered this history of rebellion as she contemplated jail as a place.

Jail as a Place of Resistance

As I am demonstrating, Mae Mallory consistently wrote in response to unfolding events. But it was a constant struggle to maintain momentum. Mae told the *Afro American*'s Bill Worthy that "she has read 'Negroes With Guns' by Robert Williams. [She] hopes herself to write a book. She [is] available to speak before groups, but assumes that by the terms of her bail, she will be confined within the state of Ohio."[15] Mae also wrote to Julian Mayfield in Ghana about her aspirations: "Maybe I told you that I am trying to write. At first I thought that jail would be the ideal place. It isn't. There is plenty [of] material for any number of books but finding the privacy and having the discipline to stick to writing is hard in jail."[16] She proudly wrote to Mabel Williams, "I am writing a little now. Articles of mine have appeared in several publications. Perhaps you have seen some, maybe *Freedomways*."[17] Through prison writing Mae achieved what public school and life circumstances prevented. She emerged as a scholar, an organic intellectual. Mallory wrote to cope and as a form of resistance to Twenty-First and Payne, the geography of domination. She wrote to survive.[18] This is summarized well in her declaration: "I intend to write a book. I will call it 'Skyscraper at 21st and Payne.'"[19]

In what follows Mae Mallory used her writing to unveil the space and place of prison as an avenue to articulate her incarcerations over the years 1957, 1958, and 1961 to 1965.[20] Mae's writing acted as a liberating tool, letting the outside world know that she is there, alive, fighting for freedom, rallying against suppression. Mae Mallory's "Skyscraper on 21st and Payne," "Open Letter to My Friends in America and Those in Foreign Lands," and *Letters from Prison* shed light on Cuyahoga County Jail as a geography of domination. In "Skyscraper on 21st and Payne," (1961) Mae writes,

> The wind moans around the 7th floor of Cleveland's skyscraper on 21st street and Payne Avenue. It sounds like the pathetic cries of a dying prehistoric animal according to Hollywood's soundtracks. These moaning sounds are

frightening to the inmates that are hearing them for the first time. This noise does not bother me. I am used to it. I have lived on the 12th floor of a New York housing project.[21]

Mae's "Skyscraper on 21st and Payne" reveals to us the Cuyahoga County Jail as a geography of domination, as described by Katherine McKittrick. McKittrick argues that the slave ship was a geography of domination that enclosed, controlled, and hid Africans' humanity, because it "'just is.' ... Those inside, [are] bound to the walls, are neither seeable nor liberated subjects." They are prisoners within a Hollywood horror movie come to life, entrapped within the carcass of the dinosaurian structure, rendered invisible, robbed of their freedom. The massive skeletal prehistoric animal encases their human intricacies and social interactions.[22]

Exhibiting her intellect and echoing *David Walker's Appeal to the Colored Citizens of the World*, Mallory's "Open Letter to My Friends in America and Those in Foreign Lands" reveals the interior of Twenty-First and Payne:

> Not out of self-pity, [but] so that you may be fully informed ... "My room is in Cell-Block 7a. It is a tiny room approximately six feet by nine. There is a metal bed with a [white] mattress. We are allowed one sheet, one limp flat pillow, one pillowcase and one unsanitary reprocessed wool blanket. We are given one bath towel a week—a whole one if we are lucky.... Since the jail furnishes no clothing the inmates must provide their own."[23]

Mallory's description of her cell and prison conditions replicates Jones's and Flynn's Alderson Prison environment, which speaks to prison's global dehumanizing efforts to strip women and girls of dignity: prison as stark, dank, colorless; women and girls ensnared in the skeletal dinosaur; prison as bleak and dark as the Hollywood horror movie that Mae paints Twenty-First and Payne to be.[24] Mae's experience is similar to that of Flynn and Jones at New York's Women's House of Detention. Flynn details deafening noises "from the shrill incessant chatter of inmates. Hysterical laughter screams of suffering addicts suddenly cut off from narcotics. The weeping and cursing of forlorn desperate women, crowded together in small quarters."[25] Mallory writes that the seventh floor was composed of "two large compartments containing thirteen tiny rooms," housing twenty-seven women and children as young as fifteen. It was a "real cellblock" locked by padlocks, with bunk beds, toilets, sinks, and steel bars dividing the cells—certainly no Technicolor movie.

> The day room is the space that is left between the rooms on either side of the area taken up by the toilet and shower. In the recreation room is a long rus-

tic table with two makeshift benches. No radio or TV set, only newspapers, if some inmate is fortunate in having the money to buy them. We are allowed playing cards, but strangely, a Monopoly set is forbidden. I had two Monopoly sets in the package room. I requested that one be given to me [which] was refused. The Chief explained that a Monopoly set contains dice. The inmates might use the dice to gamble.

Mae Mallory's own life experience in New York City's towering housing projects buffered her from fearing the roaring dinosaur edifice, yet it remained a menacing place.[26] The state imprisoned Mallory and the others because they threatened society. Instead, the prison posed a threat to them, surrounded by dangerous men and menacing prison guards *and* matrons. "There's one half white [matron] here who gives me hell. I think that she thinks I'm a Communist, so she has set herself up to be America's Number One Defender against Communism. Then sometimes she joins Sgt. John Ungary in thinking that I'm not really Communist . . . just a Black Muslim."[27]

The state used "communist" and "Black Muslim" interchangeably, defining Mae as a menacing Black radical. Politics and oppression went hand in hand in Mae's experience, making prison completely unhospitable. In "Skyscraper on 21st and Payne" Mae recalled that children and women were encircled by male prisoners: "Men are on the fourth, fifth, sixth, [and] seventh floors. They are in the cell blocks of the seventh floor. I am told those men on the eighth floor are 'probates'—mentally deranged and are thrown into cell block A and B with the other prisoners. They are strapped to their beds in lockup rooms when and if they become violent."[28]

Mae exposed an inadequate prison health care system and the health dangers the prison posed to the women.[29] The jail was overloaded; thus the threat of hepatitis contagion emerges as a recurring theme in Mae's writing, appearing as a source of distress. In her 1962 diary entries, her short story "Rev Saves a Paper Hanger Soul" (n.d.), and letters to Robert Williams and Conrad Lynn, she writes about the jail contagion.[30] In "County" (September 1, 1962) she writes that "the whole women's section of the jail was supposed to be under quarantine for a case of infectious hepatitis in cellblock B. The quarantine was already two weeks old. We were denied all visitors including lawyers."[31] The quarantine caused the women feelings of stress. "Most of us were edgy."[32]

Mae recounted in "Cuyahoga Jail" (May 16, 1962) that the building was overtaxed. "The capacity for this area is seventeen, we now have twenty one female inmates ranging in age from fifteen to fifty seven."[33] In "Rev Saves a Paper Hanger Soul" she described the "overcrowded as usual dayroom" with inmates "lounging at the cots." In "County" she discussed the overextended cellblock 7a with twenty-three stressed out and argumentative women fitting into a space for thirteen.[34] Mallory excavates and unearths Twenty-First and Payne/Pain: the pain of crushing, stifling crowds; the pain of illness due to teeming inmates within the disease-infested structure; the threat of pain given dangerous male prisoners and menacing prison guards; the pain of monotony due to rules that prevented even the minimal joy of a board game or comfortable bedding. Mae reveals a stark situation, with children imprisoned with adults—girls and women so strained by their living conditions in an overstuffed dinosaurian carcass that constant confrontation exploded. While Mae Mallory escaped the terror of the prison as a "dying prehistoric animal" and its fearful cries, she could not escape the stench of the dying beast—the carcass deteriorating, congealing, resembling Flynn's and Angela Davis's descriptions of New York's Women's House of Detention with its "consummate filth," "scurrying mice," and graffiti-inflamed walls, "dingy, dim, and dungeon like."[35] Mae describes Twenty-First and Payne similarly, with food served "in 'one big metal dog bowl just like dog food.' . . . The building is old, looks old, and smells old and musty. Funky is the way [it smells], food, beds, and a few of the matrons. Yes, this jail is really funky."[36] The prison's odors, the olfactory assault on the prisoners' humanity, made the jail a horrible environment, with everyday indignities they could not escape.

It is also significant that Mae Mallory casually mentions encountering imprisoned children as young as fifteen.[37] In a letter to Mabel Williams she writes, "As I look about me here in jail, I see so many of our young and beautiful girls, here because of prostitution. This seem to be truly the only means left for them to make a living."[38] She points to the lack of opportunities for young Black girls and women, which led them to incarceration. Mae touches on the striking and unjust system of child incarceration with adult women and men, which began during slavery, manifested with the Black codes, and continued with the 1960s law and order legislation, foreshadowing the mounting incarceration rates of Black girls and women in the twenty-first century.[39]

We see that the state criminalized and incarcerated political prisoners such as Mae Mallory, Claudia Jones, Assata Shakur, Angela Davis, and Elizabeth Gurley Flynn, among others, for their political beliefs. The police and the media harassed Shakur, defining her as "the soul of the Black liberation Army." The state arrested Angela Davis for protesting the Vietnam War (1967), for her political and socialist ideology, and for her support of George

Jackson and the Soledad brothers (1970).⁴⁰ And as I reiterate, these women wrote themselves out of prison.

Refusing to disappear, Mae unearthed the prison as a Black "geographic region," making visible her social and political history. She tells us that jail renders prisoners inhumane, subjected to daily mortification. She rejects erasure.

Fighting the White Supremacist Triumvirate

Mae Mallory's "The Gun Moll, Miss Deep South, and the Alcoholic Old Relic" and her published "Of Dogs and Men" allow us to explore how she wrote to fight white female supremacy in prison to survive her incarceration. Mae writes that the arrival of the Gun Moll, Miss Deep South, and the Alcoholic Old Relic at Twenty-First and Payne brought a cacophony of chaos. These three women, whom I call the white supremacist triumvirate, instigated an onslaught of racialized conflict and clashes. According to Mallory, before they came to jail, few if any racial ruptures occurred. Their ingress brought racialized mayhem and dissension, compounding tensions that already existed given overcrowding, not race. She indicates that such "cohorts from the deep south" boasted "of their achievement of getting the colored girls moved out of their rooms and across the hall."⁴¹ They successfully encouraged prison authorities to use racist practices of transferring African American inmates in preference to whites to relieve the overburdened prison. Their actions reveal a claim to white womanhood's privileges.⁴² Like the middle-aged white woman whom Elizabeth Gurley Flynn met at Alderson Prison in the 1950s, the Gun Moll, Miss Deep South, and the Alcoholic Old Relic used white womanhood tropes to oppress Black women prisoners. Flynn recalls that the white woman she met employed true womanhood tropes by "weep[ing] hysterically and protest[ing]" her lot of living with Black prisoners. Her actions gained her the promise from a white officer of a single room in an effort "to calm her" and protect her from contamination, the pollution of Blacks.⁴³ Comparably, by demanding that the state remove the "colored girls" from their presence, the white supremacist triumvirate argued that the very sight of Black women impinged on their womanhood and their whiteness. By demanding that the state answer their whims, they successfully negotiated their position from criminal to the southern belle fantasy trope. The southern belle fantasy trope fits within the cult of true womanhood trope of the beautiful, innocent, pure, and virginal white woman in need of protection, the antithesis of Black womanhood.[44] These tropes ignore the white supremacist savagery of the southern belle: her maintenance of white power, her subjugation of Black women, and her active participation in beating and lynching African American women, children, and men. The southern belle fantasy trope ignores the reality that not all white southern women or men descended from the mythic planter class.[45] By controlling their prison living situation through whiteness privileges bestowed on them by the state, the white supremacist triumvirate elevated their position, obscuring their low-caste status and criminality. They asserted white supremacy by positioning themselves at the center of the southern belle fantasy trope; above Black women inmates, the southern belle could not exist without oppressing Black women.[46]

At Twenty-First and Payne the new transfer scheme concocted by the white supremacist triumvirate, aided by the state, marked how they claimed whiteness and womanhood. Mae wrote that the new transfer practice broke with the previous custom of moving new inmates in preference to old, regardless of color. African American women protested that the new transfer scheme was racist. They tried to induce Chief Narducci to return to the old method. He refused. Mae recalled that because of their demands, police inflicted pain on Black prisoners by dragging two of them by their "hand[s] and feet" across the floor. Mae tried to prevent the state-sanctioned savagery. For her actions the new matron "put her feet on my pelvis bone and pushed with all her might," to crush Mae physically and emotionally. Mae Mallory fully blamed the white supremacist triumvirate for the transfer scheme, the violence, and their efforts to cause racial strife. What really incensed Mallory was their uninhibited swanking and bragging about their hand in removing the "colored girls."

> This was too much. I made a break to chase [the Alcoholic Old Relic] into her room. Instead of running into her room, she ran for The Gun Moll's room and fell. The matrons on duty were the Tom Stooge and this new white matron [who] had previously kicked me in my pelvis. They called the chief and claimed that I had beaten this Alcoholic Old Relic. This charge was substantiated by Miss Deep South and the [Gun Moll's roommate].[47]

In "Jail Is Hell" Mae recounted her treatment. "When they can't think of anything else to accuse me of [they accuse me of] hitting an old woman."[48] The prison melee illuminated several of Mae's key survival and protest strategies—her physical, psychic, and intellectual resistance to state repression. As Mallory was an advocate for self-defense, it remains unsurprising that she fought back. Before prison, on June 13, 1961, Mae used her body to fight state tyranny at the United Nations protesting Patrice Lumumba's murder.[49] By chronicling the prison melee and by physically fighting back at Twenty-First and Payne and the United Nations, Mae took a stand against white female supremacy and state domination. Mae asserted *her rights and her Black womanhood*. The prison clash also elucidated the white supremacist triumvirate's efforts to elevate their prison class status by claiming whiteness and womanhood, notwithstanding *their* criminality.

> The agitation for all this started when [the Gun Moll] helped to beat and rob an old man. [Her] take was 29 cents. [She robbed him] with her boyfriend [to] get money to divorce and exchange spouse[s]. [She] came very pregnant and boastful of the fact that [the police captured her] with two guns. Immediately, she irritated most of the inmates and expected to ride rough shod over everyone using her pregnancy as protection.[50]

According to Allison Berg and Marilyn S. Blackwell, the "Republican Mother" framework portrays white women as providing the nation with citizen sons and with daughters as wives for these citizens. They contribute to the prevention of race suicide by keeping "her body pure for racial reproduction."[51] She in effect protects the nation from the Black and southern and eastern European mothers who carelessly overprocreate.[52] For the Gun Moll this also meant discarding her criminality. The "Republican Mother," Blackwell asserts, "was charged with ensuring the virtue of future generations."[53] Eugenicist Albert Wiggam contends she becomes a vessel for the creation of a great race, the ultimate "guardian of the blood."[54] The Gun Moll redefined herself as the ultimate mother at Twenty-First and Payne, in need of protection and special treatment, because she protected the nation and the jail from African American women.

Mae Mallory presents the second member of the white supremacist triumvirate as "the Alcoholic Old Relic [who] was brought in on a drunk charge. This old relic would agitate and annoy [everyone].... This ancient one would wear hard bottom shoes at breakfast time and clomp around making as much noise as possible," deliberately disturbing the inmates.[55]

The third member of the triumvirate was "Miss Deep South." Mallory writes that she "thought [African American inmates] delighted in her talk about the nice old colored lady that used to work for her mother. This nice old colored lady died on the day of this inmate's graduation from high school."[56] With this story Miss Deep South lets Black prisoners know that she and society relegate them to low-caste worker stock, in charge of taking care of white folks. Elizabeth Gurley Flynn detailed encounters with white southern women at Alderson Prison trying to maintain white supremacy through the Mammy trope. "White women from the South were particularly obnoxious, expecting Negro women to wait on them, work for them," and sexually service them, treating African American women "rudely and contemptuously."[57]

At Twenty-First and Payne Mae Mallory discovered a way to resist white supremacy and the cacophony of chaos that was Miss Deep South and the white supremacist triumvirate. After Miss Deep South told the story of her "colored maid," Mallory wryly took great pleasure in relaying the story of *her own white manservant.* "I informed her of the drunk old white man that worked for my mother and washed our windows because we lived on the twelfth floor. This immediately caused her to dislike me."[58]

By introducing the ever-loyal and loving white manservant, Mae vanquished Miss Deep South's hyperstereotypical Black womanhood reflected through the requisite colored maid. By transforming the mammy into a white manservant, Mae defiled and despoiled the southern belle fantasy trope, emasculating white men through Black women's work, the ultimate humiliation and disgrace for white supremacists. Mallory's white manservant avenged Black women. Mae disempowered Miss Deep South and the white supremacist triumvirate, rendering them incorporeal. She destroyed all notions of the hegemonic work hierarchy of color by flipping the script with the ever-loyal white male manservant. He proved his love of the Black family in a fantastic feat of dexterity and drunken splendor by washing the family's twelfth-floor windows on the outside of the building, acting as a human crane. Mae's white male manservant puts to rest any notion that people of color belonged at the bottom rung of society, forever in love with and in the service of white folk.

"Of Dogs and Men": Mae as a Pet

While incarcerated at Twenty-First and Payne, Mae wrote "Of Dogs and Men" (1962), a groove on Robert Burns's "To a Mouse"—"The best laid schemes of mice and men / Gang oft agley [go oft awry]." Mae wrote,

> Just recently, I read of the case of a dog fighting for his life in the courts. This dog is accused of killing six sheep. The courts have ordered him to be put to death. The case is now before the Supreme Court. Chances are that this dog will be allowed to remain in its home pending the outcome of litigation.... I,

too, have a case before the Supreme Court. But look where I have to stay pending the outcome of litigation. For many months, I have been locked up in the Cuyahoga County Jail. Denied the companionship of my family and friends. This dog is actually accused of killing six sheep. I killed no one. I am guilty of no crime. The charge against me is kidnapping a white couple. This couple was protected and given safe conduct out of an enraged community. This constituted kidnapping in the eyes of the racists. This dog will probably get more consideration from the courts than I will.[59]

Mae wrote of the effort by a white supremacist woman to maintain the status quo during World War II in New York City. "An [upper-middle-class] white woman I used to babysit for when I was but a teenager once said that having me around was like having a pet."[60] This attitude likened Mae to the nineteenth-century Chinese houseboys deemed household pets and markers of wealth for white women.[61] The economic downturn of the 1930s relegated Black women to selling their labor on New York streets to predatory white women who, by having Black maids, undergirded their identity, white supremacist ideologies, and "class privilege."[62] By defining Mallory as a pet, the white supremacist woman ensured Mallory's position in the white household as the personification of the ultimate domestic trophy, stripped of humanity. Her pet status allowed the white woman to uphold hegemonic power.

In "Of Dogs and Men" Mae considers her transfiguration from human to pet and the other identities that Black domestics hold for white women. Mallory wrote: "I wondered about that statement [having me around was like having a pet]. For it was different. The usual statement of this nature concerning a Black servant goes something like 'She's Just Like One of The Family.'" Teenaged Mae Mallory also questioned the designation of "pet." "The usual American household pet is a dog. Could this woman have intended to imply that having me around the house was like having a dog around? No doubt she did!"[63] Mae learned that the dog led a better life than Black girl domestics.

Mallory shows us another way in which white female supremacists attempted to control the Black maid, through the concept of love between the Black maid and her white charges. In "Of Dogs and Men," the white children are nonentities; they do not register or play *any* role in Mae's story, contesting the notion that love exists between the Black maid and white child.[64] Mae shows us, in "Of Dogs and Men," that the true experience of Black maids is one of exploitation: "For both the lady and her dog to be dressed in mink and 'go strolling down Fifth Avenue' was considered 'smart.' But if I were paid a decent salary by her, it would be considered stupid; if I would have demanded more money, it would have been considered impudent. The dog really led the best life."[65]

Mae Mallory's experience elucidates the government's role in maintaining unfair labor practices, by defining domestic work and "babysitting" as not real work. This practice denied domestics Social Security, ensured their low-wage status, and maintained a working-class African American, Mexican, Japanese, and poor nonwhite population of workers like Mae in the United States.[66]

"Of Dogs and Men" also acted as a form of resistance to New York's white supremacist women, most specifically the woman who equated a teenaged Mae to a household pet dog in order to sustain her status. "Of Dogs and Men" taught us all that "pets" do bite and fight back. Mae recalled that the white woman she worked for lived in a "NO DOGS OR NEGROES ALLOWED" upper-middle-class apartment building. Mae heard they considered allowing dogs, but "never had I heard a conversation about allowing Negroes." She noted that some New York apartments allowed dogs to enter through the front entrance. This indulgence did not apply to African Americans. Mae began her sardonic pushback against white supremacist rules: "When I was without my little charges I was instructed to use the 'Service Entrance.' Since I did not come to service the building, I paid no heed to such instructions and went brazenly through the front door. No one raised a fuss! After all, a war was going on—and Afro-Americans were in it 'Fighting for Democracy.' Come to think of it, so were some dogs."

Mae knowingly came to the following conclusion about the binary identities assigned her: "After thinking about it and making a comparison of my life with that of the pooch's I found out that I could not only compare very well my life with this animal. I could contrast, with great similarity, the lives of Afro-Americans in general with those of America's most favorite household pets." Mae Mallory critiques the U.S. systems of inequality and determines that "interestingly enough, from the comparison, I found out that it is the dog that leads the best life. Yes, perhaps the lady was right!"[67] Mallory's assertion proved true, for teenaged Mae wore a threadbare coat while on Fifth Avenue white women and their dogs wore mink coats. Mae contested her situation as a working-class girl confined to wearing a coat unsuitable for New York weather and the utter absurdity, inhumanity, and waste of a dog and master in mink. At this point the story develops as a protest of dehumanization. Mae wrote:

> Most negroes do not choose to lead a dog's life—whether it is as a lap dog, hunting dog, or one from the kennel. They do not want scraps from the mas-

ter's table, neither crumbs, neither do we choose to be masters—only master of our fate. The thinking the Black man in America realizes [is] that he needs liberation. We live in shacks that no self-respecting dog would appreciate.[68]

Mae cleverly connects African Americans to the varying breeds of dogs while simultaneously arguing that unlike the dog, they don't want scraps in the form of substandard housing, low wages, and poverty. They don't choose supreme power overall but want agency and human rights.

Mae continues her groove on the relationship between dogs and Blacks by introducing the Show Dog. She writes that the state uses the Show Dog—African American diplomats in Africa, Asia, and Latin America—to vote against Majority World independence, exposing Black UN Special Representative Ralph Bunche as a Show Dog. Bunche refused to use UN forces to prevent Belgium's overthrow of Congo's prime minister Lumumba.[69] She reveals the complicity with hegemony that some middle-class Blacks use to gain power on the backs of the African American working class and poor. She writes that the Show Dog "shows up in Africa, Asia, and Latin America as diplomats and ambassadors . . . with lots of foolish propaganda on how well the Blackman is treated in America and 'the progress we are making.' Dogs are never made to stoop so low."[70] The relationship between African American diplomats and the State Department was a complex one, given that Blacks who wanted to serve fought on two fronts: white racism and entrée into the diplomatic corps. The Eisenhower, Kennedy, and Johnson administrations were reticent to assign ambassadorships to African Americans. They thought that Blacks could not pass security clearance without the taint of communism sullying their record. By 1962 only two African Americans held diplomatic posts: Mercer Cook in Niger and Clifton Wharton in Norway. Given the difficulty of obtaining these posts, it is questionable whether they held the type of power that Mae suggests. Perhaps Mae was talking about the cultural ambassadors sent overseas to argue that African Americans were not oppressed. This practice backfired given Birmingham's Sixteenth Street Baptist Church murders, after which Louis Armstrong refused to act as an ambassador. "Of Dogs and Men" acts as a continuation of Mae Mallory's pre-incarceration writing and advocacy, conjoining Majority World revolutions with African American civil rights. This is captured well in her statement that "the average Afro-American does not want the People's Republic of China kept out of the United Nations. He does not support the blockade of Cuba, nor does he feel the need of an Atomic War to protect imperialistic interests. It is only the Show Dog and those that aspire to be Show Dogs who support these causes."[71]

Mae indicates that instead of working to reform African American social and economic conditions, the Show Dog maintains white supremacy in the United States and across the globe in former colonies. Mae then moves beyond the Show Dog and connects the dog's life to that of the African American condition:

> The thinking Blackman in America realizes that he needs liberation . . . the same as other oppressed peoples in Asia, Africa, and Latin America. We, too live in shacks that no self-respecting dog would appreciate. We are unemployed many months of the year. There is admittedly no relief in sight from this situation. We cannot afford proper medical care. Our infant mortality rate is much higher than white citizens in America. . . . We still fill the jails and hang on trees until we are dead. Our bodies are still found in bags weighted with concrete at the bottom of rivers. Our arms, heads, and legs are still being severed from our bodies. And we are still being found in rivers—no water in our lungs—dead. These deaths are always "accidental," heart attacks, or of "natural causes." No investigations needed.[72]

Mae's observations act as a portent of the concerted effort to keep Blacks on the margins of society.[73] She sums up the African American condition and concludes, "These things shouldn't happen to a dog. But they do happen to Negroes in America."[74]

Melancholy and Dream Escape

Carole Boyce Davies notes that Claudia Jones used prison blues poetry to express intense feelings.[75] Working-class Mae Mallory's writings allowed her to escape melancholy and prison in a reimagining of McKittrick and Woods's politics of place.[76]

Her diary exposes her struggles with melancholy at Twenty-First and Payne. She wrote to express her feelings and as an escape. "The sun is shining brightly, my heart hangs heavily in my chest. I can't really define or describe this feeling—it may very well be self-pity."[77] Counter to the picturesque image that sunshine engenders, Mallory remains despondent. She begins to write herself out of her misery by recounting that the Monroe Defense Committee members protested on her behalf at a rally at a speech by Carl Weygandt, chief justice of the Ohio Supreme Court, to compel him to free her and prevent her extradition to Monroe with its southern violence.[78] After the rally Monroe Defense Committee members visited Mae and experienced castigatory harassment by a deputy who demanded that they leave. This form of maltreatment worked as a strategy to ensure that the prison was unbearable for the incarcerated and their supporters. It worked to discourage visitors. The officials used various methods to make prison life untenable. On June 23, 1962, the *Call and Post* noted that "Mrs. Ruth Stone, secretary of the committee, said the committee met last Monday with Sheriff Joseph M. Sweeney and complained of certain treatment that Mrs. Mallory has received while in jail."[79] The *Afro American* reported:

> The five-member delegation, Miss Audrey Proctor said, received a degree of satisfaction. But she claimed they were received in an undemocratic way, explaining Miss Proctor declared that an appointment for five persons was confirmed by her several days ago but only two were permitted to see the Cuyahoga County Sheriff. Miss Proctor and another MDC official Ruth Stone accused the Sheriff of curtailing Mrs. Mallory's Jail privileges.[80]

They reported that "Mrs. Stone said the committee told Sheriff Sweeney that he had 'deliberately allowed a clamp-down'" on Mrs. Mallory's privileges. This included refusing Mae's request for Black history books, providing Mae with a cot and not a bed, delivering her mail late, refusing to give Mae medical care, and allowing fruit given to her to spoil. "Mrs. Stone said that Sheriff Sweeney assured the committee that each complaint would be checked and, if true, each would be corrected."[81] *Workers World* reported these adverse circumstances and said that "Ruthie Stone and Audrey Proctor of the Monroe Defense Committee demanded that the matter be looked into immediately and that the sheriff make proper adjustments." The late mail delivery suggests that officials opened her mail and intentionally allowed her fresh produce to spoil. The MDC's meeting with Deputy Chief Carl Narducci halted these practices.[82]

Undaunted, MDC members stood their ground and stayed with Mae until the intimidation became intolerable.

> I cried out "what about freedom of speech! What about the right to assemble!" ... Ruthie dear pretty Ruthie, yelled back—"we don't have them anymore." I answered back, that must be the Gestapo. [MDC members] eventually left. They told me the Law said they had to go—"we're for you Mae—We love you Mae." I could hear them say as they slowly walked away down the street towards Superior.[83]

For a brief moment they reclaimed the space by reinscribing the politics of place as somewhere affirming, a place where they could speak out for social justice for Mae. They transformed the prison from a place of domination and subjugation to a site of resistance and agency, where they could freely talk about their efforts for Mae. Mallory rejected state sanctions on her life using tropes of freedom. Ruthie Stone responded that collectively the MDC and Mae lost their rights to free speech and assembly within the prison. Mallory pushed back with her words as she likened their encounter to Nazi Germany's slaughter of Romany, Jewish people, Blacks, and others. While she began this entry in misery and hopelessness, she writes "herself out of the state restrictions on her life." She reconfigures her melancholy as agency, reshaping it as brave and audacious and recounting the love and support emanating from MDC.

This entry reveals Mae Mallory's dream escape coping strategy. After the aborted visit by the MDC, Mallory writes that she took to bed the following morning, escaping prison through dreams.

> This morning after breakfast I went back to sleep and dreamt about Ruthie and the new apartment. In my dream Ruthie came to take me to the store to buy some fruit. We went to the store and bought fruit, then we decided not to go back to jail. [She] let me see the new apartment.... We traveled through a long narrow walkway to an elevator that was used for the store that [was] apparently in the front. I didn't get to see the rest of the apartment. I was awakened by the inmates going to the Catholic Church and the ringing of the church bells from outside.[84]

The church bells interrupted the beautiful dream escape of pretty Ruthie and fresh fruit, propelling Mallory back to the reality of mutilated fruit and "funky" prison food. The new apartment symbolized a new life, a flight from prison, but the church bells dragged Mallory back to the stark reality of the bleak jail. The church bells signified hegemonic tropes of enslavement, calling Mae back to slavery/prison, like L. Frank and Culture Clash's interpretation of the Catholic mission as a place of enslavement for Native Americans.[85] Mallory's long path to the new apartment represented another hegemonic trope: the long pathway to the apartment signified an endless path to the unobtainable—freedom. Christianity played a central role in enslavement and in hindering Mae's freedom. The bells rang her back into prison. For a brief moment dream-escaping Mae Mallory liberated herself from prison life.

Dream Escaping Twenty-First and Pain

Mae's despondency reappeared in her diary entry "Cuyahoga County Jail."

> Early morning, all the inmates are asleep. The early morning sounds are heard as a cool breeze whistles around the building. . . . I have been lying awake for a long time trying to determine whether I should get up and write or continue to lie in bed and ponder this strange feeling that seems to squeeze my heart. My heart feels as if it will very shortly stop forever.[86]

The oppressive and suffocating nature of imprisonment led to Mae's suffering. Charles Sanders wrote in the *Call and Post*, "For a Woman Like Mae Mallory—a woman with as much energy as she has racial pride—jail can be Hell. And so, it is Hell for Mae Mallory." Mae describes a gripping depression, metal weights pressing her down in bed, stealing her sleep, causing fear. The monotony of jail life, the difficulty of being "locked up" with "so many different personalities and no recreational activities," unless created by the inmates, proved unbearable for Mae. She wrote that her Supreme Court case would get a hearing on June 21, 1962, argued by Walter S. Haffner. She expressed disappointment with the date, for she anticipated that the case would be heard in the fall. Chief Justice Weygandt's disapproval of the MDC picket, the expected loss of the case, and her ultimate loss of freedom added to her misery. Mallory wrote, "It appears the powers that be do not intend to free me. How is it possible to see so much danger in me is more than I can fathom."[87] Mae's profound and heartrending despair and lack of understanding of her danger to the state give these words a special poignancy. They make clear Mae's lack of knowledge of the meticulous machinations that kept her imprisoned: Monroe's white supremacists who wanted Mae punished, her two-thousand-plus-page FBI files, the FBI defining her as a communist and enemy of the state, and the FBI disruption program keeping Mae, Robert F. Williams, the Monroe Defense Committee, and the Committee to Aid the Monroe Defendants at odds and distrustful of each other.[88]

Although despairing, Mallory wrote her way out of her hopeless state. She found rays of light recalling that a telegraph wire of support arrived from the Youngstown Steel Workers Union, frequent marchers for Mae.[89] A trade union member, Mae gained overwhelming support from Cleveland and countrywide union members, proving that the Mallory Freedom Movement was a large undertaking. The Negro American Labor Council voted unanimously to support Mae in her extradition fight. Cleveland's United Auto Workers Union and the AFL-CIO publicly opposed her extradition. The Midwest Division–Foundry Council Meeting (March 17, 1962) with two hundred delegates from Wisconsin, Michigan, Illinois, Indiana, Ohio, and Canada, voted unanimously to send a telegram to Governor DiSalle demanding that he withdraw his extradition order. They also notified the court of appeals of their opposition to Mallory's extradition. On April 28, 1962, Ford Motor Company Local 600 sent a wire calling on President Kennedy to aid Mallory and the Monroe Defendants.[90] Mae found hope in the abetment she received. "Whatever happens to me, I must say that Ted and Frances Dostal, with the support of WWP particularly, the people from Buffalo have worked harder than beavers to get me free."[91] Mae's writing and union support reveal to us how Mae dream-escaped out of despondency and found hope.[92]

The sameness of prison wore down the energy, exuberance, life, and will of Mae Mallory and other like-minded prisoners. Through dream escape the women turned into pugnacious opponents against the tediousness of jail life. They valiantly tried warding off hopelessness. The women roused Mae out of her morose state. While no recreational activities existed in jail, Mae's mates exhibited great ingenuity by creating a live fantastical dream escape through what Mae Mallory described as "the most amazing fête of creativity." They executed a surprise thirty-fifth birthday party for Mae—very much like a party that Elizabeth Gurley Flynn and Claudia Jones gave for a forlorn Black girl turning nineteen at the Women's House of Detention. Secretly Mae's mates decorated the dayroom, constructed party paraphernalia, including imaginative fabulous paper hats and "party finery," which they wore to greet Mallory. At the fête they presented Mae with "glowing candles" on a cake. They gifted her an extraordinary homemade party outfit.[93] "I seriously doubt if anyone else in history ever attended a birthday party in a costume such as I wore. I was wrapped in a large multistriped beach towel, blue rubber beach sandals on my feet, a newspaper hat, with the crown of England pasted on it covering my head. Surely it was a sight to see."[94]

Mae expressed absolute joy, a childlike innocence of wonder at the magical party. Mae and her comrades successfully escaped prison through a dreamlike and surreal construction of hypernormality. Mae discovered friendship, support, and caring. The dream escape drew Mallory out of depression and gave her a fantastical exuberance.

"Primitive-Looking"

While raising her children Mae tried mightily to instill them with race pride—to infuse Pat with a strong love of self as a beautifully dark-skinned child. Because Mae worked, her family's color caste ideology and patriarchal ideals wreaked havoc on Pat's ideas of herself as a gorgeous Black-skinned girl. The family's ideologies destroyed her light-skinned brother Butch through lessons in color caste, patriarchy, and misogyny. While Mae remained unable to protect her children from these ignorant retrograde notions, one must wonder if she buffered her child and adult self from their ignorant color caste ideals of beauty. When she looked in the mirror did she smile and see a beautifully dark-skinned zaftig woman? Did she truly love herself? Several of her prison interviews offer us a measure of understanding of this, simultaneously pointing to the outside world's response to the gorgeous Mae. What was the outside world's response to Mae? The *Call and Post*'s Charles Sanders wrote, "[Mae Mallory] talked to the *Call & Post* Tuesday in the hallway just outside her cell. Wearing bobby sox, black loafers, a too short green dress and, for some unexplained reason, two rubber bands on her left arm."[95] In this description, disdain for Mae materializes—an expectation that Mae, a prisoner with no resources or power, should look glamorous—that her appearance was inappropriate. We've seen this before. Conrad Lynn described her in masculinized terms rife with derision. Saunders and Lynn promoted the worst stereotypes of Black womanhood: the fat Black body as masculine, not worthy of respect, love, or protection because she refuses to thin down and conform to hegemonic societal norms.[96] In 1963, when meeting Mae in prison, the *Call and Post*'s Allen Howard found Mae filled with an abundance of Afrocentric self-esteem. "Despite her rift with the law, Mrs. Mallory . . . possesses a faith in human nature that is untarnished, a racial pride that is sincere and a cheerfulness that is surprising."[97] What remains clear in these interviews is Mallory's exuberant nature and Black pride. What emerges here in fact is that she safeguarded and protected herself from her family's ignorance, as an organic intellectual, reading African American and African history and literature voraciously as a free and incarcerated woman. Her erudition acted as armor.

Mae Mallory's race pride comes out in these articles, offering us a photographic snapshot in time—a picture of how Mae viewed herself. When Sanders asked Mae to tell him a little about herself, she said, "Sometimes I look at myself and wonder when all this will end. When will I be able to stop being at odds with everybody?"[98] An acute self-awareness and feelings of inadequacy are revealed. Pat told me that Mae's large personality could be off-putting. "My mother took up all the air, and people would say 'Oh, you're not like your mother' [laughing]," indicating Mae's problematic personality, traits that Pat should avoid. Mae understood her personality as something that some might identify as flawed, while others might see her as self-possessed. She opens up an avenue for thought when she says she is at odds with everybody. Does she include friends, family, society, and the law in this idea? Why wouldn't that overabundance of confidence kick in at this moment? And then she says strikingly, "I know I'm not a half-white woman. I know that I'm primitive-looking."[99]

Words assault the reader's senses. Mae reveals to us familial scars, deep lacerated wounds, bloodied badges of dishonor, left by irresponsible adults on Mae the child. In this utterance we see an unconfident, completely shattered Mae—a Mae wounded by a childhood infused with old Black Southern Baptist patriarchal norms, the color caste ideology, seared into Mae's very being. Unbelievingly and inexplicably, Mae believed that her beautiful dark skin and lovely zaftig body embodied the primitive, "little evolved," "belonging to or characteristic of an early stage of development," "CRUDE."[100] Primitive is how Mae described herself to the world, forcing us to deal with, unpack, and understand her words—words that lay bare and uncover a complex lack of self-worth and self-love, conflicting with the race pride she so proudly wore as a badge of honor. In this interview, Mae unveils to us the belief that Black beauty DID NOT INCLUDE HER—harsh lessons taught by her family and society. How could Mae feel this way? How could this be? These were generational lessons passed down to Mae and taught to her children—generational lessons she remained unable to shield herself and her children from.

Mae told Sanders, "I know that my hair is kinky, and I'm damn glad I'm like I am." The first of these two discordant phrases has the unintended effect of defining Black hair as deficient, lacking luster, shine, glamour. While she asserts that "I'm damn glad I'm like I am," she cancels her self-love out by describing beautiful nappy hair as lacking. With Mae's words we understand why she insisted that Pat press her hair in Cleveland—why that moment of insisting on the hot comb could have undone all of Abbey Lincoln's good work, of taking care of Pat's Afro and building up Pat's self-esteem—Lincoln's gently guiding Pat into personifying the quintessential Afrocentric beauty. Mae's words reveal a discomfort in her kinky hair, in an Afrocentric beauty aesthetic, her feelings of being flawed.[101]

From 1962 to 1963 Mae Mallory told Sanders and Howard that she committed herself to fighting for social justice from jail. Mallory said, "I start[ed] thinking to myself: this is not just my personal individual fight. This is a fight that I'm waging as an individual for a cause. We're all in this thing together." Mae connected her incarceration to freedom movements unfolding across the United States and the World. She said, "It doesn't matter whether we're black or half-white, good looking or primitive-looking, [with] straight hair or kinky hair." Mae unwittingly exposed color-caste lessons learned. She revealed that in her mind's eye the straight-haired, light-skinned über-mulatto *is* the quintessential Black beauty ideal. Mae unveiled ugly thoughts, lessons learned. She then combined her ideas concerning standards of beauty with political movements.

> [It doesn't matter whether we're] dirty or clean, ignorant or intelligent, we don't amount to a damn thing in Cleveland until our Black brothers win their fight in Georgia, Mississippi, Alabama and all over the world. That's the only time we'll be able to stick our chest [out] and really feel like first-class human beings.[102]

It's astonishing that Mae, who fought for human rights the majority of her adult life, who fully rejected male chauvinism, misogyny, patriarchy, and hegemony, conflated the fight for social justice with the actions of "Black brothers'" actions when she was fighting for rights from jail. She erased the reality that African American girls and women led human rights movements.

Mae expressed her commitment to fighting societal wrongs. "Being in jail made me more determined to fight against injustice. I can't change the color of my skin, but I believe I can change the things that makes dark skin uncomfortable."[103] She again uncovered lessons in color caste. Change the color of dark skin for whom? For the person inhabiting the dark skin. Change for the person casting their eyes on the Black skin, so you cover a Black-skinned child (Pat), so only the light-skinned child is viewed? Who is uncomfortable and why? Mae positions her skin color as imperfect—trauma-induced lessons. Mae's words unleash an ugly torrential history of color caste used to enslave and humiliate African Americans, Native Americans, the Romany, Okinawans, southern and eastern Europeans, dark-skinned Asians . . . in order to maintain white supremacists social order and power.[104] Sadly, I can only think of

> I'm so forlorn, Life's just a thorn,
> My heart is torn, Why was I born?
> What did I do, to be so Black and Blue?[105]

I'm glad I did not know this Mae. I'm glad I knew the Mae who reveled in Black beauty, mine, hers, Pats, and Mommy's. I am glad I knew the Mae who taught me lessons in self-love, the love of my Black skin, my Black eyes, my nappy hair. I am glad that Pat, Mae, and my mother taught me, the Black Power baby, that Black is beautiful. I am glad that I only knew the

Mae who taught my white friend Hindi these same lessons. It must have been super hard for Mae to fight these feelings, to try to instill in her children their Black beauty. Mae must have struggled mightily with dual feelings of inadequacy and Black pride, wrestling mightily to try to raise prideful children.

Fantastical Tales and Sexuality

Mae Mallory's diary allows us to explore sexuality and incarceration of women and reveals her as an adept storyteller, drawing interesting character sketches of the imprisoned. Her stories remained ripe with excitement and intrigue: stories of attempted jail breaks; narratives of raging against white supremacy within and out of prison; tales of heterosexual and homosexual love and sex. These incarcerated women endeavored to normalize their situation. Writing fantastical stories gave Mae an outlet to dream-escape prison.

Lesbian romantic or sexual relationships played a prominent role in two stories, reflecting the lived experiences of incarcerated women during Mae's time.[106] Elizabeth Gurley Flynn's experience at Alderson Prison (1950s) and Juanita Díaz-Cotto's examination of Latinas' prison experience (1970s) contextualize Mallory's stories. At Alderson Flynn encountered women in lesbian relationships replicating hyper-heterosexual normative family models. She observed hypermasculinized husbands, protectors of "idealized housewives," and "play families" of daughters and sons. Family members performed the services "traditionally accorded men on the outside (cooking, cleaning, laundry, drugs)."[107] Díaz-Cotto writes that prisoners adopted "masculinized" roles, whether straight or gay, to protect themselves. Flynn and Díaz-Cotto note that women prisoners pursued lesbian relationships but returned to their husbands and children after incarceration. Through Mae Mallory's stories we also view lesbian relationships at Cuyahoga County Jail.

> It was bitter cold. At 5 the night matron came into the cell block and called lights. [She motioned for] girls to get up and get ready for the trip to the women's penitentiary. Cold, sleepy crying women scrambled out of bed. Some were sleeping double because it was so cold, 16 degrees below zero, the coldest day recorded in the city. Some were taking advantage of the situation, sleeping double because they knew this cold night they could pursue their activities without being molested by authorities. The place was too cold to sleep, too cold to write, too cold to read. Blankets were placed on the floor under the radiators. Some girls laid on the floor near the radiator.[108]

By using coldness, these women sought warmth in each other as they escaped state-sanctioned repression, like their Chicana sisters in the 1970s who also worked to conceal their sexual encounters in prison.[109] While this short story gives a glimpse into the romantic relationships of the women at Twenty-First and Payne, Mae's "Rev Saves a Paper Hangers Soul" offers a more complex contextualized story of lesbian relations as a way to escape state domination.

She tells the story of the "the Paper Hanger," a jailhouse term meaning someone who writes bad checks.[110] We meet the Paper Hanger and her confederates, who plot to break out of prison by placing a sheet over the night matron's head. Soon the story turns to sex and longing as the Paper Hanger sexually propositions the Rev. "Rev I heard that you really save souls. I want you to save my soul, just as you saved Alice's. You must have saved her soul right." Using coded language, the Paper Hanger implies that the Rev participated in carnal relations with Alice and that she would like in on the action. "The night that you had revival, and you were saving souls; Alice came out of your room smiling. Her face was very red, looking as if she was very happy. You are an excellent soul saver. Rev, please save my soul. I have lots of money downstairs and I'll give you a hundred dollars to save me."[111] This replicates the sex-for-pay encounters Flynn observed at Alderson Prison and those written about by Juanita Díaz-Cotto.[112] Mae writes that the Rev played along with the game with no intention of getting involved in romance. She was "innocent of homosexual lovemaking. This always got a response and lots of interest whenever The Rev mentioned a soul saving meeting." The Rev's sermons and "soul saving meetings" reverberate with humor and veiled messages, as she adopts a "better laugh than cry" ideology concerning the impending women's federal penitentiary transfer. Mae makes clear that the Rev respected the lesbians in the jail and engaged in their jokes to pass the time. J. Le also proposed "turn[ing] The Rev out," given that J. Le "had been initiated into the cult of homosexuality" in Maryland prisons. The Rev went along, willing to play the butt of a joke, but not willing to participate in sex.[113] The scenes at Twenty-First and Payne mirror what Flynn saw at Alderson of women's efforts to "turn" heterosexual women.[114] "Rev Saves a Paper Hangers Soul" reveals Mae's esteem for the lesbians she encountered—her nonjudgmental and accepting attitude toward nonheteronormativity. My father says that many of the former inmates volunteered and worked with MDC given their esteem for Mae.

In "The Revival Meeting" Mallory writes that the weekends were the longest days for all the women. Mae notes that the women passed the time with a Saturday "Revival" in the overcrowded dayroom. The congregation included a multiracial, interfaith group, including a few "Jewish sisters." The Rev led the revival with an oration titled "Getting Her Entrance Papers [indictment papers] to Marysville College [Penitentiary]." The title alone induced the women's laughter; they had already shed tears over their imprisonment, their eventual transfer from Twenty-First and Payne to a federal prison, and the life circumstances that led them to incarceration. The sermon and revival meeting allowed the inmates to share laughter.[115] The Rev orated in rousing "Southern Primitive Baptist" mode, with call and response.

> One of these mornings I [am] going to be called downstairs
> Amen
> We chorused Amen.
> "There sitting on the bench in a long black robe will be the judge"
> Ah, say Amen.

The Rev is called not by God but by a judge, and not called up to heaven but down to hell. The judge represents the devil.

> We chorused Amen.
> This man is going to call my name.
> He'll say, "are you guilty of hanging some paper [writing bad checks]?
> The time has come for you to face the music. Are you going to sing?"
> Say "Amen."
> We said amen.[116]

The judge used the word "sing" as in "admit to the crime." The prisoners interpreted his command to sing as a coded spiritual with directions to freedom, escaping jail, as their forebears took flight from slavery.[117] Mae illustrates this insurgency of the inmates in the Rev's call and response: "At this point a sister burst out in song 'We Ain't Got Long to Stay Here.'"[118] The sister chose this coded song of how to abandon a slave life for the North or Canada. Rooted in Mae's story is a message of hope and freedom from Twenty-First and Payne. The revival sparked a fire within the sister who burst into song with the spiritual "Steal Away." The insurrectionary fire nourished the prisoners as they joined in song with Jesus representing freedom. "Steal away, steal away, steal away to Jesus, I ain't got long to stay here." In singing this song of hope, agency, using signs of Christianity, the women proclaimed, "We ain't got long to stay here."[119] Mae's story appears simple and humorous, but we can see implanted within her story calls for liberation, for revolution, for change. The story also brings to light the mundane ways in which the state criminalizes and incarcerates poor African American women for passing bad checks, for working illegal and illicit prostitution jobs out of necessity and desperation, because they lack legal and marketable skills. Mae continues: "The preacher said 'Amen.' She continued, 'the judge said since you have hung paper, I am going to send you to Marysville. You are going down yonder.' In true preaching style The Rev continued, 'ooh, ooh, children down yonder derrr.'"[120] By using Christianity as a freedom call, these women found a way to protest their incarceration. Although the Rev made it clear that the transfer of the Paper Hanger to the federal penitentiary would supervene, the women tried to arm her with tools to survive the penitentiary. They gave her strategies to advocate for liberation and use the insurrectionary spirit of the slaves for her emancipation. By using humor and solidarity across the races, the women discovered resiliency, hope, and dream escape.

In "Sex Love in Church," Mae wrote of romance intertwined with religion. Mallory recalled that church served the "same social function as in the free world. . . . Female inmates usually plan ahead for church, trying to be the first dressed and out of the door, since they're limited in the number that can attend." The limit on attendance caused a rush: "The men are usually in church seated and well equipped with mirrors or highly polished metal so that they [can] feast their eyes on female beauty. They can see but cannot touch. This did not escape the eyes of the Deputies who immediately called for a search. The men were searched on the spot, one at a time, but no mirrors were found."[121] The policing of the inmates even while attending church service blocked intimacy.

Not all the romantic encounters remained innocent or chaste. Mae Mallory's story "Mer Dear the Big Eyed Girl and the Rape Fantasy" offered a sordid tale of lust, violence, and the promise of prurient sex.

> A tall, slim, tan, big eyed girl called sweetly down the pipe. "Hello, Hello Daddy," she said in a syrupy Southern accent. Almost immediately a bass voice called up. "Hey Baby, what's your name?" "Mer Dear," she said, reminding me of old times. A husky voice answered, "what are your qualifications Mer Dear, who is your man?" Mer Dear answered that she had no man, that she didn't mate anymore because she enjoyed the act so well. "I want a man to make mad passionate love, caveman style, to grab [my] hair, drag [me] down an alley through broken glass, then after the bottles cut me in the ass I want you to rape me. Then you walk down the alley with a cigarette stuck

in the corner of your mouth. Then you look out the corner of your eyes, and then come back and rape me again."[122]

Perhaps Mer Dear, like many incarcerated women, experienced abuse—sexual, physical, or psychological. Johnson, Acoca, and Katz argue that the state incarcerated girls who experience abuse for participating in delinquent activities.[123] Instead of offering help to young women and girls, the state jailed them. Perhaps Mer Dear was one of these girls, perchance she just enjoyed the rape fantasy, or maybe she was just passing time.

One of the most intriguing stories of romance and betrayal at Twenty-First and Payne was that of "Christina and the Ebony Hued Man." Christina stood by the window in her cell and saw a "a long shiny new Cadillac." Out of it came a "tall Ebony Hued Man, the picture of Bond Street." Christina, Mae noted, always recognized "good clothes." We learn that she knew how the Ebony Hued Man came to own these fine things. Christina screamed out the window: "Hey baby get out of my new shoes, suit, coat and shirt, those are my rags. When I found you, you had nothing but your naked ass. Now you're driving a long Cadillac, dressed in fancy clothes, lots of money in your pocket and money in the bank. All I got from you was beatings, cuts, and bruises."[124] Although imprisoned, Christina lets us know that she paid for his fine things, and for this, her lover repaid her with violence. Christina is assertive and refuses further victimization. Christina uses her words to fight for herself, for her humanity, *and* she makes a claim on *her* property. Christina experienced abuse and that led her to incarceration.[125] What matters here in Christina's story is that she gained agency. The seemingly cultured man yelled up at Christina, "Shut up you stupid bitch," eradicating all thoughts of him as refined. Christina responded, "That's alright Daddy I'll see you in church. The prosecutor and I got together on you. You're on your way Daddy. You're going to Columbus where they won't let you wear my fine clothes. I'll be wheeling your Cadillac Daddy I'm hitting the streets after the trial." Her threats sound well thought out and planned in order to ensure his incarceration at Columbus's notorious Ohio State Penitentiary and hopefully gain her freedom. Time marched on with Christina still incarcerated, monotonously passing time until "one day after lunch as [Christina] was lying in bed browsing through 'True Story' [magazine] a voice yelled 'look out your window Mama, I got a scribe for you.' A scribe is a letter written by one inmate to another on a different floor and passed a variety of ingenious ways." Christina's predictions came true, for that "scribe" came from the jailed Ebony Hued Man, proving that karma was a chick named Christina.[126]

Mae Mallory and World Revolutions

Like Claudia Jones's poems in support of worldwide independence movements, Mae Mallory connected her incarceration to world revolutions in Asia, Africa, and Latin America. Mae wrote, "I don't believe the salvation of Black people lies with the capitalist. We can and must interpret socialism for ourselves as the Chinese, Cubans and others do for themselves."[127]

Like Mrs. Johnson and Audrey Proctor Seniors, Mae aligned with the revolutions that emerged in Asia, most specifically the success of the Chinese Revolution and the Vietnamese fight for independence. She took note of the failure of India's passive resistance. "Passive Resistance never liberated any people. Not even the people of India who represented a vast majority of their country." Mae argued against India's passive resistance in favor of China's and Vietnam's liberation models.[128]

Maoism and the People's Republic of China offered a Majority World revolutionary model: a peasant-led revolution specific to the conditions of Majority World countries and the internally colonized, like African Americans. This attracted Mallory.[129] Mae proclaimed to Robert and Mabel Williams, "What a joy the people of Asia are winning their battles against the capitalist, their stoogies and the mercenaries. This means the capitalists are being pushed back to their own shores." She aligned African Americans with these revolutions. "Our people must be made aware of the People's Republic of China and what it means to us as a people separate and apart from white capitalist racists." She notes that Chinese history "is not required reading in the schools," and Williams should lead in educating African American children on the Chinese Revolution and other world revolutions. "You are our source of information and are identified with the people of the world who are fighting for freedom and those who have won their freedom."[130] Mallory proposed a children's Majority World revolutionary curriculum, with Maoism and Asian revolutions as models for African American revolutionary movements.[131] Mae's argument for U.S. educational reform remained in line with Mrs. Johnson's educational initiatives with the aid of my parents in Monroe.

Mae dreamed of Africa and Cuba:

> The newly emerging nations of Africa would do well to heed the advice of Fidel Castro and profit from his experiences. Kwame Nkrumah's speech is certainly an indication that Afro-Americans can depend upon the African Nations to take the proper steps in the U.S. so that we can truly LIFT EVERY

VOICE AND SING TIL EARTH AND HEAVEN RING, RING WITH THE HARMONY OF LIBERTY.[132]

In her "Black Liberation Fighter Returns to the Motherland," Mae Mallory argued for the need for an African world revolution. She connected her experiences traveling in Africa to her Cleveland and Monroe incarcerations. Her African travels allowed her to remember her dream of Africa at Twenty-First and Payne (1961–1963) and in Monroe (1964). She recalled, "I used to lie awake in my jail cell and dream about Accra, Ghana. I used to dream that I was in Accra having heated discussions with Julian Mayfield. Julian Mayfield was actually in Accra. I thought that the only way I'd ever get to Accra would be in my dreams." In prison Mae dream-escaped to the colonially independent Ghana, to meet Julian Mayfield. Dream escape brought Mae a respite and allowed her to participate in world revolutions through her writing, and through a beautiful remembrance of brotherhood and sisterhood theorizing anti-colonial movements and world revolutions. Yet her thoughts while traveling in Africa reminded her of her time at Twenty-First and Payne. "Now I am thinking about my jail cell in Cleveland. . . . I certainly never dreamed I'd see Kenya except in some racist movie."[133] Kaleidoscopic thoughts of the beauty of Africa cancelled out Hollywood's African cinematic nightmares, allowing Mae to theorize world revolutions. In November 1963 Mae articulated her ideas concerning Pan-African liberation to the readers of *Africa, Latin America, Asia Revolution*. "We are watching the development in Africa. I am personally impressed with the idea of a Pan African Army to liberate the whole of Africa the way the Algerians liberated themselves."[134] Mae reveals France's broken promises of Algerian independence during World War I and after World War II. This led to the 1954 National Liberation Front (FLN) guerrilla warfare against France. Her words lead us to France's breached pledge of Algerian independence and their martial brutality against the Algerian people in the Battle of Algiers (1956–1957). She unveils France's lies of independence, which finally led them to relinquish Algiers in 1959, and to Algerian independence in 1962.[135] Mae was incredibly impressed with Algeria's revolution. By proposing a Pan-African army in line with the Algerian FLN, Mae proposed an African world revolution. Mae's plan merged with Mrs. Johnson's RAM principles concerning young people leading world revolutions.[136]

Separated in age by a decade, Johnson and Mallory merged their ideologies in theorizing U.S. and worldwide majority world independence. In Monroe in March 1964, while Mae was out on bail, she and Ethel experienced joyful laughter and hearty conversations about world revolutions at Johnson's home: "I am in Ethel Azalea Johnson's house now. They are laughing about some silly things."[137] While the times were incredibly hard, dreams of the African continent, joy, laughter, sleep, and theory comingled in these women's lives. In *Africa, Latin America, Asia Revolution* Mae continued discussing world revolutions. "It has been proven that a negotiated liberation isn't the most beneficial to the people."[138] Knowing that negotiation with the oppressor does not work, Mae underscored the need for warfare and pledged her allegiance to Majority World liberation through a Pan-African liberation army. She vowed, "My warmest regards to all the FIGHTERS of Africa. There can and will be no peace on earth until all oppression and exploitation are wiped out forever." For this reason Mae joined Mrs. Johnson's RAM, and MDC to African liberation movements. Her solidarity is clear: "May I reiterate my feelings of solidarity with the peoples of Africa against exploitation and racial bigotry. Mrs. Mae Mallory, Cleveland, Ohio U.S.A." *Africa, Latin America, Asia Revolution* made sure that their readers knew that Mae too was in a battle at Twenty-First and Pain for her mental stability while incarcerated. "Mrs. Mae Mallory is herself fighting for her life against racial bigotry" while simultaneously supporting world revolutions.[139] "These are trying times for us all especially with some irresponsible senators yelling for an invasion of Cuba. I read in *Workers World* that Fair Play for Cuba had a very nice demonstration in front of the United Nations."[140]

Before Mae's incarceration she fully supported Latin American freedom struggles, cheering Castro on in New York, attending talks such as "Caribbean Revolutionaries Speak Out! What Are the Relationships between Latin American Revolutionary Movements and the Struggle for Afro-American Liberation?," sponsored by *On Guard*. This featured Guianese revolutionary Ram John Akara, Puerto Rican liberation leaders Luis Muñoz Sullivan and Peregin Garcia, Cuban revolutionary leader Carlos Moore, Dominican liberation leader Tobias Cadral, and Haitian student Serge Sdanbal, who was most certainly fighting Duvalier's regime.[141] Transformative societies in Latin America, Cuba, and the Caribbean held a special place in Mae's heart, as Cuba did for many Black radicals.[142] Cuba permeated her writings, thoughts, and interviews. "If I had fled to Cuba, I wouldn't be facing a lynch mob and wouldn't be fighting extradition."[143] Mae thus lays bare the reality that Williams left her behind to face the wrath of the white supremacist state. Her avowal is potent. The Cuban Revolution paved the way for Williams's escape and could have paved the way for Mae to a different life, as Castro welcomed *all* revolutionaries to Cuba in his speech titled "Our Party Reflects Our Country's Recent History." "This is not only a land of Cubans it is a land of revolutionaries (*Applause*). The revolutionaries of this hemisphere, including U.S. revolutionaries, have the right to consider themselves our brothers." Castro cojoined this invitation to the U.S. radical self-defense freedom movement. "Like Williams, all those who are persecuted by the reactionaries and exploiters there can find asylum here. This is the homeland of the revolutionaries of this hemisphere."[144] This statement of solidarity allows us to truly understand what Mae missed—what Williams's rejection meant when he planted her in New York after Monroe's riot. Notwithstanding the fact that if she had made it to Cuba she would have abandoned Pat, Butch, and her mother, Mae lets us know that she missed a Cuban freedom, with Pan-African liberation ideologies that merged with her own.

As newspapers, journals, and articles were sent to Mae, she learned of the freedoms that Monroe's African Americans gained in Cuba, freedoms denied teenaged and incarcerated Mae. An image of a Monroe mother in Cuba who gave birth to her baby beside a white Cuban mother who also gave birth resonated with her. In her mind she could successfully conjoin motherhood and freedom to the Cuban Revolution. In her Cuba, Black women did not face Jim Crow segregation in birthing rooms in inferior hospitals, but rather enjoyed full freedom in giving birth beside white Cubans, and health care was free. This must have made Mae reflect on her own reality that "America has cut deep grooves into my very soul. These scars are a result of an economic system that exploited the world." Memories of her enslaved grandmother also appeared: "Scars melted my grandmother's breast when she was a young girl . . . by a jealous white mistress who didn't stop to consider my grandmother had no control over how her body was used or who used it."[145] Mae reflected on her grandmother and other African American women's forced procreation, forced sterilization, and inferior hospitals Black women were compelled to go to. As a Black feminist, Mae drew the connections with white supremacist feminist violence, her slave grandmother's reproductive rights, and African American women's reproductive rights in the 1960s. With this, she places African diasporic women at the center of her argument for the Cuban Revolution, world revolutions, and liberation struggles. All manner of thoughts most certainly popped into Mae's mind at seeing this beautiful image of a Monroe mother's freedom in Cuba—a freedom that alluded Mae.

Significantly, while Mae was incarcerated at Twenty-First and Pain, a whole movement to gain justice and freedom for Mae, Richard Crowder, and Harold Reape took shape on the national and international front. This movement positioned Mae as an international cause célèbre.

Internationalizing Mae Mallory's Case

The international media, leaders in newly independent countries, and those fighting for independence fully supported Mae Mallory and the Monroe defendants as they would later do in Angela Davis's case. The *Call and Post*'s Charles Price reported that Mallory's "attorney Haffner said in racially tinged language that the Mallory case has drawn attention in many countries, especially the 'darker' countries. They are waiting to see what we do in this struggle against discrimination." Charles Sanders wrote, "The Mae Mallory Story is known in a lot of countries of the world now." *Afro American*'s Bill Worthy noted that "[Mae Mallory] was *The* world-famous prisoner in Cuyahoga County Jail." In March 1963 the *Call and Post* pronounced, "The international publicity aroused by those who came to her rescue makes certain that the eyes of the world will be watching North Carolina justice at work, if, in the end, Mrs. Mallory has to make the trip south." Finally, in October 1964 the *Call and Post* reported that "letters of protest against her treatment have come from all over the nation, African and European countries."[146]

Mexico's people put their full support behind Mae Mallory. In *Free Mae Mallory, Letters from Prison*, flyers, and materials, the Monroe Defense Committee fully utilized all that had been published about Mae in Mexico. The *Política quince días de México y del mundo* published "Fugitive from Barbary" on November 15, 1961. They wrote that "people in China, Ghana, Cuba and Algeria wrote to Governor DiSalle to protest Mae's extradition."[147] The *Cleveland Courier* reported that "in Mexico City when President and Mrs. Kennedy visited there recently, students and peasants picketed with placards saying: 'Libertad para Mae Mallory.' Word from Red China, Egypt and Czechoslovakia has shown someone interested in her case in each of those countries."[148] The Nation of Islam's *Muhammad Speaks* informed their readers that "pleas for [Mae Mallory's] liberty from Ghana, Egypt, Jamaica, Panama, Cuba, is growing." *Muhammad Speaks* printed Chao Sze-Yuan's letter from China:

> We are indignant over the frame-up by the white supremacists on the heroic actions of Afro-Americans. As people of China who show great sympathy to Mrs. Mae Mallory, we hope you will bring our best regards to all of the Black friends who are living in poor conditions and treated brutally by the Klan-led mobs.... We protest the decision to harm this Black woman. We call upon human beings all over the world to add their voice to save this mother of two children.[149]

Nation of Islam members sent their support to Mae as she wrote to Williams that "I received a letter from Malcolm X telling me he is coming to Cleveland to visit me. Sylvester Leakes [of *Muhammad Speaks*] wrote me a long letter."[150] Notwithstanding the support she received from them, Mae felt that the Nation of Islam wasn't doing enough for her case and that they didn't credit MDC. "So far in my case the Muslims wrote a sob story but omitted the role of the MDC and what the people can do. This can't be because of poor journalist ability. They know how to write."[151] Mae again lamented the fact that *Muhammad Speaks* and the Nation of Islam in general did not mention the work of the Monroe Defense Committee or take a great interest in her case. "Of course I can understand that they want Black people to think that they are the most militant element about, they certainly have the white man upset." She felt that they only provided "lip-service, [which] wasn't necessarily for the sake of the case, but for the sake of leading their followers to believe they are doing something to help."[152] The MDC engaged in a monumental letter-writing campaign to gain allies and raise interest in Mae's case. They had allies from Mae's Harlem Crusaders such as Sylvester Leakes, a Crusaders and MDC member. My father's previous association with the Nation, Malcolm X, and Dr. Cross also led to interest by NOI, despite the rupture that occurred between my father and Cross when my father refused to join NOI. The Nation was all in for Mae and the Monroe defendants, announcing in this flyer that Ossie Davis, Ruby Dee, A. J. Muste, and David Dellinger sponsored Malcolm X, CORE's James Farmer, the *Afro-American*'s William Worthy, Bayard Rustin, and the *New York Post*'s Murray Kempton discussing "The Challenge of Racism" in New York with proceeds going to the Monroe defendants.[153] This effort crossed all boundaries of Black political movement and activism.

Mae also gained allies from the Asian American community. She wrote to her friend Lilo:

> Lilo I admire your courage. You really must be a remarkable woman, after having been in a Japanese Prison camp and still not warped by race hatred, especially in a society where it is an admirable thing to hate nonwhites.... Clarence Seniors, chairman of the MDC told me how you helped with petitions getting other groups to help and financial assistance. Please know I appreciate your efforts. How lucky I feel to have friends such as the Warders, Seniors, Durens, Andersons, and yourself. Yes Lilo, this is a struggle for the benefit of all mankind. We must succeed this time; it could be too late if we fail.[154]

Perhaps Lilo reminded Mae of her great friend Yuri Kochiyama, who also experienced the Japanese concentration camps.[155] As these articles and letters illustrate, Mae's incarceration sparked an international movement, linking her case to successful freedom and liberation movements. Mao Zedong wrote: "Robert F. Williams asked me for a statement in support of the American Negroes against racial discrimination. On behalf of the Chinese people, I wish to take this opportunity to express our resolute support for the American Negroes in their Struggle against racial discrimination and for freedom and equal rights."[156] As Mao's words illustrate, the Monroe defendants' case garnered supreme support from China. Two photographs within the pamphlet tell of the strength of the allegiance between China, the Monroe defendants, and Black freedom struggles. One image depicts Mao with the African delegation signifying the bonds built between China and African independence movements. The other shows Mabel and Robert F. Williams shaking Mao's hand, symbolizing the ties that linked Williams, the Monroe defendants, and Mao. These images symbolize the melding of Black radical freedom struggles with the Chinese Revolution and with Asian, African, and Latin American freedom struggles.[157]

Yet Robert F. Williams was slow in his support of Mae and the defendants. Mae expressed her displeasure over his silence in many of her letters to him. "I know you won't leave any stones unturned to help us. Give my warmest regards to Mabel and the Boys, also the brave Cuban People and their leader Fidel Castro. Rob I realize that you are very busy and the whole Cuban Government isn't there at your beck and call, but if you wait another year to defend your [sister] I may not be here."[158] Williams eventually championed Mae and the Monroe defendants from Havana. He advocated for Mae on his program *Radio Free Dixie*; sent out press releases and wrote to the U.S. House of Representatives on Mae's and the Monroe defendants' behalf; and campaigned for them in every issue of the *Crusader* that he published in Cuba and China.[159] Yet from 1962 until the late 1960s, Mae expressed her frustration that Williams did not write to her.

> This is the third time I have attempted to write to you. Each time I have put it off until later. Part of the reason is that I practically never hear from you. You have some responsibility to write me. I realize that you are not living in Utopia and Fidel Castro and the people of Cuba are having quite a time keeping their wonderful Revolution together in the face of the constant onslaught by Yankee imperialists and their stoogies. Neither am I unaware of the various factions that exists there and are every bit as dangerous as the despots

that were overthrown. Still, that is no reason for the lack of correspondence. In fact, that is the very reason that we should correspond more. Political direction is very important.... I believe that Fidel Castro needs you in Cuba to help fight against the deadly factions that are trying to overthrow him. I think you are in a position to play a tremendous role in maintaining the Cuban Revolution. I realize this is easier said than done. I have faith that you will conquer the situation no matter what it is.[160]

On August 17, 1964, Mae's frustration with Williams's silence exploded. She wrote, "Dear Mabel, I am totally disgusted with your husband. From now on I'll direct all mail to you alone. Regardless how much one hates to write, there is no excuse, especially now that correspondence is so necessary."[161] Perhaps he neglected Mae because of his tenuous position in Cuba given the racism of white CPUSA members who lived in Cuba. Williams found that he was under constant assault by them.[162] He wrote to Mae,

> The racist communist[s] have accomplished for the Yankee what they could never do for themselves. They have brought me to the verge of throwing in the towel. They have completely neutralized and incapacitated me. I'm just staying [in Cuba] as an ornament. I only serve to deceive revolutionaries into believing that white communists are our damned allies. Hypocrisy is one thing that I positively cannot stand.... EXILE IS HELL when the country you are exiled in is not concerned with your problems. If one must suffer and if one must fight is it better to suffer and fight where he will at least have the fellowship of his brothers and sisters.[163]

Cuba in the 1960s resonated with the memory of what happened in 1898 after the Spanish-American War—a war won when Black, mulatto, and white Cubans aligned themselves beautifully and rose up in insurrection against Spanish rule. The United States came in with their scientific racism, using craniology to measure Black Cuban generals' heads to prove their inferiority to whites. In 1898 white Americans brought Jim Crow racism to Cuba, which shattered an awesomely successful Cuban multiracial act of insurrection.[164] Similarly, in 1961 white supremacist CPUSA members and white agents provocateurs brought in their own ugly brand of racism to ensure that people like Williams and others never had a chance in Cuba. They sowed the seeds of racism already planted by years of colonization, like they did after the Spanish-American War. Because of the surveillance they experienced, Mae and many in the United States understood that freedom in Cuba was not totally free given white supremacists' machinations. Yet it did look like a utopia to Mae and others, and she encouraged Williams to stay. "When you can come back and lead the struggle as Fidel did in Cuba, remember Fidel was in exile too. I have faith that you will conquer the situation no matter what it is."[165] She could not forgive his silence. They would continue to battle in their letters and publicly in the *Crusader* into the late 1960s.[166] But at this moment in time Williams finally showed up to support Mae and the Monroe defendants publicly.

The Monroe Defense Committee also bound Mae's incarceration to Lumumba and the Belgian Congo.[167] At a rally for Mae at Reverend O. M. Hoover's Olivet Institutional Baptist Church, MDC declared in their flyer, "Don't Let Mae Mallory Suffer the Fate of Lumumba." It featured a photo of Mae and Lumumba with the caption "HEAR: Militant Mae Mallory, the Leader in the Struggle for Freedom." We see a cross-fertilization of Africa and the United States, a synthesis of people supporting Mae from all spectra of society. The other speakers included the liberal Rabbi Philip Horowitz of Brith Emeth who "called upon citizens in this country, who are interested in justice to come to the aid of Mrs. Mallory."[168] Other speakers were "militant leaders," and college students. Reflecting Mae's trade union background, the sponsors included Dr. Rolland Wolfe of Cleveland's Amalgamated Local 735, Local 1045 Autoworkers, Local 1330 Steelworkers, and Local 45 Auto workers. Ruthie Stone's Buffalo Mothers Alliance, Janet Hanson, Antioch College NAACP, Club One Thousand (a travel club), the *Los Angeles Herald Dispatch*, and Dr. Bernard Mandel also supported this electrifying rally.[169]

Mae Mallory herself intertwined her plight with the Belgian Congo. The *Call and Post*'s Charles Sanders reported that Mae lamented, "I'm caught in the web. Lumumba was caught up in a web. Where is he today? Dead. And that's just what's going to happen to me when they send me back to the oppressors in Monroe. They'll hang me for sure, or they'll let an 'accident' happen to me and say I tried to escape."[170] Her imprisonment and the extradition threat proved dangerous. She was correct in fearing a return to Monroe. Because the movement around her was global, she stood a better chance of survival. The international journal *Africa, Latin America, Asia Revolution*, which was printed in Switzerland with an international editorial board and international bureaus, took up the Monroe defendants' cause. They published articles by my father, letters from Mae, and articles about Williams. They kept Mae Mallory and the Monroe defendants' case front and center for their worldwide readership.[171] From Ghana, West Africa, Julian Mayfield advocated for Mae, keeping her name in Ghanaian and British newspapers. Mayfield wrote articles about Mae in Ghana's *Evening News* and in Claudia Jones's London-based *West Indian Gazette*. Ghana's *Evening News* and *Ghanaian Times* also published articles and editorials concerning Mae.[172]

On the world stage, Mae and the Monroe defendants case kept them at the forefront of public international discourse concerning African American freedom. Those in the United States also made sure that their case remained center stage.

The Mallory Movement: A U.S. Domestic Struggle

A publicity poster captures the ways in which the U.S. liberation struggle used culture for mobilizing liberation. Mae Mallory and the Monroe defendants drew supporters from variegated backgrounds. On April 29, 1961, Morehouse graduate and Afro-Nigerian musician Olatunji and his African Troupe, renowned African American country-blues performer Lightin' Hopkins, and Pat Mallory's music teacher, folk singer Pete Seeger, performed a benefit concert for the Monroe defendants at the Riverside Plaza Hotel.[173] The University of Michigan subscribed to the *Crusader* and *Did You Know?*, which worked to support MDC. Luminaries and ordinary people supported Mae by writing to the governor and sending donations, including African American writers Paule Marshall, Leroi Jones, and Maya Angelou; African American Scholar W. E. B. Du Bois and his wife, African American scholar and playwright Shirley Graham Du Bois; Dr. John Henrik Clarke; Dr. Ana Livia Mayfield; and James M. Russell's Freedom Fighters. African American writer James Baldwin wrote "A Personal Appeal" and contributed $250, while playwright Lorraine Hansberry contributed $150. Mae and the Monroe defendants received full support from local Cleveland disc jockey "Musically Yours" Genial Gene. Mae also received support from the cultural set and labor unions, specifically at the "Mae Mallory Benefit" held at the Local 1330 Union Hall featuring the famous funk/rhythm and blues band from El Morocco in New York City.[174] As she wrote to African American civil rights activist and comedian Dick Gregory,

> Dear Mr. Gregory, Thank you so much for your public comments [on television] about my case. It was a very courageous thing for you to do, especially since my case is symbolic of the most oppressed and those that are willing to take the most militant avenues of struggle. . . . I am not at all negating the work of the passivists but attempting to show the necessity of more militant actions, because as we strive for more important aims and goals as the situation is forcing us to do; it is the utmost importance for us to realize that passive resistance limits our effectiveness.[175]

Although she offered Gregory thanks, two days later she criticized his efforts to Mabel Williams:

> Bill Worthy got Dick Gregory to make a statement on T.V. a mild one, nonetheless he did say something. This isn't anything like the support he has given King. This does not mean that I should run to these individuals and hug their knees for recognition. Their recognition came only after we had managed to survive and carry on the fight for two years.[176]

As when she criticized the Nation of Islam, Mae felt that Gregory's efforts were not enough. Notwithstanding Mae's reproach, Gregory, the Nation of Islam, and many groups and individuals advocated for her.

In January 1963 Cleveland's Humanist Council met in the African Room of the *Call and Post* to plan a rally for Mae. Ruthie Stone's Mothers Alliance remained very active in the Mallory case, sending Mae letters and hosting a Mae Mallory benefit, the "Chicken and Chitlin" party on February 23, 1963.[177] Later that year British philosopher and humanitarian Lord Bertrand Russell wrote, "I hope that a vast movement of protest will arise on behalf of the Monroe Defendants."[178] My mother's organization Youth against War and Fascism fully supported Mae. YAWF's flyer announced, "Demonstrate to Save Mae from the KKK" at Hotel Biltmore, Forty-Third Street and Madison Avenue (10/24/63).[179] In November 1963 the *New York Times* reported that YAWF protested Mae's extradition at President Kennedy's Hilton Hotel talk.[180]

Mae remained keenly aware of the people and the machinations working to keep her incarcerated. In 1964 she wrote the following to Mabel Williams:

> Our friends, the Communist Party of America and the Socialist Workers Party told so many lies about me that the so-called liberals and some radicals would have nothing to do with me.... Somehow, the American Humanist Council heard about the case and Clarence Seniors kept after them. Finally, they decided to help.[181]

That same year Cleveland's "Afro American New Year's Party" offered live entertainment, free food, and a "whole barbecue pig." All proceeds went to Mae Mallory's defense.[182]

From the jazz community, Abbey Lincoln and her husband drummer Max Roach had always supported Mae and Pat. Before Mae went to Monroe the couple performed with African American actor and writer Ossie Davis and African American musician Charles Mingus for her Crusader Family at the Jazz Gallery on Eighth Street on May 7, 1961. The Crusader Family used the funds to support and buy arms for Negroes with Guns.[183] According to my father, Lincoln and Roach performed Max Roach and African American Broadway composer Oscar Brown's *We Insist: The Freedom Now Suite* with Coleman Hawkins and Olatunji at the Village Gate. My father and Dr. Cross attended the performance as honored guests. Clarence Seniors recalled, "We were told that the album was being dedicated to Robert Williams and his struggles." The album notes by jazz historian Nat Hentoff cite the student sit-in movement, Martin Luther King Jr., CORE, and the NAACP as the impetus for the album. No mention is made of Williams or Mae.[184] Perhaps it was not politic to mention these radicals in the notes, although they all advocated for Mae and the Monroe defendants. Notwithstanding this, Roach and Lincoln performed several benefit concerts on Mae's behalf. Gerald Quinn, chair of the New York Monroe Defense Committee, wrote to Williams: "Ossie Davis and Ruby Dee have just opened a new show on Broadway, they're giving a benefit performance for the MDC on Nov. 9th [1961]. Everybody is pitching right in and helping. Max Roach and Abbey Lincoln have offered their talents whenever they are needed." Lincoln and Roach performed at this benefit performance of Davis's Broadway show *Purlie Victorious*, starring Davis, his wife Ruby Dee, the comedian Godfrey Cambridge, Alan Alda, Beah Richards, Helen Martin, Ci Herzog, and Sorrell Booke.[185] Over the years Davis allowed the use of *Purlie Victorious* for benefits for Mae. In 1963 the Friends of Mae Mallory attended a benefit performance of *Purlie Victorious* in Buffalo, New York. Mae wrote to the *Buffalo Challenger*:

> I am indeed grateful to Mr. G. Hinton, Associate Editor of The Challenger for being instrumental in the arrangement of the Benefit. As a result of the hard work and full co-operation on the part of the FRIENDS OF MAE MALLORY, Mr. Hinton, Mr. Keller and the sympathetic theatre goers, the affair was a huge success both entertainment-wise and financially.... The author Ossie Davis and his wife have been strong supporters since the beginning of the case.[186]

It was heartening, then, when out on bail and in New York in 1964, Mae was a special guest to see Abbey Lincoln and Max Roach perform.

> I went to the Village Vanguard as a guest of Abbey Lincoln and Max Roach. They were great as entertainers. I went to talk over some things politically with them. There are a few things they said that left me worried. We are to meet again this week, maybe then they will be able to make me understand what they mean. Some of these entertainers are using the struggle and the

wrath of the people to frighten the white power-structure into giving them [entertainers] jobs. I hope this isn't the case with Max and Abbey.[187]

Cultural performers were always under surveillance by the FBI. The state surveilled the jazz couple just as heavily as they surveilled Mae. Their moral compass would not allow them to participate in the type of actions that Mae suggests, of filling their pockets on Black oppression. It's amazing that anyone during this historical period survived with their mind intact given the FBI and CIA's disruption program. Racism, surveillance, and violence remained unrelenting and soul-killing. The disruption programs had the intended effect of working to cast doubt on friendships such as Mae's with Roach, Lincoln, and Williams. Sadly, these agencies successfully pitted friend against friend. Mae received immeasurable support from numerous people, including Roach and Lincoln, as well as Black nationalist groups and organizations from around the country.

In 1961 Gerald Quinn wrote to Williams, "The Monroe Defense Committee has gotten the support of a large section of the militant Afro-Americans (including Pat Alexander of the *L.A. Herald-Dispatch*).... We plan to have a rally in two weeks in Harlem. We have already lined up all the Nationalists."[188] With this letter, the MDC announced Black nationalists' allegiance to Mae and the Monroe defendants.

An allied organization, the Deacons for Defense and Justice for the Oppressed, who "found it necessary to organize to protect civil rights workers in the South where the police and Sheriffs fail to do so," came to Cleveland under the auspices of the Friends of Mae Mallory in 1965. This symbiotic relationship between Mae and the DFD grew over the years as they would find ways to collaborate on civil rights activism.[189] Because of Mrs. Johnson and MDC, the Monroe defendants also maintained a solid relationship with the Revolutionary Action Movement. RAM's *Black America* published Max Stanford's "Free Mae Mallory" and promoted Crowder and Reape's Monroe Youth Action Committee headquarters, as well as Mrs. Johnson's *Did You Know?* Mae's relationship with RAM and Max Stanford would prove an enduring one.[190]

In November 1963 the Group on Advanced Leadership (GOAL), founded in 1962 by educator and activist Richard Henry, educator James Hurst, and others to advocate for equality in education, housing, and jobs, sponsored the Northern Negro Grass Roots Leadership Conference at King Solomon Baptist Church in Detroit. We as a family attended, and Grattan belonged to GOAL's Constitutional Committee. The two thousand conference attendees came from "11 northern cities in eight states." GOAL promoted several boycotts, including one against Cadillac initiated by Cleveland CORE and Cleveland's Freedom Fighters. GOAL demanded that Detroit public schools use textbooks that included African American history in the curriculum, "called on members to organize units of GOAL sponsored International All-Trades Union of the World in their home areas," and backed the Freedom Now Party "with the goal of getting the ballot in 1964." GOAL "supported the principle of self-defense."[191] GOAL also aligned with Majority World people's struggles: "The Northern Negro Grass Roots Leadership Conference recognizes its solidarity with the colored oppressed people of the world and aims to implement this recognition in all its future perspectives and actions, and the copies of our resolution therefore be sent to their organizations all over the World."[192]

The conference featured many speakers, including journalist and civil rights activist William Worthy, Malcolm X, and Detroit's Black nationalist Reverend Albert B. Cleage.[193] Cleage "called for a Negro commitment to settle for only total freedom," rejected the notion that "Christ taught the type of non-violence taught by Martin Luther King," and proclaimed that King's passive resistance strategy was "not the way."[194] Cleage's ideology reflected that of Mae's as her *Call and Post* interview shows, notwithstanding her atheism: "I'm on pretty good terms with the Supreme Being because I believe He doesn't want us to always be yelling at him to come down here and get these white people off us. That's something we can do for ourselves when we decide to stop letting them use our heads as ramrods. (9/22/62)[195] Mae maintained that while some Cleveland ministers came to her defense, only one had visited her in prison. She believed that Cleveland ministers saw her as "a little black Martian whom they're afraid to come near. I don't know why they're so shook up over my theory about self-defense when they can look right in the Bible and find cases where people defended themselves instead of falling down on their knees in a non-violent prayer." She exhibited her Black Southern Baptist upbringing and Bible training:

> Why look at Sampson. He took a jaw bone of an ass and beat the hell out of somebody there in the Old Testament. Look at David; he took his little old sling shot and shot the devil out of Goliath. Sampson and David didn't get on their knees and ask the Supreme Being for non-violent help: they picked up what they had at their hands to work on the enemy.[196]

Mae actually lays the groundwork for people like Cleage, whose ideologies of freedom and self-defense reflected her own. Unfortunately for Mae, being a working-class Black nationalist and a woman proved problematic for many male-centered Black Nationalists, civil rights activists, and the elite. GOAL, however, conscientiously supported Mae given the presence of Cleveland's CORE, the Freedom Fighters, my parents, and Grattan. Other speakers drew connections to Mae as Malcolm X did in his "Message to the Grassroots" speech. In it he bound the African American revolution to world revolutions, to the movement forming around Mae Mallory.

> The Black Revolution is sweeping Asia, sweeping Africa, is rearing its head in Latin America. The Cuban Revolution—that's a revolution. They overturned the system. Revolution is in Asia, is in Africa . . . [African Americans] need a Revolution. Whoever heard of a revolution where you lock arms, as Reverend Cleage was pointing out beautifully, singing "We Shall Overcome"? Just tell me. You don't do that in a revolution. . . . These Negroes aren't asking for no nation. They're trying to crawl back on the plantation. . . . All the revolutions that are going on in Asia and Africa today are based on what? Black Nationalism. A Revolutionary is a Black Nationalist.[197]

These words reflect the Mae Mallory movement, one that merged Black nationalism and international revolution. Malcolm's words created a link to Black oppression, the international freedom struggles against white supremacy, and Mae Mallory and MDC. Participants of the conference led by Grattan, my parents, Cleveland's CORE, and Cleveland's Freedom Fighters (both of which my mother was a member) resolved to fully advocate for Mae Mallory, Richard Crowder, Harold Reape, and Robert F. Williams. GOAL called on President Kennedy to allow Williams's return to the States. They stood strongly with Mae by stating, "Be it resolved that this conference go on record in support of this militant Black, grass roots freedom fighter by at least sending a telegram to Governor James A. Rhodes of Ohio demanding that Mae Mallory be given asylum in Ohio." They connected Mae and the Monroe defendants' case with all African Americans in the South as they expressed their "vital concern with the plight of our militant brothers and sisters of the South [who] are courageously fighting against racist tyranny of this country."[198] GOAL attendees then voted unanimously to enter the campaign for Mae and the Monroe defendants.[199] We see why the FBI, President John F. Kennedy, and Attorney General Robert F. Kennedy went after these radicals working for change in the United States and around the world. Their pronouncements, their advocacy, and their mission of Black liberation proved bold and brave. They threatened the very core of U.S. tyranny.

Mae Mallory, Public Speaker

In Macon, Mae Mallory's Black woman principal told the children that they must stand proud and tall and claim the world as their own. Additionally, Mae's Irish middle-school teacher showed interest in Mae because she "had found one academic mind." These teachers' influences led Mae to aspire to an academic life in the same vein as Robert F. Williams, whose aspirations were crushed by racism in the military. Poignantly, her arrest and incarceration offered her the opportunity to realize her dreams of being a writer and public speaker. Her incarceration allowed her to fully inhabit the role of public organic intellectual. In 1961 Mae embarked on her public speaking career sponsored and arranged by the Monroe Defense Committee.[200] One 1961 announcement read, "Public Rally: Come and Hear the Facts of the Monroe, N.C. Kidnapping as Told by Mae Mallory: Courageous Mother Facing Extradition to North Carolina," under the auspices of the Cleveland chapter of the Monroe Defense Committee. Cleveland's Reverend J. L. King's Phillips Memorial Baptist Church held a mass meeting "In Defense of Mae Mallory" in March 1962. The organizing committee included Walter Hogan, chair, and Ted Dostal, secretary. The meeting featured Mae recounting her experience. They included musical entertainment by "soloists and choral groups," Antioch Baptist Church's Male Chorus, Frank Clemmons, Ben Gardner, Meita Marshall, the Metropolitan Baptist Church Choir, the Comrade Singers, and the Jerusalem Gospel Chorus.[201] In 1963 Mae made bond, gaining her freedom. She sardonically wrote Williams, "When I was on the weeks 'vacation' from jail March 14 to 22, I spoke to many people. That Sunday [I spoke] to a capacity crowd in Youngstown, Ohio. That following Tuesday night I was on *The Bill Gardan Hour* [on a show] called *Apartment 13*, on station W.E.R.E."[202] In March 1963 she found herself arrested in a publicly staged spectacle, briefly curtailing her speaking tour. The *Pittsburgh Courier* reported that "carloads of white racists parked around the Courthouse Square waiting for her" as Mae and her lawyer tried to voluntarily surrender (3/30/63). Cleveland's "local Black residents were in doubt as to whether she'll ever reach the Courtroom to be tried if extradited." This staged public humiliation included "newspaper, television, and radio reporters waiting to record as [Sergeant Ungvary] and an associate swished Mrs. Mallory next door to Central headquarters." Mae told the *Pittsburgh Courier*, "I was fingerprinted [and] taken up to the fourth floor on the elevator, down a filthy corridor, through the men's section and placed in a cell. [I was] put in a paddy wagon and brought over here [to Judge John Corrigan's Court]." Corrigan ordered her returned to Monroe, while Governor DiSalle refused to intercede. He fell in line with Monroe justice. Mae told the *Pittsburgh Courier*:

> I am too numb to say anything at the moment except that I will exhaust all of the legal remedies available in the effort to gain my freedom and keep from going back to North Carolina. I have been out of jail for exactly one week. I don't know who is going to hang me first[,] Cleveland or North Carolina. . . . I have no intention of running away. If they [don't] resist in doing this cruel thing, let the onus be on them. I am going to try American justice and let the whole world see what it's like.

Her lawyer Haffner appealed, and Mae was released from jail briefly in April 1963. She reembarked on her speaking engagements.[203] A flyer announced the following event for July 14: "Come to the 'Freedom Now' Picnic in honor of Mae Mallory, Pioneer Pavilion. Mae Mallory and others will speak starting at 6pm about the Afro American Struggle for Freedom Now. Sponsored by the Youngstown Friends of Mae Mallory Committee."[204]

In 1964, on her return to Cleveland, Mae participated in a speaking tour sponsored by MDC, WWP, and YAWF. My parents, Dotty Ballan, Marianne Weismann, Ernest Weisman, and the Dostals made the tour a success. At the lectures, as part of the talks, they gave out leaflets and Mayfield's "Lynch Threat to Frameup," and they sold *Negroes with Guns* and raffle tickets to help with the defense costs. Different people took turns driving Mae to lecture sites. Ernest Weisman of Workers World and YAWF drove Mae to cities in New York and Pennsylvania. Reports were written on what worked and what didn't work.[205] They planned a West Coast tour that never took off because California colleges, universities, and bookstores didn't want to cover Mae's expenses.[206] Nevertheless, the speaking tour proved successful. The *Call and Post* announced:

> Mrs. Mallory, who is currently touring Ohio speaking on a fund-raising drive for appeal of her case. She will speak at the meeting that will begin at 8 pm. . . . Mrs. Mallory's appearance is sponsored by the Freedom Fighters, a militant civil rights group headed by James Russell. . . . Mrs. Mallory's lecture tour through Ohio will take her to the campuses of Oberlin, Hiram, Antioch, Central State, Ohio University, and Toledo University.[207]

One sees a developing speaking itinerary across numerous institutions. The *Amsterdam News* announced, "Rep Adam Powell, Harlem Rent Strike Leader, Jesse Gray, School Integrationist, Mrs. Mae Mallory, and others will speak at a rally, Powell Auditorium, 144 W. 138th Street."[208] In October 1964

Mae spoke at Reverend C. T. Nelson's Greater Friendship Baptist Church, where she gave a "moving account of Dixie's brand of lynch justice." She then went to Roxbury, Massachusetts, where she spoke at Tremont Methodist Church.[209] University sites included Columbia University, City College of New York, Hamilton University, Kent State University (sponsored by CORE), University of Pittsburgh, Bethany College, University of Cincinnati, Michigan State University, Swarthmore College, and Harvard University. After the talk at Oberlin, Ted Dostal wrote to my parents, "It was suggested that the MDC write to these 2 mothers" for Mae to give a talk at Rutgers University and Douglass College.[210] Many other groups and organizations invited Mae to speak, including New York's Unitarians. High schooler Marcia Guidoni suggested a meeting with Mae and her civil rights club in Saint Albans, Queens.[211]

Continuing as a public intellectual for Mae included founding organizations to help African Americans. In June 1964 while out on bail, Mae wrote, "Now I am back here in Harlem trying to keep things going." And so she did. From July 16 to July 22, 1964, Harlem blew up in fury, a mass uprising because white police officer Thomas Gilligan killed fifteen-year-old James Powell. [212] Mae wrote to Mabel Williams of her efforts after the riots: "The May/June 1962 issue of the *Crusader* was exceptionally good. We passed out a few thousand right after the riot. It would have been very easy to get rid of 10,000 that night. We must find a way to get about 10,000 of each issue if they continue to be as good as the last."[213] Mae continued to support Williams in this way. She attended rallies, and in Harlem she organized the Women's Committee of Harlem and Militant Black Women with Yuri Kochiyama. Echoing the thoughts swirling around given the murder of James Powell and numerous other Black women, girls, boys, and men, Mae asked on the group's flyer,[214]

> Dear Sister,
> ARE YOU—sick and tired of our children being used for target practice by the police? Irate about having to live in occupied territory? (Occupied by Murphy's Marauder's), Determined not to share your food with rats and roaches? Disgusted with "leaders" that run down town and sell-out whenever there is the slightest pressure? Do YOU LOATHE the rotten merchandize that is sold in our communities at top prices? WE CAN DO SOMETHING ABOUT THESE THINGS !!! WE MUST ORGANIZE, Meeting Time: Monday Sept 14th [1964] 8pm, Place: 212 W. 129th St. Apt 12 E.[215]

Mae maintained this pace of activism until she was reincarcerated. We see how the state worked to crush Mallory's aspirations and advocacy through incarceration and twenty-plus years of FBI surveillance. At Twenty-First and Payne, Mae positioned herself as an intellectual, writing and requesting newspapers and Black history books, only to find that Ohio County officials "refus[ed] to deliver reference volumes on Afro-American history which [she] requested."[216] Notwithstanding state oppression, Mallory's voice rose as she wrote herself out of prison contesting state-sanctioned violence. Mae Mallory, as a political prisoner trying to survive incarceration, positioned herself as an intellectual, writing to demand freedom for herself and all people of color.

Chapter 7   Audrey Proctor Seniors
Motherhood and Writing Resistance

Mommy loved Godzilla movies. Her favorite misunderstood movie monster was Mothra (1961). She would just giggle with eyes twinkling and say, "Oh Paula the Shobijin [little ladies] that summoned Mothra, OH BOY!!!! That was my favorite part of the movie!!! You know Mothra was a giant Moth," she would LAUGH. In Cleveland my mother found fun, love, and activism.... Daddy recalled, "I took Audrey to see Mary Poppins [1964]. After the movie was over Audrey was so delighted, she jubilantly asked, 'Can we see it again?'" Daddy laughed recounting this moment. "I took her to see Mary Poppins again."

In 1961 Robert F. Williams's ideology of self-defense, and the fact that he beat the Klan in Monroe and escaped Monroe to land in Castro's "racism-free" Cuba, cemented Audrey Proctor's and the Monroe Defense Committee's idolization of him. But Williams lost his shine with my mother and MDC members, given his yearlong silence about Mae Mallory's incarceration. On June 30, 1962, my mother wrote a surprising letter to Williams in Havana that illuminated her awakening social and political thought and adoption of *Cubanismo*. Audrey was deeply disappointed in Williams, for he did not keep in touch with Cleveland's MDC when he landed in Cuba. My mother felt he had completely abandoned Mae. Her letter to Williams disclosed her disapproval of his silence: "I have written before, but I don't know if the mail was confiscated or not. We in the Monroe Defense Committee have been waiting to hear word from you."[1] When Williams went into exile, my mother knew of his position within Castro's government. My father wrote in "Free Mae Mallory" that "the *Crusader* became the most outspoken Black voice in the U.S.A.—and did not flinch when it came to admiring the militant struggles of the masses in Africa, in Cuba and elsewhere in their fight for freedom."[2] My parents idolized Williams following his self-defense ideology, but my mother found fault in his non-actions concerning Mallory and the Monroe defendants. Before his exile Williams gained notoriety in Cuba for his political ideology against U.S. fascism, emerging as a "folk hero" in exile.[3] In *Our Party Reflects Our Country's Recent History* Castro described him as a revolutionary, a leader whom Cuba considered a brother who "was brutally persecuted [in the United States and] found asylum in this land."[4] According to Cynthia A. Young, the Cubans "defined [Williams] quite literally as a physical and ideological bridge between the Cuban Revolution and the Black Revolt brewing in the United States."[5] My mother anticipated that Williams would help Mallory, given his international popularity and his position as an international folk hero. Audrey blamed Mae's incarceration solely on him. "We know that Mae is in this situation because she like the rest of us in the M.D.C. believe in your ideas and what you stand for"—meaning Williams's armed resistance strategy. She continued, "Yet there are some of us who feel disappointed that no word from you has reached us. Rob, I strongly believe that you should be able to do something for Mae."[6] Proctor had not forgotten that, in anticipation of the Freedom Riders' visit, Williams publicly asked for help in the *Crusader*. He personally called Mallory for aid.[7] In the letter Audrey illumines her political ideology of self-defense and independence. My mother states that she and the Monroe Defense Committee "believe in [Williams's] ideas and what you stand for," armed self-defense and African American agency. Given MDC's effort to connect African American liberation to Majority World movements to create a national and international self-defense movement for Majority World liberation, it remains unsurprising that Audrey expected Robert to fight for Mae from Cuba and make her case an international one.[8]

In the letter she writes about the need for a united front among African Americans globally and between Williams and Mallory. "Rob the urgency for unity among Blacks as a whole is becoming increasingly necessary since it appears that the *powers that be* intend to continue to hang us separately at this time instead of [an] all out massacre like the 6 million Jews or the atomic massacre of the Japanese."[9] Like Paul Robeson, my mother recognized the links between worldwide acts of violence, fascism, and repression and those perpetrated on African Americans. She links Jewish and Japanese suffering by hegemony and white supremacists to massacres of Blacks like

Paul Robeson and Mae Mallory to maintain white power and the social order, through Red Scare tactics and law-and-order legislation.[10]

Twenty-one-year-old Audrey Proctor castigates Williams and writes, "Rob, you of all people should and do know that there isn't any justice for Blacks here in this so-called free country, and we are depending upon you and people like you to let the world know what an injustice is suffered by Mae Mallory and people like her."[11] Given Williams's own experience of battling white supremacy and the Klan in Monroe, she scathingly and sardonically takes him to task. "You should know this better than anyone. Isn't that why you are in Cuba today?" Because of his international status as a freedom fighter and folk hero in Cuba, Audrey and the MDC expected him "to help create clamor for Mae's freedom. The greater the clamor, the greater are Mae's chances for freedom, and with you in Cuba it could cause international clamor." She and the MDC counted on Williams "to reach the people of Cuba and other Latin American countries," involve them in Mae's case, and use his connections within Castro's revolutionary government. Audrey wrote, "We feel that you can do so unless you are willing to let Mae Mallory go back to Monroe and face the racist mob[s]." She contends that his inaction relays the message that he would allow Mallory to face Monroe justice, which for Black women meant rape and beatings as social control. Mae's lawyer Haffner wrote to Williams about Mae's condition in jail and his inaction:

> [Mae Mallory] is an active person and being cooped up in jail is not good for her.... [Mr. Williams] the fight in the United States of America cannot be waged from distant shores. If you prefer to remain in Havana, then you will remind me of the man who urges the other person to fight and boos if the results are not to his likings.[12]

My mother's letter let Williams know that "I understand that you have a radio program. It appears to me that you should utilize it for the benefit of Mae." She had expected him to use his 50,000-watt radio program Radio Free Dixie, which, according to Timothy Tyson, reached the South and as far as Saskatchewan, Canada.[13]

Mommy's bravery emerges as she questions Williams's commitment: "I hope you realize that there are sacrifices to be made and the few of us who are doing everything we can, just can't reach Cuba and that is why we are asking you to do it for us." Audrey relates the MDC's willingness to put themselves in physical and emotional jeopardy for Mallory's freedom and exoneration. She maintains that this commitment to social justice extended to promoting self-defense and Black human rights. MDC made great sacrifices, my father lost family connections, my mother lost a home with Auntie Gladys, members lost jobs and "respectability," and Pat Mallory lost her mother and a carefree youth. This is not to say that Robert did not make sacrifices given his Cuban and later his Chinese exile, but as far as my mother was concerned, his sacrifices had little to do with Mallory and more to do with *his own well-being*. From my mother's perspective, Williams sacrificed nothing. To add to the injury, she felt he refused to help Mae and the MDC.

Audrey Proctor did not reserve her wrath for Robert F. Williams exclusively. She attacked and condemned formal Black organizations for their complacency, acceptance of an unjust society, and dismissal of Mae Mallory. "We can't depend upon these so-called respectable Negroes and Black organizations to come to the defense of Mae." Although my mother belonged to the radicalized New Orleans NAACP, she knew that some NAACP branches and conservative groups bought into hegemony, were inadequate in fighting white oppression, and proved incredibly class-conscious. My mother knew that formal conservative Black organizations gained benefits for the Black middle and upper classes exclusively, leaving the poverty-stricken behind. These groups proved unresponsive to the needs of Mae and other working-class people, including the NAACP and Mae's Black councilman who refused to help.[14]

Audrey Proctor placed herself at the center of the Mallory case as one who would, like the Cubans, "stand up against the oppressor," all five feet, one inch and less than one hundred pounds of her. She was ready and willing to fight against repression in the United States. She knew what a horrible world Blacks lived in and wanted to make serious changes. This she endeavored to do through the Mallory case and her Cleveland activism for equitable education and voting rights. She could not understand why Williams would not take action when she and the MDC were doing so very much at such a great sacrifice. Audrey ends the letter with hope, wit, and assuaging Robert's ego, to wake his conscience.

> We all hope to hear from you as soon as possible. I am closing this letter with this thought in mind; I know that Robert Williams the man who held the Klan off for three years and the man who told his people to arm them-selves will do everything in his power to help Mae Mallory. As Always For Freedom Now Audrey Proctor.

Williams sent my mother Mao Zedong's *Little Red Book* and his *Listen Brother*, but I could not find any extant literature to prove whether Williams responded to my mother's letter privately or publicly. He did not respond to the Monroe Defense Committee. Why didn't he respond to my mother or MDC?

In 1962, a year after the riots, Williams would write of Mallory's plight from Havana in three columns for the *Crusader*. He put Mae on the front page at the center of motherhood tropes: "Tonight in the so-called free world, a mother of two children languishes in a dismal jail . . . deprived of the right and joy to give companionship and guidance to her teenage daughter." He wrote of Mae's plight notwithstanding the rupture in their relationship given his anger toward her during the Stegalls' invasion.[15] The rupture appears as one of the reasons for Williams's silence, among a myriad of other reasons including his Cuban exile. Although he had visited Cuba in 1960 and the Cuban people considered him a hero, he found himself navigating a Cuban politics where, according to Devyn Spence Benson, the new leaders refused to discuss Cuba's racial discrimination problems, which deeply disturbed him. On top of this, unsurprisingly, Williams had CPUSA foes in Cuba.[16] Another reason for Williams's yearlong silence included the FBI disruption program set in place to keep Mae and him at odds with each other. The FBI caused a decades-long rupture in their relationship. On March 29, 1967, Mae wrote to Mrs. Johnson that Williams "even accused me of being a spy for the man. Never in my life was I so insulted. Rob should be the last person to accuse me of such a thing."[17] This was an often-repeated accusation by Williams about Mae.[18] He sent a letter with these assertions to Mae and to *Crusader* subscribers. This led Yuri Kochiyama and James Foreman to question his behavior and to vouch for Mae. Yuri wrote,

> We discussed the "controversial" letter. Mae was naturally upset but could not believe that you mailed copies for Crusader readership. She asked me to bring this up to you whether it might have been the FBI or CIA who may have duplicated such and disseminated copies. Or was it to alert people everywhere to the wider implications, that everyone be more discriminatory and careful. And not be fooled nor used.[19]

Williams's actions led Yuri to end the friendship. James Foreman also wrote to Williams: "I am most interested in knowing if you wrote the letter to Mae Mallory which has your signature. If you are the author, then I am afraid you have been wrongly advised. Mae has always defended and worked in your behalf. I have the utmost confidence in her and hope that my word has some meaning to you." Not only did Williams send the letter but he expressed outward hostility toward Mae publicly in 1967 and in Dar es Salaam in 1968 and 1974 at the Sixth Annual Pan-African Conference.[20] In her letter to Mrs.

Johnson, Mae wrote that "even after I got to Africa Rob treated me like dirt under his feet. Anyone just one bit less dedicated than myself would have just forgot about Rob, and I still may have to come to this."[21]

The FBI took full advantage of the breach and worked vigorously to keep Mallory and the Monroe defendants incarcerated. They actively caused dissension within the Monroe Defense Committee, the Workers World Party, the Socialist Workers Party, and the Committee to Aid the Monroe Defendants, because of their efforts to free Mae, Harold Reape, and Richard Crowder. Believing that WWP controlled the MDC and that the SWP controlled the CAMD, the FBI worked to disrupt these organizations through phone calls, as well as through letters they sent out as if generated by the Negroes with Guns. Correspondingly, J. B. Matthews, director of research for the House Un-American Activities Committee, subscribed to all these organizations' newspapers. He joined these groups under several pseudonyms to destroy the members and the organization.[22] My parents subscribed to the *Crusader* from its inception, knew of the FBI's machinations, and knew that the FBI watched them. My parents' membership in WWP allowed them access to history as it unfolded in Cuba, leading to their knowledge of Williams's actions and nonactions.[23] Audrey and Clarence Seniors remained well versed in Cuban history and politics given their vast library. What my mother objected to most vigorously was Robert F. Williams's abandonment of Mae Mallory *and he did abandon her.*

> *As a child my mother gave me everyday lessons concerning the problems of Christianity, racism, colonialism, and imperialism. "Paula, the United States was built on racism. Racists used the Bible and Christianity to enslave African Americans. Paula, you must fight against racism and racist people. Paula, we want a just and equitable society. Colonialism and imperialism prevent equity because they were established to keep people of color in a marginal position. We must rally against colonialism, imperialism, racism, and the use of religion as a weapon of oppression and subjugation." These lessons she taught me. I grew into understanding these lessons, for they were hard, thought-provoking lessons for a young child. These lessons I carried with me throughout life.*

Cubanismo

In 1979 Fidel Castro visited New York—a momentous and exciting occasion for Mommy at thirty-nine and me, age sixteen. We watched in rapt interest as Castro was interviewed by African American television journalist Bill McCreary from The McCreary Report. *"You know, Paula, Castro would only be interviewed by a Black reporter. In New York he refused to speak English, demanding an interpreter. He came for us. The Cuban Revolution, that's the revolution to emulate!" My mother instilled in me a deep admiration of Fidel Castro and the Cuban Revolution. I looked with intense interest at our books about Castro and the revolution. So enthralled was I of the Cuban and Chinese Revolutions that as a young dancer I wrote a paper about the difference between Chinese ballet and Cuban ballet. Chinese ballet used Chinese heroines, heroes, and tales, according to a book gifted to me by a Brooklyn Friends favorite teacher. Alicia Alonso's Cuban ballet stuck to traditional ballet. It did not present the revolution. It was through Castro's visit, my mother's lessons on Cuban and Chinese revolutionary history, that my mother and I bonded over Castro and Cuban revolutionary theory.*

Fidel Castro and the Cuban Revolution represented a third-world Hollywood heroic fantasy for many African Americans and whites, and for many races, ethnicities, and classes. They worshipped Castro because they felt he symbolized the definitive Hollywood "bad boy," infused with masculinity and an insurrectionary swagger.[24] My mother so admired Fidel Castro that, according to her FBI report, her "billfold contained a photograph of FIDEL CASTRO, bearing no identifying marks."[25] The idolization of Fidel sparked the fire that led Audrey Proctor, the self-educated organic intellectual, to learn all she could about Castro's ideology and Cuba's revolution. The revolution led Blacks like Proctor to hold up Castro and the revolution as a model for social and political change. As Stokely Carmichael asserted in 1967, "Cuba had permitted us to observe many kinds of tactics employed in its struggles which we can adapt to ours," including urban guerrilla warfare.[26] The Cuban Revolution cast people of color as the heroes and white supremacists and colonialism as villains. The revolution and Castro ascended as mythic heroic representations of real social and political change, which strengthened the Black community's support of Castro, especially on his 1960 visit to New York City.

In his 1965 speech "Our Party Reflects Our Country's Recent History" Castro asserted, "We challenge [the U.S. government] to permit the representatives of the Negro or civil rights organizations in the United States to visit Cuba so that they can see how, with the disappearance of the exploitation of man by man, racial discrimination has disappeared in our country once and for all."[27] Audrey Proctor astutely linked Castro's words and actions concerning people of African descent to her letter to Williams. She linked the need for African American unity to the Cuban Revolution. My mother wrote, "Rob, I know the people of Cuba are awakened to the fact that there is no justice for Blacks unless we unite like they in Cuba did."[28] She alluded to the triumph of the Cuban Revolution because the white, Black, and mulatto Cubans stood together to beat colonialism and white supremacist oppression using Cubanismo.[29]

Proctor fully expected Williams to use Cubanismo to link Mallory's and all African Americans' freedom struggles to the broader context of anti-colonial movements, as Castro did in his 1960 *Declaration of Havana*. He extended friendship to African Americans, identified U.S. lynching as social control, discussed the "persecution" of intellectuals and workers, and condemned U.S. imperialism in Latin America, Mexico, Nicaragua, Haiti, Santo Domingo, Cuba, and Puerto Rico. Castro condemned "the outrageous treatment dealt by the Marines to our wives and daughters, as well as to the most exalted symbols of our history, such as the statue of José Martí." In this statement Castro referenced the U.S. military presence in Guantanamo Bay, the U.S. creation and training of insurgents on the island, the Agrarian Reform Law, and the nationalization of U.S. and Cuban bourgeoisie properties. According to Julio Cubría Vichot, this marked the beginning of "eliminat[ing] one of the main pillars of neocolonial domination." Fidel declared that Cuba would march "with all the world and not with just a part of it."[30] Audrey Proctor expected Williams to advocate for liberation and amalgamate Mallory's struggle to the Cuban Revolution, as Castro connected African American oppression to the Cuban Revolution and colonialism. Castro spoke at the U.N. General Assembly on September 26, 1960: "Colonies do not speak. Colonies are not recognized in the world. Colonies are not allowed to express their opinions until they are granted permission to do so." Castro illuminated the silencing of Cuba's Revolution and Black radical activists like Mae Mallory, Mrs. Johnson, Ruthie Stone, Audrey Proctor, and Clarence Seniors who advocated for change through self-defense.[31]

One of the Workers World parents took us to the "Bozo Show"—me, age six, with my friends Hindi, Nina, Susie, Sara, Eric, Jonathan, and Mallory. We sat in the dark studio on gym bleachers. One of the clowns, perhaps Bozo, gave out toys to all the white children. No toy for me. I came home and told Mommy. Mommy said, "Bozo is racist. Paula, racism is when people feel that white people are better than Blacks, that Black people are undeserving. Nobody is better than you, you are deserving. You are a pretty, smart Black girl and I love you. Bozo and those clowns are racists." Lesson in racism taught by Mommy. My mother The Colony spoke and taught me to rage. She taught me to identify racism, to rage against racism and white supremacy— to speak up and fight back. I never had to figure out what racism was. I had experienced it, and Mommy taught me to let The Colony speak.

In Audrey's letter to Williams, she exposed an ideology that corresponded with Castro's. "We must depend upon people like you, myself and others who are willing to stand up to the oppressor and those who know what a rotten society we as Blacks live in."[32] Proctor centered herself in the fight against U.S. repression, proving that colonies and its people *do speak, do rage against repression*. Through their raging, colonies like Proctor and Mae Mallory unveil "the rotten society" that they, the colonies, inhabit.

Castro asserted that the Cuban Revolution would "carry out a true program of social development," equalizing society for all classes. Castro proposed the right of the people to land, education, medical care, living wages over "starvation wages," jobs for youths, race equality, gender equality, and the right to defend their country.[33] These declarations resonated for Majority World leftists and Black radicals.

Castro's speech allowed Proctor and other Black radicals to imagine a United States where the common people eradicated racism and created an equal and just society in the mold of insurgent Cuba—a society where people like Mallory gained praise for fighting hegemonic power not incarceration. Fidel Castro's ideology and Williams's exile were the reasons that Proctor and MDC expected Williams's help, not deafening silence.

Motherhood and the Monroe Defense Committee

Cleveland-born, Brooklyn-bred. As a little girl looking through my mother's meticulous red photo album, I rummaged through the past. Me with a white diapered bum, me on our Monroe porch surrounded by smiling MDC members. Wobbly-legged me holding Daddy's leg. Rosie petitioning for Mae, her baby Nina with a beagle, photos of toddler Mallory, Sara, Eric, Hindi, Su-

sie, we were all born the same year—Workers World babies. Mae petitioning, photos of Pat, Grattan smiling and laughing. Mommy let the photos tell the story.

Fig. 8. From left, Wilbur Grattan, Mae, Paula, Libby, and Lumumba Kenyatta at the Freedom House in Monroe, North Carolina, Audrey and Clarence Seniors Collection.

We children were bright luminous stars central to our mothers' activism in Workers World and the Monroe Defense Committee. Our mothers marveled at us, and included us in their political crusades, as they worked to create a beautiful just world: "Paula, our baby here has been on many picket lines. Her first line was when she was two weeks old."[34] The Monroe Defense Committee centered Mae Mallory's case on motherhood, most certainly because Mae, my mother, Ruthie Stone, and Mrs. Johnson embodied motherhood, and because of the continual presence of neighborhood children at the Cleveland MDC's storefront office. My mother's and MDC's activism revolved around the motherist frame.[35] Ruthie Stone came to Monroe as a mother of a baby girl having already combined motherhood with activism with Buffalo's Workers World and Mothers Alliance. The newspapers reported that "fireworks broke out when Mrs. Ruth Stone, treasurer of Mothers Alliance spoke on behalf of welfare recipients" at a New York state legislature public hearing on welfare. They reported that Stone "waged war against racial discrimination" in Buffalo and the South, advocated for welfare rights, compelled Buffalo shop owners to hire African Americans, and fought against colonialism in Africa. Stone successfully combined motherhood with activism and brought these skills to Cleveland's Monroe Defense Committee.[36] Audrey and Ruthie Stone connected motherhood with activism. They ran the office and cared for Ruthie's daughter and other children from the community, including me in 1963, and teenaged Pat and Iris, *who they put to work*.[37] The *Call and Post* reported that everyday political activist "Mrs. Ruth Stone, Monroe Defense Committee Secretary organized a picket line and staged a march in front of Governor DiSalle's office in the State Capitol Building," when DiSalle decided to send Mae to Monroe.[38] According to Clarence Seniors, when MDC moved from Cleveland to Monroe to the Freedom House/MDC's office, they attracted young children. Clarence recalled fondly a little girl Jeanne, age three, whose mother dropped her off at Cleveland's MDC office. They raised her for four years until her parents claimed her. They cared for a fourteen-year-old girl who worked in the Cleveland office, making sure she stayed away from boys and men. When Ruthie left, my mother cared for her daughter until she returned for her. My parents took care of a little boy named Hazel who just showed up at Monroe's MDC office, appearing parentless. My parents loved Hazel so much that they tried unsuccessfully to informally adopt him. They fed and cared for children in both cities. MDC's environment provided a space where Audrey and Ruthie could mother, teach, and influence children as role models and everyday political activists. Through their work and everyday existence, they taught the children about equity and activism. They taught the children what repression looked like, how to fight for a just society through social and political action. I am most certain that my mother infused the children with a Black-is-Beautiful ideology.

> *My mother instilled in me an unbreakable pride in my Blackness, my dark skin, and my nappy hair. She told me regularly I was smart and pretty, ensuring that I grew up with an abundance of confidence. I grew up with Black is Beautiful dolls. A friend said, "You were so lucky to have such pretty Black dolls. My South Carolinian Black dolls were monstrous." Mrs. Alesi, Mommy's Board of Ed boss, had given me a beautiful porcelain Japanese doll, which my mother approved of. Then in a moment of what I can only guess was insanity, Mrs. Alesi gave me a white doll and a yellow pigtailed wig. "No!!! Paula, you cannot keep the doll or wig!!!" Those markers of white supremacy met the garbage chute. I am sure that Mommy gave Mrs. Alesi a lesson in the Black beauty aesthetic!! My mother was raising a revolutionary*

Black is Beautiful child. Mommy I am sure taught Cleveland and Monroe's children these same lessons.

At 220 Montgomery Street on our orange sofa, my mother taught me Black is Beautiful, leafing through Ebony, Jet, and Afro American Woman magazines. The latter's cover featured Black beauty aesthetic models, Afrocentric clothing designs by Khadejha, a story about Sojourner Truth, and Langston Hughes's and Juanita Poitier's poems. We also watched the televised Miss Black America Pageant.... Mommy and I looked at my favorite black-and-white, Black baby photo book, entranced by Black baby beauty. We read African American, Majority World, and European history; we looked at art and picture books, J. A. Rogers's 100 Amazing Facts about the Negro, The Sweet Flypaper of Life. Our library called to us. My mother's silent encouragement, quiet urging, compelling me to learn, to study them all over the course of my childhood to adulthood. I just breathed it all in. I exhaled Black, Brown, Native American, and Asian beauty. I am certain Mommy shared these lessons with Cleveland's and Monroe's children.

My mother was fully committed to the Monroe Defense Committee, Workers World Party, and the Workers World–affiliated Youth against War and Fascism. YAWF was founded in 1962 as an anti-fascist youth committee dedicated to anti-Vietnam protest, although J. B. Matthews and the FBI felt that YAWF's principal purpose was "revolutionary overthrow of American capitalism."[39] As an everyday political activist, my mother included me in *all* her political activities. The naming of children within WWP proved pivotal. I, Paula Marie, was named after Paul Robeson. Jeanette Merrill named her daughter Mallory, after Mae.[40] The multiracial nature of the MDC, WWP, and YAWF worked to educate children of these organizations about an equitable society and what the world should look like. We children knew nothing but equality from a very young age given the racial makeup and equal division of labor and power in our community.

By 1963 Audrey Proctor Seniors's political activities fit firmly within the motherist frame. She married my father in 1962, became a mother in 1963, named me after Robeson, and advocated for Mallory. Because MDC was committed to freedom for all African Americans, we as a family participated in a myriad of demonstrations for desegregation, voting rights, and equitable labor practices in Cleveland. In 1963 Mommy joined two rallies to protest President Kennedy's labor practices, carrying the sign "Subtle Discrimination Is Still Discrimination" with a child carrying the sign "Kennedy Did You Wait 100 Years."[41]

> As a little girl my mother took me on excursions that brought us to the Village. Out of the Sixth Avenue train station we passed people with eyes occluded, hands big and fat with ugly bloodied pinprick marks. Slowly they bent all the way down to ground, and as if they were a ball they bounced back up only to repeat this grotesque movement. "Mommy, why are those people doing that?" "Paula, they are nodding. They use and are addicted to the drug heroin." Because of my mother's lesson, because this scenario proved forbidding and terrifying, I never used drugs. My mother's lessons safeguarded me. I was about ten and was dropped off at home every day—a latchkey kid. My mother worked. Every day this man waited for me and "escorted" me to my door. I told her; she was beside herself. She went to her neighbors for help. A neighbor's husband threatened the man with a gun. The threat didn't dissuade him; he continued "escorting" me. My mother and I went to the police department. They told her they couldn't do anything until the man did something to me. SUDDENLY, it stopped. As a grown woman I asked my mother, how'd it stop? She said, "The police don't tolerate people who mess with children no matter the child's color. The police beat the living hell out of the man. That's how it stopped."
>
> For college I wanted to audition for North Carolina School of the Arts. My mother told me "under no circumstances will you be going there." The Greensboro Massacre (1979) and police harassment of Winston-Salem's Black Panthers informed her command. I didn't audition. On college graduation I was offered a job teaching dance at Brooklyn's South Shore High School. Mommy said, "Paula, a Black girl was raped by whites over there." I did not take the job. My mother taught me how to protect myself.

One of the most critical aspects of radical women's activism included the motherist frame as a warrant for resistance, the model that Audrey Proctor Seniors and MDC used to protect Mae Mallory. Mallory represented family, an important family member whom my mother and the Monroe Defense Committee charged themselves with caring for, mothering, and protecting. They argued that the state was unjustified in restraining Mae, that she personified womanhood and motherhood and needed safeguarding from Monroe's justice. They argued that Mallory needed protection from Monroe's political and social terror, which manifested in rape and the lynch mob as a method of social control.[42] Many people supported Mae, including the Cleveland Missionary Society who, according to my father's article "Missionary Sisters Visit Mae Mallory in Jail," visited Mae with "no doubt in their minds that this was an innocent mother suffering unmercifully in jail solely because she had the courage to withstand the humiliation, threats, [and] violence, to gain the dignity of equality and freedom."[43] While imprisoned, Mae's words accompanied the picketers on placards stating "If I Die a Piece of Freedom Dies with Me," accompanied by a noose and mock tomb, reflecting the very real danger of her extradition to Monroe.[44] By shaping the Mae Mallory case around motherhood, my parents and MDC rallied to protect African American motherhood. They linked the protection of Black motherhood to social action. Mallory's incarceration prevented her from physically nurturing or mothering her children and resonated with the history of slavery, with forced separations of mother and child, and black codes that criminalized Black women, legally sanctioning their jailing. The Monroe Defense Committee reconfigured the discourse surrounding African American women by defining Mae as the incarnation of the quintessential woman.

My mother joined numerous protests for Mae, including the multiracial Youngstown Friends of Mae Mallory Committee march in May 1963. The *Youngstown Vindicator* reported that the group marched at the Youngstown University graduation to urge Governor Rhodes, the keynote speaker, to give Mallory asylum. The accompanying photograph shows Seniors, with a slight smile, wearing a dark dress with white polka dots, a sweater draping her shoulders, a large white beaded necklace with a drop pendant, and high heels—as per usual for the glamorous Audrey. Mommy dressed elegantly on the picket line to exhibit a respect for herself and the march, and to demand reverence and human rights, tropes denied African American women. The motherist frame also emerged in protest signs carried by Black men that proclaimed the need to protect Mallory, as a mother and woman, including "No Black Man Can Walk in Freedom while a Black Woman Sits in Jail." [45] These Black men could not ignore Mallory's plight. They could not casually go on their way walking free without offering aid to an African American mother, a Black woman. While the Monroe justice system proclaimed that no Black woman could embody motherhood or womanhood, MDC firmly placed Mallory at the axis of motherhood and womanhood discourse.

What is significant about the participation of Audrey Proctor Seniors and the Monroe Defense Committee protests is their inclusion of children and teenagers of all races. As everyday political activists, my mother, Stone, and the parents and guardians of these children instilled in them a strong sense of agency and justice, as well as a liberational spirit. One 1963 photograph of an MDC march shows Audrey smiling at two joyful five-year-old girls carrying signs that read "Keep the KKK Away from Mae" and "Rhodes: Don't

Fig. 9. Butch (left), "My Mother is No Kidnapper," and Mae, "Save My Mother." Audrey and Clarence Seniors Collection.

Send Mae to the KKK."[46] This photograph indicates that their parents educated them about Mallory's imprisonment and the terror of the Klan. They taught them to RESIST.

Pat visited Cleveland regularly to see Mae. My mother put the teenaged Pat and Iris, Grattan's daughter, to work. Audrey most certainly insisted that they participate in Mae's rallies. Through Mae and my mother, Pat learned to rage against oppression. One photograph from November 18, 1961, shows Butch, 15, and a small-framed sixteen-year-old Patricia leading a protest on Mae's behalf, carrying the banner "Save My Mother."[47]

My mother took me to all the rallies for Mae in my pram, and through her educational efforts she taught me before I could even walk to advocate for justice. The U.S. government attempted to dishonor Mommy's efforts. The FBI reported that Audrey Seniors participated in a Mallory demonstration at a dedication ceremony for Cuyahoga Community College, with Governor Rhodes as the guest speaker. They reported that thirty "Black and white" MDC members, including children, participated. They mischaracterized my mother as a defiant provocateur: "Audrey Seniors [was] determined to cause an incident. Audrey Seniors deliberately pushed a baby stroller carrying her child into the police officers." The FBI then offered an unveiled threat to

Mommy and me, given their false charge of assault with a baby and carriage: "The use of restraint on the part of the officers prevented any incident."[48]

Activism in Cleveland

When Cleveland's CORE was reestablished in 1962, my mother joined. In 1963 she participated in a sit-in. According to the *Call and Post* my father stayed home "babysitting their three month old daughter." The article stated, "Miss [Ruth] Turner, chairman of the Cleveland CORE chapter, Mrs. Clarence Seniors, 22 and Bruce Melville, 22, began the sit-in demonstration in the governor's office Monday to call attention to the fair housing bill now in committee. The demonstrators said they will not budge until the bill is brought out for a vote in the Ohio House." Seniors, Turner, and Melville, a Western Reserve student, participated in this sit-in to protest the subpar and overcrowded living conditions in Cleveland's segregated Black communities. Segregated public housing and homes owned by Blacks lacked indoor plumbing. Another contributing factor included the state's use of urban renewal to destroy Black communities.[49]

> *Hindi, Sarah, Eric, Nina, my neighbor/friend Michael and I all went to Brooklyn's African American J. Marjory Jackson Studio of Music and Dance Experimental Group. The School Motto was "Our Home Away from Home is one of laughter, games, music, sharing, helping, loving, obeying, and learning to consider the rights of others." Mommy enjoyed telling me, "Paula, at Mrs. Jackson's you and a little girl jumped into the pool with all your clothes on." She would laugh!!! "Mrs. Jackson spanked you two. You didn't want to go back to school." I most certainly was not amused. "The rights of others" did not extend to me and my right to jump in the pool. Before and after school Rosie, Nina's mother, would pile us into her Volkswagen Bug. Rosie wore metal braces that attached to her red leather shoes. I asked why. She told me that she had had polio, pointing to our vaccination scar, indicating our protection. Question answered, we continued on with our day of adventure. The energetic Rosie, with her curly brown hair, glittery eyes, beaming exuberant smile, snazzy dresses, and wonderful personality, was fun. In that Bug each of us tried to avoid sitting on that big hump. No seatbelts. Rosie would move that heavy gearshift and off we'd go!!! Our graduation from Mrs. Jackson's was stupendous. All festooned in our costumes, we sang "Medley Nursery Rhymes." At our final graduation festivi-*

ties, "The Awarding of Diplomas," all bedecked in our white caps and gowns, we stood proudly on the stage as our parents beamed.

Audrey Proctor Seniors belonged to Cleveland's United Freedom Movement, which was founded on June 3, 1963, by Ruth Turner, Reverend Paul A. Younger of the Fidelity Baptist Church, and others.[50] It was a multiracial coalition of formal civil rights groups, fraternal and social organizations, and radical groups like MDC. In Cleveland over 70 percent of elementary, middle, and high school children faced segregation. Schools banned African American children from extracurricular activities and forced them to eat separately from whites.[51]

According to the *Cleveland Press*, the United Freedom Movement began Cleveland's first "Negro rights demonstration" to end segregation in the public schools, because integration negotiations between them and the school board broke down.[52] As militants became more active in the organization, the "NAACP withdrew [from the group] in 1966."[53] The United Freedom Movement fought public school segregation and worked to equalize housing and welfare and advance political participation. They worked to end discriminatory hiring practices and to obtain voting rights for African Americans. The *Plain Dealer* reported that "the Clarence Seniors's brought their infant along in a cart, [and that they were] active in the defense of Willie Mae Mallory."[54] The *Cleveland Press* ran a photograph of a UFM march whose caption read, "Youngest among pickets was Paula Seniors wheeled by her mother, Mrs. Audrey Seniors, and two white toddlers, Wilma and Matthew Shaw, possibly age three and five, who, according to Seniors, were 'veterans of civil rights demonstrations.'"[55]

The *Call and Post* reported that Mommy was "a member of CORE, NAACP, MDC, and the Freedom Fighters, [and] is an ardent freedom marcher." The article featured our family. The caption reads,

> Crawling for Freedom. Eight-months old Paula Marie Seniors crawls among picket signs in her playroom at home, 10517 Superior. While Paula can only murmur "dada," her presence on a picket line can be felt. She marched (or strolled) in her first picket line at the age of three weeks when Clevelanders conducted a sympathy march for Birmingham citizens. Since then, the tot has marched for fair housing, against de facto segregation, against Central Cadillac in Washington, D.C., and half a dozen others. The 18 lbs., 27 inch tall baby eats moderately, forgets her sleeping schedule and has never been known to cry on a picket line.[56]

Audrey Proctor Seniors emerged as an everyday political activist within the motherist frame imparting knowledge to me through picketing, including ending Cleveland school segregation. The Cleveland School Board of fifteen white people lived in the suburbs. They refused to build more schools to alleviate overcrowding, provide the Black community with proper facilities, or provide Cleveland's African American schools with qualified teachers. This school board spent significantly more on white children's education than Black children's, which led to a 40 percent dropout rate of African American junior high and high school students. By age twenty-five, most of Cleveland's African Americans had only received a two-year high school education. Cleveland maintained an abysmal record in educating Black children. By 1962, over the objections of African American parents, the Cleveland School Board initiated a ridiculous busing program, busing Black children *and* their teachers to schools that had empty classrooms.[57] My mother fought for the rights of Cleveland's children, anticipating the time when she would enroll me into an equitable public school, which would reflect her efforts for a quality education for all children. That school system would never come to fruition during her lifetime, nor mine.

As an adult, my Brooklyn neighborhood friend George told me of his childhood school desegregation experience. His complete shock at his white friends' transformation into ugly beasts screaming racial epithets at him on the desegregation bus. On graduation from Mrs. Jackson's nursery school, we all headed for kindergarten.[58] *My white friends Hindi, Sarah, Eric, Susie, and Nina went to public school. When it came to kindergarten my parents and Michael's parents could not put us in Brooklyn's public schools. Mommy told me, "Paula, white racists were beating up Black children. We could not send you to public school." Our parents had all fought mightily to desegregate public schools, yet my parents felt that public schools would provide an unsafe environment for a Black child. They searched for a school. Mommy said, "I visited Brooklyn's Montessori School and watched as a child sat there crying inconsolably." Black eyes ablaze, she continued, "Not one teacher picked that child up. We chose Brooklyn Friends—they led with kindness. We, like Robeson's mother, believed in the Quaker tradition—antiwar, peace, race equality, and social justice. As atheists we accepted Quakerism for the good of your education. We always gave you the choice to believe in God." When you are raised by atheists, it's hard to believe in God. I never did. I went to Brooklyn Friends from kindergarten to the twelfth grade. I was protected. Over those years my parents gently coached me not to discuss our religious beliefs at school. Like all the other children, I sat in the meeting in silent reflection, graduating twelfth grade a good Quaker girl.*

I loved kindergarten; I adored my warm and loving teachers, Mrs. Henry and Mrs. Kossoff. They were fun, warm, and kind. We children played the TV show Lost in Space *on the monkey bars—our spaceship. I always wanted Miguel to be Don, to my Judy. I baby crushed on Miguel. I had lots of friends including my Jamaican friend Joan and my Asian friend Gail. We would share her dried plums and dried seaweed. I shared my treats too. We talked, laughed, and played.*

In graduate school in San Diego, with its weird racial dynamics, I experienced hurtful, soul-crushing anti–Black woman racism from some Majority World graduate students—a racism I had never experienced from Majority World people growing up in Brooklyn. My first semester I found myself continually saying, "I did have colored friends in New York": my Korean friend Mija, whom I met in fourth grade, my white Jewish friend Allyson, whom I met in second grade. Crying, I shared my California experience with my Black friend Deborah who lived in Germany. She told me, "Fuck them!!! Find the white people!!" Thank goodness I befriended my ethnic Chinese Vietnamese graduate school friend Michael, my Mexican friend Alicia, my Chinese graduate school friend Lianna, my white friend Sharla, and my Costa Rican friend Ivonne and her Italian husband Eddie, my daughter's godparents, during my first year in California. These friends brought joy and humanity into my California life.

But those bizarre racial forces were killing me. One weekend I was at Coronado Beach with Brooklyn-born Park the Wonder Dog. Sitting in front of the Hotel Coronado after a day visit at the dog beach, I started playing with a little Asian boy and talking to his father. The boy's mother came out of the hotel. We got to talking about how we both grew up in Brooklyn and went to Brooklyn Friends School. SHE WAS GAIL!!!! We chatted that day. Gail and her family restored my faith in a multiracial world. My mother I am sure sent Gail and her family to me to heal, to recall those beautiful multiracial Brooklyn Friends days of Lost in Space *on our monkey bar spaceship.*

My mother educated me politically, socially, and intellectually. She raised me in a wonderful, magical, quixotic multiracial world. Youth against War and Fascism's magazine, the *Partisan*, reported that "somewhere in [Audrey's] busy schedule, she finds the time to care for a two-year old daughter, who like Audrey, is a veteran of numerous civil rights demonstrations."[59] And so we were. Beginning in 1968 she took me to Danbury, Connecticut's federal prison to visit twenty-two-year-old draft resister Eddie Oquendo of Blacks against Negative Dying, Committee for GI Rights, and YAWF. Oquendo told *Esquire*, "I support all oppressed people. A man who goes into the army, if he is Black is asked to kill his mother, brothers, sisters, like Detroit and Newark . . . I say Hell No, I Won't Go."[60] My parents sponsored the "Black Memorial March" against the Vietnam War, and Mommy and I went to anti-Vietnam War protests in New York: "Hell no, we won't go!"[61]

Fig. 10. Paula, "Hell No We Won't Go," Paula Marie Seniors Collection

I remember this moment of protesting the Vietnam War: Mommy and me in a grassy field with the other protestors, Mommy standing behind me, protecting me, her tiny hand with her plain gold wedding ring holding my hand at this march. I remember the Vietnam War as it unfolded on television: the horror of seeing children, men, and women killed, the bombs, the weaponry, the horror of the Vietnam War every night on full sickening display on TV. An antiwar lesson for sure as the war raged on and on for years, live on television. Terrifying!!!!

Audrey joined the YAWF-affiliated Prisoners Solidarity Committee and advocated for prisoners' rights, such as COINTELPRO targets Martin Sostre from Buffalo, incarcerated in 1967 for opening the Afro-Asian Bookstore, and Cleveland's Ahmed Rashad, jailed for opening the similar Afro Culture Shop and Bookstore.[62] In 1971, along with the committee, my mother created the pamphlet *Prisoners Call Out Freedom*. Perhaps she and I and our Workers World friends put it together at WWP. It detailed the abysmal conditions for Black and Hispanic prisoners at New York State's Auburn Correctional Facility: "punitive segregation," solitary confinement, and the work stoppage on November 2, 1970, that led to a prisoner rebellion two days later in which 1,700 prisoners confiscated the prison's keys, "seized the major buildings, held 35 hostages," and demanded better clothing and food, a better law library, and an end to prison guard violence. The Auburn 6—Hassan Sharrief El-Shabazz, Sharean, Kareem C'Allah, Leon Writer for the People, Aki El-Alim, and Mori—were charged with robbery and assault for the rebellion. They were beaten, maced, teargassed, and tortured by prison guards, with "the prison psychiatrist support[ing] their claim of mental torture." Through the Prisoners Solidarity Committee and YAWF Audrey helped hire lawyers for the defendants and advocated for their humane treatment.[63]

In November 1971 my mother (representing the Prisoner Solidarity Committee), along with coalition committee members (and African Americans) Mrs. Margaret Opie, coordinator of the People's Center for Peace and Justice; Dr. Willie Bryant, president of the Ossining NAACP; and John Holman of the Vietnam Veterans against the War, set out to inspect New York's Sing Sing Correctional Facility and speak with prisoners. Displeased that officials had reduced the committee to four, they maintained that "their mission was more important than pique over 'games the Man Plays.'" From the prisoners they learned of inedible food, inadequate clothing, and a subpar medical facility, which helped the committee advocate for the prisoners' rights.[64]

My mother's papers included two pamphlets detailing cases that resonated with her, given her self-defense ideology and her commitment to helping poor women: "The Right of Black Women to Defend Themselves against White Male Rape" detailed the 1974 North Carolina case of Joan Little, who murdered the white male prison guard who tried to rape her, and "The Story of Dessie Woods" detailed Woods's 1975 imprisonment in Georgia for murdering the white man who tried to rape her.[65] Through her work with the Prisoners Solidarity Committee and YAWF she advocated for prison reform and prisoner freedom.

From babyhood to adulthood we went to anti-apartheid marches, sponsored by the Workers World Party and the Youth against War and Fascism.

We protested for Cesar Chavez, Dolores Huerta, and the United Farm Workers. My mother taught me the importance of supporting causes by not buying the *delicious grapes*, showing our solidarity with the farm workers. We attended regular WWP meetings at the Twenty-Fifth Street big dusty loft with large slatted wooden floors. My mother taught me how to make copies on antiquated mimeograph copy machines, how to collate flyers and pamphlets by standing in our assigned spots and passing the papers to the next person. We signed petitions; she encouraged me and instilled in me the need to resist unjust conditions in the United States and the world.

In 1979 these lessons in protest and organization led me at age sixteen with my friend Felicia to organize a protest against the reinstatement of the draft in Washington, D.C. I don't know how we did it, but we seemed to have arranged buses or arranged for our Brooklyn Friends crew to get on the buses. We proudly participated in the protest.

My mother's social and political thought grew through her activism, her writing, and her role as a mother. Mommy positioned herself firmly at the center of African American motherhood as an organic intellectual and everyday political activist within the motherist frame.[66] For three years, my parents continued to fight Mae Mallory's extradition, while simultaneously fighting for African American equality in Cleveland.

On January 10, 1964, Monroe successfully extradited Mae and convicted her of kidnapping, with a prison sentence of sixteen to twenty years. We moved to Monroe and established Freedom House, 605 Brown Street, which, according to my father, was "heavily guarded and loaded with ammunition, guns, and rifles." The FBI reported that MDC received no support from Monroe's Black community, dismissing Negroes with Guns, Mrs. Johnson, and Monroe defendant Richard Crowder's Monroe Youth Action Committee. Crowder founded the Monroe Youth Action Committee to help young Black people and organize domestic workers into the Union County Women's League to advocate for equitable pay. The Monroe Youth Action Committee produced the newsletter *Freedom*, held study programs to teach Black history, organized desegregation demonstrations in downtown Monroe, and organized school boycotts, given Monroe had only one Black school. The FBI dismissed the Monroe Youth Action Committee because prominent African Americans like Dr. H. Creft condemned them. "Adult Negro leadership in the community does not approve of the Crowder group. Our children," he said, "are not taking part in the demonstrations."[67] Mrs. Johnson supported them, writing in *Did You Know?*, "The militant youth in Monroe need a lot of encouragement from freedom loving people everywhere, because they are surrounded with racist oppressors and Uncle Toms."[68] The FBI completely wrote off Monroe's African Americans' advocacy. The FBI reported that "information has been received that SENIORS has indicated he plans to leave Monroe in the near future and take Mae Mallory with him if he can get he[r] out on bond."[69] MDC gained Mallory's release with a $10,000 cash bond. Mae lived with our little family in Monroe and traveled widely. As the office manager of MDC, my mother created flyers discussing MDC's move to Monroe. With my father she created the pamphlet "From Lynch Threat to Frame-up" (September 16, 1964), which detailed the Monroe riot and the case against Mallory, Reape, and Crowder. My mother cleverly worked to gain international attention for the defendants and successfully publicized the case in the *Ghanaian Times* and the *West Indian Gazette*. In 1964 she helped organize Mae's national speaking tour beginning in Buffalo with a flyer that announced "Mrs. Mae Mallory, Black Freedom Fighter and Defendant in the Infamous Monroe 'Kidnapping' Case Will Also Speak."[70] My parents drafted letters soliciting speaking engagements, sent out documents concerning the tour, and thanked people for their donations.[71] Notwithstanding the repression, my parents, Mrs. Johnson, and the Monroe Defense Committee successfully made Mallory a household name.

Audrey also worked as the business manager and writer for *Did You Know?*[72] Around 1965 she joined Youth against War and Fascism, becoming the national editor of their magazine, the *Partisan*. She contributed several articles to the *Partisan* and *Did You Know?*, which offer an understanding of her social and political thought and how she wrote resistance.[73]

Writing Resistance and Saint Augustine

Ever since I was a little girl my mother inoculated me with the ideology of self-defense. "Paula, I believe in self-defense; passive resistance is ridiculous. You must always defend yourself. You never, ever let someone hit you and not hit them back." Like her idol Paul Robeson, she lived by the mantra of self-defense. Throughout my childhood my mother readily dismissed passive resistance. "Martin Luther King Jr. and his followers' passive resistance model is utterly and completely ludicrous." My mother had no regard for King and his kind.

Audrey Proctor Seniors's efforts concerning equity and social rights went beyond the Monroe Defense Committee and issues affecting Cleveland's Blacks. Through her writing in *Did You Know?* she brought attention to freedom struggles going on across the country in places such as Saint Augustine, Florida. In her article "The Open Forum" published in *Did You Know?* (April 18, 1964) she critiqued the freedom struggle in Saint Augustine, a site of intense massive resistance to desegregation of schools and public facilities. In 1964 Dr. R. N. Hayling, the African American advisor to the NAACP Youth Council and Saint Augustine's African American militant youth, a self-defense proponent, advocated for desegregation and an end to white racialized violence. The Ku Klux Klan, the John Birch Society, and white supremacist police maintained a stronghold in Saint Augustine. Sheriff L. O. Davis's "Mauncy's Raiders" terrorized the Black community. They beat Florida Normal School students during dime-store sit-ins while police watched. They kidnapped and assaulted Hayling and three others while a white woman shouted, "Kill them, castrate them." They burned Black families' homes and cars in retaliation for their children desegregating schools. President Lyndon B. Johnson and Martin Luther King Jr. refused aid. King repeatedly rebuffed Hayling's invitation to visit Saint Augustine.[74]

In response to white supremacist brutality, Hayling vowed, "I and others of the NAACP have armed ourselves. We will shoot first and ask questions later."[75] Like Monroe's Robert F. Williams, the NAACP's national office removed Hayling as advisor to the NAACP Youth Council.[76] In March 1964, similar to Williams's 1961 call on his friends, Hayling encouraged northerners to travel to Saint Augustine to participate in protest rallies with Black youth.[77] On March 29, 1964, 150 Black students marched to desegregate Ponce de Leon Motor Lodge. An interracial group led by Mrs. Mary Peabody (the mother of the Massachusetts governor) also marched separately. The police arrested half the students and Peabody.[78] Because the protesters included white folk, the media expressed great interest in the protests, not the common disinterest when the protesters and victims of white supremacist violence were African American. My mother responded to the Saint Augustine situation by writing "The Open Forum." "Wasn't it thoughtful of Mrs. Mary Peabody . . . to go to Jacksonville [Saint Augustine], Florida to help out those poor Negroes whom she said, 'needed help.' Before the proper lady from Boston decided those poor Negroes needed her help and support (it is my opinion) they were doing fine until the proper lady from Boston came."[79] Audrey's article chronicling the event exposed her radical thought through a careful analysis of Saint Augustine's freedom struggle. She revealed her support for Saint Augustine's Black militant youth, her commitment to self-defense, and her criticism of Martin Luther King Jr., the nonviolence movement, and Peabody, who represented white elite's "martyrdom" in the battle for African American rights.

Audrey sardonically admonished Mrs. Peabody, for she believed that Peabody and her ilk obscured the actions of Saint Augustine's Black youth, *who did not need her help*. My mother denounced the passive resistance movement's use of whites to gain sympathy and support, while successfully hiding African American agency and militancy. Ultimately the white liberal strategies of Peabody and her kind mischaracterized Blacks as victims as opposed to people with agency who fight back and take action for their own welfare. Audrey said that "after spending two nights and two days in jail and eating with her 'finger,'" Peabody posted bond then headed back to Boston, feeling that she "had done all she could in a good cause."[80] The *New York Times* reported that Peabody said of the St. Johns County Jail, "It is very pleasant here.... There are seven of us in one jail, all white women, and we have running water and a shower."[81] Audrey reproached Peabody: "By bringing respectability into the struggle in Jacksonville, the militant Black youth were all but forgotten. One must remember that it was the youth who took up the fight because the 'respectable leaders' of that city were somewhat slow."[82] My mother redefined respectability as a pejorative that encompassed opportunistic and self-serving white liberals like Peabody and Blacks like Martin Luther King Jr. She exposed the respectability trope as a system to keep Black radicals and militants in place, while Black leaders and white elites benefited from the trope through complacency and the maintenance of the status quo. My mother chastised "respectable leaders" for their inaction and for allowing Saint Augustine's militant Black youth to start the freedom movement and let them fend for themselves. By identifying them as militant, she revealed their self-defense stance and cast her lot and support with them.

Audrey also held the white liberal elite responsible for the aftermath of the protest. "What has happened to Jacksonville, now that Mrs. Peabody is back in Boston 'sipping tea?' We no longer hear anything about the youth who are in jail unable to post bond and leave town in a private plane." My mother let us know that the media silenced and abandoned the militant Black youth's story once whites like Peabody went back to their upper-class existence, leaving those who began the struggle behind to pick up the pieces and face white supremacists as they had done before the "good whites" visited. Audrey noted that Peabody and King "love to enjoy the compliments of 'how brave you are,' 'You really have courage,' 'I suppose that jail was simply awful.' While the poor kids are still in jail hoping that their struggle won't be forgotten as they are." My mother asserted that Peabody and King deliberately obscured the real issues of Black disenfranchisement, white supremacist violence, and the bravery of Black youth by refocusing the battle as that of elite white women's "struggle" for the "Negro" through her incarceration. My mother exposed the complicity of white liberals, Blacks like King, the state, and the massive resistance movement in successfully marginalizing Black working-class and poor communities. Audrey argued that they made a deliberate effort to prevent real social and political change. My mother then tried to recenter the story on the young people so that they are not forgotten. She proposed, "It is too bad that the militant youth of today cannot tell folks such as Mrs. Peabody to stay home and attend to her charities or her flower garden. Because folks like Mrs. Peabody and others are making sure that the struggle doesn't become a real revolution."

Writing Resistance and the Partisan

I first discovered that my mother was a member of Youth against War and Fascism and the national editor of their *Partisan* magazine through her FBI file. I later discovered that she was also the circulation manager from the J. B. Matthews Papers at Duke University. My mother never once shared this part of her life with me, of writing for the *Partisan*, or *Did You Know?* She did not tell me about her extraordinary life. The *Partisan* editors announced to readers that my mother was joining the magazine as an editor.

"INTRODUCING IN THIS ISSUE"

> Audrey Seniors is a 24-year-old New Orleans Southerner who recently returned to the Southern battlegrounds after a two-year stay in Cleveland, Ohio where, as secretary of the Monroe Defense Committee, she was actively engaged in the Mae Mallory extradition fight. Now in Monroe, North Carolina she continues her secretarial duties with the MDC while also serving as the business manager of *Did You Know?*, a militant bi-weekly Freedom publication edited by Mrs. E. A. Johnson, a long-time associate of the militant Robert Williams. Somewhere in her busy schedule she finds the time to care for a two-year-old daughter, who like Audrey is a veteran of numerous Civil Rights demonstrations.[83]

As a member of Youth against War and Fascism and as the national editor and circulation manager of the *Partisan*, Audrey Proctor Seniors committed herself fully to YAWF's tenets. In the April 1965 inaugural edition of the *Partisan*, the editors laid out their ideology:

> The history of our time is illumined in the glow of burning napalm, it is punctuated by the cries of Black children on the streets of Selma.... We identify with the force of the oppressed. We urge all sincere youth, regardless of their backgrounds, to make the same identification. *They* bombed North Vietnam; *we* must stop them. Our optimism for the future of this and all other generations is based on the confidence that the hardware and paraphernalia of the oppressors is not immovable, but the force of the oppressed rising to their freedom is irresistible.[84]

This creed aligned with my mother's stance of fighting oppression, colonialism, and hegemony. Her work with YAWF and her essays in the *Partisan* illustrate her commitment to battling U.S. and world repression. She wrote "Monroe, N.C." (April 1965) and "A Charlotte Widow" (July 1965) while living in Monroe and working on Mallory's case. The essays illuminate the African American condition in North Carolina, a state that tried to expunge African Americans through intimidation, lynching, decades-long sterilization projects (1919–1977, repealed 2003), and urban renewal's commitment to razing African American communities.[85] North Carolina's white supremacists worked to ensure Black underemployment and unemployment and the denial of social services, mirroring Cleveland. By 1963 over 50 percent of the Black population lacked a high school education because North Carolina promoted work over education, with a six-month school term.[86] State officials encouraged and helped maintain class divisions, by making economic and social deals with the African American middle and upper classes at the expense of the lower class.[87] Mommy lived in this environment and shared it with the *Partisan* readers. In "Monroe, N.C." my mother sets a moody tone. "There was no moon in sight. It had been pitch dark for some-time, and although I try not to leave the house after dark, I was at home by myself, out of cigarettes, and just had to go to the store for a pack. I had to hurry because I knew it was closing time at the store." Audrey shares the scene she happened upon:

> As I was quickly walking down the street, my attention was slightly diverted to the vacant lot adjoining the grocery building. A small group of Black men were standing there, appearing at first glance as if they were in a huddle around a bush fire to keep warm. I had seen the men many times before

during the daytime in one place or another. Most of the time they could be found on one of the main street corners in our small but unique community.

Her account reveals the utter idleness of these men. Instead of fully inhabiting their humanity and their environment, they haunt the streets of Monroe, just being. "Whether it is the coldest time of year or the hottest summer day, you can always see them outside either huddled by a fire or sitting on a huge wooden log, sometimes standing, sometimes sitting on the ground, facing the road, soaking up the sun, and surrounded by all the small children of the neighborhood."[88] While Audrey exposes their joblessness, she expresses a deep respect for them. She allows us to see hope and love as children encircle and engulf the men; with innocence, the children accept their existence.

Monroe's African American men experienced a history of economic subjugation. From the late 1800s, North Carolina Blacks competed with white workers pushed off the farms due to debt peonage. African Americans found themselves locked out of factory work, blocked from working in the textile industry, the furniture industry, and the cotton mills. White supremacist owners refused to hire Black workers, arguing that they must protect white womanhood from Black men *and* Black women.

Beneath the surface of the life scene that my mother happened upon was the stark reality of Black males' unemployed, impoverished, and homeless state—blocked from welfare aid, emasculated.[89] Seniors notes the state's complicity in keeping these Black men unemployed. "Each month the unemployment office 'officially' reports that there is no job problem here or anywhere else in Union County, North Carolina."[90] The state participated fully in spreading this false reality. Mommy had a copy of a 1963 "Population and Economy" report by Monroe's Community Planning Board, which asserted that Monroe's unemployment rates were low, no unemployment problem existed, and when unemployment occurred it was because of seasonal work, conveniently leaving out a discussion of how race impacted employment.[91] Audrey continues, "But viewing them from the community's true employment situation, there is no doubt in my mind that they have long been among the ranks of the unemployed. There is no doubt in anyone's mind that they rank among the poorest of the poor, the downtrodden, the dejected, the disinherited."[92]

My mother writes that it is not only the men that are threadbare and in disrepair; rather, the entire community is ragged, that the neighborhood's houses complement [the men's] tattered outfits. They are dark and dirty and dejected looking houses—a better description would be shacks. Many never have taken a painting. Indoor plumbing is a luxury few can afford. If there is water inside, it is usually a cold-water spigot. Jelly Coal or wood stoves supply the only warmth. They stand on dirt streets or the lowest class of roads, with no sidewalks. Trash lies there for weeks without being collected.[93]

What Audrey Seniors saw uncovered the harsh reality of Black life in Monroe. In 1963, 68.2 percent of Monroe's African American housing was substandard. The state denied Black communities basic services like trash pickup.[94]

Audrey writes about the African American neighborhood women. "Many women, some with plenty of children, occasionally stop near them to hold a conversation or call one of them to come over, but even when you are in the know it is hard to determine which of them are the wives of these seemingly homeless men."[95] These men were not merely "homeless" but sustained and preserved ties to romantic relationships, with wives, children, and families. Mommy illuminates the fact that these men most certainly were victims of the "man-in-the-house" and "substitute father" welfare laws that legally denied their comfort and love to Black women at home, because Black women could not get welfare if a man was in the house. These laws denied Black womanhood and manhood rights, working to control the Black body.[96] My mother pointed out, "Those who are more fortunate among the women find some remarkable way to take care of a house full of children on a $15 a week domestic job. Although it is a miracle how it is done (I haven't found out yet). How they still wish that they were at least on welfare."[97]

My mother lets us know that Monroe's African American women had to make it on their own in substandard low-wage jobs because of state control of their very being. White women refused to work with them in North Carolina's textile, apparel, and furniture industries. They found themselves locked out of managerial, office, and sales positions. Only one-fifth of Black women worked as professionals. Their only option was domestic labor, which didn't pay enough to support a family.[98] Audrey writes that African American women "know that if they could get any aid at all their men would have to leave for the chain gang to pay the State back for their pittance."[99] Heartrendingly she adds, "And then who would be there to give them at least the comfort of knowing that they are women and wanted."[100] She lets us know that due to their economic situation, the state controls their love lives, their relationships, and their rights as women. She tells us of the state's complicity in not only disallowing welfare and aid to Black women but also blocking the fundamental basic human need for love and the human touch. My mother continues that not only are these African American women and men forbidden basic human romantic relations, but that poverty and white supremacy kills their soul, their humanity. She shows why the men were at the store:

> The storekeeper was about to lock the doors for the night. As his assistants were taking out the garbage, I noticed the men were still there. And when I reached the checkout counter by the big store window, they seemed to be waiting in burning anticipation for something.... And then all of a sudden it happened. Before the storekeeper could get out of sight after dumping the last container of garbage, these men lit out to the trash piles so fast I was stunned. And with tears in my eyes although I've seen incidents of this nature so many times before, I realized what was going on.

Mommy was grief-stricken for the men.

> I was not looking at a pack of hungry dogs who with a decided purpose, attack our garbage cans at night and strew trash all over everywhere. I was not looking at alley cats who sometimes have the courage to attack those hungry dogs when they get there first. I was not looking at a pack of vicious, baby-eating big rats which are no strangers to tenement houses. I was looking at men, would be strong-bodied men. Men who speak back to me as I say hello to them. Respecting me as I respect them. Grown men who I see every-day.

She was bereft over their transformation into beasts, starving and ravenous. I know that my mother cried, overcome with emotion. I know that she was pained and saddened witnessing these Black men's shame, their downward spiral into the abyss of desperation. I am most certain that she counted my father and herself lucky, given their ability to support themselves and keep the state out of their lives. I know my mother questioned the humanity of the storekeeper and wondered, as I wonder now, why they did not just put the leftover food out nicely so that the men could maintain their humanity. The storekeeper participated in maintaining their wretched state. Audrey ended "Monroe" with these words. "There is no doubt in my mind that they want sincerely to be and would be good providers for their wives and children if they had a chance to make an honest living. But there is no chance for them in Monroe, or in many other Black communities across the South. There isn't even a chance to be nothing but a man."[101]

Throughout my life, I witnessed my mother's loving kindness and hospitality. When I was a little girl our Brooklyn apartment at 220 Montgomery Street was filled with friends coming for day visits and staying overnight. Workers World and YAWF member Mary Ann Weissman came to our home often. Mary Ann, like Mae, faced incarceration for protesting the court-martial of three antiwar soldiers at Fort Sill.

A Native American friend visited often; his name is lost to me in the ethers of time. One morning he entranced us with how in upstate New York he and other American Indian Movement members battled the FBI and U.S. soldiers and beat them!!! Then he and my mother got into a friendly debate. "You know," he said, "African slaves should have fought back like we did upstate." He had to have known better than to say that to Mommy—erudite, organic intellectual self-defense advocate. She said, "We did fight back— Harriet Tubman freeing slaves with her rifle, Sojourner Truth, Frances E. W. Harper, Sarah P. Remond, Nat Turner, and Blacks at Harpers Ferry like Osborne P. Anderson. We always fought back, and we fought with you my Brother and our Native Brothers and Sisters." Oh, they carried on in their who-was-the-most-fierce-warrior-against-white-oppression verbal battle, laughing and one-upping each other. He told us of his times at the UN to argue for equity, only to see how the Cold War worked . . . the American and Russian contingents were friends. He concluded that powerful whites stick together.

In Brooklyn my mother was always helping people. In 1985 I moved out of my mother's home at 20 St. Paul's Court, apartment 3G, having graduated from City College of New York. A young mother with a young son was having a very hard time emotionally and economically given her mother's death and life circumstances. My mother without hesitation gave her a home in my old room. Her son lived elsewhere. The precariousness of the woman's situation, her proximity to homelessness and inability to physically be there for her son was a concept that I did not grasp. I can't even imagine being separated from my mother. This young Brooklyn mother, I am sure, reminded Mommy of Monroe's women (1964–1965). Their similarities of circumstance resonated for my mother. I can honestly say at twenty-two I lacked compassion and was very resentful and jealous of the attention my mother bestowed on this young mother and her son. I was an obviously very self-absorbed twenty-two-year-old. I did not verbally express my feelings, but I acted out, with rudeness to my mother's guest. My mother explained to me the woman's circumstances many times. "Paula, her mother died, she has a son who she is not able to care for at this point in her life, she has nowhere to live." Then as she should have, she admonished me, "BE KIND." Mommy taught me through her actions: opening her home to the woman's young son when he visited his mother, making sure he felt cared for, making sure that this young mother maintained her relationship with her boy. My mother's conduct taught me compassion; she taught me love.

"A Charlotte Widow" reminded me of the Brooklyn mother who my own mother took in. My mother's essay weaves connecting fibers of compassion and care for the young Brooklyn mother and her son in 1985 to the women in "Monroe" in 1965 and the unemployed ravaging men. She begins, "We found [the Charlotte Widow and her five children] in very poor condition and living in unbearable surroundings—a section of Charlotte called Brooklyn. Brooklyn is 238 acres of oppression: pure alum and poverty."[102] My mother visited the Charlotte Widow under the auspices of Mrs. Johnson's Crusaders Association for Relief and Enlightenment, offering food, clothing, supplies, and enlightenment, supplying the mother's needs.[103] The Charlotte Widow was a college-educated thirty-six-year-old whose husband found himself unemployed with a heart condition before his death. Audrey writes that the family's condition proved very bleak while the husband lived. They could not pay their bills or their rent and could not feed the family. They could not "get any relief from the city. They were told that there wasn't an emergency fund to aid them as long as the father was at home."[104] Welfare workers used the "man-in-the-house" and "substitute father" rules to deny them welfare aid, encouraging the husband to abandon his family:

> The father out of desperation turned to the only other alternative he felt left for him—robbery, to feed his family. He was killed trying. In fact, it was reported that when the cop shouted to him to "Stop or I'll shoot," he said, "Go ahead and kill me." As his brother relayed around that time, "He felt that he would help them more being dead than alive. At least now they could get on welfare."

My mother selflessly helped this woman and her children. "At 36 she had given birth to ten children, two are dead and three are with relatives."[105] My mother used CARE donations, doing what North Carolina's government would not do: offering help to North Carolina's desperate.[106] Several months later my mother checked on them. She described the children in "tatters with no shoes on their feet," no money "to buy food or anything else." My mother wrote of their substandard housing and absence of medical care for an infant whose right side was paralyzed. The mother was told "there isn't anything that could be done now" for the baby. Having learned that this woman had attended two years of college, my mother noted, "If that is happening to a former two-year college 'coed' we wondered about the plight of the high school graduate; and thought to ourselves, 'Heaven help the high school drop-out!'"[107] The widow's daughter's public education proved a setup for failure.

> Her twelve-year old daughter is fast falling under the influences of the vices that are produced by the onerous environment which plagues them daily. She is getting encouragement to stay in school. [The Charlotte Widow said] "They are promoting her with D's each year, and she is learning nothing. When I questioned the teacher about passing her with D's she told me 'It is better to keep them in their age group.'"

With North Carolina's 45 percent dropout rate, by undereducating the girl, the teacher in fact encouraged her to leave school.[108] "She is quite worried about her girl and fears that she will soon run away from home for good and fall under very bad influence."[109]

Seniors offers the history of Charlotte's Brooklyn. Built in the 1800s for the "better classes" of African Americans, "[Brooklyn] is the seat of Daddy Grace's biggest kingdom, all decorated in red, white, and blue—'The House of Prayer for all Peoples.'"[110] Daddy Grace, a Cape Verdean immigrant, established his Pentecostal church in Charlotte's Brooklyn in 1923/1924.[111] My mother writes, "It is the only large Black group that gets the full cooperation and sanction of the local power structure." His members "put on a show, dressed in full 'heavenly' regalia [they] parade with pomp and ceremony.... Clearly, it is not the answer to the problems, but is a dose of narcotic medicine people take in for lack of something more meaningful and beneficial."[112] Obviously my mother felt that Daddy Grace was a charlatan who did no real good works for the majority of African Americans living in Brooklyn. I am sure he gave my mother another reason for her atheism. The Charlotte Widow lived down a dead-end street—Short Alley as my mother described it—"unpainted, shotgun houses, beer bottles, trash and filth of all descriptions. From the Alley one can see the spire of one of the finest white churches in Charlotte." My mother wrote that the Widow's social worker, acting as an urban renewal agent, tried to "get her to move out of one slum and into another where the rent is higher," but the widow told my mother, "I won't move from one house which the city is going to tear down into another which they will want to tear down within a short time after I have moved in.... They are only moving those from houses they are tearing down now. It may be another two years before they come to me."[113] The widow remained acutely aware of the urban renewal plans and how it would affect her and her children.[114] Mommy noted that Short Alley was in full view of the urban renewal projects of Charlotte: "Just a few blocks away there are new shopping centers, office buildings, an expressway and many other ultra-modern structures that blend with the old to further confuse the tattered children in the slums next door who can't seem to realize why they are as they are in the face of this progress."[115]

Notwithstanding his alliance with white power, by the 1960s the city demolished Daddy Grace's House of Prayer, razed Brooklyn using federal money, and replaced it with a city park and government plaza buildings. A visit to Charlotte in 2023 revealed a downtown mall where Brooklyn once was, a street sign reading Brooklyn Village, and the Levine Museum's virtual tour of Brooklyn.[116] My mother witnessed this urban renewal firsthand. "Before we left [the Widow] begged us to come back again and help her do what she could to get them out of this hell."[117]

In 1964 my mother continued to fight and rally for justice and human rights for African Americans in Cleveland, Monroe, the two Brooklyn's, and across the United States. She fought ferociously for Mae Mallory. Mae's white supporter Carla Hart wrote to Harry Golden in Charlotte concerning my mother.

> The Mae Mallory case pains me deeply. It reminds me of the Scottsboro case, which was a frame-up.... I think Mae Mallory was framed because she was a leader in the integration movement.... I must tell you about my visit to Monroe. The committee to defend Mae Mallory has their headquarters in a very poor run down house. The people are so sincere. The Negro woman [Audrey Proctor Seniors] who is helping Mae Mallory is 23 with a husband and a baby. They have traveled with Mae Mallory all over the country in regard to this case. This woman is one of the most intelligent women I have ever met. She has a small baby who is adorable.... This young woman in Monroe has read two of your books and liked them very much.[118]

Hart conveys my mother's intelligence, alluding to my mother's immense knowledge of socialist theory, revolutionary thought, and history. She positions my mother within the cult of true womanhood and cult of true motherhood tropes by discussing her motherhood and womanhood coupled with her activism, dismissing the state's construction of Black womanhood as deficient. Hart does not mention my mother's self-defense stance, her self-defense training by RAM, and the probability that my mother most certainly was armed. Carla Hart's letter reveals that women of different nationalities, generations, and classes built alliances to protect African American motherhood and womanhood from the state through self-defense and activism while refusing exclusion from their rights as women and mothers.

My Brooklyn

In 1965 my mother, my father, and the Monroe Defense Committee won Mallory's case due to racial discrimination in the jury selection. Our family moved to Brooklyn, New York while Mae and Pat moved back to Harlem. Mine was a different Brooklyn. But my mother never forgot Charlotte's Brooklyn and those who had to live lives like "the Charlotte Widow" and the men and women of Monroe.

Part III   Internationalizing the Struggle

Chapter 8

Pat Mallory, Black Nationalist Rebel Woman
Social and Political Awakening in Tanzania and Guyana

A memory of Ebbets Field—snazzy, jazzy nineteen-year-old Pat in her minidress sitting with me, age five, casting a shine on the room, a shine on me, showering me with affection.

In high school Pat Mallory built up her confidence and emerged as a Black Nationalist Rebel Girl, an organic intellectual, and a community feminist. Through self-healing she learned to love herself, her Black beauty, her Black aesthetic, and her intellect. As a Black Nationalist Rebel Girl Pat used education and activism as a form of self-healing. In 1963, from her prison cell, Mae took notice of Pat's blossoming persona. "Pat is threatening not to attend her graduation. She claims she does not want to sit through such a long-drawn-out affair. Her school is huge, and I admit her graduating class is large, nevertheless, I think Pat should attend." Mae disapproved of Pat's new independent spirit. "She claims that if she is forced to go, she is going to wear dungarees under her gown and a skull cap under her mortar board. Her whole gang plans to dress in this fashion. Knowing Pat and that bunch she travels with, this is the way they probably will dress. It will embarrass my mother to no end."[1]

When Pat graduated from high school, she had no plans concerning her life. She knew, like so many in the African American community, *she had to go to college or university* by the Black Mother's Decree. Mae wrote with the aspirational dreams of a mother denied a college education and a life as a scholar that "the most important thing is that she graduates. She has been accepted to Bronx Community College. I hope she will be able to bring her grades up so that she can continue in a better college for a degree."[2] Pat recalled, "When I graduated from high school, I immediately went to Bronx Community College. I was floundering. My mother wasn't there, I didn't have any direction, *but I did know I had to go to college.*"[3] As a Black Nationalist Rebel Girl, a definitive generational shift occurred with Patricia Mallory given the age differences between her and Mrs. Johnson (twenty-nine years older), Mae (eighteen years), and Audrey (five years). Audrey Proctor Seniors's sisterhood and political lessons and Mae's teachings infused Pat with an African American woman radical ideology—the impetus for an activist life. The age differences meant that Pat's experience proved radically different from these women. The education received by Johnson, Seniors, and Mae did not reflect Pat's, given their lives in activism and the racial roadblocks that prevented them from going to college. By Black Mother's Decree, Pat attended college.

Pat eventually dropped out of Bronx Community College, but she found her way back to higher education. She says, "There was an organization called Educational Alliance and they hooked you up." Pat received an associate's degree from Manhattan Community College. She attended SUNY Stony Brook "because it was like the 'Berkeley of the East,' you know. It was progressive and all this kind of stuff." At the school, students participated in sit-ins, protested for African American civil rights, and against the Vietnam War.[4] Pat fit right in. She was armed and ready to fight for social and political change within an academic framework, with like-minded Black classmates. Pat noted, "Of course, all of us were African oriented." Pat majored in anthropology with a sub-major in secondary education. She took on leadership roles: "I was the president of the Black Student Union at Stony Brook." When Pat attended college, African American and Majority World students across the country organized a network, sharing information and organizing strategies to make changes on their campuses. They went to conferences, invited speakers to their campuses, put on Black cultural events, and organized Black student unions. They demanded a more equitable education in order to "survive the white college experience," refusing exclusion at their institutions.[5] Some like at Cornell University took up arms and occupied buildings to force administrators to meet their demands.[6] These students and like-minded white students challenged administrators to increase the numbers of students of color on campus. They pushed to hire faculty of color and fought to create ethnic and African American studies departments.[7]

Pat pushed these Black political agendas at Stony Brook. She remembered, "My three roommates and a couple of us went to the president of the university and said that we needed to have more Black students."[8] Pat and her roommates' actions proved successful because "three hundred [new students] came the next year. Those students became involved. We did what people did in the 1960s on campuses." In 1968 Pat as leader of the Black Student Union/Black Students United and the other members demanded a Black studies department.[9]

> After months of patience and good faith we the Black Students United at Stony Brook . . . demand a signed agreement by the Administration to provide the necessary resources to establish a Black Institute . . . a degree-granting Institute of Black Studies . . . [with] a maximum amount of autonomy in the university system. [The institute should] provide Black students an educational standing necessary for them to assume the roles of leadership in the community, eliminating the Social, Economic, and Political problems in Black America. . . . We feel that the Black experience shall become part of the mainstream of the American Educational system.

Pat and her comrades received a Black studies department, which still exists to this day. Predating Cornell University's African American students' successful demand of African-centered dorms at Ujamaa Residential College in 1972, Pat and her classmates demanded a Black dorm (1967–1968). Pat said, "Some of the students were not as radical and they were saying 'that's like segregation,' 'you're segregating yourself.' We argued philosophical arguments about the Black dorm. Well, the white folks were glad to give us our own dorm," she laughed. "They gave us the worst dorm on the campus."[10]

Attending Stony Brook, becoming the president of the Black Student Union/Black Students United, and participating in Afrocentric student activism allowed Pat to self-heal.[11] Pat attended the Black Student Convention at Jersey City University. As minister of the Culture Committee, Pat organized an Afrocentric fashion show "to the driving rhythms of the conga drums," featuring models in dashikis, Nigerian prints, and Afrocentric jewelry.[12]

Pat wrote about the murder of Martin Luther King Jr. in her article "Where Were We?" for the *Statesman* student newspaper: "One of the things that impresses people about Stony Brook, is its progressiveness. It boasts being the 'Berkeley of the East.' What I consider progressive is not present at Stony Brook. . . . The fact that the 'moods' and dances continued after the death of Dr. King is evidence of that." Pat bemoaned the administrators' lackluster response to his murder. They lacked understanding why the

Black students mourned. Pat continued, "We still must hand in our papers, study for our midterms, in spite of the grief his death caused us." She called out the white students for their continuous partying while Black students grieved.

> Somebody asked me if I was going to a particular mood and asked another person why she looked so gloomy. Aren't these questions a bit out of place in lieu of the murder of Dr. Martin Luther King, Jr., just a few days ago? I'm sure not many people went to moods or showed their 32's when the nation mourned President Kennedy's death. And yes, I am taking the liberty of comparing King with Kennedy. They both were the best upholders of the American Dream. They were killed because of it.[13]

What remains interesting in this passage is Pat's emerging individual thought. Her ideology separated her from the ideological frame held by Mae, Mrs. Johnson, and Audrey Proctor Seniors. Pat's ideas surrounding King and Kennedy differed, for while these women were mortified by their murders, they did not believe that King or Kennedy were great men. They rejected King's passivism and called out President Kennedy and Robert F. Kennedy for their lack of support of African Americans and the incarcerated Mae. Mae said at the time that the president was "wrong as hell about keeping me in jail."[14] Pat's writing shows a shift—a growing ability to share her thoughts, feelings, and ideologies, separate as they were from those of Audrey, Mae, and Ethel. This demonstrates healthy growth in a direction different from her elders. Pat lamented white students lackluster response: "More disgusting than the general attitude of the student body was the fact that very few of them showed up at the Memorial Services. A one hour tribute seemed to have been too much to pay for a great man. Where were the wearers of the Dove? Where were the wearers of the Kennedy and McCarthy buttons?" She brought to light the controversies of the white free-love generation that existed at Stony Brook and asked, "What then is more important—a liberal stand on pot or a liberal position on freedom?" Pat reveals disappointment that Stony Brook did not live up to her expectations, that it was a microcosm embodying racism and racist ideologies of the larger world. "Several students told me of prejudice and apathy on this campus. I laughed because I thought I knew better. Now I see these accusations are true. It's foolish to expect people to pay respects to a man if they don't feel the need to. It is also deceiving for Stony Brook to proudly bear the name of a progressive institution."[15] As happens with all of us who look for a utopia in our lives, Stony Brook burst Pat's bubble. Stony Brook, the administration, and white classmates revealed themselves as cogs in the wheel of white supremacy.

Pat's Stony Brook activism highlights the role of African American women activists on college and university campuses who demanded Black studies departments and Black dormitories. Pat's activism and writing elucidates her ability to self-heal from a traumatic childhood. She used lessons given to her and Iris from Audrey Proctor Seniors in the Monroe Defense Committee; lessons learned from Mae and Mrs. Johnson of raging against injustice; lessons learned in high school and Cleveland of being exhilaratingly young and blissfully joyous. These lessons allowed her to fully immerse herself in her Black Nationalist Rebel Girl identity. They allowed her to metamorphosize into a Black Nationalist Rebel Woman. Attending Stony Brook and participating in student activism centered on Afrocentric experience restored Pat. Pat developed further by going to Tanzania and Guyana as part of her university experience. Traveling helped Pat fully develop an identity seeped in African socialism, Black nationalism, Black feminism, community feminism, to become an organic intellectual. Pat fully engaged in world revolutions.

Tanzania and Guyana

In 1961 Tanzania gained independence from Britain. With independence Prime Minister Nyerere and the Tanzanian government adopted *Ujamaa* (*Ujamaa na Kujitegemea*): extended family and self-reliance. Nyerere formalized Ujamaa in 1964 and 1967 with the Arusha Declaration.[16] Ujamaa became the foundation for African socialism, moving from being a colonial subject to an independent African nation. The government established shambas—food gardens for each home—because, as Pat recalled, "Nyerere said there's no need for anybody to starve in Tanzania, and he was correct. Because there was so much land."[17] They also established Ujamaa villages, where people lived communally, having easy access to schools and hospitals. The government took over all the schools and universities. Ujamaa villages made life easier.

African socialism appealed greatly to Pat. She recalls, "I went [to Africa] because it was African socialism. I wanted to be part of that. It was an adventure. I believed in African socialism: sharing the wealth of the nation. Taking care of people, nobody getting more than what they needed or deserved. Making sure that everyone is taken care of. Medicine was free—I was shocked."

The Tanzanian government invited African Americans to Tanzania to help build the country. According to Seth Markle, "In 1971, the Tanzanian government passed a resolution to 'establish fraternal revolutionary relations with those Black American citizens fighting for justice and human equality.'"[18] African Americans initially went to Ghana. The coup led them to abandon Ghana for Tanzania to connect the African American experience with African socialism. Lessie Tate writes that African American political refugees, intellectuals, Black nationalists, and former SNCC members moved to Tanzania. SCLC director Hosea Williams traveled to Tanzania in 1971 to link Africans and African Americans through educational and cultural exchanges. Watts, California, beauty pageant queens Essieba Hayes, Twyla Wells, and Maggie Small toured Tanzania in 1972 to conjoin African and African American women's struggles.[19] Angela Davis, Stokely Carmichael, Eldridge Cleaver, Amiri Baraka, Malcolm X, Robert F. Williams, and Stokely Carmichael visited, while Pan-Africanist scholar Walter Rodney held a professorship at the University of Dar es Salaam in 1965 and from 1969 to 1974. African American "strategically placed CIA agents" also traveled to Tanzania.[20] Having experienced state repression, Pat remained acutely aware of the machinations going on to suppress African socialism and the work of African Americans in Tanzania. Pat recalled,

> Tanzania was under attack by the West because they were not trying to be colonialized. They were talking about African socialism. The West didn't want to hear anything about that.... Nyerere was trying to get rid of capitalism and the capitalist kind of thinking. There was a lot of sabotage by people looking to gain wealth. The U.S. government sabotaged Tanzania as well. Tanzania was rich. It had diamonds, the lake was powerful, which was beautiful.

The West did not want to lose these resources. They used agent provocateurs and the CIA to spy on African Americans in Tanzania. They destabilized the country, as they did in the Belgian Congo. Notwithstanding the threat the CIA posed to African Americans, over seven hundred Blacks relocated to Tanzania, "a hotbed of Pan-African and Revolutionary activity."[21]

Mrs. Johnson's call for world revolutions and Audrey Proctor Seniors's lessons to Pat and Iris concerning world revolutions set the stage for Pat's trips to the continent. As a community feminist and organic intellectual Mae set the foundation for Pat's trip. Pat recalls that in 1968, as a member of the Republic of New Afrika, "my mother had actually gone to Africa to a conference with Rob Williams and some other people." They conferred the RNA presidency on Williams.[22] In Tanzania Mae stated that she "was granted the possibility of developing a repatriate's commune to train Blacks here for the military." She wrote, "We might yet realize an African Nation here with Rob Williams as President." She unwittingly proposed African American colonialism like that of Liberia.[23] On her way to Tanzania Mae took the Pan American Airways Africa route, stopping in Dakar, Senegal. "The air was fresh, the day young, and I'm home in Africa." The route took Mae to Monrovia, Liberia, where she recalled "the one and only great letdown and total disappointment. Liberia is a huge Firestone plantation, settled by mispatriotic Negroes who are loyal to their American slave masters." Pan Am took Mae to Accra, Ghana, and Lagos, Nigeria, where she referenced the Nigerian Civil War (1967–1970), writing, "Deep in my heart, I hope the hostilities will cease in Nigeria, and the Biafrans can go about the business of fighting the real enemy," colonialism and imperialism.[24] She traveled to Entebbe, Uganda, and Nairobi, Kenya, "the home of the Mau Mau." Mae illuminated the Mau Mau Uprising (1952–1960) where they fought European colonialists, settlers, and the British army for independence.[25] Mae asserted, "the whites told stories about the Mau Mau that they thought would make us ashamed. Instead, our chests rose proudly at the report of each racist head that was felled off his shoulders by a hard-swung panga. Kenya home of Odinga, Jomo Kenyatta." Mae wrote,

> [The] Next stop and destination was Dar-es Salaam, Tanzania. Six hundred miles per hour was not quite fast enough for me. I pushed that plane a little faster until I could see the lights of Dar-es Salaam. Finally, oh finally, I'm going to walk on real African soil and not just airport concrete. What should I do? I can't just walk-through customs like the other passengers, that would not be a fitting return after four hundred years. Should I take off my shoes and let the sand run through my toes? Should I burst out singing, laughing, or crying?[26]

As the head of the Black Student Union, Pat and her classmates "asked the school to pay for us to go to Tanzania, because we didn't pay to come here, so you all pay for us to go back. We had scholarships to go to Tanzania." Because of her connections and her travels, Mae was in a great position to help Pat and her classmates realize their African dream. Mae and Pat arranged for people to make the trip. Monroe Defense Committee members, the Republic of New Afrika's minister of state and foreign affairs Wilbur Grattan, his three sons and Iris, and Pat's classmates traveled with Pat to Tanzania. Pat remembers "two Black university staff people [went too]. I don't know if they were planted there, or whether they were sincere, but they went."

> I remember going with my mother to the airport to see Pat off. I was five and a lot of people were there to bid her safe travels to the mythical Africa. It was very exciting and thrilling. The bright whiteness of the airport terminal walls where the door led to the airplane. These were the times when you could go to the gate to see your people off. We waited for the plane to arrive. We hugged Pat and waved goodbye as she stepped on the plane. It was exhilarating.

Pat gained a rich and life-changing experience filled with adventure and fun. Pat recalls, "We went to the university with some youth group we got hooked up with. Of course all of us got proposed to." Of seeing Kilimanjaro she said, "Oh My God, it was like a vision. Sometimes it looked like you saw it and sometimes it looked like it wasn't there. It was such a beautiful thing." The lushness of Tanzania's "plants with these huge leaves, it was just amazing." Pat and her friends encountered racism and colorism, African style. Pat and her classmates found that Tanzania and the African continent were not immune to the color caste system of racial hierarchy. As Pat recalls, "We went to donate blood at the hospital. Grattan said, the newspapers were taking pictures. One of my roommates Joyce was very light-skinned and Grattan said her picture is going to be in the newspaper, *and it was*. Many of us donated blood, but they put Joyce's picture in the paper. It ran deep." The legacy of color caste, a powerful method in maintaining control over the colonized, "by allowing for and justifying unequal distribution of resources and the exploitation of the powerless," continued after Tanzania's independence.[27]

As visitors, Pat and her friends felt and also experienced the hostility and hatred that Indians held for Africans. Pat noted, "The Indians of course felt they were better than the African people." According to James Brennan, the largest population of non-African-descended people in Tanzania were Indians whose presence predated European colonialism. They practiced endogamy or *jatis*, which precluded their assimilation into Black African culture and life. They bought into colonial hegemony and held incredible wealth as landowners, craftsmen, clerks, artisans, merchants, and shopkeepers. They also worked as civil servants whom the British paid more than African civil servants. This encouraged friction and conflict between the two groups, to maintain white colonial power. The Indians believed in their superiority to the Africans. All of this walled the two groups apart.[28]

Pat said, "The Indians ran a lot of these shops, so I didn't mind stealing from the store." I looked at Pat in shock, which led her to respond. "Yeah, I stole things from the stores! *Yes, I did*!!" Pat and her friends experienced and witnessed hatred by Indians against Africans. In her youthful swagger, Pat rebelled against a Black inferiority ideology by stealing from those whom she saw as oppressors of Africans and African Americans: the Indians. Pat recounts, "They had no respect for the Tanzanians, for the Africans at all. NO RESPECT. When you lined up at the post office or the bank, they'd walk right in front of you. No respect for the fact that you were there already. They would do things like that. It was terrible."

What would lead one group of color to treat another in this manner? Classified as Native under German rule (1890–1916) but as nonnative under British rule (1916–1961), Indians sought whiteness privileges, expecting to be treated as Europeans. Between 1916 and 1920 they even petitioned to make German East Africa an Indian colony, to "share the white man's burden." Indians fully embraced a colonialist ideology and disdained Black Africans. By the time of independence, Indians controlled 80 percent of the wholesale and retail trade and did not embrace Ujamaa "nation building activities."[29]

When Pat visited Tanzania she'd encountered an Indian superiority ideology. She said, "They were placed there by the British, they viewed themselves as the merchants, they had status above the Blacks. That was my bid to even the score, stealing stuff out of their stores. Yeah, then again young, and wild." Pat says the Indians' attitude toward the Africans "was one of the reasons that Idi Amin expelled them, but that's a whole other thing." Actually, it was a very similar thing. The actions of brutal and vicious dictator Idi Amin in Uganda and Ugandan Indians' attitude paralleled the situation in Tanzania. After Tanzanian independence a great push to expel the Indians occurred. Indigenous Tanzanian Africans grew tired of the Indians' racism and rejection of Ujamaa. Although there was not a great expulsion like in Amin's Uganda, in 1969 the Tanzanian government deported some Indians, and others found themselves severely oppressed by citizens and the new government.[30]

> *I remember when Pat returned from the mythical Africa. My mother and I went to the airport. I recall the utter excitement when Pat got off the plane. Pat gave me a doll with African garb and a beautiful wooden African tea set with beautiful carvings—a teapot, teacups, and saucers just the right size for my little girl's hands. The tea set came with a beautifully carved wooden tray—colonial and imperialistic relics, a Europeanized version of an African*

doll and an African version of a European pastime: tea. I discovered that it was not just the mythical Africa but in fact Tanzania that Pat visited, as Pat told me during our talks.

Following the road map laid out to her by her mother, Audrey Proctor Seniors, Mrs. Johnson, and other Black women activists, Pat continued on her quest to see and participate in world revolutions. When Pat returned from Tanzania, she determined to travel to countries that liberated themselves from colonialism and imperialism. Pat traveled to Guyana. Like Tanzania, Guyana had a complicated history with racialized hierarchies set in place by Europeans that pitted Africans against Indians who positioned themselves above Africans.

Since its independence in 1966, the People's National Congress Party ruled Guyana. Under Prime Minister Forbes Burnham they advocated for cooperative socialism, a socialism unlike that which existed in the West or in the East. As in Tanzania, the Guyanese government courted African American Black Power militants and granted Black freedom fighters asylum while silencing Black radical scholars like Walter Rodney.[31] In 1971 Pat traveled to Guyana under Mae's influence. Pat said, "There was the connection with my mother because she was involved with the people from Guyana and ASCRIA." FBI files indicate that Mae traveled to Georgetown, Guyana, in 1970 to the Pan-African and Black Revolutionary Conference. There Mae made connections with members of the African Society of Cultural Relations with Independent Africa (ASCRIA).[32] Pat notes, "I belonged to ASCRIA, a Black liberation movement, and they were having a conference. I went to their conference and stayed with some people my mother knew in Georgetown." ASCRIA, a Guyanese left-wing socialist Black Power organization, proposed a "non-capitalist revolution," rejected the colonialist mentality of African inferiority, and promoted a "cultural revolution." They encouraged Afro-Guyanese to actively embrace their African heritage.[33] Their goal included heralding Black history, Black achievement, economic uplift, and economic independence like Tanzania's Ujamaa and U.S. Black Power movements.[34] Pat toured the country and traveled to the bush, "which was kind of scary, but that was why I was in Guyana." She learned Kwe Kwe songs and attended cultural events and meetings. The main effect of her stay in Guyana was that Pat, age twenty-six, found her beauty, finally breaking the chains of color caste. She embraced herself as a full-bodied, dark-skinned beautiful Black woman, as her self-description illustrates.

Things shifted for me. I mean dramatically shifted in 1971. In Guyana it was so hot, even your shoes were hot. When I got back to the States, we were living in the projects, I walked by the bathroom mirror, and I turned around, and I looked at myself. I was JET BLACK. I didn't realize because I'm not used to looking in the mirror. *I startled myself.* I turned around and looked at myself in the mirror *again*. I said, boy, did I get Black. I went closer, and I started smiling and my teeth were so white, and I just loved what I saw [laughter]. Every time I walked by, I would look in the mirror and I would start smiling. Oh God, it was ridiculous [laughter]. After years of trying to contradict this stuff, and resist this ridiculousness, and seeing the beauty that really is Black, it sort of sunk in. You know, yeah, that's what happened.

Beauty ideals changed during the late 1960s and 1970s with Black nationalism and the Black Power movement glorifying dark-skinned beauty. Lessons Pat learned from the Yoruba priestess Mama KeKe, Miss Natural Standard of Beauty contests, the Grandassa Models, and the Naturally Shows finally seeped into Pat's psyche, cemented by her transformation to JET BLACK. Her trip to Guyana helped Pat heal and mend from her traumatic childhood. It helped her move forward with her life, to move toward change—to move permanently to Tanzania.

In 1972 my mother wrote to Pat asking about her experiences in Tanzania. "What are you teaching? Is the living cheaper than in the States? I wish I had the do re mi to make it there for a while.... I think that the Tanzanians are going to wonder what in the hell are you people trying to say."

In 1969, at the invitation of Mae, Bob and Janet Moses moved to Tanzania to raise their family. Their daughter Maisha said, "The time in Tanzania helped my father recover from the pressures of the movement.... That kind of openness, living without pressure, was healing."[35] Like the Moses family, in 1971 Tanzania offered Pat a place of rebirth and renewal. "It was an escape, a relief to get out of the U.S. It was a change. You could just feel free.... I moved there to stay. I taught four years, well actually five years.... I think it was probably the best time of my life." Before moving to Tanzania, Pat attended New York University to receive a master's degree in primary education. In the spirit of Ujamaa, Nyerere's government invited African Americans like Pat to teach at former missionary schools established by the Maryknoll Sisters (1948, 1958). Some nuns stayed on as teachers.[36] Pat says, "I went to teach English, language, composition, and Latin in Mwanza at

Nganza Secondary School.... I just lived a life as a schoolteacher, supporting the government in that way, not taking an expatriate's salary, but being paid local wages like everyone else." In Tanzania Pat embodied an organic intellectual studying the world she adopted as her own and disseminating her ideas, thoughts, and desires to her students. She taught as a political act.[37] At first she lived with white American Maryknoll Sisters. "[Laughter] Oh my gosh, I was seething. I was not happy about that. They tried to be very friendly [even making cornbread]. I wanted that cornbread so badly. I was not eating no cornbread from no white American nuns. I was miserable." Pat soon moved into her own house on campus "surrounded by all kinds of BEASTS that would invade on occasion, baboons, snakes, hyenas, and monkeys." Pat was elated to be surrounded by nature, to escape the hustle of New York, the high-rise apartment with families stacked up on one another—to escape for a slower pace, for leisure time with nature, wildlife, flora, and fauna in all their beauty. Unrestrained from constant FBI surveillance, Pat felt free, felt alive, felt hope and joy. The Tanzanian government worked to discard the "discriminatory educational policies of British Colonial rule," the Overseas Cambridge Examination. They saw an increase in school enrollments, changing the curriculum to move beyond British and European history toward African history. Teachers like Pat worked toward these goals. Pat used Donny Hathaway's song "Magnificent Sanctuary Band" in the classroom, which was in line with Tanzanian traditions of celebrations of life through song and music. The students thrived under Pat: "I was giving them Charles Dickens, along with the African Writer's Series because that became very important too." They received high scores on national exams, earning the school and students elite status.[38]

Mass Hysteria and Other Misadventures

Pat told me that the girls became sick with mysterious ailments sweeping through Africa. In 1962, after Tanzanian independence, psychogenic illness called mass hysteria broke out in girls' schools countrywide. Girls experienced hysterical uncontrollable laughter, "pain, fainting, respiratory problems, rashes," crying for up to sixteen days, violence, and "aimless running." Mass hysteria affected thousands of children, culminating in the shutting down of fourteen schools for three months. When the girls returned to school, it occurred again.[39] Pat's students did not escape the hysteria epidemic. She said, "There was some kind of hysteria going around at one time, I thought it was because they were studying too hard." She was correct.

Mass hysteria occurred due to chronic stress, societal instability, and the "uncertainties" of Tanzanian independence.[40] Pat recalled:

> I was the teacher on duty, and somebody came to me and said somebody was crying. I went to find out what was wrong. The girl just started screaming "The Clavicle, The Clavicle AHHHHH." I was like, what's going on? What happened? And then you go to the next person, and they were screaming and carrying on. Why are all these girls screaming and running around "AAHHH"? The next day we had to take them to the doctor. They had it all in the newspaper about these girls running wild at NGANZA Secondary School. So that was an adventure.

Mass hysteria lasted for two and a half years, affecting the girls and their mothers in the villages.[41]

Patricia encountered other wild adventures like that of a girl who ran away from the school. Pat recalled, "A parent came looking for his daughter. Poor little man, no shoes, dragging himself in. He gave everybody a speech: 'I'm poor and I want my child educated. I send my child to school. I come to school and the child's not here.' Everybody just felt so bad." The girl was found by a classmate in the forest. "The next morning, we heard a girl coming down the road holding on to the runaway girl. She was just screaming in Swahili, "I FOUND HER, I'M BRINGING HER!!!" Pat relayed another story of schoolgirls missing overnight because "they went to see their boyfriends" at the boys' school. Pat assumed they "must have had a party because they did not come back until the next day." She told me of "a child who got pregnant and the mother came. She was explaining that if her daughter had told her she was pregnant, she could have gone to the doctor. The local doctor [would] have delayed the pregnancy, with their local medicines, until after she graduated. Yeah, that's very strong medicines [laughter]." The pregnancies of boarding schoolgirls proved a serious issue in Tanzania given the news coverage in the *Standard*, stories with titles like "Fight Pregnancies in Schools" and "77 Pregnant Girls."[42] It appears that the pregnancies that occurred at Pat's Nganza Secondary School proved part of a larger problem at boarding schools.

There was always something going on at the school and town. Pat recounted that one of her friends, a teacher, "*would come everyday with a story*" of events in town, such as "when your vagina started talking to you. [Pat could not contain her laughter.] You would have to wear special white beads on your wrist to make your vagina stop talking to you ... I'm telling you," Pat said, guffawing uncontrollably. Pat was involved in wild adventures. One time while driving, police holding a machete flagged her down. They asked Pat to take this woman to the police station. "This lady had cut off her husbands' head, *that night*. [Pat SMIRKED BROADLY!!! Then peals of laughter cascaded out of her mouth.] Why did I HAVE TO TAKE HER TO THE POLICE STATION!!! I was eyeing her the whole time. She was fine sitting there in the back seat. I said, Lord have mercy, get me to the police station with my head." Pat recalled that teaching at the school proved thrilling. She admits: "I did [run wild], because my mother was not there at the beginning." In 1971, Pat was in Tanzania by herself, but she said that

> it wasn't a year [before my mother came]. [Laughing hard] I knew my mother and grandmother were coming. *I did not know when they were coming.* Life was a little different because there was only one phone on the campus in the office. My mother was chomping at the bit. Got the job, got the house, let's go. She was dying to get to Tanzania, and I was vehicle to get there.

Mae told a female informant and workmates that Pat lived in Tanzania.[43] Mae had her own plans for a life in Africa. Pat felt that it involved her. Pat tried to build a life of her own, unencumbered by Mae.

Mae's U.S. Activism

After her incarceration Mae set about her life as a writer, speaker, and activist. She continued her work with the African American Committee in Defense of the Congo, the Deacons for Defense and Justice of the Oppressed, and the Revolutionary Action Movement. In 1963 the FBI and CIA targeted RAM, believing them to be "the most dangerous of all the Black Power Organizations."[44] Mae wrote to Mrs. Johnson: "Pat told me about Max [Stanford] getting his head bashed in (she called me this morning).... I suggest RAM get a lawyer for Max and Stan. The conspiracy charge is a serious one meant to intimidate them. It's meant to put them out of commission... THEY SHOULD PLEAD GUILTY TO NOTHING. The NAACP and the powers that be want a scapegoat and they're it."[45] This began the efforts to actively suppress RAM. Max Stanford, Herman Ferguson, Arthur Harris, and other members found themselves falsely accused of conspiring to kill NAACP executive secretary Roy Wilkins, National Urban League executive secretary Whitney Young, Robert Kennedy, and Martin Luther King Jr. Mae and Yuri Kochiyama's Women's Committee of Harlem took up their cause. In August 1967, under the auspices of the Women's Committee of Harlem, Mae spoke at a Brooklyn Congress of Racial Equality rally. H. Rap Brown, Paul Butel, Julian Bond II, Conrad Lynn, and Delores Costelle also spoke in support of RAMs defendants. George Todd reported in the *Amsterdam News*, "Fiery

Fig. 11. Mae Mallory, national tour,
Audrey and Clarence Seniors Collection

speaker Mae Mallory of the Harlem Women's Committee called for a Black power conference for women but explained for the benefit of the men: 'We are not trying to take away your masculinity but trying to fortify it. We need a woman's organization for the defense of Black men.'"[46]

Mae used a community feminist theoretical frame to indicate her support of the accused while underplaying her and Yuri's experiences and other African American and Japanese American women's experiences with incarceration and the Japanese concentration camps. Her strategy fit in with Ula Taylor's community feminist rhetoric and not with the explosive Black feminist that was Mae. At the rally "she said that if the trial of the 17 accused fails to result in victory in court, 'we'll damn sure take it in the streets.'"[47] Mae maintained her alliance with RAM members. They faced the accusation of plotting to poison Philadelphia police. Mae and YAWF's Deidre Griswald spoke at a 1967 Philadelphia protest. Mae wrote to Robert F. Williams:

> Max Stanford was just extradited back to N.Y. . . . You would be pleased and amazed at the support for the Black people who were arrested from the Jamaica Rifle and Pistol Club [RAM]. At the first rally in Queens there were over 2,500 people there. . . . In Philly, where Max and others were jailed there don't appear to be as much support as here in N.Y.[48]

The FBI and CIA ramped up their efforts to destroy RAM members. The FBI disseminated the following information: "On February 16, 1967, J. Edgar Hoover described the Revolutionary Action Movement as a Negro organization . . . dedicated to the overthrow of the capitalist system in the United States, by violence if necessary, and its replacement by a socialist system oriented toward the Chinese Communist interpretation of Marxism-Leninism."[49] Mae stood ready to defend RAM members while simultaneously advocating for hope. According to Lawrence H. Geller in the *Philadelphia Tribune*,

> The Final Speaker was Mae Mallory. . . . She closed the meeting by saying that "the Negro youth and colored peoples the world over want a better world than they see today, and the white world is resisting. The world doesn't belong to white people only. It belongs to all of us, and we'll either share it together or there'll be no world at all," she said, to sustained applause.[50]

Mae challenged the FBI and CIA efforts at destroying the lives of RAM members, committing herself to working for a just and equal world.[51]

In 1968 Mae continued her advocacy for African American youth by speaking at the Black Youth Education Day with Lewis Micheaux, James Foreman, Leroi Jones, and his Spirit House Movement and Players. She joined the Governing Board in Harlem of Public School IS 201 (1968): As a "a concerned parent [Mae] called upon the audience to support Ronald Evans as principal of IS 201." Echoing her Macon elementary school principal's words, she told parents that Black children must continually be told "walk with your head up, chest out to the rhythm of I'm proud to be Black, this is my world."[52] Between 1968 and 1970, while living in Cleveland, Mallory planned a speaking tour in Sweden and published her own newspaper, writing to Julian Mayfield, "My little paper may not look like much, but I take a great deal of effort. Apparently, it packs a bit of clout here in Cleveland because a white journalist referred to it from time to time in the dailies."[53] She also worked for the Economic Development Conference, involved herself with Angela Davis's case, and worked with the Republic of New Afrika with Yuri Kochiyama and Wilbur Grattan. Yuri wrote Williams, "That a tiny nation like the Republic of New Africa, born in struggle and without geographic entity, could dare call itself a nation, would have proved to the world that nationhood is more than land ownership and military might, but the throbbing pulse and spirit of a people."[54]

In 1966 in Cleveland Ahmed Rashad organized the Republic of New Afrika, with its members including Wilbur Grattan as minister of state and foreign affairs, and member of PRIDE, and Mae Mallory, "Militant Mother of New York," as consul. With the endorsement of African American mayor Carl Stokes, Rashad used the $10,300 from Cleveland: Now! to open the

Afro Culture Shop and Bookstore, where with like-minded people he held classes and programs for the African American community on Black history and culture. The police and the Subversive Activities and Special Investigation Unit worked to undermine Rashad. They harassed, surveilled, inflicted violence, paid informers, and forcibly shut down Ahmed's Afro Culture Shop and Bookstore three times. They induced his landlord to break the bookstore's lease. In 1968 they compelled the landlord of his home to evict him through a twenty-four-hour eviction notice. All these actions caused outrage in the Black community. Grattan's organizations PRIDE and Peacekeepers patrolled the community dressed in "orange armbands labeled 'The Mayor's Committee,'" to support Ahmed Rashad. On July 23 the state invaded the community, stole liquor, sexually assaulted women at the Lakeview Tavern, shot at Mayor Stokes's law director, and torched buildings. The state started a war against the Black community, engaging in a gun battle with armed-and-ready Rashad and his Black nationalist comrades.

Police refused to allow Grattan and Forest to remove people the police mortally shot, telling them to "'leave the nigger to die.' The police removed their badges and severely beat Breeze Forest."[55] Ahmed Rashad surrendered, and *they charged him with murder and sentenced him to death*. This state-sanctioned horror led Grattan and Mae to form the July 23rd Defense Committee. They raised money for Rashad's defense and worked to prevent his imprisonment and execution.[56] Through the July 23rd Defense Committee, Mae, Grattan, and the Black community fought mightily for Ahmed Rashad, speaking at a fundraising meeting at the Cory Methodist Church on May 31, 1969). The *Call and Post*'s Alvin Ward reported, "Mrs. Mallory went on to explain further amid thunderous applause 'Ahmed will not die in the electric chair.' . . . Wilbur Grattan announced, 'it is imperative that we continue with the hearing to make the public aware of the atrocities against innocent Black people that occurred July 23rd.'"[57]

When Mae and other protestors attempted to present County Prosecutor Corrigan with demands to investigate the July 23rd police violence, the state jailed Mae, sentencing her to a year in the workhouse and fining her $1,000. The *Call and Post* maintained that "Mrs. Mallory will hardly spend much time in jail, and even if she does, it will mean just another revolutionary halo around her head." The state also arrested Ted Dostal of the Monroe Defense Committee. All were charged with blocking the entrance to the Criminal Court Building.[58]

Mae and Grattan advocated heavily for Ahmed's release, speaking at rallies and organizing a letter-writing campaign. They gave testimony for the ACLU in front of the grand jury. The state locked Mae out of the courtroom.⁵⁹ In 1978 Ahmed Rashad died in prison, all because he opened a bookstore and wanted to teach Cleveland's Black community.

Mae's Tanzanian Dreams

Because of the state repression, Mae longed for Africa. In her quest to get there, Mae sold raffle tickets to raise money to build a Tanzanian nursery school under the auspices of Umoja The Wanake, The Tanzania Limited Women of Tanzania (1969).⁶⁰ By 1971 the FBI reported that Mae listed her profession as writer and speaker. Mae lived in Cleveland, attended Cuyahoga Community College, and worked as a nurse at Euclid Park Nursing Home.⁶¹ The FBI reported that

> Mallory has an intense desire to go to Africa to live. She is disturbed by events and conditions in the United States and feels that Africa holds the dream she is looking for. Mallory has been inactive in specific extremist groups, but still harbors strong personal convictions. She is not presently known to be in a leadership capacity of any extremist organization. She works steadily and takes every opportunity to work over time, and on her days off so that she can make money. [The female FBI informant reported on her] plans and desires to return to Africa to live.⁶²

They reported that she told workmates, "In a couple of years when she gets the money together, she wants to travel to Tanzania to permanently live. Mallory talks about building herself a $27,000 house which she states would be a mansion over there as compared to what it is here. Mallory does not seem to respect authority in her dealings with her fellow workers and supervisors."⁶³

In February 1972 Mae rejected capitalism, colonialism, imperialism, and the internal colony to relocate from Cleveland to Tanzania. She did what *any self-possessed African American radical woman would do when rejecting oppressive systems*: she quit her job as a nurse's aide, let the post office know she was moving but offered no forwarding address, and with great intention failed to pay her phone bill. The phone company disconnected the phone when they realized she was not going to pay the bill. As any true African American woman revolutionary leaving to join the African revolution would do, she also skipped out on her rent. The manager discovered this when he went to collect it, only to discover an empty apartment.⁶⁴ I asked Pat if she had done the same and she said, "No [laughing], I paid my bills. My mother was a gangster." Pat said, "So here my mother and grandmother come packing up their stuff to go." Pat had no idea when they would arrive, so she enjoyed her life in Tanzania, having fun and having adventures.

> I met this young man who was an area commissioner, he was political, non-essential service, BUT SLICK. He showed me around. So we had our little fling. We were getting ready to go to a party one evening. I was getting ready, and this taxi was coming up. The boarding school was seven miles out of town. First of all, there was barely a road. I think it was a one-mile road, and then nothing but dirt. Anytime there was a car coming, it was quiet. There was no electricity in the street, so you know who's coming, you heard things. I'm looking and I see this cab coming down the road stopping in front of my door. *Out comes Mae Mallory and my grandmother. Oh gosh, the jig was up. They messed up my thing.*

Pat, in her grown independent woman splendor, maintained her composure and her plans. She added, "This young man and I did go out."[65] Pat says that on her return "my mother and grandmother talked themselves a blue streak. When I got back home my mother had this talk about different countries and you don't know anything about this person, and blah, blah, blah, all of that. That was it." Pat indicates that her full independence took a slight hit when Mae and her grandmother arrived. She also suggests that she did continue to live and enjoy her life independent of her mother.

Mae's arranged teenaged marriage and teenaged motherhood left little room for the romantic. Mae committed herself to radical activism, unable to conjoin motherhood and activism. Mrs. Johnson's commitment to radical activism was cultivated early through Abbeville's community of struggle and resistance. It allowed her to conjoin her radical activism with marriage, motherhood, and moments of delight. Like Ethel Azalea, my mother, Audrey Proctor Seniors, cultivated her radical activism as a teenaged member of the radical New Orleans NAACP, which led her to radical activism in Cleveland. She nimbly conjoined it with marriage, motherhood, and joy. The generational differences marked Pat for quite a different experience from Mae, Ethel, and Audrey. Unmarried, unencumbered by children, a Black Nationalist Rebel Woman in Tanzania, Pat ably compartmentalized her life. She joined and participated in African socialism by teaching at Nganza Secondary School. Teaching was her political activism. She kept her activism and teaching separate from her social and romantic life. She lived an utterly blissful life in Tanzania.

Romance and the Big Bust

Pat enjoyed her freedom and was having fun, dating, and exploring. She told me,

> There were plenty of beautiful moments, but this one strikingly amazing moment occurred with a teacher that I came close to marrying. We were driving around Lake Victoria and it was night. The moon was yellow, and the lake was smooth as glass and black. The moon came down and it was HUGE. It just looked like it took up the whole sky and it reflected on the lake. It was just gorgeous. It was like you were on another planet or someplace else. It was most romantic. [Laughter] It was just beautiful. I said to myself I'm going to try and draw it. I have never seen anything like that since. Just Gorgeous.

Pat experienced many exciting adventures. I asked her if she thought of getting married, that many people would have found a husband in Tanzania. She answered, "Yes, I did think to get married, but I didn't find anyone I wanted to marry." Pat's yellow moon romantic adventure was important, but her most monumental romance came soon after. Pat indicates, "There was what we called The Vatican; the Catholic priests were there. These were Tanzanians. There were some whites, but the Tanzanians got involved because they got free education" and employment opportunities. Paul Kollman writes in "Generations of Catholics in Eastern Africa" that the establishment of Catholic missions in Tanzania through the White Fathers and the Spiritans of France and the German Benedictines began in the nineteenth century as a strategy for colonial rule. They centered the training on the monastic life of prayer, employment, and education, with the Spiritans participating in agricultural labor. The missions provided education, health care, orphanages, other social services, and religious indoctrination. Today 30 percent of Tanzanians are Catholic.[66] In 1959 Monsignor Blomjous established the Bukumbi Pastoral Institute, twenty miles south of Mwanza. This was Pat's Vatican:[67] "I frequented the so-called Vatican where all the priests lived, [because], number one, all of them had cars. If you needed to go to town you didn't have to necessarily stand on the road all the time, you could go to the Vatican and get a ride from one of those priests.... Listen, I could go over to the Vatican and I could have bacon [laughter]. They had food [laughing]."

It appears that like Afro-Haitians, the Tanzanians resisted full Catholic indoctrination, maintaining their African culture, social beliefs, and practices. Kollman calls this the "Africanization of the Church." Pat recounted that this included dating and marriage:

> There was one [Priest], he was really nice [and] he had a telescope. I was really into the telescope.... I heard he had children too. There were two of them that everybody knew had children. The older one decided to give up the priesthood.... One teacher got pregnant by one of the priests.... One priest who had children with one of the teachers, he didn't give up the priesthood. In fact, when he visited the States, he stayed with us.... When anybody tells me about priests, this sister knows.

I have found scant information on Tanzanian priests' dating and marriage practices, but a glimmer of understanding arises from Richard A. Schoenherr's *Goodbye Father*. Schoenherr maintains that Tanzanian bishops "petitioned Rome for a married clergy" in the 1960s–1970s and again in 1994. The issue was never resolved.[68] This was the environment in which Pat came into contact with the priests of the Vatican. I asked Pat again, "Didn't you think to get married?" She answered,

> Now let me tell you, I would have married this person except for one big snafu, he was a priest. Yeah, he was Black. I was in love with that man, and we went out on dates. That's a juicy chapter. *He was so sweet.* He asked me out. We went someplace, I don't know where the hell it was. It was far away from everything and everybody. We went on a picnic. *He was very, very sweet. I was SO in love with that man.* Yes, he was in love with me too, but we were too scared. I said okay, now this man's a priest, but if he asks, I'm there. I said I'm not making the first move... I'm not going out of bounds with this guy because he's a priest. He's got to make the first move. I think he was too shy and too scared.

Pat's concern about her reputation proved well founded given societal taboos of dating Catholic priests, the stigma attached to breaching this taboo, and the Tanzanian government's Operation Vijana (January–February 1969). Before Operation Vijana, girls, women office workers, barmaids, waitresses, and women workers in Dar es Salaam found themselves marked as prostitutes and gold diggers because they wore miniskirts. With Operation Vijana the government condemned skin bleaching and skin lightening and banned African American soul music and dancing as "bad manners" that corrupted Tanzanian youth, especially girls. They banned American dress, miniskirts, tight pants, hot pants, wigs, and even the Afro defining it as indecent and decadent, "the anathema to *Ujamaa* socialist ideals," according to Markle. Scholastica Mushi's "The Tyranny of Western Dress" noted that "these women dress in minis because they want to husk our dear husbands from us."[69] The government defined African American women as immodest, claiming in 1973 that Angela Davis was the very representative of African American women's immorality because she wore an Afro and pantsuit when visiting Tanzania.[70] With all this, it is no wonder that Pat fiercely guarded her reputation. Pat found that "everybody was out there, but I wasn't. That's the other thing, talk spreads, and I didn't want to be the one, 'look at her.' And of course, they thought we were loose anyway. 'This is an American girl—they're easy.'" Pat used Mae's and her family's lessons about propriety to protect her reputation. Notwithstanding the moral prohibitions, Pat says "*I was so in love*. He was in love with me too.... Last I heard he was a bishop." Such a sweet story of unfulfilled love.

Pat learned of these ugly ideas concerning African American women and girls when in all her innocence she went for a night out.

> I finally got a car, and I went into town by myself. There was nothing to do but go to the hotel café. You could sit there and drink and chat yourself away. The place is small, everybody knows you, they watch you. I knew some of the guys that worked at the hotel. One of them came over to me, he said, "Someone wants to meet you." I'm saying, who wants to meet me? I don't know anybody here. I am just sitting minding my business. He points to this white guy sitting at a stool at the bar. I told him, *"Don't you ever in life introduce me to somebody, particularly a white man."* I guess he thought I was a prostitute.

Pat was naïve concerning Tanzania's social norms: "I guess, what I didn't know was that as a woman by yourself, sitting there at the hotel, there was only one thing [you could be]. I learned quickly from that, that I should not go out in the nighttime, because you are giving a signal that you're a prostitute looking for a hookup." The government tried to control young girls and women by banning miniskirt wearers from bars, pombe clubs (beer clubs), and night clubs. They closed these establishments through the Intoxication Liquor Amendment. The government's efforts met with resistance; as Dr. A. J. Temu said in the 1971 *Nationalist*, "It was unfair to deny the youth in the country some kind of entertainment in the form of music and beer."[71] Pat's hotel encounter embodied the government's efforts to control women and girls legally. Notwithstanding the reality that the government invited African Americans to help build the country, they defined African Americans as a lascivious threat to Tanzania. Pat confronted an African colonialist mentality and repression that did not represent her dream of Africa—of freedom from U.S. racism. I asked Pat if the Black worker apologized to her.

I don't know if he apologized, but he was looking very sheepish. I never spoke to him again. I guess he didn't understand it. But the venom I had, because, oh, how could you? I come from a Black nationalist kind of thing, like Black power. I'm going to the motherland, and this was almost as bad as them nuns. Don't be sending no white man talking to me.

Given her Black nationalist and Black feminist metamorphosis in high school and college, Pat did not expect this mistreatment anywhere on the continent. The encounter pained her deeply and made her very angry. Because of this incident, Pat began going out with friends to manza clubs—social organizations for state employees.

The Big Bust

> I keep hearing from people in Tanzania that there is some
> slight change of attitude towards Afro-Americans.
> —**Robert F. Williams to Mae Mallory, Beijing, February 14, 1969**

In 1974 the Tanzanian government accused African Americans of being CIA spies in the Big Bust. Pat said,

> The police came to African Americans' homes and did searches. Some people got put in jail because someone found a Coca-Cola can radio. That was considered spying material. Somebody else had a telescope in their house. That was considered spy material. . . . The atmosphere was getting really negative, and people were afraid. . . . The FBI got in there. I think there were too many African Americans influencing Tanzania. I think they were afraid of us importing our revolutionary zeal.

The accusations of spying, the Big Bust, Operation Vijana, and tensions between Tanzanians and African Americans magnified the multilayered position that African Americans held in Tanzania. Given African American involvement as university students, student leaders, and ministerial advisors, their work establishing and living in Ujamaa villages and their contributions to Tanzania caused strains as well as solidarities. By 1974 the strains outweighed any solidarities.[72] Pat says, "We weren't docile. I guess something just had to be done." The CIA-orchestrated Big Bust proved to be that something.

The Big Bust coincided with the Sixth Annual Pan-African Conference, which Mae participated in and helped organize. According to the FBI report on the Tanzanian Revolution, on June 15, 1974, seven African Americans, including Queen Mother Moore of the African People's Party, said they felt that the importation of arms by African American expatriates "may have been provocation by imperialists to disrupt [the] Sixth Annual Pan African Conference." They asserted that "enemies of Africa might use the incident to stir up suspicion during the Conference."[73] The very existence of the FBI file on the Tanzanian Revolution offers validity to Pat's claim of CIA and FBI machinations against African Americans in Tanzania. The Big Bust proved very effective in fracturing alliances between African Americans and Tanzanians. In Tanzania the CIA used the same strategies that destabilized left-leaning governments in Iran, Guyana, Guatemala, and the Belgian Congo.[74] According to Godfrey Mwakikagile, "the CIA tried to undermine Nyerere's government in Tanzania in order to overthrow him."[75] They sent spies and agents provocateurs to disrupt the government, and the accusations that African Americans were spies caused dissension. Pat said, "A lot of suspicion was created. People shunned us, even at the school, they were terrified and didn't know what to think." Some Tanzanians in the school system tried to repair the fractures between African Americans and Tanzanians. Pat told me,

> It got to be so bad that on one of the national exams one of the reading passages was entitled "African Americans are your friends." Somebody tried to recover that relationship, but it never got to be repaired. People who were your friends were afraid to talk to you. They didn't want to be considered spies themselves for fraternizing with you. . . . It was time to go. I think it was the FBI and CIA.

Mae and Pat were unwilling participants in the mass exodus out of Tanzania: "My mother didn't get her contract for her job, so she had to leave. . . . My grandmother lived with me for a while getting her pension, then she left and went back to the U.S. . . . My mother didn't leave right away. She moved to Dar es Salaam and stayed there for a while."

Pat left the United States to escape state repression and the internal colony only to find that the U.S. hand was far-reaching. Americans' efforts to destroy Black people and eviscerate nations like Tanzania who successfully put down imperialism and colonialism for socialism proved effective. Pat hoped she could still make a life for herself in Tanzania teaching at Nganza Secondary School. With her mother in Dar es Salaam and her grandmother back in the States, Pat felt she could breathe, come into herself again. Pat said, "The only time I felt like a sense of me-ness was when my mother's contract was not renewed, and she stayed in Dar [es] Salaam, and I was in Mwanza. She just took up all the air. I got to see what is was like to be my own person." Pat's remaining time in Tanzania was short-lived because the Big Bust prevented her from staying. "I guess they went through the papers; they found that I didn't have my master's. When I wrote to NYU to find out what happened they said that I was short three credits." The school did not renew her contract, most certainly because of the insistence of the CIA and the FBI.

Pat tried desperately to stay on the Continent. "I stayed in Dar es Salaam for a while because *I just couldn't get on that plane and go*. I actually tried to go to Ghana and some other places." Pat tried to get a visa to stay in Ethiopia. She recalled, "I did get a visa to go to Nigeria. I went to Nigeria where my college roommate lived [with her] Nigerian [husband]. I stayed with them, trying not to go back to the States, but eventually it happened." The desperation Pat felt, of trying to escape white supremacy, surveillance, and oppression, proved profound and intense. "The next year I left, but it was very hard for me to go. They gave me a big party, a big send-off. Singing, all that kind of stuff... I cried like a baby on the train. I just couldn't look out the window. Yeah, it was really sad. I just couldn't see myself going back to the States."[76] In 1976 Pat, age thirty, returned to the United States. "I took three credits when I came back from Tanzania, finally graduated with my master's in 1976, and went on with the rest of my life."

Spiritual Awakening and Forgiveness

Pat's healing from childhood trauma took many forms. The most significant was spiritual healing and awakening rooted in Africa. Before 1974's Big Bust, Pat frequently visited Janet and Bob Moses's house in Dar es Salaam on her vacations and days off from teaching. One conversation centered on spirituality. Pat said, "I had not been raised religious or anything like that, I couldn't believe any of that stuff they were talking about really. It was spooky." The Moses family gave Pat "all this literature about the Glory and all this kind of stuff," reinforcing John Mbiti's assertion that "Africans are notoriously religious [and] notoriously metaphysical." Mbiti's claim coupled with the Moseses' conversation and her return to Mwanza would reveal Pat as a metaphysical healer of self.[77] On the three-day bus trek home, the bus got stuck. Pat stayed on the bus, where she was struck by a magical revelation. "This feeling of euphoria came over me. I was taken somewhere... AHA... I thought, 'Hear no evil, see no evil, speak no evil,' I kept hearing it over and over again, like a broken record." Pat recalled moments from her childhood: "When I was a kid at my aunt's house, she had this little knickknack with these three little monkeys: hear no evil, see no evil, speak no evil." On the bus, suddenly and inexplicably Pat longed for the monkeys and thought, "*Oh, it would be nice to have that, I would love to have that.*" On Pat's return to Mwanza she discovered that her friend sent her a gift of "beautiful Makonde carvings made of ebony [of] *these three monkeys*. I said, wait a minute, something spooky is going on here. . . . I have these monkeys to this day." This was the beginning of Pat's spiritual healing. Acting as her own metaphysical/ontological healer, Pat began the journey of spiritual self-healing. In "Pan African Metaphysical Epistemology" Denise Martin writes that in many African ontologies "the person is at the center, [as the] priestess of the universe" with "the ability to consciously direct the energies flowing through all creation."[78] Through this first Tanzanian metaphysical occurrence, Pat began to use what Martin describes as "the energy of the mind and Spirit" to heal herself from past trauma. As her own priestess, Pat directed energies to allow spiritual self-healing. Her second metaphysical experience also occurred before the Big Bust. Pat lived on campus while her friend Mom Beki lived on the other side of campus. Pat relayed to me,

> [One night] I looked out the window and *saw this stained-glass window*. There's no outdoor electricity. I'm wondering where is this stained glass coming from? Then I thought, the Vatican . . . *a reflection coming all the way from over and atop of Mom Beki's house*. Every night I would see these stained-glass windows. I was going to tell somebody, but they would think I was crazy. "I ain't telling N-O-B-O-D-Y." With my big mouth, I asked Mom Beki, "Do you see it?" She said, "Nuh uh" [laughter]. That night I got up to look for the stained-glass window. It wasn't there! *That thing was meant for me.* . . . The stained-glass window and the three monkeys made me believe there's something higher than us. There's something going on in this Earth. It's not all about people. It's about things that are happening in the atmosphere and stratosphere. Something determining stuff.

The stained-glass windows continued Pat's spiritual healing. Pat began to, as Brett Hendrickson explains, use her own energetic force "to restore balance, wellness, and wholeness" to her body.[79] She undertook her spiritual healing by drawing the connections between African metaphysical experiences, ontology, and African American Pentecostalism. These practices allowed Pat to direct energy "flowing through all creation" of the mind, body, and spirit to self-heal, restoring balance, wellness, and wholeness to her life. Pat conjoined her Black identity as a metaphysical being to Pentecostalism.[80]

The followers of Pentecostalism, which began, according to Dr. Shalanda Dexter-Rodgers, "as a reform movement within American Protestantism," were the disenfranchised and poor. They "believed that they received the 'baptism of the Holy Ghost.' Through this baptism 'the very presence and power of God now resided within them.'" Pentecostalists believed that the baptism was a "gift available to any willing believer," regardless of race, gender, or class.[81] This is very similar to what Pat experienced in Tanzania and in practicing metaphysics and Pentecostalism at Herbert Daughtry's House of the Lord Church in Brooklyn.[82] Pat recalled,

> In 2014 during convocation [at the House of the Lord], I was sitting down listening. I thought my mind was on what the preacher was saying. I looked up straight ahead above the piano player *and there were those same stained-glass windows. It sure as hell convinced me.* I was afraid to talk about it. I finally told Pastor Daughtry's wife. She said, "You need to write about what you saw and experienced. . . . *These are my metaphysical experiences."* . . . Those things happened to me in Tanzania, and they did a lot for me.

Metaphysical experiences led Pat to Brooklyn's most progressive and politically active church communities. Daughtry infused his House of the Lord Church, its members, and the Black United Front with key tenets of Pentecostalism, Black religious nationalism, civil rights activism, gender equality, antiwar advocacy, pacifism, Black diasporic rights, and the South African anti-apartheid movement. It is not by chance that Pat fused together her experience with Black nationalists who followed Pentecostalist-bred Marcus Garvey with Herbert Daughtry and Pentecostalism.[83] Daughtry's church proved the perfect place for Pat, for her growth and the nurturing of her metaphysical experiences. Her belief was confirmed when she followed Daughtry's advice: "When you're seeking something, or praying and asking God, stop, and listen and be quiet. Accept it the way it comes." This advice helped Patricia, who wanted desperately to become a mother. As a married woman, she had experienced several miscarriages. Pregnant, she longed for a message from her recently deceased grandmother to let her know that *this* child would survive *this pregnancy*, given her previous miscarriages.

> I was praying for God to give me something to remember my grandmother by. I wanted to see her face, this is how I wanted the answer, like Hollywood. I wanted to see this glow, this light. I wanted my grandmother to be there. I put this candle in front of the window, I was doing all kinds of things, just waiting for this vision [laughter]. Something came. I was being still, trying to accept whatever answer I got, but I had a picture of the answer. Something came over me and said, "This child would live." That was Aleutia. I said, ain't this a kick in the butt. He survived. There's something to some of this metaphysical stuff.

Conjoining Pentecostalism and metaphysics, Pat continued the lessons she learned in self-healing in high school, college, Tanzania, and Guyana—a place that taught her to love her Black beauty. She worked to recover from childhood trauma with all these lessons. Pat found meaning for herself in a career helping children and in raising her son Aleutia. While embracing Pentecostalism, Pat continued to consider herself an atheist.

> It's hard to talk to current atheists and have them understand, and not brush the metaphysical experiences off. Having religious people hear those experiences and understand me as an atheist where I'm coming from is [nourishing], in terms of my spiritual growth. I am comfortable that I'm not alone with this. I can feel comfortable about going ahead, knowing that my metaphysical experiences are real. I'm willing to stay open and embrace it, and just live it.

Forgiveness

Late in Mae Mallory's life, Pat challenged herself to forgive Mae.

> My mother was in a nursing home. She was always in my head. I said, how am going to tell this woman "I forgive you," because I know what it's going to be [laughter]. She was in a nursing home because she couldn't walk, not because she didn't have any brain. So I said, how am I going to do this? I figured, on the way out the door [laughing], I would tell her, because then she couldn't say anything. But she fooled me. I was going out the door and I said, "I forgive you," and she said, "FOR WHAT?" "WHAT DID I DO?" [Pat burst out in uproarious laughter]. I said, "I'll tell you when I come back." Oh gosh! No, she didn't ask for any forgiveness because she didn't think she had done anything. She thought she did what she was supposed to do. That concept was lost on her. Yeah, that was that.

Sometimes there's no reconciliation, no Hollywood ending, when it comes to our closest relationships—the ones that formed who we are. What I will say is that notwithstanding the very fractured relationship between Pat and Mae, eighteen-year-old Mae, *the child that she was, tried*. In many, many instances she failed, but she also succeeded. Mae armed Pat with some strong and important life lessons that Pat carried throughout her life. Mae tried to shelter and educate her children from corrosive ideologies of Black inferiority and a white supremacist society as an everyday political activist in the motherist frame. She showered Pat with a love of literature. Frederick Douglass's Fourth of July speech became the foundation for Pat's philosophical and political beliefs. Mae infused in Pat Black nationalism and Black pride. She taught Pat to fight for social justice and equality, to fight against misogyny, to fight all of this within a Black feminist lens. Mae's life lessons and Pat's own lessons in self-healing led her to political activism in high school and college. These lessons led Pat to Brooklyn, to Daughtry's church. Pat continues to actively participate in social justice. Pat's lessons in self-healing, metaphysics, and Pentecostalism helped her take her mother's lessons and fly in life, to find herself, to live free.

Fig. 12. Audrey Seniors (center), Women's Liberation in Support of the Black Panthers, New Haven, 1969. Photo by David Fenton/Getty.

Chapter 9

Audrey Proctor Seniors

The Grenadian and Nicaraguan Revolutions

My years in New York have been politically gratifying. They have been spent working for social change. This includes anti-racist, anti-imperialist, and anti-war work as well as work focusing on the right of women to control their own bodies.

—**Audrey, Autobiographical Notes**

The great African American scholar W. E. B. Du Bois contended in *Black Reconstruction in America* that the end of abolition democracy paved the way for U.S. imperialism overseas and led not only to the disenfranchisement of African Americans but to the massive disenfranchisement of Majority World people, whom big business deemed a cheap, indispensable labor force.[1] The response worldwide by aggrieved communities of color has been to fight white supremacy through various methods, including Marxist/socialist, Maoist, Trotskyist, Cubanismo, and African socialist ideologies. Schooled by the New Orleans NAACP, the Monroe Defense Committee, the Workers World Party, the Youth against War and Fascism, and the Black Panther Party, and following the rhetoric of her idol Paul Robeson, Audrey Proctor Seniors formulated an internationalist and Pan-Africanist worldview. She traveled to Grenada and Nicaragua to support their revolutionary movements, cofounded the New York organizations the African American Solidarity Network and the Committee in Solidarity with Free Grenada, which became the Committee for a Free Grenada when the United States invaded the island. Seniors also held membership in and worked closely with the Nicaragua Exchange.[2]

She found common bonds with the people in Grenada and Nicaragua, and through her work in these countries she realized the hope for equality in the United States that remained unrealized given the failure of the U.S. civil rights movement and civil rights laws and legislation. My mother successfully linked the struggle for African American human and civil rights to these revolutionary movements and grew as both an activist and an intellectual. Seniors's disappointment with the failures of civil rights legislation and the U.S. civil rights movement, which left working-class and poor African Americans, Latinos/as, Hispanics, and Asian Americans behind in dilapidated cities with no social services, inadequate education, and few life options except military service, compelled her to commit herself to changing society through a leftist ideology. She worked with the Coalition of Concerned Black Women, who, according to my mother, "formed around the killings [beginning in 1980] of [twenty-eight] Black children in Atlanta." The Coalition also "worked around community and neighborhood issues and around larger international issues."[3] Mommy also protested the disproportionate loss of the lives of African Americans, Majority World people, and Vietnamese during the Vietnam War, recalling, "I have worked in the movement from the early days of the civil rights movement, through the Anti–Vietnam War years up to the end of that war."[4] Audrey Proctor Seniors connected the Vietnam War to European colonialist projects in Cuba and China. In the late 1970s and 1980s she linked U.S. wars and interventions in Grenada and Nicaragua to Vietnam, Cuba, and China. She realized that Europeans ravished Majority World countries of their human and natural resources, funding these projects with U.S. dollars, instead of using these resources to prevent war and help people of color. We attended weekly protest marches against the war. As the war raged on over the years we protested at rallies and demonstrations.[5]

Perhaps my mother held strong views about war because of her family's experience in U.S. wars. She often discussed with me the fact that her grandfather had been gassed in World War I and suffered debilitating consequences. Her father fought in World War II in the name of ending fascism and oppression, only to come home to a racially fractured New Orleans. Her two brothers also did time in the military, Robert in the Korean War and Carl in the Vietnam War. Perchance these men hoped that participation in war would elevate their status in the United States, only to discover that they fought wars against people of color all in the name of "democracy," with no benefits to them or their New Orleans communities.

Having coupled African Americans' oppression and the fight against colonialism in Vietnam, Africa, Asia, and Latin America with the loss of Third World lives in war, Audrey joined international revolutionary movements in Grenada and Nicaragua in the early 1980s. Mommy felt that the options left for African Americans included looking to revolutionary governments outside of the United States for alternative methods of fighting for human rights.[6] Her work with the New Orleans NAACP, the Monroe Defense Committee, WWP, YAWF, and the Black Panthers; her anti-Vietnam protests; and her commitment to Maoism, Trotskyism, and Cubanismo exposed her to international revolutionary thought and most likely led her to Grenada and Nicaragua. She connected the repression of the Vietnamese, Cubans, Chinese, Grenadians, and Nicaraguans due to colonialism and war to the experience of African Americans, people of color in the United States, and others in the Majority World. By traveling to Grenada and Nicaragua and supporting their revolutions, my mother saw that change for African Americans, the working class, and the poor could occur.

My mother and I voted for the first time together near Church Avenue. "Paula, this vote is most important. We must vote against Reagan and the racialized violence he offers the United States and the world." My mother knew of Reagan's assault on Angela Davis in California and of the retrograde programs he put in place there. So we voted together. My ballet teacher in my first year of college, Mr. Raines, also urged us all to vote against Reagan, and once Reagan became president he warned, "You better get your education now, because Reagan is going to cut all the programs that will allow you a free and just education." And Reagan cut everything and promoted war against communities of color in the United States and around the Majority World.

The Grenadian Revolution

Grenada—"It is a lovely piece of real estate."
—**George Schultz, secretary of state, February 1984**

The Grenadian Revolution and the Sandinista Revolution were modeled after the Black Panthers and the Chinese Revolution. This most certainly resonated for Audrey Seniors given her membership in the New York Black Panthers and her understanding of revolutionary theory. In 1979 Grenada's New Jewel Movement overthrew Eric Gairy's brutal dictatorship.[7] The 1973 New Jewel Party Manifesto replicated Mao's *Little Red Book* and the Black Panther Party's Ten-Point Program with their demand: "WE WANT LAND, BREAD, HOUSING, EDUCATION, CLOTHING, JUSTICE, AND PEACE."[8] The government implemented programs mirroring Cuban Revolution initiatives. They provided low-cost housing, home improvement grants and loans, and free or reduced-fee education and textbooks through the Centre for Popular Education (originally proposed in the manifesto as freedom schools). Grenada's freedom schools mirrored African American freedom schools, Black Panther schools, and Nation of Islam schools of the Black Power era. Billboards pronounced, "Education is a right, not a privilege."[9] The establishment of these schools riffed on my mother's ideology concerning educational equity and her knowledge, for she read *Children Are the Revolution: Day Care in Cuba* and *Mao's Little Red Book*.

The government established literacy campaigns, adult education programs, and scholarships for students to study in the Soviet Union, Cuba, and Eastern Europe. They built the Bernadette Bailey Secondary School, "the second high school to be built by the state in Grenada's entire history."[10] They abandoned the *Royal Reader*, which "reflected the British way of life." Maurice Bishop asserted that the *Royal Reader* taught white supremacy, "self-hate, [and the abandonment of] our history, our culture, our value." The government created the *T. A. Marryshow Readers*, which reflected the Grenadian people's history and culture. They taught patois dialect, "the Big Drum," and dancing.[11] Like Monroe's CARE they sloganeered "Health—a Basic Human Right," offering free milk for children. They provided free or low-cost health and dental care aided by "Cuban volunteer health workers," national insurance, and the creation of at least one medical facility in each of the island's six parishes. The government established thousands of jobs in security, "infrastructural work," and youth employment projects such as the National Cooperative Development Agency. They founded coursework in agriculture, construction, "cooperative fisheries," "small scale live-stock raising," baking, "handicraft," and "professional plumbing."[12] They worked to break the chain of colonization by making Grenada "self-sufficient in food," severing their dependence on food imports from former colonizers.

Bishop's government implemented women's suffrage through the National Women's Organization, created the Maternity Leave Law, instituted equal pay for women, and established day care and preschool centers. Because of the rampant sexual exploitation of Grenada's women by Gairy, his minions, and private employers in "exchange for scholarships and employment," the government enforced women's protection against sexual exploitation, workers' rights, equal pay, and women's militia duty. These programs echoed Cuba's and Nicaragua's initiatives. All of these social changes reversed the history of neglect of Grenada's poor and working class.[13]

These advances for Grenadian women resonated with my mother, for she centered her activism on women's rights to control their bodies.[14] The inroads that the Grenadian and Nicaraguan governments made for women's rights appealed to my mother, for these rights in many cases in the United States eluded African American women and women of color.

The People's Revolutionary Government (PRG) extended the "hand of solidarity" to U.S. radical groups, Native Americans, Majority World people, and African Americans arguing that they shared a mutual cultural identity.[15] Maurice Bishop wrote, "We believe that it is very important that instead of reading the propaganda that is being circulated in America, they should come out to Grenada, come out to Cuba, come out to Nicaragua, and see for themselves. So that they can understand what is happening and as a result be in a better position to appreciate what is going on in this part of the world."[16]

When Maurice Bishop spoke at Hunter College on June 6, 1983, my mother attended and recorded his speech. That month she traveled to Grenada to support the revolution through direct action and remittances, with Cuba in her mind as the imagined ideal. She intended to travel back to Grenada on a regular basis to help with the revolution. Visiting Grenada gave Audrey hope that governments could achieve social equity, and she connected African American, Latin American, and Asian struggles for equality to a diasporic resistance and advocacy for all people of color.[17]

I remember my mother's elation and joy in going to Grenada and returning home with photographs of the revolution in motion. Mommy the avid photographer took pictures of Maurice Bishop and the New Jewel Party from the audience—Bishop at the podium, fierce-looking soldiers guarding him, genuflecting admirers. Mommy came home with photographs of cultural events of dancers doing traditional dances. My mother brought back gifts: nutmeg perfume, which thirty-four years later my three-year-old daughter lathered herself with; a doll with a hat filled with nutmeg, again a prized possession of my daughter. When Mommy was in Grenada I knew she was safe and would return, and she did. I, like Pat Mallory at age sixteen, did not understand the true dangers. I continued my daily rituals of college and dance classes after school and on weekends. I danced with Gallman's Newark Dance Theater and Pepsi Bethel's Authentic Jazz Dance Theatre, and taught dance at East New York Theatrical Workshop. I was living my life. My mother and I were both unaware of the U.S. machinations to destroy the ideal of Grenada.

The Grenadian Revolution proved a threat to the United States. Since the Grenadian government positioned themselves as internationalist; supported and recognized Puerto Rican independence, the Palestinian Liberation Organization, and Nicaragua's Sandinista Revolution; and received aid from Nicaragua, the Soviet Union, Cuba, Jamaica, and Guyana, the United States instituted a policy of aggression against Grenada and radical Caribbean and Central American governments. Given her membership in New York's Black Panthers, Workers World, Youth against War and Fascism, and the Monroe Defense Committee, my mother offered her full support for these world revolutions. She remained acutely aware of the U.S. aggression against Grenada, notwithstanding the objections of the United Nations and the Organization of American States.[18] President Reagan used the CIA to cause discord in Grenada, provided financial and martial aid to countries that supported U.S. interests, and instituted severe political and economic sanctions on Grenada and Nicaragua. October 13, 1983, marked the overthrow of the government by Bernard Coard, the minister of finance, and his compatriots.[19]

On October 19 Coard and his supporters murdered Bishop, his partner Jacqueline Creft, the minister of education, and numerous leaders in the Grenadian government. My mother drew on her personal experience in Grenada to help write "The Illegal U.S. War against Nicaragua" as the legal secretary and office manager at the Center for Constitutional Rights.[20] It stated that on "October 25, 1983, the U.S. sent 1,900 troops accompanied by a 300-man force from nearby Caribbean islands to invade Grenada, a nation of 110,000 people."[21] In 1983 the United States tried to reinstall the dictator Eric Gairy, under the guise of saving American lives and fighting communism. Gairy lost the 1984 elections.[22] The United States utilized this strategy of aggression in Majority World countries like Guatemala, Honduras, Panama, Iran, North Korea, and Chile when real political and social change occurred to create social equality—an equality that threatened U.S. interests in mining, resources, and importation of foodstuffs. The United States worked to destabilize countries. My mother read about these Majority World attempts at breaking the chains of colonialism and imperialism to create a just world. Audrey joined in protests concerning the U.S. actions.

My mother and I listened to WBAI and WLIB with horror at the reports of Bishop's imprisonment, his murder, and the invasion. A deep sense of sadness and shock overwhelmed us. Audrey turned her bereavement, grief, sadness, and helplessness into action: "Currently I am working with two different organizations. They are the Committee for a Free Grenada which was formerly the Committee in Solidarity with Free Grenada before the U.S. Invasion, and the other group is The African American Solidarity Network."[23]

Audrey Proctor Seniors committed herself fully to protesting against U.S. policies of imperialistic violence in the Caribbean, Latin America, and worldwide by working with the Committee for a Free Grenada. She helped put out the newsletter of the same moniker. My mother's African American Solidarity Network worked "to teach and involve the Black community" in issues concerning Central America and the Caribbean, and to connect the high unemployment rates of the poor, African Americans, and other Majority World peoples to U.S. investment in destabilizing Grenada and Nicaragua.[24] Ronald Reagan's policies caused African American unemployment, poverty, and homelessness rates to rise.[25]

My mother used her organizational skills and her voice to oppose the U.S. action in Grenada. She spoke at the "Grenada: The Struggle Continues" conference (March 17, 1983) at Hunter College as a Committee for a Free Grenada member.[26] She used her writing to challenge U.S. aggressive policies in Grenada in the African American newspaper the *City Sun*. The *City Sun* was a very progressive newspaper, an alternative to the conservative and, in some instances, regressive Black newspapers like the *Amsterdam News*. These retrograde newspapers did not challenge hegemony or criticize Black or white political leaders like the racist Mayor Koch.[27] My mother wrote in the *City Sun*:

> The Reagan Administration invaded the small island nation of Grenada after nearly four years of threats. History has shown us it is Blacks and the poor who are on the front lines, fighting the United States dirty wars. It is Black families who must bury their sons, and it is all of us who suffer the emotional and economic hardship of their loss to our communities. I think about the recent deaths of young Black men in Grenada and Lebanon and know that one more death is one too many.... How many young Black men are aware of how we are again to be used? Are we again willing to bear the burden and cost in lives and economic depression, so that Reagan can again tell the world how he has stomped on another small Third World country and wiped out a supposed "threat to the U.S."?[28]

Audrey understood that as in Vietnam, the U.S. government would use Blacks, the poor, and Majority World U.S. citizens for the bulk of the fighting, and that the money spent on the Grenadian invasion was appropriated from these communities. She understood the U.S. history of oppression of people of color and wanted to fight against it. With this understanding Mommy, through her activism in the United States, Grenada, and Nicaragua, advocated for more educational opportunities and chances for upward mobility for racialized minorities, the poor, and the working class.[29]

The Nicaraguan Revolution

In 1983 and 1984 the Nicaraguan government asked for volunteers to work in their coffee and cotton fields, which were "endangered by the Contra war." They asked people to come and work side by side with the Nicaraguans.[30] Like Bishop, Mao, Nyerere, and Castro, who connected U.S. imperialism to anti-colonial movements in Africa, Asia, and Latin America, the Sandinistas vowed to assist Third World anti-colonial movements and African Americans.[31] In supporting "the struggle of the Black people and all the people of the United States for an authentic democracy and equal rights," the Sandinistas, like Bishop, Castro, Mao, and Nyerere, actively pursued African American allies, encouraged them to travel to Nicaragua, and linked African American and Nicaraguan histories of oppression, colonialization, and exploitation.[32] People from around the world, over one thousand North American students, people of all races, ordinary people ranging in age from seventeen to eighty, volunteered as brigadistas.[33] Forty-four-year old Audrey Proctor Seniors, who studied Spanish in Mexico, in New York, and throughout her life, volunteered and organized brigades through the Nicaraguan Exchange, "a project of the interreligious Foundation for Community Organization," the precursor to Pastors for Peace. She also volunteered under the auspices of the African American Solidarity Network.[34] On their return home, the brigadistas formed organizations in support of the Sandinista revolution, or as in my mother's case, built and strengthened existing organizations. The brigadistas demonstrated against the war to protest Reagan's policies.[35] Jeff Jones in *Brigadista Harvest and War in Nicaragua* contends that "by the fall of 1984, the brigades had become one of the most visible—and concrete—signs of domestic opposition to the war against Nicaragua."[36] Audrey protested the war through her writing, contributing a chapter to *Brigadista Harvest*. Mommy embodied Mao Zedong's call for Third World people to rise up against colonialism, hegemony, and oppression.

My mother expressed this opposition in a Third World Brigades recruitment flyer: "As Third World people, we have a special interest in opposing U.S. policy in Central America, and exposing the system that oppresses our peoples, both at home and abroad. The harvest brigades offer us the opportunity to make a small personal public statement against the Reagan administration's continuing policy of aggression."[37] Audrey Proctor Seniors's work with the African American Solidarity Network, the Committee for a Free Grenada, and the Nicaragua Exchange, her sojourns to Nicaragua, and her organizing Third World Brigades reflected her activism. Audrey proclaimed in the *City Sun*: "The people of Nicaragua have the right to determine their own future without interference from the United States, from present or future administrations. And we have the right, duty, and obligation to say to Reagan that we refuse to fight his dirty little battle, just as Alfred Griffin did."[38] Audrey Proctor Seniors declares fullheartedly, "We have an obligation to say that our battle is not in Nicaragua, not in Grenada, not in South Africa—not anywhere, unless we go as volunteers to stand beside our brothers and sisters." Mommy connected the issues that African Americans and other people of color in the United States experienced: "Our fight is here, against an administration which has no regard for Black and Third World people, against a mayor [Koch] who disrespects all Black and Third World peoples, against a racist [New York] police force that holds Black and Third World lives in the lowest esteem, and against those whites who think nothing of shooting Blacks in the back. This is our battleground."[39]

My mother was the smartest person I know. She read voraciously. Every morning she bought the New York Times, *the* Daily News, *the* New York Post, *and the* New York Newsday. *On the days that the weekly Black newspapers the* City Sun *and the* Amsterdam News *came out, she bought those too. I tried to emulate her. My mother would talk to me, educate me about what we read. We demonstrated; we were active. We listened to protest music: "1984, a 50 años, Sandino vive," "Por Nicaragua homenaje de los artistas Latinoamericanos," Luis E. Mejia Godoy's "Yo soy de un pueblo sencillo," "Grenada the Untold Story," and other politically infused recordings. Politics was at the center of our lives.*

Audrey Proctor Seniors traveled to Nicaragua from 1984 to 1986 at the height of the U.S.-backed Contra War, to support the pragmatic Marxist and progressive Catholic Sandinista Revolution. With the revolution in 1978, the Sandinista government enfranchised Nicaraguans by redistributing the land among the people, instituted voting rights beginning at age sixteen, and created housing programs.[40] At the Center for Constitutional Rights (CCR) my mother worked on the *Espinosa v. Reagan* and *Dellums v. Smith* cases filed under the Alien Tort Claims Act "on behalf of Nicaraguan citizens and others"—children, families, doctors, teachers, and priests who were murdered, tortured, mutilated, and hacked with machetes by the Contras.[41] In "The Illegal U.S. War against Nicaragua," Audrey helped write about Dr. Myrna Cunningham, the health administrator for Zelaya province. In December 1981 Cunningham was kidnapped, repeatedly raped, beaten, and interrogated in Honduras by the Contras.[42] These incidents of violence against women by the U.S.-backed Contras greatly affected my mother given her efforts to fight for women's rights and well-being, and they made her more determined to go to Nicaragua. The Sandinista government also founded Asociación de Mujeres Nicaragüenses Luisa Amanda Espinoza (AMNLAE), named after the twenty-one-year-old combatant whom the National Guard murdered on April 3, 1970. AMNLAE's primary goals included rebuilding the country, defending the revolution, ensuring women's equality, establishing day-care centers, providing maternity leave, and enfranchising women through educational opportunities, voluntary service in the militia, and service in the police force. They also won women parity in pay.[43]

In conversations I had with my mother she told me that to see a revolution in which the working class actually benefited signaled to her that progressive change could occur in the United States. My mother told me that to participate in a successful revolution would be an extraordinary and awesome experience.

The U.S. government made a concerted effort to destroy the Sandinista government. Audrey used her power to fight these actions. When Audrey Seniors made her first trip to Nicaragua in June 1984 with the Jean Donavan Brigade, as part of the African American Solidarity Network, the United States used the Contras to engage in a war against the Sandinistas. Notwithstanding the objections of the U.S. Congress, in 1981 the Reagan administration worked to weaken the Sandinista government by suspending President Carter's plan of peaceful coexistence and economic assistance. Utilizing strategies similar to those implemented in Grenada, and ignoring the objections of the U.S. Congress, the Reagan administration used the CIA to destroy the government and gave the Contras financial and military aid, and John Negroponte, ambassador to Honduras, let the Contras use Honduras as a military training base.[44] My mother asserted in *Brigadista Harvest* that the Reagan administration "spent over 100 million dollars in its attempt to overthrow the Nicaraguan government, [while] lobbying for 14 million dollars more for this year alone [1984]."[45] She connected the Contra War to the African American condition in the United States, for she argued that while they spent millions of dollars on the war,

> the potential for a U.S. invasion and the use of Blacks to fight are too real. . . . In Black communities across the country, we have been faced with tremendous cutbacks: in healthcare, daycare, education, food stamps, grants, to higher education. Our teenagers have the highest unemployment rate in the nation. Our rate of infant mortality has risen to almost twice the rate of white infants since Reagan started cutting programs.[46]

My mother wrote of the Reagan administration's dismantling of President Johnson's Great Society Programs, created to make real social change, but mired by the Vietnam War in the 1960s and 1970s and crushed by the Reagan administration in the 1980s, with devastating results.[47] She indicates that the financial resources being spent on the Contra War could offer social aid, health services, and education to African American and Third World U.S. communities. My mother hoped that her travels to Nicaragua would transform society. She explained why she sojourned in her 1984 autobiographical notes and in *Brigadista Harvest*.

My mother knew that Nicaragua's National Guard raped and murdered U.S. white women and nuns, that the "Cult of True Womanhood" did not protect them, and that her safety as a Black woman would not be guaranteed. She knew of sixteen-year-old Brenda Rocha, Dr. Myrna Cunningham, and others who had been raped, brutalized, and murdered.[48] None of these dangers gave my strong, feisty mother pause about traveling to Nicaragua and possibly facing Contra violence. In *Brigadista Harvest* and her autobiographical notes, Audrey Seniors explained why she was determined to travel to Nicaragua: "To show my support for the Nicaraguan people, and the revolution as well as my opposition to the Reagan administration's foreign policy of support to the contra (Counterrevolutionary), I was to spend three weeks in Nicaragua, two- and one-half cutting coffee."[49] Seniors went to Nicaragua at the height of war to buttress the Sandinistas, unconcerned about the physical danger to herself there. But on her return to New York, she faced dangers as well.

My mother was fearless, brave, and courageous. She came home one day a little excited and a little flustered. She told me, "Paula, today I was followed by white male FBI or CIA agents. At first, I was a little surprised and tickled to see that I was being followed by them, but then I just kept on my way, laughing to myself." She was not afraid. She was just letting me know what was going on.

The FBI harassment of brigadistas proved such a problem that the *Brigadista Newsletter* ran the February 1985 article "FBI Alert" detailing what to do if stopped and questioned by the FBI.[50] "If an Agent Knocks: Federal Investigators and Your Rights" (March 1985), published by CCR, featured photographs of my mother in a graphic comic. She and her friends Joan Gibbs and Dorothy Zellner cowrote the pamphlet, which included the writings of Linda Backiel, Jonathan Ned Katz, Margaret L. Ratner, and the Movement Support Network. The pamphlet featured the story of a creepy FBI agent, illustrating questions such as "What is political intelligence?," "Do I have to talk to the FBI?," and "Under what laws do the agents operate?" Answers to each question are given. The FBI agent is seen following my mother down the street. She turns around and looks at him and in all her beautiful indignation with furrowed brow, gloved hand raised pointing at him, says, "I have nothing to say to you. I will talk to my lawyer."[51] The *Brigadista Newsletter*'s "FBI Update" (May 1985) featured this same photograph and quotation.[52] The twenty-plus-year government surveillance of Audrey Proctor Seniors influenced her decision to write and pose as someone being surveilled in "If an Agent Knocks." She wanted others to know what the U.S. government was capable of. Stouthearted, my mother exuded an aura of fearlessness, unconcerned about the surveillance.[53]

In the face of oppression, Audrey Seniors was excited about her trip to Nicaragua, especially because, as she wrote in *Brigadista Harvest*, "the week before, someone had attempted to snatch my bag off my shoulder, and someone else had robbed my daughter's apartment. . . . I looked forward to three weeks of feeling safe and secure, even though I knew I would be in a country at war."[54] She traveled unencumbered by fear, feeling "safe and secure" in a war zone. She was acutely aware of the dangers she faced while in Nicaragua picking coffee. Mommy wrote in "Viewpoint" for the *City Sun*, "We were reminded of the hundreds of U.S. troops stationed in nearby Honduras and the hundreds more who will soon be arriving to carry out 'war games.' . . . It is no longer a 'game.'"[55]

My mother's activism remains a brilliant and brave form of protest, self-determination, and self-defense. While in Nicaragua, Audrey Seniors toured Managua with the Asociación de Mujeres Nicaragüenses Luisa Amanda Espinoza (AMNLAE) and met with the Mothers of Heroes and Martyrs, women whose children had died in battle with Somoza or the Contras. In "Viewpoint" my mother wrote of this experience and of how one mother made an indelible impact on Seniors: "In December 1984, I made a second trip to Nicaragua, not as a visitor but as a worker on a volunteer coffee brigade. Again, I was reminded of the words of that Nicaraguan mother, whose daughter had been murdered, and of the other 8,000 men, women and children who have been killed by cold-blooded acts of violence paid for by the United States."[56] Seniors relayed the mother's message to U.S. mothers in her autobiographical notes and *Brigadista Harvest*. "[The mother] asked us to tell the mothers in the United States not to let their sons come to invade Nicaragua: 'We know what it is like to lose a child and we do not wish it to happen to anyone else.'" This mother extended fellowship mother to mother, but with steely determination and courage she warned, "If your [American] sons come here to invade us, they will be killed"—in other words, the Nicaraguan mothers *would* fight back, and the casualties would be the American visitors' *own* children. This statement greatly affected and made an incredible impression on Seniors, who wrote, "Many times since I have reflected on these words and what they mean for Black and Latino mothers and families here. History has shown in Vietnam and most recently in Grenada, that it is Blacks and the poor who are on the front line fighting the United States' dirty wars.... Black mothers must bury our sons, and all of us suffer the emotional and economic hardship of their loss to our communities," specifically Black, Latino, and poor communities.[57] Audrey Seniors felt insurmountable anguish for the mothers, while gaining strength of mind to work to transform the U.S. system of exploitation of Third World peoples.

A photograph of my indomitable mother in New York City at a summer anti-Contra demonstration shows her unsmiling with large, dark sunglasses and a silky scarf in red, her favorite color, adorning her head. She rests her left hand on her hip, while her right arm holds up a red sign that reads "No Vietnam in Central America!" This image best represents my mother's antiwar stance and how she connected the Contra War to the Vietnam War. We see in this image her unflinching dedication to ending war.

Audrey Proctor Seniors returned to the United States with a resolve to return to Nicaragua as a worker, a brigadista, to help the people decide the destiny of their country and fight U.S. hegemonic oppression. In her Volunteer Work Brigade application form, she wrote of how her travels to Nicaragua fit into the objectives of the African American Solidarity Network to educate the African American community. Seniors wrote: "I will be able to talk with groups that we are presently engaged in reaching out to, around the issues of Central America and the Caribbean. To point out the links between Central America and Blacks in the U.S."[58] As part of this mission, my mother gave interviews concerning her visit to Nicaragua and its connection to Grenada on the New York public radio station WLIB. She wrote articles for the *City Sun*, gave lectures, and spoke to African American organizations concerning Nicaragua and Grenada.

Between 1984 and 1986 Audrey Proctor Seniors worked in Nicaragua as a brigadista picking coffee to support the Sandinistas. Her brigadista application asked if she suffered from any physical ailments. She emphatically asserted no, although she suffered from kidney disease throughout her life. My mother dedicated herself to the Nicaraguan Revolution notwithstanding the hazards to herself, given her illness. Asked if she ever worked as a hard laborer, she replied, "My tendency is to say yes, having once worked as a maid in a hotel, as well as house work and all that that entails."[59] In very savvy language Audrey let the application reviewers know of the labor-intensive nature of maids' work *and* housework—work usually dismissed as easy and inconsequential, but which in fact *is* backbreaking work. We learned this from Mrs. Johnson, who wrote of her mother's dire life as a maid and the brutality of the job.[60] Maids' work and housework were debilitating to both physical health and psyche. By answering that, yes, she worked hard labor, my mother elucidated her political ideology concerning the labor of the working class and poor—that maids' work and housework are arduous and grueling work, and that those who do it should receive respect and pay. Asked why she wanted to participate in the work brigade, she wrote:

> I think that firsthand experience similar to those of the Nicaraguan people will further help to cement the friendship and understanding between the two peoples. If going on a work brigade will further the revolution and help the economy then I am willing. It will also help in educating the constituency we are reaching out to. Lastly, it should also help to keep me humble.[61]

My mother *was* humble. She worked to involve the African American community in Nicaragua and to strengthen the bonds between the two groups. As the coordinator for Third World Outreach in 1985, my mother wrote a Third World Brigade recruitment leaflet, which included this argument:

> As Third World people, we have a special interest in opposing US policy in Central America, and exposing the system that oppresses our peoples, both at home and abroad. The harvest brigades offers us the opportunity to make a small personal contribution to the Nicaraguan people, while making a much larger public statement against the Reagan administration's continuing policy of aggression.

My mother was doing it all, working at CCR, working at the Nicaragua Exchange, and attending to me as I moved toward college graduation. She compiled lists of people to contact for the Nicaragua Exchange and the African American Solidarity Network. She drafted documents for them to gain support.[62] The *Brigadista Bulletin* reported, "The Third World Brigade organizing committee is planning a tour by New York Brigadista Audrey Seniors to promote the project."[63] She was very serious about involving people of color in the issues of the U.S. war against Nicaragua, the Grenadian invasion, and the links to Black economic, political, and social suppression.

In many instances African American leftists working with white leftist organizations often found that whites undercut their efforts at organizing and other related activities. They devalued their experiences as African American subjects in the United States.[64] Similarly, in 1986 Audrey Proctor Seniors found her work undermined by a white woman of the Nicaragua Exchange named Gia. Gia placed a white woman on the Third World Brigade over a person of color, bringing to light long-standing issues between African American radicals, "white radicals," and white women who all subscribed to the "White Race First Policy" and Alvin Poussaint's White African Queen complex while professing to "help" "the colored."[65]

In the 1900s Blacks working within white organizations often found that whites undercut their organizing efforts, showed little interest in the Black condition, and maintained white supremacy within a communist/socialist framework, leading to an exodus of Black members. Comparably, Alvin Poussaint's White African Queen complex, defined as white women's fantasy of "leading Black men to freedom," fit within the "white race first policy" as white women recruits to SNCC used their sexualized relationships with Black men to gain power. Cynthia Griggs Fleming writes that they coveted Black women's leadership positions and tried to take over SNCC. For their "indiscriminate sexual behavior" they held "minor responsibilities," because as Charles Jones noted, "*White women couldn't come in and get over on their bodies alone.*"[66]

Gia's actions in undercutting my mother's authority and organizational skills by placing a white woman on a Third World Brigade replicated the White African Queen complex, the White Race First Policy, *and* the maintenance of white supremacy through a communist or socialist structure. Gia did this notwithstanding the fact that the *Brigadista Bulletin* (March 1985) noted the need for Third World Brigades because of the insensitivity and racism of White brigadistas. One Black man recounted his experience: "There was one other Black Brigadista man on my brigade, and [white] people kept calling us by each-others' name." This further illustrated the need for Third World Brigades.[67] The *Brigadista Bulletin* (October 1985) specified very clearly that the Third World Brigade was cosponsored by the African American Solidarity Network, and that

> special Brigades (Jewish, Unitarian Universalist, Third World, and Elders) are separated contingents within the larger groups, designed to provide people with shared backgrounds or interests, an opportunity to experience Nicaragua together. All brigade dates are open to all applicants, but Special Brigade contingents are open only to members of those groups.[68]

The usual white supremacist behavior occurred with Black activists in league with the Sandinistas, not afforded the same privileges as these white subgroups, given the white need to surveil and control Black people. It remains abundantly clear that Gia knew of the need for a Third World Brigade, free of the interference of white folks, their watching eyes, and sexually predatory white women in the White African Queen complex vein.

My mother was deeply offended and angry with Gia, and with a pen like a sword she wrote a scathing letter addressing her concerns. Given all we know about the FBI's infiltration of radical U.S. movements, of people like civil rights photographer/informant Ernest Withers, Black Panther Richard Aoki, and others, and the large number of entries in the FBI files of Audrey Seniors, Mae Mallory, Ethel Azalea Johnson, Clarence Seniors, and Robert F. Williams that identified women as agents/informers reporting to the FBI on their activities, it would most certainly be unsurprising if both Gia and the white female brigadista were in fact FBI agents and informants, assigned to disrupt Third World brigadista activists and report back on the politics, ideology, and the work of the Third World brigadistas.[69] Perhaps my mother suspected this, for without fear of repression, and never one to mince words, she severely chastised Gia for her transgression in a letter. "Since 1983, there have been a number of brigades to Nicaragua, (in fact you were on a brigade last year) and as Third World Brigadistas can attest, there were either a few of us or none at all. That is a total of 60 Third World Brigadistas out of 1,500 or 1 of 50."[70] My mother let Gia know that her actions were reprehensible given the overabundance of whites on the brigades and the lack of Third World brigadistas. The Brigade recruitment materials show an abundance of white faces and white people's experience, over those of people of color. My mothers' recruitment efforts and the materials she created for Third World Brigades reflects a shift in the Nicaragua Exchange.[71] Audrey Proctor Seniors revealed her commitment to building and maintaining Third World Brigades. In this exchange with Gia she exposed the problematic and harmful nature of placing a white woman on the brigade over Third World Brigadistas.

> The need to involve people of color on the issue of Nicaragua cannot be overstated. One way to do this was and is to have a special brigade of Third World people, to not only harvest the crops that need to be harvested, but to talk with Nicaraguans and learn from them. The Nicaragua Exchange is also organizing better-integrated brigades throughout the year, but the Third World brigade was a special way to meet the needs of Third World Brigadistas who wanted to work together. It is most important that we have first-hand lessons, so that we can return to our communities and talk about what we have learned.... Because we are Third World people, it is easy for us to return to our communities and raise the issue of Nicaragua, to get other people involved who might not even show up for a meeting and usually don't when whites are involved.

Seniors explained that many African Americans were distrustful of whites, white women, and their organizations, and Gia's actions confirmed the reasons why. African American Solidarity Network's Ron Ashford wrote that one of the reasons for founding the AASN included the fact that attempts to bring Blacks into "white solidarity organizations [met] with little success."[72] My mother continued in her letter to Gia, "Politically, it was (and is) a correct decision to have a Third World Brigade. The SNSP [Nicaraguan Peoples' Solidarity Committee] has in the past complained about the lack of Third World people on the brigades. They were quite pleased with the idea of a special brigade consisting of *only* Third World people.

Then she called Gia out on her racist behavior: "When you take it upon yourself to do other than what a group has agreed on, it says that you *think* that only you know what is best for the group." My mother expressed her discontentment with Gia and stated that she felt personally "betrayed by you, by your lies." My mother ended the letter with this affirmation: "But in spite of your manipulation, the brigade was a highly successful one, with Brigadistas returning saying they are ready to work toward building for next year." With a touch of very nasty venom, my mother signs the letter "Very Truly Yours, Audrey P. Seniors."

By organizing Third World Brigades, picking coffee as an "Ambassador of Peace" at the government-run La Lima Coffee Farm, and visiting political and social organizations through the Asociación de Mujeres Nicaragüense, Seniors supported the Sandinista government and came home armed with knowledge to teach African Americans and people of color of the relationship between the Contra war and the adverse conditions in their communities given the appropriation of financial and human resources from their neighborhoods to maintain the war. In her autobiographical notes (1984–1985) my mother recounted her experiences in Nicaragua and how the U.S. Contra war affected the Nicaraguan people:

> As we traveled into the mountains and beautiful countryside, passing through the picturesque city of Matagalpa, night began to overtake us. As night came, I no longer thought about the beauty of the countryside, but instead thought of the murders of the TelCor (telecommunication) workers, who were on their way to cut coffee, of the mothers who were murdered on their way to visit their sons and daughters, of the many people from the elderly to babies who were murdered by the Contra, with the backing and blessing of Reagan and his administration. I thought of the brothers and sisters in Southern Africa, the young, the old, murdered by the Contra there, dying and suffering with the backing and blessing of Reagan and his administration. I thought of all the atrocities that are carried out in Third World countries, supported with weapons and monies supplied by the United States government. These

thoughts and others ran through my mind throughout our trip on this dark highway. I no longer thought of cutting coffee.[73]

Moodily, my mother intermingled the beauty of Nicaragua with the brutality and barbarity of war—the cruelty and savagery of the murder of ordinary people, and the U.S. hand in these murders in Nicaragua and South Africa, so that the United States and Europe could seize the resources of these lands. The U.S. government's actions tried to ensure that people of color could not step out of their assigned place and would remain in low status positions. My mother never expressed fear, never mentioned the personal danger that she experienced, never let on that she might perish, might not return home, that her government and the Contras considered her an enemy. My mother instead chronicled the toll of the war on the Nicaraguan people.

In her autobiographical notes Audrey Proctor Seniors also wrote about her experience as a brigadista: "To reach La Lima's coffee fields, one must climb the mountains. The highest places I had ever climbed previously were the subway stairs in New York, certainly no mountains. I was determined to climb those mountains and more important to either lose my fear of heights or at best ignore it. Climb them I did, [but] the fear remained." A photograph of her picking coffee shows her as ebullient, bright-eyed, and smiling, wearing short Senegalese twists covered by a beige scarf, a red sleeveless T-shirt, a gold watch, a water flask, and a basket tied to her waist as she picked coffee. She teasingly sticks her tongue out. The photograph reveals her fun-loving spirit:

> Each morning we were awakened at 4 a.m. to wash, dress, breakfast, and leave for the fields by 6 a.m.... We were led to the fields by Nicaraguan workers and some militia people for our protection, since the Contras were carrying out their threats to disrupt the harvesting of the coffee and a large number of Nicaraguans had already died harvesting the coffee. Each day we were given talks by one or more of the union leaders of the UPE [Unidad de Producción Estatal]. There would always be chants and songs as we marched off to the fields.[74]

Seniors describes the Reagan administration's use of tax dollars, and social and welfare program dollars, to fund the murder of workers. My mother returned to the United States and continued her efforts on behalf of the Nicaraguan people. She received letters of thanks for her work in the coffee fields. In 1987 she helped raise $5,000 to build children's parks in Nicaragua. That same year the Nicaragua Exchange disbanded because of its very success and the formation of other aid groups. This accounts for the end of Audrey Proctor Seniors's travels to Nicaragua.[75]

Namibia, Panama, and Black Women in Defense of Ourselves

On January 22, 1987, my mother and I attended a reception honoring Oliver R. Tambo, president of the African National Congress, at a posh Atlantic Avenue loft.[76] My mother studied African history in her high school years, and her library included books and pamphlets on South Africa and the continent. Armed with this arsenal of knowledge, in 1989 Audrey Proctor Seniors traveled to the newly independent Namibia as a staff member of the International Association of Democratic Lawyers, to observe the South West Africa People's Organization's free elections.[77] Founded in 1960, "SWAPO is a national liberation movement rallying together on the basis of free and voluntary association, all freedom inspired sons and daughters of the Namibian people."[78] With independence from South Africa, SWAPO became Namibia's governing party.

> *When Mommy came home from Namibia, she was so tickled that she illegally crossed the border to South Africa. She loved meeting South African and Namibian people. She captured her visit with beautiful photographs of murals and of herself with soldiers. My mother was brave.*

That same year, when CCR sued the United States for "illegal invasion and subsequent human rights violation" against the Panamanians due to the Panama invasion, Audrey worked on that case. My mother was grief-stricken by Panamanian loss of life.[79] In 1991 her name appeared on "African American Women in Defense of Ourselves" in the *Amsterdam News* and the *New York Times*'s guest editorial, condemning Anita Hill's treatment, Clarence Thomas's sexual harassment of Hill, and his nomination to the Supreme Court.[80] Her work, her political life, and our life together of fun and activism were permanently intertwined.

One day in 1989, Mommy asked me to meet her for dinner after work. She told me in the most matter-of-fact way that she had breast cancer. I was scared and upset, she upbeat: "Stuff happens." My tough strong mother. As a little girl, I remember asking her about the square-shaped bumpy keloid scars she had on the top of her breasts. She told me that in Cleveland the doctors suspected she might have breast cancer, so they operated but found nothing. The scars to me symbolized an interesting map of my mother's life. The scars symbolized a map of freedom from cancer. It was very distressing to hear that somehow these good luck tattoos had failed. My mother's optimistic and positive attitude helped soften the horror of it all. She had a mastectomy around Christmas. Her hospital mate was a Jewish woman with a daughter. Every day we would meet and take care of our mothers and exchange Christmas and Chanukah presents. We were two daughters taking care of their mothers.

When my mother finally came home, she was out on sick leave for quite some time recovering from the surgery. She could not lift her arm and needed help getting in and out of my white Mustang. We took to driving around Brooklyn, exploring. We drove to her favorite place: the beach; to new neighborhoods like the Jewish enclave in Williamsburg, which seemed like another world compared to our Flatbush neighborhood with our beloved Prospect Park, Botanical Gardens, and Brooklyn Museum. At Coney Island we ate Nathan's hot dogs. My mother looked longingly at her favorite ride, the Cyclone roller coaster. We made the best of it. She hated the plastic surgeon and after one reconstructive surgery chose not to reconstruct her other breast. She refused to meet with the breast cancer support group, asking, "What do I have in common with those white women?" She skipped chemo and radiation treatment because of her kidney disease. The cancer never came back.

My mother's kidneys began to fail around 1991 or 1992. To prepare my mother for dialysis, they had to put a tube in her arm, but my mother was so tiny and her veins so small that her veins collapsed. They put valves in her arms many times, scarring up her arms. They finally put a tube in her neck. My glamorous mother took to wearing long-sleeved shirts to cover the scars and the tube entry. It was important to Mommy to be independent and to do things for herself and by herself. It was important for her to take separate vacations from me, especially after she went on the dialysis machine. Soon after she received her shunts and started the dialysis machine, we both traveled. My mother went to Aruba trying out how it would be to travel while on dialysis. She loved to travel overseas—Mexico, Grenada, Nicaragua, Namibia, and the Caribbean. I went to Cancun. It was difficult for my feisty mother to be confined by illness. She did not have the best time in Aruba, nor did I in Cancun, for that matter.

The Last March

My mother's last political and personal battle occurred in 1994. On October 26, 1994, the CCR's African American director, "House Negro" Ron Daniels, and the board—"white liberals" William Kunstler, Michael Ratner, Arthur Kinoy, and others—fired my mother, the office manager and secretary, after a spotless fifteen-year-record. Our friend and my mother's coworker, Joan Gibbs, told me that they ruthlessly cancelled my mother's health insurance.[81] They fired my mother, a cancer survivor with kidney disease, and retained a white woman with less longevity, who, as my mother told me, "bombed places as a member of the Weather Underground!!!" William Pleasant of the *Daily Challenge* reported that CCR's actions

> are reminiscent of Reagan's treatment of the PATCO [Professional Air Traffic Control Organization] workers in 1981 and is worse than the present mayor's treatment of city workers. For [CCR] to engage in such blatantly anti-worker actions especially firing one of its most senior workers who is disabled, is the worst form of hypocrisy, according to Joan Gibbs, a senior CCR attorney and spokesperson for the workers.

The majority of CCR's staff and lawyers formed a union and went on strike, with Joan Gibbs acting as their spokesperson. CCR fired Joan in retaliation. They went on strike for my Mommy.[82] Pleasant continued: "Seniors' firing seems to have added gasoline to the workers fire. Said Gibbs: 'Audrey Seniors, an African American, was my secretary and support of several other women attorneys. She had more seniority than anyone, but they kept a white worker with much less seniority. I believe that was not only a violation of the Americans with Disabilities Act, but Title VII also.'" The CCR demonstrators demanded that Audrey be reinstated. Joan and the United Auto Workers Union represented my mother.[83] Although very ill, my mother marched on the picket line, and I joined her as I had always marched with her throughout my life.

> *My mother never fared well in cold weather given her small frame and small hands that turned green from the cold. I bought her cashmere-lined leather gloves from Lord and Taylor to keep her hands warm ... Striking, the air was cold, so the shop owner downstairs from the Center, my mother's Korean friend, let her stay in the shop to keep warm during the strike when she got cold. She fed my mother coffee, tea, and treats. She talked to my mother and supported my mother. My mother had lots of friends ... We would go to the UAW office where she played solitaire on their computer. By this time, she was doing dialysis at home.*

The *Village Voice* reported that with "chants of 'House Negro!' 'House Negro!'" directed at Daniels, "the staff expresses particular outrage at the layoff of Audrey Seniors, calling the treatment of the [fifty-three]-year old cancer survivor with a chronic kidney condition 'heartless' and 'morally indefensible.'" My mother's humor was intact when she asked the reporter, "Who in the hell is going to hire me?"[84] Ignoring her illness as we had done since I was a child, my mother and I marched on the picket lines and participated in the two-month strike. I recall one protest where Black Panther Bobby Seale was speaking. He and Arthur Kinoy passed us. Kinoy wagged his finger disapprovingly at us, as if we were naughty children. Seale didn't skip a beat and kept walking.

I asked Joan Gibbs how the strike ended. She told me that African American Brooklyn activist Sonny Carson threatened to kill them all. That's how my mother won her job back.[85] But who really wants to go back to a place that treated you so shabbily and with such ill regard? Audrey Proctor Seniors retired due to her health and a hostile work environment.[86]

My mother had great plans for her retirement, to take ceramics classes, to take swimming lessons—she loved to swim, to travel. That summer of 1995 my magnificent fun-loving mother and I had a wonderful time together. We went shopping, we went to street fairs where she bought a painted Mexican vase and dropped it but still treasured and displayed it at home. We went to Brooklyn's African Street Festival at Boys and Girls High. I remember her fatigue climbing the steep train stairs, having to rest after climbing a few stairs. Later that week we went to the Fourth of July fireworks under the Brooklyn Bridge. My mother truly loved fireworks and got such a thrill out of watching them. She was like a kid watching the pyrotechnics, her eyes wide with wonder at the colored lights, the pop of the fireworks, the smell of the smoke. Her smile while watching this wonder beamed as bright as the fireworks. I had more fun watching her than the fireworks. She loved the sun on her face, she loved to bathe in the sun at the beach, at the park. The spring and the summer were her favorite times of the year, so maybe that is why she left me in the summer. The weather was changing, she hated the winter, so that must be why she left in the summer, her favorite time of the year.

Radicalized by the New Orleans NAACP, the Monroe Defense Committee, the Workers World Party, the Youth against War and Fascism, and the Black Panther Party, my mother used this education to rage against war and violence in the name of democracy, and against hegemonic oppression in the United States and worldwide. My mother took action, unafraid of the repercussions she might face, and advocated for equality for African Americans and people of color in the United States, the Caribbean, Latin America, and the diaspora, at the same time raising me. While many activists abandoned the struggle for human rights, my mother worked for revolutionary causes her whole life. She defiantly held aloft the banner for revolution, for self-defense, self-determination, independence, and freedom for all people. She let nothing dissuade her, not even when the FBI threatened her family in New Orleans in the 1960s, surveilled her in Cleveland, and Monroe. They surveilled her in the 1960s and 1970s in New York and followed her around New York City during her work for Grenada and Nicaragua in the 1980s. She emphatically pressed forward, keeping the banner aloft for the revolution.

My mother told the nurse the week before she died, "You get up to go even though you might not feel well. You get up to meet your friends. These are the things you do. You just do them."

Chapter 10   Radicalized Daughters Speak

Let Resistance Be Your Motto by Pat Mallory Oduba

I was asked by Paula to write a few words for the conclusion. My mother, Mae Mallory, taught me many years ago to "Let resistance be your motto," the best slogan to describe her. As much as I resented the admonitions of my mother, I took on the attitude of resistance and wore it as part of my personality. I didn't know how much I took those words to heart. It didn't occur to me that it would be an automatic response to almost everything I was asked to do. Thus, when Paula asked me to write my thoughts as a radical daughter, my first impulse was to tell Paula, "No, thank you."

Throughout life with resistance as my motto, I turned down opportunities that may have led me in another direction: writing. I found a passion for writing, but I was too unsure of myself and the success writing could offer me. I resisted. I resisted success. As a university student I resisted an opportunity to write for my school newspaper. I resisted writing a piece for a book by Toni Cade on my experience on a predominantly white college campus. As unimportant as I thought I was as a leader, I now claim my importance and my role as a leader, reversing my pattern. I accepted Paula's offer to write this conclusion.

My great-uncle, Arthur White, used to say that "we all waited on line in heaven to be born." Some people say we choose our parents. I've recently learned that when we are born we instinctively expect to be PROTECTED and PREPARED for the life we'll be living on this earth. I wonder when in heaven do we choose our parents. Do we choose what city, what country to be born in? We are taught to believe in our inferiority, that our position in this world is due to inferior genetic material, deliberately designed for the conniving greed of white supremacists who plot to steal the wealth of the planet. With these white supremacists' lessons in mind, *who* would choose to be formerly enslaved Africans in the southern states of the USA? *Who* would choose to be born and raised poor, deeply melanated, short, and fat? *Who* would choose to be born a nappy-headed girl child? *Who* would choose two poor Black parents born under similar circumstances? To top it all off—*who* would choose to be *raised radical*? *Who* would choose to be *an African American woman radical's daughter*? That was *not* the life I expected or wanted. I resented it . . . but I gradually accepted my lot. I understood my position and finally gained pride in my mother's attempt to *protect* and *prepare* me for what I needed in life. My mother prepared me to maintain and pass on the fight for my people and all people who stood on that line in heaven waiting to be born and those who are standing in line now, waiting their turn to be born.

I was raised in a *radical household* composed of my mother and my younger brother. My parents divorced when I was a toddler. My father had very little to *no* influence on my upbringing. The few encounters we had were significant and the memories are everlasting. Nevertheless, I would not recognize him if I saw him face to face. I saw him twice in my lifetime, once, when I was eight years old and the next when I was twenty-four. My brother was removed from the household by the courts when he was eleven because he was getting into trouble in the streets. Our household was reduced to just my mother and me. I thought that I was *not* protected or prepared for the life that was placed around my neck, the necks of my parents and my people in these United States. In fact, being born beautifully, deeply, and richly melanated, gorgeously short and fat, with lovely nappy hair, proved just the right material to move and shake this world, just the right ingredients needed to come out fighting as an unapologetic radical. I look at our African American politician Stacey Abrams and many other zaftig African American women making brilliant contributions to our liberation. Black women are the backbone of the world, and now society recognizes us as leaders, leading progressive change and movements in the United States and across the globe. My mother did exactly what she needed to do to protect and prepare herself, Butch, and me for a liberated life in these United States of America.

As long as I can remember, my mother was a radical. She once revealed to me that an aunt asked her, "Ain't you scared?" I never thought of my mother as afraid of anything. I saw her cry twice in the sixty-two years that I knew her: first, when Fidel Castro was addressing the United Nations and the press cut off his speech, and next at my grandmother's funeral twenty years later. Crying was a sign of weakness. We were taught not to cry. She once shared a pictorial of the brutal violence of South African apartheid with me. I was moved to tears, and she said, "There's no need to cry. You must help to change the oppression of South Africa. Crying does not help." It seemed as though she was afraid of nothing and no one, and she tried to instill that in me and Butch.

The only religion in our household was *resistance, never passive resistance*! She fervently believed and supported armed resistance to prevent the ongoing practice of lynching of our people. My mother raised money to buy arms for Blacks to protect themselves from the Klan in Monroe; she sued the New York Board of Education to end de facto segregation and *won*. She was active in organized labor and involved herself in a host of other bold activities. She fought against sexism, capitalism, racism, colonialism, and religion, particularly Christianity. She fought them all vigorously! In fact, she and Madeline Murray, the atheist who founded American Atheists, were very close friends. She had a book titled *Let Resistance Be Your Motto* and many other books about resistance. *Let Resistance Be Your Motto* always drew my attention. It became my motto. My childhood years were exciting times, and I didn't even know how much those times would play out in the rest of my life with the mantra "Let resistance be your motto."

INFLUENCES

Numerous bold and brave women including my mother changed the pattern of life in their communities. The larger news media didn't mention their activities because of racism and sexism. The media encouraged suffering peacefully.

I was the fifteen-year-old with her mother's photo posted with "Wanted" above her head in post offices around the country ... Because of my mother's incarceration, older women took me into their fold. As a young woman growing up in New York, my grandmother couldn't do a thing with me, so Nannie Murrell Bowe, who was a couple years older, helped me become a young woman. She'd sew clothes for me and show me how to wear things, wear nice dresses. She taught me how to take care of myself. So that was good. Nannie talked to me about men and sex. Nannie took me to Margaret Sanger's clinic for birth control to prevent any pregnancy. She looked out for me. Nannie saw this young teenager who could become a wreck; she was steering me in the right direction, which was good. Big sisters helped guide me through my stormy adolescence, like Audrey Seniors and Janet Jemmott [Moses], who kept me level-headed.[1] They were married, which fascinated me—to see a family, to see a wife and husband in the same home. I wondered how it would be to live in the same house with your father, given none of my friends' fathers lived with them, except for one friend. It fascinated me to see a married couple in the same home, talking very sweetly to each other. I never heard that kind of talk going on between my mother and whoever she was dating. I give credit to these women who lived with men. They seemed happy.

As a youngster I did not understand the Cold War tactics of oppression used against me and my family. My mother associated with Communist Party members; I overheard many of her conversations affirming communism. She helped organize the International Ladies' Garment Workers Union—a union tinged with communism. I did not understand Red Scare tactics that manifested in threats, insults, isolation, and my punishment at elementary school. In school they taught us that communism was something awful, but I resisted anti-communist talk. There was no reason to be loyal to the United States in my opinion, given lynching—Emmett Till—and segregation, and NO federal declaration against these injustices.

All of this would shape my being in my teen years when the 1960s Harlem Riot erupted.[2] I was in high school and independent. My mother was in Cleveland, leaving me, age fifteen, in the hands of my meek and mild grandmother Willie Lee Brown Streeter. She managed to keep me from going to jail or getting pregnant *and* I managed to graduate from high school. All she had to do was call my mother to report my teenaged behavior. Although I was out of reach from my mother given she was in jail in Cleveland and I was in New York, she still had a chilling effect on me. Her sharp tongue and a cutting glance etched in my soul, worked to get me back in line.

I was sent to a private progressive school, the Downtown Community School in what is now considered the East Village, where Pete Seeger was the school's music director. He left a wealth of folk music from around the world. At the school I befriended my African American buddy Lisa, a teenage girl, raised middle-class, from an activist household with a progressive mom like mine. Finding a like-minded teenage girl whose mom was "progressive," though not an activist, was enough for me. We became close friends and declared we were sisters. I lost close contact with Lisa. When we graduated from DCS, she went on to Music and Art High School. My other "sister," Angela Fernandes, was raised by her aunt. Her mother had passed away. We were both motherless, but her strong-willed Aunt Edna kept her in line, and me too by default. All of these women, girls, my mother, and grandmother laid the foundation for my personality, my being. With all these lessons, I was set to explore my world. I lived a life of protest.

My brother and I were de facto activists. In February 1960 my brother and I were on the picket line against segregation policies at Woolworth's on 125th Street in Harlem. It was so cold, and we were out for so long that when we got home my mother turned on the oven and we put our feet in the oven to warm them. I was sent to Highlander Folk School in Monteagle, Tennessee, for a youth gathering with Guy and Candy Carawan. We took the Greyhound bus and used the opportunity to test the new law assuring that African-heritage interstate travelers would not be relegated to the back of the bus. Notable was the fact that the African American writer Julius Lester was there as one of the adults onboard, and Fred Shuttlesworth Jr. was one of the youth.

As a college student, off I went with all my experiences as the daughter of an African American radical mother, to build my own life and face my own challenges.

I chose an ANGRY BLACK WOMAN persona. I wore it proudly. What was there to be happy about when you learned about the over four hundred years of heinous crimes committed against my people? The U.S. efforts to brainwash and turn people against each other, their stealing resources from other nations, labeling them "underdeveloped," and bragging about these robberies. Because I was Mae's daughter, I was expected to be radical. I tried to live up to that, trying to appease my mother, and those around her who expected a radicalized daughter. I was beginning to be like my mother in my attitude and radical thought. However, I did break the Mae Mallory mold of insensitivity, for I gave people space to just be, unlike my mother. I was becoming my own African American woman radical activist.

RADICAL DAUGHTER

My mother wanted her children to have a better life. I went to college, got my BA and MA, and got married to a Howard University graduate with a degree in chemical engineering. I was living that so-called middle-class life. Yet the struggle did not end with my middle-class life because classism, sexism, and internalized oppression are still ongoing battles that I engage in.

I now have a son. I have given him a radical perspective, with an emphasis on inner self-appreciation. I surrounded him with a community of people who see him as a complete human being. I ensured his agency as someone who deserves to be heard. I infused him with a strong sense of self so that he knows how great he and his people are.

As I come closer to my own life's conclusion, I have made a more cultural relationship with Christianity with the teachings of my pastor, Reverend Dr. Herbert D. Daughtry. I was led there by my mother's influence and the strong spiritual/unexplainable metaphysical situations I experienced in Africa. Those metaphysical experiences convinced me that there is a science greater than humans . . . We call it God. My resistance gets in the way of complete conviction.

Radicalized Daughter by Paula Marie Seniors

Generational differences separated Ethel Azalea Johnson (1916), Mae Mallory (1927), Audrey Proctor (1940), and Pat Mallory (1945), but their ideology of radical African American women's activism bound them together as a family. They believed in self-defense, human rights, and an end to colonialism and imperialism in the United States and worldwide. They taught us—their children Ray Jr., Pat, Butch, and me—these ideologies. Pat and I in turn have taught our children these lessons.

My mother raised me in a magical multiracial world, of protest, political education, joy, and wonder. Our motto "Joie de vivre" (joy of living) was sprinkled with hues of red, her favorite color. To be Audrey Proctor Seniors's radicalized daughter meant a life filled with immense love, joy, happiness, and activism—joie de vivre every day of our life together, talking, listening, learning, and exploring the world!!! We traveled to New Orleans, Montreal, Cape Cod, the Bahamas.

> Paula, I don't want you to have regrets in life. Anything you do you should do to your fullest ability. You should have no regrets in your life. Down the road you can say I tried my hardest, I did my best, I have no regrets.
>
> —**Audrey**

My mother didn't care what career path I chose as long as it was something I loved—something I pursued to my fullest ability. So when I decided to become a dancer she was fine with that decision, but by Black Mother's Decree I had to go to college. I had no choice, none of this "turning professional" and not going to college for me. My first choices were Purchase and Juilliard. I got into Adelphi, City College of New York, Goucher . . . I chose City College because my dance mentor Tee Ross, whom I danced with in Pepsi Bethel's Authentic Jazz Dance Theater, went there. It was an absolutely beautiful experience. My ballet teacher was Mr. Walter Raines from Dance Theater of Harlem, Stuttgart Ballet, and New York City Ballet, and Mrs. Denise Jef-

Fig. 13. Paula Marie Seniors, "Dancer as Athlete," Audrey and Clarence Seniors Collection

ferson, director of the Ailey School, taught us Martha Graham's technique. I became their baby; they pushed me and used me to demonstrate the dance combinations. I loved and respected them immensely. It was wonderful; I became very good. My first year at City College of New York my mother attended all my dance performances. I danced the Sugar Plum Fairy on pointe, won the Thelma Hill Memorial Dance Award, and made the dean's list. That summer we went to the Bahamas, the days of chartered planes, physical tickets, hotel reservations, and landline telephones. We got to the airport and realized we had left our tickets and papers on the dresser and couldn't depart. My mother called the agent, who rearranged our travel plan; we stayed at a hotel at the airport. The next day we boarded the plane. The plane ride was bumpy. My mother put on a brave face; at one point the plane dropped several feet. People screamed, we held hands, and I could see the little beads of sweat on my mother's brow. My courageous, strong mother defied fear. Neither one of us talked on that plane ride, so scared was I. Mommy the Brave. We finally made it to the Bahamas and off that dang plane. We had fun discovering the Bahamas. The flight back was a smooth one.

In my second year of college I auditioned for Juilliard and Purchase, with the help of choreography taught to me by Dr. Jill Beck, our dance history and Labanotation teacher, and Jenny who taught dance notation. I was accepted into both schools but chose to leave school and join a dance company, where I met my good friend Daryl Sneed. I also taught dance at East New York Theatrical Workshop in Brooklyn. Daryl and I danced with Alfred Gallman's Newark Dance Theater, and I finished my degree at City College. Because my mother raised me to be independent, I moved out into my own apartment.

I danced with Eleo Pomare's Dance Company and Shirley Rushing's RushingDanz while teaching dance at Red Hook Arts in Brooklyn to many children, including gutsy, spirited nine-year-old Angie, the daughter I wished for. I made a lifelong friend with the drama teacher, Verna Hampton. Dancing for Eleo was wonderful. I played Little Mahalia Jackson in *Blues for a Gospel Queen* at Brooklyn's Billie Holiday Theater and the Little Blind Girl in *Louis Braille*; I understudied in *Give My Regards to Broadway* and performed in *Little Shop of Horrors* and *The Music Man*. I performed with my great friend Angelo Adkins in *Singing in the Rain* and the European tour of *Hair*. I performed in *Ain't Misbehavin'* and *The Roar of the Greasepaint*, where I met my friend Sheryl Rifas.

Later in life I asked my mother, "Why didn't you make me go to Juilliard or Purchase, when I was accepted?" She told me, "You were always grown; nobody could tell you what to do."

When I had stalls in my career, my mother would say, "Paula, you can come back home, you can save money and you can take your dance and singing classes without stress." But because she raised an independent radical daughter, I didn't go back home. I struggled. At one point in my struggles she asked, "Are you going to be a waitress for the rest of your life?" With that question I went back to college at New York University and earned a master's in musical theater vocal performance—I didn't have a practical bone in my body. During my time at NYU I joined the picket line for my mother against the CCR in between classes.

INGRAINED IN MY DNA: SELF-DEFENSE AND ACTIVISM

While watching tributes to John Lewis with my daughter, age ten, I was SICKENED watching him get his ass kicked by white supremacists on that bridge in Alabama. His passive resistance ideology encouraged his beating. I found myself telling my daughter, "You must always fight back; you must always defend yourself." A sudden lucid realization came to me—my mother's lessons of self-defense and advocating for equality were ingrained in my DNA, as were Mae's lessons to Pat. Because of my mother's lessons I believe fullheartedly that you must defend yourself and others against violence and injustice. My mother's lessons carried me through life. In 1990–1991, during the First Gulf War, in between my professional dancing duties I protested and volunteered with an antiwar group, collating flyers. These were lessons learned from Mommy about the importance of protest.[3] I, a radicalized daughter, protest because of my mother. My experience marked a two-decade generational shift from Patricia. I always understood my mother and why we protested and loved going to protests with her. I loved the camaraderie of the movements we involved ourselves in. When Nelson Mandela was freed from prison, my mother and I both went to the celebration at Yankee Stadium—I with my friends Sharon and Carol and she with hers. We met at Mommy's home afterward and compared our experiences.

When my mother died I continued my life of activism as a graduate student in San Diego, protesting the wars in Iraq and Afghanistan. At one march the white organizers, whom I had just met, inexplicably asked me to lead the march. I declined. I could not find protests against these wars when I lived in Blacksburg, so I joined the Iraqi Veterans Against the War. While living in Charlottesville I protested the Iraq and Afghanistan war every Thursday night on the downtown corner. These were the lessons of activism and protest my mother infused in me.

BLACK PRIDE

My mother taught me of the beauty of being Black, of the beauty of Black skin, dark skin. When I was old enough to wear makeup, my mother taught me how to apply foundation a shade darker than my skin to accentuate the Africanness. As a little girl in Brooklyn in the late 1960s, we encountered many different types of people, whom I also learned from.

> *Riding the 41 bus with Mommy*
> *In Brooklyn age five, six, or seven*
> *With the funny Haitian ladies*
> *With their pale pink lipstick*
> *And their white powdered faces*
> *Not masking their brown*
> *Unmasking their brown skin*
> *Their African*
> *Their Haitian*

These ladies were the first Haitians to escape the brutal Duvalier regime for Brooklyn, exhibiting an internalized racism that I as a child did not understand. These newly arrived immigrants, while masking their brown skin and seeming quiet and meek, publicly protested the Duvalier regime.

My mother, Audrey Proctor Seniors, taught me to reject hegemonic beauty ideals—no light powder or pale pink lipstick for us. It was Black beauty aesthetic, Black is Beautiful all the way. My mother taught me a complete and total love of my Blackness.

My mother taught me lessons in compassion, how to be a better human being. My mother kept in contact with my former boyfriend. I couldn't understand why. She told me, "Paula, his mother died. I keep up with him so he knows he is not alone in this world." A lesson taught—a lesson learned. Sometimes Mommy had to reteach me empathy and compassion. In 1994, when the grunge singer Kurt Cobain committed suicide, I told my mother, "Cobain's suicide was a selfish act." She stopped me cold: "Paula, for some life becomes so unbearable, so painful, they see no options, the only way they see to relieve the pain is suicide. They aren't selfish, they are suffering. They deserve understanding and sympathy. We should have compassion for them, for what they were going through to lead them to self-destruction."

In 1994–1995 dialysis left my tiny mother's body ravaged and wrecked given the tubes put in her arms collapsing her veins, then one in her neck, and then one in her belly for dialysis at home. She had purple bruises everywhere. She wore long-sleeved and high-necked shirts to cover the tubes and bruises. I can only imagine how she must have felt, to see her beautiful body bruised and damaged by these alien tubes. I was talking to my mother and said something cruel about the way someone looked. She told me, "It's unkind to talk about people's bodies in such malicious ways." In that moment I realized that I had wounded and deeply hurt my mother. I had not recognized her changing body, had not really understood what her changing body meant to her, given the kidney disease wreaking havoc on her small frame. I felt *shame*. She went on, "You should show kindness, compassion, and understanding to people and not be so judgmental concerning the way people look." In this my mother led me to understand that her body was wrecked by kidney disease, and that the same thoughtfulness and care I showed to her, I should show for others. I hugged my mother, apologized profusely, and took this lesson from her body into my own.

When my mother was in the hospital, my aunt Doris and I were riding the crosstown bus after visiting my mother when a mentally challenged young white man got on the bus. All the white people moved away from him. He sat next to Doris and me; we did not move away. He started talking to us, and we in kind talked to him. We had a wonderful conversation. Aunt Doris and I talked about this encounter later, of the coldness of the bus riders. My mother taught me lessons in gentleness that carried me through life.

Mommy always cultivated special friendships with young people: Pat, Crystal, the woman who lived with her with the son, and in her last year of life Maha, her good friend and dialysis nurse. Maha and Mommy were truly simpatico. She loved pronouncing Maha's name like she loved pronouncing the model Vendela's name. "Maha" would roll off my mother's lips and she would giggle. When I visited my mother at her house she told me excitedly about Maha: "She's Iranian, she's working hard to get into medical school. Oh, she is so much fun to talk to, Paula." They had a very special bond.

These friendships my mother cultivated taught me about creating bonds with young people. My first beloved "adopted" daughter was Angie from Brooklyn, whom I met when she was nine as her dance teacher at Red Hook Arts. I just adored Angie, the feisty little girl who is now a mother and important within the New York City Police Department. Others include former students Dr. Santavaris Brown and Ysa Valdes from Florida Memorial College, Dr. Luvena Kopp from the College of New Jersey, and Melissa Burgess, Holli Gardner Drewry, Daveisha Gibson, Dr. Dana Volk, Desiree Turner, Drs. Lauren and Jon Catherwood Ginn, Dr. Kelly Cross, Hailey Brown (PhD candidate), Sadah Espii Proctor, Anamika Sharma, Kim Johnson, Yasmin Huggins, and Grace [Suzzannah] Sesekhalid from Virginia Tech. I have lifelong bonds with all these young people due to my mother's lessons.

LESSONS IN BLACK MOTHERHOOD

When my mother died, an insurmountable desire swept over me, an intense longing overwhelmed my whole body: I wanted to become a mother. For some women like myself there's a connection between losing our mothers and the overpowering desire to become a mother. The mothering instinct engulfs us. Before my mother died she often asked me with a mischievous grin, "When are you going to make me a grandmother?" Besides the beloved nine-year-old Angie, the mothering instinct just had not kicked in. But it overwhelmed me with her death. In graduate school I tried to adopt, but I never got a placement. Time marched on. With my second job in New Jersey, I again tried to adopt, but without permission the white social worker called my boss, who urged me to wait until I got tenure. I withdrew my application. In Blacksburg I again ran afoul with another white social worker who maliciously held up my application. On her firing the Black social worker said I was a perfect candidate and was baffled at this white woman's actions. Time moved on and I remained inconsolable in my parentless state. My friends Carole Boyce Davies and Joanne Gabbin encouraged me to try again. In 2013 I finally adopted my daughter. It took eighteen years for me to become a mother, for the powerful desire to be relieved when my beautiful daughter came into my life. I had such a beautiful childhood with my extraordinary mother, I wanted to give my daughter that same magical childhood filled with Black pride, music, singing, dancing, reading, and traveling.

Veronica Chambers in "The Myth of Cinderella" explains that in the 1970s countless Black women resisted espousing "feminism because it seemed that just when it was about to be their turn to be *Cinderella*, white women were telling them that the fantasy was all wrong."[4] There lies the dilemma of Black women and feminism, the quandary my mother found herself in. Like her friend Yuri Kochiyama, my mother Audrey Proctor Seniors did not claim feminist status while fighting for the rights of Black women and women of color. Both women felt that white feminism left women of color out of the equation and presented men as the enemy. My mother ascribed to the notion that while white women fought for abortion rights and to go to work on the backs of women of color who cared for their homes and children, Black and Majority World women battled to keep their children. As in Antonia Grace Glenn's *Ito Sisters*, when her Japanese American great-aunt gave birth, a white nurse forced the baby back in her body, causing an abortion.[5] Black and Majority World women struggled against state-sanctioned sterilization, advocated for women's rights, and promoted abortion rights. The entrenchment of white supremacist feminist racism and white supremacy, as well as U.S. racism, led my mother down her own path in which she combined the battle against racism, imperialism, and colonialism to Majority World women's rights in the United States, Grenada, Nicaragua, and worldwide. She rallied against sexism, misogyny, and patriarchy; she fought for Black and Majority World women to control their own bodies; and as she taught me, she argued that Black women were equal to men and whites. My mother took her women's work incredibly seriously, teaching me these lessons without hesitation, making sure I knew my importance, knew my options as a Black woman in this world.[6]

MOTHER'S SACRIFICES

Years ago, I requested my mother's FBI files and received no response. I requested my parents' FBI files in 2010 and 2011, which was approved, but I had yet to receive them in the mail. In 2011 I received a cryptic email from the secretary at my job to call the FBI, but no other information was given.

I called and she said, "Hi, this is [Ms. Bambi]. I am with the FBI. I need your father's waiver to release your mother's files." I asked her how large my parents file were. She said she was not finished working on them. I asked if she was a historian because it seemed to me that since the FBI is chronicling people's lives, the FBI is in fact doing the work of historians. She laughed. I then asked her if she was an FBI agent; she said she was FBI personnel. To find out that my parents' FBI files were so extensive that they couldn't just send them to me gave me the creeps, made me anxious, and exposed my mother's strength in withstanding state surveillance. I waited. One day I came home and my parents' files were sitting on the porch in a box.

My mother knew the FBI watched her. This did not deter her from a political life, or a private life. Never did the FBI impinge on our fantastic life together. Even surveilled, we lived a quixotic dream.

I think one of the biggest sacrifices my mother made in her life was *no alimony* in her divorce. She committed herself fully to me: "Ordered, Adjudged and Decreed that the plaintiff [Clarence Henry Seniors] pay as support for the infant issue of the marriage of the parties here to vis., Paula Marie Seniors her tuition at Brooklyn Friends School."[7] I didn't know anything about alimony as a child; I just knew that I went to Quaker school. I learned as an adult that women and men obtain alimony from their former spouses. Alimony didn't even appear as a notion for my mother. My mother unselfishly ensured for me a stellar education. She sacrificed for the sake of her child, with no regrets. With this divorce decree my father paid for my education from kindergarten to college, my clothes, my shoes, and my dance classes. NEVER did my mother ask for anything from my father for herself. NEVER. I sometimes wonder if she would have lived longer if she had in fact received alimony. The doctor told me when she died that she probably caught a virus as a young child, which led to her kidney failure, but I still wondered. If she had gotten alimony, would her self-care have been better? When I was twelve, my mother was pregnant. My mother told me that the baby boy was born premature and died. She grieved over her baby privately. I never saw her cry. The sacrifices my mother made proved immeasurable. She never complained or regretted her life decisions. She was proudly an African American woman radical activist.

MY MOTHER AND THE FREEDOM MOVEMENT

My mother's overall impact on the freedom movement was vast yet unrecognized. Her leftist Black nationalist ideologies and misogyny are key to why she, Ethel Azalea Johnson, Mae Mallory, Pat Mallory, and Ruthie Stone have been excluded from historical records. They went unrecognized because of their working-class backgrounds, and in Mae Mallory's case, her big personality. All of these reasons led to their omission from history books and celebrations of Black leftist activists.

My mother did not become an African American woman radical activist for recognition, fame, or money. She truly cared about this world and about the people in it. She joined political organizations.

As a member of the radical New Orleans NAACP with its communist-affiliated union members from the ILWU and the CIO, Audrey Proctor Seniors saw African American women lead. Through them she learned to lead. Seeing these Black women offered Audrey a model she could follow as she moved forward in her life as an African American woman radical activist. With the NAACP she worked to desegregate New Orleans's public and Catholic schools and advocated for equal pay for Black teachers and equalized playgrounds. She worked to desegregate stores and to end lynching and white sexualized violence against African American women and girls. Audrey worked on voter registration drives and pushed for African American history and music in the public school curriculum. Her membership meant FBI surveillance. Her membership meant erasure from the historical record. As a foot soldier for the New Orleans NAACP, her activism went unrecognized.

As a founding member of Cleveland's Monroe Defense Committee, my mother ran the office, wrote articles, and initiated voter registration drives. With the MDC, Congress of Racial Equality, and the United Freedom Fighters she made tremendous contributions to Mae Mallory's, Harold Reape's, and Richard Crowder's kidnapping cases. She with the MDC gained their freedom from jail on kidnapping charges and had the kidnapping charges dropped. My parents' impact on the lives of Mallory, Reape, and Crowder was immense. She did all of this with a baby on her hip.

In Cleveland's Congress of Racial Equality, she advocated for a fair housing bill, and with Cleveland's United Freedom Movement and Freedom Fighters she picketed to desegregate Cleveland's schools and pressed to boycott Cadillac.

In 1964, with Mae's extradition, we moved to Monroe, and through the MDC my mother worked closely with Mrs. Johnson, my adopted grandmother, on the Monroe defendants' case, as well as serving as business manager for *Did You Know?* She became a writer, both with my father Clarence Henry Seniors and on her own with the article "St. Augustine." They worked with Mrs. Johnson on her educational initiatives of Head Start, adult education, and preschool programs. With the Crusaders' Association for Relief and Enlightenment they distributed food, clothing, and enlightenment to Monroe and the surrounding area's Black community, predating the Black Panthers' free breakfast program. She made quite an unrecognized contribution to aiding African Americans in need. My mother's time working with CARE became the inspiration for her pieces "A Charlotte Widow" and "Monroe."

When Mae won her case we all moved to New York. My mother continued her activism with Workers World Party and Youth against War and Fascism, and as the editor of the *Partisan*. These advocacies changed people's lives. While my mother's life did not reach the history books created by men and conservatives, Audrey Proctor Seniors contributed to a movement led by African American women radical activists, working-class women fighting for the good.

Audrey brought to New York the lessons learned of organizing, grassroots outreach, and aid from New Orleans, Cleveland, and Monroe to Workers World, Youth against War and Fascism, the Black Panthers, and the many groups she belonged to. She advocated against the Vietnam War and all wars, and in 1968 she joined the Black Panther Party, where she befriended Afeni Shakur. With the Black Panthers, she participated in the November 1969 "Women's Liberation in Support of the Black Panthers" march to free the New Haven Nine, who included two children accused of murdering Alex Rackley. They protested COINTELPRO's use of agents provocateurs in New Haven's Black Panthers branch. The iconic photo in chapter 9 captures my mother's erasure from the historical record. The title does not reveal my mother's or any of the women's names—unnamed, unrecognized, unacknowledged. Yet she played a vital role in the Black Panther Party, WWP, and YAWF, helping bring an end to the Vietnam War. She brought focus to how wars feed colonialism and imperialism. She advocated for innocent Black Panthers. She brought forth the downfall of COINTELPRO due to the trial of the New Haven Nine.[8]

My mother committed herself to drawing African American and African diasporic people into the causes she felt were important: antiwar, anticolonialism, and anti-imperialism in the United States and overseas. She worked mightily to involve people in Grenada and Nicaragua through her work with the Committee in Solidarity with Free Grenada, Committee for a Free Grenada, African American Solidarity Network, and Nicaragua Exchange. She organized Third World Brigades to pick coffee for Nicaragua's Sandinistas. My mother got people involved in protesting the U.S. invasion of Grenada through her public talks, her pamphleteering, her grassroot recruitment efforts, and her articles for the *City Sun*.

In 1980, working with the Coalition of Concerned Black Women, she involved herself in seeking justice for the twenty-eight Black children murdered by the Klan in Atlanta. In 1989 my mother traveled to Namibia as an observer of the SWAPO free elections. In 1991 my mother joined the "African American Women in Defense of Ourselves" to condemn Clarence Thomas's Supreme Court nomination and his sexual harassment of Anita Hill.

She was loyal to her friends and family, had a great sense of humor, knew her self-worth, and was loving. My mother was such a vibrant and exuberant person who loved me, loved life, and loved people. Her love of people and her protest and activism efforts proved her biggest contribution to the freedom movement. Her contributions proved enormous, far-reaching, *unacknowledged*, and *overlooked*, with the exception of Eric Zolov and Robert H. Holden's *Latin America and the United States* (2000, 2010). They included an edited version of her chapter from *Brigadista Harvest*. They offered her recognition, *and* university professors still teach her chapter.

One Last Summer

After being reinstated at the Center for Constitutional Rights, my mother retired due to ill health and a hostile work environment. She had big retirement plans—big plans. My mother lived a very active life and enjoyed her fifty-three years of life to the fullest. Audrey Proctor Seniors loved the summer, so it is no surprise to me that her last summer was filled with pure delight. We spent time with her friends, picnicking with her friend Nadine Clark, going to Atlantic City to play the slot machines. She thrilled at the effort to increase her coffers with the one-armed bandits!! We saw *Don Juan de Marco* and *Bad Boys* and wondered why a white woman was the lead woman character in *Bad Boys* and not a Black woman. My mother kept up with Aunt Doris and her brothers, Robert, Carl, and Gary, marveling at their exciting lives. My mother truly loved and cherished her life and didn't want to leave. She fought as hard as she could to stay because she had things to do. My mother taught me so much in our wonderful, magical, quixotic multiracial world. But one thing she did not teach me was how to live without her.

My mother called me to tell me she was sick and needed to go to the hospital. We conducted our ritualized action, practiced over many years: we took a taxicab to New York University Medical Center. My mother's ill health normalized. I stayed with her that night. The next day I went to work at NYU Library as if nothing happened, although I remember feeling very poorly. But I went to work because that was part of our ritual in normalizing my mother's health. We had done this many times before. At work I received an urgent call from the doctors saying that my mother had a blood clot, and they might have to amputate her leg. I rushed to the hospital, and from that moment I never left my mother's side. This was our first time in ICU, and it was scary.

The ICU housed me, a white man watching after his wife, and a white daughter watching after her mother. The first time someone died, their large family collectively burst into tears. The daughter and I callously and arrogantly said, "Well, you could see they were dying. Their eyes were vacant like glassy-eyed dead fish." We didn't realize what was to come for us in the ICU. Every day someone died, and fear coursed through us, the Triad of Misery. Our bodies created that special pungent order that anxiety, fear, and panic imbues scared people with. One day another person died, one person too many for our miserable sorrow-filled triad. The white man frantically started praying. The white daughter took out her rosaries, fiddling with the beads and praying. I the atheist started PRAYING. WE ALL PRAYED FOR LIFE. "Mommy, please don't leave me here by myself, MOMMY!!!! PLEASE!!!" Our triad stayed at the hospital trying to look after our loved ones. WE NEVER LEFT.

I called Aunt Doris, who immediately came from New Orleans. The first day of her visit with Mommy, I told her, "Mommy looks bad, her mind is unclear, keep a brave face, please don't cry." My poor lovely sensitive aunt broke out in tears in front of Mommy, unable to control her emotions. "Doris," Mommy would say when Doris visited us in New York or we saw her in New Orleans, "You are so sensitive, you cry at the drop of a hat." They both laughed uproariously. Seeing her sister in such terrible shape, Doris couldn't come to the hospital. She stayed home and made good New Orleans food. My father visited every day. When I called Nadine she came back from her vacation. Joan pretended she was a relative to get information about Mommy. One day when Mommy was in a lucid state, she was *furious*. "Paula, that white male nurse called me 'Girl.' Oh, I laid him out." At one point Mommy was moved from ICU to the transplant unit where the baseball player Mickey Mantle received a liver transplant.

At New York University my mother had *never* had a Black doctor, or a Black nurse, for that matter. One day I sat on one of the metal beds away from my mother, crying in wretched despair. The vein doctor, who saved my mother's leg—a dark-skinned man, perhaps Southeast Asian—saw me. He gently told me, "You can't lose hope. You must continue to have hope." He soothed me with his words. I went back and sat with Mommy when allowed into her room. Every day I sat with the white daughter with the rosaries, and the white man with the wife. Every day we all *prayed*. Maha visited Mommy every day. Their bond was strong. Maha talked to my mother, she looked at my mother's charts, she talked to the doctors. One day Maha became incredibly upset looking at the charts. She couldn't believe what she saw. She talked frantically to the doctor. Oh My God, she was bereft, unable to conceal her fear and sadness. Her eyes insisted that "these charts are untrue. How can this be?" I looked on in utter disbelief and terror-filled sorrow. NO THIS CANNOT BE TRUE!!! Maha's wretchedness revealed tragedy, heartbreak.

Death is horrible. Death is ugly, ghastly, grim. When my mother was dying, they called me at home. We rushed to the hospital—Doris, my father, Nadine, and Maha. The room was dark. There were windows, but they were high, in the corner. My mother was in bed on a machine and a morphine drip, unbearably bleak in their darkness and artificial light. I wanted desperately for them to move my mother to the window. I wanted her to see the sky—to see the promise of the sun. I talked to her, told her how much I loved her, told her it was all right. I could see in her eyes when she realized she was dying, the shock, the tears. She had a tube in her mouth but she wanted desperately to tell me something. The nurse told me they could not take out the tube. OH GOD. I told her "I love you" over and over. I begged in my mind's voice, *Mommy!!! Please don't leave me here by myself!!! Mommy!!!! Please!!!!* I had to face the unbelievable realization that she would not live, would not conquer this. NO!!!! She died; I wailed. Maha cried. We were shattered. "MOMMY!!! PLEASE DON'T LEAVE ME HERE BY MYSELF!!! MOMMY PLEASE!!!!" I fainted.

It never occurred to me that my mother would die—that I would be left alone in this world. I thought she would live forever. How could she not live forever?[9]

Maha told me she just could not come to the funeral. I totally understood. Before my mother died I rollerbladed every day. Mommy got sick of me carrying the big bulky knapsack to carry my rollerblading pads. She gave me a cute little knapsack. She and Maha were on the same page. I told Maha that I rollerbladed without a helmet. "Paula, you must wear a helmet." After my mother's death, she bought me a helmet. Maha got into medical school in Grenada. Maha's Grenadian entry created a complete circle to my mother's beautiful life as an African American woman radical activist.

> *Yuri Kochiyama called me. She was yelling at me: "Why did Audrey die?" I really couldn't answer why my mother died. I didn't understand it myself.*

> But Yuri was upset, angry, demanding answers I did not have. She came to the funeral and wrote a nice letter and obituary. She wrote, "Dear Paula, how much you remind me of your mother." An excerpt from the obituary for Workers World follows:
>
> "Because we are all 'connected' by love and unity in the struggle, we know you would want to know what might have befallen a friend or comrade from the past. On August 20th we were saddened to learn of the passing of Audrey Seniors of Brooklyn, a long time dedicate who worked in the civil rights movement in Louisiana, North Carolina, Ohio, and the last 25 years in New York.... The last 15 years, she was on the staff of the Center for Constitutional Rights. She left behind her daughter, Paula, and former husband, Clarence Seniors, also an activist."

My mother used to say, "You come in this world by yourself, you die by yourself." Not true, Mommy. I came into this world with you. Mommy, you left this world with me right by your side.

When my mother died my friends Sheryl, Sharon, Derrick, Andrea, and Angelo, my aunt Doris, my uncle Carl, and my father all accompanied me to the funeral parlor. My father and I, Joan Gibbs, Dorothy Zellner, Suzanne Shende, David Lerner, Sheldon, Nadine, and many others arranged the funeral. David wanted to write an obituary for the *New York Times*, but I could barely think. It didn't happen. Joan told the CCR people who fired my mother that they were not welcome at the funeral and their safety could not be guaranteed, because the family might take physical action. At the funeral my friend Verna narrated and my friend Miron Lockett sang, as did my mentor and friend, opera singer Lynda Elliott. People shared their remembrances, which are now lost given the funeral parlor's incompetence. The place was packed.

The week after my mother died I tried to act as if nothing had happened and went back to work at the library. I thought I could pretend that I did not lose the best person in my life. I was working with the public. I nearly climbed over the desk to beat up this white girl who started screaming at me over a record album she wanted. Susan Hayes kindly hired me back in cataloging with my friends Wen Chao and Janet. Susan told me, "Paula, you have someplace to go. You can come to work whenever you want to. If you don't feel up to it you don't have to come." When I looked really bad Susan would send me home. My mother would have wondered why I could not maintain the strong Black woman persona that she instilled in me. I could not understand it either. My mother did not teach me how to live without her. My heart shattered when she died; I could not function. The pain was unbearable.

Riding the crosstown bus in Manhattan, I just started crying. This older silver-haired white woman asked, "What's wrong?" I told her my mother died. She kindly comforted me and told me about her grief when her mother died. Some other older white women on the bus joined in trying to help me. They were kind.

Because I could not sleep I took to walking at night from my Brooklyn apartment as far as I could go. When I could walk no further, I would take a cab to Broadway in the Village to a hip coffee shop with big comfy sofas. I would sit there sipping coffee, eating, and reading until the sun came up. I would go home and sleep, then wake up and rollerblade in Prospect Park until I was exhausted, then try for sleep again. This was my ritual. Rollerblading I found my dog Park, who saved me. Rollerblading I befriended a beautiful Japanese American man, Glen, at Battery Park City. Every weekend and on Fridays we'd skate, go to beautiful art exhibits at the Guggenheim, eat at different restaurants, go to outdoor concerts, dance, laugh, and have a wonderful time. We had everything in common: a love of art, music, dance, everything. He was from Hawaii, and he was an artist. He was kind, he was beautiful, he was fun. I wasn't ready. I missed out.

I didn't work full time for two years. I graduated with that musical theater degree. My father insisted I go to graduation. My friend Deborah, my father, and his new white wife came and took me out to celebrate. I walked in the restaurant looking a sight with that hood on. Deborah said, "I thought you were supposed to keep that hood."

With the encouragement of Susan Hayes, New York University Career Services, opera singer Dr. Lynda Elliott, and Emory University's Kharen Fulton, I applied to graduate school.

My mother's smile was luminescent. She made life and the world a beautiful, exciting, and joyful place. She was my inspiration, my role model. She encouraged me in all my aspirations, intellectually, culturally, socially, and politically. Life with her was an incredible, wonderful, joyous adventure. All our activities together held special significance because of her magnificent personality, her magnificent presence. My mother's life taught me to live as my mother lived, to place myself on the front lines of the struggle for social justice and equality as my mother did until the day she died.

While many Black radical, Black Power, and civil rights activists abandoned the struggle for African American and Majority World human rights, Audrey Proctor Seniors continued to work for revolutionary causes in the

United States and the diaspora. She saw the revolutionary movement not as just a Black movement but a movement for people of color, for all oppressed and marginalized peoples worldwide. She took up the banner of African American women radical activism and didn't just talk the talk but walked the walk, as George Lipsitz so often said in graduate school. My mother never became discouraged. Kidney disease and other ailments could not keep this tiny four-foot-eleven (although she insisted she was five feet one) dynamic African American radical revolutionary from participating in the struggle for freedom that Majority World people continue to fight. My mother let nothing dissuade her, not white supremacist women and men, not the FBI. Audrey rallied forward, a true rebel revolutionary. She let nothing slow her down, not the victories won with Mae Mallory and the Monroe defendants, not the final end of the Vietnam War, or the end of South African apartheid. My mother marched on in her work in Grenada, Nicaragua, and Namibia. She marched on in her last march with her coworkers when she was callously fired from the Center for Constitutional Rights. In the face of ill health, my mother marched on. And with the success of that final victory, her reinstatement at CCR, when that last struggle was over, she marched on . . .

Notes

Preface

1. Informant T-5 reported that Audrey Seniors held a Black Panther Party membership card. Audrey Seniors FBI, Black Panther Membership, 3, 3/1/71.
2. Frazier, *Harambe City*, x–xii.
3. Meier and Rudwick, *CORE*, 3.
4. Frazier, *Harambe City*, xiv–xv.
5. Ibid., xv.
6. Du Bois, *Black Reconstruction*, 711–712; Du Bois, *Souls*.
7. Frazier, *Harambe City*, xix.
8. Thermrise Khan, Seve Abimbola, Catherine Kyobutungi, Madhukar Pai, "How We Classify Countries and People—and Why it Matters," *BMJ Global Health*, vol. 7, no. 6, 2022.
9. White Rose Mission, "Appeal."
10. Moore, "Committee."
11. "Mr. Muhammad and His Moslems?" *Sepia*, 11/59*; "Mr. Muhammad Speaks," *Pittsburgh Courier*, 5/16/59*; "Mr. Muhammad's Blueprint"*; "Thumbnail Sketch," n.d.*; "Mr. Muhammad's Economical and Educational Program," *Messenger* 1, no. 1 (1959): 2–39*; Burley, *Muhammad Speaks**. Articles and documents that are found in the Audrey Seniors and Clarence Henry Seniors Collection are noted with an asterisk in the notes and bibliography.
12. Burkett, *Mind*; Kochiyama, *Passing*; *Black Panther 10 Point Program*; Carawan, "An Exciting Singer"; "Horton Visits Unions"; *Adult Leadership*; Weatherwax, *Ancient Africa*; Audrey Seniors FBI, Black Panther Membership, 3.
13. Shiek, *On Strike*; *Black Panther, San Francisco Strike*; Corker, *Black Studies*.
14. Shiek, *On Strike*; *Black Panther, San Francisco Strike*; Corker, *Black Studies*; Alridge and Young, Introduction; Kendi, *Black*.
15. Shiek, *On Strike*.
16. Aceves, *Anatomy*, 608.
17. "Strike Settlement Agreement"*; Loines and Daniels, "Statement from the Union."*
18. Foong, "Frameup in Monroe."

Introduction

1. Cobb, *This*, 7, 8–9, 157–158.
2. Ibid., 3, 5–10, 13, 16, 115–116, 140–141, 157–158, 169–170; Crosby, *Taste*, 93, 126, 169–171, 178, 180.
3. Cobb, *This*, 139, 158.
4. Ibid., 3, 5–10, 13, 16, 115–116, 140–141, 157–158, 169–170; Crosby, *Taste*, 93, 126, 169–171, 178, 180.
5. Cobb, *This*, 5–10, 13, 16, 115–116, 140–141, 157–158, 169–170; Crosby, *Taste*, 93, 126, 169–171, 178, 180; "Ethel Azalea Johnson Obituary"; "Ethel Johnson," obituary; "Dr. King's Aide Speaks Here: Role and Community Action Described at Mass Meeting," 1/17/66, UCHR; Johnson, FBI, Charlotte, 8/26/63, 3–4, Philadelphia, 8/26/63, 1–2; Johnson, FBI, Charlotte, 1/26/65; Johnson, *Did?*, 7/6/63.*
6. Snipes, "Writing," 43, 57.
7. Lipsitz, *Life*, 9–11; Gramsci, *Selections*, 9–10; Taylor, *Veiled Garvey*, 2; P. Collins, *Black*, 148; Kuumba, *Gender*, 64.

Chapter 1. Mrs. Ethel Azalea Johnson

1. Johnson, "Did?," *Crusader*, 8/8/59.
2. "NAACP Board Suspends Branch President Who Advocated Violence," *Amsterdam News*, 6/13/59; "Wilkins Moves for a Showdown in Carolina," *Amsterdam News*, 7/4/59; A. Seniors FBI, Activities, 5/10/65; C. Seniors FBI, Activities, 5/10/65.
3. Johnson FBI, 1/25/65, 6/27/63, 8/26/63, 4; Ross, "CARE."
4. T. Tyson, *Radio Free Dixie*, 199.
5. "North Carolina Leader"; Williams, "Bohemia Part II"; "NAACP Board Suspends"; "Wilkins Moves"; Committee to Combat Racial Injustice [CCRI], "Justice"; CCRI, "Committee Takes Steps"; "Committee to Combat Racial Injustice," *Carolina Times*, 12/29/58; CCRI, "Press Conference"; Morrow/CCRI, "White House"; CCRI, "Statement by Lynn"; CCRI, "Statement by Williams"; Williams to Madison, 1/3/59; CCRI, "Synopsis"; CCRI, "Facts on Cases," [1958]; CCRI, "Facts . . . Kissing Case," [1958]; Green, "Committee to Combat"; CCRI, "Exact Copy of Editorial Appearing in *Carolina Times*, January 10, 1959, Durham, N.C. Approved by Negro Leaders," 1/10/59, MSA.
6. T. Tyson, *Radio Free Dixie*, 46–47, 62–73; Young, *Soul Power*, 6, 26–27; Williams, *Negroes with Guns*, 50–51; Weissman [Lavan], *Monroe Story*, 1, 3; Williams, "Bohemia . . . Part I," 1–7.
7. T. Tyson, *Radio Free Dixie*, 51; Chester S. Davis, "Communist Front Shouts Kissing Case to World," *Journal and Sun Sentinel* (Winston-Salem, N.C.), 2/8/59, 2A, MS 425 North Carolina, CABP; Williams, "Bohemia . . . Part I," 7–8, 9–10; Williams, "1957"; Green to Lynn, 5/11/63; "Dr. Albert E. Perry," obituary; "Perry Stays in Limelight: Still Captured Razed on Negro Doctor's Farm," *Mail*, 11/24/57, UCHR, BFP; Bill Hughes, "Perry Trial, State's Witness Tells of Abortion," *Charlotte News*, n.d., box 26, Clippings Folder, BFP; "Jury of Ansonians Begins Hearing Perry Case Facts," *Mail*, 10/31/57, UCHR; "Cross-Examination Interrupted by Overnight Recess until 9:30," *Mail*, 10/31/57, UCHR; "Hospital Staff Privileges of Dr. A. E. Perry Are Suspended," news clipping, 11/21/57, UCHR; "Monroe Surgeon Says Woman 'Had Abortion,'" *Charlotte Observer*, 11/1/57, 10A, UCHR; "Medical Staff Recommended Suspension of Dr.

Perry," news clipping, 11/14/57, UCHR; "Grand Jury Returns True Bill in Case against Dr. A. E. Perry," *Charlotte Observer*, 11/28/57, UCHR; "Trial of Perry Case Likely to Continue through Friday," *Mail*, 11/31/57, UCHR; "Perry Defense May Seek New Site for Trial," news clipping, 11/26/57, UCHR; Bill Hughes, "Anson Jury Set for Perry Trial," *Charlotte News*, n.d. [1957], UCHR; "Perry Is Given Parole," news clipping, 7/1/60, UCHR; "Dr. Perry Absolved in Abortion Case," news clipping, 6/29/64, UCHR; "Medical Staff Recommended"; "Safe Robbery at Dr. Perry's Home," news clipping, 2/28/64, UCHR; Mallory FBI, 2/27–4/10/64, "Doctor's"; Johnson, "Wait," 4/24/65; Cobb, *This*, 109–110; Clarence Seniors autobiography, 72.*

8. Umoja, *We Will*, 2013; T. Tyson, *Radio Free Dixie*, 62–71; Weissman, *Monroe Story*, 1–3; Williams, "Bohemia . . . Part I," 6–7.

9. Williams, *Negroes with Guns*, 50–51; Weissman, *Monroe Story*, 1–5; T. Tyson, *Radio Free Dixie*, 80; C. Davis, "Communist Front."

10. T. Tyson, *Radio Free Dixie*, 51; Williams, *Negroes with Guns*, 51, 80; Weissman, *Monroe Story*, 1–3.

11. Weissman, *Monroe Story*, 2.

12. Williams, "Bohemia . . . Part I," 6–7.

13. Williams, *Negroes with Guns*, 51; Williams, "1957," 70.

14. Johnson FBI, 1/25/65, 2–45, 1/25/63, 1, 3/20/64, 11/8/63, 5/31/68, 1, 2, 08/26/63, 5/6/63, 6/27/63, 2–4, 3/28/66, 2, 10; "Ethel Azalea Johnson Obituary"; "Ethel Johnson"; Clarence Seniors interview, 2010; Doc to Williams, 10/5/61. According to this letter, Ray Johnson burned the *Crusader*'s mailing list.

15. Johnson FBI, 1/25/65, 2–4, 5, 1/25/63, 1, 3/20/64, 11/8/63, 5/31/68, 1, 2, 08/26/63, 5/6/63, 6/27/63, 2–4, 3/28/66, 2, 10; "Ethel Azalea Johnson Obituary"; "Ethel Johnson"; Clarence Seniors interview, 2010; Doc to Williams, 10/5/61.

16. T. Tyson, *Radio Free Dixie*, 81; Johnson FBI, 1/25/65, 5, 1/25/63, 1, 3/20/64, 11/08/63, 03/28/66, 2.

17. Weissman, *Monroe Story*, 2–3, 1; Williams, "1957," 70–71; Oakley, "When"; "Negro Ask"; "Country Club Sale Talked," news clipping, n.d., box 26, BFP; "Outlaw a Menace [the Klan]," *Monroe Journal*, box 26, Clippings Folder, BFP; Perry, "Report"; Perry, "To Parks," 6/19/57, 7/23/57.

18. Weissman, *Monroe Story*, 1–3; T. Tyson, *Radio Free Dixie*, 80; Williams, *Negroes with Guns*, 51, 57–58; C. Davis, "Communist Front"; "Mrs. Johnson," FBI, 8/26/63, "NAACP Had a Rifle Club," *Charlotte Observer* (8/25/63), Johnson FBI, 1/25/65, 15; Oakley, "When," 79–80; "Jurist Fines Gun Toting Klansman," *Louisiana Weekly*, 2/1/58, 1, 6, ARCTU.

19. Clarence Seniors autobiography; Weissman, *Monroe Story*, 3, 1; Williams, "Bohemia . . . Part I," 8.

20. Williams, "Bohemia . . . Part I," 8.

21. Ibid., 8–15, 11–12; Cobb, *This*, 11.

22. Williams, "Bohemia . . . Part I," 8–15; Cobb, *This*, 11.

23. Oakley, "When," 79–80; "Jurist Fines"; Williams, "Bohemia . . . Part I," 13–14.

24. Johnson FBI, 1/25/63, 4, 5/31/68, 4.

25. T. Tyson, *Radio Free Dixie*, 78–80, 141; Williams, *Negroes with Guns*, 50–51; "News in Brief, in North Carolina," *Southern Patriot*, 3/60; Bill Hughes, "Perry Trial May Go to Jury Today," *Charlotte News*, 11/1/57, UCHR; "Dr. Perry Absolved"; Williams, "Bohe-

mia Part II," 4–6; Hughes, "Perry Trial, State's Witness"; "Jury of Ansonians"; "Hospital Staff Privileges"; "Monroe Surgeon"; "Medical Staff Recommended"; "Grand Jury Returns"; "Trial of Perry"; "Perry Goes to Prison"; "Perry Defense"; Hughes, "Anson Trial"; Hughes, "Perry Trial May"; "Perry Is Given Parole"; State of Ohio, "In Re Mae Mallory," 5; Bill Hobbs, "Negro Asks Support Here," UNC News, 8/16/62, NNC; "Safe Robbery"; Williams FBI, 2/27–4/10/64; Gray, "Doctor's Wall Safe Cracked."

26. T. Tyson, *Radio Free Dixie*, 78–80, 141; Williams, *Negroes with Guns*, 50–51; "News in Brief, in North Carolina"; "Dr. Perry Absolved"; Williams, "Bohemia Part II," 4–6; Hughes, "Perry Trial, State's Witness"; "Jury of Ansonians"; "Hospital Staff Privileges"; "Monroe Surgeon"; "Grand Jury Returns"; "Trial of Perry"; "Perry Goes to Prison"; "Perry Defense"; Hughes, "Anson Trial"; Hughes, "Perry Trial May"; "Perry Is Given Parole"; "Medical Staff Recommended"; State of Ohio, "In Re Mae Mallory," 5; Hobbs, "Negro Asks Support Here"; "Safe Robbery"; Williams FBI, 2/27–4/10/64; Gray, "Doctor's Wall Safe Cracked"; CCRI, "Exact Copy of Editorial Published in *London News Chronicle*, Dec. 18, 1958," 12/18/58, RFWP, HRAEC; CCRI, "Committee Takes Steps"; CCRI, "Press Conference"; Morrow/CCRI, "White House"; David Hudson, "This Day in History: The Creation of Head Start," White House Archives, President Barack Obama, 5/18/2015; CCRI, "Statement by Lynn," "Statement by Williams"; Williams to Madison, 1/3/59; CCRI, "Synopsis"; CCRI, "Facts . . . Kissing Case"; CCRI, "Facts on Cases"; Green, "Committee to Combat"; CCRI, "Exact Copy . . . *Carolina Times*"; "The 'Kissing Case' and the Lives It Shattered," NPR, 4/29/2011, https://www.npr.org/2011/04/29/135815465/the-kissing-case-and-the-lives-it-shattered; "Carolina Kiss Case," *Southern Patriot*, 1/59, 3, box 14, folder 2, CABP; "The Kissing Case to Be Appealed," *Southern Patriot*, 2/59, 3, box 14, folder 2, CABP.

27. Mallory, "Memo," 196; "Robert Williams President of the Union County, N.C. NAACP." WCSCRBC; 1, 2; Williams, "Bohemia Part II," 5–6.

28. Mallory, "Memo," 196; Williams, "Robert Williams President," 1, 2; Williams, "Bohemia Part II," 5–6; "Monroe NAACP"; "NAACP: Committee," 1; Lathan, "Crusader," 65; Williams, *Negroes with Guns*, 61–62. In her memo Mallory states that Reed was raped. Others say an attempted rape occurred.

29. James, *Resisting*, 143.

30. Williams, *Negroes with Guns*, 62.

31. T. Tyson, *Radio Free Dixie*, 146, 147; Williams, *Negroes with Guns*, 62; Clarence Seniors autobiography, 9.

32. Mallory, "Memo," 204.

33. Lathan, "Crusader," 65.

34. Mallory, "Memo," 204; "Monroe NAACP"; Johnson, *Did?*, 11/7/64, 3, 6/19/65, *MMP*; Johnson, "Did?," 12/3/60, *MMP*; Johnson, "Did?," 8/7/61, *MMP*; Stanford, "Towards a Revolutionary Action Movement"; Luce, *Washington Report*, 4/11/66, 2–4; RAM, FBI, 10/64, 1–3; A. Seniors FBI Appendix, RAM, 20–21, 3/16/65, 3/6/64, 2/19/65; RAM FBI, Appendix, "Source Stated in 5/65"; Johnson, "Delegation."

35. Clarence Seniors, "Free."

36. Williams, *Negroes with Guns*, 63; Williams, "Robert Williams," 1; Mallory, "Memo," 210.

37. "NAACP Board"; "Wilkins Moves."

38. "Monroe NAACP."

39. Ibid.; Umoja, *We Will*, 50, 258; Cobb, *This*, 107–113, 129–130, 151–153.

40. Kornweibel, *Seeing Red*, 11, 54.

41. Young, *Soul Power*, 28; Weissman, *Monroe Story*, 11–12; Williams, "Bohemia Part II," 8.

42. Williams, "Cry of Death"; Williams, "Bohemia Part II," 8.

43. Johnson FBI, 6/27/63, 2–3, 8/26/63, 3/20/64, 11/8/63, 1, 1/25/63, 1, 5–6, 5/31/68, 2.

44. Young, *Soul Power*, 28; Johnson, "Did?," 12/3/60.

45. Young, *Soul Power*, 28; Johnson, "Did?," 12/3/60.

46. Garrow, *Bearing*, 325, 329–330; Ransby, *Ella Baker*, 263, 269–-271.

47. Fleming, *Soon*, 112; Cobb, *This*, 3, 5–10, 13, 16, 115–116, 140–141, 157–158; Crosby, *Taste*, 93, 126, 169–171, 178, 180.

48. Fleming, *Soon*, 112.

49. Fleming, *Soon*, 112; Cobb, *This*, 3, 5–10, 13, 16, 115–116, 140–141, 157–158; Crosby, *Taste*, 93, 126, 169–171, 178, 180.

50. Johnson, "Did?," 12/3/60.

51. Franklin, "Jackanapes," 62–63; Seth Rosenfeld, "New FBI Files, Wide Range of Black Panthers Informants Activities," *Mercury News*, 6/9/2015; Aoki FBI; Johnson FBI, 1959–-1972; Audrey Seniors FBI 1962-1973; Appendix Committee to Aid the Monroe Defendants, 3/28/65; Clarence Seniors FBI, 1959–1973; Mallory FBI 1957-1976; CAMD FBI 1961-1963, 1, 11/1/61, 1, 4/30/62, "Memorandum," 9/13/61, 1–2, 4/30/62, 5/2/62; Kornweibel, *Seeing Red*, 11, 54. Aoki's biographer Fujino disputes the claim that Aoki was an informant.

52. Johnson, "Did?," 12/3/60.

53. Blake, *Children*; Rickford, *Betty Shabazz*, 341, 344–349; "Daughters," 166–168; Pressman, "Interview."

54. Johnson, *Did?*, 4/3/65, 4.

55. Johnson, *Did?*, 11/7/64. See also Rasmussen, *American Uprising*; T. Thomas Fortune, "Race War in Alabama, Riot and Bloodshed in the Town of Blossburg," *New York Sun*, 6/28/1899; "Executed Woman to Get Pardon," *New York Times*, 8/16/2005; "South: Georgia: Posthumous Pardon," *New York Times*, 8/31/2005; Shaila Dewan, "A Crescendoing Choir from the Graveyards of History," *New York Times*, 8/21/2005, 3; Bates, *Long Shadow*, 15.

56. Johnson, death certificate; "Ethel Azalea Johnson Obituary"; "Ethel Johnson"; Johnson FBI, Connections, 6/27/1963, 2.

57. Finnegan, "Equal," 245; Ballard, *One*, 91; Dray, *At the Hand*, 226.

58. Megginson, *African American*, 92.

59. Johnson, death certificate; "Ethel Azalea Johnson Obituary"; "Ethel Johnson"; Johnson, FBI, 1/25/63, 6/27/1963, 2.

60. Johnson, "Did?," 4/29/61.

61. Du Bois, *Black Reconstruction*; Rutkoff and Scott, *Fly Away*, 48; Ballard, *One*, 134–135.

62. Du Bois, *Black Reconstruction*; Rutkoff and Scott, *Fly Away*, 48; Ballard, *One*, 134–135; W. L. Burke, "Radical," 90–92, 100, 112–113, 169; E. Foner, "South Carolina"; Painter, *Creating*, 137.

63. Bethel, *Promiseland*, 5–7, 10.

64. Lau, *Democracy Rising*, 15–16, 48, 53, 62; Finnegan, "Equal," 226–229, 246–252;

Dray, At the *Hand*, 245–250; Ballard, *One*, 156–159, 166, 186; Rutkoff and Scott, *Fly Away*, 48, 53.

65. Bethel, *Promiseland*, 7, 10; Finnegan, "Equal," 246–247; Ballard, *One*, 156; Lau, *Democracy Rising*, 15–16; Dray, At the *Hand*, 226.

66. Ballard, *One*, 156; Bethel, *Promiseland*, 39, 74–77, 128–130, 213; "Women's Class Sitting on Steps with Banner 'Esse Quam Videri, '11,'" photograph, USC, https://digital.tcl.sc.edu/digital/collection/hac/id/121/rec/1.

67. Johnson, "Did?," 4/29/61.

68. Mack, *Parlor Ladies*, 1999, 175, 151, 155–156; Megginson, *African American*, 337, 346; Rutkoff and Scott, *Fly Away*, 50; Ballard, *One*, 156; Bethel, *Promiseland*, 39, 74–77, 128–130, 213.

69. Johnson, "Did?," 4/29/61.

70. Ibid.; Lathan, "Crusader," 64.

71. Johnson, "Did?," 4/29/61.

72. Finnegan, "Equal," 245–248; Dray, At the *Hand*, 226; Ballard, *One*, 157–159; Lau, *Democracy Rising*, 15–16, 62.

73. Megginson, *African American*, 80, 92, 275, 394; Rutkoff and Scott, *Fly Away*, 36; Finnegan, "Equal," 241–243.

74. Megginson, *African American*, 243–244, 337, 342, 349, 351; Mack, *Parlor Ladies*, 129, 148–150, 152, 53, 157, 175; Bethel, *Promiseland*, 124–125, 127, 151.

75. Johnson, "As Relayed."

76. Johnson, "Did?," 9/24/60, 5.

77. Johnson, "As Relayed."

78. Johnson, "Did?," 4/29/61.

79. Williams, *Negroes with Guns*, 78; Lumumba, "Mae," 5, 23; Nelson, *Freedom Riders*; Mallory FBI, 9/7/61, 15–17.

80. Johnson, "Did?," 7/24/61, 6/26/61.

81. Johnson, "Did?," 6/26/61.

82. Johnson, "Did?," 7/31/61.

83. Johnson, "Did?," 8/7/61.

84. Ibid. The Klan regularly attacked Monroe's Black community. Williams, "Bohemia . . . Part I," "Bohemia Part II."

85. Johnson, "Did?," 7/61, 8/61, 6/21/61.

86. Mallory FBI, 9/7/61, 15.

87. "Negro," Freedom Fighter Newsletter.

88. Williams, "Join."

89. Angola's People's Movement for Liberation (1956) led the socialist independence movement (1951–1961). The CIA backed the slaughter and napalm bombing of thousands of Angolans. "Angola Profile Timeline," 3/7/2018, BBC; World Peace Foundation, "Angola: War of Independence," Mass Atrocity Endings, 8/7/2015, https://sites.tufts.edu/atrocityendings/2015/08/07/angola-war-of-independence-post-war-consolidation/.

90. Lumumba, "Mae," 2, 10, 13; Clarence Seniors interview, 6/1/20.

91. C. Levy, "Dangers," 8/21/61.

92. Williams, "Radio Free Dixie—On the Air," *Crusader*, 10/62–11/62, 8/63; Mallory, "Memo," 207–209; Lumumba, "Mae," 20; Clarence Seniors, "Free"; "Ask Kennedy to

Reveal FBI's Role in Monroe," *Michigan Chronicle*, 12/16/61; Williams, "Bohemia Part II," 11.

93. Clarence Seniors, "Free."

94. Williams, "Radio Free Dixie—On the Air," *Crusader*, 10/62–11/62, 2, 8/63, 7; Mallory, "Memo," 207–209; Lumumba, "Mae," 20; Clarence Seniors, "Free."

95. Webb, "Behind"; Lumumba, "Mae", 20–22. See also Webb, *Not*; Webb, *Special Delivery*.

96. Webb, "Behind"; Mallory, "Monroe!"; Williams to Webb, 12/19/61.

97. Williams, *Negroes with Guns*, 85; Williams, "Radio Free Dixie—On the Air," *Crusader*, 10/62–11/62, 2–3; Clarence Seniors, "Free"; Lumumba, "Mae," 20–22.

98. Alex Poinsett, "What's Behind Race Tension in Monroe, N.C.? Negroes Right to Be Human," *Jet*, 9/61, 16.*

99. "FBI Arrests Mae Mallory"; Poinsett, "What's Behind"; "An Easy Decision for Governor DiSalle," *Call and Post*, 2/10/62; "Case of Mae Mallory"; "FBI Agents Capture Wanted Woman in Cleveland Home," *Call and Post*, 10/21/61; Williams to Webb, 12/19/61; "Agrees Negroes Barred from Jury," *Chicago Daily Defender*, 2/9/66, 7; "Upset Mallory Conviction," *Chicago Daily Defender*, 2/9/66, 7.

100. "Monroe Abduction Retold," *Charlotte News*, 2/25/64, MMP.

101. Mallory, "Memo."

102. Clarence Seniors interview, 6/1/20.

103. Williams FBI, 2/21/62; Doc to Williams, 10/5/61.

104. Johnson, "The Crusader Newsletter [published] 503 Boyte Street [Johnson's home]," *Crusader*, 1/13/62, HGP.

105. Finnegan, "Equal," 248–252; Ballard, *One*, 3, 8–9, 186; Lau, *Democracy Rising*, 15–16, 62; Johnson FBI, 6/27/63, 2, 8/26/63, 1–5, 3/20/64, 1–2, 1/25/65; Rutkoff and Scott, *Fly Away*, 48, 53; Bethel, *Promiseland*, 184.

106. Clarence Seniors autobiography, 4; Johnson FBI, 6/27/63, 5/8/63, 2.

107. Finnegan, "Equal," 248–252; Ballard, *One*, 3, 8–9, 186; Lau, *Democracy Rising*, 15–16, 62; Johnson FBI, 1957–1973; Rutkoff and Scott, *Fly Away*, 48, 53; Bethel, *Promiseland*, 184.

108. American Security Council, "Revolutionary Action Movement"; "Cleveland," *Militant*, 3/22/65, JBMP; RAM, folder 8, 1963–1966, JBMP; *Black America*, Fall 1964; Stanford, "Towards a Revolutionary Action Movement"; Luce, *Washington Report*, 4/11/66, 2–4; RAM FBI, 10/64, 1–3; T. Tyson, *Radio Free Dixie*, 194; Ransby, *Ella Baker*, 215; Burlage, "Truths," 114; "Introducing," *Partisan*, 4/65; Audrey Seniors FBI, 1962–1973; Johnson FBI, 6/27/63, 2–3, 8/26/63, 3, 3/20/64, 11/08/63, 1, 1/25/63, 1, 1/25/65, 5–6; Clarence Seniors autobiography; Clarence Seniors interview, 12/31/18.

109. Stanford, "Towards a Revolutionary Action Movement."

110. Ibid., 5–6; Luce, *Washington Report*, 4/11/66, 2–4; RAM FBI, 10/64, 1–3.

111. Luce, *Washington Report*, 4/6/66, 3; "Revolutionary Action Movement," *Congressional Record* (Senate), 5/12/66, 9885, box 482, folders 8–10, JBMP.

112. Stanford, *Monthly Review*, 5/64, 5–7; Luce, *Washington Report*, 4/11/66, 2–4; RAM FBI, 10/64, 1–3; Worthy, "Red."

113. Johnson, "Burn," 9/4/65; D. Scott interview.

114. Williams and Seniors, "Monroe Defense Committee"; Johnson, "Delegation"; Johnson, "Complete Unity"; Johnson, "Did you know that in 1965"; Johnson, *Did?*,

3/4/65; Strong, "Report," 5/4/65; Strong, "Report," 4/24/65; Strong, "Why Isn't," 6/19/65; Strong, "If the U.S.," 3/66; Wheeldon, "Woman," 6/19/65, 7/24/65, 9/4/65; Johnson, "Did?", *Crusader*, 7/25/59, 9/24/60, 4/8/61; Johnson, *Did?*, 4/18/64; Johnson, "Continued," 11/65; Williams, "Sierra Maestra"; *Brief History of Cuba*, 47–50*; Williams, "Cuba and the Negro"; Williams, "See Cuba"; Williams, "Dear Friends"; Williams to *Crusader*, 10/10/60; "Group Tour"; "Dominican"; Fremantle, *Mao*, 62.*

115. Stanford, *Monthly Review*, 5/64, 5–6; Luce, *Washington Report*, 4/11/66, 2–4; RAM FBI, 10/64, 1–3; Lawrence H. Geller, "RAM Members Bolstered by Whites in Protest Meeting at City Hall," *Philadelphia Tribune*, 10/17/67.

116. Johnson, "Philadelphia," 6/15/63.*

117. "Raymond H. Johnson, 14 April 1942–9 August 1962," *Workers World*, 8/24/62, LOC; "North Carolina Leader."

118. Clarence Seniors interviews.

119. R. Johnson, "Says Save Mae," *Afro American*, 4/7/62.

120. Ibid.; "Raymond H. Johnson."

121. R. Johnson, "Says Save Mae"; "Raymond H. Johnson"; Clarence Seniors autobiography; Burlage, "Truths," 116.

122. Mallory to Lynn and Williams, 8/28/62; Mallory to Mabel Williams, 10/11/62; "North Carolina Leader"; Clarence Seniors autobiography, 38–39; Clarence Seniors interviews.

123. Mallory to Lynn and Williams.

124. Mallory to Mabel Williams, 10/11/62.

125. "Raymond H. Johnson."

126. Johnson FBI, Connections, 10/8/63, RAM, 15.

127. Mallory, "Memo," 210; MDC FBI, 10/2/61;
Audrey Seniors FBI, Appendix, MDC, 7–9, 3/4/63, MDC, 5, 3/16/65, 3/6/64, 2/19/65, Appendix, CAMD, 3/28/65; Appendix, Mothers Alliance, 8, 2/17/64; Williams to Mr. W. C., FBI, 10/12/61; Green, "Summary Report"; "Store Drops Racial Bars in Hiring," *Afro American*, 7/4/59; Westbrook, "Mrs. Ruth Stone."

128. Johnson FBI, 8/26/63, 3–4, 1/25/65, 1–2, 16; "Ethel Azalea Johnson Obituary"; "Ethel Johnson"; Johnson, "Crusaders Assn."*; Ross, "CARE"; "Head Start," *Monroe Enquirer*, 5/31/65, UCHR.

129. Johnson FBI, 8/26/63, 3–4, 1/25/65, 1–2, 16; "Ethel Azalea Johnson Obituary"; "Ethel Johnson"; Johnson, "Max Stanford Jr."*; Ross, "CARE"; "Head Start."

130. Johnson FBI, 1/29/65, 3, 1/25/63, 1, 15, 6/27/63, 1; *Black America*, Fall 1964.

131. Clarence Seniors to Ballan, 8/20/64.*

132. Clarence Seniors to Ballan, 10/18/64.*

133. Seniors to Ballan, Did?, 6/21/65.*

134. Mary [Yuri] and Bill Kochiyama, *Did?*, 9/4/65; Johnson, *Did?*, 11/7/64, 3, 6; T. Tyson, *Radio Free Dixie*, 194; Ransby, *Ella Baker*, 215; Burlage, "Truths," 114; "Introducing," *Partisan*, 4/1965; Johnson FBI, 6/27/63, 5/8/63, 3, 8/26/63, 6/27/1963, 2–3, 3/20/64, 11/8/63, 1, 1/25/63, 1, 1/25/65, 5–6; Johnson, *Did?*, 4/18/64; Johnson, *Did?*, 11/21/64, 4/3/65, 4/18/64, 4/24/65, 5/8/65, 6/5/65, 6/19/65, 7/3/65, 9/4/65, 9/65, 11/65, 11/7/65, 1/6/66, 2/19/66, 3/66, 5/66, 6/66, 6/19/66; Williams and Seniors, "Monroe Defense Committee"; Johnson, *Did?*, 2/19/66, 12/19/66; *Clarence* Seniors to Ballan, 6/21/65*; A. Seniors FBI, Activities, 7–12, 5/10/65; C. Seniors FBI, Activities, 7–12, 5/10/65.

135. Meeks, *Caribbean*, 58–59. See also Paula Marie Seniors, *Beyond*, 51, 55, 57; Ferrer, *Insurgent Cuba*, 196–97; Edward Johnson, *History*, 6; Kaplan, "Black and Blue," 219–220.
136. Ransby, *Ella Baker*, 199–200.
137. Johnson and Johnson, "Seasons Greetings."

Chapter 2. Ethel Azalea Johnson

1. Ross, "CARE"; Burlage, "Truths," 114; T. Tyson, *Radio Free Dixie*, 199.
2. Lathan, "Crusader," 62; Johnson, "Did You Know?" 7/11/59.
3. O. Patterson, *Slavery*, 38, 41–45; Moore, *Name*, 237.
4. Moore, *Name*, 232–233.
5. Johnson, "Did?," 4/29/61.
6. Lathan, "Crusader," 60–62; Johnson, "Did You Know?" 7/11/59.
7. Ibid.; T. Tyson, *Radio Free Dixie*, 199–200.
8. Johnson, "Did?," 10/22/60, *MMP*.
9. Lathan, "Crusader," 60–62, 64; T. Tyson, *Radio Free Dixie*, 199–200; Johnson, "Did?," June/July 1959, 9/5/59, 9/19/59, 8/20/60, 9/24/60, 6/5/61; Williams, "Sierra Maestra"; Williams, "Cuba"; "Africa: Tom Toms"; "Notice!! Readers"; Castro, "Fidel Castro Speaks to the Cuban People"; "Robert F. Williams, Editor"; Johnson, *"Care Packages from Abroad"*; Onyewu, "African Students"; "Dominican"; Mallory, "Fidel Castro"; "Hitler's Protégé"; Johnson, *Did?*, 4/24/65, 6/19/65, 7/24/65, 3/66, 1/69; Strong, "If the U.S."; Strong, "Report," 5/4/65; Strong, "Why Isn't"; Wheeldon, "Woman," 6/19/65; Williams, "Letter from Rob."
10. Johnson, "Did?," 4/29/61.
11. "Dominican."
12. Stanford, "Revolutionary Nationalism"; Stanford, *Monthly Review*, 5/64, 5–6; Luce, *Washington Report*, 4/11/66, 2–4; RAM FBI, 10/64, 1–3; Williams FBI, 9/25/61; A. Seniors FBI, Appendix, Youth against War and Fascism, 7, 5/31/68.
13. Johnson, *Did?*, 4/24/65.
14. Johnson, "Did?," 9/5/59.
15. Mkapa, "Leadership," 3, 4, 6, 8, 12–14, 19, 21–22, 24, 25; Graham Du Bois, "What," *Freedomways*, 205.*
16. Johnson, "Did?," 9/19/59.
17. Johnson, "Did?," 8/20/60.
18. Fox Butterfield, "2 Studies Find Laws on Felons Forbid Many Black Men to Vote," *New York Times*, 9/23/2004; Painter, *Creating*, 245; Reese, *American*, 155; Du Bois, *Black Reconstruction*, 167, 674; Franklin, *From Slavery*, 342*; M. Alexander, *New Jim Crow*, 6, 7, 9, 96, 184.
19. Johnson, "Did?," 8/20/60, 7.
20. Johnson, "Did?," 10/8/60.
21. Johnson, "Did?," 7/25/59.
22. "Tom Mboya," *Britannica*.
23. Johnson, "Did?," 9/24/60.
24. "Hitler's Protégé"; "Africa," *Crusader*, 8/27/60; Onyewu, "African Students."
25. Mallory, "Fidel Castro"; Iandolo, "Beyond the Shoe," 130–137.
26. Zedong, "Report," 3/27; Zedong, *Quotations*, 11–12.

27. Young, *Soul Power*, 156, 159; N. Perry, The *Negro National Colonial Question*, chap. 2, n. 30; Kelley and Esch, "Black," 98, 99–100, 113, 124, 125; Robinson, "Internationalism"; Mullen, *Afro-Orientalism*, 29; Horne, *Race Woman*, 175–176, 230–231, 234; Mullen, "Persisting," 252–253; R. J. Alexander, *Maoism*, 9, 25, 28, 36–37; Boyce Davies, *Left*, 125–127, 222, 227–229.

28. Ransby, *Ella Baker*, 215; Burlage, "Truths," 114.

29. Kelley and Esch, "Black," 99–100.

30. Williams, *Did?*, 10/21/64.

31. Johnson, *Did?*, 1/69.

32. President Johnson signed the 1964 Civil Rights Act, which desegregated public accommodations, protected people according to race, religion, and national origin, and offered equal job opportunities. It did not succeed fully. It didn't get rid of literacy tests or protect people against police brutality. The act led to the Voting Rights Act, the Economic Opportunity Act, and the War on Poverty, which created Head Start. Painter, *Creating*, 279–280, 368.

33. Johnson, *Did?*, 3/66.

34. "Don't Let Vietnam."

35. Johnson, *Did?*, 4/18/64.

36. Johnson, "Delegation."

37. Johnson, "Self Defense."

38. Johnson, "Delegation"; Roy Reed, "Wounded Negro Dies in Alabama," *New York Times*, 2/27/65; Robbie Brown, "45 Years Later an Apology, and 6 Months," *New York Times*, 11/15/2010; Painter, *Creating*, 275, 367–368.

39. Johnson, *Did?*, 11/7/64, DRRUC.

40. Johnson, "Delegation."

41. Johnson, "Continued."

42. Painter, *Creating*, 281–282; Franklin, *From Slavery*, 651; Hine, *African American*, 553–554.

43. Quotation from Johnson, "More Blacks." See also J. Williams, *Captain*, 31, 73, 76; Hine, *African American*, 554; Franklin, From *Slavery*, 651.

44. Bennett, *Before*, 2003, 615–616; Painter, *Creating*, 368.

45. Johnson, "Continued."

46. Williams, "Sierra Maestra"; *Brief History of Cuba*, 47–50*; Williams, "Cuba," *Crusader*, 8/20/60; Williams, "Cuba and the Negro."

47. Williams, "See Cuba"; Williams, "Dear Friends"; Williams to *Crusader*; "Group Tour."

48. Castro, "Fidel Castro Speaks to the Children," 8/6/60, 8/27/60, 9/17/60; Castro, "Fidel Castro Speaks with the People of Cuba"; Castro, "Fidel Castro Speaks to the Cuban People"; "Agrarian."

49. Castro, "Fidel Castro Speaks to the Children," 8/6/60, 8/27/60, 9/17/60.

50. "Agrarian"; World Food Programme, Cuba, https://www.wfp.org/countries/cuba.

51. Castro, "Fidel Castro Speaks with the People of Cuba"; Castro, "Fidel Castro Speaks to the Cuban People."

52. Johnson, "Did?" 2/4/61, 4/8/61; Nadasen, *Welfare Warriors*, 6, 9, 10, 47–48; Smith, *Welfare Reform*, 4–5, 87–88; Poole, *Segregated*, 9, 141, 173, 177–178, 181; Lipsitz, *Possessive Investment*, 5; E. Glenn, "Caring," 53–55; McDuffie, *Sojourning*, 113, 126–127, 132; Crow

et al., *History*, 22, 121–122, 136–138, 140–141, 144–145; North Carolina Division of Community Planning, "Population," 9/63, 3, 4–6; LeLoudis, "Leadership."

53. A. Nelson, *Body*, 90, 112; Williams, "Bohemia Part II," 8; Ross, "CARE."

54. Ross, "CARE"; A. Nelson, *Body*, 90, 112; Williams, "Bohemia Part II," 8.

55. Johnson, "Did?," 8/15/59, 12/31/60, 1/21/61, 2/4/61, 4/8/61; Johnson, *Did?*, 7/6/63; "The Members"; "Unity"; Johnson, "Thanksgiving"; Johnson, "C.A.R.E. News"; Johnson, "Citizenship"; Johnson, *Did?*, 4/18/64, 4/3/65; Williams, "Bohemia Part II," 8.

56. Johnson, "Did?," 11/11/61; "Crusaders Association"; "The Members"; Johnson, "C.A.R.E. News"; Johnson, "Care Sincerely"; Johnson, *Did?*, 7/3/65, 9/4/65, 11/65, 3/66; Johnson, "C.A.R.E. Packages Have Been Received."

57. Johnson, "On the Monroe Scene."

58. Johnson, "C.A.R.E. News."

59. Borstelmann, *Cold War*, 108; Woods, *Black Struggle*, 7, 93; Bartley, *Rise*, 74, 90–91, 187; Wilhoit, *Politics*, 112; G. Lewis, *Massive Resistance*, 40; "At Louisiana Hearing"; W. M. Rainach, "Special Note"; Weiner, *Enemies*, 175–177, 183–185, 189, 195–200, 250; Jeffreys-Jones, *FBI*, 134, 170–171.

60. Johnson, "C.A.R.E. News."

61. Ibid.

62. Johnson, *Did?*, 5/8/65; Johnson, "To Clarify!"

63. Johnson, "Did?," 12/31/60.

64. Castro, "Fidel Castro Speaks to the Children," 8/27/60, 9/17/60.

65. Castro, "Fidel Castro Speaks to the Children," 8/6/60, 8/27/60, 9/17/60; Castro, "Fidel Castro Speaks with the People of Cuba," 9/24/60; Williams, "Dear Friends"; Martin Guevara, "Cuba's Tarara Summer Camp," *Havana Times*, 4/16/2014; "Fidel, el pionero mayor," Cuba Debate, 11/28/2017, http://www.cubadebate.cu/fotorreportajes/2017/11/28/fidel-el-pionero-mayor/; "Speech Pronounced," 7/20/75; Benson, *Antiracism*, 199; Pérez, "Fidel Vive!"; Samad, "Legacy"; "Ciudad Militar," 1930–1950, photograph, UVDC; "Concrete Tanks," 1900 [Camp Columbia], photograph, MLMDC; Stables, 1905–1908, photograph, MLMDC; Storehouse, 1900–1909 [Camp Columbia], photograph, MLMDC.

66. Castro, "Fidel Castro Speaks to the Children," 8/20/60, 5.

67. H. Williams, *Self-Taught*, 72–74; Crow et al., *History*, 33, 81, 102, 123, 135–138, 140, 157–158; G. Gilmore, *Gender*, 1996, 33, 157–158; Greenwood, *Bittersweet Legacy*, 243; North Carolina Division of Community Planning, "Population," 3; LeLoudis, "Leadership," 4; Ballard, *One*, 156; Bethel, *Promiseland*, 39, 74–77, 128–130, 213; "Women's Class Sitting on Steps with Banner 'Esse Quam Videri, '11," photograph, USC, https://digital.tcl.sc.edu/digital/collection/hac/id/121/rec/1.; "10 Men, 1917," photograph, USC, https://digital.tcl.sc.edu/digital/collection/hac/id/163/rec/2; Johnson, "Did?," 4/29/61. White supremacists closed Black-founded high schools, while Rosenwald established primary schools.

68. Johnson, "Did?," 10/8/60.

69. H. Williams, *Self-Taught*, 72–74, 79; G. Gilmore, *Gender*, 33, 157–158; Greenwood, *Bittersweet Legacy*, 243; Crow et al., *History*, 81, 102, 134–138, 140; North Carolina Division of Community Planning, "Population," 3; LeLoudis, "Leadership," 4.

70. Johnson, "Did?," 10/22/60.

71. Johnson, "Local Scene"; Johnson, "Did?," 10/22/60.

72. H. Williams, *Self-Taught*, 72–74, 79; G. Gilmore, *Gender*, 33, 157–158; Greenwood,

Bittersweet Legacy, 243; Crow et al., *History*, 81, 102, 134–138, 140; North Carolina Division of Community Planning, "Population," 3; LeLoudis, "Leadership," 4.

73. Johnson, "Monroe Scene."

74. Charron, *Freedom's Teacher*, 339; Burlage, "Truths," 114; "News Release Mrs. Septima Clark."

75. Johnson, "Did You Know?," Crusader, n.d., MMP; Johnson, *Did?*, 11/7/64, 7/3/65, 5/8/65; Johnson, "To Clarify."

76. Charron, *Freedom's Teacher*, 339; Burlage, "Truths," 114; Johnson, "Did?," 10/8/60; Johnson, "Citizenship"; Johnson, "Did You Know?," Crusader, n.d.; Johnson, "Project Head Start"; Johnson, *Did?*, 6/19/65.

77. Johnson, "Citizenship"; Charron, *Freedom's Teacher*, 339.

78. Workable Program, "Report," 1–5.*

79. Johnson, "Urban Renewal."

80. Johnson FBI, 1/29/65, 3, 9, 8/26/63, 1–2, 1/25/65, 16; "Ethel Azalea Johnson Obituary"; "Ethel Johnson."

81. Johnson FBI, 8/26/63, 1–2, 1/25/65, 16; Clarence Seniors interview, 11/7/2010; Johnson, "Thanksgiving."

82. Office of Head Start, "Head Start History," last updated 6/23/2022, https://www.acf.hhs.gov/ohs/about/history-of-head-start; U.S. Department of Health and Human Services, "Head Start Timeline," https://eclkc.ohs.acf.hhs.gov/about-us/article/head-start-timeline; Hudson, "This Day"; Johnson, "Project Head Start"; Old North State Medical Society, "Program," 7, 8, 14–15, 17–18; "Head Start Fund Approved for Winchester Ave. School," *Monroe Enquirer*, 5/31/65, UCHR; "Dr. Hubert Henry Creft Sr. (1885–1966)," https://www.findagrave.com/memorial/24357531/hubert-henry-creft.

83. Johnson, "To Clarify!"; "Head Start Fund."

84. Johnson, *Did?*, 7/3/65. The following account of her efforts regarding the preschool/Head Start and all quotations come from this issue.

85. Johnson, "Did?," 8/22/59.

86. Johnson, "Did?," 10/22/60.

87. Ross, "CARE."

88. Johnson, *Did?*, 11/7/64.

89. Johnson, "Did?," 6/26/59, 7/4/59.

90. Johnson, "Did?," 7/25/59.

91. Ibid.; Johnson, "Did?," 8/59, Johnson, "Did You Know?" 7/11/59, 9/24/60, 7/4/59; "J. Ernest Wilkins"; Bennett, *Before*, 755.

92. Johnson, "Did?," 1959.

93. Johnson, "Did?," 9/12/59.

94. Johnson, "Did?," 8/27/60. All quotations on this incident come from this issue.

95. Ross, "CARE."

Chapter 3. Mae Mallory

1. Lumumba, "Mae," 17–18; Mallory, "Memo," 196.

2. "Manifesto"; "KKK" flyer; Crusaders for Freedom, "Passive Resistance"; Crusaders for Freedom, press release; Mallory, "Militant Mass Protest"; "Special Invitation"; Mallory, "On the New York Scene"; "Meetings."

3. "Benefit Performance" ticket; "Crusaders . . . Benefit Performance."

4. "Special Invitation." Born in Bessemer, Alabama, on May 22, 1927, Dr. Lonnie

Cross [Abdulalim Abdullah Shabazz] received an A.B. with honors from Lincoln University in 1949, an M.S. in mathematics from Massachusetts Institute of Technology in 1951, and a PhD in mathematical analysis from Cornell University in 1955. He was a professor and departmental chair of mathematics at Atlanta University (1957–1962 and 1986–1997), and in 1997 he was Distinguished Professor of Mathematics at Lincoln University and endowed chair at Grambling State University.

Given reprisals due to his membership in the Nation of Islam and his civil rights activism, he left Atlanta University in 1962 and directed education at Washington D.C.'s University of Islam from 1962 to 1975. "In 1992, one hundred of the African American holders of doctoral degrees could trace their academic lineage back to Shabazz or to his students." He died in 2014. "Abdulalim Abdullah Shabazz," Mathematical Association of America, https://www.maa.org/programs-and-communities/outreach-initiatives/summa/summa-archival-record/abdulalim-abdullah-shabazz.

5. Lumumba, "Mae," 17–18; "Manifesto"; "KKK" flyer; Crusaders for Freedom, "Passive Resistance"; "Special Invitation"; Lathan, "Crusader," 60; Williams, "Robert Williams"; Webb, "Behind"; "Monroe NAACP"; Clarence Seniors interview, 6/1/20; Blain, *Set the World*, 2, 188–189, 205, 31–32; Clarence Seniors interview, 6/1/20.

6. Mallory FBI, 10/11/61, "Justification," 9/8/61, 9/14/61.

7. African American Committee leaflet; "Call for Investigation"; Philip Benjamin, "400 Picket in Salute to Castro and Lumumba," *New York Times*, 2/19/61.

8. Lynn, *There Is*, 163.*

9. Clarence Seniors interview, 1/2/2009; Mallory, "Memo"; Williams, "Radio Free Dixie—On the Air," 10/62–11/62.

10. Mallory to Lynn, 9/9/62.

11. Mallory, "Memo"; Williams, "Radio Free Dixie—On the Air," 10/62–11/62, 2; "Mac Mallory Free on $10,000 Bail," reprinted from the Los Angeles *Herald Dispatch*, part 2, box 16, folder 49, HGP; Mallory, "Reverse"; Lumumba, "Mae," 17–18, 19–20; Mallory, "Monroe!"

12. Mallory, "Memo," 208; Williams, "Radio Free Dixie—On the Air," 10/62–11/62, 2.

13. Mallory, "Memo," 208.

14. Ibid., 207–210; Williams, "Radio Free Dixie—On the Air," 10/62–11/62, 2–3; Lumumba, "Mae," 17–22; Clarence Seniors, "Free"; Williams, *Crusader*, 8/63, 7; Webb, "Behind"; Williams, *Negroes with Guns*, 85; Williams FBI, 2/21/62; Doc to Williams, 10/5/61; Clarence Seniors, "From Lynch Threat"; Mallory FBI, 8/31/61, 9/1/61, 4/2/62, FBI; Williams FBI, 5/1/62, Belmont, Rosen, Williams; "Expect Ruling Soon in Mallory Case," *Call and Post*, 4/21/62, 3; Sanders, "Jail"; "FBI Arrests."*

15. Mallory to Williams, 9/11/62.

16. Oduba interviews.

17. Mallory, "Memo," 210.

18. Williams, "Radio Free Dixie—On the Air," 10/62–11/62, 2–3; Mallory, "Memo," 207–210; Williams, *Negroes with Guns*, 85; Green, "Committee to Aid"; Lumumba, "Mae," 18; Clarence Seniors, "Free"; Charles Sanders, "FBI Agents Capture Wanted Woman in Cleveland Home," *Call and Post*, 10/21/61; "Where FBI Found Woman," *Call and Post*, 10/21/61; "FBI Arrests."

19. Mallory, "Memo," 210; Al Sweeney, "Taking a Look at the Political Tote Board," *Call and Post*, 3/31/62, 2C; Sanders, "Jail."

20. "Black Zionist Stooges Lie about Mae Mallory," 4/5/62*;

"NAACP Head Claims She Refused Legal Services," *Herald Dispatch* (Huntington, W.Va.), 4/5/62, 1*; Haffner to Williams, 5/24/62.

21. J. Levy to MDC/Stone, 6/23/62; "Mallory Case"; "Mae Mallory 'Mistreated'"; "NAACP Says Mae Spurned Their Help," *Call and Post*, 3/31/62, 3A; "Store," *Afro American*, 7/4/59; Westbrook, "Mrs. Ruth Stone."

22. Mallory, "Memo," 210.

23. Golden to Robinson, 7/16/65.

24. Mallory, "Memo," 210; "Mae Mallory 'Mistreated.'"

25. Clarence Seniors autobiography.

26. Mallory, "Memo," 210; T. Tyson, *Radio Free Dixie*, 278–282, 293; Cruse, *Crisis*, 381.

27. Williams, "Radio Free Dixie—On the Air," 10/62–11/62, 2–3.

28. Clarence Seniors, "Free."

29. Bloom, *Modern*, 3, 4.

30. Mallory, "Constant Desperation," 1–4; Mallory FBI, 6/21/57, 1.

31. Lumumba, "Mae," 3.

32. Ibid., 2–3; Mallory, "Constant Desperation," 1–4; Mallory FBI, 6/21/57, 1; Manis, *Macon*, 78.

33. Oduba interviews.

34. Mallory, "Constant Desperation," 1.

35. Oduba interviews.

36. Mallory, "Constant Desperation," 1–2, 4; Tate, "Allegories," 103.

37. Oduba interviews.

38. Mallory, "Constant Desperation," 1–2, 4, 6.

39. Sudarkasa, "Interpreting," 43, 46, 48; Heinecke, "One Step," 45–46; Douglass, *Narrative*, 48, 121–122; Gutman, *Black Family*.

40. Mallory, "Constant Desperation," 3.

41. Lumumba, "Mae," 3–4.

42. Ibid., 3–4, 18.

43. Nevels, *Lynching*, 35, 71, 72, 73, 89–90.

44. Lumumba, "Mae," 4.

45. Manis, *Macon*, 56, 58; Brundage, *Lynching*, 8, 20; O. Patterson, *Rituals*, 176–179; Wells, *Red Record*, 157, 245; Markovitz, *Legacies*, 20, 22, 160n73, 162n84; Feimster, *Southern Horrors*, 159, 166, 171, 172, 173; King, *African American*, 149–151; Allen, *Without Sanctuary*, 20, 93, 94, 95, 179–180; Bloom, *Modern*, 3, 4.

46. Lumumba, "Mae," 4.

47. Ibid., 4, 6, 7.

48. Oduba interviews.

49. Mallory to Johnson, 3/29/67.

50. Mallory, "Constant Desperation," 9.

51. M. Berry, *My Face*, 52–54; Painter, *Creating*, 163; Gross, *Colored Amazons*, 40–41.

52. Mallory, "Constant Desperation," 8–9.

53. Black Panther 10 Point Program; Zedong, *Quotations*.

54. Lumumba, "Mae," 4–5.

55. Manis, *Macon*, 78–79.

56. Mallory, "Constant Desperation," 8–9.

57. Lumumba, "Mae," 1–2.

58. Ravitch, *Great School Wars*, 173–174, 241–242; Mabee, *Black Education*, 247, 249, 250, 258–259; Commission on School Integration, "Public School," 5–7.

59. Mabee, *Black Education*, 243, 261, 268; Commission on School Integration, "Public School," 11.

60. Lumumba, "Mae," 5, 6.

61. Ibid., 6–7.

62. Ibid.

63. Ibid.; Mallory FBI, 6/21/57, 2.

64. Lumumba, "Mae," 7–8.

65. Ibid., 8.

66. Ibid., 6, 8; Mallory FBI, 6/21/57, 2.

67. Lumumba, "Mae," 8–9.

68. Ibid., 8; Mallory FBI, 6/21/57, 2.

69. Lumumba, "Mae," 8–9.

70. Ibid., 9.

71. Ibid., 9, 10.

72. Ibid., 10–11.

73. Turner, *Caribbean Crusaders*, 16–18, 41, 46, 47, 87.

74. Ibid., 110; Breitman et al., *Trotskyism*, 6, 7; Makalani, *In the Cause*, 33, 39, 44, 53–54, 65–66, 73, 85.

75. Lumumba, "Mae," 10–11.

76. Mallory FBI, 5/27/59, 2, 6/21/57, 1, 4, 5, 5/28/58, 2–3, 4, 6, 28, 30, 5/29/59, 2, 6/18/62, 3–4, 7/63, 1, 6/18/62, 3, 5, 5/28/60, 3/18–5/6/60, 8/13/63, 3/27–8/8/63, 6/5/61, 5/15/61, 4/23–5/25/58, 28, 30, 5/6/58, 5/13/58, 5/16/58, 5/20/58, 4–5, 6/21/57, 5, 8.

77. Lumumba, "Mae," 10–11; T. Tyson, *Radio Free Dixie*, 190; McDuffie, "New Freedom," 95.

78. Lumumba, "Mae," 11.

79. Mallory FBI, 4/25/58, 1–2.

80. Jesse H. Walker, "Theatricals," *Amsterdam News*, 1/17/59, 16.

81. "Commission on School Integration, "Public School," 7, 11, 22, 25–26, 27; Ravitch, *Great School Wars*, 251–253, 241, 246, 247.

82. Mallory, *Letters from Prison*, 30.

83. Ibid.; Lumumba, "Mae," 12–15; Oduba interviews.

84. Lumumba, "Mae," 12–15; Mallory, *Letters from Prison*, 29–30.

85. Oduba interviews; Lumumba, "Mae," 11; Mallory, *Letters from Prison*, 29–30; David Goodman and Randy Leonard, "Truck Kills Boy, 6, as He Walks to School," *New York Times*, 2/28/2013; Matt Flegenheimer, "Fingers Are Pointed as Truck Kills Boy," *New York Times*, 3/5/2013, 5.

86. Oduba interviews; Lumumba, "Mae," 11; Mallory, *Letters from Prison*, 29–30; Goodman and Leonard, "Truck Kills Boy"; Flegenheimer, "Fingers Pointed."

87. Lumumba, "Mae," 11.

88. Mallory, *Letters from Prison*, 29–30; Oduba interviews; Lumumba, "Mae," 13.

89. Kornweibel, *Seeing Red*, xii, xiv–xv; O'Reilly, *Racial Matters*, 4–6, 12.

90. Lumumba, "Mae," 13; Mallory, *Letters from Prison*, 29–30.

91. The Welfare Department reported Mae's address as 27 Morningside Avenue. Mallory FBI, 6/21/57, 8–9, 30.

92. Mallory, *Letters from Prison*, 30; "Rev. Eugene Callender, Who Saw Potential of School Dropouts, Dies at 87," *New York Times*, 11/7/2013.

93. Mallory, *Letters from Prison*, 30.

94. P. Collins, *Black*, 148; Kuumba, *Gender*, 64.

95. Mallory, *Letters from Prison*, 30.

96. Mallory FBI, 6/5/61, 5/15/61, 5/28/58, 3-4, 4/24-25/58, 28, 30, 5/6-20/58, 4, 13-16, 4/25/58, 3-4, 5/27/59, 6/5/61, 4/28/58, 3-4, 30, 5/6/58, 13-16, 5/20/58, 4.

97. Benjamin Fine, "Negro Sues City on School Zoning," *New York Times*, 7/18/57, 1, 14; Lumumba, "Mae," 15; Back, "Still Unequal," 67-68; Mallory FBI, 5/28/58, 4; Loren B. Pope, "21 Negro Pupils Are Kept Home on Charge of Segregation Here," *New York Times*, 9/9/58; Loren B. Pope, "21 Negro Pupils Still Kept Home; City School Head to Talk to Brooklyn Parents Monday in Integration Dispute," *New York Times*, 9/10/58, 1.

98. Mallory, *Letters from Prison*, 30; Pope, "21 . . . Still Kept Home"; Oduba interviews.

99. Mallory, *Letters from Prison*, 29.

100. "Harlem Parents File for Million; Claim Asks the City to Pay for 'Segregating' Pupils—Law Suit Expected," *New York Times*, 10/29/58, 69.

101. Weiner, *Enemies*, 195-196, 198-200, 250; Jeffreys-Jones, *FBI*, 134, 171; Audrey Seniors FBI, 1962-1972, 3/28/65, 6/29/65, Appendix, Workers World, 3/4/64, 11, MDC, 3/16/65, 5, 3/6/64, 2/19/65, CAMD Appendix, 3/28/65, Appendix, MDC, 3/4/63, 7-9; Clarence Seniors FBI, 1959-1972, 3/25/65, 6/29/65; Mallory FBI, 1957-1976; Johnson FBI, 1959-1972; MDC, 1961-1965, Internal Security Miscellaneous, 10/2/61; Workers World Party FBI, 1959-1972, 9/1/61; CAMD FBI, 1961-1963, 1, 11/1/61,1, 4/30/62, "Memorandum," 1-2, 9/13/61, 4/30/62, 5/2/62.

102. Weiner, *Enemies*, 195-196, 198-200, 250; Jeffreys-Jones, *FBI*, 134, 171; Kornweibel, *Seeing Red*, xii-xiii; O'Reilly, *Racial Matters*, 8, 45; Audrey Seniors FBI, Appendix, Workers World, 3/4/64, 11, MDC, 3/16/65, 5, 3/6/64, 2/19/65, Appendix, CAMD, 3/28/65, Appendix, MDC, 3/4/63, 7-9; Clarence Seniors FBI, 1959-1972; Mallory FBI, 1957-1976; Johnson FBI, 1959-1972; MDC, 1961-1965, Internal Security Miscellaneous, 10/2/61; Workers World Party FBI, 1959-1972, 9/1/61; CAMD FBI, 1961-1963, 11/1/61,1, 4/30/62, "Memorandum," 1-2, 9/13/61, 4/30/62, 5/2/62; "Mr. Muhammad," *Sepia*, 11/59*; Mallory, United States Secret Service, 3; McDuffie, *Sojourning*, 113, 126-127, 132; Southern Negro Youth Congress FBI, SNYC; Louise Thompson Patterson FBI, 1941-1943; Gilyard, *Louise Thompson Patterson*, 261, 262, 264; Nation of Islam FBI; Highlander FBI, 1936-1941; King FBI, 1977; Rustin FBI, 1963-1966; Claudia Jones FBI, 1951-1955; Evers FBI, 1963-1964; Du Bois FBI, 1942-1960; Muhammad FBI, 1940-1963; Freedom Riders FBI, 1961-1962; Hamer FBI, 1963; Malcolm X FBI, 1953-1964; Carmichael FBI, 1964-1966.

103. Jeffrey-Jones, *FBI*, 134, 170-171, 175-177, 183-185, 189; Weiner, *Enemies*, 195-198, 250-251; Sanders, "Jail"; Liuzzo FBI.

104. Weiner, *Enemies*, 195-196.

105. Ibid.; Jeffrey-Jones, *FBI*, 170-171; Mallory, "On the New York Scene." In Greensboro "attorney Samuel Mitchell won a delay of a years' prison sentence imposed on him on charges of late filing of income tax." "News in Brief, in Greensboro, N.C.," *Southern Patriot*, 6/62, 2, CABP.

106. Mallory FBI, 6/21/57, 10, 30, 5/29/59, 6/5/61, 5/23/60, 5/28/60.

107. "Protests School, Arrested on Welfare Charge," *Amsterdam News*, 6/29/57; Mallory FBI, 5/27/59, 2, 5/28/58, 1, 5, 5/28/58– 5/28/60, 1, 6/18/62, 3.

108. Lumumba, "Mae," 15–16; Oduba interviews; Marton, "#Closerikers"; Daniel Beekman, "Spofford, aka Bridges Juvenile Center Finally Shut Down," *New York Daily News*, 3/31/2011; Conger and Ross, "Project Confirm."

109. Lumumba, "Mae," 15–16; Oduba interviews; Marton, "#Closerikers"; Beekman, "Spofford"; Conger and Ross, "Project Confirm"; Mallory FBI, 5/28/58, 1, 4, 5/28/60, 5/23/60, 6/5/61.

110. Lumumba, "Mae," 10, 15; Mallory FBI, 5/28/58, 3; Boyce Davies, *Left*, 134; W. Patterson, *Ben Davis*, 43–44, ACSC.

111. Lumumba, "Mae," 15–16; Mallory, *Letters from Prison*, 29–30; Mallory FBI, 5/28/58, 1.

112. Lumumba, "Mae," 15–16; Mallory, *Letters from Prison*, 29–30; Mallory FBI, 5/28/58, 1.

113. O'Reilly, *Racial Matters*, 8, 45; Kornweibel, *Seeing Red*, xii; Carol Cratty, "Newspaper Lawsuit Yields FBI Records from Civil Rights Era Informant," CNN, 2/25/2013; Robbie Brown, "Civil Rights Photographer Unmasked as Informer," *New York Times*, 9/13/2010, 2; "Released Documents"; Franklin, "Jackanapes," 62–63; Audrey Seniors FBI, 1962–1972; Clarence Seniors FBI, 1959–1972; Mallory FBI, 1957–1976; Johnson FBI, 1959–1972.

114. Kornweibel, *Seeing Red*, xiii; Franklin, "Jackanapes," 62–63.

115. O'Reilly, *Racial Matters*, 8, 45; Kornweibel, *Seeing Red*, xii; Audrey Seniors FBI, 1962–1972; Clarence Seniors FBI, 1959–1972; Mallory FBI, 1957–1976; Johnson FBI, 1959–1972.

Chapter 4. Audrey Proctor

1. Dubuclet interview, 2/20/2011.

2. Clarence Seniors autobiography; Romberstein, Memorandum; "Mallory Case."

3. Breitman et al., *Trotskyism*, 35–36, 203–204, 294; R. J. Alexander, *Maoism*, 36–37; Griswold, *Workers World Party*, 1, 9, 27, 29–31.

4. Griswold, *Workers World Party*, 30.

5. Marcy et al., "Statement," 1; Griswold, *Workers World Party*, 1, 9, 27, 29–31; Griswold, "Rosemary"; Greg Butterfield, "Rosemary Neidenberg: A Century of Revolutionary Struggle," *Struggle La Lucha*, 4/8/20; Deidre Griswold, "Milt Neidenberg Fought for the Liberation of the Workers and the Oppressed," *Workers World*, 2/26/2018; Breitman et al., *Trotskyism*, 31, 35–36, 203–204, 294; R. J. Alexander, *Maoism*, 36–37.

6. Deidre Griswold, "Rosemary Neidenberg: A Long and Valued Life," *Workers World*, 4/7/20; G. Butterfield, "Rosemary Neidenberg"; Brenda Ryan, "Memorial for Milton Neidenberg: Workers Pay Tribute to Revolutionary Boldness," *Workers World*, 4/6/2018.

7. Jeanette Merrill and Rosemary Neidenberg, "Mae Mallory: Unforgettable Freedom Fighter Promoted Self-Defense," *Workers World*, 2/26/2009; Mallory, "Memo," 210.

8. Hicks, "Open Letter"; Clarence Seniors autobiography.

9. Hicks, "Monroe Defense Committee Bulletin."

10. MDC FBI, 10/2/61; A. Seniors FBI, Appendix, MDC, 7–9, 3/4/63, MDC, 5, 3/16/65, 3/6/64, 2/19/65; Green, "Summary Report"; Williams FBI, Williams to Mr. W. C., 10/12/61.

11. Advertisement—Purlie Victorious; Hicks, "Dear Friend"; Hicks, "Mae," 1–2; Hicks, MDC flyer, 11/7/61; O. Davis, "Purlie."*

12. Diderich to Boyte, 9/24/61; Perry to Hicks, 9/30/62; Perry, "What Is CAMD?"; Perry, "Provisional"; Green to Lynn, 5/11/63; Baldwin, "Personal."

13. MDC FBI, 10/21/61, 11/28/61; Green, "Summary Report"; Williams to Mr. W. C.; Williams FBI, 2/13/62, 9/25/61; CAMD–SWP FBI, 2/13/62; SWP FBI Disruption Program, 2/28/64, 4/30/62, 1–2, 5/14/62, 1, 9/21/62, 1, 3/3/64, 1–6, 3/6/64, 1–2, 3/11/64, 3/16/64, 1–3, 3/17/64, 1–4, 4/10/64, 1, 4/13/64, 4/15/64, 1–4, 6/25/64, 4/23/64, 5/4/64, 1, 2/26/65.

14. Williams to Mr. W. C.; Mallory, "Memo," 210.

15. Hicks, "MDC Bulletin"; Mae Mallory, "A Letter from Prison: I Appeal to You," *National Guardian*, 11/29/62, 5, box 346, folder 1, JBMP; Clarence Seniors, "Dear Friend"; Perry to Boyte, 1/23/64.

16. Mallory, "Letter from Prison."

17. Ibid.; Hicks, "MDC Bulletin"; Clarence Seniors, "Dear Friend."

18. "Nixon, Lodge Favorite in Poll at Morris Brown," *Atlanta Daily World*, 11/1/60, 4; "Segregation in the Courts Is Being Challenged by Clarence Seniors," *Southern Patriot*, 6/60*; "$1 Million"*; "Don't Let Mae"; "Mae Mallory Speaks," *Call and Post*, 4/20/63; "Fifth Annual Luncheon"*; "Negro Files Sit in, in Atlanta," *New York Times*, 4/26/60, 30; "Suit Challenges Court Segregation," *Atlanta Constitution*, 4/26/60, 1; "Student Sues Atlanta for Millions," *Call and Post*, 5/4/60, 10D; "Cross Burning Is Tied to Student Segregation Suit," *Atlanta Daily World*, 5/10/60, 1; "Summary Judgement Asked in Court," *Afro American*, 6/18/60, 17; "Suit Hits Courtroom Bias," *Call and Post*, 6/18/60; "Atlantan to Appeal Court Jim Crow Case," *Philadelphia Tribune*, 6/23/60, 11; "Anti-Segregation Suit Is Permitted Pauper's Appeal," *Atlanta Daily World*, 7/9/60, 1; "Negro Gets Right to Appeal," *Atlanta Journal and Constitution*, 7/10/60, 11B; "Clarence Seniors, a Morris Brown College Student," *Afro American*, 7/23/60, 6; "Court Seating Case Is Today," *Atlanta Daily World*, 10/27/60; "Clarence Seniors and His Lawyers, Challenging Segregated Seating in Atlanta Court Rooms," *Atlanta Daily World*, 10/29/60; "Dismissal of Court Seating Suit Is Upheld," *Atlanta Daily World*, 11/24/60, 5; "Court Seating Verdict to Be Appealed in Georgia," *Afro American*, 12/3/60, 15; "Clarence H. Seniors, Morris Brown College Student," *Afro American*, 12/3/60, 6; "Officials Identify 77 Arrested in Sit-downs," *Atlanta Constitution*, 3/16/60, 7; "List Names of Sit-Ins Now in Jail," *New Pittsburgh Courier*, 10/29/60, 7; Sims-Alvarado, *Atlanta*, 73; M. Daniels, *Saving*, 116.

19. "Nixon, Lodge"; "Segregation in the Courts"; "$1 Million"; "Don't Let Mae"; "Mae Mallory Speaks to St. James Forum," *Call and Post*, 4/20/63; "Fifth Annual Luncheon"; "Negro Files," *New York Times*, 4/26/60; "Suit," *Atlanta Constitution*, 4/26/60; "Student Sues," *Call and Post*, 5/4/60; "Cross Burning," *Atlanta Daily World*, 5/10/60; "Summary Judgement"; "Suit," *Call and Post*, 6/18/60; "Atlantan to Appeal," *Philadelphia Tribune*, 6/23/60; "Anti-Segregation," *Atlanta Daily World*, 7/9/60; "Negro Gets Right," *Atlanta Journal and Constitution*, 7/10/60; "Clarence Seniors," *Afro American*, 7/23/60; "Court Seating," *Atlanta Daily World*, 10/27/60; "Clarence Seniors," *Atlanta Daily World*, 10/29/60; "Dismissal," *Atlanta Daily World*, 11/24/60; "Court Seating," *Afro American*, 12/3/60; "Clarence Seniors," *Afro American*, 12/3/60; "Officials," *Atlanta Constitution*, 3/16/60; "List," *New Pittsburgh Courier*, 10/29/60; Sims-Alvarado, *Atlanta*, 73; M. Daniels, *Saving*, 116.

20. Clarence Henry Seniors [as A. T. Simpson], "After One Year of Hell: Mae Mallory Is Still a Champion," *Workers World*, 10/26/62.*

21. Green, "Summary Report," 1.
22. Hicks, "Open Letter," 9.
23. Mallory to Williams, 8/16/62; Lynn to Williams, 4/14/62.
24. Green, "Summary Report," 1.
25. Hicks, "Open Letter," 4-7.
26. Hicks, MDC flyer.
27. Cruse, *Crisis*, 368–371; MDC FBI, 10/2/61; Williams FBI, 10/12/61, Williams to Mr. W. C.; Green, "Summary Report"; CAMD-SWP, 11/1/61, 1, 4/30/62, "Memorandum," 1–2, 9/13/61, 4/30/62, 5/2/62; SWP FBI, 2/13/62, FBI, 3/6/64, 1.
28. Green to Lynn, 5/11/63.
29. Cruse, *Crisis*, 368–371; MDC, FBI, 10/21/61; Williams FBI, 10/12/61, Williams to Mr. W. C.
30. Mallory, "Memo," 210; Williams FBI, Williams to Mr. W. C.
31. Mallory FBI, 8/13/63.
32. "Mae Mallory and MDC."
33. Clarence Seniors, "Dear Friend."
34. Mary and Bill Kochiyama, *Did?*, 9/4/65; Johnson, *Did?*, 11/7/64, 3–6; T. Tyson, *Radio Free Dixie*, 193, 194; Ransby, *Ella Baker*, 215; Burlage, "Truths," 114; "Introducing," *Partisan*, 4/65; Johnson FBI, 6/27/1963, 2–3, 8/26/63, 3, 3/20/64, 11/8/63, 1, 1/25/63, 1, 1/25/65, 5–6; Williams and Seniors, "Monroe Defense Committee"; Johnson, *Did?*, 4/18/64, 11/21/64, 4/3/65, 4/24/65, 5/8/65, 6/19/65, 7/3/65, 9/65, 9/4/65, 4/18/64, 11/65, 6/5/65, 11/7/65, 1/6/66, 2/19/66, 3/66, 6/19/66; Johnson, *Did?*, 7/19/66–8/66, 5/66, 3–4; "Ethel Azalea Johnson Obituary"; "Ethel Johnson"; Johnson FBI, 8/26/63, 1/25/65, 16; Johnson, *Did?*, 7/6/63; Clarence Seniors to Ballan, 10/18/64; Clarence Seniors autobiography; "The Youngest and Oldest Freedom Marchers," *Call and Post*, 11/23/63.*
35. Wilbur Grattan, "The Weekend of Political Prisoners," *Call and Post*, 5/31/69, 15A; American Security Council, "Revolutionary Action Movement"; "Cleveland Teacher Is Suspended for Black Nationalism," *Militant*, 3/22/65, box 482, RAM Folder 1963-1966, JBMP; *Black America*, Fall 1964; Clarence Seniors autobiography; "Freedom Fighters," 1; "Black Detroit Timeline: 1955–1969," *Michigan Chronicle*, 1/12/2011, A7; "Black Muslims Join New Militant Northern Negro Organization," *Chicago Daily Defender*, 11/21/63; "Asserts Negroes Excluded: Ask Board to Halt Purchases of Books," *Michigan Chronicle*, 3/31/62; Richard Gibson, "U.S. Exile Returns to Red China," *Chicago Defender*, 10/19/68, 26; "Republic of New Africa," *Call and Post*, 6/29/68; Alvin Ward, "Black Dissenters Conduct Dialogue," *Call and Post*, 5/31/69, 15A; Alvin Ward, "60 from Cleveland Attend Sessions: Gun Play, Mass Arrests, Mar Separatist Meet in Detroit," *Call and Post*, 4/5/69; Hucks, *Yoruba*, 157–158; Alvin Ward, "Witnesses Testify in the July Disturbances," *Call and Post*, 5/31/69, 16A; "Turnpike Murder—Suicide Figure Lambright Laid to Rest," *Call and Post*, 4/19/69, 1A; "Tanzania Welcomes Negro, Wife of Ambassador Says," *Call and Post*, 8/9/69; Kerr, *Derelict Paradise*, 174–175; Masotti and Corsi, *Shoot-Out*, 49–50, 74, 77*; "Masotti Report Critical, Tells Few New Facts, Disappointing," *Call and Post*, 6/7/69, 1A; "New Afrika to Test Appeal in Brooklyn Area," *Call and Post*, 3/21/69; "Grand Jury Takes No Action in Police Case," *Call and Post*, 6/14/69, 3A; Ellen Delmonte, "Whites Cheer Panther Lawyers at CWRU Rally," *Call and Post*, 12/27/69, 1A; "Lawyer Cleared of Charges," *Call and Post*, 9/20/69, 1B; "Kellog Flemings Deny Double Deals," *Call and Post*, 7/19/69, 16A; Grattan to Williams,

3/13/67; Thomas A. Julius, "Negro Labor Force in U.S. 5,925,000! Industry Finds Bias Wasteful," *Pittsburgh Courier*, 9/4/54, B9.

36. Grattan to Williams, 3/13/67.

37. "Republic of New Africa," *Call and Post*, 6/29/68; "Republic of New Afrika to Organize Black Legion," *Michigan Chronicle*, 6/29/68; Ward, "Black Dissenters"; Ward, "60 from Cleveland"; Hucks, *Yoruba*, 157–158; Kochiyama to Gaidi, Imari, Williams, 9/11/69; "TWA Refuses."

38. "Republic of New Africa"; "Republic of New Afrika"; Ward, "Black Dissenters"; Ward, "60 from Cleveland"; Gibson, "U.S. Exile"; Ward, "Witnesses Testify"; "Turnpike Murder"; "Tanzania"; Hucks, *Yoruba*, 157–158; Kerr, *Derelict Paradise*, 174–175; Masotti and Corsi, *Shoot-Out*, 49–50, 74, 77; "Masotti Report"; "New Afrika," *Call and Post*, 3/21/69; "Grand Jury Takes No Action"; Delmonte, "Whites Cheer"; "Lawyer Cleared"; "Kellog Flemings"; Dick Peery, "Mae Mallory Jailed," *Call and Post*, 6/14/69; "He Must Be Crazy," *Call and Post*, 6/14/69; "Jail Term Levied on Mrs. Mallory," *Afro American*, 6/28/69, 12; "In Cleveland Court: Find 20 Activists Guilty of Contempt," *Chicago Defender*, 6/11/69, 8; Dick Peery, "Militants Storm Corrigan's Office," *Call and Post*, 5/31/69, 1; June V. Williams, "One Woman's Opinion," *Call and Post*, 6/21/69, 5; Dick Peery, "White Racialism Surfaces at Evans Trial," *Call and Post*, 5/10/69, 1.

39. American Security Council, "Revolutionary Action Movement"; "Cleveland Teacher"; *Black America*, Fall 1964; Clarence Seniors autobiography; "Freedom Fighters"; "Black Detroit"; "Black Muslims"; "Asserts Negroes Excluded"; Gibson, "U.S. Exile"; "Republic of New Africa"; "Republic of New Afrika"; Ward, "Black Dissenters"; Ward, "60 from Cleveland"; Hucks, *Yoruba*, 157–158; Ward, "Witnesses Testify"; "Turnpike Murder"; "Tanzania"; Kerr, *Derelict Paradise*, 174–175; Masotti and Corsi, *Shoot-Out*, 49–50, 74, 77; "Masotti Report"; "New Afrika"; "Grand Jury Takes No Action"; Delmonte, "Whites Cheer"; "Lawyer Cleared"; "Kellog Flemings."

40. Mallory to Mabel Williams, 3/30/64.

41. Mallory, "Memo"; Clarence Seniors, phone interview, 9/23/2007; Cruse, *Crisis*, 381; American Security Council, "Revolutionary Action Movement"; "Cleveland Teacher"; *Black America*, Fall 1964; "Wilbur Grattan," *Fugitives*; "Wilbur Grattan," *Hearings*, 1969-1973, 4373, 5013, 1970, 54, 1973, 1053, 1054, 1056, 1058; "Wilbur Grattan, Riots," 4373; "Wilbur Grattan, Revolutionary Activities," 1056; "Wilbur Grattan, Black Panther Party"; "Wilbur Grattan," *Congressional Record*, 187; "Wilbur Grattan," *Establishing*.

42. Matthews, Reports on Workers World Party.

43. Mallory FBI, 8/13/63, 1, 3–4.

44. MDC FBI, 10/21/61.

45. Williams FBI, 10/12/61, Williams to Mr. W. C.; MDC FBI, 11/28/61; SWP FBI, 3/6/64, 1-2, 4, 6, 7, 4/3/64, 4/4/64, 4/10/64; Weissman, "Statement," 2/26/64, 1-2; Williams FBI, 4/10/64, 5/14/62, SWP; Weissman FBI, 4/14/64; "Kidnap Trial Reporter Runs into Robbery," *Charlotte News*, 2/27/64, 8A, ALUA; "Physicians Safe Rifled," *Raleigh News and Dispatch*, 2/27/64, ALUA; "Bandits Get Contents of Safe," *Greensboro Daily News*, 2/27/64, ALUA; Gray, "Doctor's Wall Safe Cracked"; "Two Bandits Rifle Negro Doctor's Safe," *Monroe Enquirer*, 2/27/64, ALUA.

46. Johnson FBI, "Doctor's," 2/27–4/10/64.

47. SWP FBI, 3/6/64, 4.

48. Ibid.; Weissman, "Statement"; Gray, "Doctor's Wall Safe Cracked"; Johnson

FBI, New York, "Doctor's," 2/27–4/10/64; Williams FBI, New York, "Doctor's," 2/27–4/10/64; "Tampering Admitted by FBI in Stegall Kidnapping Trial," *Monroe Enquirer Journal*, 4/2/75; "Dear Political," flyer; Agee, *Inside*.*

49. SWP FBI, 4/4/64/–4/10/64.

50. Weissman, "Statement," 2/26/64; "Safe Robbery at Dr. Perry's Home," news clipping, 2/28/64, UCHR; Gray, "Doctor's Wall Safe Cracked."

51. Williams FBI, 3/11/64, 2; Weiner, *Enemies*, 183–185, 189, 195–196, 198–200, 250; Jeffreys-Jones, *FBI*, 134, 170–171, 177; Agee, *Inside*; "Dear Political"; "Tampering Admitted."

52. Clarence Seniors interview, 1/2/2009.

53. Franklin, "Jackanapes," 62–63; Rosenfeld, "New FBI Files," *Mercury News*, 2015; Aoki FBI, 1962–1967; Johnson FBI, 1959–1972; Audrey Seniors FBI, 1962–1973; Clarence Seniors FBI, 1959–1973; Mallory FBI, 1957–1976; Williams FBI, 9/11/61, 9/20/61, 9/21/61, 9/22/61; CAMD FBI, 1961–1963, 1, 11/1/61, 1, 4/30/62, "Memorandum," 1–2, 9/13/61, 4/30/62, 5/2/62; MDC FBI, 1961–1965, 1, 11/1/61, 1, 4/30/62; Kornweibel, *Seeing Red*, 11, 54; Cratty, "Newspaper Lawsuit"; Brown, "Civil Rights Photographer"; "Released Documents."

54. Weiner, *Enemies*, 175–177, 183–185, 189, 195–196, 198–200, 250; Jeffreys-Jones, *FBI*, 134, 171, 177.

55. Clarence Seniors interview, 2007; Mallory FBI, Cleveland, 8/13/63, 3/27–8/8/63, 5.

56. Clarence Seniors autobiography.

57. "UFM Pickets from All Walks of Life," *Cleveland Plain Dealer*, 9/26/63, 27.*

58. Clarence Seniors autobiography.

59. Audrey Seniors FBI, 3/3/63, 1–2; "Wedding Bells. Clarence Seniors, 25, 10516 Superior, to Audrey, 21 8419 Decker," *Call and Post*, 9/8/62.

60. Clarence Seniors interview, 1/2/2009; Clarence Seniors autobiography.

61. Dubuclet interview, 3/2006. All quotations from Aunt Doris in this passage come from this interview.

62. Audrey Seniors FBI, 3/3/63, 3/4/63.

63. Mallory FBI, 8/13/63, 10/7/62, 4.

64. Audrey Seniors FBI, 5/31/68, 1; Clarence Seniors FBI, Activities, 7–12, 5/10/65, 1957–1973, Detention Communist List, 12/4/57, C; Clarence Seniors Secret Service file, FBI File, 5/20/66; Memorandum, Clarence Henry Seniors, FBI File, 7/6/66, 1–2.

65. Williams FBI, 4/15/64.

66. Clarence Seniors interview, 1/2/2009.

67. Mallory, "Memo," 210; Clarence Seniors interview; Mallory, letter/petition, 6/2/63*; Bertrand Russell's endorsement*; "Come," flyer, 7/14/63; Clarence Seniors, "Free"; Letter from Mallory and MDC; Mallory FBI, 8/13/62, 10/7/62, 4.

68. Mallory, letter/petition; Letter from Mallory, MDC, 1963; Clarence Seniors interview, 1/2/2009; Mallory, "Memo"; Clarence Seniors phone interview, 2010, "Come" flyer.

69. Castro, *Our Party*, 10/3/65, 8, 9; Castro, *Declaration*, 9/2/60; Castro, "Speech at the United Nations," 9/26/60; Lavan, *Che Guevara Speaks*; Scheer, *Diary*; Guevara, *Reminiscences*; Fremantle, *Mao*; Yu-Chang, *The Revolution*, 1962; Zedong, *Quotations*; Zedong, "Statement," 4–5; Zedong, *Statement*; *Chosen Passages*; Spencer, *Sun Yat-Sen*; Jansen, *Japanese*; Buck, *Man*; Piao, *Long Live*; *Constitution of the Communist Party*; Arévalo, *Shark*, 1961; Weglyn, *Years*.

70. Lipsitz, *Life*, 9–11; Gramsci, *Selections*, 5–6, 9–10; Melvin Tapley, "Inmates Air Grievances at a Famous Prison," *Amsterdam News*, 10/16/71, C3; Audrey Seniors FBI, Black Panther Membership, 3, 3/1/71.

71. Audrey Proctor [Seniors] birth certificate, 1940; Dubuclet interview, 2/20/2011; "Faculty," 5/24/58.

72. Audrey Proctor Seniors, Autobiographical Notes.*

73. Audrey Seniors, "My Memory Book."

74. Dubuclet interview, 2020.

75. Ibid.

76. Audrey Seniors FBI, 3/4/63, 5.

77. NAACP, "History"; Fairclough, *Race*, 48–51; Sartain, *Invisible Acts*, 93–94, 105; E. Wright FBI, New Orleans, 4/21/45, 7, 4/10/46, 1–3.

78. Sartain, *Invisible Acts*, 105, 93.

79. E. Wright FBI, New Orleans, 4/21/45, 7.

80. Ibid., 51, 58, 99, 82–83, 101–102; NAACP, "Introduction"; NAACP, "History."

81. Borstelmann, *Cold War*, 108; Woods, *Black Struggle*, 7, 9.

82. "Birds of a Feather—Key NAACP Leaders Have 'Front' Records," *Citizens' Council*, 5/57, LSUSC; "'Freedom' Red Style," *Citizens' Council*, 2/57, 2, LSUSC.

83. Dudziak, *Cold War*, 67, 124–125; Layton, *International Politics*, 93; Woods, *Black Struggle*, 2, 5; Borstelmann, *Cold War*, 65, 108; "Birds of a Feather"; Southern Lady, "Women of the South," *Citizens' Council*, 2/57, 4, LSUSC; "Current Red Activity," *Citizens' Council*, 1/58, 3, LSUSC; "Commies After It: Forced Immigration Seen as Part of Leftist Scheme," *Citizens' Council*, 1/58, 4, LSUSC.

84. G. Lewis, *Massive Resistance*, 127–128, 122.

85. NAACP, "History"; Fairclough, *Race*, 48–51; Sartain, *Invisible Acts*, 93–94, 105; E. Wright FBI, New Orleans, 4/21/45, 4/10/46; "White Bus Driver"; "Whites Assaulting"; Borstelmann, *Cold War*, 108; Woods, *Black Struggle*, 7, 93.

86. Bloom, *Modern*, vii, 3, 4; Sartain, *Invisible Acts*, 51, 58, 60, 69, 99; Fairclough, *Race*, 18–19.

87. Sartain, *Invisible Acts*, 82–83, 85, 100–102.

88. "Truman Balks at Lynch Action: Fails to Take Initiative on Plea of Crusade; Paul Robeson Leads Group in Audience with President," *Chicago Defender*, 9/28/46, 1; "American Crusade Ends with Anti-Lynch Decree," *Chicago Defender*, 9/28/46.

89. Audrey Proctor's generation admired Paul Robeson for his political stand and his artistry, as did Williams, Sidney Poitier, Harry Belafonte, and Ossie Davis.

90. "Group Sees Truman on Lynching Curb," *New York Times*, 9/24/46, 43; "To Open Crusade against Lynching," *New York Times*, 9/23/46, 16; Robeson, *Here I Stand*, 92; Paula Marie Seniors, "Jack Johnson," 165–170.

91. Paula Marie Seniors, "Jack Johnson," 165–170; Wright, *Robeson*, 13; "Group Sees Truman"; "To Open Crusade"; Robeson, *Here I Stand*, 92; "Truman Balks"; "American Crusade."

92. Woods, *Black Struggle*, 7, 93; Fairclough, *Race*, 223–225, 211; NAACP, "Introduction"; Sartain, *Invisible Acts*, 93, 105; Borstelmann, *Cold War*, 108; Bartley, *Rise*, 74, 90–99, 187; "At Louisiana Hearing"; Rainach, "Special Note."

93. Bartley, *Rise*, 90–91; *Citizens' Council*, 1/58, 3, LSUSC; Fairclough, *Race*, 199–202.

94. Bartley, *Rise*, 90–91, 135, 194–198, 209, 215, 217, 225, 228; Fairclough, *Race*, 199–202, 205–207.

95. Fairclough, 184, 192, 194–197, 209–210.
96. Ibid., 223–225, 211.

Chapter 5. Patricia Mallory

1. Painter, *Creating*, 230–231; Makalani, *In the Cause*; Berry and Gross, *Black*, 146–148.
2. Oduba interviews. All quotations from Pat are from these interviews unless otherwise noted.
3. Lipsitz, *Life*, 9–11; Gramsci, *Selections*, 9–10.
4. Blake, *Children*, 174.
5. Sudarkasa, "Interpreting," 43, 46, 48; Heinecke, "One Step," 45–46; Douglass, *Narrative*, 121–122.
6. "Girl Scout Daisy Notes," *Amsterdam News*, 5/1/65, 19.
7. "In Jail, Mrs. Mallory Slams July 4 Celebrations as 'Sham,'" *Afro American*, 7/21/62.
8. A. J. Cooper, *Voice*, 61.
9. Falk, *Rooted*, 27.
10. Gaines, *Uplifting*, 16–17; Thomas and Turner, "Race," 1, 11; Drake and Cayton, *Black Metropolis*, 496–499, 506–507.*
11. Hoose, *Claudette Colvin*, 22–23.
12. William Falk's *Rooted in Place* details the agrarian family model of patriarchy and misogyny in which Pat Mallory grew up. This model dictated Pat's place in the family as lower caste because of her gender.
13. See McDuffie, Sojourning, 143–146; Edelman, Interview 1.
14. Gaines, *Uplifting*, 135–136; McDuffie, *Sojourning*, 33.
15. Sharpley-Whiting, *Pimps Up*, 57, 81–82, 68; White, *Ar'n't I*, 50–51; W. King, "Prematurely Knowing."
16. A. Lee, "Old Woman," 83–85; Wells, "LaKeesha Walrond"; LaKeesha Walrond, lakeeshawalrondphd.com; "Maya Angelou"; Oprah Winfrey interview, 1991, https://www.facebook.com/watch/?v=1588511321183095; https://www.youtube.com/watch?v=1ObDKKW-sn8.
17. P. Johnson, *Inner Lives*, 183–189, 57–63; Sharpley-Whiting, *Pimps Up*, 57, 68, 77, 78, 81–84, 92–93, 68; Acoca, "Living," 82–83, 84; Katz, "Explaining," 31; Hernandez, "On Visual," 250; Bilksy and Chesney-Lind, "Doing Time," 31–32; C. Collins, *Imprisonment*, 53; Winfrey interview.
18. Perry-Burney et al., "Rural"; McDuffie, *Sojourning*, 33.
19. Walrond, lakeeshawalrondphd.com.
20. "Emmett Till"; Feldstein, *Motherhood*, 89–91; Richard Pérez-Peña, "Woman Linked to 1955 Emmett Till Murder Tells Historian Her Claims Were False," *New York Times*, 1/27/2017; Ed Pilkington, "Will Justice Finally Be Done for Emmett Till? Family Hopes a 65 Year Old Wait May Soon Be Over," *Guardian*, 4/25/2020; Weller, "How the Author"; Painter, *Creating*, 245; Berry and Gross, *Black*, 165–168; Emmett Till Interpretive Center, https://www.emmett-till.org; T. Tyson, *Blood of Emmett Till*, 2017.
21. Berry and Gross, *Black*, 158; McDuffie, *Sojourning*; Boyce Davies, *Left*.
22. "Mr. Muhammad," *Sepia*, 11/59*; "Mr. Muhammad Speaks," *Pittsburgh Courier*, 5/16/59*; Bennett, *Before*, 593, 577, 600–609; Painter, *Creating*, 253–256, 268–275; Hoose, *Claudette Colvin*; Berry and Gross, *Black*, 163, 169–170, 174; Ransby, *Ella Baker*; Lichtenstein et al., *Who Built America?*, 612–621; SNCC Constitution; Zinn, *Albany*, 5–8*; Williams, "Neo Barbarism."

23. Blake, *Children*, 40–41; McDuffie, *Sojourning*, 102, 187; "Daughters," 166–168; Pressman, "Interview."

24. Grattan to Williams, 3/13/67.

25. Weiner, *Enemies*, 195–196, 198–200, 250; Jeffreys-Jones, *FBI*, 134, 171; Kornweibel, *Seeing Red*, 1998; O'Reilly, *Racial Matters*, 198.

26. K. Burke, "Do I," 71–72.

27. E. Jackson, "This Is," 5*; Haviland, *James*, 2015. The Smith Act criminalized communism. See Boyce Davies, *Left*, 134; W. Patterson, *Ben Davis*, 43–44, ACSC; Flynn, *13 Communists*.

28. McDuffie, *Sojourning*, 184; Ransby, *Eslanda*, 3.

29. Harlem Education History Project, "Wadleigh Year Books" and "Wadleigh High School."

30. Mabee, "Margaret Mead," 6–8, 14; Semel and Sadovnik, "Lessons," 66, 68, 74–78, 82; "Urban Exchange," *New York Magazine*, 7/5/71; "Downtown Community School"; Gold, *Downtown*.

31. Cooper and Datnow, "African-American"; Birts, "African American"; Tatum, "Family Life"; DeCuir-Gunby et al., "African American Students."

32. Mallory to Mabel Williams, 10/11/62.

33. Anderson to Mallory, 5/15/63.

34. Bennett, *Before*, 596–597; Frazier, *From*, 623; Painter, *Creating*, 253; Hucks, *Yoruba*; Razak, "African," 6.

35. Singe et al., "Resilience," 1098, 1096; Grossman et al., *With Phoenix*, 115–116, 171–173, 178, 190.

36. "Senator Keating"; Robeson, "It's Good"; "Protest against Nuclear War"; Boyce Davies, *Left*, 143–144, 151, 210–211, 213–216, 219–220.

37. Benson, *Antiracism*, 178–179; Meeks, *Caribbean*, 59; Young, *Soul Power*, 33–34; Castro, "Speech at the United Nations," 1–2.

38. Mallory, "Fidel Castro."

39. Jo Thomas, "The Last Days of Castro," *New York Times*, 3/14/93, 2; Samad, "Legacy"; Rogo, "Brief Understanding"; Pérez, "Fidel Vive!"

40. Horton and Adams, *Unearthing*, xi–xii, 250; "South's Menace"; "Labor Colleges"; "Horton Visits Unions"; "Application Blank"; "Application for Highlander"; "Workshop"; "Community Services"; "News Release," 8/14/59; "Residential Workshop."

41. Horton and Adams, *Unearthing*, xi–xii, 250; Liveright, "Here"; "We Will"; "Southside"; "Highlander and Education"; "Application Blank"; "Application for Highlander"; "Workshop"; "Community Services"; "News Release," 8/14/59; "Residential Workshop."

42. "Highlander Work Camp Raided"; "Tragic Day for the South, the Highlander Folk School Is Closed," *Southern Patriot*, 11/61, CABP; "Federal Court Stops Highlander Investigation," *Southern Patriot*, 2/68, CABP; "Application Blank"; "Application"; "Workshop"; "Community Services"; "News Release Mrs. Septima Clark"; "News Release," 8/14/59; "Residential Workshop."

43. Diane McWhorter, "Marching in King's Shadow," *New York Times*, 10/6/2011; Job Nordheimer, "Rev. Fred Shuttlesworth, an Elder Statesman for Civil Rights, Dies at 89," *New York Times*, 10/5/2011; Meier, "Negro Protest Movements," 440.

44. Singe et al., "Resilience"; Grossman et al., *With Phoenix*, 115–116, 171–173, 178, 190.

45. See Ashe, *Hard Road*, 96–100; "The Draft, Cassius vs. Army," *New York Times*, 4/30/67; "Muhammad Ali Appeals," *Southern Patriot*, 1/68, CABP.

46. Spencer-Antoine, *Revolution*, 15, 26–27; "Mr. Muhammad," *Sepia*; Bennett, *Before*, 593, 577; "Mr. Muhammad's Blueprint"; "Thumbnail," n.d.; "University of Islam no. 2," photograph, 3, "Department Store," 8, "Dress Shop," 11, "Cleaning Plant" [dry cleaners], 12, "Grocery Store," 14, "Restaurant," 17, "Power of the Press," 20, "Barber Shop," 22, in *Messenger* 39, vol. 1, no. 1, 1959*; "Temple no. 2 Clothing Factory," "Temple no. 2 [dry] Cleaners," "Temple no. 2 Grocery and Market," "Shabazz Restaurant," *Muhammad Speaks*, 10/25/63*; "Mr. Elijah Muhammad, The Messenger of Allah," 1959, Courier, ACSC; Burley, *Muhammad Speaks*; "Thumbnail," 1959.

47. Spencer-Antoine, *Revolution*, 15, 26–28; "Mr. Elijah Muhammad, the Messenger of Allah, 1959," *Courier*, 26.*

48. Lumumba, "Mae," 17–18; "Note . . . Manifesto," 6/10/61; "KKK" flyer; Crusaders for Freedom, "Passive Resistance"; Mallory, "Militant"; "Special Invitation"; "Benefit Performance" ticket; Lathan, "Crusader," 60; Williams, "Robert Williams"; Webb, "Behind"; "Monroe NAACP"; Clarence Seniors interviews; Blain, *Set the World*, 20, 188–189, 205, 31–32; Harold Golden, "Robert Williams in China," *Carolina Israelite*, 12/64, file 100-HQ-387728 section 18, HGP; O. Muhammad, "Pan African Journal."*

49. Kochiyama, *Passing*, 2004; Fujino, *Heartbeat*, xxx, 174, 340; Collier-Thomas and Turner, "Race."

50. Taylor, *Promise*, 93.

51. Ibid., 77; Spencer-Antoine, *Revolution*, 47, 69.

52. Herb Boyd, "Black Nationalist Pioneer, Carlos Cooks," *Amsterdam News*, 2/13/2017; Cooks, *Street Speaker*; Marcus Garvey, "In Memoriam," *Garvey's Voice*, June–July 1951*; Hon. Marcus Garvey, "Greetings—1944"*; Marcus Garvey, "Negro Must Show Love in Own Ranks," *UNIA Progressive Voice*, 6/48*; Clarence Seniors, "Marcus Garvey"*; "Announcing"*; Austin, "Marcus"*; Tinson, *Radical Intellect*, 32, 39–40, 86; Ford, *Kwame Brathwaite*; Harris et al., *Carlos Cooks*; "Celebrate MARCUS GARVEY DAY, 1958," *Courier*, 1958*; "Celebrate," flyer.*

53. Rhodes-Pitts, *Harlem*, 168–169, 181; Ford, *Liberated Threads*, 46–47; Ford, *Kwame Brathwaite*, 43.

54. Cooks, *Street Speaker*.

55. Rhodes-Pitts, *Harlem*, 168–169, 181; Tinson, *Radical* Intellect, 32, 39–40, 86; Ford, *Liberated Threads*, 46–47; Boyd, "Black Nationalist"; Cooks, *Street Speaker*; Ford, *Kwame Brathwaite*, 43.

56. Singe et al., "Resilience"; Oduba interviews; Grossman et al., *With Phoenix*, 115–116, 171–173, 178, 190.

57. Raquel Laneri, "How a Harlem Fashion Show Started the 'Black is Beautiful' Movement," *New York Post*, 2/5/2018; Nnadi, "How One"; Charlayne Hunter, "Harlem Models Stress Unity Idea," *New York Times*, 6/26/71; Ford, *Liberated Threads*, 51–53, 55–58; Ford, *Kwame Brathwaite*, 3, 12–16, 41, 43.

58. Laneri, "How a Harlem Fashion Show"; Nnadi, "How One"; Hunter, "Harlem Models"; Ford, *Liberated Threads*, 51–53, 55–58; Ford, *Kwame Brathwaite*, 2019, 65–75.

59. Ford, *Liberated Threads*, 16–18, 31, 30–32, 36–37, 95, 102–109, 112; Ford, *Kwame Brathwaite*, 68; Paula Marie Seniors, *Beyond*; O. Patterson, *Slavery*; *Black Panther*, San Francisco Strike.

60. See Ford, *Liberated Threads*, 46–51; Ford, *Kwame Brathwaite*, 44, 47.

61. Bennet, *Before*, 597; Franklin, *From Slavery*, 623; Berry and Gross, *Black*, 175; Painter, *Creating*, 266–268.

62. Blake, *Children*, 174.

63. Mallory FBI, 6/21/57, 1–2, 4, 5– 8, 10, 5/28/58, 1–3, 5–6, 6/18/62, 3–4; 6/5/61, 7/63, 1, 5/27/59, 2, 5/28/60, 8/13/63, 10/11/61.

64. Frazier, *Harambe City*, 60–62; "CARE to Explain New Housing Act," *Call and Post*, 11/4/61; "2 Sit in Dark State Office to Back Bill," *Chicago Tribune*, 6/18/63, 10; "Ohioans Sit-In for Fair Housing," *Chicago Daily Defender*, 6/20/63, 6; Michney, *Surrogate Suburbs*, 2–3, 5, 179–180, 192, 196; Phillips, *Alabama North*, chap. 7, 8. See also the following articles from the 11/4/61 edition of the *Call and Post*: "No Negroes Wanted Say Hough Residents"; Charles Sanders, "Adult Education: Night High School Is 7-Year Career for Alvin Ward, Father of Six"; "Candidates Attack Present School Board"; "Coles for School Board Gets Five Endorsements"; "Parents Win Bus Transfer Issue"; "Display Ad 20"; "Cubs Billy Williams Named Rookie of Year"; "Crowe Named Cards Scout"; "Charge Wife with Slaying Husband"; "Buckeyes in Big Ten Showdown"; "Boosters Plan Big Homecoming"; "Thurgood Marshall Sworn In as U.S. Judge"; "Sigma Gamma Rho Plans Founder's Day Luncheon"; Hazelle Harding, "Peace Corps Error May Strengthen Program"; Chas H. Loeb, "Election Day, Editorial in Rhyme"; Leonard M. Hamilton, "About Your Social Security"; "Ostend St. Club Gives Record Player"; "Flora C. Green Addresses Jewelites; "Leontyne Price Lost Voice on Met Stage"; "Dog Breaks Window to Battle Rival"; Charles H. Cobb, "Witch Doctor's Trick: How to Butter Bread on Both Sides"; "Come on Let's 'Twist'"; "Eagles Motorcycle Club Plans Benefit"; Dan Day, "Capital Spotlight"; "Chesterfield Pupil Wins Drawing Contest"; A Timely Gift to Charity Hospital"; "Fun Galore aboard the S.S. Khayyam"; Connie Harper, "Nautical Nifties Greet Guests"; "Kappa Polemarch Is Founder's Banquet Speaker"; "Queen of the Kappa Carnival," advertisement; Charles Sanders, "Dismissed Engineer Is Bitter"; Lucile Selz, "Tubman: 'U.N. Must Find Spirit, Attitude, Approach'"; "Sgt. Edward Anderson," biographical cartoon; Balthrope, "Correct Etiquette."

65. "Gerald Quinn Gets Top MDC Position," *Afro American*, 6/9/62, 3.

66. "Addison Girls League Carries on Addison Tradition," *Call and Post*, 11/4/61; Jacqueline Balthrope, "Correct Etiquette," *Call and Post*, 11/4/61.

67. Allen Howard, "Mae Walks Out of Pure Hell," *Call and Post*, 3/23/63.

68. Mallory FBI, 11/23/70, 1, 11/30/70, 7, 12/10/70, 1; Clarence Seniors autobiography.

69. McDuffie, *Sojourning*, 102, 142–143, 147–148.

70. Singe et al., "Resilience"; Grossman et al., *With Phoenix*, 115–116, 171–173, 178, 190.

Chapter 6. Mae Mallory

1. Boyce Davies, *Left*, 102–103; Harlow, *Resistance Literature*, 2, xvi–xvii, xiii.

2. McKittrick and Woods, *Black Geographies*, 6.

3. O'Reilly, *Racial Matters*, 1989, 8, 45; Kornweibel, *Seeing Red*, xii; Cratty, "Newspaper Lawsuit"; Brown, "Civil Rights Photographer," 9/13/10; "Released Documents"; Franklin, "Jackanapes," 62–63; Audrey Seniors FBI, 1962–1972; Clarence Seniors FBI, 1959–1972; Mallory FBI, 1957–1976; Johnson FBI, 1959–1972; Williams FBI, 9/11/61, 9/20/61, 9/21/61, 9/22/61, "Public Statements and Speeches of Robert Franklin Williams," 7/10/61, 12–14, copy of "From Yankee Slavery to Cuban Freedom," 10/27/61.

4. Rowan, "Has Paul Robeson," *Ebony*, 10/57.*

5. Ibid.; Goodman, *Paul Robeson*, 10–14; Robeson, *Negro*, 15*; Robeson FBI, 3/16/42; "Communist Activities Paul Robeson"; "Robeson Off to Europe after 8-Year Battle," *New York Times*, 7/8/58, 8.*

6. Robeson, *Here I Stand*, 42, 92; Robeson Jr., *Undiscovered*, 287; Paula Marie Seniors, "Jack Johnson," 165–170; "Group Sees Truman"; "To Open Crusade"; "Truman Balks"; "American Crusade"; Goodman, *Paul Robeson*, 175, 178; Robeson, *Negro*; Robeson, "Paul Robeson's Column"; Robeson, "Here's My Story"; Robeson, *Freedom*; Robeson, "If Enough"; "Robeson Pushes"; "Robeson Off"; Associated Press wire photo, 1958*: "Singer Paul Robeson waves goodbye before leaving Idlewild Airport on flight to England on his first trip out of the U.S. in eight years. Until a recent court ruling, he had been unable to get a passport for refusing to sign a non-communist affidavit"; O'Reilly, *Racial Matters*, 8, 45; Kornweibel, *Seeing Red*, xii; Cratty, "Newspaper Lawsuit"; Brown, "Civil Rights"; "Released Documents"; Franklin, "Jackanapes," 62–63; Audrey Seniors FBI, 1962–1972; Clarence Seniors FBI, 1959–1972; Mallory FBI, 1957–1976; Johnson FBI, 1959–1972; Williams FBI, 9/11/61, 9/20/61, 9/21/61, 9/22/61, "Public Statements and Speeches of Robert Franklin Williams," 12–14, 7/10/61.

7. Flynn, "Horizons," 34–35, 38–39*; Boyce Davies, *Left*, 134, 185–203.

8. Flynn, *13 Communists*, 7–8, 11.*

9. Ibid., 19, 22, 23.

10. Grattan to Williams, 3/13/67.

11. Mallory to Lynn, 9/4/62.

12. Zinn, "Albany," 5–8*; Williams, "Neo Barbarism"; Lichtenstein et al., *Who Built America?*, 612–621; Bennett, *Before*, 600–609; Katzenelson, *When*, 142–173; Painter, *Creating*, 268–275; Mallory to Lynn and Williams, 8/28/62, 4; "Cops Snatch Mae," *Pittsburgh Courier*, 3/30/63, MDC, MMP; Leakes to Williams, 1/17/63; Sixteenth Street Baptist Church FBI, 9/16/63; Williams, "Press Release—Birmingham."

13. Mallory to Ballan, 5/17/63.

14. Mallory to Williamses, 6/9/64.

15. William Worthy, "Mallory Freed on $15,000 Bond," *Afro American*, 3/16/63.*

16. Mallory to Mayfield, 2/17/63.

17. Mallory to Mabel Williams, 8/20/64.

18. Lichtenstein et al., *Who Built America?*, 612–618; "2 Sit in Dark State Office to Back Bill," *Chicago Tribune*, 6/18/63; "Ohioans," *Chicago Daily Defender*, 6/20/63; "CORE Leader Sit-in Gov. Rhodes Office," *Call and Post*, 6/22/63, 4B; Worthy, "Mallory."

19. Howard, "Mae Walks Out."

20. McKittrick, *Demonic Grounds*, xxi–xxii; Glissant, *Caribbean Discourse*, 5–9, 11.

21. Mallory, "Skyscraper," 1–2.

22. McKittrick, *Demonic Grounds*, x–xi.

23. Mallory, "Open Letter," 22; D. Walker, *David*, 2000.

24. Mallory, "Open Letter," 23–24.

25. Flynn, *Alderson*, 16.*

26. Mallory, "Open Letter," 22, 23–24; Mallory, "Skyscraper," 2–3; Mallory, "Cuyahoga," 5/15/62.

27. Sanders, "Jail."

28. Mallory, "Skyscraper," 2–3; Mallory, "Open Letter," 22.

29. P. Johnson, *Inner Lives*, 278–279; Hoffman, "Hep C," 228.

30. Mallory, "Rev"; Mallory to Williams, 8/28/62; Mallory, "County," 9/1/62; Mallory to Lynn and Williams, 8/28/62; Mallory to Lynn, 9/9/62; P. Johnson, *Inner Lives*, 278–279; Hoffman, "Hep C," 228.

31. Mallory, "County," 10.

32. P. Johnson, *Inner Lives*, 278–279; Hoffman, "Hep C," 228.

33. Mallory, "Cuyahoga," 5/15/62; Mallory, "Skyscraper," 2–3.

34. Mallory, "Rev"; Mallory, "County," 10.

35. A. Davis, *Angela Davis*, 284*; Mallory, "Skyscraper," 1–2; Mallory, "Open Letter," 23–24; Mallory, *Letters from Prison*, 23–24; Flynn, *Alderson*, 16–17.

36. "Mae Mallory Mistreated," *Call and Post*, 6/23/62; Sanders, "Jail"; Mallory, "Skyscraper," 1–2.

37. Mallory, "Skyscraper," 2–3; Mallory, "Cuyahoga," 5/15/62.

38. Mallory to Williams, 10/11/62.

39. Weaver, "Frontlash," 230; Hernandez, "On Visual," 250; Bilksy and Chesney-Lind, "Doing Time," 31–32; C. Collins, *Imprisonment*, 53; Acoca, "Living," 77, 78, 92–93, 82–83, 84; Katz, "Explaining," 31.

40. Boyce Davies, *Left*, 132, 133, 134, A. Davis, *Are Prisons*, 61–62, 63, 81–82; A. Davis, *Angela Davis*, 152–156, 283–286; Flynn, *Alderson*, 9–10, 15.

41. Mallory, "County," 13–14.

42. Nevels, *Lynching*, 35, 71, 72, 73, 76, 89–90; Hunter, *To 'Joy*, 2, 115–116; Feimster, *Southern Horrors*, 142, 125, 126, 135, 141.

43. Flynn, *Alderson*, 179.

44. White, *Ar'n't I*, 29; Welter, "Cult," 152; D. Gutierrez, *Walls*, 32–33; McWilliams, *North from Mexico*, 43.

45. White, *Ar'n't I*, 29; Welter, "Cult," 152; D. Gutierrez, *Walls*, 32–33; McWilliams, *North from Mexico*, 43; Nevels, *Lynching*, 64, 74, 35, 36, 72, 89–90, 92, 71, 73, 76; Feimster, *Southern Horrors*, 142, 125, 126, 135, 137, 138, 139–140, 141, 166–167, 161, 169–170, 171, 172.

46. Nevels, *Lynching*, 35, 71, 72, 73, 89–90.

47. Mallory, "County," 12, 13–14.

48. Sanders, "Jail."

49. Lynn, *There Is*, 163.

50. Mallory, "County," 12.

51. Berg, *Mothering*, 1–2, 79; Blackwell, "Republican," 31.

52. Berg, *Mothering*, 1–2, 79; Blackwell, "Republican," 31.

53. Blackwell, "Republican," 31.

54. Wiggam, *Fruit*, 280; Blackwell, "Republican," 31; Aanerud, "Legacy," 27.

55. Mallory, "County," 12–13.

56. Ibid.

57. Flynn, *Alderson*, 178.

58. Mallory, "County," 12–13.

59. Mallory, *Letters from Prison*.

60. Mae Mallory, "Of Dogs and Men," *Workers World*, 11/23/62, 4, LCC; Mallory, "Of Dogs," in *Letters from Prison*, 25–26. See also Paula Marie Seniors, "Mae Mallory."

61. Espiritu, *Asian American*, 34–35.

62. Gore, *Radicalism*, 19, 104, 106–107, 108, 110; McDuffie, *Sojourning*, 112–113; C. Tyson, *Just as I Am*; T. Brown, *Raising Brooklyn*, 23–25, 39, 45–46, 49–51; A Negro Nurse, "More Slavery at the South," *Independent*, 1/25/12, 196–197; E. Glenn, "Caring," 46, 53–55; Boyce Davies, *Left*, 45.

63. Mallory, "Of Dogs and Men," *Workers World*.

64. E. Glenn, "Caring," 48, 46, 53–54; Childress, *Just*, 3; T. Brown, *Raising Brooklyn*, 17; 23–25, 39, 45–46, 49–51; Negro Nurse, "More Slavery"; Gore, *Radicalism*, 104, 107, 110; McDuffie, *Sojourning*, 167; Boyce Davies, *Left*, 45; Kirk Semple, "A Boon for Nannies, If Only They Knew," *New York Times*, 4/14/2011; Monique P. Yazigi, "So Hard to Find Good Employers These Days," *New York Times*, 8/15/99, 1–2; Constance Hays, "The Nanny's Life," *New York Times*, 8/28/94.

65. E. Glenn, "Caring," 48, 46, 53–54; Childress, *Just*, 3; T. Brown, *Raising Brooklyn*, 17, 23–25, 39, 45–46, 49–51; Negro Nurse, "More Slavery"; Gore, *Radicalism*, 104, 107, 110; McDuffie, *Sojourning*, 167; Boyce Davies, *Left*, 45; Semple, "Boon for Nannies"; Yazigi, "So Hard"; Hays, "Nanny's Life"; Mallory, "Of Dogs and Men," *Workers World*.

66. Roediger, *Wages*, 5; E. Glenn, "Caring," 53–55; McDuffie, *Sojourning*, 113, 126–127, 132.

67. Mallory, "Of Dogs and Men," *Workers World*, 4.

68. Mallory, "Of Dogs and Men," *Workers World*, 4; Mallory, "Of Dogs," *Letters from Prison*.

69. Iandolo, "Beyond the Shoe."

70. Mallory, "Of Dogs and Men," *Workers World*, 4; Mallory, "Of Dogs," *Letters from Prison*.

71. Krenn, *Black Diplomacy*, 94–95, 97, 115–116, 120–121, 126–128.

72. Mallory, "Of Dogs and Men," *Workers World*, 4; Mallory, "Of Dogs," *Letters from Prison*.

73. Sam Dillon, "Study Finds High Rates of Imprisonment among Dropouts," *New York Times*, 10/8/2009; Project NIA, Chicago Youth Justice Data Project; "Misplaced Priorities," NAACP, 4/2011.

74. Mallory, "Of Dogs and Men," *Workers World*, 4.

75. Boyce Davies, *Left*, 100–101.

76. McKittrick and Woods, *Black Geographies*, 6.

77. Mallory, Diary, 6/3/62.

78. Mallory FBI, 8/13/63, 1, 4. Informant CV T-2 noted that the Seniorses and the Dostals visited Mallory in jail.

79. "Mae Mallory 'Mistreated'"; Sanders, "Jail."

80. "Sheriff," *Afro American*, 6/30/62, 3.

81. "Mae Mallory 'Mistreated.'"

82. "It's a Struggle," *Workers World*, 6/22/62, 1, LOC.

83. Mallory, Diary, 6/3/62, 1–2.

84. Ibid.

85. Culture Clash, "Mission"; Frank, "II. Mission Times."

86. Mallory, "Cuyahoga," 6/17/62, 6.

87. Sanders, "Jail."

88. Golden to Robinson, 6/16/65.

89. "UAW Council Backs Mallory," *Call and Post*, 3/17/62.

90. "Group Probes Commission," *Call and Post*, 2/17/62; "UAW," *Call and Post*, 3/17/62; Mallory, "Cuyahoga"; "The President Asked to Aid N.C. Victim," *Michigan Chronicle*, 4/28/62; Mallory, "Cuyahoga," 6/17/62.

91. Mallory, "Cuyahoga," 6/17/62, 6.

92. Boyce Davies, *Left*, 100–101.

93. Mallory, "Cuyahoga," 6/17/62, 6; Flynn, *Alderson*, 17–18.

94. Mallory, "Cuyahoga," 6/17/62, 6.

95. Sanders, "Jail."

96. Lynn, *There Is*, 163; Shaw, *Embodiment*, 50.

97. Howard, "Mae Walks Out."

98. Sanders, "Jail."

99. Ibid.

100. *Merriam-Webster Dictionary*, 2020.

101. Sanders, "Jail"; White, *Ar'n't I*, 42; O. Patterson, *Slavery*, 60–62; Kelley, *Yo Mama's*, 27–28; Rooks, *Hair Raising*, 24–25; Murray, *Practical Leaflet*; Morrow, *Four*, 111; Washington, *Up from Slavery*, 98.*

102. Sanders, "Jail."

103. Howard, "Mae Walks Out."

104. Gaines, *Uplifting*, 16–17; Collier-Thomas and Turner, "Race," 11; Drake and Cayton, *Black Metropolis*, 496–499, 506–507; P. Collins, *Black*, 79–80; Rooks, *Hair Raising*, 24–25; Hoose, *Claudette Colvin*, 23–24; Hancock, *We Are*, xviii; Alt and Folts, *Weeping Violins*, 2; Quintana and Gray, *Gitano*, 13–14; Frasier, *Gypsies*, 144, 164–165, 169; Barany, *Gypsies*, 95, 86; Paula Marie Seniors, "Exile"; Ensted, *Ladies*, 27.

105. Andy Razaf, lyricist, Fats Waller, composer, "Black and Blue," Mills Music, 1929, SCRBC.

106. Flynn, *Alderson*, 159–160, 178, 179; Díaz-Cotto, *Gender*, 298–299; Díaz-Cotto, *Chicana Lives*, 253–255.

107. Díaz-Cotto, *Gender*, 298–299; Díaz-Cotto, *Chicana Lives*, 253–255.

108. Mallory, Diary, 1/24/63, 15.

109. Díaz-Cotto, *Chicana Lives*, 245–247.

110. "Paper Hanger," UrbanDictionary.com.

111. Mallory, Diary, n.d. [1963], 1–2.

112. Díaz-Cotto, *Gender*, 298; Díaz-Cotto, *Chicana Lives*, 254–255; Flynn, *Alderson*, 161, 178.

113. Mallory, Diary, n.d. [1963].

114. Flynn, *Alderson*, 162.

115. Mallory, "Rev," 1–5.

116. Mallory, Diary, n.d. [1963].

117. R. Gutierrez, *When Jesus*, 134–135.

118. Mallory, Diary, n.d. [1963], 2–3.

119. R. Gutierrez, *When Jesus*, 134–135.

120. Mallory, "Rev," 4.

121. Mallory, "Sex."

122. Mallory, "Mer Dear."

123. Acoca, "Living," 82–83, 84; Katz, "Explaining," 31; P. Johnson, *Inner Lives*, 183–189, 57–63.

124. Mallory, "Christina," [1961–1963], 1, 2.
125. Acoca, "Living," 82–83, 84; Katz, "Explaining," 31; P. Johnson, *Inner Lives*, 183–189, 57–63.
126. Mallory, "Christina," 3–4.
127. Mallory to Williams, 2/29/68.
128. Kelley and Esch, "Black," 159; Young, *Soul Power*, 156, 159.
129. Kelley and Esch, "Black," 159; Young, *Soul Power*, 156, 159.
130. Mallory to Williamses, 6/9/64.
131. Kelley and Esch, "Black," 98–100, 113, 124, 125; Robinson, "Internationalism," 260–276; Mullen, *Afro-Orientalism*, 29; Mullen, "Persisting," 252–253; R. J. Alexander, *Maoism*, 9, 25, 28, 36–37.
132. Mallory, "Fidel Castro."
133. Mallory, "Black Liberation"; Freedman and Molteno, *Zed Pan Africa*, 106, 119, 138, 144.*
134. Mallory, "Letter to the Editor"; Mallory to Gibson, *Africa*, 8/24/63.
135. Freedman and Molteno, *Zed Pan Africa*, 77, 97, 103, 107, 121, 150*; Verges, "People's Victory"*; "Algerian War," *Encyclopedia Britannica*, https://www.britannica.com/event/Algerian-War.
136. Stanford, "Revolutionary."
137. Mallory to Mabel Williams, 3/30/64.
138. Mallory, "Letter to the Editor"; Mallory to Gibson, 8/24/63.
139. Mallory, "Letter to the Editor."
140. Mallory to Williams, 9/11/62.
141. "On Guard," n.d. [1961].
142. Thomas, "Last Days"; Samad, "Legacy"; Pérez, "Fidel Vive!"
143. "Mallory Case."
144. Castro, "Our Party," 9.
145. Mae Mallory, "Black Liberation Fighter Returns to the Motherland," *Workers World*, 8/5/68, 5, MMP, JBMP.
146. Charles Price, "Freedom Rider, Mallory Case Spotlighted at Cory Forum," *Call and Post*, 3/31/62; Sanders, "Jail"; Worthy, "Mallory"; "Case of Mae Mallory"; "Mae Mallory Speaks at Greater Friendship," *Call and Post*, 10/17/64, 12A.
147. Clarence Seniors, "Free."
148. "Jail Fails to Damp Mrs. Mallory's Spirit," *Cleveland Courier*, 8/62, in "Clippings."
149. "From Mexico to Ghana Free Mae Mallory! Cry Now International," *Muhammad Speaks*, 9/20/62, in "Clippings."
150. Mallory to Robert Williams, 8/16/62, 9/11/62.
151. Mallory to Anderson, 5/13/63.
152. Mallory to Dearest, 5/18/63; Mallory to Jeanne, 6/23/63.
153. "Hear Malcolm X."
154. Mallory to Lilo, 5/18/63.
155. See Kochiyama, *Passing*; A. Glenn, *Ito Sisters*; Fujino, *Heartbeat*; Lisa Hung, "The Last Revolutionary," *East Bay Express*, 3/2002; Okihiro, *Margins*; Saxton, *Indispensable Enemy*; Weglyn, *Years*.*
156. Zedong, "Statement," 1.

157. Ibid.

158. Mallory to Robert Williams, 8/16/62.

159. Williams to Nix, 3/8/62; Williams to Kowalski, 3/8/62; Williams, "Statement," 1963; Williams press releases, 2/29/64, 5/7/63, 4/9/64, 2/23/62, 7/6/62, 10/16/62; Williams press release, Havana, Cuba, n.d.; Williams, "Protest," 1964; Williams to Primer, 1962; Williams press conference request; Williams, "Radio Free Dixie Transcript," 11/9/62, 12/28/62, 11/11/62, 3/1/63, 3/5/63, 3/8/63, 3/15/63, 3/22/63, 3/29/63, 4/12/63, 4/26/63, 5/3/63, 1/10/64, 1/17/64, 1/24/64, 2/7/64, 2/24/64.

160. Mallory to Williamses, 6/9/64.

161. Mallory to Mabel Williams, 8/17/64.

162. Williams to Mallory, n.d. [1961–1963]; "The Violent Crusader: American Communists Are Racists, Williams Charges," news clipping, 2/17/66, UCHR.

163. Williams to Mallory, n.d.

164. Paula Marie Seniors, *Beyond*; Ferrer, *Insurgent Cuba*, 1999, 196–197; Edward Johnson, *History*, 6, SCRBC; Kaplan, "Black and Blue," 219–220.

165. Mallory to Williamses, 6/9/64.

166. Williams to Mallory, 4/21/69; Kochiyama to Rob Williams, 7/15/69; Foreman to Williams, 8/3/69.

167. Johnson, "Did?," 9/24/60; Peck, *Lumumba*; Peck, *Lumumba, la mort*.

168. "Don't Let Mae"; Levenson, "Congregation Brith Emeth," 127, 131; "Rabbi Philip Horowitz," *Jewish News*, 10/4/11; "Ohio Gov Asks FBI Probe," *National Herald Dispatch*, n.d., in "Clippings."

169. "Don't Let Mae"; Levenson, "Congregation Brith Emeth," 127, 131; "Rabbi Philip Horowitz."

170. Sanders, "Jail."

171. Mallory, "Pan African"; Clarence Seniors, "Free"; "Robert F. Williams Speaks."

172. "From Mexico"; "Jail Fails"; "Editorial: Save Mae Mallory," *Evening News* (Accra, Ghana), 4/17/63; Julian Mayfield, "Save Mae Mallory! Frame-up in Monroe," *Evening News* (Accra, Ghana), 3/29/62, MDC folder 1, JBMP; Julian Mayfield, "Why They Want to Kill Mae Mallory," *Evening News* (Accra, Ghana), 3/31/62; "Julian Mayfield," *Los Angeles Herald Dispatch*, in "Clippings"; "Julian Mayfield," *Evening News* (Accra, Ghana), in "Clippings"; Julian Mayfield, "The Monroe Kidnapping," *West Indian Gazette*, 11/61; "Mae Mallory's Case Is a Blot on American Conscience," *Ghanaian Times*, 7/13/63, JMP, SCRBC; Julian Mayfield, "Open Letter to an American Governor," *Ghanaian Times*, 6/24/63, Monroe Defense Committee, box 1, MMP; Clarence Seniors, "From Lynch Threat."

173. "Olatunji" flyer; Oduba interviews; "Talking Union"; "Pete Seeger, Champion of Folk Music and Social Change Dies at 94," *New York Times*, 1/29/2014, A20; Herb Boyd, "Babatunde Olatunji Memorialized as 'God's Gift to the World,'" *Amsterdam News*, 5/1/2003, 4; "The Mission of Olatunji and His Drums of Passion," *Pittsburgh Courier*, 2/10/62, 5; Hodges and Mazzocchi, "Lightnin' Hopkins"; O'Brian and Ensminger, *Mojo Hand*; Olatunji, *Beat*; Govenar, *Lightnin'*; Wolfgang Saxon, "Sam Lightnin' Hopkins: Blues Singer and Guitarist," *New York Times*, 2/1/82; Melvina Reynolds, "The Battle of Monroe," RFWP, MMP.

174. Weber to Johnson, 10/20/61; Clarence Seniors, "Free"; Baldwin, "Personal"; Williams FBI, 3/11/64, 2; MDC, press release; Angelou, *Heart*, 198; "Humanist Council Plans a Rally for Mae," *Call and Post*, 1/26/63, 13C; Hicks, "Dear Friend"; Seniors to

Russell, 8/13/64*; Mallory to Hansberry, 6/1/63; Funk Music Hall of Fame, "The Moroccos: Dayton Ohio's First Funk and R&B Band 1956 to 2018," 1/29/2020, https://www.youtube.com/watch?v=LIgJESio_a8.; Mae Mallory Benefit.

175. Mallory to Gregory, 6/1/63.
176. Mallory to Mabel Williams, 6/3/63.
177. Rita to Mallory, 1963; Scott to Mallory; McRae to Mallory; Spruill to Mallory; Mallory to Jones, Mothers Alliance; Mallory to McCarroll.
178. "Mae Mallory's Case."
179. YAWF, "Demonstrate."
180. Homer Bigart, "President Speaks: Urges Restoration of Cuts—Honored by Protestants Here Kennedy Fights for Foreign Aid in Speech," *New York Times*, 11/9/63; Mallory to Mabel Williams, 8/17/64.
181. Clarence Seniors, "Free"; Baldwin, "Personal"; Williams FBI, 3/11/64, 2; MDC, press release; Angelou, *Heart*, 198; "Humanist Council"; Mallory to McCarroll.
182. "Afro American New Year's Party."
183. "Benefit Performance," program.
184. Clarence Seniors autobiography; Brown et al., *We Insist*.*
185. Quinn to Williams, 10/14/61; O. Davis, "Purlie"*; "Purlie Victorious Benefit"; "Mae Mallory Benefit of Purlie Victorious," *Buffalo Challenger*, 7/17/63, MMP.
186. Mae Mallory, letter to the *Buffalo Challenger*, 7/22/63, MMP; "Mae," 8/17/63, MMP.
187. Mallory to Mabel Williams, 8/20/64.
188. Quinn to Williams, 10/14/61.
189. "Deacons," n.d. [1965]; Alvin Ward, "Defense Deacons Raise Funds Here," *Call and Post*, 11/27/65, 4A; "Deacons," 1963 flyer; Deacons FBI Files, "Fund raising 10/24/65," 6–9, "President of the DDJ in Louisiana," 10/23/65, 3–4, "Confidential Deacons of Defense and Justice," 11/24/65, 1, 2, 5, "Changed Deacons of Defense and Justice," 11/9/65, 1; "Deacons for Defense Leader Here Wed. October 27th," *Buffalo Challenger*, 10/21/65, Buffalo, N.Y. Organization, folder 2–7, MMP.
190. *Black America*, November/December 1963*; *Black America*, Fall 1964; Mallory to Robert Williams, 8/28/67.
191. Sanders, "Jail"; "Freedom Fighters."
192. "Freedom Fighters."
193. Ibid.; Sanders, "Jail."
194. "Freedom Fighters."
195. Sanders, "Jail."
196. Ibid.
197. Malcolm X, *Grass Roots*.*
198. "Freedom Fighters."
199. "Black Detroit," *Michigan Chronicle*, 1/12/2011; "Black Muslims," *Chicago Daily Defender*, 11/21/63; "Asserts," *Michigan Chronicle*, 3/31/62.
200. Lumumba, "Mae," 1–2, 6–7.
201. "You Can Help Free Mae Mallory: Attend the Mass Meeting in Defense of Mae Mallory at the Phillips Memorial Baptist Church," in "Clippings."
202. Mallory to Williamses, 4/10/63.
203. "Cops," *Pittsburgh Courier*, 3/30/63, MMP; "Freed on Bond."
204. Youngstown Ohio Organizations; "Front Groups Committee."

205. Weissman to Weissman, 10/64*; Ballan to Clarence Seniors, 10/5/64*; Steinberg to Seniors, 10/7/64*; Fragment notes on Mae Mallory's lecture tour*; Seniors to Keleher, 10/64*; Weissman to Clarence Seniors, 11/9/64*; Ballan to Clarence Seniors, 11/8/64*; Clarence Seniors to Wright, 10/20/64.*

206. Blanchfield to Clarence Seniors, 9/23/64*; Ballan to Clarence Seniors, 11/6/64*; D. Smith to MDC, 11/13/64*; Clarence Seniors to Ballan, 11/13/64*; Clarence Seniors to Beyers, 10/20/64*; Clarence Seniors to Althaus, 10/20/64*; Clarence Seniors to Wiebe, 10/20/64*; Ballan to Althaus, 10/5/64.*

207. Clarence Seniors to Russell, 8/13/64.*

208. "Rep. Powell Speaker at Sunday Rally," *Amsterdam News*, 9/26/64.

209. "Mae Mallory Speaks," *Call and Post*, 10/17/64; Clarence Seniors to Lee, 10/6/64.

210. Dostal to Clarence Seniors, n.d. [1964]*; Ballan to Clarence Seniors, 10/5/64*; Clarence Seniors to Keleher, 10/7/64*; Dostal to Clarence and Audrey Seniors, n.d. [10/64].*

211. Bletter to Mallory and Seniors, 9/21/64*; Sidofsky to Clarence Seniors, 9/27/64*; Hopkins to Clarence Seniors, 9/30/64*; Steinberg to Clarence Seniors, 10/7/64*; Clarence Seniors to Guidoni, 10/26/64.*

212. *Police Terror*; "Says Harlem Disorders No Race Riot," *Afro American*, 8/8/64, 12; "Clerics Join Hands to Combat Race Riot Strife," *Amsterdam News*, 8/1/64, 29; Jesse H. Walker, "Not a Race Riot," *Amsterdam News*, 7/25/64, 30; "Harlem Race Riot," Britannica.com.

213. Mallory to Mabel Williams, 8/17/64.

214. Mallory to Williamses, 6/9/64; Mallory to Mabel Williams, 8/17/64.

215. Mallory and Kochiyama, "Organization."

216. "It's a Struggle Just to Get Fresh Fruit in Jail! Mae Wins Round with Ohio Sheriff," *Workers World*, 6/22/62, 1, LOC; Al Sweeney, "I Lived," 184.

Chapter 7. Audrey Proctor Seniors

1. Proctor to Williams.
2. Clarence Seniors, "Free."
3. T. Tyson, *Radio Free Dixie*, 228, 291.
4. Castro, "Our Party," 1965, 8, 9.*
5. Young, *Soul Power*, 25.
6. Proctor to Williams, 6/30/62.
7. Lumumba, "Mae," 18; Williams, "Join."
8. Mallory FBI, 8/13/63; "Mae Mallory and MDC"; Green, "Summary Report."
9. Proctor to Williams, 6/30/62.
10. Weaver, "Frontlash," 236–237, 240–241; Du Bois, *Black Reconstruction*, 342; M. Alexander, *New Jim Crow*, 40; Paula Marie Seniors, "Transforming"; A. Davis, *Are Prisons*, 25, 26, 28–29, 33–34, 94.
11. Proctor to Williams, 6/30/62. All Proctor quotations in this passage come from this letter.
12. Haffner to Williams, 8/1/62, 12/22/65.
13. T. Tyson, *Radio Free Dixie*, 287.
14. Hoose, *Claudette Colvin*, 52–54, 58–60, 65–78; P. Hendrickson, "Ladies," 288, 298; Mallory, "Memo," 210; Mallory to Robert Williams, 8/16/62; "NAACP Says Mae Spurned Their Help," *Call and Post*, 3/31/62; "Mallory Defense Group Speaks Up," *Call*

and *Post*, 4/7/62, 3C; Price, "Freedom Rider"; "Mae Mallory and MDC"; Len Watkins, "'DiSalle Has Doomed Me,' Insists Mae Mallory," *Call and Post*, 2/17/62; "Now Just What Did N. Carolina's Governor Say to Gov. DiSalle?" *Call and Post*, 2/17/62; "Names in the News: DiSalle Agrees to Send Mae to Monroe," *Michigan Chronicle*, 2/24/62, 8; Al Sweeney, "A Summer of Political Lull May Be Prophetic," *Call and Post*, 7/14/62, 2C; Haffner to Williams, 5/24/62; Anderson to Williams, 5/29/62; "A Stone's Throw: Is JFK Losing Colored Vote?" *Afro American*, 11/24/62, 5; "Easy Decision," *Call and Post*, 2/10/62; Sweeney, "Taking a Look," *Call and Post*, 3/31/62; "Perk Seeks to Reverse DiSalle Mallory Ruling," *Call and Post*, 2/17/62, 8A; Al Sweeney, "Thanks to Mallory, DiSalle Recognizes the Negro Vote," *Call and Post*, 3/24/62, 2C.

15. Williams, "Radio Free Dixie—On the Air," October/November 1962, 1–2; Williams, "Hands"; Williams, "On the Monroe Scene."

16. Williams, "Why"; Williams, "Dear Friends"; Williams, "Cuba and the Negro"; Williams, "See Cuba"; Williams, "Sierra Maestra"; Benson, *Antiracism*, 167, 170–171, 278; Williams to Mallory, "Exile."

17. M. Mallory to Ethel Johnson, 3/29/67.

18. Williams to Mallory, 4/21/69; Kochiyama to Rob Williams; Foreman to Williams, 8/3/69.

19. Kochiyama to Rob Williams.

20. Foreman to Williams, 8/3/69; Williams to Mallory, "Exile"; Williams to Golden; Haffner to Williams, 12/22/65; "Williams Assails Racism in Cuba," *Charlotte Observer*, 9/27, RFWP; Williams to Mallory, 4/21/69; Kochiyama to Rob Williams; Mallory to Williamses, 6/9/64; Mallory to Robert Williams, 8/16/62; Mallory to Mabel Williams, 8/17/64.

21. M. Mallory to Ethel Johnson, 3/29/67.

22. Williams, FBI Files, Airtel.

23. Clarence Seniors, "Free."

24. Young, *Soul Power*, 33–34.

25. MDC, FBI, 11/29/63, 1–2.

26. Woods, *Black Struggle*, 250.

27. Castro, "Our Party," 8.

28. Proctor to Williams, 6/30/62.

29. Meeks, *Caribbean*, 58–59.

30. Castro, *Declaration*; Vichot, *Brief*, 54–57; Mills, *Listen**; Miller, *90 Miles**; Kenner and Petras, *Fidel**; Elliot and Dymally, *Fidel Castro**; Lavan Weisman, *Che Guevara Speaks*; Scheer, *Diary**; Guevara, *Reminiscences*.*

31. Castro, "Speech at the United Nations," 4.

32. Proctor to Williams, 6/30/62.

33. Castro, "Speech at the United Nations," 5, 7–9, 10, 14–16, 25–26, 30; Castro, *Declaration*, 10, 12.

34. Mallory to Dearest, 5/18/63.

35. Mallory, "Memo," 210; Clarence Seniors interview, 9/23/2007; Kuumba, *Gender*, 64, 19, 57.

36. Westbrook, "Mrs. Ruth Stone"; Quinnette M. Westbrook, "The Mothers Alliance," *New Pittsburgh Courier*, 11/5/60; "Store," *Afro American*, 7/4/59; "Witness Assail Work Relief Plan," *Afro American*, 1/7/61; "N.Y. Mothers Back Struggle for Equality," *Afro American*, 10/8/60.

37. Clarence Seniors interview, 1/2/2009; Oduba interviews.
38. P. Collins, *Black*, 148; "Mallory Case."
39. YAWF FBI, 10/67, 1–2; "Front Groups Committee"; "Activities"; *Congressional Record* (House), 5/10/65; "Workers World," *Peacemaker*; "YAWF Forums."
40. Robeson, *Here I Stand*; Graham, *Paul Robeson*.*
41. Audrey Seniors FBI, 3/3/63, 1–2; "Wedding Bells," *Call and Post*, 9/8/62; Audrey Seniors, "Kennedy," photograph, 1963*; Audrey Seniors, "Jack," photograph, 1963*; "UFM Pickets," Cleveland *Plain Dealer*, 9/26/63*; "250 Picket School Board Quietly," *Cleveland Press*, 9/28/63, 11*; "Youngest"; "Don't Let Mae"; "Public Rally," *Call and Post*, 11/25/61; Len Watkins, "100 March to City Jail in Sympathy for Mae," *Call and Post*, 4/6/63; "UFM," *Encyclopedia of Cleveland History*, https://case.edu/ech/articles/u/united-freedom-movement-ufm.
42. Mallory, "Memo," 210; Clarence Seniors interviews; Kuumba, *Gender*, 64, 19, 57; T. Tyson, *Radio Free Dixie*, 278–282, 293, Cruse, *Crisis*, 381; Williams, *Crusader*, October/November 1962, 2.
43. Clarence Seniors, "Missionary Sisters."
44. Mallory scrapbook, 1961–1965.
45. "Rain Can't Crimp Spirits at Commencement," Youngstown *Vindicator*, 5/29/63*; Demonstration in Youngstown, 5/28/63, Clarence Seniors scrapbook, news clipping*; Paula Marie Seniors, *Beyond*, 26, 148.
46. "Rain Can't Crimp Spirits at Commencement," Youngstown *Vindicator*, 5/29/63*; Demonstration in Youngstown, 5/28/63, Clarence Seniors scrapbook, news clipping*; Paula Marie Seniors, *Beyond*, 26, 148.
47. P. Mallory, "Save My Mother."*
48. MDC FBI, 10/31/62, 3/12/1964, 16.
49. "CORE," *Call and Post*, 6/22/63; "Youngest"; "Ohioans"; "2 Sit"; Frazier, *Harambe City*, 60–63; "No Negroes."
50. "Civil Rights Group to Unveil a Plan," *Call and Post*, 6/22/63, 1; "UFM Pickets"; "250 Picket."
51. "Civil Rights," *Call and Post*, 6/22/63; "UFM Pickets"; "250 Picket"; Frazier, *Harambe City*, 62, and the following articles from *Call and Post*, 11/4/61: "Candidates"; "Coles"; Sanders, "Adult Education"; "Parents."
52. "Civil Rights," *Call and Post*, 6/22/63; "UFM Pickets"; "250 Picket"; Frazier, *Harambe City*, 62, and the following articles from *Call and Post*, 11/4/61: "Candidates"; "Coles"; Sanders, "Adult Education"; "Parents," "Civil Rights," *Call and Post*, 6/22/63; "Protest Parade July 14," *Call and Post*, 6/29/63, 1A; "Agreement," *Call and Post*, 8/10/63; "A Crack in a Stubborn Wall?" *Call and Post*, 8/10/63, 2C; "UFM Plans Workshop at Antioch," *Call and Post*, 12/12/64, 5A; "School Boycott Proves 92% Effective," *Call and Post*, 4/25/64, 1A.
53. "UFM," Ohio Historical Society*; "UFM," *Encyclopedia of Cleveland History*.
54. "UFM Pickets."
55. "250 Picket."
56. "Youngest."
57. Frazier, *Harambe City*, 62, and from *Call and Post*, 11/4/61: "Candidates"; "Coles"; "Adult"; "Parents."
58. J. Marjory Jackson graduation program, 6/23/68, Ellen Cohen Collection.

59. "Introducing," *Partisan*, 4/65.

60. "Youth," YAWF; "Free," YAWF; Geller, "RAM Members"; Yuri Kochiyama, "Prejudice Hit in Draft Case," *National Guardian*, Youth against War and Fascism, 1966–1967, box 587, JBMP; Editorial Staff Audrey Seniors, *Partisan*, Fall 1967, 1–2, JBMP; "Mrs. Maryann Weissman, 29 of New York Leads Members of Youth against War and Fascism from Court Martial Room in Fort Sill, Oklahoma," *Star Ledger*, 6/2/67, Youth against War and Fascism folder 2, 1966–1967, JBMP; "Refused to Obey Order, War Foes Chant, but GI's Guilty," *Star Ledger*, 6/2/67, Youth against War and Fascism folder 2, 1966–1967, JBMP; "Army Punishes Young Socialist Who Refused to Show Literature," *New York Times*, 6/2/67, YAWF folder 2, 1966–1967, *JBMP*; Vogel, "Hell"; "Activities"; *Congressional Record* (House), 5/10/65; WWP, 10/67, 1959–1969, JBMP; Romberstein, "Memorandum"; "YAWF Forums"; "Anti-Vietnam"; Oquendo, "American Negro."

61. "Join," flyer.

62. *"Prisoners Call Out Freedom"*; Sostre, *Letters from Prison.**

63. *"Prisoners Call Out Freedom,"* April 1971, 5, 7–9, 14–17; "6 Inmates as Auburn Indicted for Role in November Rioting," 1/27/1971, *New York Times*, 33.

64. Tapley, "Inmates Air Grievances."

65. "Story of Dessie Woods," 1–5, 11–17; Lukata, "Right of Black Women," 1–3, 6–7.

66. P. Collins, *Black*, 148.

67. Johnson, *Did?*, 7/6/63; Moorer, "Monroe Youth Organize"; "Collecting Kidnap Bonds Probably in Final Stage," *Monroe Enquirer*, 7/26/68, MMP, RFWP.

68. Clarence Seniors autobiography; Socialist Workers Party, Airtel; Johnson, *Did?*, 7/6/63; "Collecting."

69. Socialist Workers Party, Airtel.

70. Seniors and Seniors, "Chairman"; Moorer, "Monroe Youth Organize"; "Monroe School's Boycott Appears to be Weakening," *Charlotte Observer*, 9/4/63, 3A, Monroe Youth Action Committee, 1963, box 347, folder 1, JBMP; Johnson, "Inevitable Change"; Johnson, "Monroe, N.C."; "Collecting."

71. Seniors and Seniors, "Chairman"; Moorer, "Monroe Youth Organize"; "Monroe School's Boycott"; Johnson, "Inevitable Change"; Johnson, "Monroe, N.C."; "Collecting"; *"Deacons for Defense," Buffalo Challenger*, 10/21/65, MMP; Clarence Seniors to Shaver, 9/20/64, 12/16/64; Seniors and MDC, "Dear Friend," 2/9/65, 5/14/65, 8/30/65; Seniors and MDC, "Dear Friend," 2/1/64; "Mae Mallory Speaks," *Call and Post*, 4/20/63; "Don't Let Mae."

72. "Introducing," *Partisan*, 4/65; Audrey Seniors FBI, "Miscellaneous Activities," 3/16/65.

73. Seniors, "Monroe, N.C."; *Audrey Seniors*, "A Charlotte Widow"; Audrey Seniors FBI, Audrey Seniors member of the Editorial Staff of the Partisan, 3, 3/1/71.

74. A. Seniors, "Open Forum"; Garrow, *Bearing*, 316–317; Jules Loh, "St. Augustine Quiet," *Atlanta Journal and Constitution*, 7/5/64, box 26 Clippings Folder, BFP.

75. A. Seniors, "Open Forum"; Garrow, *Bearing*, 316–317; Loh, "St. Augustine Quiet."

76. A. Seniors, "Open Forum"; Loh, "St. Augustine Quiet"; Garrow, *Bearing*, 325, 329–330.

77. Garrow, *Bearing*, 316–317.

78. Ibid., 317–318; Colaiaco, *Martin Luther King Jr.*, 99; "Mother of Massachusetts Governor Jailed in Florida: Gov. Peabody's Mother Jailed in Sit-In," *New York Times*, 4/1/64, 1.

79. A. Seniors, "Open Forum."

80. Ibid.

81. "Mother of Massachusetts Governor."

82. A. Seniors, "Open Forum."

83. "Introducing," *Partisan*, 4/65.

84. Ibid., 5.

85. Roberston, "N.C. Republicans"; Kessel and Hopper, "Victims"; State of North Carolina, "Welcome"; Begos et al., *Against Their Will*;

David Zucchino, "Sterilized by North Carolina, She Felt Raped Once More," *Los Angeles Times*, 1/25/2012; Stowe, *Inherit*, 18–19; Workable Program, "Report"*; Hanchett, *Sorting Out*, 249–250; Greenwood, *Bittersweet Legacy*, 1; Dallam, *Daddy Grace*, 135–138. Between 1929 and the 1990s, when it finally became illegal, over 76,000 people were sterilized against their will.

86. Crow et al., *History*, 136–138, 140; North Carolina Division of Community Planning, "Population," 9/63.

87. Crow et al., *History*, 136–138, 140–141, 144.

88. Audrey Seniors, "Monroe, N.C."

89. Poole, *Segregated*, 178, 180; North Carolina Division of Community Planning, "Population," 4–6; Crow et al., *History*, 22, 121–122, 145–146.

90. Audrey Seniors, "Monroe, N.C."

91. North Carolina Division of Community Planning, "Population," 5.

92. Audrey Seniors, "Monroe, N.C."

93. Ibid.

94. North Carolina Division of Community Planning, "Population," 22; Crow et al., *History*, 195.

95. Audrey Seniors, "Monroe, N.C."

96. Nadasen, *Welfare Warriors*, 6, 9, 10, 12, 47; Poole, *Segregated*, 141, 173, 177–178; Lipsitz, *Possessive Investment*, 5; E. Glenn, "Caring," 53–55; McDuffie, *Sojourning*, 113, 126–127, 132; Crow et al., *History*, 136–138, 140–141, 144; Smith, *Welfare Reform*, 4, 6, 87–88.

97. Audrey Seniors, "Monroe, N.C."

98. G. Gilmore, *Gender*, 22–23; Crow et al., *History*, 119–120, 146; North Carolina Division of Community Planning, "Population," 4.

99. Audrey Seniors, "Monroe, N.C."

100. Ibid.

101. Ibid.

102. Audrey Seniors, "Charlotte Widow." See also Sigler, "Daddy Grace," 67–77; Dallam, *Daddy Grace*.

103. Johnson, "Did?," 12/31/60; Johnson, *Did?* 7/6/63, 11/7/64; Johnson, "Did?," n.d.; "The Members"; "Crusaders Association"; T. Tyson, *Radio Free Dixie*, 203.

104. Audrey Seniors, "Charlotte Widow"; Nadasen, *Welfare Warriors*, 6, 9, 10, 12, 47; Smith, *Welfare Reform*, 4, 6, 87–88; Poole, *Segregated*, 141, 173, 177–178; Lipsitz, *Wages*, 5; E. Glenn, "Caring," 53–55; McDuffie, *Sojourning*, 113, 126–127, 132; Crow et al., *History*, 136–138, 140–141, 144.

105. Audrey Seniors, "Charlotte Widow."
106. Johnson, "Did?," 12/31/60, 7/6/63; Johnson, *Did?*, 11/7/64, 11/65, 7/3/65, 9/4/65, 3/66; "Johnson, "Did?," 11/11/61; "Crusaders Association"; "The Members"; "Crusaders," 4/15/61; T. Tyson, *Radio Free Dixie*, 203; Johnson, "Care Sincerely"; Johnson, "C.A.R.E. News" ; Johnson, "Did?," 10/21/61; Johnson, "Did?," 1/21/61; "C.A.R.E. Packages."
107. Audrey Seniors, "Charlotte Widow."
108. H. Williams, *Self-Taught*, 72-74, 79; G. Gilmore, *Gender*, 33, 157-158; Greenwood, *Bittersweet Legacy*, 243; Crow et al., *History*, 81, 102, 134-138, 140; North Carolina Division of Community Planning, "Population," 3; LeLoudis, "Leadership," 4.
109. Audrey Seniors, "Charlotte Widow"; Sigler, "Daddy Grace," 67-77; Dallam, *Daddy Grace*; L. Davis, *Daddy Grace*.
110. Audrey Seniors, "Charlotte Widow."
111. L. Davis, *Daddy Grace*, x; Dallam, *Daddy Grace*, 7, 34-35, 39-40, 78, 112, 137; Sigler, "Daddy Grace," 67-68, 71, 77.
112. Audrey Seniors, "Charlotte Widow."
113. "Secrets of Daddy Grace," *Afro American*, 3/5/60*; Audrey Seniors, "Charlotte Widow."
114. Hanchett, *Sorting Out*, 127-133, 249; Dallam, *Daddy Grace*, 34-35, 39-40, 78, 112, 135-138; Sigler, "Daddy Grace," 67-68, 71, 77.
115. Audrey Seniors, "Charlotte Widow."
116. Ibid.; Hanchett, *Sorting Out*, 249-250; Greenwood, *Bittersweet Legacy*, 1.
117. Audrey Seniors, "Charlotte Widow."
118. Hart to Golden.

Chapter 8. Pat Mallory, Black Nationalist Rebel Woman

1. Mallory to Ellie, 6/19/63.
2. Ibid.
3. Oduba interviews. All quotations from Pat are from these interviews unless otherwise noted.
4. "Homecoming at Stony Brook: A Sign of a Changed Campus," *New York Times*, 11/8/84; Jeremy Kline, "Politics," *Statesman*, 10/28/2014, SUNYSBA; Jon Friedman, "Letter," *Statesman*, 8/27/2017, SUNYSBA; Dawson, *Paul Lauterbur*, 693.
5. Kendi, *Black*, 109, 112- 113; Shiek, *On Strike*; Black Panther, *San Francisco Strike*; Corker, *Black Studies*; Alridge and Young, Introduction.
6. Kendi, *Black*, 109, 112- 113; Shiek, *On Strike*; Black Panther, *San Francisco Strike*; Corker, *Black Studies*; Alridge and Young, Introduction.
7. Shiek, *On Strike*; Black Panther, *San Francisco Strike*; Corker, *Black Studies*; Alridge and Young, Introduction; Kendi, *Black*, 108-109, 113-114, 120-121, chapter 6-8; Painter, *Creating*, 315-316, 333.
8. See Tina Myerson, "Administration," *Statesman*, 12/10/68, SUNYSBA; Dwight Loines, "Administrative," *Statesman*, 4/15/69, SUNYSBA.
9. "To All," *Statesman*, 2/7/69, SUNYSBA; "Progress," *Statesman*, 4/15/69, SUNYSBA; Calvin Canton, "Black Studies," 4/15/69; "Reflections," 4/15/69, *Statesman*, SUNYSBA.
10. See "Plan Black Halls for Next Year," *Statesman*, 5/6/70, SUNYSBA; "There Will Be a Meeting at 8 p.m. in A & B Lounge, Black Dorm," *Statesman*, 9/29/70, SUNYSBA;

"Welcome to Ujamaa!" [Ujamaa Residential College], https://cornell.campusgroups.com/urc/home/.

11. Singe et al., "Resilience."

12. P. Jackson, "Struggle," 4/15/69, SUNYSBA; Hoffman, "African Culture," *Statesman*, 11/22/68, SUNYSBA.

13. P. Mallory, "Where?," *Statesman*, 4/23/68, 13, SUNYSBA.

14. Sanders, "Jail."

15. P. Mallory, "Where?"

16. Tate, "Power," 149, 170; Assenoh, *African*, 120-122*; Markle, "Book Publishers"; Brennan, *Taifa*, 127, 163, 166, 198-199, 187; Ivasca, "Cultured States," 189, 191; Markle, *Motorcycle*, 117.

17. See Verges, "People's Victory."

18. Markle, "Book Publishers"; Ivasca, "Cultured States," 188-191.

19. "Afro-Americans Seek Links with Africa," *Nationalist*, 7/71; "Black Women in the Struggle," *Nationalist*, 3/25/72.

20. Tate, "Power," 164-166; Ivasca, "Cultured States," 68-69, 71, 79-81, 188-191, 201-202; Markle, *Motorcycle*, 125-126; "Back to Africa," *Sepia*, 8/69, 47-50*; Mwakikagile, *Relations*, 236-239; R. Lewis, *Walter Rodney's*, 43.

21. Ivasca, "Cultured States," 68-69, 79-81, 201-202; Markle, *Motorcycle*, 125-126; Verges, "For the Independence."*

22. See Gibson, "U.S. Exile," *Chicago Defender*, 10/19/68; "Williams Conferred in Dar es Salaam with Mrs. Mae Mallory," *Chicago Defender*, 10/19/68, 26; Letter to Robert Williams, 4/21/69; Mallory to Robert Williams, 7/7/68; Mallory FBI, 6/10/68, 1-2, 6/20/68, 1, 7/18/68, 1-2, 8/15/68, 1, 8/30/68, 3-6, 2/4/72, 3; "Republic of New Afrika," *Michigan Chronicle*, 6/29/68; "Ex-NAACP."

23. "Republic of New Afrika"; Mallory FBI, 8/15/68, 1, 8/30/68, 3-6, 2/4/72, 3; Mallory to Williamses, 6/9/64.

24. Mallory, "Black Liberation."

25. Freedman and Molteno, *Zed Pan Africa*, 118, 138.*

26. Mallory, "Black Liberation."

27. Lewis et al., "Historical," 21-24, 25.

28. Brennan, *Taifa*, 3, 49-51.

29. Ibid., 51-53, 176-189.

30. Ibid., 183; "Asians Tell of Brutality," *Sunday News*, Tanzania, 10/1/72, 1; "U.S. Accepts Asians," *Sunday News*, Tanzania, 10/1/72; "U.K. Read to Try for U.N. Debate on Asians [expelled from Uganda]," *Daily News*, Tanzania, 10/3/72.

31. Tate, "Power," 164-166; Ivaska, *Cultured*, 68-69, 71, 79-81, 188-191, 201-202; Markle, *Motorcycle*, 125-126; "Back," *Sepia**; Mwakikagile, *Relations*, 239; "Black Women"; R. Lewis, *Walter Rodney's*, 43.

32. Mallory FBI, 11/23/70, 1, 12/10/70, 1.

33. Quinn, *Black Power*, 144, 137-141; *Toward a Revolutionary*.*

34. Quinn, *Black Power*, 137-141.

35. Blake, *Children*, 38-39, 43.

36. *Buffaloes*, 8-9, 83-84, 102-115; Maryknoll Sisters, "History"; Lernoux, *Hearts*, 209, 211-215; Hill Fletcher, Mothering as Metaphor, 15.

37. Lipsitz, *Life*, 9-11; Gramsci, *Selections*, 9-10.

38. *Buffaloes*, 107-108, 213; Markle, *Motorcycle*, 80.

39. Kokota, "Episodes"; Holmes, "1962 Laughter Epidemic"; Ebrahim, "Mass Hysteria," 7/1/68; Dossey, "Strange Contagions," 118.

40. Holmes, "1962 Laughter Epidemic."

41. Kokota, "Episodes"; Holmes, "1962 Laughter Epidemic"; Ebrahim, "Mass Hysteria"; Dossey, "Strange Contagions," 118.

42. "Fight Pregnancies in Schools," *Standard*, 7/3/71; "77 Pregnant Girls," *Standard*, 7/28/71.

43. Mallory FBI, 2/4/72, 3, 3/9/72, 2–3, 1/17/73, 2/8/68, 2, 5/10/68, 2/26/70, 8, 11, 5/10/68, 6/10/68, 1–2, 12/16/71, 2, 12/27/71, 2, 3/17/71, 3, 6/10/69, 1–2, 3/13/70, 1–4.

44. "Revolutionary," [RAM] FBI, n.d.; "Max Stanford."

45. Mallory to Johnson, 6/9/63.

46. George Todd, "250 Attend Rally Assailing White Power: H. Rap Brown, Bond Not There," *Amsterdam News*, 8/19/67, 23; Kochiyama to Mabel Williams, 9/3/69.

47. Todd, "250 Attend"; Kochiyama to Mabel Williams, 9/3/69.

48. Mallory to Robert Williams, 8/28/67.

49. "Revolutionary," FBI, n.d.; "3 Charges Voiced in RAM Case," *Long Island Press* (Jamaica, N.Y.), 1/16/68, RAM, JBMP; "Exclusive: Black Power Militants Are Now Speaking of the 1967 Newark and Detroit Race Riots as Mere 'Rehearsals,'" *Long Island Press* (Jamaica, N.Y.), 1/10/68, RAM, JBMP; "15 in RAM Deny New Charge," *Long Island Press* (Jamaica, N.Y.), 1/10/68, RAM, JBMP; "Lawyer for RAM Suspects Asks, Jury of Their Peers," *Long Island Press* (Jamaica, N.Y.), 1/18/68, RAM, JBMP; "Reindicted for 'Criminal Anarchism,'" *National Guardian*, 1/27/68, RAM, JBMP; "Congressional"; "Revolutionary," FBI, 2/28/69, JBMP; "Violence in the Age of Overkill," *Washington Report*, 9/23/68, 2, RAM, JBMP; "Organizations," FBI, 9/18/68, RAM, JBMP; "New York Jury," *Exclusive*, 6/19/68, JBMP; "Agent Sheds Cover, Testifies," *Guardian*, 6/15/68, 4, RAM, JBMP; "Ferguson, Guilty, Is Freed on Bail," *New York Times*, 6/16/68, JBMP; "RFK," 6/15/68, *Human Events*, JBMP; "Kennedy Put on Death List by Philadelphia, Police Say," *Philadelphia Bulletin*, 6/6/68, RAM, JBMP; "Max Stanford"; "Firebrand or Educator? Herman Benjamin Ferguson," *New York Times*, 2/28/68, RAM, JBMP; "Conspiracy Suspects Bail to 100Gs," *Long Island Press* (Jamaica, N.Y.), 2/28/68, RAM, JBMP; Luce, "Is the U.S.," *Human Events*, JBMP; "RAM," *Congressional Record*, 4/25/68, JBMP; "Quick Arrests Called Vital in Terror-Plot Case," *New York Times*, 5/18/68; Mallory to Robert Williams, 8/28/67.

50. Geller, "RAM Members."

51. Gibbs interview, 5/3/2021. Herman Ferguson was exiled in Guyana and returned to the United States in 1989. Joan Gibbs represented him, with the aid of my mother, her legal secretary. They successfully won all the cases against him.

52. "Malcolm X Memorial at IS 201," *Amsterdam News*, 2/17/68; Sarah Slack, "IS 201 'Happening,'" *Amsterdam News*, 2/24/68.

53. Mallory to Mayfield, 8/25/70.

54. Kochiyama to Brothers Gaidi, Imari, and Sister Mabel Williams, 9/11/69; Kochiyama to Mabel Williams, 9/10/69, 9/11/69.

55. Mallory to Robert Williams; "Republic of New Afrika," *Michigan Chronicle*, 6/29/68; Grattan, "Weekend," *Call and Post*, 5/31/69; Ward, "Black Dissenters," *Call and Post*, 5/31/69; Gibson, "U.S. Exile"; Ward, "Witnesses," *Call and Post*, 5/31/69; "Turnpike Murder," *Call and Post*, 4/19/69; "Tanzania," *Call and Post*, 8/9/69; Hucks, *Yoruba*, 157–158; Ward, "60," *Call and Post*, 4/5/69; Kerr, *Derelict Paradise*, 174–175; Masotti and

Corsi, *Shoot-Out*, 49–50, 74, 77; "Masotti Report," *Call and Post*, 6/7/69; "New Afrika," *Call and Post*, 3/21/69; J. Davis, "FBI's War"; Beckles, "Black Bookstores."

56. Ward, "Witnesses"; Delmonte, "Whites Cheer," *Call and Post*, 12/27/69; "Lawyer," *Call and Post*, 9/20/69; "Kellog Flemings," *Call and Post*, 7/19/69.

57. Ward, "Witnesses."

58. "He Must Be Crazy," *Call and Post*, 6/14/69; Peery, "Mae Mallory," *Call and Post*, 6/14/69; "Grand Jury," *Call and Post*, 6/14/69; "Jail," *Afro American*, 6/28/69; "In Cleveland," *Chicago Defender*, 6/11/69; Ward, "Witnesses"; Peery, "Militants," *Call and Post*, 5/31/69.

59. "Tanzania"; "Jail," *Afro-American*, 6/28/69; J. Williams, "One," *Call and Post*, 6/21/69; "Grand Jury," *Call and Post*, 6/14/69; Delmonte, "Whites Cheer"; Peery, "White Racialism," *Call and Post*, 5/10/69.

60. "Tanzania"; "Jail"; J. Williams, "One"; "Grand Jury"; Delmonte, "Whites Cheer"; Peery, "White Racialism"; Mallory FBI, 5/10/68; "Call for Investigation"; Mallory to Mayfield, 3/12/69; Mallory to Mayfield, 8/25/70; "Republic of New Africa"; Ward, "Black Dissenters"; Grattan, "Weekend"; Gibson, "U.S. Exile"; Ward, "Witnesses"; "Turnpike Murder"; Ward, "60"; Kerr, *Derelict Paradise*, 174–175; Masotti and Corsi, *Shoot-Out*, 49–50, 74, 77; "Masotti Report"; "New Afrika"; "Grand Jury"; "Lawyer"; "Kellog Flemings"; Peery, "Mae Mallory"; "He Must Be Crazy"; "In Cleveland"; Peery, "Militants."

61. Mallory FBI, 2/4/72, 3, 3/9/72, 2–3, 1/17/73, 2/8/68, Rabble Rouser Index, 2/8/68, 2, 5/10/68, 2/26/70, 8, 11, 6/10/69, 1–2, 3/13/70, 1–4, 12/27/71, 2, 3/17/71, Racial Matters Black Nationalist Tendency, 3.

62. Mallory FBI, 12/16/71, 2, 12/27/71, 2.

63. Mallory FBI, 2/4/72, 3.

64. Ibid.; Mallory FBI, 3/9/72, 2, 5/10/68, 12/27/71, 1, 2/1/73, 1–2, 1/17/73, 2, 4/30/73, Key Extremist, 7/8/75, 4/16/74.

65. Mallory FBI, 2/4/72, 3, 3/9/72, 2, 5/10/68, 12/27/71, 1, 2/1/73, 1–2, 1/17/73, 2, 4/30/73, Key Extremist, 7/8/75, 4/16/74.

66. See Kollman, "Generations," 415, 417–419, 422–423.

67. de Jong, *Challenge*, 43.

68. Schoenherr, *Goodbye Father*, 2002, 176–177.

69. Ivaska, *Cultured*, 96–98, 103, 107–113; Rosita Sweetman, "What Really Is a Prostitute?" Women's Special Page, *Sunday News*, Tanzania, 10/1/72, 11; Scholastica Mushi, "The Tyranny of Western Dress," *Standard*, 4/6/72, 6.

70. Ivaska, *Cultured*, 60, 68–69, 79–81, 105; Markle, *Motorcycle*, 125–126; Ivaska, "Movement," 201–202; Mushi, "Tyranny"; Ivaska, "Movement," 201–202.

71. "Leaders Accused of Encouraging Mini-Skirts," *Nationalist*, 10/22/71; Sweetman, "What Really"; "Nightclub Ban Will Not Lower Crime Rate," *Standard*, 7/18/71.

72. Ivaska, *Cultured*, 71–72.

73. "Black American Community," FBI, 6/17/74.

74. Iandolo, "Beyond the Shoe," 130–136; Peck, *Lumumba*; Peck, *Lumumba, la mort*; "New Revolt in Congo," *Workers World*, 1/23/64, 4, LOC; Eleanor Stephens, "Phony 'Mercy Mission' to Congo Is Crude Cover-Up for U.S. Invasion," *Workers World*, 11/27/64, 1, LOC.

75. O'Reilly, *Racial Matters*, 8, 45; Kornweibel, *Seeing Red*, xii; Cratty, "Newspa-

per Lawsuit"; Brown, "Civil Rights Photographer"; "Released Documents" ; Franklin, "Jackanapes," 62–63; Peck, *Lumumba*; Peck, *Lumumba, la mort*; "New Revolt"; Stephens, "Phony"; 41; Mwakikagile, *Relations*, 236–240.

76. O'Reilly, *Racial Matters*, 8, 45; Kornweibel, *Seeing Red*, xii; Cratty, "Newspaper Lawsuit"; Brown, "Civil Rights Photographer"; "Released Documents"; Franklin, "Jackanapes," 62–63; Peck, *Lumumba*; Peck, *Lumumba, la mort*; "New Revolt"; Stephens, "Phony"; 41; Mwakikagile, *Relations*, 236–240.

77. Martin, "Pan African," 209.

78. Ibid.

79. B. Hendrickson, "Metaphysical Healing."

80. Martin, "Pan African," 209.

81. Dexter-Rodgers, "Pentecostalism"; D. Daniels, "Pentecostals"; "Herbert Daughtry"; Michelle Stoddart, "Reverend Herbert Daughtry Talks about Civil Disobedience," *Everybody's Brooklyn*, 5/31/99, 18.

82. Martin, "Pan African."

83. "Herbert Daughtry"; Stoddart, "Reverend Herbert Daughtry"; Dexter-Rodgers, "Pentecostalism," 277–279; D. Daniels, "Pentecostals"; C. Seniors, "Marcus Garvey"*; Austin, "Marcus"*; Garvey, "Negro," 6/48*; "In Memoriam," June–July 1951; Garvey, "Greetings—1944"*; "Marcus Garvey Speaks," *Garvey's Voice*, June–July 1951.*

Chapter 9. Audrey Proctor Seniors

1. Du Bois, *Black Reconstruction*, 630–631.

2. "Audrey Seniors, a Member of the Dec. 18 La Lima Brigade."*

3. Audrey Seniors, Volunteer Work Brigade application*; Bailey, "Atlanta Child Murders"; Baldwin, *Evidence*, 1985; Headley, *Atlanta*. African American Wayne Williams was convicted for two murders. My mother and I along with James Baldwin and many other Blacks disbelieved Williams's guilt, believing that the Klan killed all the children.

4. Audrey Seniors, Volunteer Work Brigade application.

5. "Hell," Photograph, PMSC.

6. Audrey Seniors, Volunteer Work Brigade application.

7. Ferguson, *Grenada*, ix; Martin and Williams, In *Nobody's*, 3–5; Clark, "Second Assassination," 28–30, 32; G. Williams, *U.S.-Grenada*, 23, 20–25, 28–31, 33, 163; Brizan, *Grenada*, 348–349; O'Shaughnessy, *Grenada*, 1–2, 77–79; Marquez, "Grenada," 6–8*; Schoenhals and Melanson, *Revolution*, 32–33; Burrowes, *Revolution*, 29; Jacobs, "W. Richards Jacobs"; EPICA, *Grenada*, 54–56; M. Wright, "Grenada," 21–25.

8. Zedong, *Quotations*"; P. Foner, *Black Panthers*, 78*.

9. EPICA, *Grenada*, 85; M. Wright, "Grenada," 22–23; Brizan, *Grenada*, 348–349.

10. EPICA, *Grenada*, 85; M. Wright, "Grenada," 22–23; Brizan, *Grenada*, 348–349.

11. EPICA, *Grenada*, 81–82, 84–85; M. Wright, "Grenada," 22–23.

12. EPICA, *Grenada*, 74–87; Martin and Williams, *In Nobody's*, 3–5, 49–51, 61, 70–76, 77–81, 146, 167–169, 174–177; Bishop, "In Nobody's Backyard," 4/13/79, 117–118; Ferguson, *Grenada*, 8–9; Sherman and Crozier, *Grenada*, 86–87, 91–98; Seabury and McDougall, *Grenada*, 217–221, 222–229; Marquez, "Grenada," 8–9; Schoenhals and Melanson, *Revolution*, 48–54; O'Shaughnessy, *Grenada*, 105–106; Jacobs, "W. Richards Jacobs"; M. Wright, "Grenada," 22–23.

13. Seabury and McDougall, *Grenada*, 97–100; M. Wright, "Grenada," 22–23.
14. Audrey Seniors, "Autobiographical Notes."
15. Bishop, "In Nobody's Backyard," 4/13/79, 117–118; Martin and Williams, In *Nobody's*, 101.
16. Bishop, "In Nobody's," 4/13/79, 117–118; Martin and Williams, In *Nobody's*, 101.
17. Maurice Bishop Speech.*
18. Payne et al., *Grenada*, 148; R. Lewis, *Walter Rodney's*, 225; W. Gilmore, *Grenada*, 27–28; G. Williams, *U.S.-Grenada*, 43–54, 169–170; Sherman and Crozier, *Grenada*, 43–44, 18–21, 23–28, 50–51; O'Shaughnessy, *Grenada*, 3–4, 10–11; Burrowes, *Revolution*, 31–32; Jacobs, "W. Richards Jacobs."
19. Rose, *Dependency*, 354; Payne et al., *Grenada*, 81–87, 106, 57–59, 130–131, 135–136, 148, 149, 151, 154–155, 158–161; "Grenada Revolution," "Maurice Bishop," www.paradise-inn-carriacou.com/grenada; Marquez, "Grenada," 8; Martin and Williams, *In Nobody's*, 178–181; W. Gilmore, *Grenada*, 28–29, 30–32, 36–38; Ferguson, *Grenada*, ix, 1–3, 13–14; G. Williams, *U.S.-Grenada*, 82–84, 92–95, 148–149, 156–157, 166–168; O'Shaughnessy, *Grenada*, 2–3, 11, 21–27; Schoenhals and Melanson, *Revolution*, 71–81; Burrowes, *Revolution*, 66, 79–83.
20. Audrey Seniors, résumé, n.d.; Audrey Seniors, business card.*
21. "Illegal U.S. War," 10.*
22. O'Shaughnessy, *Grenada*, 1–2, 77–79; Hugh O'Shaughnessy, "Obituary: Sir Eric Gairy," *Independent*, 8/25/97; Associated Press, "Sir Eric Gairy Former Leader of Grenada," *Los Angeles Times*, 8/25/97; France Presse Agences, "Eric Gairy, 75, Former Premier of Grenada, Ousted in 1979," *New York Times*, 8/25/97.
23. Audrey Seniors, Volunteer Work Brigade application.
24. *Committee for a Free Grenada Newsletter*, 2/84, 4/84, 9/84.*
25. Hine, *African American*, 580–581; Bennett, *Before*, 666, 669, 670, 674–675; Lipsitz, *Possessive Investment*, 84.
26. "Grenada," 3/17/84, Hunter College.*
27. Dawkins, *City Sun*, 116–117, 120–121, 124, 137.
28. Audrey Seniors, "Viewpoint," *City Sun*, 2/7/85.*
29. "Audrey Seniors, a Member of the Dec. 18 La Lima Brigade."
30. J. Jones, *Brigadista Harvest*, xvii.*
31. Borge et al., *Sandinistas*, 21; Zedong, "Statement," 4–5, ACSC; Zedong, *Statement*, 1–4*; Castro, "Our Party," 5, 8–9; Castro, *Declaration*, 5–9, 10, 12–13; Max Frankel, "Cuban in Harlem: He Balks at East Side Bill and Spurns U.S. Offer on Quarters," *New York Times*, 9/20/60, 1; Castro, "Speech at the United Nations," 5, 7–9, 10–13, 14–16, 21–22, 30.
32. "Historic Program," 21.
33. "Volunteer" flyer, n.d.; Audrey Seniors, "Dear Friends . . . Third World Brigade"; International Work Brigade flyer, 10/10/85; Asato, "Third World."
34. "Volunteer" flyer, n.d.; Audrey Seniors, "Dear Friends . . . Third World Brigade"; International Work Brigade flyer, 10/10/85; Asato, "Third World"; Ashford, "Statement"; "Volunteer" flyer; International Work Brigade flyer; Pastors for Peace, Interreligious Foundation for Community Organization, https://ifconews.org/about-us/.
35. "Volunteer" flyer; Audrey Seniors, "Dear Friends . . . Third World Brigade"; International Work Brigade flyer; Asato, "Third World."

"Volunteer" flyer; Audrey Seniors, "Dear Friends . . . Third World Brigade"; International Work Brigade flyer; Asato, "Third World"; Ashford, "Statement"; "Volunteer" flyer; International Work Brigade flyer; Pastors for Peace.

36. J. Jones, *Brigadista Harvest*, xxvii–xxviii.

37. Audrey Seniors, "Dear Friends . . . Third World Brigade."

38. Audrey Seniors, "Viewpoint"; "Armed Forces," *Jet*, 6/4/84. Black Muslim Griffin, age twenty-two, refused to fight in Grenada and Lebanon. His religious beliefs prevented him from firing on Muslims.

39. Audrey Seniors, "Viewpoint."

40. AASN, n.d. [1984–1985]*; T. Walker, *Nicaragua*, 10, 95; Monterrey and Pineda, *Nicaragua*, x, 90–92, 97–98; LaRamée and Polakoff, "Evolution," 179–180; Jayko, *Introduction*, 5.

41. "Illegal U.S. War," 8–12.

42. Schaap and Schaap, "Nicaragua," 10.*

43. AASN, n.d. [1984–1985]*; T. Walker, *Nicaragua*, 10, 95; Monterrey and Pineda, *Nicaragua*, x, 90–92, 97–98; LaRamée and Polakoff, "Evolution," 179–180; Jayko, *Introduction*, 5; Borge, *Women*.

44. Rose, *Dependency*, 355; Payne et al., *Grenada*, 57–59; Jean Donavan Brigade*; "Illegal U.S. War," 6.

45. Rose, *Dependency*, 355; Payne et al., *Grenada*, 57–59; Jean Donavan Brigade*; "Illegal U.S. War," 6; Audrey Seniors, "Audrey Seniors," in *Brigadista*, 133.

46. Rose, *Dependency*, 355; Payne et al., *Grenada*, 57–59; Jean Donavan Brigade*; "Illegal U.S. War," 6; Audrey Seniors, "Audrey Seniors," in *Brigadista*, 133; Audrey Seniors, "Viewpoint."

47. Carr, *Colorblind Racism*, x; Omi and Winant, *Racial Formation*, 1, 147–148; Jones et al., *Created Equal*, 641, 644; Helene Cooper, "Obama Cites Limits of U.S. Role in Libya," *New York Times*, 3/28/2011; Eric Lipton, "Clinton and Gates Defend Mission in Libya," *New York Times*, 3/27/2011; Mark Landler and Steven Erlanger, "Obama Seeks to Unify Allies as More Airstrikes Rock Tripoli," *New York Times*, 3/22/2011; Michael D. Shear, "Obama Defends 'Limited' Role in Libya," *New York Times*, 3/28/2011; Erick Schmitt, "U.S. Gives Its Air Power Expansive Role in Libya," *New York Times*, 3/28/2011.

48. Schaap and Schaap, "Nicaragua," 10; "Illegal U.S. War," 8–12.

49. Audrey Seniors, "Autobiographical Notes"; Audrey Seniors, "Audrey Seniors," 133.

50. "FBI," 5, *Brigadista* 13, February 1985.

51. Seniors et al., "If an Agent Knocks," 3–5.*

52. "FBI," *Brigadista* 5.

53. Seniors et al., "If an Agent Knocks."

54. Audrey Seniors, "Audrey Seniors," 133.

55. Audrey Seniors, "Viewpoint."

56. Ibid.

57. Audrey Seniors, "Audrey Seniors," 132–133.

58. Audrey Seniors, Volunteer Work Brigade application.

59. Ibid.

60. Johnson, "Did?," 4/29/61, 9/24/60.

61. Audrey Seniors, Volunteer Work Brigade application.

62. Audrey Seniors, "Third World"; "Audrey Seniors, a Member of the Dec. 18 La Lima Brigade"; "Third World Brigade Co-sponsored by Afro-American Solidarity Network," *Brigadista* 18, 8/85, 3.*

63. "Audrey Seniors to Promote the Project," *Brigadista* 16, 6/85, 5.

64. Boyce Davies, *Left*, 229; Turner, *Caribbean Crusaders*, 16, 46–47, 87; Young, *Soul Power*.

65. "Audrey Seniors, a Member of the Dec. 18 La Lima Brigade"; Boyce Davies, *Left*, 229; Breitman et al., *Trotskyism*, 31, 23, 27–28; Turner, *Caribbean Crusaders*, 16–18, 46, 47, 77–78, 86, 87, 51–52, 53, 17; Poussaint, "Stresses"; Fleming, *Soon*, 117–118, 128–129, 136–139.

66. "Audrey Seniors, a Member of the Dec. 18 La Lima Brigade"; Boyce Davies, *Left*, 229; Breitman et al., *Trotskyism*, 31, 23, 27–28; Turner, *Caribbean Crusaders*, 16–18, 46, 47, 77–78, 86, 87, 51–52, 53, 17; Poussaint, "Stresses"; Fleming, *Soon*, 117–118, 128–129, 136–139.

67. "Audrey Seniors, a Member of the Dec. 18 La Lima Brigade"; Boyce Davies, *Left*, 229; Breitman et al., *Trotskyism*, 31, 23, 27–28; Turner, *Caribbean Crusaders*, 16–18, 46, 47, 77–78, 86, 87, 51–52, 53, 17; Poussaint, "Stresses"; Fleming, *Soon*, 117–118, 128–129, 136–139.

68. "Third World Brigade."

69. Cratty, "Newspaper Lawsuit"; Brown, "Civil Rights Photographer"; "Released Documents"; Franklin, "Jackanapes," 62–63; Audrey Seniors FBI, 1962–1972; Clarence Seniors FBI, 1959–1972; Mallory FBI, 1957–1976; Johnson FBI, 1959–1972; Williams FBI, 9/11/61, 9/20/61, 9/21/61, 9/22/61, "Public Statements and Speeches of Robert Franklin Williams," 12–14, 7/10/61.

70. Audrey Seniors to Gia.* All references to Seniors's letter to Gia are to this letter.

71. Audrey Seniors, "Third World"; "FBI," *Brigadista*, 2/85, 5; "FBI," *Brigadista*, 5/85; Asato, "Third World"; "Audrey Seniors, a Member of the Dec. 18 La Lima Brigade."

72. Ron Ashford, "Statement African American Solidarity Network," n.d. [1984 or 1985].*

73. Audrey Seniors, "Autobiographical Notes"; Audrey Seniors, "Audrey Seniors."

74. Audrey Seniors, "Autobiographical Notes"; Rivera, "Labor Relations," 262; Deere and Marchetti, "Worker-Peasant," 53.

75. Lampson to Audrey Seniors, 1/6/87; Seniors et al. to Brigadistas, 2/23/87; Lampson, Promoter Social Chale Maslam; "Dear Friends, In June the Nicaragua Exchange will Close."

76. American Committee on Africa, "Reception," n.d. [1987].*

77. "Report from the War Zone"; Seniors' International Association of Democratic Lawyers Membership Card, n.d.*; "SWAPO Constitution"*; "A Trust Betrayed: Namibia"*; "United Nations Council for Namibia."

78. "SWAPO Constitution."

79. Center for Constitutional Rights, "*Salas v. United States*."

80. "African American Women in Defense of Ourselves," Guest Editorial, *Amsterdam News*, 10/26/91, SCRBC; "African American Women in Defense of Ourselves," *New York Times*, 11/17/91, reprinted in *Essence*, 3/92, 56.

81. Gibbs interview, 2019; Seniors business card; William Pleasant, "Class Conflict at Center for Constitutional Rights," *Daily Challenge*, 10/27/94, SCRBC.

82. Pleasant, "Class Conflict"; "Memo to All Board Members," 10/20/94.*

83. Pleasant, "Class Conflict"; Herb Boyd, "Ron Daniels Denies Charges of Elitism, Job Layoffs," *Amsterdam News*, 11/19/94, 23, SCRBC; William Pleasant, "Ron Daniels, Baltimore Confab Blasted," *Daily Challenge*, 11/17/94; Sarah Smith, "Street Beat, Constitutional Crisis," *Village Voice*, 10/26/94, SCRBC.

84. S. Smith, "Street *Beat*."

85. Carson, *Education**; Marc Santora, "Sonny Carson, 66, Figure in 60's Battle for Schools Dies," *New York Times*, 12/23/2002; Herb Boyd, "Remembering Sonny Carson," *Michigan Citizen*, 1/18/2003; "Brooklyn Warrior Sonny Abubadika Carson Lives," *Amsterdam News*, 5/28/2015.

86. "Strike Settlement Agreement"; Loines and Daniels, "Statement"; R. Daniels, "Memorandum" to Seniors, "Separation Package."*

Chapter 10. Radicalized Daughters Speak

1. Janet Jemmott, a member of SNCC, married Bob Moses, taught in Tanzania, and is a pediatrician in the United States. Scant information exists concerning Nanny Murrell except that she signed "All Jim Crow Practices Abolished by Revolution" (*Militant*, 1961; "Janet Jemmott," https://snccdigital.org/people/janet-jemmott/) and "Cuba, a Declaration of Conscience," with my father and Dr. Cross.

2. *Police Terror**; "Harlem Race Riot," Britannica.com; Lancaster, "O'Hair"; Elder, "Why Madalyn Murray O'Hair."

3. Michael R. Gordon, "Bush Sends U.S. Force to Saudi Arabia," *New York Times*, 8/8/90; "12,000 in 7 States Strike RCA Plants," *New York Times*, 6/2/70; "RCA Strike," *New York Times*, 6/3/70.

4. Chambers, "Myth"; Dowling, *Cinderella Complex*, 26–27, 31, 38–39, 95; Sarah Kershaw, "Rethinking the Older Woman–Younger Man Relationship," *New York Times*, 10/14/2009; C. Lee, *For Freedom's Sake*, 5, 85, 21–22; Crawley et al., *Gendering Bodies*, 171–172; Gutman, *Black Family*, 1976, 75–76, 469; Carby, *Reconstructing*, 18, 38; White, *Ar'n't I*, 29, 42; D. Berry, *Swing*, 78–79; W. King, *African American*, 140–141; Browning, "Anti-Miscegenation," 31; Barnett, "Anti-Miscegenation"; A. Davis, *Women*, 90–98, 202–206, 210, 213–221, 230–232, 237–239; Roberston, "N.C. Republicans"; Kessel and Hopper, "Victims"; State of North Carolina, "Welcome"; Begos et al., *Against Their Will*; Zucchino, "Sterilized."

5. A. Glenn, *Ito Sisters*, 2017.

6. For a comprehensive discussion of white supremacist feminists see Paula Marie Seniors, "Reconfiguring," 187–196; E. Glenn, "Caring and Inequality"; A. Glenn, *Ito Sisters*, 2017.

7. "Audrey Seniors, Plaintiff."

8. Sheehy, "Consequences"; Neil MacFarquhar, "Harold M. Mulvey, 68, Judge at Tense Black Panther Trials," *New York Times*, 3/1/2000.

9. Audrey Seniors, death certificate.

Bibliography

Manuscript Collections Abbreviations

ACSC	Audrey Seniors and Clarence Henry Seniors Collection (to be deposited at Tamiment Library, New York University). Sources marked with an asterisk (*) in the notes and bibliography belong to this collection.
ALUA	Archives of Labor and Urban Affairs, Walter P. Reuther Library, Wayne State University
APTP	Alexander Pierre Tureaud Papers, Amistad Research Center, Tulane University, New Orleans, Louisiana
BFP	Boyte Family Papers, David M. Rubenstein Rare Book and Manuscript Library, Duke University Libraries
CABP	Carl and Ann Braeden Papers, Betsey B. Creekmore Special Collections and University Archives, University of Tennessee Libraries, Knoxville
CCRI	Committee to Combat Racial Injustice
CFF	Crusaders for Freedom, MMP
DRRUC	Dodd Reading Room, University of Connecticut
FBIRTV	FBI Records: The Vault
FOIA	FBI Freedom of Information Act
GLWP	George Lavan Weissman Papers, Walter P. Reuther Library, Archives of Labor and Urban Affairs, Wayne State University
HGP	Harry Golden Papers, J. Murrey Atkins Library Special Collections, University of North Carolina, Charlotte
HRAEC	Highlander Research and Education Center, New Market, Tennessee
JBMP	J. B. Matthews Papers, David M. Rubenstein Rare Books and Manuscript Collection, Duke University
JMP	Julian Mayfield Papers, Schomburg Center for Research in Black Culture
LOC	Library of Congress, Washington, D.C.

LSUSC	Louisiana State University Special Collections, Baton Rouge
MLMDC	Merrick Library, University of Miami Digital Collections, Camp Columbia
MMP	Mae Mallory Papers, Walter P. Reuther Library, Archives of Labor and Urban Affairs, Wayne State University
MSA	Michigan State University Archives
NNC	North Carolina Collection, Louis Round Wilson Library Special Collections, University of North Carolina, Chapel Hill
	Committee to Aid the Monroe Defendants
	Ephemera Monroe Defense Committee
NOPL	New Orleans Public Library
PMSC	Paula Marie Seniors Collection (to be deposited at Tamiment Library, New York University)
PRDA	New York University Digital Archives. Freedom. Paul Robeson Collection
RAM	Revolutionary Action Movement
RFWP	Robert F. Williams Papers Bentley Historical Library, University of Michigan, Ann Arbor
SCRBC	Schomburg Center for Research in Black Culture
SUNYSBA	Special Collections and University Archives, State University of New York, Stony Brook
TLRWLA	Tamiment Library and Robert F. Wagner Labor Archives, New York University Library
	Mildred McAdory Edelman, Oral History Project Interview
	Ventana Cultural Workers in Solidarity with Nicaragua Collection
UCHR	Union County Heritage Room, Monroe, North Carolina
UNCUV	Underground Newspaper Collection, University of Virginia
USC	Harbison Agricultural College Photograph Collection, South Carolina Library, University of South Carolina Digital Collection
WCSCRBC	Robert F. Williams Collection, Schomburg Center for Research in Black Culture
YAWF	Youth against War and Fascism

Books, Book Chapters/Excerpts, and Reports/Pamphlets

A Brief History of Cuba: From Columbus to the 21st Century. Havana: Editorial Capitan San Luis, 2017.

Aceves, William J. *The Anatomy of Torture: A Documentary History of Filartiga v. Pena-Irala*. Boston: Brill, 2007.

Acoca, Leslie. "Living on the Outside." In *Girls, Women, and Crime: Selected Readings*, edited by Meda Chesney-Lind and Lisa Pasko. Thousand Oaks, Ca.: Sage, 2004.

Agee, Philip. *Inside the Company: CIA Diary*. New York: Bantam, 1975.*

Alexander, Michelle. *The New Jim Crow: Mass Incarceration in the Age of Colorblindness*. New York: New Press, 2010.

Alexander, Robert J. *Maoism in the Developed World*. Westport, Conn.: Praeger, 2001.

Allen, James, ed. *Without Sanctuary: Lynching Photography in America*. Santa Fe: Twin Palms, 2000.
Alridge, Delores P., and Carlene Young. Introduction to *Out of the Revolution: The Development of Africana Studies*. New York: Lexington, 2003.
Alt, Betty, and Sylvia Folts. *Weeping Violins: The Gypsy Tragedy in Europe*. Kirksville: Missouri University Publishing Association, 1996.
Angelou, Maya. *The Heart of a Woman*. New York: Random House, 1981.
Arévalo, Juan José. *The Shark and the Sardines*. New York: Lyle Stuart, 1961.*
Asch, Moses, and Alan Lomax, eds. *The LeadBelly Songbook*. New York: Oak Publications, 1962.*
Ashe, Arthur. *A Hard Road to Glory: A History*. New York: Amistad, 1988.
Assenoh, A. B. *African Political Leadership: Jomo Kenyatta, Kwame Nkrumah, and Julius Nyerere*. Malabar, Fla.: Kreiger, 1998.*
Bailey, Ura Jean. "The Atlanta Child Murders and the Black Caucus of SRCD." In *Our Children Too: The History of the First 25 Years of the Black Caucus of the Society for Research in Child Development, 1973–1977*, edited by D. Slaughter-Defoe, A. M. Garrett, and A. O. Harrison-Hale. Monographs of the Society for Research in Child Development. Boston: Blackwell, 2006.
Baldwin, James. *Evidence of Things Not Seen*. New York: Holt, Rinehart & Winston, 1985.
Ballard, Allen B. *One More Day's Journey: The Story of a Family and a People*. New York: McGraw-Hill, 1984.
Barany, Zoltan. *Gypsies: The East European Gypsies: Regime Change, Marginality and Ethnopolitics*. Cambridge: Cambridge University Press, 2001.
Bartley, Numan V. *The Rise of Massive Resistance: Race and Politics in the South during the 1950s*. Baton Rouge: Louisiana State University Press, 1969.
Bates, Daisy. *The Long Shadow of Little Rock*. New York: David McKay, 1962.*
Bennett, Lerone. *Before the Mayflower: A History of Black America*. New Millennium ed. Chicago: Johnson, 2003.
Benson, Devyn Spence. *Antiracism in Cuba: The Unfinished Revolution*. Chapel Hill: University of North Carolina Press, 2016.
Berg, Allison. *Mothering the Race: Women's Narratives of Reproduction, 1890–1930*. Urbana: University of Illinois Press, 2001.
Berry, Daina Ramey. *Swing the Sickle for the Harvest Is Ripe*. Urbana: University of Illinois Press, 2007.
Berry, Daina Ramey, and Kali Nicole Gross. *A Black Women's History of the United States*. Boston: Beacon, 2019.
Berry, Mary Frances. *My Face Is Black Is True: Callie House and the Struggle for Ex-Slave Reparations*. New York: Knopf, 2005.
Bethel, Elizabeth Rauh. *Promiseland: A Century of Life in a Negro Community*. Philadelphia: Temple University Press, 1981.
Bilksy, Brian, and Meda Chesney-Lind. "Doing Time in Detention Home: Gendered Punishment Regimes in Youth Jails." In *Razor Wire Women: Prisoners, Activists, Scholars and Artists*, edited by Jodie Michelle Lawston and Ashley E. Lucas. New York: State University of New York Press, 2011.
Blackwell, Mary S. "The Republican Vision of Mary Palmer Tyler." In *Mothers and

Motherhood: Reading American History, edited by Rima D. Apple and Janet Golden. Columbus: Ohio State University Press, 1997.

Blain, Keisha N. *Set the World on Fire: Black Nationalist Women and the Global Struggle for Freedom*. Philadelphia: University of Pennsylvania Press, 2018.

Blake, John. *Children of the Movement*. Chicago: Chicago Press Review, 2004.

Bloom, Harold. *Modern Critical Interpretations: Narrative of Frederick Douglass*. New York: Chelsea, 1988.

Borge, Tomás, Carlos Fonseca, Daniel Ortega, Humberto Ortega, and Jaime Wheelock. *Sandinistas Speak*. New York: Pathfinder, 1982.*

Borge, Tomás. *Women and the Nicaraguan Revolution*. Atlanta: Pathfinder, 1983.*

Borstelmann, Thomas. *The Cold War and the Color Line: American Race Relations in the Global Arena*. Cambridge: Harvard University Press, 2001.

Boyce Davies, Carole. *Claudia Jones beyond Containment*. Burbury, Ghana: Ayebia, 2011.

———. *Left of Karl Marx: The Political Life of Black Communist Claudia Jones*. Durham: Duke University Press, 2007.

Breitman, George, Paul Le Blanc, and Alan Wald. *Trotskyism in the United States: Historical Essays and Reconsiderations*. Atlantic Highlands, N.J.: Humanities Press, 1996.

Brennan, James. *Taifa: Making Nation and Race in Urban Tanzania*. Columbus: Ohio University Press, 2012.

Brizan, George. *Grenada: Island of Conflict*. London: Zed, 1984.

Brown, Tamara Mose. *Raising Brooklyn: Nannies, Childcare, and Caribbean's Creating Community*. New York: New York University Press, 2011.

Brundage, W. Fitzhugh. *Lynching in the New South: Georgia and Virginia, 1880–1930*. Urbana: University of Illinois Press, 1993.

Buck, Pearl. *The Man Who Changed China: The Story of Sun Yat-sen*. New York: Random House, 1953.*

The Buffaloes: A Story Commemorating Maryknoll Society's 50 Years in Tanzania, 1946–1996. Tanzania, 1997.

Burke, Kimberly. "Do I Have to Stand for This?" Riverside Unit Texas, 2002. In *Interrupted Life: Experiences of Incarcerated Women in the United States*, edited by Rickie Solinger, Paula C. Johnson, Martha L. Raimon, Tina Reynolds, and Ruby C. Tapia, 71–72. Berkeley: University of California Press, 2010.

Burke, W. Lewis, Jr. "The Radical Law School: The University of South Carolina School of Law and Its African American Graduates, 1873–1877." In *At Freedom's Door: African American Founding Fathers and Lawyers in Reconstruction South Carolina*, edited by James Lowell Underwood and W. Lewis Burke Jr. Columbia: University of South Carolina Press, 2000.

Burkett, Randall, ed. *The Mind of Carter G. Woodson: As Reflected in the Books He Read and Published. A Catalog of the Library of Carter G. Woodson and the Association for the Study of African American Life and History*. Atlanta: Emory University Press, 2006.

Burlage, Dorothy Dawson. "Truths of the Heart." In *Deep in Our Hearts*. Athens: University of Georgia Press, 2000.

Burley, Dan, ed. *Muhammad Speaks to the Blackman*. Vol. 1, no. 1, 1960.*

Burrowes, Reynold A. *Revolution and Rescue in Grenada: The U.S. Caribbean Invasion*. New York: Greenwood, 1988.

Carby, Hazel. *Reconstructing Womanhood: The Emergence of the Afro-American Woman Novelist*. Oxford: Oxford University Press, 1987.

Carr, Leslie. *Colorblind Racism*. New York: Sage, 1997.
Carson, Sonny. *The Education of Sonny Carson*. New York: Norton, 1972.*
Charron, Katherine Mellen. *Freedom's Teacher: The Life of Septima Clark*. Chapel Hill: University of North Carolina Press, 2009.
Cobb, Charles E. *This Non-Violent Stuff'll Get You Killed: How Guns Made the Civil Rights Movement Possible*. New York: Basic Books, 2014.
Cohen, Lizbeth. *Making a New Deal: Industrial Workers in Chicago, 1919–1939*. New York: Cambridge University Press, 1990.
Colaiaco, James A. *Martin Luther King Jr.: Apostle of Militant Nonviolence*. New York: St. Martin's, 1988, 1993.
Collins, Catherine Fisher. *The Imprisonment of African American Women: Causes, Conditions, and Future Implications*. Jefferson, N.C.: McFarland, 1997.
Collins, Patricia Hill. *Black Feminist Thought: Knowledge, Consciousness, and the Politics of Empowerment*. New York: Routledge, 1991.
Constitution of the Communist Party. Peking: Foreign Languages Press, 1969, YAWF Imprint.*
Cooper, Anna Julia. *A Voice from the South*. New York: Negro Universities Press, 1892, available at Documenting the American South, https://docsouth.unc.edu/church/cooper/menu.html.
Cooper, Robert, and Amanda Datnow. "African-American Student Success in Independent Schools: A Model of Family, School, and Peer Influence." In *Schooling Students Placed at Risk: Research Policy and Practice in the Education of Poor and Minority Adolescents*, edited by Mavis G. Sanders. New York: Routledge, 2000.
Crawley, Sarah L., Lara J. Foley, and Constance L. Shehan. *Gendering Bodies*. Lanham, Mass.: Rowman & Littlefield, 2008.
Crosby, Emilye. *A Taste of Freedom: The Black Freedom Struggle in Claiborne County, Mississippi*. Durham: University of North Carolina Press, 2005.
Crow, Jeffrey J., Paul D. Escott, and Forla J. Hatley. *History of African Americans in North Carolina*. Raleigh: Division of Archives and History, North Carolina Department of Cultural Resources, 1992.
Cruse, Harold. *The Crisis of the Negro Intellectual*. New York: William Morrow, 1967.*
Culture Clash. "The Mission." In *Life, Death and Revolutionary Comedy*. New York: Theatre Communication Group, 1998.
Dallam, Marie W. *Daddy Grace: A Celebrity Preacher and His House of Prayer*. New York: New York University Press, 2007.
Daniels, David D., III. "Pentecostals: African American." In *African American Traditional Religions*, edited by Charles H. Lippy. Washington, D.C.: CQ, 2010.
Daniels, Maurice Charles. *Saving the Soul of Georgia: Donald L. Hollowell and the Struggle for Civil Rights*. Athens: University of Georgia Press, 2013.
Davis, Angela. *Angela Davis: An Autobiography*. New York: Random House, 1974.*
Davis, Angela. *Are Prisons Obsolete?* New York: Seven Stories, 2003.
———. *Women, Race, and Class*. New York: Vintage, 1980.
Davis, Lenwood. *Daddy Grace: An Annotated Bibliography*. Santa Barbara, Ca.: ABC-CLIO, 1992.
Dawkins, Wayne. *City Sun: Andrew W. Cooper's Impact on Modern-Day Brooklyn*. Jackson: University of Mississippi Press, 2012.
Dawson, Joan M. *Paul Lauterbur and the Invention of MRI*. Boston: MIT Press, 2003.

de Jong, Albert. *The Challenge of Vatican II in East Africa: The Contributions of Dutch Missionaries to the Implementation of Vatican II in Tanzania, Kenya, Uganda, and Malawi, 1965–1975*. Nairobi: Paulines, 2004.

Dexter-Rodgers, Shalanda. "Pentecostalism." In *The Great Migration: A Historical Encyclopedia of the American Mosaic*, edited by Steven A. Reich, 277, 279–280. Santa Barbara, Ca.: Greenwood, 2014.

Díaz-Cotto, Juanita. *Chicana Lives and Criminal Justice: Voices from El Barrio*. Austin: University of Texas Press, 2006.

———. *Gender, Ethnicity, and the State*. Albany: State University of New York Press, 1996.

Douglass, Frederick. *The Narrative Life of Frederick Douglass*. 1845; New Haven, Conn.: Yale University Press, 2001.

Dowling, Colette. *The Cinderella Complex: Women's Hidden Fear of Independence*. New York: Summit, 1981.

Drake, St. Clair, and Horace R. Cayton. *Black Metropolis: A Study of Negro Life in a Northern City*. Chicago: University of Chicago Press, 1945, 1993.*

Dray, Philip. *At the Hand of Persons Unknown: The Lynching of Black America*. New York: Random House, 2002.

Du Bois, W. E. B. *Black Reconstruction in America, 1860–1880*, New York: Athenaeum, 1935*; New York: Free Press, 1997.

———. *The Souls of Black Folk*. 1903, available at Documenting the American South, https://docsouth.unc.edu/church/duboissouls/dubois.html.

Dudziak, Mary L. *Cold War Civil Rights: Race and the Image of American Democracy*. Princeton, N.J.: Princeton University Press, 2000.

Elliot, Jeffrey M., and Mervyn Dymally. *Fidel Castro. Nothing Can Stop the Course of History*. New York: Pathfinder, 1986.*

Ensted, Nan. *Ladies of Labor, Girls of Adventure*. New York: Columbia University Press, 1999.

EPICA Task Force. *Grenada: The Peaceful Revolution*. Washington, D.C.: Ecumenical Program for Interamerican Communication and Action, 1982.*

Espiritu, Yen Le. *Asian American Women and Men*. Thousand Oaks: Sage, 1997.

Fairclough, Adam. *Race and Democracy: The Civil Rights Struggle in Louisiana, 1915–1972*. Athens: University of Georgia Press, 1995.

Falk, William. *Rooted in Place: Family and Belonging in a Southern Black Community*. New Brunswick, N.J.: Rutgers University Press, 2004.

Feimster, Crystal N. *Southern Horrors: Women and the Politics of Rape and Lynching*. Cambridge, Mass.: Harvard University Press, 2009.

Feldstein, Ruth. *Motherhood in Black and White: Race and Sex in American Liberalism, 1930–1965*. Ithaca: Cornell University Press, 2000.

Ferguson, James. *Grenada: Revolution in Reverse*. Rugby, U.K.: Latin America Bureau, 1990.

Ferrer, Ada. *Insurgent Cuba: Race, Nation and Revolution, 1868–1898*. Chapel Hill: University of North Carolina Press, 1999.

Finnegan, Terrence. "'The Equal of Some White Men and the Superior of Others': Masculinity and the 1916 Lynching of Anthony Crawford in Abbeville County, South Carolina." In *Men and Violence: Gender, Honor, and Rituals in Modern Europe*

and America, edited by Pieter Spierenburg. Columbus: Ohio State University Press, 1998.
Fleming, Cynthia Griggs. *Soon We Will Not Cry: The Liberation of Ruby Doris Smith Robinson*. Lanham, Md.: Rowman & Littlefield, 1998.
Flynn, Elizabeth Gurley. *The Alderson Story: My Life as a Political Prisoner*. New York: International, 1963.*
———. *I Speak My Own Peace*. New York: Masses & Mainstreams, 1955.*
———. *13 Communists Speak to the Court*. New York: New Century, 1953.*
Foner, Eric. "South Carolina's Black Elected Officials." In *At Freedom's Door: African American Founding Fathers and Lawyers in Reconstruction South Carolina*, edited by James Lowell Underwood and W. Lewis Burke Jr. Columbia: University of South Carolina Press, 2000.
Foner, Philip, ed. *The Black Panthers Speak: The Manifesto of the Party: The First Complete Documentary Record of the Panthers Program*. Philadelphia: Lippincott, 1970.*
Ford, Tanisha C. *Kwame Brathwaite: Black Is Beautiful*. New York: Aperture, 2019.
———. *Liberated Threads: Black Women, Style, and the Global Politics of Soul*. Chapel Hill: University of North Carolina Press, 2015.
Frank, L. "II. Mission Times." In *Acorn Soup: Drawings and Commentary*. Berkeley: Heyday, 1999.
Franklin, John Hope. *From Slavery to Freedom*. New York: Knopf, 1947; New York: McGraw-Hill, 2010.*
Franklin, V. P. "Jackanapes: Reflections of the Legacy of the Black Panther Party for the Hip Hop Generation." In *Message in the Music: Hip Hop, History, and Pedagogy*, edited by Derrick P. Alridge and James B. Stewart. Washington, D.C.: Association for African American Life and History Press, 2010.
Frasier, Angus. *The Gypsies*. New York: Oxford University Press, 1992.
Frazier, Nishani. *Harambee City: The Congress of Racial Equality in Cleveland and the Rise of Black Power Populism*. Fayetteville: University of Arkansas Press, 2017.
Freedman, Henry, and Robert Molteno. *Zed Pan Africa Handbook*. Secaucus, N.J.: Cinnamon, 1981.*
Fremantle, Anne. *Mao Tse-tung: An Anthology of His Writings*. New York: New American Library, 1962.*
Fujino, Diane. *Heartbeat of Struggle: The Revolutionary Life of Yuri Kochiyama*. Minneapolis: University of Minnesota Press, 2005.
Gaines, Kevin G. *Uplifting the Race: Black Leadership, Politics, and Culture in the Twentieth Century*. Chapel Hill: University of North Carolina Press, 1996.
Garrow, David J. *Bearing the Cross: Martin Luther King Jr. and the Southern Christian Leadership Conference*. New York: William Morrow, 1986.
Gilmore, Glenda Elizabeth. *Gender and Jim Crow: Women and Politics of White Supremacy in North Carolina, 1895–1920*. Chapel Hill: University of North Carolina Press, 1996.
Gilmore, William C. *The Grenada Intervention: Analysis and Documentation*. New York: Facts on File, 1984.
Gilyard, Keith. *Louise Thompson Patterson: A Life of Struggle for Justice*. Durham, N.C.: Duke University Press, 2017.

Glenn, Antonia Grace. *The Ito Sisters: An American Story*. Oakland: Unwashed Masses, 2017.

Glenn, Evelyn Nakano. "Caring and Inequality." In *Women's Labor in the Global Economy: Speaking in Multiple Voices*, edited by Sharon Harley. New Brunswick, N.J.: Rutgers University Press, 2007.

Glissant, Edouard. *Caribbean Discourse: Selected Essays*. Charlottesville: University Press of Virginia, 1989.

Gold, E. J. *Downtown Community School, Camp Woodland, Camp Woodstock*. Nevada City, Ca.: Gateway, 2014.

Goodman, Jordan. *Paul Robeson: A Watched Man*. London: Verso, 2013.

Gore, Dayo. *Radicalism at the Crossroads: African American Women Activists in the Cold War*. New York: New York University Press, 2011.

Govenar, Alan. *Lightnin': His Life and Blues*. Chicago: Chicago Press Review, 2010.

Graham, Shirley. *Paul Robeson: Citizen of the World*. New York: Julian Messner, 1948.*

Gramsci, Antonio. *Selections from the Prison Notebooks*. Edited by Quintin Hoarse and Geoffrey Nowell Smith. New York: International, 1971.

Greenwood, Janette Thomas. *Bittersweet Legacy: The Black and White Better Classes in Charlotte, 1850–1910*. Chapel Hill: University of North Carolina Press, 1994.

Griswold, Deidre. *Workers World Party and Its Front Organizations: A Study Prepared by the Minority Staff of the Committee on Internal Security*. House of Representatives, 93rd Congress, 1st Session. Washington, D.C.: Government Printing Office, April 1974.

Gross, Kali. *Colored Amazons: Crime, Violence, and Black Women in the City of Brotherly Love, 1880–1910*. Durham: Duke University Press, 2006.

Grossman, Frances K., Alexandra B. Cook, Selin S. Keple, and Karestan C. Koenen. *With Phoenix Rising: Lessons from Ten Resilient Women Who Overcame the Trauma of Childhood Sexual Abuse*. San Francisco: Jossey-Bass, 1999.

Guevara, Ernesto Che. *Reminiscences of the Cuban Revolutionary War*. New York: Monthly Review, 1968.*

Gutierrez, David. *Walls and Mirrors: Mexican Americans, Mexican Immigrants, and the Politics of Identity*. Berkeley: University of California Press, 1995.

Gutierrez, Ramon. *When Jesus Came the Corn Mothers Went Away*. Stanford: Stanford University Press, 1991.

Gutman, Herbert. *The Black Family in Slavery and Freedom*. New York: Vintage, 1976.

Hanchett, Thomas W. *Sorting Out the New South City: Race, Class, and Urban Development in Charlotte, 1875–1975*. Chapel Hill: University of North Carolina Press, 1998.

Hancock, Ian. *We Are the Romani People*. Paris: Centre de recherches tsiganes, 2002.

Harlow, Barbara. *Resistance Literature*. New York: Methuen, 1987.

Harris, Robert, Nyota Harris, and Grandassa Harris. *Carlos Cooks and Black Nationalism from Garvey to Malcolm*. Dover, Mass.: Majority, 1992.

Headley, Bernard. *The Atlanta Youth Murders and the Politics of Race*. Carbondale: Southern Illinois University Press, 1998.

Hernandez, Lillian. "On Visual Politics and Poetics." In *Razor Wire Women: Prisoners, Activists, Scholars and Artists*, edited by Jodie Michelle Lawston and Ashley E. Lucas. New York: State University of New York Press, 2011.

Hill Fletcher, Jeannine. *Motherhood as Metaphor: Engendering Interreligious Dialogue*.

Bordering Religions: Concepts, Conflicts, and Conversations. New York: Fordham University Press, 2013.

Hine, Darlene Clark. *The African American Odyssey.* 2nd ed. Upper Saddle River, N.J.: Prentice Hall, 2002.

"The Historic Program of the FSLN" (1969, 1982). In Borge et al., *Sandinistas Speak.**

Hodges, Graham Russell, and Jay Mazzocchi. "Lightnin' Hopkins." In *Encyclopedia of African American History: 1896 to Present, from the Age of Segregation to the Twenty-First Century,* edited by Paul Finkelman. New York: Oxford University Press, 2013.

Hoffman, Johanna. "Hep C, Pap Smears, and Basic Care: Justice Now and the Right to Family." In *Interrupted Life: Experiences of Incarcerated Women in the United States,* edited by Rickie Solinger, Paula C. Johnson, Martha L. Raimon, Tina Reynolds, and Ruby Tapia. Berkeley: University of California Press, 2010.

Horne, Gerald. *Race Woman: The Lives of Shirley Graham Du Bois.* New York: New York University Press, 2000.

Horton, Miles, and Frank Adams. *Unearthing Seeds of Fire: The Idea of Highlander.* Winston Salem, North Carolina: Blair Reprint, 1989.*

Hoose, Phillip. *Claudette Colvin: Twice Toward Justice.* New York: Melanie Kroupa, 2009.

Hucks, Tracey E. *Yoruba Traditions and African American Religious Nationalism.* Albuquerque: University of New Mexico Press, 2012.

Hunter, Tera W. *To 'Joy My Freedom: Southern Black Women's Lives and Labors after the Civil War.* Cambridge: Harvard University Press, 1997.

The Illegal U.S. War against Nicaragua. Center for Constitutional Rights Legal Educational Pamphlet, 12/83.*

Ivasca, Andrew. "Cultured States: Youth Gender and Modern Style in 1960s Dar Es Salaam." In *Transnational Histories of Youth in the Twentieth Century,* edited by Richard Ivan Jobs and David M. Pomfret. New York: Palgrave Macmillan, 2015.

Jacobs, W. Richards. "W. Richards Jacobs Grenada's Ambassador to Cuba." In *The Grenada Revolution at Work,* n.d., 11–12.*

James, Joy. *Resisting State Violence: Radicalism, Gender and Race in U.S. Culture.* Minneapolis: University of Minnesota Press, 1996.

Jansen, Marius B. *The Japanese and Sun Yat-Sen.* Cambridge, Mass.: Harvard University Press, 1954.*

Jayko, Margaret. Introduction to Borge, *Women and the Nicaraguan Revolution.**

Jeffreys-Jones, Rhodri. *The FBI: A History.* New Haven: Yale University Press, 2008.

Johnson, Edward A. *The History of the Negro Soldiers in the Spanish American War, and Other Items of Interest.* Raleigh: Capital Printing, 1899; New York: Johnson Reprint, 6, SCRBC.

Johnson, Paula C. *Inner Lives: Voices of African American Women in Prison.* New York: New York University Press, 2002.

Jones, Jacqueline, Peter H. Wood, Thomas Borstelmann, Elaine Tyler May, and Vicki Ruiz. *Created Equal: A Social and Political History of the United States, Brief Edition.* Vol. 2, *From 1865.* New York: Pearson Longman, 2005.

Jones, Jeff, ed. *Brigadista Harvest and War in Nicaragua: Eyewitness Accounts of North American Volunteers Working in Nicaragua.* New York: Praeger, 1986.*

Kaplan, Amy. "Black and Blue on San Juan Hill." In *Cultures of United States Imperialism*. Durham: Duke University Press, 1993.

Katz, Rebecca S. "Explaining Crime and Resistance in the Context of Victimization Experience." In *Girls, Women, and Crime: Selected Readings*, edited by Meda Chesney-Lind and Lisa Pasko. Thousand Oaks: Sage, 2004.

Katznelson, Ira. *When Affirmative Action Was White*. New York: Norton, 2006.

Kelley, Robin D. G. *Yo Mama's Diskfunctional: Fighting the Culture Wars in Urban America*. Boston: Beacon, 1998.

Kelley, Robin D. G., and Betsey Esch. "Black Like Mao: Red China and Black Revolution." In *Afro Asia: Revolutionary and Political and Cultural Connections between African Americans and Asian Americans*, edited by Fred Ho and Bill V. Mullen. Durham: Duke University Press, 2008.

Kendi, Ibram H. [Ibram X. Rogers]. *The Black Campus Movement: Black Students and the Racial Reconstruction of Higher Education, 1965–1972*. New York: Palgrave Macmillan, 2012.

Kenner, Martin, and James Petras, eds. *Fidel Castro Speaks*. New York: Grove, 1969.*

Kerr, Daniel R. *Derelict Paradise: Homelessness and Urban Development in Cleveland, Ohio*. Amherst: University of Massachusetts Press, 2009.

King, Wilma. *African American Childhoods: Historical Perspective from Slavery to Civil Rights*. New York: Palgrave, 2005.

Kochiyama, Yuri. *Passing It On: A Memoir*. Los Angeles: Asian American Studies Center, 2004.

Kornweibel, Theodore. *Seeing Red: Federal Campaigns against Black Militancy, 1919–1925*. Bloomington: Indiana University Press, 1999.

Krenn, Martin L. *Black Diplomacy: African Americans and the State Department, 1945–1969*. London: M. E. Sharpe, 1999.

Kuumba, M. Bahati. *Gender and Social Movements*. Lanham, Md.: AltaMira, 2001.

Lavan, George [George Weissman]. *Che Guevara Speaks*. New York: Grove, 1967.*

LaRamée, Pierre M., and Erica G. Polakoff. "The Evolution of the Popular Organizations in Nicaragua." In *The Undermining of the Sandinista Revolution*, edited by Gary Prevost and Harry E. Vanden. New York: St. Martin's, 1997.

Lathan, Rhea Estelle. "Crusader: Ethel Azalea Johnson's Use of the Written Word as a Weapon of Liberation." In *Women and Literacy: Local and Global Inquiries for a New Century*, edited by Beth Daniell and Peter Mortensen. London: Lawrence Erlbaum, 2007.

Lau, Peter F. *Democracy Rising: South Carolina and the Fight for Black Equality since 1865*. Lexington: University Press of Kentucky, 2006.

Layton, Azza Salama. *International Politics and Civil Rights Policies in the United States, 1941–1960*. Cambridge: Cambridge University Press, 2000.

Lee, Andrea. "An Old Woman." In *Sarah Phillips*. Boston: Northeastern University Press, 1984.

Lee, Chana Kai. *For Freedom's Sake: The Life of Fannie Lou Hamer*. Urbana: University of Illinois Press, 1999.

Lernoux, Penny. *Hearts on Fire: The Story of the Maryknoll Sisters*. New York: Orbis, 1993.

Lewis, George. *Massive Resistance: The White Response to the Civil Rights Movement*. London: Holder Arnold, 2006.

———. "White South, Red Nation: Massive Resistance and the Cold War." In *Massive Resistance: Southern Opposition to the Second Reconstruction*, edited by Clive Webb. New York: Oxford University Press, 2005.

Lewis, Kelly M., Solette Harris, Christina Camp, Willbrord Kalala, Will Jones, Kecia L. Ellick, Justie Huff, and Sinead Younge. "The Historical and Cultural Influences of Skin Bleaching in Tanzania." In *The Melanin Millennium: Skin Color as 21st Century International Discourse*, edited by Ronald E. Hall, 21–25. London: Springer, 2013.

Lewis, Rupert Charles. *Walter Rodney's Intellectual and Political Thought*. Kingston, Jamaica: University Press of the West Indies, 1998.

Lichtenstein, Nelson, Susan Strasser, Roy Rosenzweig, Stephen Brier, and Joshua Brown. *Who Built America? Working People and the Nation's Economy, Politics, and Society since 1877*. 2nd ed. New York: St. Martin's, 2000.

Lipsitz, George. *A Life in the Struggle: Ivory Perry and the Culture of Opposition*. Philadelphia: Temple University Press, 1988.

———. *The Possessive Investment in Whiteness: How Whites Profit from Identity Politics*. Boulder: Westview, 1998.

Lu Hsun. *Chosen Passages from Lu Hsun: The Literary Mentor of the Chinese Revolution*. Edited by Hsueh-Feng. New York: Cameron, 1964.*

Lynn, Conrad. *There Is a Fountain: The Autobiography of a Civil Rights Lawyer*. Westport, Conn.: Lawrence Hill, 1979.*

Mabee, Carleton. *Black Education in New York State from Colonial to Modern Times*. Syracuse, N.Y.: Syracuse University Press, 1979.

Mack, Kibibi Voloria C. *Parlor Ladies and Ebony Drudges: African American Women, Class, and Work in a South Carolina Community*. Knoxville: University of Tennessee Press, 1999.

Makalani, Minkah. *In the Cause of Freedom: Radical Black Internationalism from Harlem to London, 1917–1939*. Chapel Hill: University of North Carolina Press, 2011.

Manis, Andrew, M. *Macon Black and White: An Unutterable Separation in the American Century*. Macon: Mercer University Press and the Tubman African American Museum, 2004.

Markle, Seth M. *A Motorcycle on Hell Run: Tanzania, Black Power, and the Uncertain Future of Pan-Africanism, 1964–1974*. East Lansing: Michigan State University Press, 2017.

Markovitz, Jonathan. *Legacies of Lynching: Racial Violence and Memory*. Minneapolis: University of Minnesota Press, 2004.

Martin, Tony, and Dessima Williams. *In Nobody's Backyard: The Grenada Revolution in Its Own Words*. Vol. 1, *Revolution at Home*. Dover, Mass.: Majority, 1983.

Maurice Bishop Speaks: The Grenada Revolution, 1979–1983, Edited by Bruce Marcus, and Michael Taber. New York: Pathfinder, 1983.

Masotti, Louis H., and Jerome Corsi. *Shoot-Out in Cleveland: Black Militants and the Police*. New York: Praeger, 1969.*

McDuffie, Erik. *Sojourning for Freedom: Black Women, American Communism, and the Making of Black Left Feminism*. Durham: Duke University Press, 2011.

McKittrick, Katherine. *Demonic Grounds: Black Women and the Cartographies of Struggle*. Minnesota: University of Minnesota Press, 2006.

McKittrick, Katherine, and Clyde Woods. *Black Geographies and the Politics of Place*. Boston: South End, 2007.

McWilliams, Carey. *North from Mexico: The Spanish-Speaking People of the United States.* New York: Greenwood, 1968.

Meeks, Brian. *Caribbean Revolutions and Revolutionary Theory: An Assessment of Cuba, Nicaragua, and Grenada.* Kingston, Jamaica: University of West Indies Press, 2001.

Megginson, W. J. *African American Life in South Carolina's Upper Piedmont, 1780–1900.* Columbia: University of South Carolina Press, 2006.

Meier, August, and Eliot Rudwick. *CORE: A Study in the Civil Rights Movement, 1942–1968.* New York: Oxford University Press, 1973.

Michney, Todd M. *Surrogate Suburbs: Black Upward Mobility and Neighborhood Change in Cleveland, 1900–1980.* Chapel Hill: University of North Carolina Press, 2017.

Miller, Warren. *90 Miles from Home: The Truths from Inside Castro's Cuba.* Greenwich, Conn.: Crest, 1961.*

Mills, C. Wright. *Listen Yankee: The Revolution in Cuba.* New York: Ballantine, 1960.*

Monterrey, Glenda, and Amada Pineda. "Women in the Revolution." In *Nicaragua: A New Kind of Revolution*, edited by Philip Zwerling. Westport, Conn.: Lawrence Hill, 1985.

Moore, Richard. "The Name 'Negro'—Its Origin and Evil Use." In *Richard B. Moore, Caribbean Militant in Harlem: Collected Writings, 1920–1972*, edited by Joyce Moore Turner and W. E. B. Turner. Bloomington: Indiana University Press, 1972.

Mullen, Bill V. *Afro-Orientalism.* Minneapolis: University of Minnesota Press, 2004.

———. "Persisting Solidarities: Tracing the Afro Asian Thread in U.S. Literature and Culture." In *AfroAsian Encounters: Culture, History, Politics*, edited by Heike Raphael-Hernandez and Shannon Steen. New York: New York University Press, 2006.

Mwakikagile, Godfrey. *Relations between Africans and African Americans: Misconceptions, Myths, and Realities.* Johannesburg: Pan African, 2006.

Nadasen, Premilla. *Welfare Warriors: The Welfare Rights Movement in the United States.* New York: Routledge, 2006.

Nelson, Alondra. *Body and Soul: The Black Panther Party and the Fight against Medical Discrimination.* Minneapolis: University of Minnesota Press, 2011.

Nevels, Cynthia Skove. *Lynching to Belong: Claiming Whiteness through Racial Violence.* College Station: Texas A&M University Press, 2007.

O'Brian, Timothy J., and David A. Ensminger. *Mojo Hand: The Life and Music of Lightnin' Hopkins.* Austin: University of Texas Press, 2013.

Okihiro, Gary. *Margins and Mainstreams: Asians in American History and Culture.* Seattle: University of Washington Press, 1994.

Olatunji, Babatunde. *The Beat of My Drum: An Autobiography.* Philadelphia: Temple University Press, 2005.

Omi, Michael, and Howard Winant. *Racial Formation in the United States: From the 1960s to the 1980s.* New York: Routledge, 1994.

O'Reilly, Kenneth. *Racial Matters: The FBI's Secret File on Black America.* New York: Free Press, 1989.

O'Shaughnessy, Hugh. *Grenada, Revolution, Invasion and Aftermath.* Bury St Edmunds, U.K.: St Edmundsbury Press, 1984.

Painter, Nell. *Creating Black Americans: African American History and Its Meaning.* New York: Oxford University Press, 2007.

Patterson, Orlando. *Rituals of Blood: The Consequences of Slavery in Two Centuries.* New York: Civitas, 1999.

———. *Slavery and Social Death: A Comparative Study*. New York: Routledge, 1982.
Payne, Anthony, Paul Suggon, and Tony Thorndike. *Grenada: Revolution and Invasion*. New York: St. Martin's, 1984.
Peery, Nelson. *The Negro National Colonial Question*. Chicago: Create Space Independent, 1975.
Phillips, Kimberly L. *Alabama North: African American Migrants, Community, and Working-Class Activism in Cleveland, 1915–1945*. Urbana: University of Illinois Press, 1999.
Piao, Lin. *Long Live the Victory of People's War!* Peking: Foreign Languages, 1968.*
Police Terror in Harlem. Pamphlet, July 1964, Harlem Defense Council, 1–11.*
Poole, Mary. *The Segregated Origins of Social Security: African Americans and the Welfare State*. Chapel Hill: University of North Carolina Press, 2006.
Quinn, Kate. *Black Power in the Caribbean*. Gainesville: University Press of Florida, 2014.
Quintana, Bertha, and Lois Gray. *Gitano: The Gypsies of Southern Spain*. New York: Holt, Rinehart & Winston, 1972.
Ransby, Barbara. *Ella Baker and the Black Freedom Movement: A Radical Democratic Vision*. Chapel Hill: University of North Carolina Press, 2003.
———. *Eslanda: The Large and Unconventional Life of Mrs. Paul Robeson*. New Haven: Yale University Press, 2014.
Rasmussen, Daniel. *American Uprising: The Untold Story of America's Largest Slave Revolt*. New York: Harper Collins, 2011.
Ravitch, Diane. *The Great School Wars: A History of the New York City Public Schools*. Baltimore: Johns Hopkins University Press, 2000.
Razak, Ariska. "African Religions-In-Diaspora." In *Encyclopedia of Women in World Religion: Faith and Culture Cross History*, edited by Susan de Gaia. Denver: ABC-CLIO, 2019.
Rhodes-Pitts, Sharifa. *Harlem Is Nowhere: A Journey to the Mecca of Black America*. New York: Little, Brown, 2011.
Rickford, Russell J. *Betty Shabazz: A Remarkable Story of Survival and Faith Before and After Malcolm X*. Naperville, Ill.: Sourcebooks, 2003.
Robeson, Paul. *Here I Stand*. New York: Othello Associates, 1958; New York: Beacon, 1988.*
———. "It's Good to Be Back." In *Paul Robeson Speaks*, edited by Philip Sheldon Foner, 478–480. New York: Citadel, 2002.*
———. *The Negro and the Soviet Union*. New York: New Century, 1950.*
Robeson, Paul, Jr. *The Undiscovered Paul Robeson: An Artist's Journey, 1898–1939*. New York: Wiley, 2001.
Robinson, Greg. "Internationalism and Justice: Paul Robeson, Asian and Asian Americans." In *AfroAsian Encounters: Culture, History, Politics*, edited by Heike Raphael-Hernandez and Shannon Steen. New York: New York University Press, 2006.
Roediger, David. *Wages of Whiteness: Race and the Making of the American Working Class*. London: Verso, 2007.
Rooks, Noliwe. *Hair Raising: Beauty, Culture, and African American Women*. New Brunswick, N.J.: Rutgers University Press, 1996.
Rose, Euclid. *Dependency and Socialism in the Modern Caribbean: Superpower Intervention in Guyana, Jamaica, and Grenada, 1970–1985*. Lanham, Md.: Lexington, 2002.

Rutkoff, Peter M., and William B. Scott. *Fly Away: The Great African American Cultural Migrations.* Baltimore: Johns Hopkins University Press, 2010.

Sartain, Lee. *Invisible Acts: Women of the Louisiana NAACP and the Struggle for Civil Rights, 1915–1945.* Baton Rouge: Louisiana State University Press, 2007.

Saxton, Alexander. *Indispensable Enemy: Labor and the Anti-Chinese Movement in California.* Berkeley: University of California Press, 1971.

Scheer, Robert, ed. *The Diary of Che Guevara.* Introduction by Fidel Castro. New York: Bantam, 1967.*

Schoenhals, Kai P., and Richard A. Melanson. *Revolution and Intervention in Grenada: The New Jewel Movement, the United States, and the Caribbean.* Boulder, Co.: Westview, 1985.

Schoenherr, Richard A. *Goodbye Father: The Celibate Male Priesthood and the Future of the Catholic Church.* Oxford: Oxford University Press, 2002.

Seabury, Paul, and Walter A. McDougall, eds. *The Grenada Papers.* San Francisco: ICS Press, 1984.

Seniors, Audrey Proctor. "Audrey Seniors." In *Brigadista Harvest and War in Nicaragua: Eyewitness Accounts of North American Volunteers Working in Nicaragua.* New York: Praeger, 1986.*

Seniors, Paula Marie. *Beyond Lift Every Voice and Sing: The Culture of Uplift, Identity, and Politics in Black Musical Theater.* Columbus: Ohio State University Press, 2009.

———. "Exile and Erasure in Cinderella: The African American Cinderella and the Asian Prince." In *Images That Injure,* edited by Susan Dente. Westport: Praeger, 2011.

———. "Jack Johnson, Paul Robeson and the Hyper Masculine African American Übermensch." In *Harlem Renaissance, Politics, Arts, Letters,* edited by Jeffrey O. G. Ogbar. Baltimore: John Hopkins University Press, 2010.

———. "Mae Mallory and 'the Southern Belle Fantasy Trope' at the Cuyahoga County Jail 21st and Payne/'Pain.'" In *From Uncle Tom's Cabin to The Help: Critical Perspectives on White-Authored Narratives of Black Life,* edited by Claire Oberon Garcia, Vershawn Ashanti Young, and Charise Pimentel. New York: Palgrave Macmillan, 2014.

———. "Reconfiguring Black Motherhood: Michelle Obama and the Mom in Charge Trope." In *Michelle Obama's Impact on African American Women and Girls,* edited by Paula Marie Seniors, Michelle Duster, and Rose Thevenin. London: Palgrave Macmillan, 2018.

———. "Transforming the Carmen Narrative: The Case of Carmen the Hip Hopera." In *Message in the Music: Hip Hop, History, and Pedagogy,* edited by Derrick P. Alridge and James B. Stewart. Washington, D.C.: Association for African American Life and History, 2010.

Sharpley-Whiting, T. Denean. *Pimps Up, Ho's Down: Hip Hop's Hold on Young Black Women.* New York: New York University Press, 2007.

Shaw, Andrea Elizabeth. *The Embodiment of Disobedience: Fat Black Women's Unruly Political Body.* Lanham, Md.: Lexington, 2006.

Sherman, Sir Alfred, and Brian Crozier, eds. *The Grenada Documents.* London: Sherwood, 1987.

Sigler, Danielle Brune. "Daddy Grace: An Immigrant's Story." In *Immigrant Faiths: Transforming Religious Life in America,* edited by Karen I. Leonard, Alex Stepick, Manuel A. Vasquez, and Jennifer Holdaway. Walnut Creek, Ca.: AltaMira, 2005.

Sims-Alvarado, Karcheik. *Atlanta and the Civil Rights Movement, 1944–1968*. Charleston, S.C.: Arcadia, 2017.
Smith, Anna Marie. *Welfare Reform and Sexual Regulation*. Cambridge: Cambridge University Press, 2007.
Snipes, Wilson Currin. "Writing about People." In *Writer and Audience: Forms of Non-Fiction Prose*. New York: Holt, Rinehart & Winston, 1970.
Sostre, Martin. *Letters from Prison*. Philosophical Society, State University of New York at Buffalo, Martin Sostre Defense Committee, 1968, 1969.*
Spencer, Cornelia. *Sun Yat-sen: Founder of the Chinese Republic*. New York: John Day, 1967.*
Spencer, Robyn C. [Robyn Spencer-Antoine]. *The Revolution Has Come: Black Power, Gender, and the Black Panther Party in Oakland*. Durham, N.C.: Duke University Press, 2016.
Stowe, Gary. *Inherit the Land: Jim Crow Meets Miss Maggie's Will*. Jackson: University of Mississippi Press, 2007.
Sudarkasa, Niara. "Interpreting the African Heritage in Afro-American Family Organization." In *Black Families*, edited by Harriette Pipes McAdoo. Beverly Hills: Sage, 1981.
SWAPO *Constitution of the South West Africa People's Organization*. Published by the SWAPO Department for Publicity and Information, Provisional Headquarters, Lusaka, Zambia, 1976, 1981.*
Sweeney, Megan. "'I Lived That Book!' Reading behind Bars." In *Interrupted Life: Experiences of Incarcerated Women in the United States*, edited by Rickie Solinger, Paula C. Johnson, Martha L. Raimon, Tina Reynolds, and Ruby Tapia. Berkeley: University of California Press, 2010.
Tate, Claudia. "Allegories of Black Female Desire; or, Rereading Nineteenth Century Sentimental Narratives of Black Female Authority." In *Changing Our Own Words*, edited by Cheryl A. Wall. New Brunswick, N.J.: Rutgers University Press, 1989.
Taylor, Ula Yvette. *The Promise of Patriarchy: Women and the Nation of Islam*. Chapel Hill: University of North Carolina Press, 2018.
———. *The Veiled Garvey: The Life and Times of Amy Jacques Garvey*. Chapel Hill: University of North Carolina Press, 2003.
Tinson, Christopher M. *Radical Intellect: Liberator Magazine and Black Activism in the 1960s*. Chapel Hill: University of North Carolina Press, 2017.
Toward a Revolutionary Socialist Guyana: Principles and Programs of the Working People's Alliance. Pamphlet, n.d.*
A Trust Betrayed: Namibia. United Nations, 1974.*
Turner, Joyce Moore. *Caribbean Crusaders in Harlem*. Urbana: University of Illinois Press, 2005.
Tyson, Cicely. *Just as I Am*. New York: Harper Collins, 2021.
Tyson, Timothy B. *The Blood of Emmett Till*. New York: Simon & Schuster, 2017.
———. *Radio Free Dixie: Robert F. Williams and the Roots of Black Power*. Chapel Hill: University of North Carolina Press, 1999.
Umoja, Akinyele. *We Will Shoot Back: Armed Resistance in the Mississippi Freedom Movement*. New York: New York University Press, 2013.
United Nations Council for Namibia. Published by the United Nations Department of Public Information.*

Walker, David. *David Walker's Appeal to the Coloured Citizens of the World*. Edited by Peter P. Hinks. University Park: Pennsylvania State University Press, 2000.
Walker, Thomas. *Nicaragua in Revolution*. New York: Praeger, 1982.
Washington, Booker T. *Up from Slavery: An Autobiography of Booker T. Washington*. New York: Bantam, Doubleday, Doran, 1929.*
Weatherwax, John M. *Ancient Africa*. ASALH Press, n.d.*
Webb, Constance. *Not without Love: Memoirs*. Hanover, N.H.: Dartmouth College, 2003.
———. *Special Delivery: The Letters of C. L. R. James to Constance Webb, 1939–1948*. Hoboken, N.J.: Blackwell, 1995.
Weglyn, Michi. *Years of Infamy: The Untold Story of America's Concentration Camps*. New York: Morrow Quill, 1976.*
Weiner, Tim. *Enemies: A History of the FBI*. New York: Random House, 2013.
Wells, Ida B. *A Red Record from Selected Works of Ida B. Wells*. Edited by Trudier Harris. New York: Oxford University Press, 1991.
White, Deborah Gray. *Ar'n't I a Woman? Female Slaves in the Plantation South*. New York: Norton, 1985.
Wiggam, Albert Edward. *The Fruit of the Family Tree*. Indianapolis: Bobbs-Merrill, 1924.
Williams, Gary. *U.S.-Grenada Relations: Revolution and Intervention in the Backyard*. New York: Palgrave, 2007.
Williams, Heather Andrea. *Self-Taught: African American Education in Slavery and Freedom*. Chapel Hill: University of North Carolina Press, 2005.
Williams, John A. *Captain Blackman*. Minneapolis: Coffee House, 1972, 1988, 2000.
Williams, Robert F. *Negroes with Guns*. New York: Marzani & Munsell, 1962.*
Woods, Jeff. *Black Struggle, Red Scare: Segregation and Anti-Communism in the South, 1948–1968*. Baton Rouge: Louisiana State University Press, 2003.
Wright, Charles H. *Robeson: Labor's Forgotten Champion*. Detroit: Balamp, 1975.
Young, Cynthia A. *Soul Power: Culture, Radicalism, and the Making of a U.S. Third World Left*. Durham: Duke University Press, 2006.
Zedong, Mao. *Quotations from Chairman Mao Tse Tung [Little Red Book]*. Peking: Foreign Language, 1st ed., 1966.*
———. *Statement Calling on the People of the World to Unite to Oppose Racial Discrimination by U.S. Imperialism and Support the American Negroes in Their Struggle against Racial Discrimination*. Peking: Foreign Languages, 1964.*
Zinn, Howard. *Albany: A Study in National Responsibility*. Southern Regional Council, 1962.*

Manuscript Collections, Archival Documents, FBI Files, Correspondence, Interviews

"Activities: The Workers World Party, Both by Itself and through Its Youth Arm. Youth Against War and Fascism." Workers World Party Folder 1959–1969, box 571, folder 9, JBMP.
Adult Leadership Here Is Highlander. 4/57, vol. 5, no. 10, box 3035, Highlander Folder 1959–1965, box 3027–3035, CABP.
"Africa: Toms Toms and Uncle Toms." *Crusader*, 8/27/60, MMP.
African American Committee in Defense of the Congo leaflet. Box 2, folder 2-2, MMP.

"The Afro American New Year's Party—The 1964 Year of Rededication." Monroe Defense Committee, box 1, folders 1–9, MMP.
"Agrarian." Crusader, 1960, MMP.
American Committee on Africa and the Africa Fund. "Reception Honoring Oliver R. Tambo, President, African National Congress," n.d. [1987].*
American Security Council. "Revolutionary Action Movement." 10/12/64, RAM, folder 8, box 482, RAM Folder 1963–1966, JBMP.
Anderson, Charles. "Forecast Storm." 1963, MMP.
———. Letter to Mae Mallory, 5/15/63, MMP.
———. Letter to Robert Williams, 5/29/62, RFWP.
"Announcing Grand Opening of the Garvey International Library and Educational Institution." Flyer, 8/16/59.*
"The Anti-Vietnam Agitation and the Teach-In Movement: The Problem of Communist Infiltration and Exploitation, A Staff Study Prepared for the Subcommittee to Investigate the Administration of the Internal Security Act and Other Internal Security Laws to the Committee on the Judiciary United States Senate." 10/22/65, 211, box 587, YAWF Folder 1963–1965, JBMP.
Aoki, Richard Matsui. FBI, 1962–1969, FBIRTV. https://vault.fbi.gov/richard-m.-aoki.
"Application Blank." Workshops on Citizenship and Integration. 1958, HRAEC.
"Application for Highlander Youth Project July 6–August 16, 1960." HRAEC.
Asato, Linda. "Third World Harvest Brigade Visits Nicaragua." *Unity Newspaper*, 1/31/86, Ventana Cultural Workers in Solidarity with Nicaragua Collection, box 3, tam. 121, TLRWLA.
"At Louisiana Hearing: Ex-Red Brands NAACP as Vehicle for Communism." *Citizens' Council* 2, no. 7, 4/57, 1, 3, LSUSC.
"Audrey Seniors, a Member of the Dec. 18 La Lima Brigade." *Brigadista Bulletin: A Newsletter of the North American Brigades* 14 (3/85), 4, TLRWLA.*
"Audrey Seniors to Promote the Project." *Brigadista Bulletin: A Newsletter of the North American Brigades* 16 (6/85), 5, TLRWLA.
Austin, Columbus A., Sr. "Marcus Auberlius Garvey, a Condensed Biographical Sketch of the Black Moses." A Documentary Works and Aims of the United African Nationalist Movement, 1958.*
Baldwin, James. "A Personal Appeal from James Baldwin February 1, 1964." Ephemera on the Monroe Defendants, NNC.
Ballan, Dorothy. Letters to Clarence Seniors, 10/5/64, 11/6/64, 11/18/64.*
———. Letter to Keith Althaus, Hamilton College, 10/5/64.*
"Benefit Performance." Ticket number 395, box 2, Crusaders for Freedom Folder, CFF, MMP.
"Benefit Performance by Abbey Lincoln, Max Roach, Ossie Davis, Charles Mingus at the Jazz Gallery 8th Street Near 1st Avenue, Sunday May 7th 1961." Program, Crusaders for Freedom NYC 1960–1961, folder 2-10, MMP.
Bertrand Russell's endorsement. 6/2/63, part 2, box 16, folder 49, HGP.*
Black America. November/December 1963, 2.*
Black America. Fall 1964, box 482, RAM Folder 1963–1966, JBMP.
"Black American Community in Tanzania." FBI, 6/17/74, Julian Ellison, Owusu Sudakai, Muhammed Ahmad, Irving Davis, Muhammad Kenyata, and Imamu Baraka, FOIA.

Black Panther 10 Point Program. *The Black Panther*, Special Collections and University Archives, Virginia Tech University.
Blanchfield, Jim. Letter to Clarence Seniors, 9/23/64.*
Bletter, Gloria. Letter to Mae Mallory and Clarence Seniors, 9/21/64.*
Brown, Oscar, Max Roach, and Abbey Lincoln. *We Insist Freedom Now Suite*. Candid Records, 1960.*
By Memorial Trustees. "Medical Staff Privileges of Dr. Perry Are Revoked." [1957,] UCHR.
"Call for Investigation of the Murders of Pierre Mulele, and Lumumba." African American Committee in Defense of the Congo, box 2, folder 2, MMP.
Canton, Calvin. "Black Studies in Sept. 1969." *Statesman*, 4/15/69, 3, SUNYSBA.
Carawan, Guy. "'An Exciting Singer,' Exclusive Management Paul Endicott." Flyer, HRAEC.
Carmichael, Stokely. FBI, 1964–1966, FBIRTV. https://vault.fbi.gov/Stokely%20 Carmichael.
Castro, Fidel. *Declaration of Havana*, 9/2/60 (Published by the 26th of July Movement of the United States).*
———. "Fidel Castro Speaks to the Children." *Crusader*, 8/6/60, 8/20/60, 8/27/60, 9/17/60, MMP.
———. "Fidel Castro Speaks to the Cuban People." *Crusader*, 12/17/60, MMP.
———. "Fidel Castro Speaks with the People of Cuba." *Crusader*, 9/24/60, MMP.
———. "Our Party Reflects Our Country's Recent History: Our Country's Recent History Report by Commandant Fidel Castro, Closing the Ceremony of Presentation of the Central Committee of the Communist Party of Cuba at the Chaplin Theatre in Havana, the 3rd of October 1965." Ediciones en Colores, Havana, 1965.*
———. "Speech at the United Nations, General Assembly Session, 9/26/60." Fair Play for Cuba Committee, 1960.*
———. "Speech Pronounced by the Commander in Chief Fidel Castro Ruz, First Secretary of the Central Committee of the Community Party of Cuba and Prime Minister of the Revolutionary Government, at the Inauguration of the 'José Martí' Pioneer Camp. Tarara, July 20, 1975, 'Year of the First Congress.'" http://www.cuba.cu/gobierno/discursos/1975/esp/f200775e.html.
"Celebrate MARCUS GARVEY DAY." Flyer, 1959.*
"Ciudad Militar (Camp Columbia), Quemados de Marianao." Circa 1930–1950, University of Virginia Digital Collection, https://search.lib.virginia.edu/catalog/uva-lib:2231190.
"Clippings." In Mallory, *Letters from Prison*.
"Come to the 'Freedom Now' Picnic in Honor of Mae Mallory." Flyer, 7/14/63, Youngstown Ohio Organizations 1961–1963, box 2, folder 2-26, MMP.
Committee for a Free Grenada Newsletter. 2/84, 4/84 (vol. 2, no. 1), 9/84 (vol. 2, no. 2).*
Committee to Aid the Monroe Defendants. FBI, 1962, reel 16, reel 25, RFWP.
———. A. Seniors FBI, Appendix Committee to Aid the Monroe Defendants, 3/28/65, FOIA.
———. FBI, 1961–1963, 1, 11/1/61, 1, 4/30/62, "Memorandum," 1–2, 9/13/61, 4/30/62, 5/2/62, RFWP.
Committee to Combat Racial Injustice. "Committee Takes Steps to Free Children in Carolina Kissing Case." 12/19/58, RFWP, HRAEC.

———. "Facts on Cases in Monroe, N.C." [1958], RFWP, HRAEC.
———. "Facts on Cases in Monroe, N.C., 'Kissing Case.'" [1958], RFWP, HRAEC.
———. "Justice." 12/18/58, RFWP, HRAEC.
———. "Press Conference on Carolina Kissing Case." 12/29/58, RFWP, HRAEC.
———. "Statement by Conrad Lynn on Dec. 31, 1958 Press Conference." 12/31/58, RFWP, HRAEC.
———. "Statement by Robert F. Williams on Dec. 31, 1958 Press Conference." 12/31/58, RFWP, HRAEC.
———. "Synopsis of the Events in Monroe, N.C." RFWP, HRAEC.
"Community Services and Segregation Workshop, Highlander Folk School." 5/17-29/59, HRAEC.
"Communist Activities Paul Robeson, American Committee to Save Refugees United American Spanish Aid Committee." San Antonio, Texas, 3/16/42, 4-5, part 1A, FBIHQ file 100, FOIA.
"Concrete Tanks used by Both Camp Columbia and Mariano in Havana Cuba." 1900, MLMDC, https://digitalcollections.library.miami.edu/digital/collection/cubanphotos/id/7631/rec/1.
"Congressional Record Extensions of Remarks—RAM." 2/12/68, E706, RAM, JBMP.
Congressional Record. House, 5/10/65, 9644, Workers World Party Folder 1959-1969, Matthews box 571, folder 9, JBMP.
Cooks, Carlos A. *The Street Speaker.* Vol. 1, no. 3, Freedomarchives.org, http://www.freedomarchives.org/Documents/Finder/DOC32_scans/32.Various.BLM.Street.Speaker.1956.pdf.
"Crusaders Association for Relief and Enlightenment Will Meet Sunday April 23rd." *Crusader,* 4/15/61, MMP.
Crusaders for Freedom. Press Release. Harlem, NYC, 5/17/61, MMP.
Crusaders for Freedom NYC. "Passive Resistance Is a Fraud. Now Is the Time to Strike Back." 1960-1961, folder 2-10, CFF, MMP.
"Crusaders for Freedom Present a Benefit Performance for Robert F. Williams, President of the Monroe N.C. Chapter." Flyer, box 2, Crusaders for Freedom Folder, MMP.
"Cuba, a Declaration of Conscience." Signed by Nanny Murrell, Lonnie Cross, Clarence Seniors and others. Pioneer Publishers, 6/61.*
Daniels, Ron. Memorandum to Audrey Seniors, "Separation Package." 2/9/95.*
"Deacons for Defense and Justice Defenders of the Oppressed." Flyer, 1963, Buffalo, N.Y. Organization, folder 2-7, MMP.
"Deacons for Defense and Justice Defenders of the Oppressed." Flyer, n.d. [1965], Buffalo, N.Y. Organization, folder 2-7, MMP.
Deacons for Defense FBI Files. RFWP.
"Dear Friends, In June the Nicaragua Exchange Will Close." *Brigadista Bulletin: A Newsletter of the North American Brigades* 33 (5/87), 1-4, TLRWLA.
"Dear Political Rights Defense Fund Supporter." Flyer, 7/22/75, RFWP.
Diderich, Paul. Letter to Harry C. Boyte, 9/24/61, Correspondence Folder 1961-1963, BFP.
Doc to Rob Williams. 10/5/61, reel 1, RFWP.
"Dominican Liberation Movement's 'Appeal to Human Rights.'" *Crusader,* 7/17/61, HRAEC, RFWP, MMP, HGP.

"Don't Let Vietnam Become Another Korea." Youth Against War and Fascism, n.d. [1964], 1963–1965, folders 3–5, box 587, JBMP.
Dostal, Ted. Letter to Clarence and Audrey Seniors, n.d. [1964].*
———. Letter to Clarence Seniors, n.d. [10/64].*
"Downtown Community School." Norman Studer Papers, M.E., SUNYSBA.
"Dr. Albert E. Perry, Jr. (1921–1972)." Obituary, UCHR.
Du Bois, W. E. B. FBI, 1942–1960, FBIRTV. https://vault.fbi.gov/
Dubuclet, Doris Proctor. Interviewed by Paula Marie Seniors, New Orleans and phone interviews, 2006, 2011, 2019–2020.
Edelman, Mildred McAdory. Oral History Project Interview 1, TLRWLA.
"Editorial Staff Audrey Seniors." *Partisan* 3, no. 2 (Fall 1967): 1–2, Youth against War and Fascism folder 2, 1966–1967, JBMP.
"Ethel Azalea Johnson Obituary, The Family Program." n.d. [1985], Rhea Lathan. Florida State University.*
"Ethel Johnson." Obituary, news clipping, 1985, UCHR.
Evers, Medgar. FBI, 1963–1964, FBIRTV. https://vault.fbi.gov/Medgar%20Evers.
"The Faculty of the Joseph S. Clark Senior High School Requests the Honor of Your Presence at the Senior Prom." Audrey Seniors, "My Memory Book," 5/24/58, PMSC.
"FBI Alert." *Brigadista Bulletin: A Newsletter of the North American Brigades* 13 (2/85), 5, TLRWLA.
"FBI Update." *Brigadista Bulletin: A Newsletter of the North American Brigades*, 15, 5/85, TLRWLA.
"Fifth Annual Luncheon Honoring 'Woman of the Year' Mrs. Septima Poinsette Clark, and 'Man of the Year' Dr. Donald Szontha Harrington, Waldorf Astoria." Utility Club, 6/4/60, 1–2, 8.*
Flynn, Elizabeth Gurley. "Horizons of the Future for a Socialist America." Communist Party, 1959.*
Foreman, James. Letter to Robert Williams, 8/3/69, RFWP.
"Free Political Prisoners." Youth against War and Fascism folder 2, 1966–1967, JBMP.
"FREED ON BOND APRIL 1963." Monroe Defense Committee, 5/31/63, box 1, folder 1–9, MMP.
"Freedom Fighters, Resolution Passed at the Northern Negro Grass Roots Leadership Conference." Detroit, November 9–10, 1963, box 2, folder 2–19, MMP.
Freedom Riders. FBI, 1961–1962, FBIRTV. https://vault.fbi.gov/freedom-riders.
Friedman, Jon. "Letter to the Editor: The Times Have Changed." *Statesman*, 8/27/2017, SUNYSBA.
"Front Groups Committee against War and Fascism." Cleveland, Ohio, Youngstown, Ohio, Workers World Party Folder 1959–1969, box 571, folder 9, JBMP.
Gibbs, Joan. Interviewed by Paula Marie Seniors, New York, 2019–2021.
Golden, Harold. Letters to Arthur Robinson, 6/16/65, 7/16/65, part 2, box 16, folder 16:50, HGP.
Grattan, Wilbur. Letter to Robert Williams, 3/13/67, RFWP.
Green, Berta. "Committee to Aid the Monroe Defendants." 11/61, Committee to Aid the Monroe Defendants folder, NNC.
———. "Committee to Combat Racial Injustice, Detroit Michigan, Fact Sheet on the Kissing Case." N.d. [1958], MSA.

———. "Summary Report on CAMD." 4/1/64, 1, MSA.
———. Letter to Conrad Lynn, 5/11/63, reel 1, RFWP.
"Grenada: The Struggle Continues." 3/17/84, Hunter College.*
"Group Tour of Havana." *Crusader*, 10/22/60, 5, box 1, Crusader 1960–1965, MMP.
Haffner, Walter S. Letters to Robert Williams, 5/24/62, 8/1/62, RFWP.
———. Letter to Robert Williams, 12/22/65.*
Harlem Education History Project. "Wadleigh High School and Junior High School." https://educatingharlem.cdrs.columbia.edu/omeka/wad.
———. "Wadleigh Year Books." http://educatingharlem.cdrs.columbia.edu/omeka/wad_yb.
Hart, Carla. Letter to Harry Golden, [1964 or 1965], part 2, box 16, folder 50, HGP.
Hamer, Fannie Lou. FBI, 1963, FBIRTV. https://vault.fbi.gov/fannie-lou-hamer.
"Hear Malcolm X, James Farmer, William Worthy, Bayard Rustin, Executive Secretary." N.d., HRAEC.
"Hell No We Won't Go." Photograph, PMSC.
Hicks, Calvin. "Dear Friend." 9/20/62, reel 1, RFWP.
———. "Dear Friend." Monroe Defense Committee, 10/13/61, box 346, folder 1, JBMP, BFP.
———. "Mae Mallory Released: We Will Fight the Extradition." 10/21/61, 1–2, box 346, folder 1, JBMP, BFP.
———. "Monroe Defense Committee Bulletin." 1962, folder 1, box 346, JBMP, BFP.
———. Monroe Defense Committee Flyer. 11/7/61, JBMP, BFP.
———. "An Open Letter to Sponsors, Friends, Contributors, Interested Persons, Monroe Defense Committee." Monroe Defense Committee box 346, folder 1, JBMP, BFP.
"Highlander and Education for SNCC and COFO." *Highlander Reports*, August 1961–December 1964, Highlander Folder 1959–1965, CABP.
Highlander Folk School. FBI Files, 1936–1941, FBIRTV. https://vault.fbi.gov/Highlander%20Folk%20School.
"Highlander Work Camp Raided." 1963, Highlander Reports II, August 1961–December 1964, Highlander Folder, 1959–1965, CABP.
"Hitler's Protégé." *Crusader*, 4/29/61, MMP.
Hoffman, Nancy. "African Culture Comes to SUSB." *Statesman*, 11/22/68, 5, SUNYSBA.
Hopkins, Al. Letter to Clarence Seniors, Monroe, N.C., 9/30/64.*
"Horton Visits Unions." *Highlander Fling* 2 (1/39), 2, box 3041, CABP.
International Work Brigade. Flyer, 10/10/85, box 3, tam. 121, TLRWLA.
"Introducing in This Issue Audrey Seniors." *Partisan* 1, no. 1 (4/65), FBI, UNCUV, PMSC, FOIA.*
J. Marjory Jackson Experimental Group. Graduation Program, Brooklyn, New York, 6/23/68, Ellen Cohen Collection.
"Jack, Bob, Ted, We want . . . [freedom, justice, equal rights]." Photograph, 1963.*
Jackson, Esther Cooper. "This Is My Husband: Fighter for His People, Political Refugee." National Committee to Defend Negro Leadership, 1953, 5.*
Jackson, Philip A. "Struggle for Freedom." *Statesman*, 4/15/69, 2, SUNYSBA.
Johnson, Ethel Azalea. "As Relayed to Me by a Negro Maid." *Crusader*, 10/1/60, 5, box 1, *Crusader* 1960–1965, MMP.

———. "Burn Baby Burn." *Did You Know?*, 9/4/65, MMP.
———. "C.A.R.E. News." *Crusader*, 12/23/61, NNC, HGP.
———. "Care Packages from Abroad." *Crusader*, 11/12/60, MMP.
———. "C.A.R.E. Packages Have Been Received." *Crusader*, 4/15/61, MMP.
———. "C.A.R.E. Sincerely and Gratefully Thanks the Following Groups and Individuals." *Crusader*, 1/13/62, HGP.
———. "Citizenship School Report July 1964–June 1965." King Center, Atlanta, SCLC Papers, subgroup E, series 3, box 155, folder 5.
———. "Complete Unity, Dedicated Struggle, Total Victory, for Worlds Oppressed Peoples!" *Did You Know?*, 3/66, MMP.
———. "The Continued Psychological War." *Did You Know?*, 11/65, MMP.
———. "The Crusader Newsletter." *Crusader*, 1/13/62, HGP.
———. "The Crusaders Assn. for Relief and Enlightenment (CARE) Is in Great Need of Used Clothing, etc." *Did You Know?*, 7/6/63.*
———. "Crusaders Association for Relief and Enlightenment on Behalf of the Needy Afro-Americans Wishes to the Monroe Defense Committee." *Crusader*, 11/11/61, HGP.
———. Death Certificate, State of Michigan Department of Health, 6/26/1985, Rhea Lathan. Florida State University.*
———. "A Delegation of Black Youths from Monroe Was Represented at the Largest Stop the War in Vietnam Demonstration." *Did You Know?*, 4/24/65, MMP.
———. "Did You Know?" *Crusader*, n.d., 1959, June/July 1959, 6/26/59, 7/4/59, 7/25/59, 8/59, 8/8/59, 8/15/59, 8/22/59, 9/5/59, 9/12/59, 9/19/59, RFWP, 7/11/59, HGP, NNC.
———. "Did You Know?" *Crusader*, 8/20/60, 9/17/60, 8/27/60, 9/24/60, 10/8/60, 10/22/60, 10/29/60, 12/3/60, 12/31/60, 1/21/61, 2/4/61, 4/8/61, 4/15/61, 4/29/61, 6/21/61, 6/26/61, 7/61, 7/24/61, 7/31/61, 8/61, 8/7/61, MMP, 11/11/61, NNC, HGP, 6/5/61, 1, Martin Luther King Jr. Center, Atlanta, Georgia, SCLC Papers, subgroup E, series R, box 155, folder 22.
———. *Did You Know?*, 4/18/64, 3/4/65, 4/3/65, 7/24/65, 6/5/65, 7/3/65, 9/4/65, 9/65, 1/6/66, 2/19/66, 5/66, 6/19/66, 7/19/66–8/66, 12/19/66–1/67, MMP, CABP, 11/21/64, 11/7/65, 6/66, 1/69, DRRUC, RFWP, HRAEC.
———. "Did You Know Is a Factual Report of News from Behind the Headlines Trying to Publish Bi-monthly on Contributions." *Did You Know?*, 7/6/63, MMP, RFWP, HRAEC.*
———. "Did you know that in 1965 the cost of fighting the war in Vietnam . . ." *Did You Know?*, 3/66, MMP.
———. "Ethel A. Johnson Publisher." *Did You Know?*, 6/15/63.*
———. FBI, 1959–1972, FOIA.
———. FBI, Charlotte, 1/25/63, Connections MDC, Philadelphia; Charlotte (Guy Hill Cox Jr.), Security Matter Miscellaneous, 4; (Guy Hill Cox Jr.), "Synopsis." 1, 3/20/64, Charlotte, Philadelphia, 11/8/63, 1, Charlotte, 1/26/65 (Guy Hill Cox Jr.), Connections with RAM, 3/28/66, Charlotte (Guy Hill Cox Jr.), Background, 2, 5/31/68, Charlotte (Guy Hill Cox Jr.), Johnson, Copy to Secret Service, 4, Charlotte (Guy Hill Cox Jr.), Johnson, Succinct Summary, 2, Connections with the Monroe Defense Committee, 10, FOIA, 6/27/63, Ethel Azalea Johnson, IS-Cuba, 1–4, Philadelphia, 2–4, Philadelphia, Memorandum 2–3, Connections, 2, Fort McPherson, Ga.

1/29/65 (Guy Hill Cox, Jr.), 3, "Mrs. Johnson Reports That the Monroe NAACP Had a Rifle Club," *Charlotte Observer* (8/25/63), New York, 2/27–4/10/64, "Doctor's Wall Safe Cracked," 5/6/63, Philadelphia, 2–4, IS-Cuba, 2, Philadelphia, 5/8/63, 8/26/63, Philadelphia, Charlotte, Confidential Security Matter, 1–4 (Guy Hill Cox Jr.), FOIA.

———. FBI, 1/25/65, Philadelphia, Charlotte (Guy Hill Cox Jr.), Johnson, Confidential, Security Matter, 2–4; Charlotte (Guy Hill Cox Jr.), Johnson Connections to Williams, 5–6, FOIA.

———. "The Inevitable Change." *Did You Know?*, 6/15/63.*

———. "Lest We Forget." *Did You Know?*, 6/15/63.*

———. "The Local Scene." *Did You Know?*, 11/7/64, 3, 6, DRRUC.

———. "Max Stanford Jr. and Stan Daniels Representatives of RAM." *Did You Know?*, 7/6/63.*

———. "Monroe, N.C." *Did You Know?*, 7/6/63, MMP, RFWP, HGP.*

———. "More Blacks Are Being Killed in Vietnam Than Whites, and in America Too!" *Did You Know?*, 3/66, MMP.

———. "On the Monroe Scene." *Crusader*, 12/2/61, NNC, HGP.

———. "Philadelphia, Penn." *Did You Know?*, 6/15/63.*

———. "Project Head Start." *Did You Know?*, 5/8/65, MMP.

———. "Self Defense, Is Common Sense." *Did You Know?*, 11/7/64.

———. "Thanksgiving Day, Monroe, N.C. Style." *Crusader*, 12/2/61, NNC, HGP.

———. "To Clarify!" *Did You Know?*, 6/19/65, MMP.

———. "Urban Renewal Strikes Again." *Did You Know?*, 11/7/64, RFWP.

———. "Wait till Next Election," *Did You Know?*, 4/24/65, MMP.*

Johnson, Ray, and Ethel Johnson. "Seasons Greetings." *Did You Know?*, 1966–1967, HRAEC.

"Join and Support the Black Memorial March." Flyer, Blacks Against Negative Dying, Movement for Puerto Rican Independence, Black Brotherhood Improvement Association, Dominican Youth Federation, Liberator Magazine, Harlem Unemployment Center, n.d. [1967], JBMP.

Jones, Claudia. FBI, 1951–1955, FBIRTV. https://vault.fbi.gov/Claudia%20Jones%20.

"Kennedy Did You Wait 100 Years?" Photograph, 1963.*

King, Martin Luther, Jr. FBI, 1977, FBIRTV. https://vault.fbi.gov/Martin%20Luther%20King%2C%20Jr.

"KKK Attempts to Murder Robert Williams." Flyer, 7/10/61, Crusaders for Freedom NYC 1960–1961, folder 2-10, MMP.

Kline, Jeremy. "Politics at Its Finest: A Voting Scandal at Stony Brook University." *Statesman*, 10/28/2014, SUNYSBA.

Kochiyama, Mary [Yuri]. Letter to Brothers Gaidi, Imari, and Sister Mabel Williams, 9/11/69, reel 4, RFWP.

———. Letters to Mabel Williams, 9/3/69, 9/10/69, 9/11/69, reel 4, RFWP.

———. Letter to Rob Williams, 7/15/69, reel 4, RFWP.

Kochiyama, Mary [Yuri], and Bill Kochiyama. *Did You Know?* 9/4/65, MMP.

"Labor Colleges Fight to Raise Living Standards of South." Southern Resident Labor Colleges II 1930s, Box Highlander 1930s, 3044, CABP.

Lampson, Alicia Carter. Promoter Social Chale Maslam, n.d. [1987], PMSC.

———. Letter to Audrey Proctor Seniors, 1/6/87, PMSC.

Leakes, Sylvester. Letter to Robert Williams, 1/17/63, RFWP.
Letter from Mae Mallory and the Monroe Defense Committee. Buffalo, N.Y. Organization 1963, box 2, folder 2-7, MMP.
Letter to Robert Williams from the Tanzanian Ministry of Foreign Affairs. 4/21/69, RFWP.
Levy, Charles. "The Dangers of Non-Violence." *Crusader*, 8/21/61, 5, MMP.
Levy, James E. Letter to Monroe Defense Committee and Ruthie Stone, 6/23/62.*
Liuzzo, Viola. FBI, 1965-1972, FBIRTV. https://vault.fbi.gov/Viola%20Liuzzo.
Liveright, A. A. "Here Is Highlander: Twenty-Five Years of Leadership Training for Democratic Living." *Adult Leadership Here is Highlander*, 4/2/57, Highlander Folder 1959-1965, box 3036, CABP.
Loines, Dwight. "Administrative Mentality Lacks Humanity." *Statesman*, 4/15/69, SUNYSBA.
Loines, Dwight, and Daniels, Ron. "Statement from the Union and Management of CCR." 12/8/94.*
Luce, Phillip Abbott. *Washington Report*, 4/6/66, 3, RAM, KIC Document 1, JBMP.
———. *Washington Report*, 4/11/66, 2-4, Uhuru Folder, JBMP.
———. "Is the U.S. Facing Insurrection?" *Human Events*, 3/23/68, 184, RAM, JBMP.
Lumumba, Malaika. "Mae Mallory Interview." 2/27/70, Ralphe J. Bunche Oral History Project, Moorland-Spingarn Research Center, Howard University.
Lynn, Conrad. Letter to Robert F. Williams, 4/14/62, RFWP.
"Mae Mallory and the Monroe Defense Committee." 1962-1963, folder 1-9, MMP.
"Mae Mallory Benefit Cabaret Dance, Featuring the Famous El Morocco's, Local 1330 Union Hall." 11/24/62.*
Mae Mallory Scrapbook. 1961-1965, PMSC.
Malcolm X. FBI, 1953-1964, FBIRTV. https://vault.fbi.gov/malcolm-little-malcolm-x, https://vault.fbi.gov/Malcolm%20X.
———. *Grass Roots Speech*. Paul Winley Records, 1963.*
Mallory, Mae. "Christina and the Ebony Hued Man." [1961-1963], box 1, Mae Mallory Writings, MMP.
———. "Constant Desperation." Mae Mallory Writings, 1962-1963, box 1, Folder 1-6, MMP.
———. "County." 9/1/62, box 1, Mae Mallory Writings 1-6, Diary, MMP.
———. "Cuyahoga County Jail." 5/15/62, 4, box 1, Mae Mallory Writings 1-6, MMP.
———. "Cuyahoga County Jail." Monday 6/17/62, 6-7, [Diary], Mae Mallory Writings 1-6, box 1, MMP.
———. Diary. 6/3/62, box 1, Mae Mallory Writings 1-6, 1-2, MMP.
———. Diary. Thursday 1/24/63, box 1, Mae Mallory Writings 1-6, 15, MMP.
———. Diary. N.d. [1963], box 1, Mae Mallory Writings 1-6, 1-2, MMP.
———. FBI, 1957-1976, FOIA.
———. FBI, 6/21/57, New York, 1, 4; [Redacted SA], Administrative, Affiliation Communist Party Movement, Connections Communist Party, Security Matter, 1, 4, 5, 8, 10, FOIA.
———. FBI, New York (Paul Neumann), 4/23-25/58, 5/27/59, 2, 5/29/59, Affiliation with CP Fronts, Background, Character, Miscellaneous, Alias, Security Matter, 1-6, 3-4, 13-16, 20, 28, 30, FOIA.

———. FBI, 5/6/58 to 5/20/58 (Paul J. Neumann), 1–6, 4–5, Security Matter, FOIA.
———. FBI, 3/18–5/6/60, 5/23/60, 5/28/60, 5/15/61, 6/5/61 (Robert V. Walker), Security D, FOIA.
———. FBI, 3/18/60–3/3/68, 8/31/61, 9/1/61, 9/7/61, 15–17, 8/13/62, 4, 10/7/62, 4, 12/10/70, 2/26/70, 8, 11, 3/9/72, 2–3, FOIA.
———. FBI, Charlotte, 4/2/62, Letter to Director from SAC Charlotte, FOIA.
———. FBI, Cleveland, 8/13/63, [Redacted SA], Details, Secret, 10/7/62 (CV T-2), 3/27–8/8/63, 4, [Redacted SA], Details, Secret, 10/7/62 (CV T-2), 11/23/70, 1, 12/16/71, 2, 12/27/71, 2, 1/17/73, 2/1/73, 1–2, 4/16/74, 7/8/75, FOIA.
———. FBI, Cleveland, 3/17/71 (SA George J. Steinback), Racial Matters Black Nationalist Tendency, 3, FOIA.
———. FBI, Cleveland, 4/30/73, Key Extremist, FOIA.
———. FBI, Mae Mallory, Monroe Defense Committee 1962–1963 folder 1–9, MMP, FOIA.
———. FBI, New York, 6/21/58, Mallory, Administrative, Affiliation with the Communist Movement, Evidence of Membership in the Communist Party, 1–2, 5, 8, FOIA.
———. FBI, New York, 10/11/61, Mae Mallory, "Justification for Continuation of Technical Microphone surveillance." Initial authorization and installation, 9/8/61, 9/14/61; Technical microphone surveillance, FOIA.
———. FBI, New York, Cleveland, 6/18/62 (SA Redacted), Affiliation with the Communist Movement, Evidence of Membership in the Communist Party, Security Matter, 3–4, FOIA.
———. FBI, New York, 2/8/68, 2, Mallory, Rabble Rouser Index, FOIA.
———. FBI, New York, 5/10/68, 1–2, 6/10/68, 1–2, 6/20/68, 1, 7/18/68, 1–2, 8/15/68, 1, 8/30/68, 3, 6/10/69, 1–2, FOIA.
———. FBI, New York, 3/13/70 (James L. Lott), 1–4, FOIA.
———. FBI, New York, Mallory, 11/30/70, 7, FOIA.
———. FBI, Ohio, 7/63 (SA Redacted), Mallory, Security Matter-C, 1, FOIA.
———. FBI, United States Department of Justice, Federal Bureau of Investigation, 5/10/68, FOIA.
———. United States Secret Service, 3/17/71, FOIA.
———. FBI, Washington, D.C., 2/4/72, 3, FOIA.
———. "Fidel Castro in New York 1960." *Crusader*, Crusaders for Freedom NYC, 1960–1961, folder 2-10, MMP.
———. "I Was One of the Harlem Nine." In *Letters from Prison*.
———. Letter to Charles Anderson, 5/13/63, MMP.
———. Letter to Sam and Dottie Ballan, 5/17/63, MMP.
———. Letter to Dearest Friends, 5/18/63, Mae Mallory Collection 1963, Correspondence 1–2, MMP.
———. Letter to Ellie, 6/19/63, MMP.
———. Letter to Richard Gibson, Member Editorial Board, African Revolution, 8/24/63, MMP.
———. Letter to Dick Gregory, 6/1/63, MMP.
———. Letter to Lorraine Hansberry, 6/1/63, MMP.
———. Letter to Jeanne, 6/23/63, MMP.
———. Letters to Ethel Azalea Johnson, 6/9/63, 3/29/67, MMP.

———. Letter to Jones, Mothers Alliance, 5/23/63, MMP.
———. Letter to Lilo, 5/18/63, MMP.
———. Letter to Conrad Lynn, 9/4/62, 9/9/62, reel 1, 3–4, RFWP.
———. Letter to Conrad Lynn and Robert Williams, 8/28/62, RFWP.
———. Letters to Julian Mayfield, 2/17/63, MMP, 3/12/69, 8/25/70, JMP, SCRBC.
———. Letter to Toby McCarroll, 6/9/63, MMP.
———. Letter to Mabel Williams, 10/11/62, 3/30/64, 8/17/64, 8/20/64, RFWP, 6/3/63, MMP.
———. Letter to Mabel and Rob Williams, 4/10/63, 6/9/64, reel 1, RFWP.
———. Letter to Robert Williams, 2/29/68, 7/7/68, MMP, 8/16/62, 8/28/62, 9/11/62, 8/28/67, reel 1, RFWP.
———. Letter/petition, 6/2/63, part 2, box 16, folder 49, HGP.*
———. *Letters from Prison by Mae Mallory: The Story of a Frame-up*. Monroe Defense Committee, 1963, SCRBC, JMP, WCSCRBC, RFWP.*
———. "Memo from a Monroe Jail." *Freedomways* 4, no. 2 (Spring 1964), HGP.*
———. "Mer Dear the Big-Eyed-Girl and the Rape Fantasy." Diary, 1/24/63, box 1, MMP.
———. "Militant Mass Protest Causes NAACP to Abandon Rally and Turn It Over to Robert Williams." Crusaders for Freedom NYC 1960–1961, folder 2-10, CFF, MMP.
———. "Monroe! Mississippi! Murder!" Monroe Defense Committee, 10/8/62, 2.*
———. "Of Dogs and Men." In *Letters from Prison*, 25–26.
———. "On the New York Scene." *Crusader*, 3/26/60, RFWP.
———. "Open Letter to My Many Friends in America and Those in Foreign Lands." In *Letters from Prison*.
———. "Rev Saves a Paper Hangers Soul." Diary, n.d. [1963], Mae Mallory Collection, box 1, Mae Mallory Writings 1–6, 6, MMP.
———. "Reverse Freedom Ride." N.d. [1964], part 2, box 16, folder 49, HGP.
———. "Sex, Love in Church." Diary, n.d. [1963], Mae Mallory Collection, box 1, Mae Mallory Writings 1–3, MMP.
———. "Skyscraper on 21st and Payne." Mae Mallory Writings, 1962–1963, box 1, folder 1-6, MMP.
Mallory, Mae, and Mary [Yuri] Kochiyama. "Organization of Militant Black Women." Flyer, 1964, box 2, folder 2-20, MMP.
Mallory, Pat. "Where Were We?" *Statesman*, 4/23/68, 13, SUNYSBA.
"Manifesto Crusaders for Freedom—Outline." 6/10/61, Crusaders for Freedom NYC 1960–1961, folder 2-10, MMP.
Maurice Bishop Speech. Hunter College, 6/5/83.*
Matthews, J. B. Reports on Workers World Party, 11/67, Workers World Party Folder 1959–1969, box 571, folder 9, JBMP.
McRae, Mary. Letter to Mae Mallory, Mothers Alliance Movement, Buffalo, N.Y. Organization 1963 folder 2-7, MMP.
"Meetings of Afro-Americans, 311 136th Street." 6/14/61, Afro Americans–N.Y.C. 1961, folder 2-4, MMP.
Mejia Godoy, Luis E. "Yo soy de un pueblo sencillo." *Ocarina*.*
"The Members of the Crusaders Association for Relief and Enlightenment (C.A.R.E.) wish to thank the many friends," *Crusader*, 10/21/61.

"Memo to All Board Members." Center for Constitutional Rights, 10/20/94.*
Monroe Defense Committee. FBI, 1961–1965, A. Seniors, 3/25/65, 6/29/65; C. Seniors, 3/25/65, 6/29/65; Cincinnati, 11/29/63, 1–2; Cleveland, 10/31/62, 10/2/61; Internal Security Miscellaneous, 11/28/61; Internal Security, 3/12/1964 (William W. Patton), 16, FOIA.
———. Press Release, 10/14/63, box 346, Monroe Defense Committee June 1963–1964, JBMP.
"Monroe NAACP Defies National Office Decision on Williams." 1210, n.d. [1959], Robert F. Williams Collection, Miscellaneous American Letters and Papers, box 16, JMP, WCSCRBC.
Moore, Richard B. "Committee to Present the Truth about the Name 'Negro.'" The History and Culture of African Peoples lecture series, 4/14/62.*
Moorer, Marti. "Monroe Youth Organize." Progressive Labor Pamphlet, July–August 1963, 14, Monroe Youth Action Committee folder 1, box 347, JBMP.
Morrow, E. Frederic, and Committee to Combat Racial Injustice. "White House Deplores, but Will Not Intervene in 'Carolina Kissing Case.'" 12/19/58, RFWP, HRAEC.
"Mr. Muhammad's Blueprint." N.d.*
Muhammad, Wallace Fard. FBI, 1940–1976, FBIRTV. https://vault.fbi.gov/Wallace%20Fard%20Muhammed.
Murray, Margaret James [Mrs. Booker T. Washington]. *Practical Leaflet No. 1*, n.d., Hampton University Archives.
Myerson, Tina. "Administration Examines Admission Policy." *Statesman*, 12/10/68, 5, SUNYSBA.
Nation of Islam. FBI, 1964, FBIRTV. https://vault.fbi.gov/Nation%20of%20Islam.
"National Association for the Advancement of Colored People: Committee on Branches, Roy Wilkins, Executive Secretary Complainant against Robert F. Williams." 1, Robert F. Williams Collection, Miscellaneous American Letters and Papers, box 16, WCSCRBC.
National Association for the Advancement of Colored People. "History of the New Orleans Branch, 1915–1990: 75 Years of Perseverance and Courage." N.d. [1990], Amistad Research Center, Tulane University, New Orleans, Louisiana.
———. "Introduction." Federal Bureau of Investigation, "Communist Infiltration of the National Association for the Advancement of Colored People in New Orleans Division." 3/30/48, Internal Security, reel 1, New Orleans Public Library.
"The Negro." *Freedom Fighter Newsletter*, 6/5/63.*
"Negro Ask Full Use of Recreation Facilities: NAACP Delegation Makes Demands of City Council at Tuesday Night Meeting." N.d., box 26, BFP.
"A New York Jury Convicted Two 'RAM' Negroes of Plotting to Assassinate Civil Rights Leaders Roy Wilkins and Whitney Young." *Exclusive: A Digest and Analysis of Washington Intelligence for Limited Distribution*, 6/19/68, RAM, JBMP.
"News Release August 14, 1959." HRAEC, box 3, CABP.
"News Release Mrs. Septima Clark, Director of Education at Highlander Folk School, has announced that the school will hold its workshop on Citizenship Schools on September 4th to 7th." 8/14/59, Highlander Folk School, Monteagle, Tenn., HRAEC.
"1984, a 50 años, Sandino vive." Enigrac-PE-7001, 1984.*

North Carolina Division of Community Planning, Monroe Planning Board. "Population and Economy." September 1963, digitized by State Library of North Carolina.

"Note Outlining the Manifesto of the Crusaders for Freedom." 6/10/61, Crusaders for Freedom NYC 1960–1961, folder 2-10, MMP.

"Notice!! Readers in the New York Area: Lecture on Cuba." *Crusader*, 10/29/60, MMP.

Oduba, Pat Mallory. Interviews with author, Charlottesville, Virginia, 2015, 2019–2021.

"Olatunji and His African Troupe, Lightning Hopkins, Pete Seeger Benefit Concert." Flyer, 4/29/61, CABP.

Old North State Medical Society. "Program: Sixty-Third Annual Meeting: Old North State Medical Society, Organized 1887, the Oldest Negro Medical Society in the World." Vol. 63 (6/6/50), Document no. 28-063, 14–15, 17–18, North Carolina History of Health Digital Collection, https://dc.lib.unc.edu/cdm/compoundobject/collection/nchh/id/974466/rec/5.

"On Guard, Friday June 23, 8 p.m. Tuscan Building. Sponsored by On Guard Committee for Freedom." N.d. [1961], N.Y.C. Pamphlets 1961–1965, box 2, folder 2-18, MMP.

Onyewu, Nicholas D. Ukachi. "African Students See Khrushchev in New York." *Crusader*, 10/8/60, MMP.

Oquendo, Eddie. "The American Negro." *Esquire*, 11/67, Youth against War and Fascism, 1966–1967, box 587, JBMP.

"Organizations Advocating Violence—RAM." FBI, 9/18/68, 11, RAM, JBMP.

"Patricia Mallory, Miss au Naturale, Women's Committee of the Harlem Unemployment Center. Annual Steer-B-Que Bus-Outing & Dance Booklet." 7/30/66, p. 4, box 2, folder 2-25, 1965–1966, MMP.

Patterson, Louise Thompson. FBI, 1941–1943, Digital Archives Washington State University.

Patterson, William. *Ben Davis Crusader for Negro Freedom and Socialism*. New York: New Outlook, 1967.*

Perry, Albert E., Jr., MD. Letter to Calvin Hicks, 9/30/62, RFWP.

———. Letter to Harry Boyte, 1/23/64, BFP.

———. "Provisional Executive Committee of The Committee to Aid the Monroe Defendants." 5/11/63, RFWP, MMP.

———. "A Report." 1957, Committee on Recreation and Welfare of Union County, box 28, BFP.

———. "To Parks and Recreation Commission." 6/19/57, 7/23/57, Committee on Recreation and Welfare of Union County, box 28, BFP.

———. "What Is CAMD?" Flyer, Committee to Aid the Monroe Defendants, n.d., RFWP.

"Plan Black Halls for Next Year." *Statesman*, 5/6/70, SUNYSBA.

"Por Nicaragua homenaje de los artistas Latinoamericanos." *Ocarina*, 1983.*

"*Prisoners Call Out Freedom*." Prisoners Solidarity Committee, April 1971.*

"Progress in Black Studies at S.B." *Statesman*, 4/15/69, 2, SUNYSBA.

"Protest against Nuclear War." Flyer, 3/24/63, Youth against War and Fascism, 1963–1965, box 587, JBMP.

"Purlie Victorious Benefit." Flyer, box 346, MDC folder 1, JBMP.

Quartermasters Stables, Camp Columbia, 1905–1908. Available at Merrick Library, University of Miami.

Quinn, Gerald. Letter from New York Monroe Defense Committee to Rob Williams, 10/14/61, RFWP.

W. M. Rainach, W. M. "A Special Note to Louisianans." *Citizens' Council* 2, no. 6 (3/57): 3, LSUSC.

"RAM." *Congressional Record*, 4/25/68, E3364, JBMP.

Razaf, Andy, lyricist, and Fats Waller, composer. "Black and Blue." Mills Music, 1929, SCRBC.

"Reflections on Our Struggles at Stony Brook." *Statesman*, 4/15/69, 7, SUNYSBA.

"Residential Workshop on Community Services and Segregation." 5/17–24/59, Highlander Folk School, Monteagle, Tenn., HRAEC.

Revolutionary Action Movement. FBI, Appendix RAM, "Source Stated in 5/65," RFWP.

———. FBI, 1964, 10/64, JBMP.

"Revolutionary Action Movement, FBI, Activities Directed Toward the Administration." House Committee on Internal Affairs, 3/29–5/1/73, 1056, JBMP.

"Revolutionary Action Movement Summary of Activities." FBI Report, n.d., 2/28/69, RAM, JBMP.

"RFK a RAM Target." *Human Events*, 6/15/68, 3, RAM, JBMP.

Rita to Mae Mallory, Mothers Alliance Movement, Buffalo, N.Y. Organization 1963 folder 2-7, MMP.

"Robert F. Williams, Editor of the Crusader to Speak in New York Feb. 9." *Crusader*, 2/4/61, MMP.

Robeson, Paul. FBI, 3/16/42, part 1A, FBI HQ File 100.

———. *Freedom*. 2/51–8/55, PRDA.

———. "Here's My Story." *Freedom*, 1951–1955, PRDA.

———. "If Enough People Write Washington I'll Get My Passport in a Hurry." *Freedom*, July–August 1955, PRDA.

———. "Paul Robeson's Column." *Freedom*, 11/50, PRDA.

"Robeson Pushes Passport Fight: Support Needed." *Freedom*, July–August 1955, PRDA.

Romberstein, Herbert. Memorandum to Donald T. Appell, Workers World Party Convention 1960. *Peacemaker*, 12/18/65, Workers World Party Folder 1959–1969, box 571, folder 9, JBMP.

Rustin, Bayard. FBI 1960–1969, FBIRTV. https://vault.fbi.gov/bayard-rustin.

Scott, Daryl. Telephone interview with author, spring 2022.

Scott, Harvey. Letter to Mae Mallory, Mothers Alliance Movement, Buffalo, N.Y. Organization 1963 folder 2-7, MMP.

"Senator Keating Pounds the War Drums." Flyer, Youth against War and Fascism, 1963–1965, box 587, JBMP.

Seniors, Audrey Proctor. "Audrey Seniors, Plaintiff, against Clarence Seniors, Final Judgment of Divorce (Personal Services)." 12/8/70.*

———. Audrey Seniors FBI, Activities, 7–12, 5/10/65, Appendix, Monroe Defense Committee, 7–9, 3/4/63, Monroe Defense Committee, 3/16/65, 3/6/64, 2/19/65, Appendix, Mothers Alliance, 8, 2/17/64, Workers World, Appendix, 11, 3/4/64, Appendix, RAM A, 20–21, 3/16/65, 3/6/64, 2/19/65, Appendix, Youth Against War and Fascism, 7,

5/31/68, Audrey Seniors Black Panther Membership, 3, 3/1/71, Audrey Seniors member of the Editorial Staff of the Partisan, 3, 3/1/71, "Miscellaneous Activities, RE *Did You Know?*, 6–7, 3/16/65, 5/31/68, 1, FOIA.
———. "Autobiographical Notes." n.d. [1970s–1980s], PMSC.
———. Birth certificate, 1940, PMSC.
———. "A Charlotte Widow." *Partisan*, 7/65, 10–12, UNCUV.
———. "Dear Friends . . . Third World Brigade." Nicaragua Exchange letter, n.d., TLRWLA.
———. Death certificate, 1995, PMSC.
———. FBI, 1962–1973, 1963–1965, 3/3/63, Cleveland (William W. Patton), Security Matter—WWP, 1–3, FOIA.
———. International Association of Democratic Lawyers Membership Card, n.d., PMSC.
———. Letter to Gia, 1/23/86, Nicaragua Exchange Letterhead.*
———. Letter to Pat Mallory, Pat Mallory Oduba Collection.
———. Letter to Robert Williams, 6/30/62, reel 1, 1–2, RFWP.
———. "My Memory Book." 1958, PMSC.
———. "Monroe, N.C." *Partisan*, 4/65, 5, UNCUV.
———. Nicaragua Exchange Flyer for Third World Outreach.*
———. "The Open Forum." Did You Know?, 4/18/64, MMP.
———. Résumé, n.d., PMSC.
———. "Third World Brigade Flyer." Nicaragua Exchange, 1985–1986, TLRWLA.
———. Volunteer Work Brigade Application, 1984–1985.*
Seniors, Audrey Proctor, Theresa Delgadillo, Daryll Williams, Victor Sanchez, Victor, and Amilcar Shabazz. Letter to Brigadistas, 2/23/87, PMSC.
Seniors, Audrey Proctor, Joan Gibbs, Dorothy M. Zellner, Linda Backiel, Jonathan Ned Katz, Margaret L. Ratner, and the Movement Support Network. "If an Agent Knocks: Federal Investigators and Your Rights." Educational pamphlet, Center for Constitutional Rights, photographs by Maddy Millier, March 1985, 3–5.*
Seniors, Clarence Henry. Autobiography, 1997–2010.*
———. Clarence Seniors FBI, Activities, 7–12, 5/10/65, 1959–1973, Detention Communist List.
———. "Dear Friend." 1962, MDC folder 1, box 346, JBMP, BFP.
———. Flyer to "Dear Friend." 2/1/64, part 2, box 16, folder 50, HGP.
———. Flyers to "Dear Friend." 2/9/65, 5/14/65, 8/30/65, NNC.
———. "Free Mae Mallory!" Reprinted from *Africa, Latin America, Asia Revolution*, part 2, box 16, folder 49, 11/63, HGP.*
———. "From Lynch Threat to Frame-up." [A. Seniors] 9/16/64, Ephemera on the Monroe Defendants, NNC.
———. Interviews by Paula Marie Seniors, Charlottesville, Virginia, 2007–2010, Newark, New Jersey, 2010, Greensboro, North Carolina, 2018, 2020.
———. Letter to Keith Althaus, 10/20/64.*
———. Letters to Dottie Ballan, 8/20/64, 10/18/64, 11/13/64, 6/21/65.*
———. Letter to Robert H. Beyers, 10/20/64.*
———. Letter to Marcia Guidoni, 10/64.*
———. Letter to Brian R. Keleher, Michigan State University, 10/7/64.*

———. Letter to William Lee Jr., 10/6/64.*
———. Letter to James M. Russell, 8/13/64.*
———. Letters to Mr. J. Shaver, 9/20/64, 12/16/64, NNC.
———. Letter to Richard Wiebe to arrange "a schedule of Mrs. Mallory's appearances on the West Coast," 10/20/64.*
———. Letter to Bob Wright, Civil Rights Coordinating Committee, Harvard University, 10/20/64.*
———. "Marcus Garvey." Unpublished essay, n.d. [1958 or 1959].*
———. "Missionary Sisters Visit Mae Mallory in Jail." From *Story of a Frameup*, 35–36, box 6, folder 5, JMP.
Seniors, Clarence Henry, and Audrey Proctor Seniors. "Chairman: Clarence Seniors Mallory on National Tour." Monroe Defense Committee, flyer, 9/22/64, JMP, WCSCRBC.
Sidofsky, Arthur. Letter to Clarence Seniors, 9/27/64.*
Sixteenth Street Baptist Church Bombing. FBI, 9/16/63, FBIRTV. https://vault.fbi.gov/16th%20Street%20Church%20Bombing%20.
Smith, Dee. Letter to the Monroe Defense Committee, 11/13/64.*
Socialist Workers Party, Airtel to Director, FBI, from SAC, Charlotte, Socialist Workers Party—IS-SWP, Disruption Program, reel 25, Robert Williams FBI Files, RFWP.
Socialist Workers Party, FBI, New York, 4/3/64, SWP Disruption Program.
Socialist Workers Party, FBI, New York, 4/4–10/64, 4/30/62, 1–2, 5/14/62, 1, 9/21/62, 1, 3/3/64, 1–6, 3/6/64, 1–2, 3/11/64, 3/16/64, 1–3, 1, 3/17/64, 1–4, 4/10/64, 1, 4/13/64, 4/15/64, 1–4, 6/25/64, 4/23/64, 5/4/64, 1, 2/26/65, RFWP. SWP Disruption Program, A. Seniors FBI File, 1962–1972, FOIA.
Southern Negro Youth Congress FBI Files. TLRWLA.
"South's Menace to Nation's Wage Standards Leads Liberal Group to Seek Wider, Support of Labor Colleges." *Southern Labor Colleges*, 1930, no. 1, Highlander Folk School, Monteagle, Tenn., Commonwealth College, Mena, Arkansas, 1930s, CABP.
"The Southside Voter Education Program." *Highlander Reports III*, 8/61 to 12/64, Highlander Folder 1959–1965, box 3025, CABP.
"Special Invitation from Dr. Lonnie Cross of Atlanta University." 6/7/61, Crusaders for Freedom NYC 1960–1961, folder 2-10, MMP.
Spruill, Vera. Letter to Mae Mallory, "Chicken and Chitterling Party in support of Mae." Mothers Alliance Movement, Buffalo, N.Y. Organization 1963 folder 2-7, MMP.
Stanford, Max. "Towards a Revolutionary Action Movement." *Monthly Review*, 5/64, 5–13, RAM box 482, folders 8–10, JBMP.
———. "Revolutionary Nationalism, Black Nationalism, of Just Plain Blackism. Towards Revolutionary Action Movement Manifesto." 1963, 3, NNC.
State of Ohio Cuyahoga County. "In Re Mae Mallory Petitioner-Appellant vs. Joseph M. Sweeney Sheriff of Cuyahoga County, Ohio Respondent–Appellee, in the Court of Appeals no. 25965, Brief and Assignment of Error on Behalf of Petitioner-Appellant," 5, MMP.
Steinberg, Jonathan. Letter to Clarence Seniors, 10/7/64.*
"Storehouse at Camp Columbia in Havana, Cuba." 1900–1909, MLMDC.
"Strike Settlement Agreement." 1–9, 12/8/94.*

Strong, Anna Louise. "If the U.S. Makes War on China." *Did You Know?*, 3/66, MS 0425, 1947–1967, box 3, folder 48, CABP.
———. "Report." *Did You Know?*, 4/24/65, MMP.
———. "Report on the Spreading War in Indo China." *Did You Know?*, 5/4/65, MMP.
———. "Why Isn't China Worried?" *Did You Know?*, 6/19/65, MMP.
Student Non-Violent Coordinating Committee. "Constitution (as revised in Conference, 4/29/62." CABP.
"There Will Be a Meeting at 8 p.m. in A & B Lounge, Black Dorm." *Statesman*, 9/29/70, SUNYSBA.
"Third World Brigade." *Brigadista Bulletin: A Newsletter of the North American Brigades* 22 (1/86), 2, TLRWLA.
"Third World Brigade Co-sponsored by Afro-American Solidarity Network." *Brigadista Bulletin: A Newsletter of the North American Brigades* 18 (8/85), 3.*
"A Thumbnail Sketch." *Messenger of Allah*, 1959, Courier.*
"A Thumbnail Sketch of the Messenger, Mr. Elijah Muhammad." *Messenger of Allah*, n.d.*
"To All the Administrators at Stony Brook, From Black Students United." *Statesman*, 2/7/69, SUNYSBA.
"TWA Refuses Flight to Black Man." Flyer, RFWP.
"United Freedom Movement." Ohio Historical Society.*
"Unity." *Crusader*, 10/21/61.
Vogel, Eddie. "Hell No We Won't Go—Joel Meyers." Youth against War and Fascism folder 1968, JBMP.
"Volunteer Work Brigades to Nicaragua." Flyer, n.d. [1984–1985], box 3, TLRWLA.*
"We Will, Education for Integration in Our Residence Sessions, in Our Field Program, in Our Community." *Highlander Reports*, *Highlander Reports* 2, 7/56, Highlander Folder 1959–1965, box 3032, CABP.
Webb, Constance. "Behind the Iron Curtain the Community Speaks." 1211, Robert F. Williams Collection, Miscellaneous American Letters and Papers, box 16, WCSCRBC.
Weber, Edward. Letter to Mrs. Johnson, 10/20/61, RFWP.
Weissman, Ernie. Letter to Clarence Seniors, 11/9/64.*
———. Letter to Maryann Weissman, 10/64.*
Weissman, George Lavan. FBI, 4/14/64, box 1, folder 4, GLWP.
———. *The Monroe Story*. N.d. [1961, 1962], box 1, folder 35, GLWP.
———. "Statement by George L. Weissman." 2/26/64, box 1, folder 35, 1–2, GLWP.
"Welcome to Ujamaa!" [Ujamaa Residential College], https://cornell.campusgroups.com/urc/home/.
Wheeldon, B. M. "A Woman Looks at New China." *Did You Know?*, 6/19/65, 7/24/65, 9/4/65, MMP.
"White Bus Driver Attacks Leola Triplet." Letter to Alexander Pierre Tureaud, 6/13/45, series IV, APTP.
"Whites Assaulting Black People." Letter to Alexander Pierre Tureaud, 9/18/49, series IV, APTP.
White Rose Mission and Industrial Association. "An Appeal to Our Friends." 4/6/10, White Rose Mission and Industrial Association Collection, SCMS 565, SCRBC.

"Wilbur Grattan." Black Panther Party, Cleveland, 1967–1973. 12/22/69, Department of Justice, Cleveland File, FBI, Kansas State University.

"Wilbur Grattan." *Congressional Record*, 1/6/69.

"Wilbur Grattan." "Establishing a National Commission on the Causes and Prevention of Violence," White House Executive Order 11412, 6/30/68.

"Wilbur Grattan." "Hearings, Reports and Prints of the House Committee on Internal Security." Vol. 1, 1969, 4373, vol. 5, 1969–1973, 1970, 5013, 1973, 1053, 1054, 1056, 1058, 6/25/73, 6/25/73, 1056.

"Wilbur Grattan." Montgomery, Alabama, Selma, Alabama, 1/29/31, *Fugitives Wanted by Police*, vol. 2, no. 4, U.S. Bureau of Investigation, J. Edgar Hoover, Director, Washington, D.C., 4/1/33, 30.

"Wilbur Grattan, Revolutionary Activities Directed toward the Administration," House Committee on Internal Affairs, 3/29–5/1/73.

"Wilbur Grattan, Riots, Civil and Criminal Disorders." Committee on Government Operations, Permanent Sub-Committee on Investigations, 1969.

Williams, Robert F. "Bohemia Freedom Struggle in the Free World Part I." 1–7, RFWP.

———. "Bohemia Part II: Freedom Struggle in the Free World." RFWP.

———. *Crusader*, 8/63, 7, part 2, box 62, folder 26, HGP.

———. "The Cry of Death." *Crusader*, 8/13/60, MMP.

———. "Cuba." *Crusader*, 8/20/60, MMP.

———. "Cuba and the Negro." *Crusader*, 8/27/60, MMP.

———. "Dear Friends, My Recent Trips to Cuba." *Crusader*, 10/10/60, MMP.

———. FBI, reel 16, RFWP, 1961–1965 (Detention Communist List), reel 25, 4/10/64, 4/15/64, Airtel to Director, Charlotte, Disruption Program, 2/13/62, Charlotte, 2/21/62, "Committee to Aid the Monroe Defendants, 5/14/62, Disruption Program Memo, Memo to the Director of the FBI, 3/11/64, 2, 5/1/62, Mr. Belmont, A. Rosen, Williams, New York, Williams, Socialists Workers Party, Disruption, Memo to the Director of the FBI 3/11/64, 2, Reel 25, New York, Robert Williams, Socialist Workers Party IS-SWP Disruption Program, 9/25/61, "Robert Franklin Williams Unlawful Flight to Avoid Prosecution," 10/12/61, Williams to Mr. W. C. [Redacted], from Mr. F. J. Baumgardner, RFWP; FBI, 9/11/61, 9/20/61, 9/21/61, 9/22/61, RFWP; "Public Statements and Speeches of Robert Franklin Williams," 12–14, 7/10/61, copy of "From Yankee Slavery to Cuban Freedom," 10/27/61, WCSCRBC.

———. "Hands across the Mason-Dixon." *Crusader*, 5/62, RFWP.

———. "Join the Operation Big Switch! All American Crusade for Freedom." *Crusader*, 8/21/61, MMP.

———. "Letter from Rob." *Crusader*, 11/21/64, HRAEC.

———. Letter to *Crusader*, 10/10/60, 5, box 1, *Crusader*, 1960–1965, MMP.

———. Letter to Harry Golden, n.d., RFWP.

———. Letter to Hon. Frank Kowalski, U.S. House of Representatives, 3/8/62, RFWP.

———. Letter to Mr. Blaine M. Madison, Commissioner, State Board of Correction and Training, Raleigh, North Carolina, 1/3/59, RFWP, HRAEC.

———. Letter to Mae Mallory, n.d. [1961–1963], RFWP.

———. Letters to Mae Mallory, 2/14/69, 4/21/69, RFWP.

———. Letter to Mae Mallory, "Exile Is Hell." N.d. [1961–1963], RFWP.

———. Letter to Hon. Robert C. N. Nix, U.S. House of Representatives, 3/8/62, RFWP.

———. Letter to Primer Congreso Nacional A.J.R., 1962, RFWP.
———. Letter to Constance Webb, 12/19/61, RFWP.
———. "Neo Barbarism." n.d., 5, RFWP.
———. "1957: The Swimming Pool Showdown." *Southern Exposure* 3, no. 2 (1980): 70, NNC.
———. "On the Monroe Scene." *Crusader*, 1962, RFWP.
———. Press Conference Request, n.d., RFWP.
———. Press Releases, 2/23/62, 7/6/62, 10/16/62, RFWP.
———. "Press Release—Birmingham 16th Street Church Bombing, Murder of Medgar Evers, Civil Rights Bill." 1963, RFWP.
———. Press Release, Havana, Cuba, n.d., RFWP.
———. Press Releases, Havana, Cuba, 5/7/63, 2/29/64, 4/9/64, RFWP.
———. "Protest the Ban Press Release." 1964, RFWP.
———. "Radio Free Dixie—On the Air." *Crusader*, 10/62–11/62, 2, 8/63, 6–7, HGP.
———. "Radio Free Dixie Transcript on Mae Mallory and Monroe." 11/9/62, 12/28/62, 3/1/63, 3/5/63, 3/8/63, 3/15/63, 3/22/63, 3/29/63, 4/12/63, 4/26/63, 5/3/63, 1/10/64, 1/17/64, 1/24/64, 2/7/64, 2/24/64, RFWP.
———. "Robert Williams President of the Union County, N.C. NAACP." Document 1, 2, n.d. [1959], Miscellaneous American Letters and Papers, box 16, WCSCRBC.
———. "See Cuba for Yourself." *Crusader*, 10/6/60, MMP.
———. "Sierra Maestra: The Face of Cuba." Reprinted from *Lunes de revolución* in *Crusader*, 8/13/60, HRAEC.
———. "Statement of Robert F. Williams." Press release, Havana, Cuba, 1963, RFWP.
———. "Why I Am Going to Cuba." *Crusader*, 6/60, HRAEC.
Williams, Robert, and Audrey Seniors. "Monroe Defense Committee." *Did You Know?*, 11/21/64, MS OH25, box 3, folder 48, CABP.
Workable Program for Monroe, N.C. "Report Prepared by the Mayor's Advisory Committee on the Workable Program May 1960." Box 28, Racial Folder, BFP.*
"Workers World." *Peacemaker*, 12/18/65, 10/67, Workers World Party Folder 1959–1969, box 571, folder 9, JBMP.
Workers World Party. FBI, 1959–1972, 9/1/61, RFWP, A. Seniors FBI File, FOIA.
"Workshop on Integration, Highlander Folk School." [Attendees from New York City, Knoxville, Tenn., Columbia, S.C., Conway Ark., Charlotte, N.C.], June 15–21, 1957, HRAEC.
Worthy, William. "The Red Chinese American Negro." *Esquire*, 10/64, 174–175, RAM folder 8, JBMP.
Wright, Ernest. FBI, NOPL, 4/21/45.
"YAWF Forums: The Court Martial of Private Stapp." 1967, YAWF folder 2, box 571, Duke University Youth against War and Fascism, 1966–1967, JBMP.
Youngstown Ohio Organizations. 1961–1963, box 2, folder 2-26, MMP.
"Youth against War and Fascism." Youth against War and Fascism folder 2, 1966–1967, JBMP.
Youth against War and Fascism. FBI Files, 1967.
———. FBI, 1–2, 10/67, JBMP.
———. "Demonstrate to Save Mae from the KKK." Flyer, October 24, 1963, Hotel Biltmore. YAWF, 1963–1965, JBMP.

Zedong, Mao. "Report on an Investigation of the Peasant Movement in Hunan" (March 1927). In *Quotations from Chairman Mao Tse Tung*, 11–12.

———. "Statement by Comrade Mao Tse-Tung Chairman of the Central Committee of the Communist Party of China in Support of the Afro-American Struggle against Violent Repression." 4/16/68.*

Journals, Dissertations, Periodicals, Media, Microfilm, Websites

Aanerud, Rebecca. "The Legacy of White Supremacy and the Challenge of White Anti-racist Mothering." *Hypatia* 22, no. 2 (Spring 2007): 27.

"All Jim Crow Practices Abolished by Revolution." Signed by Nanny Murrell, Lonnie Cross, Clarence Seniors, and others. *Militant* 25, no. 17 (4/24/61).

"Armed Forces." *Jet*, 6/4/84.

Back, Adina. "Still Unequal: A Fiftieth Anniversary Reaction on *Brown v. Board of Education*." *Radical History Review* 90 (Fall 2004): 67–68.

Barnett, Larry D. "Anti-Miscegenation Laws." *Family Life Coordinator* 13, no. 4 (1964): 95–96.

Beckles, Colin. "Black Bookstores, Black Power, and the FBI: The Case of Drum and Spear." *Journal of Black Studies* 20, no. 2 (1996): 64–71.

Begos, Kevin, Danielle Deaver, John Railey, and Scott Sexton. *Against Their Will: North Carolina's Sterilization Program and the Campaign for Reparations*. Apalachicola, Fla.: Gray Oak Books, 2012.

Birts, Angela R. "The African American/Black Racial Tapestry: Black Adolescents' Private Independent School Experiences and Racial Identity Development." PhD diss., San Jose State University, 2017.

Black Panther, San Francisco Strike. California Newsreel, 1969.

Brooklyn Friends School. "Camilla Church Green '60 (Alumni/ac Reflections)." https://vimeo.com/236132617.

Browning, James R. "Anti-Miscegenation Laws in the United States." *Duke Bar Journal* 1, no. 1 (1951): 26–41.

"The Case of Mae Mallory." *Call and Post*, 3/30/63, 2C.

Center for Constitutional Rights. "*Salas v. United States*." Last updated 10/8/2007. https://ccrjustice.org/home/what-we-do/our-cases/salas-v-united-states.

Chambers, Veronica. "The Myth of Cinderella." *Newsweek*, 11/3/97, 78.

Clark, Steve. "The Second Assassination of Maurice Bishop." *New International: A Magazine of Marxist Politics and Theory* (1987).

Collier-Thomas, Bettye, and James Turner. "Race, Class, and Color: The African American Curse on Identity." *Journal of American Ethnic History* 14, no. 1 (1994): 5–31.

Commission on School Integration. "Public School Segregation and Integration in the North." Special issue, *Journal of Intergroup Relations* (1963).

Conger, Dylan, and Timothy Ross. "Project Confirm: An Outcome Evaluation of a Program for Children in the Child Welfare and Juvenile Systems." *Youth and Juvenile Justice* 4, no. 1 (2006): 97–115.

Corker, Niya. *Black Studies*. Niya Corker and Jean Richard Boden, producers, 2007.

"Daughters of Malcolm X and MLK Stage-Struck Duo." *Ebony*, 5/79, 166–168.

Davis, Joshua Clark. "The FBI's War on Black-Owned Bookstores." *Atlantic*, 2/19/2018.

Davis, Ossie. "Purlie Told Me!" *Freedomways*, Spring 1962, 155–159.*

DeCuir-Gunby, Jessica T., Pamela P. Martin, and Shauna M. Cooper. "African American Students in Private, Independent Schools: Parents and School Influences on Racial Identity Development." *Urban Review*, 3/2012, 113–132.

Deere, Carmen Diana, and Peter Marchetti. "The Worker-Peasant Alliance in the First Year of the Nicaraguan Agrarian Reform." *Revolutionary Nicaragua* 8, no. 2 (1981): 40–73.

"Don't Let Mae Suffer the Fate of Lumumba: Mass Freedom Rally." *Call and Post*, 3/3/62.

Dossey, Larry. "Strange Contagions: Of Laughter, Jumps, Jerks, and Mirror Neurons." *Journal of Science and Healing* 6, no. 3 (2010): 118–128.

Du Bois, Shirley Graham. "What Happened in Ghana." *Freedomways*, 1966.*

Ebrahim, G. J. "Mass Hysteria in School Children: Notes on Three Outbreaks in East Africa." *Clinical Pediatrics* 7, no. 7 (1968): 437–438.

Elder, Sean. "Why Madalyn Murray O'Hair Was the Most Hated Woman in America." *Newsweek*, 3/17/2017.

"Emmett Till." *Jet*, 9/15/55, 6–9.

"Ex-NAACP Leader Meets with Separatists in Tanzania." *Jet*, 7/11/68.

"FBI Arrests Mae Mallory." *Afro American*, 10/21/61, 1.*

Foong, Yie. "Frameup in Monroe: The Mae Mallory Story." PhD diss., Sarah Lawrence College, 2010.

Gray, Don. "Doctor's Wall Safe Cracked, N.Y. Trial Reporter Only Person Home." *Charlotte Observer*, 2/27/64, To the Director of the FBI from SAC New York, "Socialist Workers Party," FOIA.

"Grenada Revolution." https://carriacou.biz/grenada-history/the-grenada-revolution/.

"Harlem Race Riot of 1964." Britannica.com, https://www.britannica.com/event/Harlem-race-riot-of-1964.

Heinecke, Craig. "One Step Forward: African-American Married Women in the South, 1950–1960." *Journal of Interdisciplinary History* 31, no. 1 (Summer 2000): 43–62.

Hendrickson, Brett. "Metaphysical Healing and Health in the United States." *Religion Compass* 8, no. 11 (11/17/2014).

Hendrickson, Paul. "The Ladies before Rosa: Let Us Now Praise Un-famous Women." *Rhetoric and Public Affairs* 8, no. 2 (Summer 2005): 287–298.

"Herbert Daniel Daughtry." Available online at *Gale in Context Biography*.

Holmes, Tao. "The 1962 Laughter Epidemic of Tanganyika Was No Joke." Atlas Obscura, 1/15/2016, https://www.atlasobscura.com/articles/the-1962-laughter-epidemic-of-tanganyika-was-no-joke.

Hughes, Bill. "Perry Trial, State's Witness Tells of Abortion." *Charlotte News*, n.d. [1957], box 26, Clippings Folder, BFP.

Iandolo, Alessandro. "Beyond the Shoe: Rethinking Khrushchev at the Fifteenth Session of the United Nations General Assembly." *Diplomatic History* 41, no. 1 (1/1/2017): 128–154.

"J. Ernest Wilkins." Mathematicians of the African Diaspora, http://www.math.buffalo.edu/mad/PEEPS/wilkns_jearnest.html.

Kessel, Michelle, and Jessica Hopper. "Victims Speak Out about North Carolina Sterilization Program, Which Targeted Women, Young Girls and Blacks." *MSNBC*, 11/7/2011, http://rockcenter.msnbc.msn.com/news/2011/11/07/8640744-victims

-speak-out-about-north-carolina-sterilization-program-which-targeted-women-young-girls-and-blacks.

King, Wilma. "'Prematurely Knowing of Evil Things': The Sexual Abuse of African American Girls and Young Women in Slavery and Freedom." *Journal of African American History* 99, no. 3 (Summer 2014): 173–196.

Kokota, Demobly. "Episodes of Mass Hysteria in African Schools: A Study of Literature." *Malawi Medical Journal*, 9/23/2011, 74–77.

Kollman, Paul. "Generations of Catholics in Eastern Africa: A Practice-Centered Analysis of Religious Change." *Journal for the Scientific Study of Religion* 51, no. 3 (2012): 412–428.

Lancaster, Katherine. "O'Hair, Madalyn Murray (1919–1995)." Texas State Historical Association, Handbook of Texas, last updated 7/14/21. https://www.tshaonline.org/handbook/entries/ohair-madalyn-murray.

LeLoudis, James L. "Leadership and Politics in the War on Poverty: The Case of the North Carolina Fund." *Popular Government*, Spring/Summer 2003, 2–13.

Levenson, Alan T., "Congregation Brith Emeth and Rabbi Philip Horowitz." *Ohio History* 120 (2013): 118–138.

Lukata, Yakina. "The Right of Black Women to Defend Themselves against White Male Rape." T. Gathering, 1975.

Mabee, Carleton. "Margaret Mead Progressive and a 'Pilot Experiment' in Interracial Education: The Downtown Community School." *New York History* 65, no. 1 (1/84): 4–31.

"Mae Mallory 'Mistreated,' Says Group." *Call and Post*, 6/23/62.

"Mallory Case Heads for U.S. High Court." *Call and Post*, 7/7/62.

Mallory, Mae. "Letter to the Editor." *Africa, Latin America, Asia Revolution*, 11/63.*

———. "A Pan African Army." *Africa, Latin America, Asia Revolution*, 11/63.*

Marcy, Sam, Vincent Copeland, Jack Wilson, Ronald Jones, and Dorothy Flint. "Statement." *Workers World, Workers World Party and Its Front Organizations: A Study Prepared by the Minority Staff of The Committee on Internal Security*. House of Representatives, Ninety-Third Congress. Washington, D.C.: Government Printing Office, 1974.

Markle, Seth. "Book Publishers for a Pan African World: Drum and Spear Press and Tanzania's Ujamaa Ideology." In "Rethinking Pan-Africanism for the 21st Century," edited by Jonathan B. Fenderson, Anthony Ratcliff, and Christopher M. Tinson, special issue, *Black Scholar* 37, no. 4 (2008), 16–26.

Marquez, Roberto. "Grenada: History, Neo-Colonialism, and Culture in the Contemporary Caribbean." *Contribution in Black Studies: A Journal of African and Afro-American Studies* 6, no. 1 (1983): 8–9.*

Martin, Denise. "Pan African Metaphysical Epistemology: A Pentagonal Introduction." *Journal of Pan African Studies* 2, no. 3 (3/15/2008): 209–227.

Marton, Janos. "#Closerikers: The Campaign to Transform New York City's Criminal Justice System." *Fordham Urban Law Journal* 45, no. 2 (1/1/2018): 499–570.

Maryknoll Sisters of St. Dominic. "History." https://www.maryknollsisters.org/about-us/history/.

"Maurice Bishop." https://carriacou.biz/maurice-bishop/.

"Maya Angelou from Silence of Rape to Voice of Compassion. I am here. life." YouTube, https://www.youtube.com/watch?v=stAOpg71vK4.

McDuffie, Erik S. "A 'New Freedom Movement of Negro Women': Sojourning for Truth, Justice, and Human Rights during the Early Cold War." *Radical History Review* 101 (5/1/2008): 81–106.

Meier, August. "Negro Protest Movements and Organizations." *Journal of Negro Education* 32, no. 4 (Autumn 1963): 437–450.

"Misplaced Priorities: Over Incarcerate Under Educate." NAACP, Prison Policy Initiatives, April 2011, https://www.prisonpolicy.org/scans/naacp/misplaced_priorities.pdf.

Mkapa, Benjamin William. *Leadership for Growth Development and Poverty Reduction: An African Viewpoint and Experience*. Commission on Growth and Development. Washington, D.C.: International Bank for Reconstruction and Development/The World Bank on Behalf of the Commission of Growth and Development, 2008, 19–79.

Muhammad, Ozier. "Pan African Journal." *Black World/Negro Digest*, 10/74, 77.*

Nelson, Stanley. *Freedom Riders*. American Experience, PBS, 2011.

Nnadi, Chioma. "How One Photographer Captured the Soul of the Black Is Beautiful Movement." *Vogue*, 2/2/2018.

"North Carolina Leader Loses Job." *Southern Patriot*, 1/66, CABP.

Oakley, Christopher Arris. "'When Carolina Indians Went on the Warpath': Showdown at Hayes Pond, the Media, the Klan, and the Lumbees of North Carolina Testimonials from the Fayetteville Observer Fiftieth Anniversary Commemoration of the Klan-Lumbee Clash." *Southern Cultures* 14, no. 4 (Winter 2008): 55–84.

"$1 Million Suits Hits Segregated Atlanta Courts." *Jet*, 5/12/60.*

Panton, Rachel. "Transformative Learning and the Road to Maternal Leadership." *New Directions for Teaching and Learning* 147 (2016): 19–25.

Peck, Raoul. *Lumumba*. Zeitgeist Video, 2000.

———. *Lumumba, la mort d'un prophète*. Velvet Film, 1990; California Newsreel, 1992.

Pérez, José. "Fidel Vive! A Cuban American Activist Reflects on El Comandante." *Root*, 12/4/2016.

Perry-Burney, Gwendolyn, Norma D. Thomas, and Traci L. McDonald. "Rural Child Sexual Abuse in the African American Church Community: A Forbidden Topic." *Journal of Human Behavior in the Social Environment* 24, no. 8 (November 2014): 986–995.

Poussaint, Alvin. "The Stresses of the White Female Worker in the Civil Rights Movement in the South." *American Journal of Psychiatry* 123, no. 4 (10/66): 401–407.

Pressman, Gabe. "Interview: Attallah Shabazz Talks about Her Father, Malcolm X." Channel 4 News, 2/20/2005.

Price, Susan. "Alumni Profile: Camilla Church Green '60." Brooklyn Friends School, 8/18/2015. https://brooklynfriends.org/camilla-church-greene-60/.

Project NIA. Chicago Youth Justice Data Project. 2010. http://www.chicagoyouthjustice.com/.

"Public Rally: Come and Hear the Facts of the Monroe, N.C. Kidnapping as Told by Mae Mallory: Courageous Mother Facing Extradition to North Carolina." *Call and Post*, 11/25/61.

"Released Documents Detail FBI Informant's Role." *Chicago Sun-Times*, 4/1/2013.

"Report from the War Zone: Namibia." *Southern Africa* 14, no. 4 (July/August 1981): 19–20.

Rivera, Carlos Alá Santiago. "Labor Relations during the Sandinista Government." *Caribbean Studies* 24, nos. 3/4 (1991): 241–265.

Roberston, Gary D. "N.C. Republicans Divided on Sterilization Payments." *Winston-Salem Journal*, 6/19/2012.

"Robert F. Williams Speaks from Peking." *Africa, Latin America, Asia Revolution* 1, no. 7 (11/63): 84–87.*

Rogo, Paula. "A Brief Understanding of Why Africans Are Hailing Castro as a Hero." *Essence*, 11/28/2016.

Ross, Vivian. "CARE Helps Blacks Help Themselves." *Charlotte Observer*, 9/5/71, UCHR.

Rowan, Carl T. "Has Paul Robeson Betrayed the Negro?" *Ebony*, 10/57, 2.*

Samad, Anthony Asadullah. "The Legacy of Fidel Castro: A Black Globalist Viewpoint." *Ebony*, 11/28/2016, 4.

Sanders, Charles. "Jail Is Hell: Mallory Moans in Cell." *Call and Post*, 9/22/62.

Schaap, Ray, and Bill Schaap. "Nicaragua under Siege: CIA's Secret War Escalates." *Covert Action Information Bulletin*, no. 18, Winter 1983.*

Semel, Susan F., and Alan R. Sadovnik. "Lessons from the Past: Individualism and Community in Three Progressive Schools." In "Education and the Liberal Communitarian Debate," edited by Dale T. Snauwaert and Paul Theobald, special issue, *Peabody Journal of Education* 70, no. 4 (Summer 1995): 55–85.

Singe, Anneliese A., Ashlee Garnett, and Dara Williams. "Resilience Strategies of African American Women Survivors of Child Abuse: A Qualitative Inquiry." *Counseling Psychologist* 41, no. 8 (2012): 1093–1124.

Shiek, Irum. *On Strike: Ethnic Studies, 1969–1999*. Center for Asian American Media, 2008.

State of North Carolina. "Welcome to the Office of Justice for Sterilization Victims." Last updated June 2014. https://ncadmin.nc.gov/about-doa/special-programs/welcome-office-justice-sterilization-victims.

"The Story of Dessie Woods." National Committee to Defend Dessie Woods, 1977, 1978.

"Talking Union with Pete Seeger." *Working USA*, 4/30/98, 66–73.

Tate, Lessie. "The Power of Pan Africanism: Tanzanian/African American Linkages, 1947–1997." PhD diss., University of Illinois, 2015.

Tatum, Beverly Daniel. "Family Life and School Experience: Factors in the Racial Identity Development of Black Youth in White Communities." *Journal of Social Issues* 60, no. 1 (2004): 117–135.

"Tom Mboya." Encyclopedia Britannica, https://www.britannica.com/biography/Tom-Mboya.

"UFM." *Encyclopedia of Cleveland History, Case Western University*, https://case.edu/ech/articles/u/united-freedom-movement-ufm.

"The Urban Exchange." *New York Magazine*, 7/5/71.

"Urges Use of Unions, Ballots in Bigot Fight." *Call and Post*, 2/11/56, 3A.

Verges, J. M. "For the Independence of the Congo." *Africa, Latin America, Asia Revolution* 1, no. 9 (1/64): 14–15.*

———. "The People's Victory in Zanzibar." *Africa, Latin America, Asia Revolution* 1, no. 9 (1964): 6–10.*

Weaver, Vesla M. "Frontlash: Race and the Development of Punitive Crime Policy." *Studies in American Political Development* 21 (Fall 2007): 230–265.

Weller, Sheila. "How the Author Timothy Tyson Found the Woman at the Center of the Emmett Till Case." *Vanity Fair*, 1/26/2017.

Wells, Veronica. "LaKeesha Walrond Used Her Childhood Sexual Abuse to Inspire a Children's Book *My Body Is Special.*" *Madamenoire*, 12/2017.

Welter, Barbara. "The Cult of True Womanhood: 1820–1860." *American Quarterly* 18, no. 2 (Summer 1966): 151–174.

Westbrook, Quinnette. "Mrs. Ruth Stone, Treasurer of the Mothers Alliance Spoke on Behalf of Welfare Recipients." *New Pittsburgh Courier*, 1/7/61, 4.

Wright, Michael Frank. "Grenada: The Events, The Future." *Contribution in Black Studies: The Black Scholar* 14, no. 6 (November/December 1983).*

Index

Abbeville/Promise Land, South Carolina, 10, 16, 20, 21, 35, 40, 42, 44, 106, 110, 239; African American women-marriage, 22; domestics, 22, 23; education, 21–22, 47, 106; enslaved Africans, 9, 10, 20, 21, 37, 40, 42, 63, 112, 163, 168, 214, 275; free Africans, 10; Ferguson Academy/Harbison College, 21; Industrial Union of Abbeville County, 21; laundresses, 22, 23; lynching, 22; mass exodus, 22, 29; motherhood in, 20–24, 60, 61; nursemaids, 23; Philadelphia (Sister City), 22, 29; Promise Land High School, 21, 22; Unions, 23; war industry jobs, 23
Abrams, Stacey, 275
Afghanistan, 282
AFL-CIO, 155
Africa. *See* anti-colonial revolutions/anti-Colonial movements
Africa, Latin America, Asia Revolution, 173
African American Committee in Defense of the Congo, 57, 234
African American freedom struggles, 34, 40
African American history books/classes, 4, 50, 105, 141, 153, 183, 287, 288
African American ministers, 17, 19, 48, 178
African American political refugees, 226
African American soldiers, 42
African American Solidarity Network, 251, 256, 257, 258, 260, 263, 264, 265, 267, 288
African American womanhood, 58, 105
African American women/Black women, 3; gendered racism, xxi, 43; "girl," 3; low-wage jobs, 212; murder of, 106; Patriarchy, xxi, 4, 61, 65, 70, 112, 113, 127, 137, 157, 159, 285;

plight of, 22, 43, 212; sexual violence, 106, 115, 287; stereotypes, 157; teachers, xx, 11, 45, 46, 47, 48, 49, 66, 67, 105, 106, 107, 120, 131, 180, 201, 232, 287; working class, 12, 83, 287. *See also* misogyny; patriarchy; rape
"African American Women in Defense of Ourselves," 269, 289
"African American Women Radical Activists," 1, 2, 61, 83, 106, 108, 191, 196, 268, 288
African Americans/Black, 35, 36
African Blood Brotherhood, 53, 72, 80; Harlem, 19; Tulsa, 19
African-centered ideology, 5
African-centered pride/self-worth/education, 35, 36, 50, 51
African labor leaders, 38
African National Congress, 269
African Nationalist Pioneer Movement, 128
African People's Party, 244
African socialism, 3, 5, 225, 226, 239, 251
African Society of Cultural Relations With Independent Africa (ASCRIA), 230
African Union, 39,
Afro American (Baltimore), 31, 111, 131, 141, 169, 170
Afro Asia, 38
Afro Asian Bookstore, 204
Afro-Cubans, 42, 46
Afro Culture Shop and Bookstore, 204, 237
Afrocentric beauty, 158
Afrocentric ideology, 16; pro-black ideology, 35
agent provocateurs, 16, 18, 94, 95, 130, 172, 226, 244, 288
Al-Azhar University (Cairo, Egypt), 50

Alabama, 19, 26, 41, 90, 112, 116, 122, 124, 159, 281
Albany Movement, 140
Alda, Alan, 176
Alderson Prison, 142, 145, 148, 160, 161
Aleutia, 247, 248, 278
Alexander, Kelly. 14
Ali, Muhammad, 126
"All I Could Do Was Cry," 17, 18
Amalgamated Local 735 (Cleveland), 173
ambassadors and diplomats, 151. *See also* Bunch, Ralph; Cook, Mercer; Show Dogs; Wharton, Clifton;
American Humanist Council (Cleveland), 174, 175
American imprisonment rates, 38; education over incarceration, 39
American Indian Movement, 214
American Legion, 11
Amsterdam News, 76, 78, 181, 234, 257, 259, 269
Angeleri, Sandra, xii, xxi, xxii
Angelou, Maya, 115, 174
Angola. *See* anti-colonial revolutions/anti-colonial movements
anti-colonial revolutions/anti-colonial movements, 30, 40, 54; Africa, 4, 16, 30, 37, 151, 152, 165, 166, 171, 179, 185, 252, 258; Algeria, 98, 166, 169; Angola, 20, 26, 30; Asia, 16, 30, 37, 151, 152, 165, 171, 179, 252, 258; Belgian Congo, 37, 39, 57, 151, 173, 226, 244; Caribbean, 4, 30, 72, 167, 256, 257, 263, 270, 271; China, 16, 30, 37, 53, 90, 98, 139, 151, 165, 169, 171, 252, 253; Chinese Revolution, 30, 40, 99, 165, 171, 190, 253; Congo, 30, 39, 40, 57, 151, 234; Cuba, 16, 37, 39, 40, 44, 131, 151, 169, 171, 172, 173, 185, 186 189, 190, 191, 252, 253, 255, 256; Institute of Science and Technology, 45; Cuban Revolution, 30, 37, 42, 43, 45, 98, 123, 124, 165 167, 168, 172, 179, 185, 190–192, 253; Dominican Republic, 37; Ghana, 109, 116, 122, 166, 169, 173, 226, 227; Grenada, 251, 252, 253, 255; Guyana, 225, 230, 244, 256; Haiti, 191; India, 38, 165; Jamaica, 256; Kenya, 30, 37, 38, 39; Latin America, 4, 16, 17, 30, 37, 124, 139, 151, 152, 165, 167, 171, 179, 186, 191, 252, 255, 257, 258; Mexico, 191; Nicaragua, 191, 251, 252, 253, 255; Puerto Rico, 191, 256; Santo Domingo, 191; Vietnam, 30, 37, 38, 42, 122, 165, 195, 210, 252, 253, 257, 263

anti-colonialism (ist), 288; ideologies, 16, 34, 37
anti-imperialism (ist), 16, 34, 54, 288
anti-intellectual, 61, 66
anti-male supremacy ideology, 69
Antioch Baptist Church Male Chorus, 180
anti-racist ideology, 16
anti-war, 4, 41, 16, 288
Aoki, Richard Matsui, 18, 94, 266
armed self-defense, 2, 12, 56, 91, 185, 276; armed self-defense guard, 15
Aruba, 270
"As Relayed to Me by a Negro Maid," "Did You Know" (1960), 23
Asa Lee. *See* Ethel Azalea Johnson
Ashford, Ron, 267
Asia. *See* anti-colonial revolutions/anti-colonial movements
Asian Americans, 170, 252
atheist, 126, 201, 248, 276, 290
Auburn Correctional Facility, 204
Austin, Texas, 11
Attucks, Crispus, 51

Backiel, Linda, 261
Baker, Ella, 73, 76, 87, 116
Baker, Lena, 19
Baldwin, James, 174
Ballan, Dottie and Sam, 33, 140, 181
Balthrope, Jacqueline, 131
Banneker, Benjamin, 51
Baraka, Amiri, 226
Bates, Daisy, 19
Benedict, Ruth, xviii
Belgian Congo. *See* anti-colonial revolutions/anti-Colonial movements
Benson, Devyn Spence, 188
Berg, Allison, 147
Bernadette Bailey Secondary School, 254
Bethany College, 182
Bevel, James, 95
Big Bust, 243–245
Big Four, 30; Farmer, James 30, 170; King Jr., Martin Luther, 2, 19, 24, 30, 78, 87, 95, 106, 117, 176, 178, 206, 207, 208, 223, 224, 234; Wilkins, Roy, 15, 30, 80, 234; Young, Whitney, 30, 234
Bishop, Maurice, 254, 255, 256, 258
Brooke, Sorrell, 176
Black America, 33
Black Beauty Aesthetic/contests (Black

aesthetic Beauty), 35, 108, 113, 128–129, 132, 133, 158, 159, 160, 194, 195, 221, 231, 248, 283
Black conservatives, 17, 19, 44
Black disenfranchisement, 209
Black elites, 19, 58
Black female body, 61
Black feminist power, 102, 249
Black identity theories, 50
Black inferiority, 36, 229, 248
Black is Beautiful, 35, 50, 159, 194, 195, 282, 283
Black Liberation Movement, 89, 230
Black male body, 17
Black male supremacy, 114, 127
Black men, 4, 14, 17, 21, 31, 36, 49, 56, 58, 72, 73, 197, 210, 211, 213, 235, 257, 265
Black militant ideology, 11
Black militants, 95, 98, 208
Black Mother's Decree, 221, 222, 279
Black Nationalism/Nationalist, 3, 12, 30, 32, 38, 40, 42, 48, 54, 73, 122, 127, 132, 177, 178, 179, 225, 226, 231, 237, 249
Black Nationalist Rebel Girl, 3, 109–136
Black Nationalist theoretical frame, 81, 92, 286
Black Nationalist tropes, 128
Black Panther Party/Black Panthers, xiv, xx, xxi, xvii, 18, 44, 66, 80, 94, 251, 253, 272, 288; New Haven, 250, 288; New York, xvii, xx, xxi, 3, 80, 99, 118, 253, 254, 256, 258, 288; provocateurs, 18, 80, 94, 95, 130, 172, 226, 244, 288; Ten Point Program, 253; Winston Salem, 196
Black Power movements, xviii, xix, 21, 35, 88, 106, 138, 159, 230, 231, 234, 235, 243, 254, 293; history, xix
Black Reconstruction in America, xix
Black resistance to trauma, 140, 141
Black Rhetoric/ Black Power Rhetoric, 35, 37
Black Student Union, xxi, 222, 223, 227
Black Students United, 223
Black studies, xiv, xvii, xviii, xx, xxi, 225; Black studies department, 223; Black studies scholarship, xix
Black teachers, 46, 180, 287; firing of, 11, 49
Black United Front, 247
Black women's body, 58, 168
Blacks. *See* African Americans
Blacks Against Negative Dying, 203
Blackwell, Marilyn S., 147
Blossburg, Alabama (1899), 19
body resistance, 63–64, 67, 140, 141
Bond, Julian II, 234

Bowe, Nannie Murrell, 276
Bowler, Jack, 51
Brigadista Bulletin, 264, 265
Brigadista Harvest, 260, 261, 262, 289
Brigadista Newsletter, 261, 262
brigadistas, 263, 268
Brooks, Bertha Mae, 11
Brown, H. Rap, 234
Brown, Oscar, 176
Brown vs. Board of Education, 1954, 11, 74
Bryant, Willie: Ossining NAACP, 204
Budapest, Marxist/Leninist (1920–1989), 38
Buffalo Challenger, 176
Bunche, Ralph, 151
"Burn, Baby Burn," 30
Burnham, Dorothy and Louis, 116, 124, 139
Burnham, Forbes, 230
Burroughs, Nannie Helen, 51
Butler, Dorothy, 131

Cade, Toni, 274
Cadillac Automobile Company, Detroit, 11, 178
Call and Post, 58, 59, 90, 95, 132, 153, 155, 157, 169, 173, 175, 178, 181, 194, 199, 200, 237
Callender, Eugene, 76, 79, 80
Cambridge, Godfrey, 176
Campbell, Grace, 19, 20
Canada, 28, 156, 162, 186,
capitalism, 195, 226, 238, 276
Carawan, Guy and Candy, xx, 124, 278; Black protest music classes, xx
CARE House, 2, 33, 44, 50; African American history courses, 50; programs, 16
Caribbean. *See* anti-colonial revolutions/anti-Colonial movements
Carmichael, Stokely, 190, 226
Carolina Laundry and Cleaners, 10
Carson, Sonny, 272
Carter, Jimmy, 260
Castro, Fidel, 39, 43, 45, 99, 106, 123, 165, 168, 171–173, 184–186, 190–192, 258, 275
Center for Constitutional Rights (CCR), xix, xxi, xxii, 256, 259, 261, 264, 269, 292, 294; firing/reinstatement of Audrey Seniors, 270–272, 281, 289. *See also* white liberals
Center for Popular Education, 254
Central America, 256, 257, 258, 263, 264
Chambers, Veronica, 285
Charlotte, North Carolina, 10, 13, 14, 41, 215, 218
Chavez, Cesar, 205

children's rights, 4
Chile, 256
China. *See* anti-colonial revolutions/anti-colonial movements
Chinese Revolution, 30, 40, 99, 165, 171, 190, 253
CIA, 94, 177, 188, 226, 234, 235, 236, 243, 244, 256, 260, 261
CIO, 105, 287
Citizen's Council, 11, 44, 105
City College of New York, 182, 214, 279, 280
City Sun, 257, 258, 259, 262, 263, 288
Civil Liberties Union (New York), xxi
civil rights/human rights, xix, 1, 2, 3, 4, 5, 48, 54, 57,64, 83, 92, 93, 105, 107, 109, 116, 124, 151, 159, 279, 181, 191, 222, 252, 266; civil rights activism, xix, 44, 47, 96, 97, 116, 124, 174, 177, 178, 247, 293; conservative activists, 19; demonstrations, 200, 202, 209; gradualism, 1. *See also* Charlotte, North Carolina; Citizenship School
Civil Rights Bill, 41
civil rights movement, 1, 4, 77, 94, 252, 292
Citizenship School, xx, 2, 33, 47
Clark, Marion, 76
Clark, Septima 47, 87,
Clarke, John Henrik, 57, 174
Clay, Mr. and Mrs., 13
Cleage, Albert B., 178, 179
Cleaver, Eldridge, 226
Clemmons, Frank, 180
Cleveland, Ohio, xiii, xv, 1, 29, 31, 59, 60, 80–86, 88–95, 96, 99, 108, 111, 130–132, 141, 155, 158, 159, 166, 167, 169, 170, 175, 177, 178, 179, 180, 181, 184, 187, 192,193, 194, 195, 196, 198, 199–206, 209, 210, 217, 225, 236, 237, 238, 239, 269, 273, 277, 288; Club One Thousand, 173; Cuyahoga County Jail, xxii, xxii, 68, 137, 141, 142, 149, 153, 155, 160, 169, 183; school desegregation, 3, 201, 287
Cleveland Press, 200
Coalition of Concerned Black Women, 252, 289
Coard, Bernard, 256
Cobb, Charles E., 2, 4
COINTELPRO, (Counter Intelligence Program), 77, 78, 79, 137, 138, 203, 288
Cold War, 71, 91, 214, 277
College of Ethnic Studies, San Francisco State College, xx, xxi

Collins, Patricia Hill, 5
colonialism, 4, 16, 30, 37, 38, 42, 54, 189, 190, 191, 194, 210, 227, 228, 230, 238, 244, 252, 253, 256, 258, 276, 279, 285, 288;
color caste code/ideology, 112, 113, 127, 157, 158, 159, 228, 230
Columbia University, 182
Colvin, Claudette, 112, 113, 116
Comintern, 38, 72
Commission on School Integration (New York), 74
Committee for a Free Grenada, 251, 256, 257, 258, 288
Committee for GI Rights, 203
Committee in Solidarity with Free Grenada, 251, 256, 288
Committee to Aid the Monroe Defendants, 18, 28, 38, 44, 80, 85–89, 91–94, 155, 189
Committee to Combat Racial Injustice, 10, 14, 15
Committee to Present the Truth About the Name 'Negro,' xx
communism, communist, 14, 44, 71, 75, 83, 92, 104–108, 116, 143, 151, 256, 277; ideology, 11
communist detention list, 12
Communist Dominated World Federation of Trade Unions. *See* World Federation of Trade Unions
Communist Party (CPUSA), 51, 71–73, 76, 78, 79, 80, 89, 99, 104, 105, 106, 107, 113, 116, 118, 119, 124, 132, 172, 175, 188, 277; betraying blacks, 72
community-based movements, 2
community feminist, 5, 10, 116, 122, 134, 221, 226, 235
Community Forum, 33
Congress of Industrial Organizations, 11, 90
Congress of Racial Equality (CORE), xiii, xviii, 18, 24, 90, 99, 170, 176, 178, 179, 182, 199, 200, 287; Brooklyn, 234
Connor, Bull, 140
Continental Insurance Company, 10
Contra War, 258, 259, 260, 261, 262, 263, 267, 268
Cook, Mercer, 151
Copeland, Vincent, 84
Corbain, Kurt, 283
Cornerstone Baptist Church, 44
Corrigan, John, 180–180, 237
Costelle, Delores, 234

386   INDEX

Council of African Affairs, 107
Crawford, Anthony, 21, 29
Creft, Hubert Henry, Jr., 48, 49, 205
Creft, Jacqueline, 256
Crosby, Emilye, 2
Cross, Lonnie, xx, 57, 84, 87, 170, 176
cross-racial solidarity, 17; class alliances, 38
Crowder, Richard (Yusef), 29, 32, 33, 53, 85, 86, 89, 91, 94, 168, 177, 179, 189, 205, 206, 287; Monroe Youth Action Committee, 177, 205
Crusader (newspaper), 2, 10, 16–20, 28, 29, 35, 37, 42, 44, 52, 78, 171, 173, 174, 182, 185, 188, 189
Crusader Family/Crusaders for Freedom, 3, 13, 26, 57, 123, 127, 170, 175
Crusaders' Association for Relief and Enlightenment (CARE), 2, 33, 42–45, 46, 57, 127, 170, 171, 175, 215, 254, 287–288
Cruse, Harold, 94
Cuba, xiv, xviii, 16, 28, 30, 34, 35, 37, 39, 40, 42, 43, 45, 53, 59, 67, 90, 98, 121, 124, 125, 184, 185, 186, 255, 256; Cubanismo, 3, 5, 30, 34, 38, 42–45, 66, 92, 99, 184, 190–192, 251, 253. *See also* anti-colonial revolutions/anti-Colonial movements
"Cult of True Womanhood," 261
cultural hegemony, 37
cultural performers, 177
Cunningham, Myrna, 259, 261
Cunningham, Noelie, 104
Cuyahoga Community College, 198, 238
Cuyahoga County Jail (Twenty-First Street and Payne/Pain), xxii, xxii, 68, 137, 141, 142, 149, 153, 155, 160, 169, 183

Da Silva, Denise Ferreira, xii, xxi, xxii
Daily Challenger, 271
"Dangers of Non-Violence," Levy, 27
Daniels, Ron, xxii, 270
Dar es Salaam, 188, 226, 241, 244, 245
dark-skinned, 112
Daughtry, Herbert, 247, 249, 279
Davies, Carole Boyce, xxii, xxiii, 137, 152, 285
Davis, Angela, 4, 144, 169, 226, 236, 242, 253
Davis, Ben, 79
Davis, Ellsworth, 131
Davis, Ossie, 57, 170, 175, 176
Deacons for Defense, 177, 234
Dee, Ruby, 170, 176
Defense Guard (Monroe), 12, 13, 15, 27

Dellinger, David, 170
Denetdale, Jennifer, xix
desegregate a swimming pool (Monroe), 12
desegregation case, 73–77, 116, 117, 119
Detroit, Michigan, 11, 42, 53, 177, 178, 203
Diaz-Cotto, Juanita, 160, 161
Dickinson, Gloria, xxii
Did You Know (newsletter), 2, 9, 10, 16–20, 23, 27, 29, 32, 33, 35, 37, 40, 41, 44, 47, 48, 51, 52, 174, 177, 206, 207, 209, 287
DiSalle, Michael V., 84, 90, 156, 169, 181, 194
disenfranchisement, 209, 251
Disruption Programs, 18, 177
Dominican Liberation Movement, "Appeal to Human Rights," 38
Dominican Republic. *See* anti-colonial revolutions/anti-Colonial movements
Dostal, Fran and Ted, 84, 90, 95, 156, 180, 181, 182, 237
Douglass, Frederick, 63, 111, 122, 248–249
dream escape writings, 137–183
DuBois, Shirley Graham, 98, 116, 138, 174
Du Bois, W. E. B., xvii, xviii, xix, 21, 51, 67, 98, 107, 116, 174, 251
Dubuclet, Doris Proctor, 96
Dunham, Katherine, 51

Ebony, 113, 195
Economic Development Conference, 236
Edelman, Millie McAdory, 73
Education, 46, 48; African American history text books, 178; Abbeville, 21–22, 47, 106; Brooklyn, 66–69; desegregation, 104; Michigan, 178; New York City, 3, 73–77; over incarceration, 39; segregation, 74; vocational, 68
educational inequalities, 50
educational initiatives, 45–52
Eisenhower, Dwight D., African American ambassadors and diplomats, 151
enslaved. *See* slaves
Eolis, Sharon Martin, 95
Esquire, 203
Ethnic Studies, xvii, xviii, xx; Ethnic Studies College, xxi; Ethnic Studies Scholarship, xix;
equality, 9, 34, 38, 39, 42, 52, 53, 65, 66, 69, 71, 75, 79, 105, 109, 138, 139, 177, 192, 195, 197, 201, 205, 226, 234, 249, 251, 255, 256, 260, 272, 281, 293

Espinoza, Luisa Amanda, 260, 262
Euclid Park Nursing Home, 238
European imperialist projects, 4
Evans, Ronald, 236
Evening News (Ghana), 173

Farmer, James, 30, 170
FBI, 13, 18, 24, 28, 29, 44, 48, 59, 71, 72, 75, 76, 80, 85, 86, 92, 93, 94, 177, 183, 188, 189, 195, 198, 206, 214, 234, 235, 236, 294
FBI files, xxiii, 95, 104, 155, 230, 266, 285, 286
FBI harassment, 96–98, 104–108, 119, 130, 261, 262, 273
FBI informants (followed by number), 238; Aoki, Richard Matsui, 18, 94, 266; CE-T, 29; CVT-1, 104; CVT-2, 97; PhT-3, 29; Spingarn, Joel Elias, 18; T-1, 32; T-4, 76, 77; T-8, 73; Withers, Ernest C., 94, 266
Ferguson, Herman, 234
Fernandes, Angela, 277
Fidelity Baptist Church, 200
Filartiga, Dolly, xxi
Fleming, Cynthia Griggs, 17, 265
Flint, Dorothy, 84
Florida International University, xxii
Florida, Jacksonville (Saint Augustine), 17, 206–208
Florida Memorial College, xxii
Florida Normal School, 207
Flynn, Elizabeth Gurley, 138, 139–140, 144, 145, 148, 156, 160, 161
Foong, Yie Yin: "Frame Up in Monroe: The Mae Mallory Story," xxii, xxiii
Ford Motor Company, 156
Foreman, James, 24, 27, 188, 236
Foundation for Community Organization, 258
Fowler, James Bonard, 41
France, 166, 240
Franklin, V. P., 18
Frazier, Garrison, 21
Frazier, Nishani, xviii, xix
Freedmen's Bureau, 46
Freedom Fighters, 10, 26, 91, 174, 181, 230; Cleveland, 29, 90, 99. 178, 179, 200, 287
Freedom Now Party, 178
Freedom Riders, Monroe, 24, 25, 26, 27, 58, 85, 88, 129, 185
Freedom School, 77, 117, 254
Freedomways, 141
Freeman, Don, 29, 91, 92, 94

friends of Mae Mallory, 98, 176, 177, 181, 197
From Uncle Tom's Cabin to The Help, xxii
Fulton, Kharen, xiii, xxi, 293,

Gabbin, Joanne, 285
Gairy, Eric, 256
Gambia, 20
Gandhi, Mahatma, 18
Gardner, Ben, 180
Garret, Ramona, 80
Garrett, Pam, 80
Garvey, Marcus, 128, 129, 247
Geller, Lawrence H., 236
gender equality/inequality, 65, 69, 247
gendered racism, xxi
Gene, Genial ("Musically Yours"), 174
Georgia, 47, 55, 56, 61, 62, 64, 66, 67, 68, 75, 112, 140, 159, 204
Ghana, 28, 59, 90, 98, 109, 116, 122, 141, 166, 169, 173, 226, 227, 245
Ghanaian Evening News, 173
Ghanaian Times, 173, 206
GI Bill, 11
Gia, 264–267
Gibbs, Joan, xix, xxii, 261, 271, 272, 290, 292
Golden, Harry, 60, 217
Gramsci, Antonio, 5
Grandassa Models, 129, 131, 231
Grattan, Iris, 90, 132, 133, 134, 198, 227
Grattan, Wilbur, 90, 91, 92, 94, 117, 118, 132, 139, 177, 179, 198, 227, 228, 236, 237
Gray, Jesse, 181
Greater Friendship Baptist Church, 182
Green, Bertha, 86, 88, 89, 93
Gregory, Dick, 174, 175
Grenada, xiv, xxii, 4, 251, 252, 253, 255, 259, 260, 263, 270, 273, 285, 288, 294; Bernadette Bailey Secondary School, 254; Bishop, Maurice, 254, 255, 256, 258; Center for Popular Education, 254; Committee for a Free Grenada, 251, 256, 257, 258, 288; Committee in Solidarity with Free Grenada, 251, 256, 288; Creft, Jacqueline, 256; Gairy, Eric, 256; healthcare in, 254; National Cooperative Development Agency, 254; National Women's Organization, 254; New Jewel Party Manifesto, 253, 255; People's Revolutionary Government, 255; revolution, xxi, 253–258, 264; women's rights, 254–255

Griswold, Deidre, 84, 235
Group on Advanced Leadership (GOAL), 90, 177, 178
Guatemala, 77, 256
Guidoni, Marcia, 182
Guy, Sallie, 20
Guyana, 109, 221–249, 256; Indians against Africans, 230; People's National Congress Party, 230

Haffner, Walter S., 155
Haffner, William, 59, 169, 181, 186
Hansberry, Lorraine, 174
Hanson, Janet, 173
Hare, Nathan, xx
Harlem, xix, xx, 3, 13, 19, 26, 55, 56, 57, 73, 75, 76, 77, 113 118, 120, 123, 125, 126, 127, 128, 129, 130, 170, 177, 278, 181, 182, 218, 234, 235, 236, 277, 278, 280; killing of James Powell, 182; Liberation Bookstore, xx; Parents Club, 76; Riot, 277; Women's Committee, 235
Harlem Nine, 74, 116–118
Harlow, Barbara, 137
Harris, Arthur, 234
Hart, Carla, 217, 218
Harvard University, 182
Hawkins, Coleman, 176
Hayes, Susan, xxi, 292, 293
Hayling. Robert. B., 17, 207
hegemony, 24, 37, 57, 76, 105, 128, 137, 149, 151, 154, 157, 159, 185, 187, 210, 228, 257, 258, 263, 272, 283
Henry, Richard, 177
Hentoff, Nat, 176
Herald Dispatch, 59
Herzog, Ci, 176
Hicks, Calvin, 85, 86, 88, 130
Highlander Folk School, Monteagle Tennessee, xix, xx, 47, 87, 124, 278. *See also* Citizenship School
Hill, Anita, 269, 289
Hinton, William A., 51
Hogan, Walter, 180
Holman, John, Vietnam Veterans Against the War, 204
Holman Methodist Church, 39
Holt, Len, 78
Honduras, 256, 259, 260, 262
Hoover, J. Edgar, 75, 77, 236

Hoover, O. M., 173
Hopkins, Lightin,' 174
Horowitz, Rabbi Philip, 173
Horton, Myles, 124
House of Prayer for all Peoples, 216, 217
House of the Lord Church, Herbert Daughtry, 247, 249, 279
House Un-American Activities Committee, 106, 107, 131, 189
housing segregation, 74
Howard, Allen, 157, 158
Huerta, Dolores, 205
human rights. *See* civil rights
Hungary/Hungarians, 39, 72
Hurst, James, 177
Huttig, Arkansas, 19

ILWU, 105, 287
imperialism(ist), xx, 4, 16, 40, 54, 189, 191, 227, 230, 238, 244, 251, 256, 258, 279, 285, 288
Indians against Africans, 229, 230
Indigenous Lumbee victory, 13
inequality, 34, 50, 65, 66, 150
informers, 16, 237, 266
Institute of Black Studies, 223
insurgency, 20, 24, 162
integration, 48, 49, 74, 77, 105, 107, 122, 124, 181, 200, 217
internal colony, 42, 43, 238, 244
International All-Trades Union of the World, 178
International Association of Democratic Lawyers, 269
International Ladies' Garment Workers Union, 277
International Revolutionary Movements, 4, 179, 252
Internationalism (st), 4, 30, 37, 251, 255
Iran, 17, 77, 244, 256
Iraqi Veterans Against the War, 282

Jackson, Esther Cooper, xviii, 116, 119
Jackson, Jimmy Lee, 41
Jamaica, 90, 169, 235, 256
James, C. L. R., 28
James, Joy, 14
Japanese American concentration camps, xvii, xviii
Jean Donavan Brigade, 260
Jerusalem Gospel Chorus, 180

Jet, 28, 113, 116, 195, 231
Jim Crow, 24, 32, 42, 53, 69, 76, 89, 168, 172
John Birch Society, 207
Johnson, Ethel Azalea, xiii, xxi, 1, 2, 4, 5, 9–54, 109, 110, 116, 129, 165, 166, 167, 188–189, 206, 209, 222, 224, 225, 226, 230, 234, 239, 264, 266, 279, 286; Abbeville, 10; Asa Lee, 3, 16; "As Relayed to Me by a Negro Maid," "Did You Know" (10/1/1960), 23; CARE House, 16, 33, 44, 50; Carolina Laundry and Cleaners, 10; Citizenship School, 2; Continental Insurance company, 10; Crusader (newsletter), 16; *Crusader* (newspaper), 2, 10, 29; Crusaders' Association for Relief and Enlightenment (CARE), 2, 33, 42–45, 46, 50; 57, 215; "Did You Know" column, 2, 9, 10, 16–20, 23, 27, 29, 32, 35, 37, 50; FBI files, 29, 266; Head Start program, 2, 48 49, 50, 287; internationalist ideology, 30; Malcolm X scholarships, 50; Monroe Defense Committee (MDC), 2, 32–34, 85, 91, 177; Monroe NAACP, 12, 57; Negroes With Guns, 9–16; organic intellectual, 5, 34, 40; Philadelphia, 29, 30, 32; radicalization of, 5; religiosity, 27; Revolutionary Action Movement, 2, 29–32; Seaboard Air Line Railroad, 10; self-defense ideology, 2, 10; surveillance of, 18; Paula Marie Seniors's adoptive grandmother, 1, 33, 287; self-defense advocate, 2, 191; *Uhuru* newsletter, 29
Johnson, Hilliard, 20
Johnson, Lyndon B., 41, 207; African American ambassadors and diplomats, 151; War on Poverty/Great Society, 48, 261
Johnson, Raymond (Ray), 10, 28
Johnson, Raymond Jr., 10, 30, 31, 34; Drowned, 32
Jones, Charles, 265
Jones, Claudia, xvii, 116, 138, 139–140, 144, 152, 156, 165, 173
Jones, Leroi, 50, 88, 94, 174, 236
Jones, Ronald, 84
Jones, Rudolph, 131

Katz, Jonathan Ned, 261
Kempton, Murray, 170
Kennedy, John F., 156, 169, 175, 179, 195, 224; African American ambassadors and diplomats, 151

Kennedy, Robert F., 179, 224, 234
Kenya, 30, 37, 38, 39, 166, 227; Kenya Federation of Labor/Anti-Colonial Federation of Labor, 39; Jomo, Kenyatta, 38, 227. *See also* anti-colonial revolutions/anti-colonial movements
Kenya African Union, 39
Kenyatta, Jomo, 38, 227
Khruschev, Nikita, 39, 40
Kinoy, Arthur, xxii, 271, 272. *See also* white liberals
King, Coretta Scott, 95
King, J. L., 180
King, Martin Luther Jr., 2, 24, 30, 87, 95, 117, 175, 176, 206, 207, 208, 209, 223, 224, 234; passive resistance/nonviolence, 19, 106, 178; tax harassment, 78
King, Martin Luther III, 117
King, Mrs. Slater, 140
Kiser, Amos, 26
Kissing Case, Monroe, North Carolina, 13–14, 58,
Kochiyama, Bill, 33
Kochiyama, Yuri (Mary), xvii, 33, 57, 171, 182, 188, 234, 235, 236, 285, 291
Kollman, Paul, 240, 241
Korean War, 11, 252
Ku Klux Klan, 11, 12, 15, 22, 27, 28, 31, 89, 105, 107, 169, 175, 184, 186, 197, 198, 207, 276, 289; Indigenous Lumbee victory, 13
Ku Klu Klan couple (Mr. and Mrs. G. Bruce Stegall), 1, 28; Motorcade, Monroe, 13
Kumba, M. Bahati, 5
Kunstler, William, xxii, 29, 91, 92, 94. *See also* white liberals

La Lima Coffee Farm, 267, 268
labor activism, xix
Ladner, Joyce, 17, 18
Latin America. *See* anti-colonial revolutions/anti-Colonial movements
Latin Americans, Latin American Student Organizations, xx
Latinas' prison experience, 160
Lavan, George. *See* George Weisman
Leakes, Sylvester, 57, 94, 170
leftist ideologies/theories, 4, 38, 54, 252
lesbian relationships, 160; "Rev Saves a Paper Hanger Soul," 161
Lester, Julius, 278
"Let resistance be your motto," 276

Levy, Charles M., 27
Lewis, John, 281
Liberia, 227
Lilo, 170, 171
Lincoln, Abbey, 57, 128–129, 132, 158, 175, 176, 177
Lipsitz, George, xii, 5
Little, Joan, 204
Little Rock Nine, 116
Liuzzo, Viola, 78
Local 1045 Autoworkers, 173
Local 1330 Steelworkers, 173, 174
Local 45 Autoworkers, 173
Los Angeles Herald Dispatch, 173, 177
Louisiana Slave Revolt (1811), 19
Louisiana Weekly, 104
Lowry, John, 24, 29, 60, 85, 86, 89, 91, 92, 94
Luce, Albert, 30
Lumumba, Malaika, 62
Lumumba, Patrice, 39, 40, 57, 151, 173
Lynn, Conrad, 1, 14, 32, 57, 58, 59, 89, 140, 143, 157
Lyons, Thelma, 76, 80

Macon, Georgia, 61, 62, 66
Majority World, xx, 3, 4, 34, 37, 39, 40, 99, 151, 165, 166, 167, 178, 185, 192, 195, 202, 222, 251, 252, 253, 255, 256, 257, 285, 293, 294; Majority World Education, xx, xxi; Majority World revolutionary theory, 34
Malcolm X, xx, 50, 55, 88, 117, 126, 127, 140, 170, 178, 179, 226; Liberation School, 127; Malcolm X Scholarships, 50
Mallory, Mae, xix, xxi, 3, 4, 26, 27, 29, 53, 54, 55–81, 92, 95, 129, 182, 217, 230, 279, 286–287; African American Committee in Defense of the Congo, 234; arranged marriage, 110; Keefer Mallory 70; Arrest, Cleveland, 29, 31, 59, 66, 68, 80, 88, 180, 237, 287, 288; New York, 78, 79, 80, 85, 130; beauty and political movements, 158, 159; "Black Liberation Fighter Returns to Motherland," 166; child neglect charges, 79, 111, 114–115, 119, 130–134; Communist Party, 71–73, 75, 79; Crusader Family/Crusaders for Freedom in Harlem, 3, 13, 26, 57, 123, 127, 170, 175; Cuyahoga County Jail, xxii, 68, 137, 141, 142, 143, 144, 149, 153, 155, 160; Deacons for Defense, 177, 234; Desegregation case (New York), 3, 76, 116–118; Dream Escape writings, 137–183; Economic Development Conference, 236; educational advocacy, 73–77; Euclid Park Nursing Home, 238; extradition to Monroe, 181; fantastical tales and sexuality, 160–164: "Christina and the Ebony Hued Man," 164, "Mer Dear the Big Eyed Girl and the RapeFantasy (Space between rape and fantasy)," 163–164, "Rev Saves A Paper Hanger Soul," 161, 163, "Sex Love in Church," 163; FBI files, xxiii, 78, 155, 230, 238, 266; *Free Mae Mallory*, 28, 60, 169, 185; friends of Mae Mallory, 177; grand larceny/fraud charge, 78, 79; Guyana, 230; Cleveland, 89–90, 137, 149, 166, New York, 118–121, 142, international support, 169–174, 206; Keffer Mallory, Jr., (Butch), 70, 74, 79, 110, 112, 113–115, 117, 118, 121, 130, 157, 168, 275, 276, 279; kidnapping, 1, 28, 29, 31, 32, 53, 59, 60, 66, 80 86, 93, 149, 180, 206, 287: extradited and convicted, 205; Mallory Freedom Movement, 155; melancholy, 152; *Memo from a Monroe Jail*, 14, 28; Monroe Defense Committee, xiii, xiv, xvii, xix, xxi, xxiii, 1, 2, 3, 18, 29, 32–34, 38, 40, 53, 82–95, 97, 99, 129, 130, 152, 155, 169, 170, 180, 184, 185, 188, 189, 196, 206, 209, 218, 225, 227, 287; National speaking tour, 206; "Of Dogs and Men," 148–152; organic intellectual, 5, 61, 110, 117, 140, 141, 157, 180, 226; organizations opposing extradition, 155; Pan-African and Black Revolutionary Conference, 230; parents, 62, 63; Patricia Mallory Oduba, xix, xxiii, 70, 109–134, 222, 224, 225, 227; Petitions for Mae Mallory release, 98; political prisoner, 3, 77–81, 138–141, 183; primitive looking, 157–160; prison brutality, 146, prison life, 142–144, 153, 155, 160; reincarceration, 182–183; release from prison, 91, 119, 181, 206; school curriculum reform, 74; speaking tour, 180–183, 206, 234, 235, 236; radicalization of, 5, Republic of New Africa, 91; Revolutionary Action Movement (RAM), 234; Saint Augustine, Florida, 206–209; school desegregation (Cleveland), 3; self-awareness/pride, 157, 158; self-defense advocate, 1, 2; separation from children, 197; surveillance, 18; Tanzania, 234, 238, 239, 243, 244; tax harassment, 78, 118; Women's House of Detention (New York), 142, 144; Woolworth's protest (Harlem), 57;

Mallory, Mae (continued)
  Youngstown Friends of Mae Mallory, 98, 179, 197
Mallory, Keefer Jr., (Butch), 70, 74, 79, 110, 112, 113–114, 115, 121, 130, 157, 168, 275, 276
Mallory, Keefer, Sr., 70
Mallory, Patricia, (Pat). *See* Oduba, Pat Mallory
Mama KeKe, 122, 125, 231,
Mammy Trope, 148
Mandel, Bernard, 173
Mandela, Nelson, 282
Mao, 34, 40, 41, 99, 171, 187, 253, 254, 258
Maoism, 3, 5, 30, 38, 40, 41, 42, 66, 92, 98, 165, 251, 253
Marcus Garvey Day, 128
Marshall, Meita, 180
Marshall, Paule, 174
Marshall, Thurgood, 131
Marti, Jose, 191; Radical Nationalist Model, 34
Martin, Denise, 246
Maryknoll Sisters, xii, 231, 232
Matthews, J. B., 189, 195
Matthews, Victoria Earle, xix
Mau Mau Uprising, 227
Mauney, Chief, 13, 27, 28,
Marxism, 34, 42, 259
Marxism-Leninism Communist Party, 84, 89, 235, 251
Massachusetts, Tremont Methodist Church (Roxboro), 182
Matthews, J. B., 92
Mayfield, Ana Livia, 174
Mayfield, Julian, 13, 14, 26, 28, 57, 58, 121, 141, 166, 173, 181, 236
Mboya, Tom, 39
McCarthyism, 116
McCreary, Bill, 190
McKay, Claude, 52, 53
Medlin, Lewis, 14
Meeks, Brian, 34
Meharry Medical School, 11, 48
Meier, August, xviii
Melville, Bruce, 199
Memo from a Monroe Jail, Mallory, 14, 28
Merrill, Jeanette, 85, 195
Meredith, James, 42
Metropolitan Baptist Church Choir, 180
Mexico, 169, 270
Micheaux, Lewis, 236

Michigan State University, 182
Midwest Division-Foundry Council Meeting, 155–156
Mikko, 84–85
Militant Black Women, 182
Military Intelligence Division (MID), 16, 138
military service (African American), 42
Mingus, Charlie, 57, 175
Minh, Ho Chi, 38
misogyny, xxi, 61, 65, 69, 113, 114, 127, 157, 159, 249, 285, 286
Miss Natural Standard of Beauty contests, 128, 231
Mississippi, 19, 26, 28, 116, 159; Hernando, 42; Poplar, 122
Mitchell, Samuel, 78
Mobley, Ora, 57
Monroe, North Carolina, 1, 2, 9, 10, 13, 14, 16, 24, 25, 26, 28, 29, 31, 32, 33, 36, 38, 43, 46, 52, 61, 83, 86, 93–94, 180, 181, 186, 205, 209, 210, 211, 213, 217, 273, 287; Angola of America, 26; Black Baptist church, 45; Black men/women and unemployment, 210–213; Citizen and Adult Education Program, 47, 48; Committee to Aid the Monroe Defendants, 18, 28, 38, 44, 80, 86, 93, 155, 189; desegregation, 206; education, 206; food/clothing assistance, 45; Freedom House, 205; Freedom Riders, 24, 25, 26, 27; Riot, 24–29; voter registration, 47, 287; youth unemployment, 25; Monroe Defendants, 54, 85, 88, 89, 92, 94, 98, 138, 156, 169, 170, 171, 173, 174, 175, 176, 177, 179, 185, 189, 287, 294; kidnapping charge, 1, 28, 29, 32, 53, 60, 86, 287
Monroe Defense Committee (MDC)-New York, 29, 86, 88, 89, 93, 94, 98, 130, 131, 176
Monroe Defense Committee (MDC)-Cleveland, 1, 18, 29, 31, 83, 84, 85, 86, 88, 89–95, 131, 132, 180, 184, 193, 194, 195, 197, 200, 237, 287
Monroe Kissing Case, 13–14, 58,
Monroe Master Plan, 47
Monroe Rifle Club, 15
Monroe Riot, 24–29, 206
Monroe Youth Action Committee, 177; *Freedom*, 205
Montgomery Bus Boycott, 116
Monthly Review, 30
Moore, Queen Mother, 57

Moore, Richard B., xx; Committee to Present the Truth about the Name 'Negro,' xx; *The Name "Negro"—Its Origin and Evil Use*, 36
Morton, David, 85
Moses, Bob and Janet, 117, 231, 245, 276
motherhood, 3, 14–24, 54, 58, 60, 69, 70, 76, 79, 81, 83, 110, 111, 114, 116, 118, 168, 184, 188, 192–199, 205, 218, 239, 284; tropes, 54, 188, 217
motherist frame, 5, 24, 58, 61, 73, 76, 112, 193, 195, 196, 197, 201, 205, 248
Mother's Alliance (Buffalo), 32, 59, 84, 95, 173, 175, 193
Mothers of Heroes and Martyrs, 262
Movement Support Network, 261
Moynihan Report, 74–75
Muhammad Speaks, 170
multi-racial community, 66
murders, 16, 129, 151, 224, 267, 268
Murray, Madeline, 276
"The Myth of Cinderella," 285

Namibia, xxi, 269, 270, 289, 294
Nat Turner, 9, 10, 18, 51, 214
The Nation of Islam, xx, 3, 4, 30, 116,126, 127, 128, 129, 169, 170, 175, 254; schools, 254
National Association for the Advancement of Colored People (NAACP), 2, 3, 10, 11, 12, 14, 16, 17, 18, 24, 44, 56, 59, 60, 73, 75, 80, 83, 93, 96, 97, 98, 99, 101, 104, 107, 116, 131, 173, 176, 187, 200, 204, 207, 234, 253, 272, 287; agent provocateurs, 16, 18, 198; Antioch College NAACP, 173; Education Committee, 76, 77; informers, 16, 59, 80; national office, 15, 16, 24; New Orleans, Louisiana, 3, 83, 97, 98, 104, 105, 116; New York, 76; Monroe, North Carolina, 2, 10, 11, 12, 14, 15, 47, 56, 57, 60; Ossining, 204
National Cooperative Development Agency, 254
National Liberation Front, 166
National Security Council, 77
National Women's Organization, 254
Nationalist, 242
Nationalists. *See* Black Nationalists
Native Americans, 154, 159, 255
Negro, 35
Negro American Labor Council, 155
Negroponte, John, 260
Negroes With Guns (pamphlet), 181

Negroes With Guns (movement), xiii, 1, 2, 3, 9–17, 24, 26, 30, 38, 40, 45, 49, 52, 53, 54, 57, 58, 80, 83, 116, 123, 129, 141, 176, 181, 189, 205; *Crusader* newspaper, 2; Monroe Rifle Club, 12, 13
Nigger. *See* African Americans
Negresses. *See* African Americans
Nehru, Jawaharlal, 38
Neidenberg, Rosie and Milt, 84, 85
Nelson, C. T., 182
New Haven Nine, Rackley, Alex, 288
Nkrumah, Kwame, 38, 165
New Jersey, Rutgers College and Douglass College, xxii, 182
New Jewel Party Manifesto, 253
New Orleans Association for the Advancement of Colored People (NAACP), 3, 83, 97, 98, 104, 105, 116, 187, 239, 251, 272, 287
New York, 181, Brooklyn, 214–218; Buffalo, 206; Harlem, 116–118, 177, 182; public school IS, 201, 236
New York Civil Liberties Union, xxi
New York Daily News, 259
New York Newsday, 259
New York Post, 170, 259
New York State, Auburn Correctional Facility, 204; Sing Sing Correctional Facility, 204
New York Times, 175, 208, 259, 269, 292
New York University, 231, 281, 289, 290, 293
Nganza Secondary School, 232, 233, 239, 244
Nicaragua, xii. xxi, 4, 191, 251, 252, 253, 254, 255, 256, 257, 258, 259, 250, 260, 261, 264, 265, 267, 268, 270, 273, 285, 288, 294; Center for Constitutional Rights (CCR), xix, xxi, xxii, 256, 259, 289, 292, 294; Foundation for Community Organization, 258; Myrna Cunningham, 259; National Guard, 261; Pastors For Peace, 258; women's rights, 260
Nicaraguan Exchange, 251, 258, 264, 266, 268, 288; Gia, 264–267
Nicaraguan People's Solidary Committee, 267
Nicaraguan Revolution, xxi, 251, 258–268
Nigeria, 109, 174, 223, 227, 245
nonviolence/passive resistance movement. *See* passive resistance
North Carolina, 43, 90, 169, 181, 196, 209, 210–213; Black communities in, 10, 210–213; Charlotte, 10, 13, 14, 215; Brooklyn section,

North Carolina (*continued*)
 214–217, 218; House of Prayer for All
 Peoples (Daddy Grace), 216, 217; Joan
 Little, 204
North Carolina College for Negroes, 11, 30
North Carolina Council on Human Relations,
 48
North Korea, 256
Northern Negro Grass Roots Leadership
 Conference, 90, 177, 178
Nyerere, Julius, 225, 226, 231, 244, 258

Oberlin College, 182
Oduba, Patricia Mallory, (Pat), xix, xx, xxiii,
 1, 3, 5, 33, 35, 55, 59, 70, 83, 88, 90, 108,
 118, 125, 129, 157, 159, 168, 174, 187, 198,
 221–249, 255, 274–279, 286; abandoned by
 mother, 69, 79, 111, 114–115, 119, 130–134;
 abuse, 114–115, 231; African Society of
 Cultural Relations With Independent
 Africa (ASCRIA), 230; Afrocentric
 beauty, 158; Aleutia, 247, 248, 278;
 ANGRY BLACK WOMAN, 278; atheist,
 248, 276; Ayoka, 125; Black Nationalist
 activities, 125–129; Black nationalist
 rebel girl, 3, 107–134, 221, 225, 239; Bronx
 Community College, 222; Catholic Priests,
 240–241; Cleveland, Ohio, 1, 83; community
 feminist, 122, 134; Crusaders for Freedom,
 123; Dar es Salaam, 245; Downtown
 Community School, 120–121, 122, 277;
 family life, 275–277; FBI surveillance,
 232; Grandassa Models, 129, 231; Guyana,
 221–249; Harlem Nine, 116–11; high school
 leadership roles, 122; Highlander Folk
 School, 124; lawsuit for desegregation case,
 73, 116, 117, 119; leftist Black nationalist
 identity, 122; Maryknoll Sisters, xii, 231;
 Mwanza, 244, 246; nuclear war protests,
 123; organic intellectual, 122, 134, 221, 225,
 232; radical daughter, 274, 275, 278; spiritual
 healing, 245–248, 279; SUNY Stony Brook,
 xv, xxi, 222–225: Black Student Union/Black
 Students United, 222, 223; colorism, 228;
 Yoruba culture, 125, 126
Ohio, Cleveland, 1, 3, 29,68, 81, 89–95,
 131–132, 159, 173, 177, 178, 179, 180, 181, 205;
 Youngstown, 181
Olatunji (African Troupe), 174, 176
Olivet Institutional Baptist Church, 173
Operation Big Stick, 26

Opie, Margaret, People's Center for Peace and
 Justice, 204
Oquendo, Eddie, Blacks Against Negative
 Dying, 203; Committee for GI Rights, 203
organic intellectual, 5, 34, 40, 61, 76, 99, 110,
 116, 117, 122, 134, 140, 141, 157, 180, 183, 190,
 205, 214, 221, 225, 226, 232
Organization of Afro American Unity, xx
Organization of American States, 256
Oxner, Mildred, 49

Palestinian Liberation Organization, 256
Pan-African: Alliances to African Americans,
 39; army, 166; and Black Revolutionary
 Conference, 230; Communist Party, 80;
 ideologies, 37, 40; Liberation, 37, 53, 166,
 167, 168; Union of Journalists, 38
Pan-Asian Liberation, 37, 53
Pan-Latin American Liberation, 37, 167, 168
Panama, 169, 256, 269
Panamanian invasion, xxii, 269
Patterson, Orlando, 36
Partisan Magazine, 3, 202, 206, 209, 210, 288
passive resistance/nonviolence movement, 1,
 2, 16, 17, 18, 19, 24, 27, 55, 106, 129, 140, 165,
 174, 178, 206, 208, 276, 281
patriarchy, xxi, 4, 61, 62, 65, 70, 112, 113, 127,
 137, 157, 158, 159, 285
Peabody, Mary, 207, 208, 209; Ponce de Leon
 Motor Lodge protest, 207
Peery, Nelson, 40
Pentecostalism, 246–249
People's Center for Peace and Justice, 204
People's Defense League, 104
People's Movement of Angola, 26
People's National Congress Party, 230
People's revolutionary Government, 255
Perry, Albert E., 11, 12, 13, 86, 94; Bertha Mae
 Brooks, 11
Philadelphia Tribune, 236
Phillips Memorial Baptist Church, 180
Pittsburgh Courier, 180, 181
Plain Dealer, 92, 200
political ideology/activism, xxi, 5, 47, 52, 54,
 71, 75, 76, 98, 99, 107, 112, 138, 185, 239, 249,
 264
political prisoners, 3, 77–81, 138–145
Ponce de Leon Motor Lodge (Florida), 207
Poussaint, Alvin, 265
Powell, Adam Clayton, 78, 181
Powell, James, 182

Price, Charles, 169
PRIDE, 90, 91, 236
prison blues writing, 137, 152
prisoner reform/freedom, 204
Prisoners Solidarity Committee, 99, 203, 204
pro-Black language. *See* Black rhetoric
pro-Black Rhetoric. *See* Black rhetoric
Proctor, Bertha and Robert, 96, 100, 102
Proctor family, New Orleans, 96–98
Progressive Educational Association, 104
Progressive Labor Movement, 32
Project Head Start, 48
Promise Land, South Carolina. *See* Abbeville
Prosser, Gabriel, 51
Prosser, Martin, 51
Provocateurs, 16, 18, 80, 94, 95, 130, 172, 226, 244, 288
Puerto Rico, 122, 125, 191, 256

Quarterman, Ola Mae, 140
Queen Mother Moore, 127, 244,
Quinn, Gerald, 176, 177
Quixotic, 202, 286, 289

race history, xix
Rackley, Alex, 288
racism, xix, xxi, 16, 31, 34, 38, 40, 49, 60,61, 67, 69, 72, 76, 99, 109, 124, 151, 167, 170, 172, 177, 180, 184, 189, 192, 202, 224, 228, 229, 242, 265, 276, 283, 285
radical activism, 5, 11, 17, 34, 54, 61, 80, 81, 98, 99–104, 107, 108, 109, 192, 196, 239, 279, 287, 288, 294
radical Reconstruction, 21
radicalism, 36, 49, 53, 83, 107, 139
Radio Free Dixie, 171, 186
Rainach, William M., 105
Randolph, A. Philip, 85
Range, William Clarence, 62
Ransby, Barbara, 34
rape: African American women, 2, 14, 16, 58, 196, 204; fantasy, 164; for game, 14, 15; Lillie Mae, 13
Rashad, Ahmed, 91, 204, 236–238
Ratner, Margaret L., 261
Ratner, Michael, xxii, 270
Ravitch, Diane, 74
Reagan, Ronald, xx, 253, 256, 257, 258, 259, 260, 264, 267, 268
Red Scare, 75, 84, 105, 131, 138, 186, 277

Republic of New Africa (RNA), 90, 91, 226, 227, 236
resistance: literature, 137; movements, 105, 196, 206, 274
Rhodes, James A., 179, 198
Richards, Beah, 175
Robinson, Arthur, 60
religiosity, 21, 27, 36, 38
Reagan, Ronald, xx, 257
Reape, Harold, 29, 32, 33, 53, 85, 86, 89, 91, 94, 168, 177, 179, 189, 206, 287
Reclaiming Dine History, xix
Reed, Mary Ruth, 14–15, 58
Republic of New Africa, 236
respectability trope, 208
Revolutionary Action Movement (Monroe, North Carolina, Philadelphia, Pennsylvania), 2, 16, 29–32, 33, 38, 40, 49, 53, 90, 92, 130, 166, 167, 177, 217, 234, 235, 236; Third Force or movement, 30
Rhodes, Jim, 197
Rhodesia, 131
Roach, Max, 57, 128, 175, 176, 177
Robeson, Paul, 98, 106, 107, 116, 138–140, 185, 186, 195, 206, 251
Robeson, Paul Jr. 119
Rocha, Brenda, 261
Rodney, Walter, 226, 230
Rogers, J. A., 195
Rogers, Johnny, 91, 94
Roosevelt, Theodore, 26
Rudwick, Eliot, xviii
Russell, Bertrand, 98, 175
Russell, James M., 174, 181
Russell, Ruth, 120
Russia, 84, 119
Rustin, Bayard, 85, 170

Saint Augustine, Florida, 206–209
Saloon, Mary, 64, 67
San Francisco State College, Strike, xx; Third World Liberation Front, xx, xxi
Sanders, Charles, 155, 157, 158, 169, 173
Sandinista Revolution, 253, 256, 258, 259
Sandinistas, 258, 259, 260, 261, 263, 265, 267, 288
Sarah Lawrence College, xxii
Satter, Beryl, xix
Scarification, 84
Seaboard Air Line Railroad, 10
Seale, Bobby, 94, 272

Schomburg, Arturo, xviii
Seeger, Pete, 120, 174, 277
segregation, 16, 19, 24, 32, 46, 67, 69, 74, 77, 79, 87, 104, 106, 107, 124, 168, 200, 204, 223, 276, 277, 278
segregationist policies, 24; transit laws, 104; voter registration, 104
self-defense/Black self-defense, 1, 2, 3, 10, 13, 16–20, 24, 26, 27, 30, 31, 38, 40, 44, 45, 48, 49, 52, 53, 54, 56, 57, 58, 80, 83, 85, 88, 99, 101, 106, 116, 123, 129, 141, 168, 176, 178, 206, 208, 214, 217, 279, 281; ideology, 3, 9, 20, 38, 40, 61, 63, 185; self-defense policy, 15, 41
self-worth/pride, 24, 157, 249
Senegal, 20, 227, 268
Seniors, Audrey Proctor, xvii, xxi, 1, 4, 53, 54, 55, 80, 82–108, 109, 110, 129, 132, 133, 134, 153, 165, 181, 184–218, 222, 225, 230, 239, 251–273, 276, 279; Aruba, 270; Ambassador of Peace, 267, anti-Vietnam War, 99; Black Panthers, xxi, 99, 271; Center for Constitutional Rights: xix, 256, 259, 261, 264, 269, firing/reinstatement of, 270–272, 289, 292, 294, "A Charlotte Widow," 210, 215, 216, 218, 287; Cleveland, Ohio, 81, 82, 83, 99, 184, 187, 199–206, 273, 287; Communist affiliations, 97, 99, 104–108, 287; death, 282, 291–292; *Did You Know* (newsletter), 10, 33, 90, 206, 207, 209; divorce, 286; education, 102–104; family in military, 252; family rejection, 187; FBI files, 95, 104, 189, 209, 266, 285–286; FBI harassment, 96–98, 104–108, 273, 287; "Free Mae Mallory" pamphlet, 98; Freedom Fighters, 99, 179; Freedom House, 205; Funeral, 292; Grenada, 255–257, 270, 273; hospitalization, 290–291; lawsuit (Atlanta), 87; library, 99; Maoism, 98; Mexico, 270; Monroe Defense Committee, xxi, 3, 32, 60, 83, 91, 98, 99, 184, 206; Monroe, N.C., 210; motherhood, 184–218; music, love of, 103; Namibia, 294: travels to, 269, 270; New Orleans Association for the Advancement of Colored People (NAACP), 3, 98–108, 116, 253, 287; Nicaragua, 273; Open Forum, The, 207; organic intellectual, 99, 190–192, 205, 214; parents, 100, 102; political activist, 99, 101; *Prisoners Call Out Freedom*, 204; Prisoners Solidarity Committee, 99, 204; radical activism, 99–104; radicalization of, 5, 99, 27; religion, rejection of, 104; retirement, 272, 289; self-defense advocate, 2, 98, 101, 217, 273; social theorist, 98–99; Workers World Party, xxi, 98, 99; Youth Against War and Fascism, 99, 206,209, 210. *See also* United Freedom Movement

Seniors, Clarence Henry, xvii, xx, 1, 9, 13, 32, 53, 54, 95, 96, 116, 137, 175, 176, 181; arrest, 87; *Did You Know* (newsletter), 10, 33 90, 287; family rejection, 97–98, 187; FBI Files, 189, 266; Freedom Fighters, 179; Monroe Defense Committee, 3, 32, 87, 88, 89, 90, 91, 194, 206; self-defense advocate, 2, 191; Workers World Party, 84; working Class, 45, 101

Seniors, Paula Marie, 5, 53, 90, 95, 184–218, 279–294; Adoption of daughter, 284–285; atheist, 290; City College of New York, 279, 280; *From Uncle Tom's Cabin to the Help*, xxii; Greneda, xxii; "joy of living" motto, 279; radicalized daughter, 279, 281, 282

sexism, 111, 115, 276, 278, 285
Shabazz, Adbulalim Abdullah. *See* Lonnie Cross
Shabazz, Betty, 117
Shakur, Afeni, 288
Shakur, Assata, 144
Shaw, B. F., 14
Show Dogs. *See* ambassadors and diplomats; Bunche, Ralph; Cook, Mercer; Wharton, Clifton
Shuttlesworth, Fred Jr., 278
Shuttlesworth, Fred Sr., 124
Sierra Leone, 20
Simpson, A. T., 88
Simpson, David, 14
Sing Sing Correctional Facility, 204
Sit-iners, 18, 26
Sixteenth Street Baptist Church (Ala.), 140, 151
Sixth Annual Pan-African Conference, 188, 243, 244
slaves, enslaved, 9, 10, 20, 21, 37, 40, 42, 63, 112, 163, 168, 214, 275; former slaves, xix; light skinned vs. dark skinned, 112; revolts, 19
Smith, Mary Louise, 116
Smith Robinson, Ruby Doris, 17
Snipes, Wilson Currin, 4
social action, 5, 16, 61, 197
social contestation, 5

social equality, 256
social justice, 35, 104, 137, 158, 159 186, 201, 249, 293
Socialism (ist), 3, 4, 5, 38, 42, 53, 92, 139, 165, 225, 226, 230, 239, 244
Socialist-Black Nationalist theoretical frame, 81
Socialistic theories/ideology of equality, 18, 66, 99
Socialist Workers Party, 12, 38, 66, 84, 86, 92, 175, 189
Sostre, Martin, Afro-Asian Bookstore, 203–204
South Africa, xxi, 247, 259, 268, 269, 276, 294
South African anti-apartheid movement, 247, 276
South Carolina, 21, 29, Abbeville, 10, 16, 20, 21, 22, 23, 24, 29, 35, 40, 42, 44, 47, 61, 106,110, 239; radical reconstruction, 21; University of South Carolina Law School, 21
South West Africa People's Organization (SWAPO), 269, 289
Southern Baptist, 61, 62, 66, 158, 178
Southern bell fantasy trope, xxii, 145, 146, 148
Southern Christian Leadership Conference (SCLC), 2, 17, 41, 80, 116, 124, 226
Southern Negro Youth Congress, 116
Soviet Bloc countries, 37, 39, 43; Hungary, 39
Soviet Union, 37, 38, 105, 138, 139, 254, 256; housing, 39; imprisonment, 39
Spanish American War, 172
Spencer-Antoine, Robyn C., 126
"Sphere of Highly Politicized Scholarship," xix
Spies, 18, 77, 80, 243, 244
Spingarn, Joel Elias, 16, Informant, 18
St. Johns County Jail (Florida), 208
Stanford, Max, 29, 53, 95, 177, 234, 235
State Surveillance, xviii, 286
Stegall, G. Bruce, 28, 29, 60, 188
Stevens, Hope, 85,
Stokes, Carl, 236, 237,
Stone, Ruthie, 1, 2, 32, 59, 60, 83, 85, 87, 91, 95, 98, 129, 153, 154, 173, 175, 191, 193, 194, 197, 286
Stony Brook (SUNY), xv, xxi, 222 223, 224, 225
Streeter, Willie Lee, 62, 63, 65, 69, 70, 277
Student Nonviolent Coordinating Committee (SNCC), 2, 17, 18, 24, 30, 87, 116, 117, 129, 226, 265,
Studer, Norman, 120
Swarthmore College, 182

Tambo, Oliver R., 269
Tanzania, xiii, 4, 221–249; African American spies and threat to, 242, 243, 244; The Big Bust, 243–245; Catholic Priests, 240–241; Indians against Africans, 228, 229; Maryknoll Sisters, xii, 231, 232; mass hysteria, 232–234; Operation Vijana, 241, 243; Sixth Annual Pan African Conference, 243, 244; social norms, 240–242. *See also* Ujammaa
Tanzanian Revolution, 244
Tate, Claudia, 62
Tax harassment, 78, 79, 118
Taylor, Ula, 5, 235
Tempia (cousin), 63–64
Temu, A. J., 242
Third Force movement, 30
Third World, 252, 257, 258, 259, 261, 263, 264, 265, 266, 267
Third World Brigades, 258, 264, 265, 266, 267, 288
Third World Brigadistas, 266
Third World Liberation Front, xx, xxi
Third World Outreach, 264
Thomas, Clarence, 269, 289
Thompson, Hanover, Monroe Kissing Case, 13–14
Till, Emmett, 116, 130, 277
Todd, George, 234
Tom Toms, 39
Trotskyist/Maoist Workers World Party, 1, 3, 18, 83–84, 85
Trotskyists (ism), xvii, 3, 5, 34, 38, 41, 42, 84, 89, 92, 151, 253,
Tshombe, Moise, 39
Tubman, Harriet, 10, 30, 50, 51, 214
Tureaud, Pierre, 106
Turner, James, 112
Turner, Nat, 9, 10, 18, 51, 214
Turner, Ruth, 199, 200
Twenty-First Street and Payne/Pain. *See* Cuyahoga County Jail
Tyson, Timothy, 10, 186

Uganda, 227, 229,
Uhuru newsletter, 29
Ujamaa, 225, 229, 230, 231, 241, 243; Residential College, 223
Umoja, Akinyele, 11
Uncle Toms, 39, 44, 206
Union County Women's League, 205, 296

unions, 105, 106; members, 75, 105, 106, 155, 287
United African Nationalist Movement, 128
United Auto Workers Union, 11, 91, 155, 271
United Farm Workers, 205
United Freedom Movement, xix, 34, 40, 99, 138, 155, 158, 168, 200, 208, 286–289
United Nations Session, 39, 57, 131, 147, 167, 191, 156, 275
United States House of Representatives, 171
Universal Negro Improvement Association, 131
University of California, San Diego, Ethnic Studies Department, xviii
University of Cincinnati, 182
University of Dar es Salaam, 226
University of Medina (Saudi Arabia), 50
University of Michigan, xv, 174
University of Pittsburgh, 182
urban renewal, 47, 131, 199, 210, 216, 217,
urban revolts, Detroit, 42; Newark, 42; Watts, 42

Vesey, Denmark, 20, 51
Vichot, Julio Cubría, 191
Vietnam. *See* anti-colonial revolutions/anti-colonial movements
Vietnam War, 3, 30, 41, 42, 99, 114, 126, 133, 144, 165, 203, 222, 252, 261, 263, 288
Vietnamese Liberation Movement, 30
Vietnam Veterans Against the War, 204
Village Voice, 271
Volunteer Work Brigade, 263
voter registration, 32, 47, 90, 105, 124, 129, 178, 287

Walrond, Lakeesha, 115
Ward, Alvin, 237
Washington, Booker T., 50
Washington Post, 131
Wattley, Parnella, 57
Watts, Rowland, 85
WBAI (radio station), 256
Webb, Constance, 28
Weisman, Ernest, 181
Weisman, George, (George Lavan), 12, 86, 88, 89, 93, 94,
Weisman, Mary Ann, 95, 181, 214
Wells, Ida B., xvii, 51
W.E.R.E. (radio station), *The Bill Guardan Hour*, 180

West Indian Gazette, 173, 206
Weyandt, Carl, 152, 155
Wharton, Clifton, 151
White, Arthur, 274
White, Georgia, 14–15, 58
White, Walter, 80
white fascists, 17, 21
white liberals, xxii, 208, 209, 270
white power, 21, 72, 93, 146, 177, 186, 217
White Race First Policy, 72, 265
White Rose Industrial Home, (Matthews), xix
white superiority tropes, 69
white supremacist triumvirate, 145–148; "The Gun Moll, Miss Deep South, and the Alcoholic Old Relic," 145
white supremacist women, 24, 64, 68, 69, 76, 145, 147, 148,149, 150, 168, 265, 294
white supremacists, xvii, xix, 3, 10, 11, 13, 15, 16, 17, 19, 20, 21, 22, 23, 24, 25, 27, 32, 35, 36, 45, 47, 48, 50, 53, 58, 64, 72, 78, 87, 92, 105, 107, 129, 140, 148, 150, 155, 159, 167, 168, 169, 172, 185, 190, 192, 172, 207, 209, 210, 224, 265
white supremacy, xx, 2, 24, 40, 45, 58, 116, 146, 148, 152, 160, 179, 186, 192, 213, 224, 245, 251, 254, 265, 285; violence, 12
white womanhood tropes, 145
Wilkins, J. Ernest, 51
Wilkins, Roy, 15, 30, 80, 234
Williams, Hosea, 226
Williams, Mabel (Robinson), 12, 16, 57, 58, 121, 141, 144, 165,171, 172, 175, 182
Williams, Robert F., 2, 4, 10, 12, 14, 16, 24, 27, 29, 30, 31, 33, 39, 40, 43, 45, 56, 57, 60, 83, 87, 98, 139, 140, 141, 143, 155, 167, 168, 171–173, 177, 179, 180, 184, 186, 188, 192, 207, 209, 226, 227, 235, 236; blacklisted, 13; blamed for Mae's incarceration, 185, 189; Canada, 28; Chinese exile, 187; Cuba, 28, 53, 59, 184, 185, 186, 187, 188; FBI files, 266; Ghana, 59; Detroit, 53; kidnapping charges, 28, 53; Ku Klux Klan, 184; and Radio Free Dixie, 171, 186; tax harassment, 78
Wilson, Jack, 84
Winfrey, Oprah, 115
Winters, Gladys, 83
Withers, Ernest C., 94, 266
WLIB (radio station), 56, 256, 263
Wolfe, Rolland, 173
Women's Committee of Harlem, 182, 234
Women's House of Detention (New York), 79, 118, 142, 144, 156

Women's rights, 4, 254, 255, 260, 285
Woods, Dessie, 204
Woodson, Carter G., xvii
Woolworth's segregation policies, 57, 278
Workers World, 31, 32, 88, 153, 214
Workers World Party (Trotskyist, Maoist), xii, xvii, xxi, 1, 3, 18, 32, 33–34, 59, 66, 84, 89, 90, 92, 95, 98, 118, 123, 130, 181, 189, 193, 195, 204, 251, 272, 288, 292
working-class/poor, 3, 4, 12, 17, 19, 83, 84, 101, 121, 151, 252, 253, 254, 257, 260, 264, 257, 264, 288
World Federation of Trade Unions, 38
World Revolutions, 4, 5, 34–54, 165–168, 179, 225, 226, 230, 256
World War I, 16, 166, 199, 252
World War II, xviii, 11, 100, 109, 149, 166, 252
Worthy, Bill (William), 141, 169, 170, 175, 178
Wright, Ernest J., 104

Yoruba Temple, 3, 4, 122, 125–126
Young, Andrew, 95
Young, Cynthia A., 17, 185
Young, Whitney, 30, 234
Younger, Paul A., 200
Youngstown Friends of Mae Mallory, 98, 181, 197
Youngstown Steel Workers, 155
Youth Against War and Fascism (YAWF) (Trotskyist, Maoist), xvii, 3, 38, 41, 95, 99, 175, 181, 195, 202, 203, 204, 206, 209, 210, 214, 235, 251, 253, 256, 272, 288; anti-Vietnam War protests, 41; *Partisan Magazine*, 3, 202, 206, 209, 210, 219, 288
youth-centered ideology, 30, 51
Youth Rebellion, Third World Liberation Front, xx
youths, militant Black, 19, 30, 206, 207, 208, 209

Zedong, Mao, 40, 99, 171, 187, 258
Zellner, Dorothy, 261, 292
Zuber, Paul, 76, 77, 119

www.ingramcontent.com/pod-product-compliance
Lightning Source LLC
Chambersburg PA
CBHW020217240426
43672CB00006B/336